The Fourth Amendment

The Fourth Amendment

Original Understandings and Modern Policing

Michael J. Z. Mannheimer

University of Michigan Press
Ann Arbor

Published in the United States of America by the
University of Michigan Press
Printed and bound by CPI Group (UK) Ltd, Croydon, CR0 4YY

First published August 2023

A CIP catalog record for this book is available from the British Library.

Library of Congress Control Number: 2023934618

ISBN 978-0-472-07633-8 (hardcover : alk. paper)
ISBN 978-0-472-05633-0 (paper : alk. paper)
ISBN 978-0-472-90371-9 (open access ebook)

DOI: https://doi.org/10.3998/mpub.12158575

The University of Michigan Press's open access publishing program is made possible thanks to additional funding from the University of Michigan Office of the Provost and the generous support of contributing libraries.

For my family

Contents

Acknowledgments

This book owes its life to the help and support of people too numerous to name. I thank all those who have given me feedback on the various articles of mine over the years that contributed content to this undertaking as well as those who graciously gave me feedback on chapters of this book, including Miriam Baer, Will Baude, Will Berry, John Bickers, Russell Christopher, Laurence Claus, Tom Davies, Don Dripps, Brenner Fissell, Barry Friedman, Mike Gentithes, Adam Gershowitz, Lauryn Gouldin, David Gray, Rachel Harmon, Steve Henderson, Carissa Hessick, Brooks Holland, Renée Hutchins, Lea Johnston, Ken Katkin, Orin Kerr, Kit Kinports, Craig Konnoth, Rob Leider, Wayne Logan, Paul Marcus, the late Dan Markel, Richard McAdams, Alan Michaels, Rob Mikos, Jamelia Morgan, Ngozi Okidegbe, Larry Rosenthal, Meghan Ryan, Laurent Sacharoff, Ric Simmons, David Sklansky, Chris Slobogin, the late Mark Stavsky, James Stern, Seth Stoughton, George Thomas, Matt Tokson, John Valauri, Jonathan Witmer-Rich, Ilan Wurman, and Ekow Yankah.

I owe a special debt of gratitude to two of my teachers: the late John Arthur of SUNY-Binghamton (now Binghamton University), who got me started on my journey of discovery by introducing me to the debates between the Federalists and the Anti-Federalists; and Akhil Amar of Yale Law School, who, in addition to being one of the leading scholars on the history of both the Fourth and Fourteenth Amendments, taught a seminar on the Bill of Rights during his visit at Columbia in the fall of 1993, and who first made me realize that the Bill of Rights is partly about federalism.

I also thank two of my deans, Judy Daar and Jeff Standen, for wisely telling me that the time had come in my career to write a book, and to Northern Kentucky University for approving the sabbatical leave during the 2020–21 academic year that led to the research necessary for chapters 6 through 11. I also thank Carol Bredemeyer, Carol Furnish, and Tobe Liebert for their impeccable skills at finding sources I was unable to locate and their ability to beg, borrow, or steal—well, beg or borrow anyway—those sources on my behalf.

Some material in chapters 2 through 5 has previously been published in a different form in the following: *Decentralizing Fourth Amendment Search Doctrine*, 107 Ky. L.J. 169 (2019); *The Local-Control Model of the Fourth Amendment*, 108 J. Crim. L. & Criminology 253 (2018); *The Contingent Fourth Amendment*, 64 Emory L.J. 1229 (2015); and *Cruel and Unusual Federal Punishments*, 98 Iowa L. Rev. 69 (2012).

Introduction

The Upside-Down Fourth Amendment

The constitutional constraints on policing, properly understood, can be summed up in one simple concept: the police must obey the law. This idea is not new. Anthony Amsterdam proclaimed it some fifty years ago when he wrote in his seminal law review article, *Perspectives on the Fourth Amendment*, that, in his view, "the fourth amendment requires all police search and seizure activity to be regulated by legal directives that confine police discretion within reasonable bounds."[1] The idea has come roaring back recently as scholars, led by Barry Friedman, tout the idea of *democratic policing*, "the idea that the people should take responsibility for policing, as they do for the rest of their government, and that policing agencies should be responsive to the people's will."[2] While the idea is not new, its connection to the original understandings of the Fourth and Fourteenth Amendments has gone largely unexplored. This book fills that gap. Its central thrust is that what the framers and ratifiers of both Amendments had in mind when they contemplated constitutional search-and-seizure constraints was something very close to democratic policing as a constitutional imperative.

In a legal system that sanctifies the rule of law, the idea that police and other governmental officials must obey the law should be non-controversial. Yet this concept has largely eluded the courts because they have misunderstood the Fourth Amendment, the Fourteenth Amendment, and the relationship between the two. The Fourth Amendment, adopted in 1791 and applicable only to the federal government, provides:

> The right of the people to be secure in their persons, houses, papers, and effects, against unreasonable searches and seizures, shall not be

> violated, and no Warrants shall issue, but upon probable cause, supported by Oath or affirmation, and particularly describing the place to be searched, and the persons or things to be seized.[3]

Section 1 of the Fourteenth Amendment, adopted in 1868 and applicable to the States, provides:

> All persons born or naturalized in the United States, and subject to the jurisdiction thereof, are citizens of the United States and of the state wherein they reside. No State shall make or enforce any law which shall abridge the privileges or immunities of citizens of the United States; nor shall any State deprive any person of life, liberty, or property, without due process of law; nor deny to any person within its jurisdiction the equal protection of the laws.[4]

Both of these provisions are critical to understanding the constitutional constraints on policing because courts have held that the Fourteenth Amendment "incorporates" the Fourth Amendment, or makes it applicable to the States.

To see how far our current law has strayed from the simple edict that government officials must obey the law, consider a pair of cases coming from state justice systems, where only the Fourteenth Amendment technically applies. *Virginia* v. *Moore*,[5] decided in 2008 by a vote of 8-1 (Justice Ruth Bader Ginsburg concurred only in the result), stemmed from an arrest made by two police officers in Portsmouth, Virginia. The officers stopped David Lee Moore on suspicion that Moore was driving with a suspended license. The suspicion turned out to be correct and the officers arrested Moore. They searched his person incident to the arrest, permitted by black-letter Fourth Amendment law, and found crack cocaine and enough cash to raise the inference that Moore was no mere user. He was subsequently charged with possession with intent to sell.

But there was a problem with the arrest. Driving with a suspended license was a misdemeanor under Virginia law. State law generally forbade the arrest of someone suspected of committing a misdemeanor and required that a summons be issued instead, so the officers violated state law in making the arrest. Had they abided by state law and merely issued Moore a summons, as the Court had held in a previous case, they could not have searched him and the drugs never would have been discovered. Moore's position was straightforward: the failure of the officers to follow state law constituted an "unreasonable seizure" in violation of the Fourth Amendment, and so the evidence discovered as a result had to be suppressed. The Court disagreed. Failure to abide by state law on arrests does not make an arrest unconstitutional.

Contrast this with the equally lopsided *Chandler* v. *Miller*,[6] decided in 1997. The Court there in an 8-1 decision held unconstitutional a Georgia statute requiring that candidates for certain state offices undergo a drug urinalysis test and certify that the results were negative. The statute specified that the tests had to be performed at a state-approved lab, had to test for five specific types of drugs, and had to conform to federal or state standards regarding such tests. The Court held that the government interest in drug-testing political candidates did not outweigh the candidates' privacy interests, so the test could not be required absent individualized suspicion of wrongdoing. The Court found the drug-testing scheme more about appearances than actually preventing the harms associated with drug use: "[T]he candidate drug test Georgia has devised diminishes personal privacy for a symbol's sake."

Civil libertarians might cheer the decision in *Chandler* and bemoan the decision in *Moore*. "Law and order" conservatives might have the opposite reaction. But both decisions—the state-friendly *Moore* as well as the individual-rights-friendly *Chandler*—are exactly wrong. The Court got these cases wrong because it forgot which constitutional provision it was interpreting: the Fourteenth Amendment, not the Fourth, which applied only indirectly. In neither case did the Court pose the correct question, which is whether Moore or Chandler had been deprived "of life, liberty, or property, without due process of law." Both were obviously deprived of liberty: Moore was taken into custody by agents of the State of Virginia; Chandler was forced to forfeit his privacy and personal autonomy by undergoing a urinalysis test by the State of Georgia. By what stretch of the English language can we say that Moore's arrest, *in violation of state law*, afforded him "due process of law," while the government-ordered analysis of Chandler's urine, *in full compliance with state law*, did not? Yet the Court has expressly endorsed just that result by relying on the "reasonableness" language of the Fourth Amendment: "Just as a search authorized by state law may be an unreasonable one under that amendment, so may a search not expressly authorized by state law be justified as a constitutionally reasonable one."[7] Barry Friedman's response to *Moore* says it best: "What?"[8]

The root of the problem is the idea of "jot-for-jot incorporation": that the Fourteenth Amendment places the exact same constraints on state governments that the Fourth does on the federal government. Once one gets away from the "due process of law" language that seems to decide both *Moore* and

Chandler and instead focuses on whether the seizure of Moore or the search of Chandler was, as the Fourth Amendment puts it, "unreasonable," one can understand the Court's mistake. The Court has held that "reasonable" generally means, in the law enforcement context (as in *Moore*), based on probable cause and, sometimes, a warrant. Outside of that context (as in *Chandler*), "reasonable" means that it passes the court's estimation of whether the intrusiveness of the search or seizure is outweighed by the government interest, taking into account the effectiveness of the search or seizure. If the question is whether state officials acted "reasonably" in these cases, then both decisions are defensible. But when Virginia or Georgia officials act, the pertinent constitutional provision does not require reasonableness; it requires "due process of law." That language should force us to ask whether state agents followed the law of the State. However, as *Moore* and *Chandler* show, the Supreme Court has held that state law is pretty much irrelevant.

Even when the Fourth Amendment applies directly, unmediated by the Fourteenth, and the Court looks at the right language, it still gets things wrong. That is because "unreasonable" is best understood in a similar way, as "*inconsistent with state law.*" Yet the Court has determined that what makes a search by *federal* agents reasonable has little if anything to do with state law either. In *Olmstead* v. *United States*,[9] decided in 1928, Olmstead was convicted of violating the National Prohibition Act, based in part on telephone conversations intercepted by the use of phone taps. Federal prohibition agents, without obtaining a warrant, had surveilled Olmstead's telephone communications by placing phone taps on his lines. Officers accessed these lines in places not owned or controlled by Olmstead: the basement of an office building and the street near his home. In so doing, the agents violated a Washington state law making it a misdemeanor to "intercept . . . the sending of a message over any . . . telephone line." The Court gave short shrift to the argument that this rendered the agents' actions unconstitutional and upheld Olmstead's conviction.

Fast-forward ninety years to 2018. Federal prosecutors obtained cell site location information (CSLI) via court orders obtained under the federal Stored Communication Act, to determine Timothy Carpenter's whereabouts on about 130 different days. This evidence tended to show that Carpenter was in the vicinity of nine retail outlets in Michigan and Ohio at the times they were robbed. The evidence helped prove Carpenter guilty of the robberies and send him to prison for life. The Court ruled in *Carpenter* v. *United States*[10] that obtaining CSLI for such a lengthy period without a warrant violated the Fourth Amendment, because, although people turn over such information to their cellular service automatically through their ownership of a cell phone, they retain a reasonable expectation that that information will go no further than the cell phone company. As Justice Neil Gorsuch pointed out in his dissent, the Court came to this conclusion without any analysis of whether Carpenter had any right under Ohio or Michigan law to keep his CSLI private.[11]

Thus, as in *Moore* and *Chandler*, which dealt with acts of *state* officials, compliance by *federal* officials with state law is neither necessary nor sufficient for compliance with the Fourth Amendment. In *Olmstead*, federal officials violated state law but, the Court held, acted in compliance with the Fourth Amendment. In *Carpenter*, federal officials may or may not have complied with state law, but the Court held that they violated the Fourth Amendment; state law was irrelevant. *Olmstead*, *Chandler*, *Moore*, and *Carpenter* are symptomatic of a larger problem. All four of these cases turn Fourth and Fourteenth Amendment principles on their head because they ignore the key question: did government officials obey the law?

To be fair, the courts do get some things right. For example, they correctly posit that the lodestar of the Fourth and Fourteenth Amendments is the placing of limits on individual-officer discretion. Officers, of course, must be permitted some discretion in enforcing the law and keeping public order because those tasks require some flexibility. Kenneth Culp Davis observed many years ago:

> Elimination of all discretionary power is both impossible and undesirable. The sensible goal is development of a proper balance between rule and discretion. Some circumstances call for rules, some for discretion, some for mixtures of one proportion, and some for mixtures of another proportion. In today's American legal system, the special need is to eliminate *unnecessary* discretionary power, and to discover more successful ways to confine, to structure, and to check necessary discretionary power.[12]

Assuming police are adhering to the law, the big question for constitutional restrictions on governmental searches and seizures is how much discretion we permit police officers to exercise on their own behalf in determining whether to search or to seize.

But courts have fumbled that question. They have tried to implement the Fourth Amendment's first clause, the Reasonableness Clause, by positing elaborate rules, some drawn from the common law of 1791, some from general privacy principles, some from their own predilections, that are unform across the Nation. One school of thought holds that the Reasonableness Clause controls officer discretion by requiring that searches and seizures always, as far as is practicable, be authorized only by judicial warrant. Another school of thought posits that officer discretion is cabined by the prospect of damage awards after the fact by a judge or jury for unreasonable warrantless searches, reasonableness to be determined in the common-law method, by the accretion of cases.

Both schools of thought rely on judicial control of executive discretion, whether before the fact (by warrants) or after (by damage awards). There seems to be no room in either school for the idea that legislatures and other politically accountable bodies should play a part in the control of individual-officer discretion. After all, if the goal really is control of discretion, an officer could legitimately search or seize even without judicial warrant, as long as she obeys specific search-and-seizure rules enacted by a democratically elected body or promulgated by a politically accountable agency. Likewise, adherence to such rules might be thought not only sufficient but also necessary; no matter how reasonable her actions might later seem to a judge, they must be authorized by law.

I will suggest that, based on the original understandings of the Fourth and Fourteenth Amendments, constitutional restrictions on searches and seizures are first and foremost dictates that executive officials obey laws and other rules that are specific enough to cabin their discretion. The Fourth Amendment, through its reasonableness requirement, requires that federal officials follow state law. What makes a search or seizure "unreasonable," I will contend, is that it is impermissible under the law of the State where the search or seizure occurred. At the founding, those who pressed for a Bill of Rights were not trying to hold federal agents to uniform search-and-seizure principles across the Nation. They were trying to hold them to the limitations on searches and seizures established by the laws of the several States. In this way, the people's security in their persons, houses, papers, and effects were protected to the extent that the people themselves decided, through state constitutions, statutes, and court decisions, they should be protected.

When it comes to the States, the Due Process Clause requires that state officials follow state law. At the time the Fourteenth Amendment was ratified in 1868, the concerns were very different from those in 1791. In the aftermath of the Civil War, formerly enslaved persons were subjected to the "Black Codes," separate sets of rules to govern the behavior of Black Americans. Some provisions explicitly differentiated between the races, subjecting Black people to stricter constraints or harsher punishment than similarly situated whites. Some provisions, notably the vaguely worded vagrancy statutes, were racially neutral but were used almost exclusively against Black people. If a free Black person were found not hard at work, he or she might be arrested and convicted as a vagrant, and sentenced to a period of labor, their services to be rented out to a white person. Worse, Black people (and, to a lesser extent, loyal whites and Northerners) in the South were subjected to atrocious acts of violence, often by state officials, that were obviously illegal under state law—murder, kidnapping, rape, robbery, assault, burglary, arson, and more—but that largely went unpunished. Through this reign of terror and the enforcement of the Black Codes, local officials were able to subordinate the newly free Black people and, in effect, reinstitute slavery in a different guise.

The Fourteenth Amendment was designed to end these practices. The Amendment requires that legislation be facially race neutral. But, given the extraordinary discretion provided by the race-neutral vagrancy statutes and the extra-legal violence meted out by state officers, more than race-neutral legislation was needed. The framers and ratifiers of the Fourteenth Amendment knew that state law could not protect Black people if the law was simply ignored and that even race-neutral laws that granted excessive discretion to executive officials could be used for discriminatory purposes. They enacted the Due Process Clause to meet these concerns. The idea of "due process of law" instantiates the idea of the rule of law that has guided the English and American legal systems for centuries. Inherent in the concept of the rule of law is the notion that law is made by legislatures (and sometimes by judges) and merely enforced by executive officers. "Due process of law," then, primarily means pursuant only to duly promulgated laws, not the whim of executive officials.

Thus, while constitutional constraints on searches and seizures are ostensibly about rights, they are driven largely by structural concerns: federalism in the case of the Fourth Amendment and separation of powers in the case of the Due Process Clause. The Fourth Amendment was driven largely by a desire to keep search-and-seizure policy in the hands of the States rather than the federal government, and the Fourteenth Amendment was driven largely by a desire to keep such policy-making in the hands of legislatures rather than executive officials. These ideas are in line with recent scholarship that has begun to question the sharp dichotomy in constitutional law between rights and structure, and to rediscover the linkages between them.[13] In isolating a powerful theme of federalism in the Fourth Amendment and separation of powers in the Fourteenth, this book sets forth a new model for

Fourth Amendment law—the Local Control Model—by which searches and seizures by both federal and state officials are regulated primarily by local, democratic controls: searches and seizures by both federal and state officials must be consistent with state law, and executed in a way that is nondiscriminatory and which limits individual-officer discretion to the extent possible. In this way, individual rights are protected by structural principles. Just as federalism and separation of powers operate to secure human freedom at the wholesale level in the Constitution generally by diffusing power to make governmental oppression more difficult, the Fourth and Fourteenth Amendments do so at the retail level in the particular context of searches and seizures. These principles drive the remainder of the book.

Chapter 1 discusses the two dominant models of the Fourth Amendment: the "Warrant Model" (that warrants are presumptively required for all searches and seizures) and the "Reasonableness Model" (that searches and seizures are subject to a generalized reasonableness standard that sometimes but does not always require warrants). It surveys the historical evidence for each and finds that each has some support in the historical record but that neither view is fully consistent with the original understanding of the Fourth Amendment.

Chapter 2 offers an alternative to these two dominant models of the Fourth Amendment: the "Local Control Model," that all federal searches and seizures must abide by state and local search-and-seizure law, policy, and norms. It will suggest that the Local Control Model is the most consistent with the original understanding of the Fourth Amendment, using evidence from the episode in American history most responsible for our Fourth Amendment, the writs of assistance controversy of the 1760s, in which the colonists recoiled at the use of a type of general warrant (one authorizing too broad a search on too scanty a basis) by the British. This chapter then shows that two other episodes straddling ratification of the Constitution also support the Local Control Model.

Chapter 3 focuses on the Anti-Federalists, who demanded that a Bill of Rights be added to the Constitution in exchange for ratification in several key States, including Massachusetts, New York, and Virginia. It shows that the Anti-Federalists viewed individual rights and federalism to be intertwined, and contends that they advocated tying some individual rights at the federal level to state protections, so that the application of some federal constitutional rights might vary by State. This chapter contends that the Fourth Amendment requirement of reasonableness represents a specific instance of the calibration of federal rights to state norms that the Anti-Federalists sought.

Chapter 4 tackles what the courts call the "What is a search?" question, and lends further support to the notion developed in Chapters 2 and 3 that search-and-seizure policy was to be developed at a state and local level. It will show that, because the Fourth Amendment reserved search-and-seizure policy to the States, the question of whether federal conduct impinges on our "persons, houses, papers, [or] effects" so as to implicate the protections of the Fourth Amendment was to be determined by state law and, where state law was unclear, by the verdicts of local juries. It will also suggest that the resurgence of a "trespass" account of the search question (that a search occurs where police commit a physical incursion on property) is a welcome innovation in the law. But it also suggests that the divergence between that account and the idea that a search occurs where police infringe upon a "reasonable expectation of privacy" has been overstated. Both, when properly understood, are supported by the original understanding of the Fourth Amendment.

Chapter 5 will add to the evidence that the original understanding supports the Local Control Model of the Fourth Amendment by focusing on the issue of what made a search or arrest lawful or unlawful during the framing period (from about 1760 to about 1790). It will show that, while search-and-seizure rules were in the main consistent, at the fringes they changed over time and across jurisdictional borders. This supports the notion that the framers and ratifiers of the Fourth Amendment understood that what was a reasonable search or seizure would also change over time and across borders, and that the lawfulness of federal searches or seizures would thus be contingent on the law of the state where the search or seizure occurred.

Chapter 6 jumps to 1866 and explores the historical backdrop that led to the adoption of the Fourteenth Amendment. It lays out the two main concerns for the Amendment's proponents. First, they wanted to protect Black Southerners from the post–Civil War Black Codes, discriminatory laws that applied only to them as well as vagrancy and other criminal provisions that were race neutral on their face but were used overwhelmingly against Black people in an effort to reinstitute slavery. Second, they wanted to protect Black Southerners, and to a lesser extent loyal white Southerners and Northerners in the South, from the horrific violence against them, much of it perpetrated or at least facilitated by state agents, that swept the South after the war.

Chapter 7 examines whether and to what extent the Reconstruction-era Republicans, the framers and ratifiers of the Fourteenth Amendment, understood it as applying the Fourth Amendment to the States. It concludes that, even if the Fourteenth Amendment was understood as applying some constraints on the search-and-seizure power of the States, the framers and ratifiers of the Amendment also understood it to be a moderate provision that would preserve our country's essential federal structure.

Chapter 8 lays out the difficult nature of incorporation of the Fourth Amendment against the States. First, one must reconcile the Reconstruction-era Republicans' desire to constrain the southern States' power to conduct arbitrary searches and seizures with their intention of largely preserving local control of search-and-seizure policy. Second, one must mesh the Republican view of the Bill of Rights as merely declaratory of pre-existing, natural rights with the more hardheaded views of the founding-era Anti-Federalists that natural rights are only as robust as the positive-law provisions that give them life. Finally, one must contend with the seeming impossibility of applying to the States a provision that is so predominantly about federalism. These paradoxes can be resolved with an approach that posits freedom from arbitrary searches and seizures as an essential right of American citizenship but that allows for variation among the States as to how to best implement this basic right, so long as the States abide by equality and due process principles. This approach would require that state officials not discriminate when searching and seizing, of course. But it would go further and require that state executive officials adhere to state law when searching and seizing, and, as a corollary, forbid overly broad grants of discretion to such officials. These are the principles of ***nondiscrimination***, ***legality***, and ***nondelegation***.

Chapter 9 further explicates these three principles and their relationship to constitutional constraints on searches and seizures.

Chapter 10 begins to re-examine Fourth Amendment doctrine based on these three principles. It contends that the Court has correctly focused on the dangers of broad individual-officer discretion. However, it has failed to fully appreciate that detailed legislative and administrative directions can serve the same discretion-narrowing function as warrants, and it has paid too little deference to state legislative judgments about search-and-seizure policy.

Chapter 11 highlights several failings of the Court's Fourth Amendment jurisprudence that are most salient for modern policing and that are directly traceable to the Court's failure to appreciate the significance of the Fourteenth Amendment: its refusal to tie the "What is a search?" question to legality; its abdication of the responsibility to limit police discretion in the areas of traffic stops, arrests for minor crimes, and stops on less than probable cause to arrest; and its effective preemption of state law governing police use of force.

It should be noted at the outset that this book is concerned with rights rather than remedies. The Supreme Court has held that when the constitutional right against unreasonable searches and seizures is violated, the remedy is often exclusion of the evidence unlawfully obtained from the prosecutor's case at trial against the victim of the unlawful search or seizure.[14] This "exclusionary rule" is what makes the Fourth Amendment relevant to criminal cases; but for this rule, violations of the Fourth Amendment could be remedied only through civil actions. This book does not take on directly the propriety of the exclusionary rule, which remains controversial.[15] However, the concept of "due process of law" encompasses both rights and remedies: where police conduct violates state law, due process of law may yet be provided by a state-law remedy for that unlawful conduct. For that reason, I will address the exclusionary rule briefly in Chapter 10, suggesting that it is justified to the extent that state-law remedies are inadequate to provide "due process of law."

~

IN A DEMOCRACY, the people are sovereign. This means that politically accountable legislators make the law and executive officials enforce it. The framers and ratifiers of the Fourth Amendment emphasized the first part of this truism, that decisions on as potent a weapon as governmental searches and seizures must be made by local lawmakers because they are more politically accountable than a distant central government. The framers and ratifiers of the Fourteenth Amendment agreed, but they emphasized the second part, that searches and seizures must be executed according to law, on a basis of equality, and with limited discretion in the hands of the law enforcers. The Supreme Court's Fourth Amendment jurisprudence is deeply flawed because it has gotten away from these principles. This book provides a map for an alternative Fourth Amendment jurisprudence more sensitive to the original understandings of the Fourth and Fourteenth Amendments.

PART I

The Fourth Amendment

Original Understandings

One

Two Models of the Fourth Amendment

The central puzzle of the Fourth Amendment has always been what the relationship is between its two clauses. The first, the Reasonableness Clause, demands that all governmental searches and seizures of "persons, houses, papers, and effects" be reasonable. The second, the Warrant Clause, spells out three requirements that must be met before a warrant may be issued: probable cause, oath or affirmation, and particularity. Essentially, two views of the Fourth Amendment have emerged, each emphasizing one of these two clauses: what I call the "Warrant Model," that warrants are presumptively required for all searches and seizures; and what I call the "Reasonableness Model," that searches and seizures merely have to reasonable, which sometimes but not always requires obtaining a warrant. This chapter briefly discusses the two models, weighs the historical support for each view, and determines that each has some historical support but that neither is the best interpretation of the historical data.

The Two Dominant Models of the Fourth Amendment

The Warrant Model posits that a warrant must be used in order to render a search or seizure reasonable, at least presumptively. The Warrant Model essentially creates a third clause of the Fourth Amendment, one that joins the other two and says, in effect, "searches and seizures performed without warrants are generally unreasonable." This view reads the Fourth Amendment as creating a "warrant-preference rule," at least for searches of homes and other premises and private spaces: a warrant is required unless there is good reason for not getting one. As Justice Felix Frankfurter, writing for himself and Justice Robert H. Jackson in a dissent, put it:

> When the Fourth Amendment outlawed "unreasonable searches" and then went on to define the very restricted authority that even a search warrant issued by a magistrate could give, the framers said with all the clarity of the gloss of history that a search is "unreasonable" unless a warrant authorizes it, barring only exceptions justified by absolute necessity.[1]

The Reasonableness Model, by contrast, emphasizes the Amendment's Reasonableness Clause. This view contends that the reasonableness of searches and seizures is generally to be measured independently of whether a warrant was used, the Warrant Clause telling us only what requirements must be met if a warrant is used.

The U.S. Supreme Court has never clearly settled upon either view. As Justice Antonin Scalia put it, the Court has "lurched back and forth between imposing a categorical warrant requirement and looking to reasonableness alone."[2] While the Warrant Model became ascendant before the late 1960s, the Reasonableness Model has seen a resurgence since then, and the debate continues. Different members of the same Court express the Fourth Amendment's central requirement in terms of either the Reasonableness Model or the Warrant Model, depending on his or her preferences. Indeed, one can often discern from a Supreme Court opinion whether a Fourth Amendment claimant will win or lose based on whether, at the outset of its Fourth Amendment analysis, the Court describes the Amendment's requirements in terms of the Reasonableness Model or the Warrant Model. To take one example, here is how the majority opinion in *City of Los Angeles* v. *Patel*, written by Justice Sonia Sotomayor, explained the provision's requirements: "Based on th[e] constitutional text, the Court has repeatedly held that searches conducted outside the judicial process, without prior approval by a judge or a magistrate judge, are *per se* unreasonable subject only to a few specifically established and well-delineated exceptions."[3] Predictably, the Court found a Fourth Amendment violation. And here is how Justice Scalia in dissent described the same requirements:

> [I]n an effort to guide courts in applying the Search-and-Seizure Clause's indeterminate reasonableness standard . . . we have used the Warrant Clause as a guidepost for assessing the reasonableness of a search, and have erected a framework of presumptions applicable to broad categories of searches. . . . Our case law has repeatedly recognized, however, that these are mere presumptions, and the only constitutional *requirement* is that a search be reasonable.[4]

The result is an uneasy truce. The Warrant Model has technically won out but the warrant requirement is shot through with so many different exceptions that one could argue that the Reasonableness Model is truly ascendant.

For example, the Court has permitted warrantless arrests when made in public, requiring warrants only when police forcibly enter a private premises to make an arrest.[5] As for searches, the Court has required a warrant for entry into private premises or a search of personal items but has recognized a number of exceptions to this requirement. Police may enter or search private spaces if there is an exigency, that is, where circumstances are fast-moving and do not allow time for police to stop and get a warrant. There are essentially four different varieties of exigency: imminent loss or destruction of evidence; imminent loss of a suspect; hot pursuit of a suspect; and an imminent dangerous situation.[6] Another commonly invoked exception to the warrant requirement is the search-incident-to-arrest exception. When a police officer makes a custodial arrest, the officer may search the person of the suspect plus anything within her immediate control without a warrant, and even without probable cause to search.[7] Police may generally also search automobiles without a warrant as long as there is probable cause to do so.[8] And, of course, police do not need a warrant or even any suspicion of wrongdoing if they have consent to search.[9] Other exceptions to the so-called warrant requirement will be discussed later in the book. If there is a "warrant requirement," it has so many exceptions that it is difficult, at least descriptively, to characterize the Fourth Amendment as setting forth a warrant-preference rule.

Normatively, however, which approach is more consistent with the history behind the adoption of the Fourth Amendment? As Justice Frankfurter put it, the Fourth Amendment cannot "be read as [it] might be read by a man who knows English but has no knowledge of the history that gave rise to the words."[10] All agree that the Warrant Clause clearly forbids general warrants, and history supports the notion that, by 1791, general warrants were almost uniformly seen as unlawful. A second point of agreement is that the main impetus behind the Fourth Amendment was to curb the power of executive officials, mainly customs officials and excisemen (tax collectors), by sharply limiting their discretionary authority. Beyond that, unfortunately, the historical evidence regarding what else the Fourth Amendment requires is ambiguous. The question really boils down to what the framers and ratifiers of the Fourth Amendment saw as the primary mechanism for curbing executive discretionary authority: ex post jury trials, as the Reasonableness Model fans think, or ex ante judicial supervision, as Warrant Model adherents claim. Adherents of each view can find some support in the historical record surrounding adoption of the Fourth Amendment. But neither tells the full story.

History and the Reasonableness Model

The idea that history supports a model of the Fourth Amendment that downplays warrants and plays up reasonableness has been most completely and robustly set forth by Akhil Amar. In his seminal piece, *Fourth Amendment First Principles* and in follow-up pieces,[11] he argued not only that warrants were not generally required for searches and seizures at the time of the adoption of the Fourth Amendment, but that warrants were actually disfavored, because a warrant immunized the government official from a later lawsuit for trespass.

Amar first staked out the textual high ground: "The words of the Fourth Amendment really do mean what they say. They do not require warrants, even presumptively, for searches and seizures."[12] After all, the negative phrasing of the Warrant Clause ("*no* warrants shall issue") itself suggests that the Amendment should be read as disfavoring, not favoring, warrants.[13] He also pointed out that a number of different types of warrantless searches and seizures were permissible in 1791: arrests, searches incident thereto, and searches aboard ships, for example. He further asserted that searches performed without warrants could be justified ex post if contraband or stolen items were found.[14]

Amar argued that the language of the Fourth Amendment disfavors warrants for good reason: warrants were issued by judges in ex parte proceedings (that is, where only the government was represented) "and had the purpose and effect of precluding any common law trespass suit the aggrieved target might try to bring before a local jury." Regulation of federal searches and seizures, he argued, would come about as a result of after-the-fact remedial action by local juries in tort suits. He cited, for example, the remarks of a Pennsylvania Anti-Federalist that if a federal constable with a warrant to search "for stolen goods, pulled down the clothes of a bed in which there was a woman and searched under her shift," the only recourse for the victim would be a jury award.[15] As such, warrants were a bad thing, not a good thing, given that they immunized officers from suit even where a search or seizure turned out to be flagrantly unreasonable. Amar concluded "that the ultimate touchstone of the Amendment is not warrants, but reasonableness."[16]

As persuasive as this account seems at first blush, it is flawed when one digs deeper. As will be seen, during the writs-of-assistance controversy in colonial North America in the 1760s, specific warrants, those based on individualized suspicion and drafted with particularity, were generally held up by the colonists as the sine qua non of a lawful search. If Amar's account were correct, James Otis, the attorney for the Boston merchants who first fought the writs of assistance in 1760, should have argued that British customs agents were entitled to no warrants at all. Instead, he argued that they were entitled to specific warrants. Likewise, colonial courts should not have offered to issue writs of assistance as specific warrants, as several did. Rather, they should have refused to issue writs at all.

Even putting this to one side, Amar's historical account is implausible. The keystone of his claim that warrants were disfavored is that the bulk of search-and-seizure policy was to be determined ex post by juries on a case-by-case basis. But, as will be shown in Chapter 5, intricate sets of rules—common-law and statutory—regarding when warrants were and were not required were already in place at the time of the adoption of the Fourth Amendment. These rules allowed arrests and searches without warrants in some circumstances and required warrants in others. True, where there was no warrant to immunize the person conducting the search or seizure, the jury determined whether the search or seizure was reasonable. But to say that the common law posited the jury as the architect of search-and-seizure policy captures only a piece of the picture, and minimizes the extent to which the common law kept a good many cases from juries by providing for search and seizure via warrant.

Moreover, the founding generation understood as well as we that tort suits are a blunt instrument of regulation and that after-the-fact remedies could offer only imperfect redress.[17] Indeed, this very argument was made amid the writs-of-assistance controversy, likely by Otis himself, in a column published in the *Boston Gazette* on January 4, 1762. Otis asked what "reparation" a petty officer would make "after he has put a family . . . to the utmost confusion and terror [without] just grounds of suspicion." He continued,

> is it enough to say, that damages may be recover'd against him in the law? I hope indeed this will always be the case;—but are we *perpetually* to be expos'd to outrages of this kind, & to be told for our *only* consolation, that we must be *perpetually* seeking to the courts of law for redress? Is not this vexation *itself* . . . ?

Otis also pointed out that some intangible harms, such as poor treatment by a petty executive officer during a search, were non-compensable: "[M]ay we not be insolently treated by our *petty tyrants* in *some* ways, for which the law prescribes no redress?"[18]

The risk of under-deterrence is amplified when one considers how unlikely it was that the victim of a purportedly unlawful search would bring a tort action. Amar can point to only a handful of reported cases in British North America in which such an action was brought. If Amar were correct, "there should be thousands of such cases, and evidence of them should be easy to find. The only evidence so far produced is [a] 'smattering of nineteenth-century cases,' . . . not the avalanche of cases that a flourishing system would generate."[19] The showcase litigation for his theory, instead, is the Wilkesite cases, a series of litigations brought in Britain against Crown officials (discussed in chapter 2). The plaintiffs in those cases, however, were a prominent Member of Parliament and his close associates. Moreover, the discovery of incriminating evidence was often an absolute defense in such a suit. As the court remarked in one of those cases, *Entick* v. *Carrington*, in explaining why general warrants had been in use for so long without being legally challenged: "It must have been the guilt or poverty of those upon whom such warrants have been executed, that deterred or hindered them from contending against the power of [an executive official], or such warrants could never have passed for lawful till this time."[20] Much as the Wilkesite cases might have set a precedent and deterred future Crown officials from violating the rights of all British subjects, it is unlikely that search-and-seizure law can be fine-tuned based solely on tort suits brought by the well-placed few with the resources and wherewithal to bring such actions.

History and the Warrant Model

Those who advocate for the Warrant Model agree that history offers a guide. But they tend to pull the camera back on the specific practices of the framers in order to view the general zeitgeist during the framing period vis-à-vis search-and-seizure policy. As Justice Frankfurter remarked, the Fourth Amendment "was the answer of the Revolutionary statesmen to the evils of searches without warrants and searches with warrants unrestricted in scope. Both were deemed 'unreasonable.'"[21] It would make little sense to think that Americans during the framing period reacted so violently to general warrants yet calmly accepted searches and seizures performed with no warrant at all. The chief vice of both general warrants and warrantless searches and seizures is that they afforded unlimited discretion to low-level executive officials: constables, customs collectors, and excisemen. Both general warrants and unwarranted searches and seizures "place[d] the liberty of every man in the hands of every petty officer."[22] Thus, the argument goes, "The Fourth Amendment was . . . adopted for the purpose of checking discretionary police authority."[23] The idea was to "'place[] the magistrate as a buffer between the police and the citizenry.'"[24] Thus, to Warrant Clause advocates, the Fourth Amendment is largely about controlling executive discretion through judicial superintendence.

But while a preference for judicial oversight of petty executive authority can be gleaned from the colonial opposition to writs of assistance and general search warrants, such a preference cannot be stated as a general rule applicable to all searches and seizures. First, warrantless arrests were common during the framing period. As long as a felony had in fact been committed, and there were reasonable grounds to believe the arrestee had committed it, warrantless arrest was perfectly acceptable. Indeed, even the felony-in-fact requirement was breaking down during the late eighteenth century; some authorities believed that a warrantless arrest could be made on probable cause both that a felony had been committed and that the arrestee had committed it. Additionally, warrantless arrests for felonies could be made in most jurisdictions based on "[t]he common fame of the country," that is, based on general reputation.[25] Moreover, in most jurisdictions warrantless arrest of a person who was actually guilty of a felony was always justified, even if based upon no suspicion at all. Warrantless arrests could also be made in some jurisdictions for such lesser offenses as vagrancy, "disturbing the Minister in Time of Divine Service," "profane[] swear[ing]," "begging," prostitution, fortune-telling and practicing other "crafty science," "'hawking' and 'peddling,'" and violations of the Sabbath. None of these crime categories requires the kind of swift action that would make obtaining a warrant impracticable, at least not as a general matter. The law was unclear even as to whether a warrant was needed to make a forcible entry into a home to arrest. Based on this evidence, adherents of the Warrant Model have a tough row to hoe in claiming that the Fourth Amendment was understood in 1791 as generally requiring warrants for seizures.

Warrant Model proponents are on somewhat firmer footing when it comes to searches, but even here they falter. Even assuming that warrants were consistently thought during the framing period to be required for searches of dwellings, there was no universal rule beyond the home. As we will see in chapter 5, customs statutes enacted by Maryland, North Carolina, and Virginia during the 1780s required that officials obtain a warrant to enter into "warehouses" and "storehouses" as well as dwellings. But customs statutes in Massachusetts and Pennsylvania during the same period permitted warrantless searches of such premises, requiring warrants only for searches of houses. Fans of the Warrant Model cannot explain why, within a span of ten years, warrantless searches of non-dwelling premises went from legitimate policy choice to constitutional boogeyman.

More broadly, the views of those who advocate a Warrant Model of the Fourth Amendment are in very serious tension with the fact that the Amendment was directed to the federal legislative branch, not the executive or the judicial. When James Madison initially proposed the Bill of Rights in the House of Representatives, he contemplated that its provisions would be interspersed, each tacked onto the provision of the body of the Constitution it was meant to alter, rather than added as a separate set of provisions at the end. The Fourth Amendment was not intended to be added to Article II, which one might expect if it were primarily a check on the executive. Nor was it destined for Article III, which one would imagine it would be if intended as a direction to judges. Rather, it was originally contemplated that the Fourth Amendment would find a home in Article I, § 9, along with the other prohibitions on the legislative branch.[26] This tells us something very significant. The Amendment is not a direction to judges about when to issue warrants or to executive officials about how to search and seize. It is a constraint on *Congress'* power to make law regarding searches and seizures.

That power lay with state legislatures, judges, and juries. For Reasonableness Model adherents are correct that after-the-fact tort suits would regulate federal searches and seizures at least some of the time. Much of search-and-seizure law was judge-made, so the framers and ratifiers of the Fourth Amendment understood that enforcement would sometimes come through ex post tort actions. Those actions would primarily be brought in state court, under state common law, state constitutions, state statutes, and local ordinances.[27] The upshot is that *federal* officers would be controlled by *state* law. The Fourth Amendment, it turns out, is as much about constitutional structure—federalism—as it is about rights.

Conclusion

Something is missing from both dominant accounts of the Fourth Amendment. If one reads the Amendment as requiring warrants whenever it is possible to get one, an entire clause is missing. Moreover, this account cannot explain why some warrantless searches and seizures were permitted at common law at the time of the framing, even where getting a warrant would have been possible. On the other hand, those who try to explain the Amendment as requiring only reasonableness have in view a version of reasonableness that mostly leaves search-and-seizure policy up to juries. But an intricate set of rules kept many of these cases from ever getting to juries, and juries were considered no more effective than they are today in deterring and providing restitution for misconduct. While the Fourth Amendment calls for reasonableness, the framers and ratifiers did not contemplate a free-wheeling reasonableness standard that left weighing of costs and benefits to juries in the run of cases. When they spoke of reasonableness, they meant the reason of the common law. And the common law, as we will see, is the law of the State where the search or seizure occurs.

Two

The Local Control Model of the Fourth Amendment

The fundamental flaw in both the Warrant Model and Reasonableness Model is that each posits a Fourth Amendment that provides a single, uniform set of rules and standards. However, history provides a third model of the Fourth Amendment that generally has been overlooked. The framing generation did not demonstrate an overriding preference for warrants, but neither did they wish to subject federal searches and seizures to a general requirement of reasonableness. Rather, what they contemplated was local control over federal searches and seizures. This third model—the Local Control Model—enjoys the most historical support. That is, the best way to understand the Fourth Amendment, as a historical matter, is as a reservation of local control over federal searches and seizures. While there was a general consensus by 1791 that general warrants—those not based on individualized suspicion of wrongdoing by a particular person—were unlawful, search-and-seizure rules were, in other respects, to be controlled by state law.

This chapter reviews the thirty-year period surrounding adoption of the Fourth Amendment, addressing first the two episodes most directly relevant to the Amendment's original meaning: the British Wilkesite cases and the American writs-of-assistance controversy, both occurring in the 1760s. The Wilkesite cases are best known for their denigration of general warrants under English common law. What gets lost in this interpretation is the fact that British courts were generally willing to recognize general warrants that were authorized by Parliament. The Wilkesite cases were more about the requirement of democratic controls on searches and seizures than they were a wholesale rejection of general warrants. The American writs-of-assistance controversy has also been misinterpreted, as a unified, continent-wide push-back by the colonists against the whole concept of the general warrant. But general warrants were in wide use by the colonies themselves until the 1780s. What the colonists objected to was subjection to search-and-seizure policies dictated by a distant central government in which they had no say. What they sought was local control of searches and seizures by democratically elected and accountable local officials.

This chapter then turns to the immediate post-Revolution period, the years leading up to and just after ratification of the Fourth Amendment. This theme of local control resurfaced twice more, strengthening the inference that the Fourth Amendment was about preserving such control over central authority vis-à-vis searches and seizures.

The Wilkesite Cases and the Writs-of-Assistance Controversy

No two historical episodes are as important to understanding the Fourth Amendment as the Wilkesite cases in Britain and the writs-of-assistance controversy in the American colonies. The Wilkesite cases can be read as rejecting general warrants even if authorized by statute. However, they can also be read to stand for the proposition that warrants unauthorized by law, whether by statute or common law, are void. These cases were arguably about democratic controls over the power to search and seize. The writs-of-assistance controversy took this idea one step further. It was not enough that executive search-and-seizure activities be authorized by law. They must be authorized by *local* law. Together, these events stand for the proposition embodied in the Fourth Amendment that search-and-seizure authority must be subject to local democratic controls.

Democratic Control of Search-and-Seizure Policy: The Wilkesite Cases

The Wilkesite cases were named for John Wilkes, a dissident Whig Member of Parliament. Though they occurred in Britain, they had a tremendous impact on this side of the Atlantic.[1] The trouble started when King George III and his ministers got wind of a tract known as *The North Briton No. 45* that was highly critical of his government. The King and his men considered this to be sedition. Separately, an associate of Wilkes, John Entick, was suspected of publishing another supposedly seditious piece, *The Monitor*. Lord Halifax, one of the King's secretaries of state, issued general warrants for the arrest of anyone involved in the production, printing, and circulation of *No. 45* and *The Monitor*, and the seizure of their papers. Crown agents armed with these general warrants ultimately arrested forty-nine suspected authors, printers, and vendors of the two tracts, including Wilkes and Entick. The agents ransacked the arrestees' homes and gathered up personal papers, looking for evidence of their ties to the allegedly seditious tracts. Wilkes, Entick, and others later successfully sued Halifax and the King's agents. The government eventually paid about £100,000 in judgments and court costs, an enormous sum equivalent to over £18 million (about $25 million) in 2020.[2]

The Wilkesite cases are typically cited for the proposition that general warrants were illegal under British common law, which is true. In *Wilkes* v. *Wood*, Lord Chief Justice Pratt declared that to permit the breaking into a home by force and seizing of papers "upon a general warrant . . . where no offenders names [*sic*] are specified in the warrant, and therefore a discretionary power given to messengers to search wherever their suspicions may chance to fall . . . is totally subversive of the liberty of the subject" and "contrary to the fundamental principles of the constitution."[3] In *Money* v. *Leach*, the judges of King's Bench "were clear and unanimous in opinion" that a warrant that does not name or describe the person to be arrested such that the "judging of the information should be left to the discretion of the officer" is illegal.[4]

What is often overlooked, however, is that the judges came to this conclusion only after concluding that the general warrants issued in those cases were not authorized by statute. The *Money* court, for example, first asked whether Halifax was authorized by an Act of Parliament to issue the warrants. The judges conceded that "there are many cases where particular Acts of Parliament have given authority to apprehend, under general warrants." However, there was no "Act of Parliament which warrants this case." Only then did the court consider whether the general warrant could "stand upon the principles of common law."[5]

It is true that adherents of seventeenth-century jurist Sir Edward Coke believed that not even Parliament could alter some fundamental aspects of the common law. It is also true that Pratt reflected this belief in the *Wilkes* case when he suggested that "not [even] an Act of Parliament itself, is sufficient to warrant any proceeding contrary to the spirit of the constitution."[6] Thus, some followers of the Wilkesite cases could have read them for the principle that general warrants could not be authorized by statute. Certainly, this was true in America, where Coke's hold on the legal imagination was strong, in contrast to Britain, where William Blackstone's view of Parliamentary supremacy—that nothing, not even the common law, bound Parliament—was more influential. The point is that the Wilkesite cases held only that the searches there were unlawful because not authorized by statute.

Thus, the Wilkesite cases do indeed stand for the proposition that, by the 1760s, general warrants were considered unauthorized by common law in Britain. However, what gets lost is the idea that general warrants might well be legal if authorized by Parliament. The furor over these cases represents a particular instance of the centuries-long power struggle in Britain between the Crown and Parliament. The controversy over general warrants, dating back at least to the Tudor and Stuart regimes of the sixteenth century,[7] was a struggle over the use of the general warrant by the Crown and the efforts by Parliament to reign in this power. But Parliament did not take the position that general warrants could never be used; it merely sought to reserve to itself the authority to determine when they were appropriate. General warrants were acceptable "so long as Parliament had laid down the law."[8] Even when Parliament in April 1766 attempted to pass a statute condemning general warrants—an effort that failed—it was careful to reserve its own power to authorize them: the motion was "to declare all General Warrants, for seizing and apprehending any person or persons, to be illegal, *except in cases provided for by act of [P]arliament.*"[9]

The Wilkesite cases thus limited the prerogative of the executive in favor of the legislature. They stand for the proposition that the search-and-seizure power is so great, so potentially destructive of liberty in the hands of the executive, that it must be tightly controlled by the democratically elected legislature. So understood, these cases are limited in their application to the United States. The framers and ratifiers surely did not mean to place ultimate control of searches and seizures in the *national* legislature, as in Britain, given that the Amendment was understood as a constraint on Congress itself. But in light of the fact that general warrants continued to be authorized by colonial and state legislatures even after the War for Independence,[10] it appears that the Wilkesite cases were not understood to mean that such warrants could never be used. Instead, the Wilkesite cases are best understood as expressing the sentiment that search-and-seizure activity must be controlled by the democratic process. Examination of the writs-of-assistance controversy will show that only a democratic process that is truly representative and accountable would do the trick. Control over searches and seizures had to be not only *democratic* but *local.*

Local Control of Search-and-Seizure Policy: The Writs-of-Assistance Controversy

I will spend a bit more time discussing the writs-of-assistance controversy of the 1760s because it is almost uniformly thought to be the single most important episode in colonial history to shed light on the meaning of the Fourth Amendment.[11] There is also a direct causal link between this controversy and American Independence, which came in the next decade. As John Adams would later write, it was in the cauldron of the writs-of-assistance controversy that "'the child Independence was born.'"[12] A close examination of this episode shows that the touchstone of the colonists' complaints about the writs was the loss of local control over search-and-seizure policy: that despite their unquestionable legality in England, the writs were illegal in the colonies. Moreover, not every colony agreed that the writs were unlawful, and they were actually issued in Massachusetts, New Hampshire, New York, and South Carolina.

Writs of assistance were akin to general search warrants. However, they were especially pernicious in at least three respects. First, they could be obtained by customs officials as a matter of course, without any allegation of illegal activity. Second, judges were required to issue them and had no further role in overseeing their execution. Finally, they did not expire upon seizure and return of stolen or untaxed goods, as with an ordinary warrant, but instead were operative until six months after the death of the monarch under which they were issued.

Such writs were used in Massachusetts beginning in 1755 by customs officials searching for untaxed goods. However, a controversy arose with the death of King George II in late 1760, and the consequent expiration of all extant writs of assistance in the spring of 1761. When new writs were requested in Massachusetts by English authorities, a group of Boston merchants resisted and hired prominent Boston attorney James Otis to represent them. In the proceeding before the Massachusetts Superior Court that became known as *Paxton's Case*, Otis eloquently pointed out the perniciousness of general warrants and offered a persuasive defense of specific warrants as an alternative. He argued that in the case of felony, "an officer may break" into a dwelling only "by a Special Warrant to search such a House, sworn to be suspected, and good Grounds of suspicion appearing."[13]

Paxton's Case is best viewed as the culmination of a century-long push in Massachusetts toward local control of search-and-seizure policy. Otis's legal arguments in favor of specific warrants were severely flawed. As the

Wilkesite cases tell us, general warrants in England were legal as long as they were authorized by Parliament. General warrants and writs of assistance were the norm in Britain, not an aberration. Indeed, the writ of assistance was an example given in the Wilkesite case of *Money* v. *Leach* of a general warrant authorized by Parliament.[14] Moreover, it was unmistakably clear that English law applied to Massachusetts in that respect. Otis's mistake—or, perhaps, his gambit—was to conflate established English law with evolving Massachusetts law. The colony had, over the course of the prior century, become increasingly hostile toward general warrants, culminating in legislation in 1756 that "abandon[ed] general warrants in favor of warrants founded on some elements of particularity."[15] Otis's argument ignored the growing gulf between Massachusetts law and English law. Only according to the law of Massachusetts were specific warrants favored.[16] Perhaps unsurprisingly, Otis lost and the Massachusetts Superior Court ruled that writs of assistance could issue.

In a January 4, 1762, *Boston Gazette* piece, Otis attempted to support his argument that customs officials in Massachusetts should be required to use specific warrants, despite the fact that they were permitted to use general warrants in England. His argument focused on the relative degree of control over customs officials in the respective locales. In England, he pointed out, customs officials were subject to the complete control of the court of exchequer, even extending to physical discipline when necessary: "In *England* the exchequer has the power of controuling them in *every respect*; and even of *inflicting corporal punishment upon them for mal-conduct*." As such, they were accountable to the court of exchequer, and were called to account on a weekly basis for their conduct. Accordingly, the people had effective control over customs officials in England and had "a short and easy method of redress, in case of injury receiv'd from them." But no such "*checks and restrictions*" existed in Massachusetts, "and therefore the writ of assistance ought to be look'd upon as a *different thing* there, from what it is here." As Otis put it, the writ of assistance gave the customs officer greater power in Massachusetts than in England, "*greater* because UNCONTROUL'D—and can a community be safe with an uncontroul'd power lodg'd in the hands of *such* officers[?]"[17]

The writs-of-assistance controversy was not primarily, as is generally thought, a dispute over a particular type of search-and-seizure practice. It was primarily a dispute over who gets to decide what those practices will be: a distant central government or a local, politically accountable one. Britain's position was that Parliament remained sovereign over the colonies despite their lack of representation in that body because "Parliament and colonial legislatures cannot simultaneously reign supreme." Though the colonies were not represented in Parliament, Britain justified central control of search-and-seizure policy on "the idea of one indivisible location for the sovereignty of a nation, Parliament being that location."[18]

What Americans complained about was not general searches per se but their "lack of voice in the decision about when and how searches may happen." They revolted against the writs primarily because "their existence and content were determined by a legislative process in which the colonists had no voice."[19] This was Otis's chief complaint. As the Wilkesite cases showed, even general warrants were acceptable so long as they were authorized by Parliament. The real complaint was not so much with general warrants, which continued to be issued widely in the colonies, but with the prescription of such warrants by Parliament rather than by colonial legislatures. It was only when general warrants "loomed from a foreign quarter and threatened [the] political autonomy" of the colonists that such warrants were suddenly seen as a threat to their liberties.[20] What was critical was not that the writs acted as general warrants but "that the expanded jurisdiction of the writs was authorized by an unrepresentative British Parliament increasingly seen as lacking sovereign authority over America."[21]

Indeed, colonial judges issued general warrants even as colonists railed against British writs of assistance. As Andy Taslitz pointed out: "Despite growing condemnation of general searches by intellectuals and even by the judiciary, the typical searches actually authorized by colonial judges and legislatures at the time were every bit as general as those under the writs of assistance."[22] General warrants continued to be issued regularly by local, colonial judges right up until the break with England, and judges in at least five States continued to issue them after the Revolutionary War.[23] The nominal dispute over the writs masked the much larger conflict over political representation, which ultimately exploded into violence at the Lexington town green.[24] The writs were merely a symptom. The disease was loss of local, democratic controls over executive officials.

In the colonial response to *Paxton's Case*, too, we see a dramatic push toward local control of search-and-seizure policy. Not only did the local responses generally frustrate the policy of the central government, but the responses differed in important respects by colony. In Massachusetts, a legislative response was attempted. The legislature there passed a bill in March 1762 to nullify the decision in *Paxton's Case* by essentially transforming writs of assistance into specific warrants. The bill would have "limited the duration of writs of assistance to seven days, based them on oath, and required that they designate the informer, the accused owner of contraband, and the alleged place of concealment."[25] Although the measure was vetoed by the governor, it stands as an example of "an effort to compel British customs officers to observe the restraints on searches that their local counterparts already accepted."[26]

Responses in other colonies were varied. After passage of the Townshend Acts in Britain in 1767, which endowed colonial courts with jurisdiction to issue writs of assistance, most of the colonial judiciaries were forced to confront the issue, and they did so in diverse ways. In one group of colonies—Connecticut, Maryland, Pennsylvania, and Rhode Island—judges either refused to grant the writs, ignored requests for them, or engaged in dilatory tactics in the hopes that customs officials would give up. Courts in Maryland chose largely to ignore the requests.[27] The Rhode Island Superior Court used indefinite delay to frustrate customs officials.[28] Like those in its neighbor to the east, judges in Connecticut also delayed in considering the writs, though arguably this was in a good-faith effort to determine their legality.[29] Judges in Connecticut later rejected requests for writs, offering instead to issue them as specific warrants, as did judges in Pennsylvania.[30]

By contrast, judges in another group of colonies—Virginia, Georgia, New York, and South Carolina—were more moderate, or at least more equivocal, in their responses to requests for writs. Virginia courts, taking a middle-of-the-road approach, granted writs that were general but were acceptable to colonial sensibilities in other respects: they were of definite duration rather than perpetual and were issued only when based on sworn allegations.[31] The judges of Georgia expressed a willingness to issue general writs, but refused to do so unless the need arose in a particular case.[32] In South Carolina, judges initially avoided responding to requests for writs of assistance while privately concluding that they were illegal. However, in 1773, the newly reconstituted high court of South Carolina ruled the writs legal and issued a number of them.[33] In New York, the situation was reversed: judges there initially issued writs, later practiced the same kind of intransigence seen in Rhode Island, and finally outright refused to issue them.[34]

Though it is tempting to see the colonial opposition as monolithic, the record discloses a more nuanced picture. Not all judges asserted colonial independence from the Crown, and those that did varied in their approach.[35]

Judicial intransigence in some colonies was accompanied by foot-dragging and interference by executive officials. In one instance, faced with indefinite delay by the Rhode Island Superior Court in considering writs, customs officials went to the governor, only to be delayed further by the actions of the governor, the judge advocate, and a deputy sheriff. Ultimately, a writ was issued as a specific warrant, but night fell before it could be executed, allowing locals to remove the sought-after contraband.[36] In Connecticut, the chief justice who had politely declined to issue the writs based on doubts about their legality also served as lieutenant governor of the colony. And when the British attempted to remove him from office based on the notion of separation of powers, the people of the colony blocked the attempt. In Pennsylvania, the chief justice sought and obtained the opinion of the colony's attorney general, who agreed with him that the writs were illegal. In Virginia, the governor himself was on the court that permitted general but limited writs.[37]

As had occurred in Massachusetts, colonial legislatures sometimes became involved. For example, in Connecticut, the chief justice, opining that "the superior court could do nothing contrary to the sense of the people," suggested that the General Assembly of the colony take up the issue of the legality of the writs. The General Assembly took the chief justice up on his proposal, appointed a committee to study the question, and ultimately punted based on the committee's conclusion that the matter "properly belonged to the Superior Court." Privately, however, the General Assembly "advised the judges not to grant the writs."[38]

Accordingly, the writs-of-assistance controversy represents an episode in which local control over search-and-seizure policy was strongly asserted against the central government, in this case the Crown. *Paxton's Case* clearly held the writs to be legal in Massachusetts, and the Townshend Act clearly extended their legality to the rest of the colonies. Yet centralized search-and-seizure policy was frustrated, and local policy made supreme, by the actions of local legislative, executive, and judicial officials. It is tempting to look back upon the writs-of-assistance controversy and see a widespread revolt by the colonists against the use of general warrants. With all the benefits of hindsight, we know that the colonists did unite in revolt in the following decade. We also know that general warrants were widely deemed unlawful by 1791, as their prohibition in the Fourth Amendment demonstrates. Yet general warrants were not universally reviled on this side of the Atlantic in the 1760s. Some States continued to use them even after Independence. And, as shown above, general warrants were issued to Crown officials in half—five out of ten—of the colonies for which data are available. A more nuanced view of the writs of assistance controversy shows that it was largely about holding Crown officials to local standards. True, the specific issue raised by the writs-of-assistance controversy—the legality of general warrants—was ultimately settled in a uniform way by the Fourth Amendment's Warrant Clause. However, the controversy stands for the more general proposition that the colonists sought not continent-wide rules, but local control of Crown officials.

The colonial response during the writs of assistance episode also tends to refute the argument of Reasonableness Model advocates that warrants were seen during the framing period as a bad thing, not a good thing. First, Otis's central argument in *Paxton's Case*—the initial colonial response to British assumption of power to obtain writs of assistance—was not that British officers must act without warrants and hold themselves vulnerable to suit. Rather, it was that they must obtain specific warrants. After Otis lost, the attempted legislative response in Massachusetts was in the same vein: to allow only those writs of assistance that met the requirements of limited duration, oath, and specificity. Moreover, of the four colonies with the strongest judicial reaction against issuing writs, judges in two (Connecticut and Pennsylvania) issued them or offered to issue them as specific warrants instead. Their response was not anti-warrant.

In short, the dispute over the writs of assistance was superficially about the search-and-seizure policy of the British Empire. But too sharp a focus on the propriety of the writs themselves ignores the real issue: political representation. Again, Taslitz: "British search and seizure policies and practices were . . . inextricably intertwined with conflicting and changing understandings of the meanings of political 'representation' and associated, if implicit, notions of voice, autonomy, and inclusion."[39] The writs-of-assistance controversy supports the notion that the Fourth Amendment was designed, not to enshrine particular search-and-seizure rules on a nationwide basis, but to ensure that those rules would be formulated by localized, politically accountable decision-makers, not central planners.

From Empire to Confederation to Republic

Following Independence, two more episodes occurred that demonstrate that local democratic control, not warrants or generalized reasonableness, was the lodestar for the freedoms enshrined in the Fourth Amendment. First, in the Articles of Confederation period, the brief period in the 1780s after the Revolutionary War but before the Constitution, much of the state legislation ratifying a proposed 1783 confederal impost explicitly held federal officers to the search-and-seizure restrictions in the respective States. Then, two pieces of early federal legislation explicitly held federal officers to the standards of the States in which they operated, demonstrating that such a patchwork approach was unremarkable in the early Republic and suggesting that adherence to state law was the touchstone of reasonableness.

Local Control Under the Confederation: State Legislation Ratifying the Proposed 1783 Confederal Impost Resolution

Americans continued after the Revolution and before ratification of the Constitution to assert local control over search-and-seizure policy. Specifically, during the Articles of Confederation period, state legislation ratifying a proposed 1783 confederal impost resolution demonstrates the importance of state control over search-and-seizure rules. On April 18, 1783, the Confederation Congress recommended that it be granted the power to levy duties on some imports, such as rum, tea, sugar, coffee, wine, and molasses.[40] Because it would grant a new power to the Congress not contained in the Articles, the resolution required ratification by each and every State before it could take effect. The ratifying legislation tells us much about the way the rights ultimately expressed in the Fourth Amendment in 1791 were viewed within the previous decade.

Eight of the States that passed legislation ratifying the confederal impost included what can be called "mini bills of rights" that explicitly required that the confederal government abide by certain search-and-seizure rules in enforcing the impost regulations.[41] Five—Georgia, Massachusetts, New Hampshire, South Carolina, and Virginia—required the confederal government to obtain a search warrant, though not necessarily a specific one, in order "to break open any dwelling house, store or ware-house."[42] Pennsylvania's legislation was less protective than this baseline, requiring a warrant (again, not necessarily a specific one) only for "dwelling house[s]."[43]

The other two States that enacted explicit search-and-seizure constraints on the confederal government—North Carolina and Rhode Island—imposed more stringent requirements. First, they included *all* premises within the prohibition.[44] Additionally, these two States required that such warrants be specific: Rhode Island required that the warrant "particularly discriminat[e] the dwelling-house, store, ware-house, or other building,"[45] and North Carolina provided that a warrant could be granted with regard to "such house" where uncustomed goods were suspected of being.[46]

Three States imposed search-and-seizure constraints by generally requiring that the confederal government follow the respective state constitutions and laws in collecting the impost. Delaware required that "such rules and ordinances for collecting and levying the . . . duties . . . *be not repugnant to the constitution and laws of this state*,"[47] and Maryland similarly required that "such ordinances, regulations and arrangements . . . for the faithful and punctual payment and collection of the . . . duties . . . *shall not be repugnant to the constitution of this state*."[48] Because the Delaware and Maryland constitutions required the use of specific warrants, their legislation ratifying the confederal impost required the same.[49] Connecticut's legislation imposed constraints on the central government in a more roundabout way by directing its citizens to adhere to confederal impost regulations except to the extent that they were "inconsistent with the constitution and internal police of this state."[50]

Finally, New York's conditional ratification, which the confederal Congress rejected, required that its own officials, who obviously would have to abide by state law, enforce the impost. Only New Jersey imposed no constraints on the search-and-seizure authority of confederal officials in enforcing the proposed impost legislation.[51]

In sum, ten of the thirteen States in ratifying the proposed confederal impost regulation of 1783 required confederal authorities to obtain warrants supported by oath[52] in collecting the impost. Four of those ten—Delaware, Maryland, North Carolina, and Rhode Island—required, expressly or by necessary implication, that those warrants be specific, while the other six did not. The States also differed as to whether any types of premises could be searched warrantlessly: Pennsylvania's warrant requirement applied only to dwellings; Georgia, Massachusetts, New Hampshire, South Carolina, and Virginia applied their requirement to stores and warehouses in addition to dwellings; North Carolina and Rhode Island applied it to all buildings; and it is unclear how far Delaware's and Maryland's respective warrant requirements extended. While nine of these ten required that searches be conducted in daytime, it is unclear whether Delaware did.[53] Of the three that did not require warrants, two required that collectors of the impost adhere to state law generally: Connecticut, by authorizing its residents to ignore any impost regulations inconsistent with state law, and New York, by requiring that the enforcers of the impost be state agents.

Thus, as late as 1786 (when legislation was enacted in the final State, Rhode Island)—three years before the Bill of Rights was drafted and five years before it was ratified—a patchwork of search-and-seizure rules, different in significant respects, was contemplated. This crazy quilt of rules that varied by State meant that *national* officials were to be constrained in different parts of the country in different ways depending upon the State in which they acted. Accordingly, Americans of that period were quite accustomed to the idea that national officials would be subjected to different search-and-seizure rules on a State-by-State basis. Indeed, this was, in essence, already the case. Anyone committing a trespass, confederal official or not, would be liable to suit under whatever state law applied. The impost ratification legislation was simply explicit in preserving the status quo.

The idea was so non-controversial that the confederal Congress readily accepted the search-and-seizure constraints that came as conditions accompanying the ratifications of eleven of the twelve States that imposed them. It was only when New York demanded that the collectors of the impost in that State be state employees that the Congress balked, deeming confederal superintendence over the impost collectors to be "an essential part of the plan."[54]

One might argue that this arrangement under the Articles of Confederation is weak evidence of what was contemplated by the Constitution. The Constitution, after all, was developed as an antidote to the anemic government under the Articles, a centralizing force in stark contrast to the decentralizing Articles. This assertion, however, misses the entire point of the Bill of Rights. As will be explored more fully in the next chapter, the Bill was a concession to the Anti-Federalist opponents of the Constitution who had feared that it would consolidate too much power in the hands of the federal government at the expense of the States. While the Constitution represented an advancement toward centralization, the Bill of Rights represented a countervailing step back toward the kind of decentralization epitomized by the Articles. In much the same way that the centripetal forces of the Constitution were a reaction to the decentralizing tendencies of the Articles, pulling the Nation together, the centrifugal forces of the Bill of Rights were a reaction to the centralizing tendencies of the Constitution, allowing for differentiation by States to be preserved. As the Constitution drew the Nation in and imposed uniformity, the Bill of Rights carved out spheres where variety and diversity could thrive.

Finally, observe that the States' conditional ratification of the 1783 confederal impost legislation demonstrates a clear preference for warrants, further undermining the claim of Reasonableness Model adherents that warrants were actually disfavored by the framers and ratifiers of the Fourth Amendment. Ten of the thirteen States implicitly or explicitly required that confederal officers obtain warrants prior to searching or seizing. These measures were passed in order to hem in the authority of confederal excise collectors, not to immunize them from suit. If Reasonableness Model proponents were correct, those States would have forbidden the use of warrants, leaving confederal officers open to common-law tort suits for trespass in state courts.

Thus, in the decade before the Fourth Amendment was adopted, the warrant was viewed primarily as a constraint on central authority, not a get-out-of-jail-free card.

Local Control Under the Republic: Contingent Federal Search-and-Seizure Authority in Early Legislation

Two early pieces of federal legislation, the Judiciary Act of 1789 and the Militia Act of 1792, specifically granted federal officers the same search-and-seizure authority that analogous state officers had under the laws of the respective States. Thus, federal legislation expressly calibrated a federal officer's search-and-seizure authority to the laws of the State in which he acted. Once again, this time following ratification of the Constitution, we see the assertion of local norms binding actors of the central government vis-à-vis search and seizure. While this falls short of definitive proof that the Constitution requires compliance with state law, the absence of any statutory language setting a constitutional floor strongly implies that Congress meant these statutes to track the constitutional limits on federal search-and-seizure authority. That is, by following state law, federal officials were necessarily acting reasonably under the Fourth Amendment.

Section 33 of the Judiciary Act of 1789, enacted by the First Congress, provided that

> for any crime or offence against the United States, the offender may, by any justice or judge of the United States, or by any justice of the peace, or other magistrate of any of the United States where he may be found *agreeably to the usual mode of process against offenders in such state* . . . be arrested.[55]

Although directed to judicial officers, not executive officials, the term "usual mode of process" was understood by contemporary lawyers as referring to arrest warrants. Thus, Congress essentially authorized arrest by warrant by federal officers and "assumed the applicability of state laws and practices" to regulate such arrests.[56]

Then, in 1792, the Second Congress passed the Militia Act, section 9 of which granted federal marshals and their deputies "the same powers in executing the laws of the United States, as sheriffs and their deputies in the several states have by law, in executing the laws of their respective states."[57] While section 33 of the Judiciary Act dictated that federal power to issue and execute arrest warrants would track state law, the Militia Act provided that federal power to otherwise search and seize would generally do so as well, except as provided by more specific federal legislation, such as the Collection Act of 1789 and the Excise Act of 1791.[58]

It is true that ordinary citizens already had the same common-law power to make arrests as did constables and sheriffs, and that federal marshals and their deputies had no less inherent authority than private persons.[59] However, as of 1792, there was sufficient dispute over whether and to what extent common-law precepts applied to the new federal government that it would have been unclear the extent to which, if at all, ordinary citizens could make warrantless arrests for *federal* crimes. Given this lack of clarity, Congress granted federal officers the express authority to arrest for federal crimes that matched the power to arrest for state offenses.

In addition, the 1792 Act grants federal officers *all* "the same powers in executing the laws" enjoyed by state officers, including several powers generally denied to ordinary citizens. For example, state officers generally enjoyed the power to execute search warrants, whereas private persons did not.[60] In addition, eighteenth-century justice of the peace manuals took pains to differentiate between the arrest powers of government officials and those of private persons. So, for example, one such manual published in the same year of the Militia Act stated that "all persons" must apprehend a felon if the felony is committed in their presence, but only "a watchman may arrest a night walker" and only "a constable may *ex officio* arrest a breaker of the peace in his view."[61] Likewise, while private persons could halt an ongoing affray, they had no power to break doors to a private home to stop the affray or to arrest the affrayers once the tumult had concluded. Those powers lay exclusively with state officers.[62]

Moreover, although private persons and state officials alike could arrest for felonies, state officials generally had greater power to break doors to arrest for felonies than did private persons. In particular, a private person could not break doors to arrest "barely upon suspicion of felony," while "a *constable* in such case may justify."[63] While an ultimate finding of guilt of the arrestee could retroactively justify the private person's breaking of doors in such an instance, one could hardly say that the power of the private person and the state official were equivalent: only the latter could, on suspicion of felony, break doors to arrest even an innocent person. Thus, the 1792 Act clothed federal officers with precisely the same law enforcement powers as their state counterparts.

In sum, while the Fourth Amendment would dictate that a federal warrant must be particularized, founded upon oath, and issued only on probable cause, the Judiciary Act of 1789 and the Militia Act of 1792 together provide that state law would determine when a warrant was needed, how it must be executed, whether and to what extent an arrestee's person and effects could be searched, and so forth. And this state of affairs existed continuously from the earliest days of the Republic until the mid-1930s, when Congress first explicitly granted federal officers general search-and-seizure authority untethered to underlying state law.[64]

One might argue that, because the 1789 and 1792 Acts require federal officers to follow state law, the Fourth Amendment cannot impose that requirement, for then the legislation would be superfluous. But the Amendment establishes a rule of limitation, while the legislation is a grant of power. The legislation granted federal executive officers search-and-seizure power up to the limits of the Amendment. Absent the legislation, federal officers would have had no special powers to search or seize beyond that which was provided to ordinary citizens in each State. In effect, these provisions prohibited the States from treating federal officials as private persons and instead gave them the same search-and-seizure authority as state officials. But the Fourth Amendment prohibited Congress from going further than that.

No discussion of early federal search-and-seizure law would be complete without reference to three other early federal statutes. The Collection Act of 1789 permitted customs searches of ships without a warrant based on "reason to suspect" that goods subject to duty were concealed therein.[65] The Act of August 4, 1790, permitted warrantless and suspicionless searches of ships.[66] The Excise Act of 1791 permitted searches of "houses, store-houses, warehouses, buildings and [other] places" without warrant if those premises were registered as places where distilleries were located.[67] If these Acts shed light on the meaning of the Fourth Amendment, they would cut against the claim that the Amendment ties the search-and-seizure authority of the federal government to that of each respective State. And, indeed, the Court and a number of scholars have argued that the Acts tell us how the Fourth Amendment should be interpreted, based on the following syllogism: the same men who drafted these statutes also drafted the Fourth Amendment; they would not have drafted statutes that they believed violated the Fourth Amendment; therefore, we must assume that the men who drafted the Fourth Amendment believed that it permitted the searches authorized by the statutes.[68]

However, any inference that legislation passed by early Congresses was necessarily constitutional butts up against perhaps the most famous Supreme Court case in U.S. history, *Marbury* v. *Madison*, in which the Court famously declared unconstitutional another provision of the Judiciary Act of 1789.[69] Such an inference also butts up against the verdict of the court of history that the Fugitive Slave Act of 1793 and the Alien and Sedition Acts of 1798 were likewise unconstitutional.[70] Regarding the latter, Justice David Souter wrote in 1992: "If the early Congress's political actions were determinative, and not merely relevant, evidence of constitutional meaning, we would have to gut our current First Amendment doctrine to make room for political censorship."[71] Regarding the former, Judge Abram Smith of the Wisconsin Supreme Court wrote in 1854: "It is a remarkable fact that the most startling deviations from strict constitutional limits occurred in the very earliest years of the republic."[72]

Moreover, the syllogism itself is faulty because, while federal statutes are drafted by Congress and signed by the President, constitutional amendments are drafted by Congress *and ratified by the States.* Interpreting a constitutional provision requires consulting not just the Members of Congress who voted for it but the members of the legislatures of the three-fourths of the States that ultimately ratified it. And in the special case of the Bill of Rights, though we have little direct evidence of the understandings of the ratifiers, statements by the Anti-Federalist critics of the Constitution during the ratification debates stand in as a surrogate. The understandings of the Anti-Federalists loom large for, as we will see in Chapter 3, the Federalist-dominated Congress proposed the Bill of Rights solely to fulfill a pre-ratification promise to them. While Congress chose the precise wording of the amendments, the ideas that those words represent were dictated to Congress by the Anti-Federalists. House member James Madison drafted the Bill, yes, but in an important sense he merely held the pen through which the thoughts of men such as Patrick Henry, George Mason, and Melancton Smith flowed. As Justice William Brennan once instructed, an amendment to the Constitution cannot be treated

> simply as an Act of Congress, as to whose meaning the intent of Congress is the single touchstone. Both the Constitution and its Amendments . . . became supreme law only by virtue of their ratification by the States, and the understanding of the States should be as relevant to our analysis as the understanding of Congress. This observation is especially compelling in considering the meaning of the Bill of Rights. The first 10 Amendments were not enacted because the Members of the First Congress came up with a bright idea one morning; rather, their enactment was forced upon Congress by a number of the States

> as a condition for their ratification of the original Constitution. To treat any practice authorized by the First Congress as presumptively consistent with the Bill of Rights is therefore somewhat akin to treating any action of a party to a contract as presumptively consistent with the terms of the contract.[73]

To use Gerard Bradley's Melvillesque analogy, "the intentions of the whale (the anti-federalists) are more important than those of the ship's crew (the First Congress, especially Madison)."[74] In interpreting the Fourth Amendment, the views of the First Congress are of secondary importance.

In any event, the early federal acts permitting warrantless and even suspicionless shipboard searches likely tell us, if anything, that such searches were simply not seen as implicating the Fourth Amendment at all. It is true that some Americans of that period viewed ships as akin to dwellings in terms of searches and that the years of the writs-of-assistance controversy saw "ardent public hostility" toward shipboard searches.[75] However, Tom Davies has argued powerfully that ships were not viewed by the framing generation as falling within the "persons, houses, papers, and effects" formulation of the Fourth Amendment. If so, shipboard searches would have been viewed, not as "reasonable," but as not governed by the Fourth Amendment at all. According to Davies, ships were seen as governed by admiralty law, a branch of civil law outside the common-law protections afforded by the Fourth Amendment. As Davies noted, not a single Supreme Court case between 1789 and 1925 involving seizure of a ship so much as mentions the Fourth Amendment, powerful evidence that ships were viewed as simply falling outside the Amendment's terms.[76] Whether the early customs statutes reflect a consensus that the Fourth Amendment was inapplicable to shipboard searches, or were simply instances of early Congresses reading the Fourth Amendment in a stingy, pro-Federalist manner, they tell us little about the original understanding of the Amendment.

The 1791 Excise Act, by contrast, clearly implicated the Fourth Amendment because it applied to searches and seizures on land.[77] But this Act was bitterly opposed by Anti-Federalists and "was widely perceived as overly intrusive of privacy."[78] According to Francis Wharton: "A majority of the southern and western members [of Congress], even before the bill was passed, proclaimed an organized agitation for its repeal."[79] The few statements we have of House members debating the search provisions of the 1791 Act illustrate this: Virginia Anti-Federalist Rep. Josiah Parker objected to the provisions regarding "the mode of collecting the tax" as being "hostile to the liberties of the people." In vivid terms, he warned that the collections provisions would "let loose a swarm of harpies, who, under the denomination of revenue officers, will range through the country, prying into every man's house and affairs, and like a Macedonian phalanx bear down all before them." Rep. James Jackson, an anti-administration Federalist from Georgia, also opposed the Act as "unfriendly to the liberties of the people."[80] Even some generally pro-administration Federalists were against the Act on constitutional grounds. Rep. John Steele of North Carolina, for example, complained that the proposed Act would subject citizens "to the most unreasonable, unusual and disgustful situation of having their houses searched at any hour of the day or night."[81]

After the Act became law, it "triggered apocalyptic protests"[82] and "was assailed violently from the country at large."[83] Maryland, North Carolina, Pennsylvania, and Virginia "united in solemn declarations of rooted dislike, and of resistance" amounting to, in some cases, "nullification."[84] Delegates from Pennsylvania's western counties remonstrated to Congress that "[i]t is insulting to the feelings of the people to have their . . . houses . . . ransacked."[85] An essay in a New York newspaper, apparently reprinted from a North Carolina paper, objected that, pursuant to the Act, "every citizen's house in the United States, is liable to undergo the insult of a search." The essay continued that the Act "lays open the peaceable dwellings of the inhabitants of a country to the entrance, insults and rudeness of a set of unprincipled excisemen," and "disturb[s] the peace and happiness of their families by the entering, searching and ransacking their houses and closets, by a set of rude and insulting excisemen."[86]

Those familiar with the Whiskey Rebellion of 1794 know that the opposition to the 1791 Excise Act soon turned violent. Barely three months after the Act went into effect, the collector of revenues for Pennsylvania's western counties was attacked by a mob of "armed men, who stripped him, cut off his hair, tarred and feathered him," and stole his money and his horse. After a complaint was filed against members of the mob in federal court, a man attempting to serve the papers relating to the litigation was himself tarred and feathered, had his horse and watch stolen from him, and was blindfolded and tied up in the woods for five hours. These acts of domestic terrorism continued in western Pennsylvania for three years until, in 1794, opposition ripened into the Whiskey Rebellion, an armed uprising put down only when President Washington called in the militia.[87] The acts of the western Pennsylvania insurgents of the early 1790s belie any notion that the provisions of the 1791 Excise Act represent anything resembling a national consensus on the meaning of the Fourth Amendment.

The point here is not that the Excise Act was unconstitutional because it sparked violent protest. And, to be clear, the Act was opposed not just because of the way the tax was collected but also because of the tax itself. The point is simply that we cannot assume that the Excise Act was constitutional simply because it was enacted by the same Congress that proposed the Fourth Amendment. Pro-administration Federalists, who desired to empower the federal government, constituted a majority of the First Congress. But Anti-Federalists constituted a sizable minority.[88] Much of the legislation considered in the First Congress was seen as carrying over the issues from the ratification debates, particularly on the question of federalism. Fundamental questions about the nature of the young Republic were inherent in virtually every issue debated in the First Congress, and debate revolved around a Federalist/Anti-Federalist axis.[89]

Moreover, the 1791 Excise Act was the handiwork of none other than Treasury Secretary Alexander Hamilton, whom Anti-Federalists despised. Indeed, opposition to Hamilton was one point around which Anti-Federalists could rally; they generally voted as a united bloc against his proposals. Together with anti-administration Federalists, they sometimes came close to defeating those proposals.[90] It blinks reality to think that there existed any consensus view that the intrusive search provisions of an Act whose architect was the hated Secretary of the Treasury were constitutional.

In the First Congress, the Bill of Rights and ordinary legislation were on two different tracks. The Bill, though necessarily blessed by the Federalist majority, was an Anti-Federalist project. Statutes, by contrast, generally subordinated the concerns of the minority Anti-Federalists as part of the Federalist project of building a powerful central government. This gives us good reason to resist the facile notion that the expansive federal search authority created by the First Congress was necessarily consistent with the Fourth Amendment. It is not only, as Tracey Maclin put it, that "early Americans did not always practice what they preached";[91] it is also that they were preaching from two different pulpits.

But one can hardly say the same of the local-control provisions of the 1789 Judiciary Act and the 1792 Militia Act. By declining to establish federal search-and-seizure rules, and instead calibrating federal rules to those of each respective State, Congress avoided the kind of controversy—culminating in armed rebellion—engendered by the Excise Act. Unlike that Act, the local-control provisions of the Judiciary and Militia Acts represented a consensus view of Federalists and Anti-Federalists alike.

Of course, these statutes are evidence only of what members of the early Congresses believed the Fourth Amendment *permitted*, not what they thought it *required*. One might argue that compliance with section 33 of the Judiciary Act of 1789 or section 9 of the Militia Act of 1792 might put a federal officer afoul of the Fourth Amendment if a State's search-and-seizure rules fell below some constitutional minimum set by the Fourth Amendment. But notice what the statutes do not say: they do not authorize federal officials to follow state law *unless it would violate the Constitution to do so*. They authorize federal officials to follow state law, full stop. Compare this with the language of section 34 of the Judiciary Act of 1789, commonly known as the Rules of Decision Act, which does contain such a proviso: "[T]he laws of the several states, *except where the constitution, treaties or statutes of the United States shall otherwise require or provide*, shall be regarded as rules of decision in trials at common law in the courts of the United States in cases where they apply."[92] Congress could equally have provided in its next-door neighbor, section 33, that any federal "offender may . . . agreeably to the usual mode of process against offenders in such state . . . be arrested, *except where the constitution, treaties or statutes of the United States shall otherwise require or provide*." That they did not strongly suggests that federal marshals could not possibly violate the Fourth Amendment if they followed state law because by following state law they were necessarily abiding by the Fourth Amendment.[93] An "unreasonable" search or seizure was one that was inconsistent with state law.

Even to speak of government officials "violating the Fourth Amendment" is a prochronism that would have made no sense in 1791 because, to the framers and ratifiers, an individual federal officer could not possibly violate the Fourth Amendment. He could violate only state law. An officer's misconduct was not considered an illegal act by the government; it was merely an instance of personal misconduct to be redressed by state tort or criminal law. As Tom Davies wrote:

> [T]he officer exercised sovereign power when he executed a legal warrant, and he also exercised official authority deriving from his own office when acting without a warrant but within the lawful bounds of that office. . . . However . . . an officer's conduct *ceased to be official* if he exceeded his lawful authority; then he committed only an "unlawful" *personal* wrong for which he was subject to forcible resistance and trespass liability just as if he held no office at all.[94]

Only Congress could violate the Fourth Amendment, either by purporting to authorize the issuance of general warrants or permit warrantless actions by federal officers inconsistent with state law, either of which would ostensibly immunize federal officers from suit, thereby displacing state law governing searches and seizures. Again, that is why Madison's initial version of the Amendment was to be placed in Article I. The Amendment preserves the power of each State to prescribe search-and-seizure rules within its borders by subjecting even federal officers to its own law.

Conclusion

A common thread runs through the writs-of-assistance controversy of the 1760s, the state impost law ratifications of the 1780s, and the early federal legislation of the 1790s: local control over search-and-seizure policy. If this view is correct, then Reasonableness Model adherents and Warrant Model advocates are each partly right and partly wrong. The Fourth Amendment does subject federal officials to a standard of reasonableness, not a regime of warrants. But it is not a freestanding reasonableness standard to be constructed freehand by unelected federal judges. It is a standard of reasonableness tied to and established by local law: statutes enacted by local legislatures, common-law doctrines determined by local judges, and normative judgments made by local juries. By the same token, the Fourth Amendment does sometimes require that federal officials use warrants, but only when, and only to the extent that, their state counterparts also fall under this obligation. Both the Reasonableness and the Warrant Model correctly home in on the key aim of the Fourth Amendment: the control of executive discretionary authority to search and seize. But that control would not necessarily be maintained by a strict warrant requirement enforced by judges ex ante nor by a reasonableness requirement enforced by juries ex post, but by a regime of local democratic controls on federal officers.

These attempts to reserve local control of search-and-seizure policy dovetail almost perfectly with the Anti-Federalist impetus behind the Fourth Amendment. It was these opponents of the Constitution who ultimately compromised, demanding a Bill of Rights with robust protections for state norms as the price for their acquiescence to union. They demanded that certain spheres of human activity be carved out of the centralization agenda of the Federalists and be retained for local control. One of those areas, because of the grave potential for abuse, was search-and-seizure law. It is to this story that we now turn.

Three

The Anti-Federalists and the Fourth Amendment

This chapter focuses on the Anti-Federalists. It was these opponents of the Constitution who ultimately compromised, demanding a Bill of Rights with robust protections for individual rights and state norms as the price for their acquiescence to union. They demanded that certain spheres of human activity be carved out of the centralization agenda of the Federalist champions of the Constitution and be retained for local control. One of those areas, because of the grave potential for abuse, was search-and-seizure law. In chapter 2, we explored the writs-of-assistance controversy and two other attempts in early American history to preserve local control of search-and-seizure policy. These attempts dovetail almost perfectly with the Anti-Federalist impetus behind the Fourth Amendment.

This chapter will first introduce the political agenda of the Anti-Federalists and the vital role they played in the adoption of the Bill of Rights. It will then discuss the Anti-Federalists' view of the deep interconnections between state sovereignty and individual liberty, which led them to demand that state common-law protections of liberty be preserved. It then discusses their state-centered, proto-Realist view of the common law, and how this view came to dominate political and legal discourse shortly after the founding. Finally, it discusses how the Anti-Federalists' view of the common law and of the interconnections between federalism and rights translates into a view of the Fourth Amendment that emphasizes local control of search-and-seizure policy rather than either warrants or general reasonableness.

Who Were the Anti-Federalists and Why Do We Care?

The first order of business is to explore why exactly we should care what the Anti-Federalist opponents of the Constitution wrote and said about constitutional restrictions on federal search-and-seizure authority. After all, the Anti-Federalists lost the ratification battle. But "we distort history when we ignore the losers in a conflict, because losing movements are forces which at every moment have influenced the final outcome."[1] Too many scholars of the Bill of Rights have ignored the influence of the Anti-Federalists.

The Bill of Rights was added to the Constitution as an implicit condition for ratification. Without the promise of such a bill, ratification almost surely would have failed. The Anti-Federalists initially were in the majority in Massachusetts, New Hampshire, New York, North Carolina, and Virginia.[2] Indeed, in New York, popular sentiment was opposed to ratification by a margin of greater than two to one.[3] The Federalists soon realized that they would need to promise the adoption of a bill of rights shortly after ratification in order to ensure that the Constitution would be ratified. In Massachusetts, the first State in which the Constitution met with serious opposition, ratification would have been impossible had the Federalists not agreed to propose amendments to Congress.[4] Likewise, "the Federalists of Virginia realized that they were not a commanding majority and would have to compromise to avert rejection of the Constitution or irresistible demands for its radical modification."[5] That compromise consisted of a promise of a bill of rights, and even with that promise, the vote was a close one: 89 to 79.[6]

Virginia and New York, the tenth and eleventh States to ratify, were particularly critical. Although the Constitution technically went into effect when the ninth State to ratify, New Hampshire, did so on June 21, 1788, a Union without New York and Virginia would have been almost inconceivable. Without New York, which separated New England from the rest of the young nation, and Virginia, which included the present States of West Virginia and Kentucky and stretched from the Atlantic to the Mississippi, the Union would have been left in three noncontiguous pieces, and deprived of almost 30 percent of its population and one of its busiest ports.[7] Only by pledging to advance the adoption of a bill of rights as one of the first orders of business of the new government did the Federalists secure ratification by swaying a sufficient number of moderate Anti-Federalists in these two States to their fold.

By "moderate Anti-Federalists," I refer to those who were at first opposed to the Constitution but ultimately voted for it based on the promise of a bill of rights. While hard-line Anti-Federalists voted against the Constitution in the ratifying conventions, and were thus not a party to the compromise, the moderates were. At the New York ratifying convention, following ratification by ten other States, these more moderate Anti-Federalists sought not outright rejection of the Constitution but "assurances that the defects of the proposed Constitution could be remedied."[8]

Thus, we have to look to men like Melancton Smith, the leader of the moderate Anti-Federalist faction at the New York ratifying convention.[9] Alone among the leaders of the Anti-Federalist cause in New York, Smith possessed "a sufficient degree of moderation to recognize the crisis that exclusion from the Union might produce."[10] Aside from the "economic and political chaos" that would result from New York's being left out of the Union, rejection of the Constitution also risked secession of the southern part of the State, including New York City.[11] Smith and his allies thus favored union but based only on the prospect of amending the Constitution to better reflect the legitimate state sovereignty concerns of the Anti-Federalists. Accordingly, the convention reached a compromise that the Constitution would be ratified but would also be accompanied not only by proposed amendments, as in Massachusetts and Virginia, but also by a letter sent to the other States calling for a second convention at which amendments could be considered. Smith ultimately voted in favor of ratification, taking eleven other moderate Anti-Federalists with him. The final vote for ratification in New York was 30–27.[12] We have Smith to thank, as much as Madison or Hamilton, for the Nation as we know it today. Because that small band of moderate Anti-Federalists led by Smith formed the fulcrum upon which ratification, and a viable Union, turned, their views should be considered paramount when interpreting the Bill of Rights.

Even after Virginia and New York ratified and the First Congress was in session, "[r]atification remained incomplete, revocable, and precarious." In addition to New York, three other States had coupled their ratification with a proposal for a second constitutional convention, which might start pulling threads from the delicate fabric of compromises struck in Philadelphia. Had an adequate bill of rights not been quickly adopted, "a second convention might have . . . gutted the Constitution" via much more radical changes in the constitutional structure.[13] James Madison viewed the result of the New York ratifying convention—ratification coupled with proposed amendments and a call for a second convention—"to be a complete victory for the Antifederalists."[14] The Bill of Rights was necessary, in Madison's words, "in order to extinguish opposition" to the new Constitution.[15]

For Madison, the issue was one of political life or death. The future President saw that he needed to back the proposed amendments following ratification or risk political suicide. In his home State of Virginia, the Anti-Federalists had only gained in power since ratification.[16] The Virginia legislature rejected Madison's bid for a U.S. Senate seat and instead chose two Anti-Federalists to fill the positions. Through what we would today call "gerrymandering," his political enemies almost succeeded in keeping him out of the U.S. House of Representatives as well. He won election to the House only because he made a commitment to his constituents to pursue a bill of rights. Madison "readily admitted that he would not have been elected without a Federalist commitment to amendments, nor would Virginia have ratified the Constitution in the absence of that commitment."[17] He felt duty bound to follow through on this pledge. Moreover, at the time he proposed the Bill of Rights in the House, North Carolina and Rhode Island still had not ratified, and one prominent Federalist from North Carolina informed him that the State would refuse ratification unless amendments were forthcoming.[18] In his speech introducing the Bill in the House, Madison invoked the need to entice these last two States into the Union.[19] And he conceded privately that the Bill of Rights was a "direct response[] to these political pressures."[20]

In short, the Bill of Rights was attributable almost entirely to the Federalists' efforts to placate moderate Anti-Federalists. As Murray Dry put it: "[W]hile the Federalists gave us the Constitution, the Anti-Federalists gave us the Bill of Rights."[21] For these reasons, "Anti-Federalist political thought is essential to understanding the meaning of the Bill of Rights."[22] That explains why the Supreme Court has cited the Anti-Federalists when interpreting virtually every provision of the Bill of Rights.[23] Thus, when interpreting the Bill, we must look to what men like moderate Anti-Federalist leader Melancton Smith sought to accomplish with it.

Incorporation of the Anti-Federalist worldview into our interpretive strategies suggests a view of the Bill of Rights that looks to *state* law as the benchmark for *federal* rights, at least where the capacious language of the Bill cries out for a benchmark. In the words of Robert Palmer: "The Antifederalist origin to the demand for a Bill of Rights dictates a state-oriented approach to the Bill of Rights."[24] This is because of the Anti-Federalist view that individual liberty is tied to state power.

The Anti-Federalist Notion of State Sovereignty as a Guarantor of Individual Liberty

The Anti-Federalists opposed the Constitution because they feared that its concentration of power in the central government would lead to both the annihilation of the state governments and the destruction of individual liberty. They believed that the proposed new central government would draw power away from the States, leaving them weak and enervated, leading to infringement of the rights of their citizens. This sounds odd to modern ears because we tend to view individual rights as being in tension with government power. But the Anti-Federalists saw things differently. They saw responsive, accountable state government as the guardian of liberty. The threat to freedom came, not from government in general, but from centralized government. The Anti-Federalists viewed the States as the protectors of individual rights.[25] Every State recognized the individual rights of its citizens through a constitution, bill of rights, or a very strong common-law tradition.[26] State power and individual rights were intertwined in their minds: the States were positioned as the guarantors of freedom as against any central government, be it the British Empire, the Confederation Congress, or the proposed federal government.

The central innovation of the Constitution was that the new federal government could act directly upon the people—it could require or forbid conduct by individuals, so long as it was within the federal government's enumerated powers—unlike the Confederation government, which could act only on the States. A new central government that could act directly upon the citizenry without having to go through the States would be able to bypass all state-level protections of liberty. The greatest fear of the Anti-Federalists, spurring them to demand a federal bill of rights, was that the state constitutions and bills of rights would be ineffectual to protect the citizenry from the new federal government's exercise of broad new powers. Of particular concern were the Necessary and Proper Clause, which gives an open-ended means by which Congress can effectuate its enumerated powers, and the Supremacy Clause, which explicitly subordinates state norms to federal power.[27] And because the federal government would be acting directly upon the citizenry, state constitutions, bills of rights, and common-law protections were no barrier. The new government could simply sidestep the protections that had developed through centuries of Anglo-American law, such as the right to a jury trial and the privilege against self-incrimination. Preservation of individual freedom was thus inextricably linked to the preservation of state power; states' rights and individual rights were intertwined.[28]

Anti-Federalist George Mason summed up these concerns in the very first sentence of his *Objections to the Constitution of Government Formed by the Convention*.[29] Mason, who attended the Constitutional Convention but refused to sign the Constitution, published his *Objections* before the ink was dry on the Constitution, and his *Objections* became "the first salvo in the paper war over ratification."[30] Mason's *Objections* were second only to those of Elbridge Gerry in their significance and influence among other Anti-Federalists.[31] Mason began his *Objections* this way: "There is no Declaration of Rights; and the Laws of the general Government being paramount to the Laws and Constitutions of the several States, the Declaration of Rights in the separate States are no Security."[32] Thus, Mason's very first reason for opposing the Constitution was that, because the Supremacy Clause subordinated state bills of rights, these were "no [s]ecurity" against the federal government.

The concern that the Constitution would weaken state governments and neuter their bills of rights to the detriment of individual liberty was echoed by Anti-Federalists in state ratifying conventions and political tracts up and down the continent. At the Pennsylvania convention, Robert Whitehill said that the Constitution would be "the means of annihilating the constitutions of the several States, and consequently the liberties of the people" and that "the dissolution of our State constitutions will produce the ruin of civil liberty."[33] In one widely read tract, Pennsylvania Anti-Federalist Centinel (George or Samuel Bryan) echoed these sentiments, writing that "the general government would necessarily annihilate the particular [i.e., state] governments, and . . . the security of the personal rights of the people by the state constitutions [would be] superseded and destroyed."[34] Similarly, in the Virginia ratifying convention the following June, Patrick Henry (of "Give me liberty or give me death" fame) declared that the Constitution would "annihilate[]" the state government, leaving it powerless, rendering the state bill of rights a barrier only against a "weakened, prostrated, enervated State Government," and therefore a nullity.[35] Likewise, at the New York ratifying convention, Thomas Tredwell expressly tied the loss of state power to the loss of individual liberty when he lamented: "Here we find no security for the rights of individuals, no security for the existence of our state governments; here is no bill of rights, no proper restriction of power; our lives, our property, and our consciences, are left wholly at the mercy of the [national] legislature."[36]

The Federalist response to this position is telling. The Federalists initially opposed adding a bill of rights for two related reasons. First, they maintained that a bill of rights was unnecessary because the powers of the federal government were limited and enumerated; the Constitution would give it no power, for example, to authorize general warrants because that was not one of the powers vested by Article I. As Federalist James Wilson put it in the Pennsylvania ratifying convention, the proposed federal government was one of "particularly enumerated" powers, and thus "there can be no necessity for a bill of rights, for . . . the people never part with their power."[37] Second, the Federalists argued that listing certain rights would be dangerous to liberty because such an enumeration would imply the nonexistence of other rights. Wilson again:

> [I]n a government consisting of enumerated powers . . . a bill of rights would not only be unnecessary, but . . . highly imprudent. . . . If we attempt an enumeration [of rights], every thing that is not enumerated is presumed to be given. The consequence is, that an imperfect enumeration would throw all implied power into the scale of the government, and the rights of the people would be rendered incomplete.[38]

Wilson's arguments became the Federalist party line and eventually made their way into Federalist No. 84.[39]

Part of the necessity argument was that state constitutions and bills of rights would be fully effective in guarding liberty. To the extent that the federal government did overextend its powers, they asserted, the state constitutions and bills of rights would act as a buffer between the government and the people, even absent a federal bill. For example, when the issue first arose at the Constitutional Convention on September 12, 1787, Federalist Roger Sherman brushed aside the suggestion that a federal bill was needed, arguing: "The State Declarations of Rights are not repealed by this Constitution; and being in force are sufficient."[40] Sherman believed that the state constitutions and bills of rights would operate even against the federal government to preserve individual liberty.

This belief was echoed by Federalist Edmund Randolph at the Virginia ratifying convention the following year. Arguing specifically against the need for a provision barring general warrants, he stated:

> That general warrants are grievous and oppressive, and ought not to be granted, I fully admit. . . . But we have sufficient security here. . . . Can it be believed that the federal judiciary would not be independent enough to prevent such oppressive practices? If they will not do justice to persons injured, *may they not go to our own state judiciaries, and obtain it?*[41]

Thus, Randolph believed that the general common-law bar on general warrants would be sufficient, even absent a written bill of rights, to prevent federal judges from issuing them. And, if that were not enough, actions could be brought in state court.

But the Anti-Federalists were not convinced. They wanted to make explicit what Sherman and Randolph believed was implicit in the Constitution. For example, Anti-Federalist Agrippa (James Winthrop of Massachusetts), as part of a proposed set of amendments to the document, suggested that the Constitution expressly provide that state bills of rights stand as a barrier between the federal government and the individual:

> Nothing in this constitution shall deprive a citizen of any state of the benefit of the bill of rights established by the constitution of the state in which he shall reside, and such bills of rights shall be considered as valid in any court of the United States where they shall be pleaded.[42]

In a similar vein, an amendment proposed by Melancton Smith at the New York ratifying convention and included in the proposals the State made to Congress as part of its ratification would have required all federal officers "to be bound, by oath or affirmation, not to infringe the constitutions or rights of the respective states."[43]

The initial failure of ratification in Massachusetts, New Hampshire, New York, North Carolina, and Virginia stemmed in large part from the Anti-Federalists' belief that, without an explicit provision such as Agrippa's or Smith's proposal, state constitutions and bills of rights were no protection against the proposed federal government. And the disagreement between the Federalists and Anti-Federalists on this issue has much to do with the very distinct views of the common law the two groups entertained.

The Anti-Federalist Conception of Common Law

The Bill of Rights was designed in large part to constitutionalize common-law restrictions on government. To support their arguments against British rule, the colonists turned time and again to the rhetoric of the "common-law rights of Englishmen." The Anti-Federalists continued this tradition in extolling the common law as establishing their rights. For example, immediately after asserting that state bills of rights were "no [s]ecurity" against the proposed federal government, George Mason in his *Objections* expressly invoked the common law: "Nor are the people secured even in the Enjoyment of the Benefits of the common-Law."[44] By "unreasonable searches and seizures," then, the framers and ratifiers of the Fourth Amendment were referring to those that violated "the reason of the common law."[45]

But the "common law" in 1791 was a notoriously slippery notion. Though it is something of an oversimplification, two views of the common law have historically competed for dominance. What we can call a "pre-Realist" view posited that common law existed "in the air," as it were, and that the task of the judge was to "discover" it. On this view, common law was uniform across jurisdictions and divorced from policy concerns and political will. This is the view of the common law that Justice Oliver Wendell Holmes derisively dismissed as "a brooding omnipresence in the sky."[46] The competing, Realist view, which ultimately won out, is that judges make the common law instead of discovering it, and that the common law varies across jurisdictions based on their respective political needs. Because Legal Realism did not achieve full victory until the first half of the twentieth century, conventional wisdom maintains that the pre-Realist view of the common law was dominant in the eighteenth century. For example, Justice Antonin Scalia wrote that, at the founding,

> the prevailing image of the common law was that of a preexisting body of rules, uniform throughout the nation (rather than different from state to state), that judges merely "discovered" rather than created. It is only in th[e] [twentieth] century, with the rise of legal realism, that we came to acknowledge that judges in fact "make" the common law, and that each state has its own.[47]

Yet the conventional wisdom glosses over a distinct ideological split in the way the common law was viewed at the time of the founding. That split can be traced to the duality contained in the most important passage from our Declaration of Independence:

> We hold these truths to be self-evident, that all men are created equal, that they are endowed by their Creator with certain *unalienable Rights*, that among these are Life, Liberty and the pursuit of Happiness.— That *to secure these rights, Governments are instituted* among Men, deriving their just powers from the consent of the governed.[48]

Read closely, this passage presents two ideas that are in some tension with one another. On the one hand, all enjoy the "rights[] [of] life, liberty and the pursuit of happiness" as *natural-law* rights, those given to us by nature and that pre-exist any government. But, on the other hand, "secur[ing] these rights" requires *positive law*—constitutions, statutes, and judicial decisions—promulgated through popular sovereignty, "governments . . . deriving their just powers from the consent of the governed." As David Bogen has put it:

> Under the Declaration of Independence, the concept of "inalienable rights" contained reference to natural and positive law. Rights were asserted as universal principles of natural law. . . . Nevertheless, "inalienable rights" also had a positive law aspect, for their content in specific applications was derived from colonial versions of the rights of Englishmen in England. Furthermore, the form that the protection of citizens' security, liberty, and property took was that of existing positive law. . . . Thus, any claim by a citizen of a fundamental right carried with it both a natural law reference and a reference to existing positive law.[49]

The best example of this duality, perhaps, is that of private property: the Constitution secures our right to "property" against government infringement in several different places, and the right to the fruits of one's labor is generally seen as a "natural right," existing independent of government; yet property is largely defined by law.[50]

The pre-Realist view described above by Justice Scalia was, as he put it, "prevailing" only among Federalists. The Federalists of the 1790s focused on the concept of common-law rights as deriving from higher law, the law of nature. As such, they viewed the common law, and common-law rights in particular, not as transient but as fixed, existing "in the air" rather than being tied to sovereignty. Observe, for example, the statement of Federalist Theophilus Parsons at the Massachusetts ratifying convention explaining that a federal bill of rights was unnecessary because if "Congress [were] to infringe on any one of the natural rights of the people . . . the act would be a nullity, and could not be enforced."[51] The remarks of Randolph and Sherman discussed above suggesting that a bill of rights was unnecessary are also indicative of the general Federalist position on the common law. The notion that common-law rights simply exist, rather than representing the relationship between an individual and a particular sovereign, explains Randolph's remark that federal judges, presumably applying general common law, would disallow general warrants, even without an express prohibition at the federal level.

But imputing this view of the common law to the entire founding generation is an error, for it "would have been foreign to many of the men who had clamored for a bill of rights in the 1780s."[52] By the late eighteenth century, there were sharp disputes over the nature of the common law, and what we can call a "proto-Realist" view of the law—one predicting the twentieth century's Legal Realist movement—had seeped into the American understanding of the nature of law. The acknowledgement that common-law judges made law rather than simply discovered it "began in the 1780s and was well underway in the 1790s."[53] In particular, the Anti-Federalists were able "to intuit the idea [Wesley] Hohfeld would resurrect and refine after the heyday of natural-rights talk in the mid-nineteenth century," of "[p]articularistic customs, charters, and the like [that] gave distinct persons or entities distinct rights or privileges against distinct entities, but not others."[54] While the Anti-Federalists' mission was to secure as against the federal government the common-law rights of Englishmen, the Anti-Federalists were under no illusion that the common law was the same in the United States as it was in England, or that it was the same in every State.

They also knew that natural rights were of no use without positive law to implement them.[55] After all, natural rights by definition attached to humans throughout the globe (or, at least, given heavily ingrained notions of white supremacy at the time, throughout Europe) but only Englishmen were thought to enjoy robust protection of these rights.[56] Once again, George Mason summed up the Anti-Federalists' proto-Realist stance in the first paragraph of his *Objections*. Immediately after invoking the common-law rights of Englishmen, he wrote that "the common-Law . . . *stands here upon no other Foundation than it's* [*sic*] *having been adopted by the respective Acts forming the Constitutions of the several States*." That is to say, even the common law, that great source of English liberty, has no authority unless adopted as positive law: it has "no other [f]oundation."[57]

The Anti-Federalists opposed the notion of a general common law for obvious reasons given their general stance on federal power. They saw the invocation of a general common law as a mechanism by which the proposed federal government could assert power far beyond that which it was granted in the Constitution. Since the common law was formed over centuries and encompassed strictures relating to all manner of human activity, the existence of a general common law would allow the federal government to effectively regulate all human endeavors. What good were the limitations on the legislative power contained in Article I, they argued, if power could be smuggled into the federal government through Article III via the notion of a general common law?

In Anti-Federalist writings about the need for a bill of rights, the idea that the common law had no effect until adopted as positive law was often expressed alongside the cognate idea that there were as many different versions of the common law as there were common-law jurisdictions. For example, "A Maryland Farmer" (believed to have been John Francis Mercer) explicitly noted that even the common-law rights of Englishmen are inapplicable unless they have been adopted as part of the positive law. And, he recognized, they differed from State to State. He wrote:

> If a citizen of Maryland can have no benefit of his own bill of rights in the confederal courts, and there is no bill of rights of the United States—how could he take advantage of a natural right founded in reason, could he plead it and produce Locke, Sydney, or Montesquieu as authority? How could he take advantage of any of the common law rights, which have heretofore been considered as the birthright of Englishmen and their descendants, could he plead them and produce the authority of the English judges in his support? Unquestionably not, for *the authority of the common law arises from the express adoption by the several States* in their respective constitutions, and that *in various degrees and under different modifications.*[58]

Here we have a frank recognition that common-law rights have no authority whatsoever in the courts aside from their "express adoption by the several States." Although Maryland Farmer did refer to "natural right[s] founded in reason," one is impotent to invoke these rights without the positive law to operationalize them. In court, with the powerful central government bearing down upon the lone citizen, he needs to cite some legal provision, not a political philosopher.

Just as telling was the Federalist response: echoing Sherman and Randolph, Federalist writer Aristides (Alexander Contee Hanson) asserted that "the party injured [by a general warrant] will most clearly have redress in a state court."[59] For Federalists, the common law existed in the ether, for anyone in any court in any State to invoke as protection against any government. They did not understand the more modern notion of common law as a set of reciprocal rights and obligations between specific parties, which could change and even disappear depending on the parties involved. The Anti-Federalists did.

The Rejection of a General Criminal Common Law

Of particular note is Maryland Farmer's observation that the common law exists "in various degrees and under different modifications" in every State. Soon after ratification, the dispute between Federalists and Anti-Federalists would focus on the existence *vel non* of a general federal common law and, in particular, a federal common law of crime. In that debate, Anti-Federalists and their immediate political descendants, Jeffersonian Republicans, reiterated Maryland Farmer's view of a differentiated rather than uniform common law.

The dispute over the existence of a federal criminal common law was publicly aired for the first time by Justice Samuel Chase in *United States* v. *Worrall*,[60] a scant seven years after the Bill of Rights was ratified. Worrall was prosecuted in federal court for attempting to bribe a federal Commissioner of Revenue. But because there was no federal statute making such bribery a crime, prosecutors had to rely on federal criminal common law. Justice Chase would have none of it. He opined that "the United States, as a Federal government, have no common law." Although each of the former colonies had adopted English common law, each adopted only "so much of the common law as was applicable to their local situation and change of circumstances." Chase saw the common law as instrumental and diverse, not declaratory and uniform, encapsulating the Anti-Federalist/Republican understanding:

> [E]ach colony judged for itself what parts of the common law were applicable to its new condition; and in various modes by legislative acts, by judicial decisions, or by constant usage, adopted some parts, and rejected others. Hence, he who shall travel through the different States, will soon discover, that the whole of the common law of England has been nowhere introduced . . . and that there is . . . a great and essential diversity in the subjects to which the common law is applied, as well as in the extent of its application. The common law, therefore, of one State, is not the common law of another.[61]

The *Worrall* opinion would become the cornerstone of the Republican position against a federal common law. The language of that opinion was echoed later the same year by Republican House Minority Leader Albert Gallatin in the debates over the Alien and Sedition Acts, when he stated that "[t]he common law of Great Britain received in each colony, had in every one received modifications arising from their situation . . . and now each State had a common law, in its general principles the same, but in many particulars differing from each other."[62] Thomas Jefferson expressed much the same thought in a 1799 letter to Randolph, denouncing the idea of federal common law as an "audacious, barefaced and sweeping pretension" that threatened the existence of independent state courts and legal systems. Compared to the assertion of a federal common-law jurisdiction, even the reviled Alien and Sedition Acts were "unconsequential" and "timid things."[63] Likewise, in a letter the following year, Jefferson wrote that

> if the principle were to prevail of a common law being in force in the U.S. (which principle possesses the general government at once of all the powers of the state governments; and reduces us to a single consolidated government) it would become the most corrupt government on the face of the earth.[64]

In instructing its U.S. Senators, the Virginia legislature decried "the monstrous pretensions resulting from the adoption of th[e] principle" that "the common law of England is in force under the government of the United States."[65] And Federalist-turned-Republican James Madison wrote of the differentiated nature of the common law less than a decade after having successfully secured ratification of the Bill of Rights. In his 1800 follow-up to the Virginia Resolutions, which savaged the Alien and Sedition Acts, Madison wrote:

> In the state prior to the Revolution, it is certain that the common law, under different limitations, made a part of the colonial codes. But . . . it was the separate law of each colony within its respective limits, and was unknown to them, as a law pervading and operating through the whole, as one society.
>
> It could not possibly be otherwise. The common law was not the same in any two of the colonies; in some the modifications were materially and extensively different.[66]

Soon after, in the election of 1800, the Federalists were soundly defeated, in part because of the "political backlash" triggered over their support for the concept of common-law crimes.[67] The *Worrall* opinion then provided a framework for the Republicans' successful attempt to repeal the Judiciary Act of 1801, which had enhanced the power of the federal judiciary.[68] In only a few years, the American update of Blackstone, penned by St. George Tucker, could confidently proclaim the absurdity of maintaining that all of the States followed a single, uniform common law:

> [I]t would require the talents of an Alfred to harmonize and digest into one system such opposite, discordant, and conflicting municipal institutions, as composed the codes of the several colonies at the period of the revolution. . . . In vain then should we attempt, by any general theory, to establish an uniform authority and obligation in the common law of England, over the American colonies.[69]

Finally, in 1812, the Supreme Court weighed in and endorsed the Anti-Federalist/Republican view, at least insofar as rejecting the idea of a general federal criminal common law, observing that the common law "var[ies] in every state in the Union."[70]

Implicit in the idea of a differentiated common law is that the common law can change over time as a well as across boundaries. Because the Anti-Federalists, and later the Republicans, recognized that the common law of England was adopted in each colony and State only insofar as it cohered with local conditions, they also recognized that the common law is capable of changing with those conditions. "By 1791 . . . 'a commonly understood concept of "common-law" had become that of a process characterized by occasional flexibility and capacity for growth in order to respond to changing social pressures, rather than that of a fixed and immutable body of unchanging rules.'"[71] Common law, to them, was the positive law articulation of natural-law principles, to be adopted, amended, adapted, or sometimes even abrogated, just like statutory law.[72]

Thus, we see the nub of the Anti-Federalists' complaint about the unamended Constitution. As Mason argued in his *Objections*, the common-law rights of Englishmen "stand[] . . . upon no other Foundation than [their] having been adopted" as the positive law in "the Constitutions of the several States." Common-law rights have no separate existence independent of the body of the rest of the common law, and the body of the common law exists, as Maryland Farmer wrote, "in various degrees and under different modifications" in the different States. And those common-law rights could change and develop over time, adapting to new needs and circumstances. But because there was no common law of the United States as a whole, there were no common-law rights to restrain the proposed central government. What the Anti-Federalists sought, it appears, was the application of common-law rights, *as adapted by the respective States*, to that government. What the Anti-

Federalists sought in the Fourth Amendment in particular was to subject the central government to each State's restrictions on searching and seizing, as they might develop over time. Statements made by the Anti-Federalists regarding federal search-and-seizure authority bear this out.

The Anti-Federalist Push for Constraints on Federal Search-and-Seizure Authority

Some have suggested that the Fourth Amendment was designed to target only general warrants, "unreasonable" merely being a reference to such warrants. It is true that, during the ratification period, Anti-Federalists specifically criticized the proposed Constitution for its lack of a prohibition of warrants that were too general or otherwise promiscuous. Federal Farmer, for example, identified as among "the rights of freemen . . . freedom from hasty and unreasonable search warrants, warrants not founded on oath, and not issued with due caution, for searching and seizing men's papers, property, and persons."[73]

But they also criticized the Constitution's failure to address searches and seizures more generally. As William Cuddihy put it,

> the debate of 1787–88 had a wider focus. The general warrant was no longer the only kind of unreasonable search. The ratifying conventions and pamphleteers increasingly spoke in the plural, of unreasonable searches and seizures. General excise searches and search warrants issued groundlessly were condemned almost as much as the general warrant.[74]

The Anti-Federalists repeatedly expressed anxiety at leaving search-and-seizure policy in the hands of a powerful central government. Yes, they demanded a prohibition on general warrants, as a consensus had developed by 1791 that such warrants were unlawful. But their concern went beyond the idea that warrants be specific, and encompassed anxiety over federal executive officers' search-and-seizure authority more generally. And consistent with their views of common-law rights more broadly, the Anti-Federalists did not seek uniform and unchanging rules on federal search-and-seizure authority. Rather, their goal appears to have been procedural rather than substantive: to maintain the primacy of state search-and-seizure law vis-à-vis federal officials.

Recall, for example, Maryland Farmer's observation that "the authority of the common law arises from the express adoption by the several States in their respective constitutions, and that in various degrees and under different modifications." He almost immediately gave as an example the absence from the proposed Constitution of a ban on general warrants: "To render this more intelligible—suppose for instance, that an officer of the United States should force the house . . . of a citizen, by virtue of a general warrant, I would ask, are general warrants illegal by the constitution of the United States?"[75] Read in light of Maryland's constitutional prohibition on general warrants, and his "various degrees and . . . different modifications" language, Maryland Farmer's concern appears to be not so much with imposing a universal ban of general warrants but rather with requiring federal officers to respect Maryland law. Of course, the Fourth Amendment ultimately did ban general warrants across the board. But this does not take away from the fact that the focus of Maryland Farmer's pre-ratification concern was not the absence of a uniform rule but the potential conflict between the Maryland rule forbidding general warrants and a federal rule permitting them.

Patrick Henry in the Virginia ratifying convention was particularly outspoken about the need to constrain federal agents by state law when searching and seizing. He despaired over the potential loss of local control over searches and seizures. He observed that state legislation had been passed in Virginia "to suppress the[] iniquitous speculations and cruel extortions" of local sheriffs who had "committed the most horrid and barbarous ravages on [the] people." This was possible because the Virginia legislature could keep a "watchful eye" on the sheriffs. But what if federal officers were to inflict such indignities on Virginians? Henry raised the specter of federal officers searching with impunity through every inch of the people's dwellings, of "harpies . . . aided by excisemen, who may search, at any time, your houses, and most secret recesses." No longer would the state legislature be empowered to prevent these indignities; state constitutions and bills of rights would be ineffectual in holding federal excisemen to account for their actions in searching for untaxed goods. Instead, Virginians would have to appeal to the national legislature, which, because of its great distance, would be unable to maintain tight control of federal officers in the field: "[I]f sheriffs, thus immediately under the eye of our state legislature and judiciary, have dared to commit these outrages, what would they not have done if their masters had been at Philadelphia or New York?"[76] Thus, Henry argued that the national legislature and federal judges would be far less inclined to constrain federal officers, and far less capable of doing so, through legislation and common-law rulemaking than were the state legislature and state judges. The premise of this argument is a common refrain among the Anti-Federalists, that local control enhances the accountability of government actors while centralized power weakens political accountability.[77] Consequently, according to Henry, nothing would "tie [the] hands" of federal tax collectors and excisemen.[78]

Henry's prescription for this problem was that such searches and seizures should be subject to state regulation. He raised the specter of a federal "exciseman . . . demand[ing] leave to enter [ones] cellar, or house, by virtue of his office." He explained that he was unwilling to abide by such a potentiality "without any reservation of rights or control."[79] Similarly, he warned that if an aggrieved person were to go to the federal courts in "Philadelphia or New York . . . there [he] must appeal to judges sworn to support this Constitution, *in opposition to that of any state*."[80] Thus, Henry argued that adoption of the Constitution without a bill of rights would free federal officers from any constitutional constraint on searching and seizing that would otherwise exist under state law. His prescription for that problem was a "reservation of rights" and "control," pursuant to what ultimately became the Fourth Amendment, to retain the buffer provided by state constitutions. This meant local control—legislative and judicial—of federal officials, such as that which had taken place in Virginia years earlier, in the form of local refusal to issue writs of assistance, perfectly legal under English law, but which conflicted with local sensibilities.

Henry's comments are critical to understanding the Anti-Federalist position on searches and seizures. The ultimate fear was unbridled executive discretion, law enforcement officers running rampant, committing "iniquitous speculations," "cruel extortions," and "horrid and barbarous ravages." But the prescription he sought is entirely unfamiliar to today's Fourth Amendment doctrine. He sought not the specific protections of judicial superintendence of executive officials through ex ante warrants or ex post jury awards, but local, democratic controls more generally. Henry's solution was more procedural than substantive. He sought to control federal officers' search-and-seizure authority through restrictions based on state law, not by any universal rules.

Consider also the warnings of Massachusetts Anti-Federalist John DeWitt about the authority that Congress would give to federal tax collectors under the proposed Constitution:

> They are to determine, *and you are to make no laws inconsistent with such determination*, whether such Collectors shall carry with them any paper[] purporting their commission, or not—whether it shall be a general warrant, or a special one—whether written or printed—

> whether any of your goods, or your persons shall be exempt from distress, and in what manner either you or your property is to be treated when taken in consequence of such warrants. They will have the liberty of entering your houses by night as well as by day for such purposes.[81]

DeWitt, like Maryland Farmer and Henry, was primarily concerned with local control of search-and-seizure policy, and only as an ancillary matter with any particular aspect of that policy. Congress, he warned, is "to determine" all of the rules attending searches and seizures, "*and you are to make no laws inconsistent with such determination.*" Read this language in the light shone by Massachusetts's unsuccessful attempt to legislatively overturn the result in *Paxton's Case*, and its later reservation of local search-and-seizure law as applied to national officials in its legislation ratifying the 1783 confederal impost. The problem, according to DeWitt, was not simply that federal search-and-seizure policy might contain features disliked by Bay Staters. The real problem was that Massachusetts would be unable—as it had done in 1783 and attempted to do in 1762—to pass legislation to do something about it. DeWitt's admonition was thus aimed not simply at the prospect of Congress' formulating search-and-seizure policy that would be antithetical to general common-law principles. Rather, he cautioned his fellow Bay Staters that they would be unable, via the typical routes of judicial and legislative rulemaking, to require federal officials to follow *Massachusetts* law: "you are to make no laws inconsistent with [Congress's] determination."

Another variation on this theme is seen in Federal Farmer's explicitly linking a demand for limitations on federal search-and-seizure authority with an invocation of Magna Carta's "law of the land" provision.[82] In suggesting various amendments to the Constitution, he proposed

> that all persons shall have a right to be secure from all unreasonable searches and seizures of their persons, houses, papers, or possessions; and that all warrants shall be deemed contrary to this right, if the foundation of them be not previously supported by oath, and there be not in them a special designation of persons or objects of search, arrest, or seizure: and *that no person shall be exiled or molested in his person or effects, otherwise than by the judgment of his peers, or according to the law of the land.*[83]

Thus, Federal Farmer specifically conjoined the requirements of a specific warrant, supported by oath, with the common-law constraint, stemming from Chapter 29 of Magna Carta, that no person be deprived of liberty or property other than "according to the law of the land."

This is significant because by "the law of the land," Federal Farmer was likely referring not to general or natural law but to the law of particular States. "Law of the land" provisions in early colonial and state legislation generally referred to the law of a specific jurisdiction. At least seven colonies were home to iterations of Chapter 29 that referred specifically to the laws of those jurisdictions.[84] Several post-1776 state constitutions contain "law of the land" provisions that also likely referred to state positive law.[85] Additionally, although his identity is still unclear, Federal Farmer is now believed to have been none other than Melancton Smith of New York.[86] And, as previously noted, Smith proposed an amendment that would have required that federal officers "be bound, by oath or affirmation, not to infringe the constitutions or rights of the *respective* states." Such an amendment would have done expressly what the Fourth Amendment does by implication: hold federal officers to the different search-and-seizure standards enshrined in the constitution of each "respective" State. In short, Federal Farmer's proposal of a proto–Fourth Amendment, linked to a reiteration of Magna Carta's "law of the land" provision, effectively meant and would have been understood as meaning that no one could be searched and seized other than by the law of the State where the search or seizure occurred.

The Anti-Federalists and the Reasonableness and Warrant Models

We can now go back and judge the two dominant models of the Fourth Amendment examined in chapter 1, the Reasonableness Model and the Warrant Model, in light of the Anti-Federalist impetus for the Bill of Rights in general and the Fourth Amendment in particular. The statements of Anti-Federalists such as John DeWitt, Patrick Henry, Federal Farmer, and Maryland Farmer, along with the more general sentiments of the Anti-Federalists, largely refute both the Reasonableness Model and the Warrant Model. Taking into account the complete historical picture, a local-control model is superior to a historical model that posits warrants as the touchstone of Fourth Amendment protection, on the one hand, or one that holds the federal government only to some nebulous standard of reasonableness, on the other.

One need go no further than the statements of DeWitt and Henry to undermine the claim that the framers and ratifiers of the Fourth Amendment were exclusively concerned with general warrants and were unperturbed by warrantless searches. Notice several things about the enlightening passage from DeWitt. First, he expressed anxiety that federal tax collectors might have a "paper purporting their commission," i.e., a warrant, "*or not.*" That is, he expressed a concern that tax collectors might act without warrant at all, in addition to expressing the concern that such a warrant might be "general" rather than "special." Moreover, he expressed concern about "whether any of [one's] goods, or . . . persons shall be exempt from distress." Again, this goes beyond a concern regarding the specificity of warrants and suggests that there might be limitations on how "goods" and "persons" can be searched or seized even with a warrant. DeWitt may have had in mind the precept, drawn from *Entick* v. *Carrington*, that seizure of "mere evidence" of a crime, even pursuant to warrant, was unlawful.[87] Furthermore, DeWitt worried about the manner in which persons and property are "to be treated when taken in consequence of such warrants." Again, the concern is not just with general warrants but also with the way in which warrants were to be executed. Finally, he expressed a concern about nocturnal searches, which again goes to the execution of warrants as opposed to their generality or specificity.

Henry, too, was worried not only about a federal official's use of general warrants, but also with his not obtaining a warrant at all and executing a search "by virtue of his office." Henry chose his words carefully. By describing a potential warrantless search by a federal excise collector as being "by virtue of his office," he deliberately evoked the *ex officio* (that is, warrantless) searches by British customs officials in the 1740s and 1750s that incensed the people of Massachusetts and were a prelude to the writs of assistance controversy.[88] To those who clamored for federal constitutional protection against unreasonable searches and seizures, "an ex officio search and a writ of assistance search were two different sides of the same coin" because "[b]oth allowed broad, discretionary . . . power without any requirement of specific cause or judicial oversight."[89] Like DeWitt, Henry also stoked fears of nocturnal searches, by conjuring up images of federal "harpies . . . assisted by excisemen[,] 'who may search, *at any time.*'"

On the other hand, the confidence of Warrant Model adherents in judicial control of executive officers is in sharp tension with the deep suspicion that the Anti-Federalists felt toward the prospect of a federal judiciary. It is true that colonial judges largely (though not uniformly) sided with the colonists during the writs of assistance controversy. However, these were the forerunners of *state* judges; federal judges were another matter. A continual Anti-Federalist complaint was that "[t]he Constitution creates a powerful judicial branch that threatens the integrity of the state courts."[90] Indeed, the major conflict during the first twenty years of the Republic over the existence of federal common law stemmed at least in part over Anti-Federalist, and then Republican, distrust of federal judges. As Henry warned in his speech referenced above, federal judges would be "sworn to support this [federal] Constitution, in opposition to that of any state, and . . . may also be inclined to favor their own officers."[91] Placing limits on federal executive officers that were to be enforced by federal judges would have been, to the Anti-Federalists, putting the foxes in charge of the henhouse. The notion that judicial oversight of executive discretion was the central goal of the Fourth Amendment is a creation of the twentieth century, not the eighteenth.

The Anti-Federalists saw judicial superintendence of executive officers not as an independent good but as an adjunct of federalism. Recall that Patrick Henry expressed support for the idea that local sheriffs be kept "under the eye of [the] state legislature and judiciary." But the Anti-Federalists did not trust the federal legislature and judiciary to similarly restrain federal officers. Rather, the idea was to restrain federal executives via the state legislature and judiciary, the former by formulating search-and-seizure policy, and the latter by providing remedies for trespass and, in doing so, building upon the common law of search and seizure. This, after all, was how the writs of assistance controversy played out in most of the colonies: local legislatures and judiciaries constraining the executive power of the Crown. It was also at the heart of the state legislation ratifying the proposed federal impost in the 1780s, which would have forced state search-and-seizure policy upon confederal enforcement officers. And it would become the strategy of section 33 of the Judiciary Act of 1789 and section 9 of the Militia Act of 1792, which required that federal agents generally abide by state statutory and common law when they search and seize.

To the Anti-Federalists, the Bill of Rights was largely about self-government and local control of the policies that affected people most directly. As Gerard Bradley cogently observed, "'the right of the people,' specified by the fourth amendment," meant "an individual's 'right' to be governed by laws . . . favored by the community's desire and political authority to enact them."[92] Search-and-seizure law is fundamentally about striking an appropriate balance between liberty and security. And the Anti-Federalists saw this as fundamentally a matter for each "community's desire," not national policy.[93]

By 1791, a consensus had developed throughout the United States that general warrants were unlawful. Thus, the Fourth Amendment specifically bans them. But no similar consensus had developed on many of the other issues of search-and-seizure policy that had arisen, such as when warrants are needed. On issues such as these, the history surrounding the adoption of the Fourth Amendment points most strongly not toward a general warrant requirement nor toward a general reasonableness standard, but to a regime of local control of federal officials. It was a regime that most closely aligned with the demands of the Anti-Federalists, whose support ultimately was necessary to form the Union. And it was a regime that Americans in 1791 would have been used to.

Conclusion

The battle over ratification resulted in the constitutionalization of some common-law rights in the Bill of Rights. If, at least for the Anti-Federalists, these common-law rights had no existence separate and apart from their adoption in the States, and if the common law differs in every State and can change over time, then it follows that the common-law rights adopted as the federal Bill of Rights also might vary by State and over time. As chapter 5 will show, search-and-seizure authority during the colonial period and immediately post-Independence did differ in some respects by colony (and then by State) and over time. But first, chapter 4 will explore how the framers and ratifiers of the Fourth Amendment contemplated that both state positive law and the customs and usage from which it sprang would dictate the metes and bounds of the interests that the Amendment would protect from infringement.

Four

Original Understandings and Fourth Amendment Search Doctrine

The framers and ratifiers of the Fourth Amendment would have understood it to preserve state common-law causes of action against government officials who infringe upon "persons, houses, papers, [or] effects" through "unreasonable searches [or] seizures." Modern doctrine breaks this down into two questions: Was there a search or seizure? And, if so, was that search or seizure reasonable? A person is seized when their liberty of movement is infringed either by physical force (e.g., a police officer tackles a suspect) or by a submission to a show of authority where a reasonable person in the circumstances would not feel free to go about their business (e.g., a motorist stops when a police car signals it to pull over).[1] The "search" question has been more complicated and requires an extended discussion. Thus, this chapter addresses the original understanding of what made something a search while the next chapter discusses the original understanding of what made a search or seizure reasonable.

This chapter will first provide a brief synopsis of Fourth Amendment search doctrine. The Supreme Court has used two different methodologies to answer the search question. Prior to 1967, courts tended to look at whether a trespass—a physical intrusion without consent—had occurred. Between 1967 and 2012, courts instead looked to whether, in the words of Justice John Marshall Harlan II's concurring opinion in the landmark case of *Katz* v. *United States*, a person's "reasonable expectation of privacy" had been breached.[2] And since 2012, the courts have used both approaches.

This chapter will then show that the framers and ratifiers of the Fourth Amendment understood its protections in a way that bridges the gap between the trespass and the "reasonable expectation of privacy" approaches.

What have been characterized as distinct touchstones, trespass and reasonable expectations of privacy, are not as different as they appear at first blush. It is more accurate to describe them as representing two stages in the development of the same root idea: established societal norms governing security against intrusions upon persons and property. Reasonable expectations of privacy depend largely on "customary social usage,"[3] that is to say, social norms, understandings, and expectations governing how individuals conduct themselves vis-à-vis their fellow individuals' claims to security from intrusions. But the common law of trespass, as the framers and ratifiers of the Fourth Amendment understood it, developed from that selfsame "customary social usage." Expectations of privacy, on the one hand, and trespass, on the other, while they may be two distinct species, derive from the same family of concepts. They represent different points on an evolutionary spectrum. What begins as social practice evolves into social understanding and expectation, which sometimes morphs into enforceable rights and interests, which often hardens into positive law. What we know as "expectations of privacy" merely constitute the precursor to a matrix of enforceable legal rights. What we know as "trespass" is simply the fully formed product of that evolutionary process.

Finally, this chapter will show that the framers and ratifiers of the Fourth Amendment, particularly the Anti-Federalists, understood that process to be decentralized. Whether we are talking about customary social norms as forming the backbone of the reasonable expectation of privacy test or as evolving into positive law, those norms, expectations, and positive laws are different in different places and at different times. Different States will have different statutory and common law reflecting those norms and expectations that change over time. And the framing generation understood that when the law is unclear, local juries would be tasked to determine the nature of those norms and expectations. Once again, we see the differentiated nature of the common law lead to a differentiated and decentralized Fourth Amendment.

A Synopsis of Modern Search Doctrine

To fully understand what the framers and ratifiers understood to be government conduct that overly intrudes upon individual interests, it will be necessary to make a quick detour to briefly examine current doctrine. Although we are still addressing only the Fourth Amendment, which applies directly only to the federal government, this discussion must yield to the reality that the Court has treated federal and state cases identically. Thus, despite the fact that I will refer to some state cases to illustrate how Fourth Amendment search doctrine has developed, the reader should keep in mind the central premise of this book, developed in Part II, that state cases should be treated differently than federal cases. In any event, much of what I say here is also relevant in state cases, given the conclusion I draw in Part II that the central constitutional constraint on state agents is that they, like their federal counterparts, must abide by state law.

Fourth Amendment search doctrine has developed in essentially three distinct stages. In the older cases, the Supreme Court tied the concept of a Fourth Amendment search to the common-law concept of trespass, an incursion onto one's property, whether land (real property) or movable items (personal property). A physical trespass, and only a physical trespass, could constitute a search for Fourth Amendment purposes. *Olmstead* v. *United States*, discussed briefly in the Introduction, provides the paradigmatic example. There, remember, federal agents had tapped the suspects' telephone lines without any physical intrusion onto their property, real or personal. The Court held that the Fourth Amendment was not implicated because there was no search or seizure, given that "[t]here was no entry of the houses or offices of the defendants."[4]

This trespass doctrine was relatively easy to apply but led to odd results. Take, for example, the cases of *Goldman* v. *United States*[5] and *Silverman* v. *United States*.[6] In *Goldman*, the Court held that there was no Fourth Amendment search when federal agents, lawfully present in an office, pressed up against the wall to an adjoining office a device to listen in to conversations taking place there. By contrast, in *Silverman*, the Court held that a Fourth Amendment search occurred when federal agents inserted a "spike mike," a microphone attached to a foot-long spike, into a wall separating the defendant's home from a vacant row house, because the spike mike intruded slightly over the property line and actually touched a heating duct in Silverman's home.[7]

The Court eventually became dissatisfied with the formalism of this approach, and also became concerned that advancing technology would outstrip privacy protections if inexorably tied to physical trespass. After all, as *Goldman* and *Olmstead* demonstrate, the government could listen in on the most intimate details of private life using common twentieth-century technology without ever conducting a physical trespass. In dissent in *Olmstead*, Justice Louis Brandeis predicted with stunning accuracy the rise of the computer age: "Ways may some day be developed by which the government, without removing papers from secret drawers, can reproduce them in court, and by which it will be enabled to expose to a jury the most intimate occurrences of the home."[8] So, in *Katz* v. *United States*, the Court overruled both *Goldman* and *Olmstead*.

Katz had been convicted of several federal gambling offenses based in part on statements he made while making a phone call from a public telephone booth (remember those?). The statements were overheard by federal agents via an electronic listening device they had attached to the outside of the booth. Were the Court to adhere to its prior decisions, it would have had to have held that no search had occurred. After all, if agents did not perform a search when they attached a listening device to the wall separating Goldman's office from one to which they had lawful access, no search occurred where the device was attached to the outside of a public phone booth. Instead, the Court forged a new path. The Court focused on the assumptions and expectations that people entertain regarding their retention or abandonment of privacy when they act in certain ways. As the Court put it: "One who occupies [a telephone booth], shuts the door behind him, and pays the toll that permits him to place a call is surely entitled to assume that the words he utters into the mouthpiece will not be broadcast to the world."[9] Or, as Justice Harlan put it in his concurrence, in a formulation that later assumed the status of controlling law: "[T]here is a twofold requirement, first that a person have exhibited an actual (subjective) expectation of privacy and, second, that the expectation be one that society is prepared to recognize as 'reasonable.'"[10] The first prong is virtually always satisfied so that, for all intents and purposes, the test is whether the government breached a reasonable expectation of privacy.[11] This "reasonable expectation of privacy" standard decouples the Fourth Amendment from physical trespass, such that a common-law trespass is neither necessary nor sufficient to constitute a Fourth Amendment search.

Finally, and most recently, the Court has added back in the notion that a trespass can constitute a search, so that a search occurs where there is an infringement of one's reasonable expectation of privacy *or* an unlicensed physical intrusion. In *United States* v. *Jones*, decided in 2012, federal agents had attached to Jones's wife's car an electronic device to monitor its movements through a Global Positioning System ("GPS") for twenty-eight days, obtaining evidence that was later used to convict him of federal narcotics charges. The Government argued that the placement of the GPS device on the car and the subsequent tracking of Jones did not constitute a search.[12]

The Court rejected this argument. But rather than deem the government conduct a search on the ground that it breached Jones's reasonable expectation of privacy, the Court, surprisingly, invoked its earlier cases by holding that the agents' conduct was a search because they "physically occupied private property for the purpose of obtaining information."[13] This older "physical intrusion" test, the Court informed us, was not laid to rest by *Katz* but had merely lain dormant for forty-five years: "[T]he *Katz* reasonable-expectation-of-privacy test has been *added to*, not *substituted for*, the common-law trespassory test."[14] Like the parrot in the famous Monty Python sketch, the trespass approach was not dead but had merely been resting. Thus, the Court resurrected—or at least awoke from its long slumber—the physical intrusion test exemplified by *Silverman*.

The Court subsequently applied this physical intrusion test in *Florida* v. *Jardines*. There, two Florida police officers entered onto Jardines's property with a drug-sniffing dog, and approached the front door of Jardines's house via the driveway and a paved walkway. The dog alerted the officers to the presence of illegal narcotics inside the house, leading to a search warrant and, ultimately, the filing of state drug charges against Jardines. Once again, the Court found that a Fourth Amendment search had occurred based on the "physical intrusion" theory advanced in *Jones*. The officers conducted a search when "they gathered . . . information by physically entering and occupying the [curtilage of Jardines's home] to engage in conduct not explicitly or implicitly permitted by the homeowner." Because there was undoubtedly a physical entry upon Jardines's land without his express consent, the only question was whether his consent could be implied. The Court conceded that "background social norms" permit people to approach a front door, knock, and ask to speak to the occupant, and a police officer can do the same "because that is 'no more than any private citizen might do.'" But those same "background social norms" do not invite a visitor or, therefore, a police officer, to approach the front door, fail to knock, and instead look for information about the premises. "There is no customary invitation to do *that*."[15]

Pre-*Katz* cases, while they relied on common-law notions of trespass, did not look to the actual positive law of trespass. *Goldman*, for example, did not mention trespass at all, except in putting to one side an earlier, ancillary intrusion into one defendant's office which did not lead to the gathering of any evidence.[16] Even *Silverman*, which seems most clearly to equate physical intrusion with a Fourth Amendment search, went out of its way to distance the constitutional inquiry from one focusing on "whether or not there was a technical trespass under the local property law." Further, *Silverman* cautioned that the Fourth Amendment search question was "not inevitably measurable in terms of ancient niceties of tort or real property law." The decision distinguished between "the technicality of a trespass . . . as a matter of local law" and "the reality of an actual intrusion into a constitutionally protected area."[17] Likewise, in *On Lee* v. *United States*, where a government informant entered the defendant's business premises and secretly permitted a government agent to listen in on their conversation through an electronic device, the Court rejected the idea that "the niceties of tort law[,]" with its "fine-spun doctrines[,]" govern the Fourth Amendment search question.[18] Thus, prior to 1967, the Court's methodology was to calibrate Fourth Amendment doctrine to a general trespass-like analysis, not the actual law of trespass.[19]

The *Katz* approach is also not closely tethered to the positive law. Under *Katz*, police might violate the law and not violate the Fourth Amendment. For example, in *California* v. *Greenwood*, the Court held that police did not conduct a search when they sifted through the defendant's garbage, placed at curbside for pickup, and found evidence of a crime.[20] Contrarily, police might abide by positive law and still violate the Fourth Amendment. Thus, in *Kyllo* v. *United States*, the Court held that use of a thermal imaging device to determine the relative amounts of heat emanating from someone's home was a search, despite that its use was not barred by law.[21] *Katz* looks beyond the positive law foundation for sources of legitimate expectations of privacy in general "concepts of real or personal property law or [in] understandings that are recognized and permitted by society."[22] The Court looks to "customary social usage," "widely shared social expectations," and "commonly held understanding[s]" about mutual rights and obligations in order to determine what expectations of privacy are reasonable, justifiable, or legitimate.[23]

This detour into current doctrine behind us, let us now return to the framing period to address which of these two methodologies is more consistent with the Fourth Amendment's original meaning.

What Was a Search in 1791?

At one level, it is easy to answer the question "What was a search to the framers and ratifiers of the Fourth Amendment?" The word "search" likely bore its plain meaning: "an examination of an object or space to uncover information."[24] However, this plain meaning approach doesn't get us very far, because once one determines that police conduct was a "search" of one's "person[], house[], papers, or effects," the key question then becomes whether the search was reasonable. As in a game of Whack-a-Mole, we can smash the search question into oblivion by appealing to plain meaning, but the question just arises again through the reasonableness inquiry. Either way, as we will see, it comes down to the same question: did the searcher violate the law?

Better, then, to divide the question in two, as the Court has done: First, has the searcher acted inconsistently with a law that applies to everyone? And second, if she has, does the law give her special authorization to do so? Again, here we deal only with the first question.

A key element of a law violation at the time of the founding was a trespass, or an unauthorized incursion onto someone's person or property. Before the advent of modern technology, there was no other way of gathering information than by making an incursion into a physical space. The purpose of the warrant at common law was to turn what would otherwise be a trespass into a judicially authorized incursion into property, privacy, or liberty. Thus, it is not surprising that originalists such as Justices Antonin Scalia, Clarence Thomas, and Neil Gorsuch have been fierce critics of *Katz* and have advocated a return to a trespass-centered, pre-*Katz* approach. The flaws of the *Katz* test, in their view, are essentially threefold. First, the test is divorced from the text and history of the Fourth Amendment.[25] Second, they have viewed the test as circular, in that it extends constitutional protection to those expectations of privacy, and only those expectations of privacy, that we generally believe are protected.[26] Finally, and perhaps worst of all, they have viewed the test as anti-democratic because it allows unelected federal judges to import their policy preferences into law by declaring their own expectations of privacy to be those that are reasonable.[27] As Justice Scalia put it, the Fourth Amendment

> did not guarantee some generalized "right of privacy" and leave it to this Court to determine which particular manifestations of the value of privacy "society is prepared to recognize as 'reasonable.'" Rather, it . . . le[ft] further expansion to the good judgment, not of this Court, but of the people through their representatives in the legislature.[28]

A trespass-based approach, by contrast, supposedly has none of these flaws. First, it is consistent with the text and history of the Fourth Amendment, given that the Amendment speaks of "persons, houses, papers, and effects," and given that the types of intrusions that gave rise to the Amendment were uniformly common-law trespasses to these interests. Second, a trespass-based approach is ostensibly not circular because it is determined exogenously. Whether government conduct is a search is contingent on whether such conduct by private persons would be considered a tortious interference with persons, things (as lawyers say, "chattels"), or land. By tying the search question to some positive law outside the Constitution itself, a trespass-based approach avoids circularity. Finally, such an approach ostensibly limits judicial discretion. By tying the meaning of the Fourth Amendment's terms to physical trespasses, the argument goes, judges cannot smuggle into constitutional law their own subjective views of the proper balance between liberty and security. Moreover, the common law of trespass, having evolved over the centuries, has gained wide acceptance and legitimacy as law. Trespasses to persons, chattels, and land are clear, it is argued, leaving little or no room for judges to insert their own policy preferences over those of the people who have formed and come to accept the law of trespass.

These arguments have some appeal to an originalist. As we have seen, the Fourth Amendment was understood in 1791 as preserving common-law rights against federal officials engaged in searching and seizing. One very useful weapon for keeping government officers in check was the common-law suit. As Jerry Mashaw has explained: "Customs officers seized property, held goods in shoreside warehouses, refused to return or release bonds, and held ships in port. A host of standard common law actions—trespass, trover, debt, detinue, assumpsit, or the like—were available to test the legality of these official actions."[29] After the Constitution was adopted, "Congress seems to have presumed that [federal] officers could and would be sued in state courts in common law actions."[30] As the previous chapter explored, the Fourth Amendment was designed to preserve this status quo.

However, to argue that Fourth Amendment searches are limited to physical trespasses is to take the only type of interference with "persons, houses, papers, and effects" that was possible in 1791 and to make it the sine qua non today, when many other types of intrusions are possible. Technology has evolved since 1791 to permit interference with those interests that do not involve some physical trespass to land, chattel, or person. And the law has evolved with it, to encompass modern torts that do not involve physical trespass. For example, in some States it is unlawful to secretly record someone without their consent, no matter where the conversation takes place. Confining Fourth Amendment searches to physical trespasses, because that was the only type of search that could have occurred in 1791, is a bit like excluding automobiles from the coverage of the Fourth Amendment because they did not exist in 1791. Not even the most zealous originalist takes that position. Instead, we argue by analogy: cars did not exist in 1791 but horse-drawn carriages and sailing ships did. Likewise, recording devices did not exist in 1791 but that does not mean that the Fourth Amendment has nothing to say about them.

Originalist judges have recognized this. The Court's decision in *Kyllo* v.

United States involved police use of a thermal imaging device which could determine how much heat was escaping from particular parts of a house. Justice Scalia, writing for the Court (including Justice Thomas), acknowledged that, in order to "assure[] preservation of that degree of privacy against government that existed when the Fourth Amendment was adopted," the Court must sometimes go beyond the notion of physical trespass. Accordingly, the Court held that use of a thermal imaging device to obtain details from within a home was a Fourth Amendment search, despite the absence of any physical trespass: "Where . . . the Government uses a device that is not in general public use, to explore details of the home that would previously have been unknowable without physical intrusion, the surveillance is a 'search.'"[31] As the *Kyllo* Court recognized implicitly, to say that the Fourth Amendment protects only against physical intrusions conflates the specific type of action the framers and ratifiers had in mind in 1791 with their more general understanding of what the Amendment accomplished. The Fourth Amendment preserves common-law protections against federal officials who undertake unreasonable searches and seizures of the people's persons, houses, papers, and effects. But the Fourth Amendment evolves with the common law upon which it is premised. As Justice Scalia wrote in a later case: "There is nothing new or surprising in the proposition that our unchanging Constitution refers to other bodies of law that might themselves change." Thus, a Fourth Amendment that dynamically incorporates the underlying common law "presents no problem for the originalist."[32]

However, an originalist account of the Fourth Amendment must still use the framers' and ratifiers' view of the common law in 1791 as the jumping-off point. For even if they understood the Fourth Amendment as dynamically incorporating the common law, a deeper exploration into how they viewed the nature of the common law is required. While Federalists and Anti-Federalists disagreed in some respects on the nature of the common law, all agreed in 1791 that the common law sprang from custom and long usage.

The Common Law as Customary Social Usage

For centuries before the framing period, English jurists understood the common law as encompassing—indeed, consisting of—custom. Custom was, in the words of Friedrich Hayek, "grown law,"[33] arising organically from the people, who gave it their tacit consent by following and applying it, until it became standardized and uniform, and assumed the mantle of law. Custom was seen as law even before it was ever adopted by statute or judicial decree.

Even prior to formal lawmaking and law-enforcing mechanisms, humans were governed by custom.[34] This had been recognized as far back as the Code of Justinian, written in the sixth century AD, which stated that "[c]ustom of long standing is rightly regarded as law."[35] Early English jurists Ranulf de Glanvill and Henry de Bracton recognized this in the twelfth and thirteenth centuries, respectively, as seen in the titles of their respective treatises: Glanvill's *The Laws and Customs of England* and Bracton's *Treatise on the Laws and Customs of the Realm of England*.[36] Sixteenth-century jurist Christopher St. German carried forward this idea of "custom as a source of law" in his text *Doctor and Student*.[37]

In the seventeenth and eighteenth centuries, English jurists built upon this custom-based view of English common law. Sir Edward Coke, the great jurist of seventeenth-century England, reaffirmed and expanded upon this view of the common law through a historical lens as the accumulation of hundreds of years of custom and usage. Coke espoused "the theory that the common law [w]as a body of principles, concepts, rules, and procedures that originated in a remote past."[38] No one really knew how the common law developed, but the metaphorical idea of "immemorial usage" as the foundation of custom was central to Coke's view of the law.[39] Later jurists, such as Coke's pupil John Selden and Selden's own student, Matthew Hale, emphasized the law's evolutionary nature.[40] Hale in particular built upon the idea that the obligation of the common law came from its democratic origins and acceptance by the people, not its mere antiquity.

At the time of the framing period, the common law was seen as indistinguishable from custom. Coke's, Selden's, and Hale's view of English common law as the end product of centuries of custom and usage found expression during the framing period in the works of William Blackstone, whose influence on the framers and ratifiers of the Constitution and Bill of Rights was most profound. Blackstone essentially equated the common law with custom. He declared that the common law could be divided into three parts. First, "General customs . . . are the universal rule of the whole kingdom, and form the common law, in its stricter and more usual signification." Second, there are "[p]articular customs[] which for the most part affect only the inhabitants of particular districts." Finally, there are "[c]ertain particular laws . . . used by some particular courts." Thus, Blackstone equated "general customs" with "the common law, properly so called"; the "general immemorial custom" was the "chief corner stone of the laws of England."[41] As Carol Rose observed, "British jurisprudes [understood] that a general custom, the 'custom of the country,' is none other than the common law itself."[42]

Blackstone endorsed Hale's understanding of the truly democratic foundation of custom as law. As Blackstone wrote, custom becomes law by a process of long social usage that culminates in its universal acceptance in the polity. Customs that become law properly so-called "receive their binding power, and the force of laws, by long and immemorial usage, and by their universal reception throughout the kingdom." As he put it, "the goodness of a custom depends upon it's having been used time out of mind; or, in the solemnity of our legal phrase, time whereof the memory of man runneth not to the contrary."[43]

One purpose served by the long-usage requirement was to ensure that the resulting common law was good, true, and pure, for if a maxim or rule could survive for a lengthy period, one could be reasonably assured that it met the requirements for reason. On this view, most often associated with Coke, English law "by many successions of ages . . . ha[s] been fined and refined by an infinite number of grave and learned men, and by long experience grown[] to such a perfection."[44] As Gerald Postema put it: "Time provides the opportunity for continuous testing, adjusting and refining of the law through deliberation and argument."[45] "Law," in Coke's memorable aphorism, "is the perfection of reason."[46]

The more practical reason for a long-usage benchmark has to do with consent. If a rule or maxim could survive to be handed down from generation to generation, that was a sign that it had gained the general assent of the community, justifying its nature as binding law.[47] In this way, the process of custom attaining the force of law was considered profoundly democratic. The durability and longevity of a custom were thought to stand in as a surrogate for more formal democratic mechanisms. As Blackstone wrote: "[T]he written law binds us for no other reason but because it is approved by the judgment of the people, therefore those laws which the people have approved without writing ought also to bind every body."[48]

Yet, at the same time, British jurisprudes understood that custom was constantly evolving in an attempt to balance stability with adaptability to change. This recognition that the common law evolved with custom was also consent-based and democratic in origin. That people be ruled by their own hands and not the dead hand of the past, the law must change as custom does to fit the changing needs of the polity.[49] In a continuing feedback loop, the people shaped the rules while the rules "shape[] the dispositions, beliefs and expectations of the people."[50] By accommodating the consent implicit in generations of usage with the current needs of the polity, custom represents the highest value of English liberty: self-government. As

Blackstone put it: "[I]t is one of the characteristic marks of English liberty, that our common law depends upon custom; which carries this internal evidence of freedom along with it, that it probably was introduced by the voluntary consent of the people."[51]

How did yesterday's custom become today's law? Lon Fuller compared the formation of law from habit and custom to "the mode in which a path is formed across a common."[52] Or think of a major four-lane highway near where you are sitting. It might have begun thousands of years ago as a path trod through the woods by mammoths or buffalo in search of water and food. Perhaps premodern hunters of the large game cut the path more clearly and deeply with their footsteps and primitive tools. Then maybe the path became an artery between native settlements or trading posts. When Europeans took the land, they adopted the path, clearing and smoothing it further for travel by horse and carriage. Finally, the path was paved for use by automobiles and widened to accommodate heavy traffic. The transformative process by which custom becomes law is similar. It was summed up in this way by a late seventeenth-century treatise on customary law:

> When a reasonable Act once done is found to be good, and beneficial to the People, and agreeable to their nature and disposition, then do they use it and practise it again and again, and so by often iteration and multiplication of the Act, it becomes a Custom; and being continued without interruption time out of mind, it obtaineth the force of a Law.[53]

The complex process begins with individual practices, "tangible forms rather than as abstractions,"[54] as persons living together in a society learn to balance their individual needs with those of the community. When humans repeatedly face the same environmental stimuli, we start to offer the same response over and over again, as a way to save our time and energy.[55] Practice leads to imitation by others. As Hayek put it: "[A]bstract rules are learnt by imitating particular actions, from which the individual acquires 'by analogy' the capacity to act in other cases on the same principles."[56] The hydraulic pressure of conformity leads to widespread adoption of a social norm, at least "where no great principle is involved."[57] The impulse to conform one's actions to the prevailing norms powerfully achieves something close to consensus, which we call custom. This consensus leads to expectations and pressures that the norms and customs will be adhered to—"interactional expectancies," in Fuller's term[58]—along with informal sanctions for non-compliance.[59] In this way, custom becomes not merely regular or habitual but normative, not merely an *is* but an *ought*.[60]

Critically, custom often comes to be treated as enforceable law. Initially, pressure to conform to custom comes only by way of morals and imitative pressure. Yet, eventually, some customary rules are cloaked with the mantle of law.[61] For example, rules regarding the security, alienability, and heritability of land all developed as customary rules. By 1135, these customs had become sufficiently developed and standardized that they could properly be called law.[62] These customary rules were fully enforceable in the local courts, further fortifying and perpetuating these customs.

However, despite its status as enforceable law, affirmation of custom as law in the courts is the exception, not the rule. That is to say, custom generally exists as a form of law even without the imprimatur of a judicial ruling or jury verdict. This is because, while disputes occur, they do not often give rise to a legal action.[63] Because custom arises primarily from "convention rather than conflict," custom grows primarily from the people, and only secondarily from the pronouncements of a lawgiver.[64] And even where cases are brought, they often are disposed of without any legal ruling on the merits.[65]

Legal rights and interests, therefore, exist even without formal court rulings.[66] Indeed, in the development of the common law, intercession by a judge was simply seen as an affirmation of customary norms that had already formed, for "it is precisely because judges were intimately familiar with the complex 'texture [of] human affairs' . . . that they were best equipped to bring . . . disagreements to a reasonable resolution."[67] Thus, notwithstanding the claims of John Austin and Jeremy Bentham, the fathers of modern positive law thinking, who believed that "[c]ustom is not law by itself . . . but becomes law only upon it being duly adopted by judges,"[68] the generally accepted notion of custom in English law was that it "was constantly followed and obeyed before ever judicial authority had pronounced upon it."[69] The Austinian claim "that custom 'is not law' until it has been pronounced upon by a Court" is a fallacy, or at least was thought so during the framing generation. To them, "[c]ustom [wa]s the first and most essential law."[70]

In England, the mass of custom throughout the realm was amalgamated and made more or less uniform by the twelfth and thirteenth centuries. The ascension to the throne of Henry II in 1154 is typically viewed as the beginning of this amalgamation process. Prior to that time, "most criminal and civil matters were within local or feudal, and not royal, jurisdiction."[71] Henry II created a centralized court, which eventually evolved into what are now called the Court of Common Pleas and the Court of King's Bench. By establishing jurisdiction in these central courts, Henry II unified the general customs of the realm, essentially creating the concept of English common law. The final step in the process is the codification of some customs into statutory law.

Thus, the common and statutory law we know today is the end product of a long, slow, iterative evolutionary process centered around custom and usage. First, individuals developed methods of accommodating the demands of society with their own desires by adopting practices in certain recurring situations. Second, the most useful and normatively attractive of these practices were repeated, imitated, and adopted while others fell by the wayside. Third, through this process of repetition, imitation, and adoption, practices attained the status of custom. Fourth, the recognition of custom established rights and interests that were legally enforceable. Finally, some of those legal rights and interests were recognized by courts and legislators. Modern law, then, still encompasses much ancient custom.

The Originalist Connection between the Trespass Test and the Expectations Test

This background on the common law behind us, we can now see that the framers and ratifiers of the Fourth Amendment likely contemplated both something like the Court's trespass test as well as something akin to the Court's "reasonable expectation of privacy" test. I say "something like" the trespass approach because the Court's Fourth Amendment "trespass" cases have not relied, as the framers and ratifiers contemplated, on compliance with the positive law of each State as the touchstone. And I say "something akin" to the *Katz* approach because the framers and ratifiers likely would posit the test not as whether an expectation was reasonable but whether it found expression in the customs and norms of the community where the putative search occurred.

As we have seen, an unreasonable search or seizure to the framers and ratifiers of the Fourth Amendment meant one that was inconsistent with state law. This concept is capacious enough to find room for both a trespass-like approach and an expectations-based approach. However, the framers and ratifiers would take issue with the Court's current trespass-based approach in two respects. First, rather than rely on general trespass principles, as the Court has done, the Fourth Amendment was understood in 1791 as subjecting federal officers to the law of each State. If search-and-seizure rules were to be enforced in large part by after-the-fact lawsuits, then the constraints on federal officers would have to differ by State, like the law by which those suits would be decided. Second, there is no reason to limit Fourth Amendment doctrine to "trespasses." Trespass just happened to be the appropriate cause of action for an intrusion at the time the Amendment was adopted. The Amendment stands for the larger principle that state law in general, not just one particular cause of action, would remain as a protection against federal officers engaged in searches and seizures. Thus, any positive law violation, whether or not it is deemed a "trespass," that infringes our security in our "persons, houses, papers, [or] effects" can be said to implicate the Fourth Amendment.

On the other hand, the framers and ratifiers would also accept something like a *Katz*ian approach that recognizes Fourth Amendment rights even where one could point to no positive law grounding one's expectation of privacy. Such an expectation could be based in the social norms, customs, and "interactional expectancies" of the community. But this view would diverge from current law in two ways. First, once again, the framers and ratifiers would not understand that the same customs, norms, and expectations governed the whole nation but that they differed by State. Second, they would not recognize such customs, norms, or expectations as such but only to the extent that they had hardened into enforceable rights and interests that a court could recognize.

This last point might seem oxymoronic. If I have an enforceable right, doesn't that mean that I am relying on a precept that has crossed over from mere custom or norm to positive law? Not necessarily. If we follow Austin and Bentham, positive law does not exist until a court or legislature declares it to be so. But our review of the development of the common law showed that enforceable rights and interests can exist before that time. After custom finds wide enough acceptance through practice to become law, but before that law ripens into legislation or reported cases, it exists in the practices and experiences of people living together in a society. The law assigns rights and duties long before they are solidified in litigation and legislation. As Steven Sachs wrote: "A rule of customary law doesn't have to wait for a judge's ruling to make it so, any more than a rule in a pickup [basketball] game waits around to be born when a referee first applies it."[72]

Or, to use another sports analogy, consider ownership rights in balls batted into the stands at baseball games. Suppose three spectators at a baseball game, Felipe, Jesus, and Matty, go for a lazy foul ball hit in their general direction. Jesus grasps the ball and momentarily has it under his control, but just as he grasps it, Matty, in a bona fide effort to catch the ball, jostles Jesus enough so that the ball pops out of his hands. Felipe then grabs the ball and maintains control over it. Who owns the ball? Prior to 2002, the most the law could tell us was that a ball hit into the stands during a baseball game became the property of the fan who caught it.[73] That doesn't much help us here: did Jesus catch the ball or did Felipe? But there is, in fact, a "common law of baseball," as it were, and it is based on custom. When a court finally addressed this issue in 2002, in litigation over Barry Bonds's record-breaking 73rd home run ball, estimated at the time to be worth upwards of $1 million, it focused on the norms of baseball fandom in fashioning a legal rule: "The custom and practice of the stands creates a reasonable expectation that a person will achieve full control of a ball before claiming possession."[74] It is not as if there was no law on the ownership of balls batted into the stands until the judge signed his name on this order. It is just that the law had never been declared by a court or legislature. Baseball fans had come to a general, if tacit, agreement on the issue long before Bonds hit his home run. It was only when that high-stakes event occurred that someone tried to challenge that tacit agreement.

Like the fish that does not realize it is surrounded by water, we do not pay attention to these informal but (sometimes) legally enforceable rules because we are immersed in them. The "common law of the laundromat" tells us whether and when it's okay to remove someone's clothes from a dryer. The "common law of the supermarket" guides us in moving another shopper's cart when it is blocking our way. The "common law of the parking lot" tells us not to take a space that another driver is waiting for with her turn signal on. And on and on.

This is the point at which the trespass test and the expectations test merge, for even cases decided under the trespass idea often have to rely on the sorts of customs, norms, and expectations that form the backbone of the common-law methodology familiar to the framers and ratifiers of the Fourth Amendment. Take the two cases that the Court used to revive the trespass methodology from its long slumber, *United States* v. *Jones* and *Florida* v. *Jardines*. In each, there was a physical intrusion onto private property for the purpose of seeking information: in *Jones*, a GPS transmitter was placed surreptitiously on an automobile;[75] in *Jardines*, police took a drug-sniffing dog to the front door of a home to detect drugs within.[76] Given these clear physical intrusions, the real issue in each case lay elsewhere. The main issue in *Jones* was, in essence, whether the placement of the device was de minimis—that is, too trivial to be legally cognizable[77]—while *Jardines* came down to whether there was implicit consent to the intrusion.

But these issues of de minimis intrusion and implied license boil down to questions about social expectations, understandings, and norms. For instance, one could argue that the placing of the GPS device on the vehicle in *Jones* while it was parked in a public lot, although a technical physical intrusion, was no greater an intrusion than the common practice of placing a restaurant take-out menu under the car's windshield wiper. Whether the latter practice is acceptable can be answered only with respect to prevailing social norms. As with the foul ball example, it is extremely unlikely that such a norm will have ever hardened into case law. What are the odds that an aggrieved driver will sue over a take-out menu, much less take the issue on appeal where it might result in a reported decision? But such a norm is recognizable as a norm nonetheless.

Likewise, *Jardines* devolves into questions about societal expectations. What divided the Court there was not whether there was a physical intrusion into a constitutionally protected area for the purpose of gathering information: all agreed that the police officer and his canine companion breached the curtilage of a private home in order to detect odors coming from within. The only issue was whether the breach was implicitly consented to because, by having a walkway leading up to his front door, Jardines implicitly licensed others, including strangers, to travel the route to his front door and stay for a short time without knocking. Resolution of that issue hinged entirely on societal norms, customs, and understandings.

The *Jardines* Court began its discussion by quoting language from its 1922 decision in *McKee* v. *Gratz* that "[a] license may be implied from the habits of the country."[78] It acknowledged that customarily there is an implicit license for strangers "to approach the home by the front path, knock promptly, wait briefly to be received, and then (absent invitation to linger longer) leave." But, it continued, there is no customary license to approach the front door of a house via the front path and refrain from knocking, and instead "explore the area around the home in hopes of discovering incriminating evidence."[79] For his part, Justice Samuel Alito in dissent agreed that whether a license could be implied hinged on social customs and norms. He conceded, for example, that it is not customary to visit another's home in the dead of night. He merely disagreed that the police in *Jardines* went against the grain of societal customs and norms: "As I understand the law of trespass and the scope of the implied license, a visitor . . . is not necessarily required to ring the doorbell, knock on the door, or attempt to speak with an occupant." And he provided his own examples of such customs and norms permitting visitors to approach the door without knocking in order to seek information, such as the motorist approaching to discern a house number not easily observable from the roadway.[80] Thus, what separated the majority from the dissent in *Jardines* was their respective discernment of prevailing social norms and customs relating to visiting a stranger's home, not whether such norms are relevant.

Thus, the "trespass" question at the heart of both *Jones* and *Jardines* can be answered only in terms of societal norms, understandings, and expectations surrounding de minimis intrusions on personal property and the scope of the implied license to approach one's front door, respectively, whether or not reflected by positive law. That is to say, the analysis in cases that, like *Jones* and *Jardines*, involve physical intrusions to personal property often devolve into a very *Katz*-like methodology. This methodology mirrors the common-law approach familiar to the framers and ratifiers.

Conversely, some cases explicitly decided under the *Katz* approach can be seen as turning on whether the suspect had, not just a reasonable expectation of privacy in the thinner sense, but an enforceable legal right to exclude. Take *Bond* v. *United States*, where the Court held that bus passengers had a reasonable expectation that their soft luggage would not be physically manipulated in an exploratory manner, so that when a police officer did so for the purpose of discovering information, he conducted a search.[81] Like *Jones*, *Bond* involved what one might deem a de minimis intrusion on personal property, one that neither damaged it nor detracted from its value. And like *Jardines*, one could frame the question in *Bond* as the scope of the implied license that bus passengers give to other passengers to touch their stowed luggage. Either way, the question can be answered only with reference to the prevailing social norms.

Bond also demonstrates that the societal norms that undergird the *Katz* test do not necessarily boil down to the subjective preferences of a majority of the Supreme Court. To see why, imagine that the duffel bag in that case had been massaged forensically by another bus passenger rather than a police officer, and that Bond had caught her in the act. One would suppose that our hypothetical Bond might have every right under the applicable state law to demand that the other passenger stop and to use force if she persisted. By contrast, Bond almost certainly would not have had any right to forcibly prevent a fellow passenger from simply moving his bag to make room for her own luggage. One could reach these conclusion even if there were no cases on point stemming from civil or criminal litigation.

The third-party consent cases, and particularly *Georgia* v. *Randolph*,[82] also hinge on social norms. The *Randolph* Court held that where one co-occupant (Mrs. Randolph) consented to entry by police and one (Mr. Randolph) objected, the objection trumped the consent and police should not have entered. What separated the majority and the dissent, which would have held to the contrary, was their respective understanding of social norms and customs that govern in this situation when entry is requested not by a police officer but by a private citizen. At its foundation, *Randolph*, like *Jardines*, is a case about license: does a third party have license to enter premises when one occupant consents and one objects? And as in *Jardines*, the question can be answered only in terms of prevailing social norms. The *Randolph* Court began with the observation that co-occupants typically operate under certain understandings "about their common authority when they share quarters." One of those understandings is that "any one of them may admit visitors, with the consequence that a guest obnoxious to one may nevertheless be admitted in his absence by another." However, the Court wrote, understandings change when the objector is present. Where one occupant has invited the guest inside but another is standing there and "saying, 'stay out' . . . no sensible person would go inside," absent "some very good reason." The "customary social understanding" under those circumstances, then, is that there is no license to enter.[83]

General acquiescence to this norm might confirm and fortify the norm to the point where it might have matured into a cognizable legal right even without reported appellate decisions. Imagine, for example, that the person requesting entry in *Randolph* had not been a police officer but instead a friend of Mrs. Randolph's. Had Mrs. Randolph invited her friend inside the house, and had Mr. Randolph objected, and had the friend entered, would the friend be civilly or criminally liable for trespass? And would Mr. Randolph have been within his rights to forcibly remove the guest? Neither the majority nor the dissent cited any cases in which this issue arose. But just because there may not be any reported appellate decisions does not mean that there is no law.

In short, the connection between the "reasonable expectation of privacy" test and the trespass test is close and strong. What connects them is the common-law process of rule development described earlier in this chapter, which was well known to the framers and ratifiers of the Fourth Amendment. From an originalist perspective, we can think of a search as a quest for information conducted contrary to law, broadly conceived—that is, law in whatever stage of evolutionary development—protecting us from intrusion in our "persons, houses, papers, and effects" from other individuals. An attempt to gather information in such a way implicates the Fourth Amendment. An attempt to do so that is unauthorized by law—by warrant or otherwise—violates the Fourth Amendment.

Decentralizing the Fourth Amendment Search Inquiry

One critical move remains. As discussed in previous chapters, the framers and ratifiers of the Fourth Amendment, at least the Anti-Federalists, understood that the customary social understandings that form the backbone of the common-law rules protecting us from incursions by others will sometimes differ by State and even by locality. One might say that like all politics, all searches are local (both overstatements, to be sure, but that will be addressed later). Thus, the Fourth Amendment search inquiry should be decentralized.

Fourth Amendment doctrine, whether expressed through the "trespass" approach or the "reasonable expectation of privacy" cases, manifest a distinct aversion to having Fourth Amendment rights hinge on local conditions. The decoupling of Fourth Amendment search doctrine from local positive law began as far back as *Olmstead* v. *United States*, the 1928 wiretapping case, in which the Court cared not one whit about the fact that the federal agents there had committed a criminal offense under the laws of Washington.[84] Across decades of cases, we see an almost fetishistic obsession with national uniformity: the Court's caution in *Silverman* v. *United States* that it was not calibrating the Fourth Amendment search question to "local law";[85] the Court's back-of-the-hand rejection in *California* v. *Greenwood* of the idea that the Fourth Amendment search question might "depend[] on the law of the particular State";[86] and the Court's punctilious avoidance in *Florida* v. *Jardines* even of the use of the term "trespass."[87]

But the original understanding of the Fourth Amendment shows that this obsession with national uniformity is misguided. At the time of the framing, both custom and law were understood as differing by locale. Even under the centralized system of common law in England, unified for most purposes in the early Middle Ages, some customs were strictly local in nature. Blackstone recognized this, writing that the unwritten law of England "includes not only general customs, or the common law properly so called; but also the particular customs of certain parts of the kingdom." According to Blackstone, even after the bulk of common law was aggregated and unified, "particular counties, cities, towns, manors, and lordships, were very early indulged with the privilege of abiding by their own customs."[88] These local customs often spring from, and are preserved because of, local conditions not generally shared.

And, of course, common law in the United States turns out not to be so "common" at all. With thirteen States at the time of the founding we had thirteen different versions of the common law. Looking to underlying positive law to determine the metes and bounds of the Fourth Amendment requires acceptance of the idea that what is a search in one State might not be a search in another because the social norms that are reflected in positive law will often differ by State. William Baude and James Stern, who elaborated upon a "positive-law model" of the Fourth Amendment, observed that application of such a model would often have to be "jurisdiction-specific."[89] A 2007 Note in the Harvard Law Review by Yaakov Roth similarly observed: "It is likely that commonly held understandings about privacy do indeed differ by state, and dynamic incorporation [of state law] would allow the Fourth Amendment to reflect these nuances."[90] Justice Gorsuch has suggested an approach whereby the Fourth Amendment search inquiry depends in part on "state-created rights."[91] Again, the framers and ratifiers of the Fourth Amendment, or at least the Anti-Federalists who demanded a Bill of Rights, understood the common law as differing by State.

The first place for courts to look is state positive law, which should be familiar to local police, lawyers, and judges, even in federal court. Take, for example, the Supreme Court's so-called "spy" cases, such as *On Lee* v. *United States*, discussed briefly above. In these cases, a government operative, a pretended friend of the suspect, wore a wire and secretly recorded or transmitted their conversation, and the suspect's words were then used against him at trial. The Court has held that this activity does not constitute a search because one who speaks indiscreetly to a friend takes the risk that the friend is secretly recording one's comments or secretly allowing a third party to listen in.[92] But would that not depend on the underlying state law? Some States are so-called "one-party" States that allow recordings of conversations as long as one party to the conversation—the one doing the recording—consents. But other States are two-party States, which outlaw recordings unless *all* parties to the conversation consent. If I am in a one-party State, I am on notice that I might be recorded without my consent, even by someone I consider a friend, and I take the risk that this might occur. But can it really be that I take that risk if the person to whom I am speaking commits a criminal offense by recording me? Following that path to its natural conclusion would lead to the destruction of privacy rights even in the home, given the possibility, however remote, that a criminal intruder will enter.

These are cases in which state law is clear. But in cases such as *Bond*, *Jardines*, *Jones*, *Randolph*, and many others, there often will be no positive law on point and the question of customary social usage is a close one. What to do in that situation? State and local custom should be consulted by courts to help decide difficult cases such as these. The very fact that the Court was closely split in many of these cases is perhaps a clue that these questions are not amenable to a simple answer satisfactory to 330 million people spread across fifty States. After all, when the Court in *McKee* v. *Gratz* wrote that "[a] license may be implied from the habits of the country,"[93] a line repeated in *Jardines*, it surely used "country" in its more colloquial sense to mean "region," the first definition provided in the Webster's Dictionary in use at the time,[94] rather than the Nation as a whole.

But how to determine "the habits of the country" when there is no legislation or reported cases on the issue? The answer is to fall back on that centuries-old, tried-and-true mechanism of common-law development: the jury. After all, the original understanding of the Fourth Amendment was precisely that juries would enforce search-and-seizure constraints on federal agents by awarding damages in common-law suits whenever they breached those constraints. And specific protection by a bill of rights for jury trials in civil cases was a key demand of the Anti-Federalists, a demand which ultimately begat our Seventh Amendment.[95]

Where legal standards are stated in generalities, such as the negligence standard in tort, we have historically trusted juries to apply these abstract standards to the concrete facts of actual cases. It is entirely consistent with this history to ask juries to draw lines when it comes to contestable assertions of infringement of security in our "persons, houses, papers, and effects," and to separate mere annoyances that must be tolerated from true abridgments of incipient legal interests. A local jury is the best measure we have for determining local custom regarding the metes and bounds of our security against intrusion when positive law is unclear. This tracks what was done at common law. According to Blackstone, establishment of the existence of a particular custom and its applicability to the dispute at hand was a two-step process. First, where a local custom was alleged, it was treated as a question of fact to be proved to a jury like any other factual question. Then, the court had to determine the legal validity of the custom.[96] Somehow, we have lost that first step.

This approach would allow Fourth Amendment law to recognize interests that communities generally recognize but that, for whatever reason, have not adequately been expressed in positive law. It also recognizes the fact that social norms are constantly evolving.[97] When courts decide that there is or is not a reasonable expectation of privacy in a particular context, that decision is more or less final: it is given *stare decisis* effect—that is, treated as binding precedent—unless and until a later court determines that the heavy presumption against overruling precedent has been satisfied.

By contrast, a jury verdict on an evolving social norm is necessarily more tentative. A jury in another case in a different court is never bound to come to the same conclusion.[98] At the same time, the requirement of judicial ratification at the second step ensures that custom not be too out of line with the positive law of the State.

Providing for a jury mechanism to the Fourth Amendment search inquiry in close cases ameliorates *Katz*'s worst flaws: its disregard of text and history, its circularity, and its undemocratic nature. First, jury determination of the liability of government officials for unreasonable searches and seizures was precisely what was contemplated by the framers and ratifiers. Moreover, unlike the *Katz* test, a model that utilizes juries in close cases avoids circularity by tying Fourth Amendment interests to something outside the Fourth Amendment itself: the law and social custom of the local community. Most importantly, engrafting the jury into the Fourth Amendment search inquiry takes unelected federal judges out of the business of divining the reasonable expectations of privacy of ordinary people, and instead directly asks the people themselves. A bottom-up system in which local judges and juries determine whether law enforcement violated state law, sometimes based on local custom, is much truer to the 1791 understanding of local democratic controls over searches and seizures, as opposed to the top-down system we currently have in which nine unelected, unrepresentative federal judges decide for the rest of us how long is too long to linger before someone's front door without knocking or how much manhandling of a duffle bag is too much.[99]

I am hardly the first to suggest entrusting Fourth Amendment questions to a jury where positive law provides no clear answer. The last two decades have seen a surge of scholarship touting the jury's historic role as a populist and democratic organ of our criminal justice system.[100] Some scholars have specifically advocated involving the jury in the determination of Fourth Amendment issues.[101] Some have even advocated the creation of the "suppression jury," a jury specially impaneled to determine Fourth Amendment issues raised by suppression motions in criminal cases.[102] In a fit of extrajudicial candor, Justice Scalia, probably the most influential Justice on Fourth Amendment issues in many decades, said just about as much: "I just hate Fourth Amendment cases. I think it's almost a jury question—whether this variation is an unreasonable search and seizure."[103]

This is not to deny a place for some nationwide Fourth Amendment rules. After all, not all politics is local and neither are all searches. Online conduct, for example, crosses state lines (and international boundaries) almost instantaneously. Moreover, our activity online has been around long enough for certain related norms to develop, but is new enough for those norms not to have developed in any kind of state-specific way. But nationwide rules on searching in cyberspace would be consistent with the Fourth Amendment in any particular State only to the extent they are not inconsistent with state law.

Again, there is an analogue in the development of common-law doctrine that the founding generation would have been aware of where uniformity was required: the *lex mercatoria*, or law merchant. The law merchant was developed by and for merchants and others engaged in commercial transactions and was historically seen as a "local" branch of common law. Blackstone described the law merchant as "a particular system of customs used only among one set of the king's subjects" that was "different from the general rules of the common law . . . yet ingrafted into it."[104] In the Middle Ages, once trade began taking place beyond the borders of a borough and even across national boundaries, disputes could not be settled by reference to law and custom that had developed purely to address local issues like landownership and use. Merchants, who best understood commercial activity and had a heightened interest in an efficient commercial system, developed their own laws and customs to govern such transactions.

The development of norms in cyberspace seems directly analogous to this medieval development of a branch of law created by and applicable to merchants.[105] It may be, then, that the guideposts we look to in determining the contours of computer searches are, first, the national legislation that has sprung up around this new technology, and second, the general norms of online activity. While these norms have been influenced from above by national decision-makers, they have also been influenced from below, by private companies and individuals heavily involved in online activity, so-called "norm proselytizers."[106] Again, so long as these laws and norms are not in conflict with a particular State's law, they would also be consistent with the Fourth Amendment.

Conclusion

Custom forms a bridge between social norms and positive law. In much the same way, custom provides an accommodation between the reasonable expectation of privacy test and a trespass-based approach to Fourth Amendment search doctrine. There are deep connections between the two approaches and, in fact, are really just different manifestations of the same basic inquiry. The framers and ratifiers would have been comfortable with both approaches, provided that the Fourth Amendment question is grounded in the law, whether fully formed or incipient, and is decentralized for determination on a State-by-State, or even community-by-community, basis by local judges and juries. In Hayekian terms, search-and-seizure rules should be the product of spontaneous order, not central planning. That is, at least, what the Anti-Federalist framers and ratifiers of the Fourth Amendment envisioned in their quest for a reservation of local control of federal search-and-seizure policy.

Five

The Contingent Common Law of Searches and Arrests

While the previous chapter addressed the original understanding of the "search" question, this chapter addresses the original understanding of what made a search or seizure reasonable. We saw in chapter 4 that the differentiated nature of the common law in 1791, and the Anti-Federalist recognition of that differentiation, meant that a federal officer conducts a search when she intrudes upon someone's person, house, papers, or effects for purposes of obtaining information in a way that would be forbidden by state law, broadly conceived, when performed by a private citizen. Seizures are comparatively easier to define: a seizure is a restraint on a person's liberty to come and go as they wish, either by physical constraints or by a show of authority to which the person submits.[1]

In this chapter, we go to the next question: assuming the officer's actions constitute a search or a seizure, is it a reasonable one? As I suggested in chapter 2, the framers and ratifiers of the Fourth Amendment did not expect that federal officers would always need a warrant based on probable cause in order to search or seize, but they also did not want federal officers loosely bound by an amorphous concept of reasonableness. Instead, I suggested that they sought to bind federal officers to follow state law on searching and seizing, which they recognized could change across borders and over time. In this chapter, I present specific evidence that search-and-seizure law differed across jurisdictional boundaries and over time in important respects during the crucial period from about 1760 to about 1790. Although search-and-seizure law in North America during that period was marked by a great deal of consistency, which one would expect given that it all emanated from English common law, that consistency masks some important differences among jurisdictions.

The Contingency of Search-and-Seizure Rules in 1791

A look at the common law of searches and seizures circa 1791 reveals that while many general principles were universal, the common law was to a large extent indeterminate. As a great many scholars such as Tom Clancy, Morgan Cloud, Donald Dripps, and David Sklansky have pointed out, there are essentially three reasons for this. First, the common law of search and seizure in 1791 was underdeveloped, given "the limited range of questions that eighteenth-century judges and commentators asked about searches and seizures."[2] Second, while the law was uniform in some respects, there were also significant differences of opinion, and "[m]any of the principles that remain today as core search and seizure concerns were being litigated at that time."[3] Finally, "[s]earch and seizure law was dynamic"; it evolved as new rules were adopted and old ones discarded, both judicially and legislatively.[4] In short, to the extent that it was clear at all, "search-and-seizure rules . . . varied from colony to colony and from decade to decade."[5] A good deal of this differentiation can be seen in the "Justice of the Peace" manuals from that era.

The Justice of the Peace Manuals

The Justice of the Peace manuals were "how-to" manuals derived from treatises by English jurists such as William Blackstone, William Hawkins, and Matthew Hale, and "addressed . . . legal matters relevant to justices of the peace and other parish and county level officers, including constables."[6] This guidance was essential because constables were chosen from among the citizenry and had no formal training in law enforcement. Even justices of the peace did not need to be attorneys, so they, too, required the guidance provided by these manuals. The manuals often contained a substantial amount of information on arrests, searches, warrants, and the duties of the constable. Tom Davies has observed that "[t]hese were probably the sources regarding criminal procedure that were most accessible to members of the Framers' generation."[7] And John Conley's research suggests that for the justices of the peace, these manuals were the "primary source of legal reference."[8]

My focus here is on the Justice of the Peace manuals published from 1761 to 1795, in the three decades or so prior to and just after the adoption of the Bill of Rights, because they shed substantial light on American sensibilities about search-and-seizure policy at the time the Fourth Amendment was adopted. Importantly, different versions of the manuals were used in different colonies and States at different times during the founding period. That very fact suggests differentiation over time and across borders. As Davies put it: "Given the locations at which American versions of justice of the peace manuals were printed, as well as statements in the various prefaces, it appears that they were often oriented to particular colonies/states."[9] Specifically, I will be making reference to the following ten manuals, listed in chronological order. Where it is not obvious from the title, I have noted parenthetically the jurisdiction(s) toward which the manual was directed:

- William Simpson, The Practical Justice of the Peace and Parish-Officer, of His Majesty's Province of South-Carolina (1761)
- James Parker, Conductor Generalis: Or, the Office, Duty and Authority of Justices of the Peace, High-Sheriffs, Under-Sheriffs, Coroners, Constables, Gaolers, Jury-Men, and Overseers of the Poor (1764) (New Jersey)
- Joseph Greenleaf, An Abridgement of Burn's Justice of the Peace and Parish Officer (1773) (Massachusetts)
- James Davis, The Office and Authority of a Justice of Peace (1774) (North Carolina)
- Richard Starke, The Office and Authority of a Justice of Peace Explained and Digested, Under Proper Titles (1774) (Virginia)
- The Conductor Generalis: Or, the Office, Duty and Authority of Justices of the Peace, High-Sheriffs, Under-Sheriffs, Coroners, Constables, Gaolers, Jury-Men, and Overseers of the Poor (1788) (New York)[10]
- The South-Carolina Justice of Peace (1788)[11]
- The Conductor Generalis: Or, the Office, Duty and Authority of Justices of the Peace, High-Sheriffs, Under-Sheriffs, Coroners, Constables, Gaolers, Jury-Men, And Overseers of the Poor (1792) (New Jersey, New York, and Pennsylvania)
- Eliphalet Ladd, Burn's Abridgement, or the American Justice; Containing the Whole Practice, Authority and Duty of Justices of the Peace (2d ed. 1792) (New Hampshire, Massachusetts, and Vermont)
- William Waller Hening, The New Virginia Justice (1795).

It should be noted at the outset that there are substantial similarities among the justice of the peace manuals. Moreover, many of the differences take the form, not of outright contradiction, but of omission of material in one manual that appears in another, or equivocation on a legal point in one that is stated more forthrightly in another. Yet the authors of these manuals were, for the most part, experienced lawyers and judges. As good lawyers know, omission of terms or conditions from any legal document can be highly significant, and equivocal directives give actors far more discretion than those stated more definitively. The question is how these differences in wording, when translated into action by real justices and constables, would have played out in real life, for, as we saw in the previous chapter, common-law doctrine was inextricably and symbiotically intertwined with custom and usage; conduct often determined law as much as law dictated conduct. However minor the differences in the manuals were, they likely resulted in different customs—and therefore different law—when operationalized by legal actors.

During the framing period, there were at least ten significant search-and-seizure issues on which the law differed based on location and time period, the first nine attributable to differences in the manuals and the British authorities on which they were based, and the tenth reflecting a difference in state customs statutes, an area not covered by the manuals or treatises.

The Felony-in-Fact Requirement for Warrantless Arrests

The law in 1791 was clear that reasonable grounds for suspicion that the potential arrestee had committed the felony in question were necessary to arrest him without a warrant. But one area where the law was in flux was with respect to the anterior question: did there have to have been, in fact, a felony at all; or were reasonable grounds for suspicion as to the commission of a felony sufficient there as well? The former is known as the "felony-in-fact" requirement. The 1780 English case *Samuel* v. *Payne* held that there was no felony-in-fact requirement; reasonable grounds of suspicion both that a felony had been committed and that the suspect had committed it were generally sufficient for a warrantless arrest.[12] Given that the case was decided eleven years prior to adoption of the Fourth Amendment, one might think that that ends the matter.

However, not all the framers and ratifiers of the Fourth Amendment would have even been aware of *Samuel* v. *Payne*. News, of course, traveled more slowly back then, and the case was decided in the midst of the American Revolution, when the future framers and ratifiers of the Fourth Amendment had other things on their mind. And for those who even knew about the ruling, as Davies pointed out, Americans of that time period would have viewed *Samuel* v. *Payne* "to be a novel English ruling" rather than a statement of settled principles.[13] The opinion itself acknowledges this in noting that "the present case . . . is . . . the first determination of the point."[14] Indeed, the trial judge in that case had held that a felony in fact was indeed a requirement for a warrantless arrest, but the judges of the King's Bench collectively disagreed and granted a new trial.[15] Unless the trial judge were guilty of the sheerest incompetence—unlikely, given that it was the esteemed Lord Mansfield—the abrogation of the felony-in-fact requirement was hardly settled law.

The justice of the peace manuals bear this out. Of the five that postdate the decision in *Samuel* v. *Payne*, only the 1795 Virginia manual even discussed the possibility that reasonable probable grounds of suspicion of a felony are generally sufficient justification for an arrest, even if no felony had in fact been committed. This discussion immediately followed a reiteration of the more conventional rule: "[G]enerally, no . . . cause of suspicion . . . will justify an arrest, where in truth no such crime hath been committed."[16] Thus, the Virginia manual set forth two inconsistent rules without picking a side. More significantly, the two manuals published in 1792—by which time a dozen years had passed since the decision in *Samuel* v. *Payne* and it likely would have been known to at least some American lawyers—did not mention that decision at all and set forth only the more conventional rule.[17]

The felony-in-fact requirement was also a rule that Americans were slow to discard. As late as 1814, courts held that a warrantless arrest could take place only if a felony had in fact been committed, irrespective of the suspicions of a constable.[18] *Holley* v. *Mix*, an 1829 New York case, appears to have been the first on this side of the Atlantic to decide that a police officer could make a warrantless arrest based only on reasonable grounds, rather than certainty, that a felony had been committed.[19]

Breaking of Doors to Arrest

The common law also differed over the issue of what circumstances permitted the breaking of doors to make an arrest. At least three distinct positions are evident. The strictest rule was the one advocated by Lord Edward Coke, William Hawkins, Richard Burn, and Michael Foster, that not even a warrant permitted breaking of doors of a dwelling to make an arrest before indictment; rather, breaking of doors was permitted only after the arrestee had been indicted, and then only with an arrest warrant.[20] This rule was discussed but not necessarily endorsed by the 1764 New Jersey manual, the 1773 Massachusetts manual, the 1788 New York manual, and the 1792 New England and mid-Atlantic manuals, which stated that "where one lies under a probable suspicion only, and is not indicted, it seems the better opinion at this day (Mr. Hawkins says) that no one can justify the breaking open of doors in order to apprehend him."[21]

However, each of these manuals immediately went on to suggest a second, more moderate rule, that a pre-indictment warrant justified breaking of doors to make an arrest: "But lord Hale, in his history of the pleas of the crown, says, that upon a warrant for probable cause of suspicion of felony, the person to whom such warrant is directed, may break open doors to take the person suspected."[22] As the manuals suggest, this was the position taken by Matthew Hale.[23] The 1761 and 1788 South Carolina manuals took this position unequivocally and did not even suggest the stricter rule: "[U]pon a warrant for probable cause of suspicion of felony, the person to whom such warrant is directed may break open doors to take the person suspected."[24]

Finally, William Blackstone took the view that no warrant was necessary at all to make an in-home arrest for a felony, so long as the felony-in-fact requirement had been satisfied. In a section regarding "[a]rrests by officers, without warrant," he wrote that "in case of felony actually committed [the constable] may upon probable suspicion arrest the felon; and for that purpose is authorized (as upon a justice's warrant) to break open doors."[25] The 1774 Virginia manual adopted this position, stating that doors could be broken without a warrant to arrest one who either has been indicted or "who is known to have committed [t]reason, or [f]elony."[26] This view was so widely adhered to as late as 1761 that an attorney in the Boston writs-of-assistance case in that year could state with confidence: "Every Body knows that the subject has the Priviledge of House only against his fellow subjects, not vs. the King either in matters of Crime or fine."[27]

Thus, at least three common-law rules on breaking of doors to make an arrest coexisted at around the same time: permitted with a warrant and only after indictment; permitted with a warrant either before or after indictment; and permitted without a warrant if a felony in fact had been committed.

Issuance of Arrest Warrant Prior to Indictment

The common law also differed over a similar issue: whether an arrest warrant could be issued before indictment. The 1764 New Jersey manual, the 1773 Massachusetts manual, the 1788 New York and South Carolina manuals, and the 1792 mid-Atlantic and New England manuals mentioned an extreme limitation advocated by Coke: that an arrest warrant could not be issued prior to indictment. These manuals strongly suggested that Coke ought not be followed, but they again did not explicitly pick a side in this controversy, stating:

> Lord Hale proves at large, contrary to the opinion of lord Coke that a justice hath power to issue a warrant to apprehend a person suspected of felony, before he is indicted. . . .
>
> . . . I think, says [Hale], the law is not so, and the constant practice in all cases hath obtained against it, and it would be pernicious to the kingdom if it should be as lord Coke delivers it. . . .
>
> Mr. Hawkins likewise seems to be of the same opinion against lord Coke, but delivereth himself with his wonted caution and candour: It seems probable, he says, that the practice of justices of the peace in relation to this matter, is now become a law, and that a justice may justify the granting of a warrant for the arrest of any person, upon strong grounds of suspicion, for a felony or other misdemeanor, before any indictment hath been found against him.[28]

The 1761 South Carolina and 1774 Virginia manuals adopted the more lenient rule without hesitation: "A Justice hath power to issue a warrant to apprehend a person suspected of felony, before he is indicted."[29]

Grounds for Warrantless Arrest

The common law also varied widely with respect to the grounds for making a warrantless arrest. For example, among the traditional causes of suspicion that would justify warrantless arrest was "[t]he common Fame of the Country."[30] This was listed as the very first ground for a warrantless arrest in seven of the manuals.[31] Yet it was omitted from the 1761 South Carolina manual and the 1774 North Carolina and Virginia manuals.[32] In addition, four of the manuals (the 1773 Massachusetts, 1788 South Carolina, 1792 New England, and 1795 Virginia manuals) permitted the warrantless arrests of nightwalkers[33]—literally, those caught walking around at night, which, in a time before artificial lighting, was highly suspicious—whereas the other six did not.[34] And even where there was agreement that nightwalkers could be arrested warrantlessly, there was some dispute over who had the power to make such arrests. According to George Thomas: "Coke said that only watchmen could make night-walker arrests [while Matthew] Bacon claimed . . . that any person could arrest a 'Night-Walker.'"[35] Moreover, nine of the ten manuals permitted warrantless arrest of vagrants,[36] but the 1774 Virginia manual did not.[37]

Finally, the common law of 1791 also diverged on whether a warrantless arrest could be made for a minor crime committed in the presence of the officer. Both Blackstone and Edward East implied that warrantless arrest power for misdemeanors extended only to those involving breach of the peace in the presence of the officer.[38] Yet Matthew Hale wrote that a constable could make a warrantless arrest "for breach of the peace and some misdemeanors, less than felony," though he did not specify what misdemeanors would qualify.[39] And Hawkins agreed that a warrantless arrest was justified for a misdemeanor that was "scandalous and prejudicial to the public," but he, too, did not specify what that meant.[40]

Authority to Search Incident to Arrest

Another significant difference among the manuals is that only two, the 1764 New Jersey manual and one version of the 1788 New York manual, mention the authority for police to perform a "search incident to arrest," a warrantless search of the person of the arrestee and his immediately surrounding area upon arrest. Only these two manuals reprinted an excerpt of an instructional essay for constables by English justice of the peace and former high constable Saunders Welch.[41] The 1758 Welch excerpt has been cited as authority that the Fourth Amendment permits searches incident to arrest.[42] Welch observed that the law allowed the constable "to disarm and bind his prisoner" upon arrest. He elaborated:

> [A] thorough search of a felon is of the utmost consequence to your own safety, and the benefit of the public, as by this means he will be deprived of instruments of mischief, and evidence may probably be found on him sufficient to convict him, of which, if he has either time or opportunity allowed him, he will be sure to find some means to get rid of.[43]

By stark contrast, the other manuals, including the 1792 revision of the 1764 manual and the other version of the 1788 New York manual, do not contain the Welch excerpt or any other reference to searches incident to arrest.[44] This suggests two possibilities. One is that searches incident to arrest were so well entrenched and so well known that most of the manuals did not bother even to mention them. The other is that searches incident to arrest were not universally considered customary. Indeed, the tone of Welch's essay suggests that he wrote it precisely because constables were *not* conducting these searches, and the preface to the 1764 New Jersey manual, which includes the excerpt, characterizes it as "a curious tract."[45] It may be that the Welch excerpt, and search-incident-to-arrest authority, was included tentatively in the 1764 edition as a sort of curiosity and rejected in other manuals as an outdated or foreign oddity. Conversely, it may have been characterized as "curious" precisely because Welch considered it necessary to remind constables to perform a search that ensured their own safety. Whatever the reason, the authority of a constable to search incident to arrest is nowhere mentioned in the other manuals. Thus, even if searches incident to arrest were well entrenched by this period, an unknowing constable going by the book—and remember that constables were just ordinary citizens conscripted into law enforcement for a short period of time—might not have exercised search-incident-to-arrest authority.[46]

Liability for Fruitless Forcible Entries

Another difference of opinion in the common law relates to whether it addresses liability for two kinds of fruitless forcible entries. Seven of the ten manuals provided that if a prospective arrestee is thought to be in the house of a third party, and one breaks doors to apprehend him, but the prospective arrestee is not there, the one who attempted to make the arrest is liable to the owner in trespass. Generally, some of the Justice of the Peace manuals say that if the person to whom a warrant is directed "break[s] open the house of another to take [the felon] he must at his peril see that the felon be there; for if the felon be not there, he is a trespasser to the stranger whose house it is."[47] In a similar vein, these manuals provided that if a private person (but not a constable) breaks doors to make an arrest upon mere suspicion of a felony, but the arrestee turns out to be innocent, the person who made the arrest is liable for damages. They state that

> it seems that he that arrests as a private man barely upon suspicion of felony, cannot justify the breaking open of doors to arrest the party suspected, but he doth it at his peril, that is if in truth he be a felon, then it is justifiable, but if he be innocent, but upon a reasonable cause suspected, it is not justifiable.
>
> But a constable in such case may justify.[48]

The 1761 South Carolina manual and the 1774 North Carolina and Virginia manuals contained no such restrictions,[49] indicating that the law in these colonies either gave those making arrests more leeway to be in error or was simply unclear. However, by 1788 and 1795, liability in such situations apparently was sufficiently clear in South Carolina and Virginia, respectively, to call for inclusion of these provisions in the manuals published in those years.[50]

Nocturnal Arrests and Searches

The law also differed with respect to nocturnal arrests and searches. Most explicitly allowed nocturnal arrests, on the theory that if an arrest were not made immediately when proper grounds appear, the putative arrestee might escape: "An arrest in the night is good . . . else the party may escape."[51] The 1761 South Carolina manual did not explicitly mention nocturnal arrests.[52] However, by 1788, South Carolina had apparently adopted the majority rule on nocturnal arrests.[53]

As for nocturnal searches, we see more variations on the theme. The 1774 North Carolina manual restated Hale's disapproval of nocturnal searches as "very inconvenient" if not "unlawful":

> Lord Hale says, it is convenient that such Warrant do require the Search to be made in the Day Time; and though I will not affirm, says he, that they are unlawful without such Restriction, yet they are very inconvenient without it; for many times under Pretence of Searches made in the Night, Robberies and Burglaries have been committed, and at best it creates great Disturbance.[54]

In a different vein, the 1764 New Jersey, 1773 Massachusetts, and 1788 South Carolina and New York manuals generally barred nocturnal searches but permitted such searches when there was "positive proof" that stolen goods were in a premises, based on the same "exigent circumstances" theory set forth for nocturnal arrests. They added to the above language: "But in case not of probable suspicion only, but of positive proof, it is right to execute the warrant in the night time, lest the offenders and the goods also be gone before morning."[55] This language was retained in the 1792 New England and mid-Atlantic manuals.[56]

In another variation, the 1774 Virginia manual also cited the same page of Hale's treatise but summarized Hale's caution in a way that presumably granted authorities more wiggle room: "[I]t is better to require the Search to be made in the Day Time, *unless it be in particular Cases*."[57] The 1795 Virginia manual, by contrast, did not contain this proviso and instead, like the 1774

North Carolina manual, recited Hale's bare admonition against nocturnal searches.[58] Finally, the 1761 South Carolina manual did not mention nocturnal searches at all.[59] Thus, different jurisdictions, at different times, had different degrees of robustness and clarity with regard to their attitude on nocturnal searches.

Guilt of the Arrestee as an Absolute Defense

The common law also appears to have differed over whether the guilt of the arrestee was an absolute defense to a subsequent tort action for trespass, false imprisonment, battery, and the like. Put another way, the issue was whether a factually guilty arrestee could sue in tort based on an improper arrest. Traditionally, "an officer could justify a felony arrest if the arrestee was actually guilty of the felony for which the arrest was made."[60] That traditional rule is suggested in most of the manuals: in listing out various grounds for a warrantless arrest, these manuals began by categorizing the grounds as "the causes of suspicion, which are generally agreed to justify the arrest *of an innocent person*."[61] This wording implies that arrest of a guilty person was always justified. However, language in the 1774 Virginia manual suggests that even a guilty person could sue for trespass if no grounds for arrest existed: it described the acceptable grounds for arrest as the "Causes of Suspicion to justify *an Arrest*," full stop.[62]

Seizure of Private Papers

Entick v. *Carrington*,[63] discussed in chapter 2 and well known to the framers and ratifiers of the Fourth Amendment, strongly suggested that seizure of private papers, even via warrant, was illegal. Thirty years after *Entick* was decided, the 1795 Virginia manual became the first to suggest that officers could not seize private papers, even with a specific warrant. The manual extensively discussed *Entick* for the proposition that "a warrant to seize and carry away papers [is] illegal and void."[64] The manual recited the holding of *Entick* with no editorial comment, strongly suggesting, though never saying outright, that the author agreed with that holding. Donald Dripps has read this as "expressly prohibit[ing] warrants for papers."[65] By sharp contrast, even the other manuals published in the 1790s did not cite *Entick* or any other case for the proposition that search warrants for private papers were illegal.[66] It appears, but is admittedly not certain, that the 1795 Virginia manual barred searches and seizures of private papers, and that the others either permitted them or took no position.

Excise and Customs Searches of Non-Dwelling Premises

One final difference in the law of searches and seizures among different States had to do with excise and customs searches: searches for goods that had been smuggled or hidden to avoid paying customs duties or excise taxes. This type of search was unknown to the common law because common-law searches typically had stolen goods as their target, so searches for taxable and dutiable items were governed by statute instead and the Justice of the Peace manuals did not mention them. All jurisdictions that had such statutes required warrants for entering a dwelling. The difference is that in Maryland, North Carolina, and Virginia, a warrant was needed to enter all other premises on land as well. A 1781 Virginia impost statute required that collectors of the impost obtain a warrant to search "any house, warehouse or storehouse."[67] A 1784 North Carolina statute was identical to Virginia's in that respect.[68] A 1784 Maryland impost statute required a warrant for entry into "any house, warehouse, storehouse, or cellar."[69]

By contrast, Massachusetts and Pennsylvania required that officials obtain warrants in order to enter dwellings to search for smuggled items but did not require warrants to enter any other premises. A 1780 Pennsylvania statute establishing an impost provided that collectors of the impost could, without a warrant, "enter any ship or vessel, *and into any house or other place* where he shall have reason to suspect that any goods, wares or merchandise, liable to the . . . duty, shall be concealed, and therein to search for the same." The Act made clear that, in order to search a dwelling, a warrant was required, thus permitting warrantless searches of "other place[s]."[70] Likewise, Massachusetts enacted an impost in 1783 that allowed collectors of the impost to enter without a warrant "into [a] vessel or float, *store, building or place* (dwelling-houses excepted) and there to search for" any goods taken there in violation of the law. Again, the Act made clear that a warrant was required to search a dwelling.[71]

Although the Warrant Clause of the Fourth Amendment would ultimately dictate a national standard regarding the contents of federal search warrants, it says nothing about when warrants are required. In the years leading up to the adoption of the Amendment, and even during the ratification debates themselves, the States differed starkly over as significant an issue as whether warrants were required to search non-dwelling premises.[72]

The Significance of Differences in the Law of Search and Seizure during the Framing Period

The differences across geographic boundaries and over time in the common law of search and seizure, particularly as demonstrated by the justice of the peace manuals, are all the more striking given that virtually all of these manuals stemmed from the same source: most "drew heavily on [Richard] Burn's English manual."[73] Instead of simply parroting Burn, the manuals tended to add their own flourishes or emphasis, or omit material from Burn. Indeed, the very fact that different manuals were used in different sections of North America and were periodically updated belies any notion that the laws were uniform or static. As Conley noted, "the main reason for revised editions rested on an editor's conscientious attempt to maintain the book's currency."[74] Thus, the differences among them appear to be the result of conscious picking and choosing of the various aspects of Burn to fit the particular jurisdiction at a particular time.

One might argue that these manuals cannot show search-and-seizure law as it was actually practiced by colonial and early state constables and justices of the peace. But of course no extant source can do this. As Davies put it: "So far as I know, we have no historical sources that preserve systematic evidence of practice; hence, it is not possible to demonstrate to what extent framing-era practice comported with doctrine."[75] Moreover, differences among the manuals probably understate the extent to which practice diverged from policy. For example, although all the manuals provide that "hue and cry"—by which offenders were pursued and arrested immediately after an offense was committed—was a sufficient ground for arrest, the use of this procedure appears to have varied by State and was used rarely in Virginia.[76]

One might argue that differences among the different manuals is less the result of policy preferences of a particular jurisdiction and more the result of either carelessness or an intent to convey the same exact information in slightly different terms. But the editors of these manuals were, in most cases, experienced lawyers, judges, and justices of the peace. Davis was "a prominent attorney, member of the council, and a justice of the peace" in North Carolina. "Greenleaf was . . . a justice of the [p]eace for Plymouth County, Massachusetts." Grimké was not only a Cambridge-educated lawyer and a justice of the peace but was also a judge on the South Carolina superior court. Hening was an attorney "who served on the Privy Council and as a clerk of the Chancery Court" in Virginia. Simpson was Chief Justice of South Carolina.[77] Moreover, their intent of keeping their manuals up to date through a process of inclusion and exclusion is manifested, at least in some cases, by their prefatory remarks, such as Ladd's expression of gratitude to "those gentlemen of the profession, who have . . . furnished him with alterations which have been made in American Jurisprudence."[78] Thus, it is more plausible that these editorial decisions were deliberately made than that these legal experts included or omitted material carelessly or arbitrarily. As Conley put it, "[e]ach editor used his own judgment to delete or add material" and each "emphasized different themes or concerns by his decision to include or exclude certain material."[79]

It could also be argued that simple omissions from one manual should not necessarily be interpreted as disagreements with other manuals that contain the omitted material, absent an express statement of disagreement. Yet one would naturally expect such disagreements to typically take the form of omissions rather than explicit statements of disagreement. For example, in a section listing the types of authority to make warrantless arrests, one would not expect a manual to expressly state that there is no authority to arrest a nightwalker or vagrant. Instead, one would expect to see exactly what one sees in some of the manuals: a failure to mention this authority at all. And as legal experts, the editors of these manuals would likely understand the significance of such an omission.

Moreover, the generally light editing that occurred between editions of the justice of the peace manuals makes all the more significant the changes that were made. For example, the 1764 and 1792 versions of *Conductor Generalis* were virtually identical. Not only that, but the later version retained the earlier edition's references to the King, to English statutes, and to other terms peculiar to English legal culture, such as "member[s] of parliament," "peers," and "knights,"[80] nearly a decade after the Treaty of Paris officially ended the American Revolution. As Conley wrote, "even after the Revolution the editors [of *Conductor Generalis*] refused to Americanize the manual."[81] This is suggestive of a strong resistance to change when updating the manual. Accordingly, omissions, such as the failure of the 1792 version to reprint the Saunders Welch excerpt that had appeared in the 1764 edition justifying search-incident-to-arrest authority, are significant.

In any event, the *reason* that certain rules were omitted or included in the various manuals is far less important than the *fact* that they were omitted or included. The function of these manuals, after all, was to inform eighteenth-century justices of the peace and constables, who generally lacked any formal legal training, how to do their jobs. Assuming that the manuals performed this function, we also have to assume that the various omissions and inclusions were manifested in the day-to-day practices of justices and constables. Diligent justices of the peace and constables, in consulting a manual to determine whether, for example, a vagrant or nightwalker could be arrested without a warrant, would have come to different conclusions based on where they were. A risk-averse justice consulting a manual to determine whether he could issue a pre-indictment arrest warrant, and a risk-averse constable doing the same to determine whether he could break doors to serve such a warrant, would have come to different conclusions depending on whether they were in Massachusetts in 1773, Virginia in 1774, or South Carolina in 1788. Cautious constables in the 1760s might not search incident to arrest except in New Jersey, where the applicable manual explicitly gave them that authority. We can only assume that the directives of the manuals, or the absence thereof, thus became the common law of the jurisdiction through custom and usage. Whatever the extent of the differences in search-and-seizure *doctrine*, search-and-seizure *practice*, as evidenced by these manuals, differed by colony and State, and over time.

Granted, those differences were relatively few and at the margins. Yet, likewise, only the tiniest fraction of DNA makes the difference between a human being and a bonobo. Like the building blocks of life, the common law is intricate, and its intricacy is founded upon "its ability to comprehend a variety of exceptions to a general rule."[82] And as any first-year law student knows, learning the law is all about learning when to apply the rule and when the exception. That one jurisdiction applies the rule when another applies the exception is not a trivial matter.

Some of the issues on which these manuals differed geographically and temporally are the same as or closely analogous to Fourth Amendment issues that confound and divide modern courts. For example, the issue of whether a warrantless arrest is justified for a minor crime divided the Court 5-4 in *Atwater* v. *City of Lago Vista*[83] and is analogous to the still-controversial 1968 decision in *Terry* v. *Ohio*,[84] permitting temporary detention upon reasonable suspicion of commission of a crime.[85] Whether and to what extent the general bar on nocturnal searches allowed for an exception when there is "positive proof . . . lest the offenders and goods also be gone before morning,"[86] is closely analogous to modern disagreements over whether and to what extent exigent circumstances can justify warrantless intrusions into dwellings[87] or the failure of police to knock and announce their presence.[88] Whether and to what extent state officials were liable for trespass when they broke doors of a third party's dwelling to arrest someone who turned out not to be present calls to mind the ongoing debate over what level of suspicion is required on the part of the police regarding the putative arrestee's presence in order to break doors to make an arrest.[89] The omission or inclusion of a "common fame of the country" ground for arrest is redolent of modern-day disputes over whether and to what extent hearsay information is sufficient to justify an arrest.[90] And a divided Court decided only in 1980 that the Fourth Amendment requires a warrant to make a forcible, at-home arrest absent exigency.[91]

Yes, some general principles were fairly well uniform at common law, as they are today. But it is because those principles are relatively uncontroversial that they are not typically misunderstood by police or contested by lawyers. It is instead the granular, and contestable, details of how search-and-seizure law is operationalized that occupy the time of modern lawyers and judges. It is on some of those details that the common law of 1791 differed.

Conclusion

In the next chapter we will move from 1791 to 1866, so this is a good place to briefly sum up the lessons of Part I of this book. First, the framers and ratifiers of the Fourth Amendment understood that transgressive searches and seizures by federal officials would be remedied at least in part by after-the-fact lawsuits based on the common law of tort. Second, they understood, or at least the Anti-Federalists did, that the common law of tort, including specific aspects of the rules of searching and seizing, differed by State, which would mean that federal officers would potentially be subject to different rules depending on the State. Third, this understanding dovetails with the Anti-Federalists' main concern in this area, which was to assert local, democratic controls over search-and-seizure policy in the face of the potential preemption of this field by the new, powerful, less accountable federal government. Fourth, the Anti-Federalist worldview should play a major role in interpreting the Bill of Rights, which was a concession to them for ultimately agreeing to ratification over their strong reservations. Finally, the assertion of local, democratic controls over searching and seizing best explains the critical writs-of-assistance controversy that led directly to the adoption of the Fourth Amendment.

If the Fourth Amendment is primarily a federalism provision that preserves local control of searches and seizures, then how can we possibly apply it to the States? The short answer is that we can't. But we don't have to, because the Fourth Amendment does not really apply to the States; the

Fourteenth Amendment does. When we speak of the Fourth Amendment, or any part of the Bill of Rights, as applying to the States, we are using a kind of shorthand. Problems occur because we have used this shorthand for so long that we forget we are using it. The next three chapters will try to create space between the Fourth Amendment and the Fourteenth in the hopes that we can remember that the principles of the former apply, if at all, only by virtue of the latter.

PART II

The Fourteenth Amendment

Original Understandings

Six

The Historical Backdrop of the Fourteenth Amendment

Having looked at the original understanding of the constitutional constraints on *federal* search-and-seizure authority, this part of the book now turns to the original understanding of what, if any, constraints are placed on the *States* in that area. From 1791 until 1868, the Fourth Amendment applied only to the federal government. The U.S. Supreme Court's unanimous decision in *Barron* v. *City of Baltimore* in 1833 made this clear.[1] The question is whether and to what extent the Fourteenth Amendment, adopted in 1868, altered that arrangement. Because most law enforcement takes place at the state level, the question of "incorporation" of the Fourth Amendment against the States by the Fourteenth is central to the issues raised by modern policing.

In the wake of the Civil War, the country adopted the Thirteenth, Fourteenth, and Fifteenth Amendments. The Thirteenth, ratified in 1865, abolished slavery and the Fifteenth, adopted in 1870, gave Black men the right to vote throughout the United States. But we are primarily concerned with the Fourteenth, ratified in 1868, section 1 of which provides:

> All persons born or naturalized in the United States, and subject to the jurisdiction thereof, are citizens of the United States and of the State wherein they reside. No State shall make or enforce any law which shall abridge the privileges or immunities of citizens of the United States; nor shall any State deprive any person of life, liberty, or property, without due process of law; nor deny to any person within its jurisdiction the equal protection of the laws.[2]

These four clauses are known as the Citizenship Clause, the Privileges or Immunities Clause, the Due Process Clause, and the Equal Protection Clause, respectively. The original understanding of what constraints, if any, these clauses place on the States vis-à-vis search-and-seizure authority is the subject of this chapter and the next two.

The purpose of this part of the book is to question the conventional thinking that the Due Process Clause of the Fourteenth Amendment applies the Fourth Amendment to the States in the exact same way it applies to the federal government. For far too long, we have ignored the fact that in state cases, courts are interpreting the Fourteenth Amendment, not the Fourth. We have accordingly paid far too much attention to 1791 and far little to 1868.[3] Andy Taslitz highlighted this deficiency:

> Understanding the meaning of today's Fourth Amendment . . . requires study of the evolving meanings of search and seizure during the fight to end slavery, for it was that fight that motivated and defined the drafting and ratification of the Fourteenth Amendment. . . . The Framers of the nineteenth century matter, therefore, as much as those of the eighteenth.[4]

Determining whether and how the Fourteenth Amendment applies search-and-seizure constraints to the States will require a deep dive into what the framers and ratifiers of that Amendment understood. But the short answer, I suggest, is this: the Fourteenth Amendment is best understood as leaving much of search-and-seizure law to local control so long as local officials (1) do not discriminate, (2) obey the law, and (3) are not given excessive discretion. This view best honors the general understanding of the framers and ratifiers of the Fourteenth Amendment, and the compromise they struck between radical centralization and radical decentralization. In this respect, the Fourteenth Amendment, like the Fourth, is a local control provision, but with the guide rails of due process and equal treatment.

But getting there requires that we proceed in steps. As Michael Kent Curtis wrote: "The meaning of the amendment should be sought in the abuses that produced it and in the political and legal philosophy of those who proposed it."[5] This chapter explores the former, while the next two chapters will look at the latter. Specifically, chapter 7 studies the specific question of whether and to what extent the framers and ratifiers of the Amendment understood it as applying the Fourth Amendment to the States. And chapter 8 attempts to translate that understanding into usable legal standards. But first, we will look at the historical backdrop of the Fourteenth Amendment, focusing on the evils that the framers and ratifiers of the Amendment meant to address. These break down into two general categories. First, there were the "Black Codes," laws passed by virtually every former rebel State that not only drew legal distinctions between the races, but also included ostensibly race-neutral vagrancy laws that were enforced largely against Blacks. Second, there was the problem of violence against and other mistreatment of Black people, Southern whites who had remained loyal to the United States, and relocated Northerners, including both physical violence and forcible searches of homes and seizure of property.[6]

Congress tried to ameliorate this situation in three overlapping ways. First, it created and then expanded the jurisdiction of the Bureau of Refugees, Freedmen and Abandoned Lands—the "Freedmen's Bureau" for short—to protect formerly enslaved people, Southern loyalists, and relocated Northerners. The Bureau had been created in March 1865. A bill to extend the life of the Bureau indefinitely and extend its coverage to aid freedmen even in loyal States was passed by Congress but vetoed by President Andrew Johnson in February 1866. Second, Congress passed the Civil Rights Act of 1866 to forbid many forms of state discrimination against Black people, ensuring that they could buy, hold, and sell property, enter into contracts, sue and be sued and testify in court, and be subject to the same criminal punishments as whites. Finally, Congress proposed, and the States ratified, the Fourteenth Amendment. In essence, the Fourteenth Amendment constitutionalized the Civil Rights Act, and both were tools to ensure that the rights of people of color, loyal whites, and Northerners would be protected even after the army and Freedmen's Bureau were gone.[7]

The Historical Context of the Fourteenth Amendment

Following the Civil War, which cost about 750,000 lives according to modern estimates, the Southern States lay bloody and prostrate, eager for readmission into the Union. President Johnson, who succeeded to the Presidency after the assassination of President Abraham Lincoln, was also eager for reunion. The Thirty-Ninth Congress was more circumspect. Even after the Thirteenth Amendment was ratified and slavery abolished, Congress refused to seat the putative Senators and Representatives of the eleven States formerly in rebellion until it was satisfied that doing so would not lead to disastrous consequences, including a takeover of the federal government by the former rebels—who were overwhelmingly Democrats—in a coalition with Northern Democrats. Because most of the Senators and Representatives outside the South were Republicans, and because the eleven former rebel States were not represented in Congress, both the Senate and the House were overwhelmingly Republican: thirty-seven to nine in the Senate, with two members of third parties; and 132 to forty in the House, with eleven members of third parties. Republicans ranged, however, from the more conservative (i.e., closest to the Democrats), to the moderate, to the most progressive group, the Radicals.[8]

Johnson was a Democrat, chosen by the Republican Lincoln to be his Vice President in order to unify the country. By late 1865, however, it was becoming clear that the Democrat in the White House and the Republican-led Congress would not work well together. One particular sore point was that Johnson had issued a general amnesty in the spring of 1865 that had had the effect of pardoning large numbers of former rebels so long as they took an oath of allegiance to the United States. As a result, some congressional Republicans were already distrustful of Johnson when the Thirty-Ninth Congress convened in December 1865. The rift between the President and Congress deepened when Johnson vetoed the Second Freedmen's Bureau Bill. Still, Johnson maintained enough influence with the legislative branch that eight Senators who had voted for the bill switched their votes after the veto, preventing a congressional override.[9] The rift was all but complete when Johnson vetoed the Civil Rights Bill on March 27, 1866, which the Republicans in Congress quickly overrode.[10] The Republicans, with supermajorities in both houses, knew that if they stuck together, they could do essentially whatever they wanted.

The Republicans had essentially four concerns, which mirror what would become the first four sections of the Fourteenth Amendment. First, they worried that in the former slave States, Black people, loyal whites, and relocated Northerners would be deprived of their basic rights. Second, because slavery had been outlawed, former slave States would, ironically, be entitled to greater representation in Congress: during slavery, enslaved persons counted as three-fifths of a person for purposes of calculating state populations for apportioning Representatives in Congress; with the abolition of slavery, former slaves would count in full, boosting the representation in Congress of former slave States. Moreover, because Black people could not vote, this change would have the perverse consequence of enhancing the power of Southern whites while keeping Southern Blacks disenfranchised. Third, there was a question of whether and to what extent former rebels should themselves be permitted to vote and to hold office; Northerners were understandably wary of opening the doors of Congress to former Confederate soldiers and their supporters. Fourth, Congressional Republicans wanted to ensure that the debts the U.S. had run up during the war would be honored while at the same time ensuring that Confederate debts, including the billions of dollars invested in human slavery that had vanished overnight, were not. Although it is only the first of these issues—the rights guaranteed against deprivation by the States—that directly concerns us, it is important to know about the other explosive issues that came to be resolved by the Fourteenth Amendment.

To address these issues, Congress appointed a Joint Committee on Reconstruction—sometimes referred to as "the Committee of Fifteen"—comprising six Senators and nine members of the House. Republicans outnumbered Democrats on the Joint Committee twelve to three. It was this committee that proposed the measures that ultimately became the Fourteenth Amendment. The Committee also broke up into four subcommittees, each of which gathered evidence regarding conditions in the former rebel States. The committee issued a twenty-eight-page report, signed by all but one of the Republican members, in June 1866. Later that month, the three Democrats issued their own fourteen-page minority report.

Notice that the political dynamic was essentially the opposite of what it had been during the framing and ratification of the Bill of Rights. In 1787–88, states-rights-oriented moderate Anti-Federalists held the cards; they would make the difference between ratification and non-ratification. They demanded a national bill of rights, predicated on the idea that the States were the guarantors of civil liberty and that constraints on the federal government were needed to track the rights observed by the States. In 1866–68, the roles were reversed. Congress was controlled by the more nationalistic Republicans, heirs to the Federalists. The Democrats, heirs to the Anti-Federalists, held sway only in the former insurrectionist States, which were at the mercy of the rest of the Union.[11] As much as the Anti-Federalists were in the driver's seat in terms of the Bill of Rights, so were the Republicans in terms of the Fourteenth Amendment. Where the Bill of Rights was a concession paid by the nationalist Federalist party to the localist Anti-Federalists, the Fourteenth Amendment was the mirror image: the price paid by localist Democrats to nationalist Republicans for readmission of the Southern States into the Union.[12] Anti-Federalists dictated the terms upon which the Union would be created; Republicans dictated the terms upon which the Union would be restored. While we look to the Anti-Federalists in interpreting the Bill of Rights, we look to the Republicans in interpreting the Fourteenth Amendment.

First, we need know what conditions in the South the Republicans were trying to fix.[13] Much of what we know about the immediate postwar South comes from Major General (later Senator and then Secretary of the Interior) Carl Schurz. President Johnson sent Schurz through the South on a fact-finding tour, culminating in a lengthy report submitted to the President and thence to Congress in December 1865.[14] We also know a good deal from the hearings held by the subcommittees of the Joint Committee in the first half of 1866. Also instructive are reports of various agents of the Freedmen's Bureau, collected in congressional reports in 1866 and 1867. Finally, there were a number of accounts written by private individuals who traveled through the South after the war.[15] These sources all tell us that the sentiment outside the South regarding the need for the Fourteenth Amendment was triggered primarily by the passage of Black Codes in many former rebel States and the violence against Black people, loyal whites, and Northerners in those States.[16]

The Black Codes

Perhaps the most important trigger for the Fourteenth Amendment was the enactment of new Black Codes in Southern States following the abolition of slavery. Nine of the eleven former rebel States—plus Kentucky, a slave State that had remained loyal—enacted such measures in 1865 and 1866. Most of the new statutes made explicit distinctions based on race. A few were facially race neutral, but it was well known that they were enforced in a racially discriminatory manner. Northerners decried both types of provisions, and both types precipitated passage of the Fourteenth Amendment. Obviously the Fourteenth Amendment was aimed at race-conscious legislation. To provide insight into what the Amendment was thought to bar beyond explicit distinctions based on race, I focus on the race-neutral provisions and the Northern reaction to them.

The race-neutral laws that sparked the greatest outrage in the North were undoubtedly the vagrancy laws. Nearly every State that had been in rebellion enacted a new vagrancy statute in late 1865 or early 1866.[17] Florida's law was typical: "[E]very able-bodied person who has no visible means of living, and shall not be employed at some labor to support himself or herself, or shall be leading an idle, immoral or profligate course of life, shall be deemed to be a vagrant."[18] Some laws specifically targeted those moving from place to place, such as Georgia's, which included "wandering or strolling about in idleness" as part of the definition of the offense;[19] Kentucky's, which forbade "loitering or rambling about";[20] and North Carolina's, which singled out "sauntering about without employment."[21] These definitions were both broad, covering conduct engaged in by many, and lacking in clarity. Thus, even industrious Black people could be swept up in these statutes' capacious language. W. E. B. DuBois, in his classic *Black Reconstruction in America*, recounted testimony of New Orleans Freedman's Bureau employee Thomas Conway that he had released numerous Black men from the city jails "who were industrious and who had regular employment."[22] Likewise, a Freedmen's Bureau officer reported in December 1865 that New Orleans police, under an order from the Chief of Police to arrest vagrant Black people in the city, were intentionally arresting non-vagrants.[23]

Although each of the vagrancy statutes was facially race neutral, it was well known that they were aimed at Black people.[24] Of the Alabama law, Major General Wager Swayne, Assistant Commissioner of the Freedman's Bureau there, commented: "No reference to color was expressed in terms, but in practice the distinction is invariable," and "it would be difficult to tell the wickedness to which they have been and still are instrumental."[25] Contemporaneous reports of enforcement of the vagrancy laws suggest that, while there were vagrants of both races, the laws were used almost exclusively on Black people. A witness before the Joint Committee testified that in Virginia:

> There is nothing said about a white man being a vagrant if he stands around and begs for drinks; but for a black man there is a great deal of legislation necessary. [W]hen they were making so much to do about the idleness of negroes, I could see others who did not claim to be negroes doing the same thing.[26]

The mayor of one Mississippi city used the vagrancy law to "round[] up hundreds of freedmen in early 1866" in order to force them to enter into labor contracts or become street sweepers for the city.[27]

Perhaps the best indication that the vagrancy laws were aimed at the formerly enslaved was the fact that every State's law but North Carolina's had hiring-out provisions, whereby the sentence for vagrancy (either directly or upon inability to pay a fine) was the hiring out of the convicted vagrant to the highest bidder for a period of time, usually up to a year but sometimes more.[28] Five States provided that county prisoners could be used on public works projects, building roads and bridges, rather than being hired out.[29] It was understood that provisions such as these were intended to apply almost exclusively to Black people.[30] Although States had once hired out vagrants of both races, they had done so on a much smaller scale, and the practice as to whites was on the downswing by the start of the Civil War.[31] After the war, hiring out of mostly Black vagrants skyrocketed. In one incident in October 1866, unusual only "in its magnitude and gross irregularity," police in Nashville, over the course of a few days, arrested twenty-seven Black men as vagrants. All were convicted and fined and, unable to pay their fines, were hired out to local whites to work on cotton plantations in Northern Mississippi.[32] In postbellum Texas, only about a third of prisoners in the state penitentiary were Black, but Black people constituted "nearly 90 percent of those leased out for railroad labor."[33] These hiring-out provisions were a response to the language of the Thirteenth Amendment, which outlawed "slavery [and] involuntary servitude, *except as a punishment for crime whereof the party shall have been duly convicted*."[34] As a result, "local jails became labor-hiring centers where employers secured the services of convicts at bargain rates,"[35] and sheriffs in some places controlled, and profited from, a large organized market in Black labor.[36]

Although vagrancy statutes were of ancient vintage and existed outside the South, courts in other parts of the country tended to use vagrancy laws more sparingly.[37] Moreover, the new Southern statutes tended to call for harsher penalties than before and the hiring-out provisions were new.[38] So were provisions in States such as Florida and Louisiana allowing "vagrants to escape punishment by posting bond," thereby allowing white people to generally avoid being hired out while forcing impoverished Black persons to have their white employers post a bond for them in exchange for agreeing to a period of unpaid labor in order to pay off the bond.[39] The discriminatory intent stands to reason: "Since all [the States] had had adequate vagrancy laws before the war, the new statutes were not necessary except as a way of warning blacks that idleness would not be tolerated."[40] And unlike vagrancy provisions in other parts of the country and at previous times in our history these Southern vagrancy laws, as we will see, were "envisioned as the foundation for an entire labor system."[41]

Many Southerners openly admitted that the vagrancy statutes were used as a tool predominantly against Black people. Consider these contemporaneous observations from the pages of a Southern business journal:

> Vagrant laws are hardly needed by the whites, and they sleep upon our statute books. The white race is naturally provident and accumulative, and but few of them thieves. They have many wants, and to supply those wants, generally labor assiduously and continually. Little legal regulation is needed to induce white men to work. But a great deal

> of severe legislation will be required to compel negroes to labor as much as they should do, in order not to become a charge upon the whites. We must have a black code, and not confound white men with negroes, because one in a thousand [white men] may be no better than the negroes.[42]

One prominent Alabamian said: "'We have the power to pass stringent police laws to govern the negroes—This is a blessing—For they must be controlled in some way or white people cannot live amongst them.'"[43] In the summer of 1866 in Texas, the only State not to have yet passed a new vagrancy statute, "conservative whites were demanding the arrest of idle, vagrant, and suspicious Negroes."[44] Texas legislators obliged, "'publicly admit[ing] that they intended the proscriptions to apply exclusively to blacks.'"[45]

The vagrancy laws were not the only way that Southerners swept Black people into the convict-leasing market. Alongside the racist view of Black people as idlers, there grew a complementary racist idea of the Black person as a petty criminal who made a living of poaching and pilfering.[46] In response, some States changed their definitions of criminal trespass and enhanced the punishments for this petty crime.[47] Some adopted severe punishments for such crimes as "the unauthorized removal of timber, berries, agricultural products, or [other items] from the land of another."[48] The Texas "legislature revised [the penal laws] with an eye toward ensnaring blacks," as shown by its focus on the theft or destruction of livestock.[49] General George E. Spencer, stationed in Alabama, testified about a "large number of negroes" arrested, mostly for "trivial offences," such as "breaking a plate" and "throwing a stone at a sheep."[50] Some Black people were likely guilty of these petty offenses, but whites who were similarly guilty often went unpunished.[51]

The effort to keep Black Southerners in economic subordination by charging them with petty offenses entailed, in some cases, a dramatic restructuring of property law. Prior to the war, law and custom in the South largely kept private but unenclosed land open for all comers to hunt, fish, and forage, and graze livestock. Fence laws had put the burden on landowners, often at great expense, to fence in their land lest it become, in essence, common property for all to use and enjoy.[52] After the war the former rebel States enacted stringent trespass laws aimed at the supposedly larcenous Black race.[53] Georgia banned hunting on Sundays and required that private property be fenced in, but only in counties with large numbers of Black people.[54] One Mississippi statute "ma[de] it a misdemeanor to hunt on privately owned land without consent in all counties outside the [largely white] southeastern piney woods and the northeastern hills." Alabama and Virginia accomplished much the same thing through home rule provisions that allowed counties to enact their own new fence and stock laws.[55] These laws not only added to the petty offenses that could be hung around the necks of Black people, subjecting them to the convict-leasing system, but also, by limiting the ability of Black people to hunt, fish, and forage, tended to force them to work on plantations for whatever wages they could get.[56]

Cheap Black convict labor was also used for public works. At one point, "[o]ver 90 percent of the cases before the Montgomery Mayor's Court involved blacks and high fines were set for petty offenses in order to get recruits for the [chain] gang." When Richmond, Virginia instituted the chain gang in December 1866, it had fourteen convicts; twelve were Black men.[57] Author J. T. Trowbridge, happening upon an all-Black chain gang, learned that its members had been convicted of "disorderly conduct, vagrancy, . . . petty theft," selling "farm produce within the town limits" outside of the marketplace, and "using abusive language towards a white man."[58]

These vagrancy provisions and petty crime statutes were to be enforced by local law enforcement—police in more densely populated areas, and militia companies elsewhere—that was entirely white and often manned by former Confederate soldiers.[59] Louisiana presents a prime example. In one parish, law enforcement officers loyal to the U.S. "were all successively removed, and in their places were appointed disloyal men, all of them identified with secession and rebellion."[60] In New Orleans, the chief detective had served in the rebel army and the chief of police, though a westerner, was reportedly "a worse rebel at heart than any born at the south."[61] The Louisiana governor appointed in Rapides Parish a sheriff who was formerly a captain in the Confederate cavalry, a constable who had served as a lieutenant in a company of Confederate guerrillas, and six or seven captains of the militia, only one of whom was a loyalist.[62] The state militia consisted almost entirely of former rebel soldiers.[63]

North Carolina was also particularly problematic in this respect. One North Carolina sheriff, a former Confederate guerilla, was described by a minister as "one of the most hostile men, an out-and-out rebel."[64] The police in that State were often former rebel soldiers, "generally commanded by former Confederate officers." The state militias were repackaged forms of the "'county patrols' or 'paddyrollers' in ante-bellum days," which had been used to detain and question enslaved persons who were away from their plantations, and to mete out punishment in the form of whippings and beatings in the case of those found without a proper pass. By the end of 1865, the New

Hanover County militia was fully under the control of former Confederate officers and was essentially a reincarnation of a Confederate company. In Wilmington, both the new town marshal and the new chief of police were former Confederate generals, and the police chief packed the ranks of the force with former Confederate soldiers.[65] Much the same was true across the South.[66] It is thus unsurprising that Black Southerners became targets of the local police forces.

The vagrancy statutes were an essential part of a systematic attempt to effectively re-enslave Black people. British journalist Sidney Andrews quoted a lawyer in Arkansas, one of the two former rebel States that did not enact a Black Code, who spoke of efforts by the state legislature to reduce the Black population to a condition of slavery using the state penal code, such as by making it a crime to break a labor contract: "It'll be called 'involuntary servitude for the punishment of crime,' but it won't differ much from slavery."[67] This quasi-slavery was effected by statutes that allowed for only a short amount of time between the expiration of one work contract and the necessity of entering into a new one, leaving the freedmen almost no bargaining power. In addition, combinations of employers agreed to keep wages barely above a subsistence level.[68] Any Black person who rejected the paltry terms offered by their former slave-master would have to travel abroad to find a better deal; unemployed and homeless, he would thus subject himself to arrest as a vagrant.[69] Major General Alfred H. Terry of the Freedmen's Bureau cited this coercive effect of the Virginia vagrancy statute in his order forbidding its enforcement.[70] The goal of the vagrancy statutes was "to use the authority of the state to ensure white employers' control over ex-slave laborers and consign freedpeople to economic dependence and social subordination."[71]

Statutory provisions for selling Black convicts at public outcry were generally viewed outside the South as attempts to re-enslave Black people in a new guise.[72] Representative John F. Farnsworth of Illinois expressed the frustration of those who thought they so recently had disposed of slavery once and for all:

> We adopted an amendment to the Constitution that slavery should not hereafter exist in this country except as a punishment for crime. Yet we find those States now reducing these men to slavery again as a punishment for crime, and declaring for every little petty offense the black man may commit that he shall be sold into bondage. So that even that constitutional provision which we made, and which was intended to knock the shackles off every man who was not guilty of

> crime in the United States, is avoided and got around by these cunning rebels.[73]

To many outside the South, the Black Codes represented "the South's categorical refusal to accept the verdict of the Civil War, a vindictive effort to thwart justice, and a conspiracy to retain the Negro in virtual slavery or peonage."[74]

It is undisputed that the Fourteenth Amendment and its coordinate legislation were in large part spurred by outrage over the Black Codes.[75] Much of the testimony before the Joint Committee related to the discriminatory enforcement of the vagrancy laws and other provisions.[76] Congressmen and Senators repeatedly denounced the Black Codes and the vagrancy provisions on the floor of Congress.[77] Northern newspapers railed against the "odious vagrant law[s]."[78] Republican journalist Horace Greeley was quoted as saying that the North must not "'remove the iron hand from the rebels' throats'" lest they again attempt to enslave the Black race.[79] Thousands of everyday Northerners engaged in petition- and letter-writing campaigns to congressmen demanding more protection for Southern Black people by the federal government.[80] "By early 1866, all mainstream Republicans were committed to the view that federal action was needed to protect the newly freed slaves from the predations of the Black Codes."[81] Historians regard the Black Codes as essentially a "but-for cause" of the Fourteenth Amendment.[82]

The race-based aspects of the Codes were an obvious target. But, importantly, the unequal enforcement of supposedly race-neutral laws in the Black Codes was also a prime concern. As Senator Lyman Trumbull of Illinois said, "if the States and local authorities, by legislation *or otherwise*, deny the[] rights [of person and property], it is incumbent on us to see that they are secured.[83] Massachusetts Senator Henry Wilson likewise praised General Grant's Order No. 3, which, as Wilson put it, "allows no law to be *enforced* against [the freedmen] that is not *enforced equally* against white men."[84] Wilson later quoted approvingly from a letter from General Swayne in Alabama that "'the law, by whomsoever made *and administered* . . . shall be faithfully *and equally applied* to all men without distinction on account of color.'"[85] Representative Samuel Moulton of Illinois said that the Second Freedmen's Bureau Bill was necessary in part because of state statutes that declare the Black man to be "a vagabond, a vagrant" which "do not operate against the white men." Continuing, Moulton said that the Bill would be operative "only . . . where the black man is discriminated against, *or* where any attempt is made to enforce unjust and unequal local civil laws against him."[86] Illinois Representative Burton C. Cook, in condemning the vagrancy laws, said that they "operate[]

upon [the freedmen] as upon no other part of the community."[87] During the ratification period, an editorial in the New York *Tribune* stated that the Amendment would "extend equal protection of the laws, not only in cases where the laws are unjust and unequal, but in cases where people are denied equal treatment in spite of state laws," because "[t]he laws might be fair and just, *but their execution might not be.*"[88] As historian Robert Harris wrote, the Fourteenth Amendment was aimed in part at "'forbidding the States in the future to enact unequal laws or *to enforce laws otherwise valid with an evil eye and an unequal hand.*'"[89]

Violence against Black People, Loyalists, and Northerners in the South

The second main impetus behind the Fourteenth Amendment was the violence inflicted in the former slave States on Black people in particular, but also on loyal whites and Northerners who had relocated to the South.[90] As Frederick Douglass put it in 1867: "Peace to the country has literally meant war to the loyal men of the South, white and black."[91] Reports by visitors from outside the South as well as the testimony of witness after witness before the Joint Committee revealed shocking accounts of violence against these three groups, especially the formerly enslaved.[92] Much of this violence was exacted by or with the acquiescence of local law enforcement and militias or quasi-governmental units such as citizen patrols. The culmination of this violence was the well-publicized massacres of Black people and white loyalists in Memphis and New Orleans in the spring and summer of 1866, just as the Amendment was being approved by Congress and sent to the States for ratification.

A particular object of the former rebels' ire were Southern loyalists, whom they viewed as traitors to the cause of Southern independence. Carl Schurz encountered much talk in "many different places and by . . . many different persons" in the South that as soon as they once more gained control of their government and their society, Southern Unionists would not be permitted to remain in peace.[93] Violence against loyal Southerners was not infrequent.[94] The former rebels also despised Northerners, particularly Union soldiers. Schurz reported, eight months after Lee's surrender, "there are still localities where it is unsafe for a man wearing the Federal uniform or known as an officer of the Government to be abroad outside of the immediate reach of our garrisons." Shootings of soldiers and other government workers "was not unfrequently reported."[95]

Southern "animosity against 'Yankee interlopers' [wa]s only second to their hostile feeling against the negro." It was Black Southerners who received, as Schurz later put it, "the first fury of the reactionary movement." Schurz saw for himself "the lifeless bodies, the mangled limbs, the mutilated heads, of not a few of the victims," producing a "dark drama of blood and horror which makes the heart sick."[96] Violence against Black people in parts of the South immediately after the war, according to Eric Foner, "reached staggering proportions," almost always with whites as the perpetrators.[97] Black Southerners were robbed; they had their homes and schools demolished and burned to the ground;[98] they were beaten, whipped, and tied up by their thumbs;[99] they were hanged, shot, drowned, stabbed, and poisoned, by the thousands.[100]

Critically, law enforcement officers were very often among the perpetrators of this violence.[101] North Carolina police tied Black people up by the thumbs and savagely whipped them.[102] One police sergeant took a Black man into custody, tied his hands behind his back, and brutally pistol-whipped him.[103] The same sergeant whipped a freedman so severely "that from his neck to his hips his back was one mass of gashes," rendering him "insensible."[104] One Bureau employee recounted an incident in which a police officer hit a Black woman over the head on the street, knocking her out cold.[105] The police in New Orleans in the summer of 1865 "conducted themselves towards the freedmen, in respect to violence and ill usage, in every way equal to the old days of slavery."[106] For example, one New Orleans officer went up and down the street near police headquarters, bashing in the head of every Black man, woman, or child that he passed.[107] Police in one North Carolina county were accused of committing multiple crimes, including four murders, in July 1865. The alleged culprits included a police captain who was arrested but released and never brought to trial, and who had allegedly ordered his men to shoot Black people suspected of theft.[108] Brevet Lt. Col. W. H. H. Beadle, testifying before the Joint Committee, regarded the Wilmington, North Carolina, police as "the hardest and most brutal looking and acting set of civil or municipal officers [he] ever saw," who terrorized Black people and loyal men. He observed one strike a small, frail Black woman over the head with his baton, rendering her unconscious. The perpetrator, his partner, and other witnesses claimed that the woman attacked first and so the officer's actions were ruled self-defense and he was not charged. Police in the city beat a Black man so brutally he had to be hospitalized. Beadle said that there were numerous such cases, usually with police claiming that the Black victim had committed a minor offense.[109] One Kentucky town marshal, according to the Freedmen's Bureau, was "very prompt in shooting the blacks whenever an opportunity occurs.'"[110]

Much of the violence was also committed by militias and quasi-governmental citizen patrols of the type that had existed in the days of slavery.[111] "'Organized patrols, with negro hounds, ke[pt] guard over the thoroughfares,'" shooting or hanging freedmen unfortunate enough to be found.[112] One citizen patrol in South Carolina tied up a freedwoman and whipped her severely, and one town patrol broke up a ball held by Black residents and flogged one man savagely.[113]

Southerners were particularly eager to have their state militias reorganized in order to reassert total control over Black lives as in the antebellum days.[114] As Carl Schurz put it:

> This concentration of organized physical power in the hands of one class will necessarily tend, and is undoubtedly designed, to give that class absolute physical control of the other. The specific purpose for which the militia is to be reorganized . . . is the restoration of the old patrol system which was one of the characteristic features of the régime of slavery.[115]

Militiamen were utterly vicious toward Black people. Senator Wilson read on the floor of Congress from a letter by a Freedmen's Bureau officer in Mississippi that "'[n]early all the dissatisfaction that now exists among the freedmen is caused by the abusive conduct of the militia.'"[116] Even the conservative Governor Humphreys of the State "'admitted . . . that two companies of the militia had sworn . . . that they would "drive out the thieving Yankees and shoot the niggers."'"[117] General Swayne in Alabama noted that "'[e]very species of outrage is committed under the[] [militia] in some counties.'"[118] General Howard said that in South Carolina "'much complaint reached [him] of the misconduct of these militia companies toward the blacks,'" that they were "'heaping upon [the freedmen] every sort of injury and insult, unchecked.'"[119] A Freedmen's Bureau officer wrote that murders of Black people were being reported to his office almost every day, "many of which are perpetrated by the militia or black cavalry, as they are called, who . . . are particularly adapted to hunting, flogging, and killing colored people."[120] Schurz informed President Johnson that the militias "'indulged in the gratification of private vengeance, persecuted helpless Union people and freedmen, and endeavored to keep the plantation negroes in a state of virtual slavery.'"[121] In Mississippi, "militia men patrolled the country . . . flogging and maltreating in almost every way the freedmen, and in some cases Union men."[122] In one case there, a Black man was accosted by militiamen who threw him down and kicked and stomped on him, breaking his breastbone.[123] In Amite County, Mississippi, one company of militiamen were responsible for severely flogging three Black women, possibly killing one of them, in one night.[124] Violence and other mistreatment by militias, organized patrols, and government officials was especially pernicious because, as one observer put it, "[t]hey give the color of law to their violent, unjust, and sometimes inhuman proceedings."[125] This reign of terror by citizen militias threatened "a sort of permanent martial law over the negro."[126]

Virtually all of the violence against Black people, loyalists, and Northerners went unpunished. Again, local law enforcement was infiltrated in many places by ex-rebels. Police, sheriffs, and justices of the peace were "extremely reluctant to prosecute whites accused of crimes against blacks."[127] Of the 237 "outrages" committed by whites against Black people in Kentucky from June 1 to October 31, 1866, not a single perpetrator was arrested or punished by state authorities.[128] At one point, the army declared martial law in parts of Florida because so many crimes against Black people and soldiers had gone unaddressed by local authorities.[129] The Joint Committee on Reconstruction observed that "local authorities are at no pains to prevent or punish" the many "acts of cruelty, oppression, and murder."[130]

When whites were prosecuted for violence against Black people, loyalists, and Northerners, they were usually acquitted. The Assistant Commissioner of the Bureau in South Carolina could point to only a single case in which a white man was convicted of murdering a formerly enslaved person, while the rest had "escaped punishment either by the failure of the grand jury to [indict] them, or, if tried, they were acquitted."[131] And if a white man was somehow convicted for a crime against a Black person, the sentence imposed was sure to be ridiculously lenient: fines of five cents, a dollar, five dollars for serious assaults, one minute of imprisonment for a murder.[132] Prospects for justice for loyalists were little better; federal Judge John C. Underwood testified that in Virginia "a Union man could [not] expect to obtain justice in the courts . . . certainly not if his opponent was a rebel."[133] The Report of the Committee of Unreconstructed States, issued at a convention of Southern loyalists in September 1866, spoke of "the triple guard" protecting rebel offenders: "disloyal magistrates, disloyal grand juries, [and] disloyal petit juries."[134] And these were cases of ordinary white citizens. There appear to have been no prosecutions of law enforcement officials or militiamen.

Law enforcement also began searching the homes of Blacks people without any pretense of legal authority. Sometimes this was done purely to harass and inflict violence on the formerly enslaved.[135] Often officials were searching for guns. Antebellum paranoia about slave insurrection morphed into unfounded fears of a Christmas 1865 uprising by freedmen. Because of these fears, Black people across the South were barred from owning firearms and other weapons.[136] In Alabama, this led to the creation of special militia companies and "squads of special constables, with arbitrary powers," filled with "lawless characters" who went about searching Black homes for arms.[137] Citizen patrols did the same in Virginia[138] as did the regular militia in Mississippi.[139] Police in other areas went about searching Black homes for guns, often in nighttime raids.[140] In some instances, Black people were killed or maimed after refusing to allow searches of their homes.[141]

Given the racist trope of freedman as petty thief, these searches quickly became an opportunity for police to ransack homes and seize more than weapons:

> Once the practice of raiding Negro dwellings became established . . . the police and militia by no means confined themselves to a search for arms. They began seizing "stolen" property as well. Since the Negroes had owned no property at the end of the war when they were freed, the police felt justified in assuming that any property they found in the possession of a Negro was stolen unless the Negro could prove otherwise.[142]

In Mississippi, militiamen and others "claiming to be agents of the state" plundered the houses of Black people in an ostensible search for arms.[143] In North Carolina, the limited search for arms by squads of local police often became an orgy of violence in which "[h]ouses of colored men [were] broken open, beds torn apart and thrown on the floor, and even trunks opened and money taken."[144] On Christmas Eve, whites in Alabama, acting "under alleged orders from the colonel of the county militia, went from place to place, broke open negro houses and searched their trunks, boxes, &c.," not only seizing firearms but also robbing the occupants blind.[145] In Texas, government patrols not only disarmed the Black residents but also "frequently robbed them of money, household furniture, and anything that they could make of any use to themselves."[146] The New Hanover County, North Carolina, militia "'visited and pillaged'" virtually every house on one particular street in a Black neighborhood.[147]

Black persons' freedom of movement was also seriously curtailed in some places by white authorities. In the antebellum era, a pass system prevailed, whereby enslaved persons found away from their plantations without a pass were seized and subjected to corporal punishments. The system survived the war and now armed militias and patrols were performing the same function. One witness testified that, in parts of Alabama, "the roads and public highways are patrolled by the State militia, and no colored man is allowed to travel without a pass from his employer."[148] Senator Trumbull read a letter from a Freedmen's Bureau officer in Texas that in some parts of the State "'the pass system is still in force, and when a freedman is found at large without a pass, he is taken up and whipped.'"[149]

The murders, rapes, assaults, tortures, home invasions, robberies, and other atrocities committed by or with the acquiescence of Southern law enforcement were well known to Congress and the public during the framing and ratification of the Fourteenth Amendment. Although the Report of the Joint Committee was not completed until June 8, 1866, after much of the debate on the Amendment in Congress had already taken place, it was widely available during the ratification period as "the official explanation and defense of the amendment."[150] In July 1866, Congress ordered 100,000 copies to be printed, and some of the testimony was quoted at length in at least one ratification document, a report of the House of Representatives of Massachusetts.[151] Moreover, the actual testimony was available beforehand, the most damning of which was "printed verbatim in many of the larger newspapers."[152] A number of Representatives referred in floor speeches to the testimony before the Joint Committee; a few quoted it at length.[153] And, of course, the testimony was known to the committee members themselves. It was they who were in the process of drafting what became the Fourteenth Amendment while testimony was still being taken. There is thus a deep connection between the tales of mistreatment in the South and the original understanding of the Fourteenth Amendment:

> The evidence of individual invasions of the rights of Negroes particularly, but also of loyalists . . . was not fortuitously brought forward as an unimportant incident of other matters regarded as primary. [T]he evidence was deliberately adduced by the committee for its bearing upon a principal feature of the proposed amendment, the precise wording of which was at the very moment under discussion by the committee.[154]

News of these atrocities was also well known to Congress and the public because of the Schurz Report, released just before Christmas, 1865. When it was transmitted to the Senate, it was ordered to be printed and copies circulated, Radical Republican Senator Charles Sumner stating that "the Senate could not listen to anything of more importance than this accurate, authentic, most authoritative report with regard to the actual condition of things in those States."[155] "By the time that Congress adjourned for the Christmas holidays, people were reading it in their newspapers," in many instances published in full.[156] Senators and Representatives were soon citing it in their speeches in Congress.[157] In short, the report contributed a great deal to opinions about the South by the rest of the country.[158]

Then, in May and July 1866, massacres of Black people in Memphis and New Orleans led by law enforcement in those cities thrust state-sponsored Southern racial violence into the spotlight once more. The violence in Memphis resulted from tensions between the city's growing Black population in South Memphis, including Black soldiers from nearby Fort Pickering, and the city's mostly Irish police force.[159] The tensions came to a head on May 1, 1866. What began as a race riot between the city's Black civilians and soldiers, on the one hand, and the city's white police and residents, on the other, turned into a massacre of Black people. By the following evening, two whites and forty-six Black people—fourteen of whom were soldiers—had been killed, seventy-five people, mostly Black, were injured, one hundred Black people had been robbed, and five or six Black women raped. The white mob burned down at least ninety-one homes (possibly over one hundred), between eight and twelve schools, and four churches, and caused a total of $130,981 in property damage, over $2 million in today's dollars. No white person was ever charged with a crime in relation to the massacre. Altina L. Waller has estimated that almost 40 percent of the white rioters were policemen, firemen, or other city employees.

Less than three months later, the violence visited upon the Black population of Memphis was repeated in New Orleans, again with state agents taking a leadership role in the bloodshed.[160] On July 30, 1866, loyalists, including many Black men, attempted to reconvene a constitutional convention that had been suspended in 1864, in order to amend the state constitution to both enfranchise Black men and disenfranchise former rebels. Lieutenant Governor Albert Voorhies, Mayor John T. Monroe, and other whites in the city viewed this convention as essentially a coup in the making. Monroe, an ex-Confederate, had discharged all Union men from the police force, replacing them with former rebels. Sheriff Harry Thompson Hayes, formerly a Confederate brigadier general, had as his deputies a large number of Confederate veterans, and he swore in a posse of additional deputies in anticipation of the loyalists' convention.

Soon after the convention began at noon on July 30, groups of mostly

Black supporters and white opponents, many of whom had been drinking, clashed outside the convention hall. Notified of the violence, Police Chief Thomas E. Adams ordered his men—heavily armed, many intoxicated, virtually all predisposed to violence toward Black people and white loyalists—to the scene. What began as a firefight between police and the Black men and white loyalists escalated quickly into "an absolute massacre."[161] Police and white citizens teamed up to brutally shoot and beat to death Black men and white loyalists both inside and outside the convention hall, a killing spree that lasted into the night.

All told, ten police officers were wounded, two seriously, and one died of sunstroke; one white civilian also died from a stray bullet. But casualties of Black people and white loyalists remain unknown to this day. Some have estimated that thirty-seven to forty-seven were killed and 150 to 300 were wounded. Three whites were among the dead and seventeen among the wounded on the loyalist side; the rest were Black. To add insult to injury, police arrested 265 loyalists, virtually all of them Black, for rioting and unlawful assembly. No white citizen or police officer was charged.

The massacres in Memphis and New Orleans were well publicized throughout the country and sparked outrage outside the South.[162] At least two Members of Congress mentioned the Memphis massacre, which occurred before Congressional approval of the Fourteenth Amendment, in debate.[163] The New Orleans massacre "became a national scandal, particularly when it became clear that state officials had led the attack."[164] The latter "was one of the most heavily covered events of 1866," often reported together with news regarding the 1866 election.[165] The U.S. House of Representatives held hearings on the Memphis massacre, resulting in a 394-page report issued on July 25, 1866.[166] The New Orleans massacre resulted in another investigation by the House, which issued a 668-page report.[167] The military conducted its own investigation of the New Orleans massacre, resulting in another 290 pages of documents and testimony.[168]

The constant reports of violent oppression of Black Southerners had their biggest effect on moderate Republicans, some of whom had at first supported President Johnson's plan to restore the Southern States quickly.[169] "[T]he persistent complaints of persecution forwarded to Washington by Southern blacks and white loyalists altered the mood in Congress by eroding the plausibility of Johnson's central assumption—that the Southern states could be trusted to manage their own affairs without federal oversight."[170]

More than just the violence, the celebration of that violence by many

Southerners convinced even ambivalent Northerners that drastic measures were required to guarantee the security of Black Southerners, white Southern loyalists, and relocated Northerners. The New Orleans massacre

> increased the perception in the North that white southerners were determined to unleash a reign of terror on the recently emancipated slaves. The barrage of self-congratulatory editorials in southern newspapers, which praised whites in New Orleans for giving a "salutary warning" that the South would never submit to Yankee rule, strengthened this conviction and persuaded northern voters that the South had refused to accept the verdict arrived at by four years of a bloody war.[171]

During the critical fall 1866 election, Republicans pointed to the New Orleans massacre to demonstrate the necessity of renewed protections for Southern Black people and loyalists in the form of the Fourteenth Amendment.[172] Schurz, in a campaign speech in early September, no doubt had Memphis and New Orleans in mind when he referred to "wholesale butcheries in broad daylight and under the inspiration of the constituted authorities."[173] As will be examined in more detail in the next chapter, Republicans won the 1866 elections handily. References to Southern violence continued into the ratification process itself, as when Governor Oliver P. Morton of Indiana declared in urging ratification by the state legislature:

> By the unrestrained slaughters of Memphis and New Orleans; by the unpunished murder of loyal men; by the persecution and exile of those who adhered to the Union [the South is] fast proving that the extraordinary powers of the Constitution must be summoned to cure the evils under which the land is laboring.[174]

Governor Lucius Fairchild of Wisconsin had a strikingly similar message for that State's legislature:

> With the massacres of Memphis and New Orleans before our eyes, and with the blood of thousands of union men—murdered because they were union men—crying aloud to us for vengeance, we continued to offer the[] [Southern States] full restoration of political rights upon the terms embodied in this resolution. It was hoped that the sober,

> second thought of the now ruling class at the south would lead to the acceptance in good faith of these terms. Events have proved that the hope was without foundation.[175]

Historians and legal theorists, regardless of their views on the incorporation question, agree that violence in the South was a major impetus for the Fourteenth Amendment.[176] To be sure, conservative politicians of the age claimed that reports of violence in the South were exaggerated.[177] The Schurz Report was claimed to be biased.[178] Even those more sympathetic to the plight of Southern Blacks expressed some skepticism.[179] And not all of the testimony before the Joint Committee on Reconstruction and the other evidence adduced by Congress paints as bleak a picture as that emphasized here.[180] Yet the preponderance of the testimony given before the Joint Committee on Reconstruction (weighing in at close to 700 pages), in addition to the reports from the Freedmen's Bureau agents reprinted in Congressional documents, repeats over and over the tales of unspeakable savagery in the South.[181] Certainly, the blood-stained streets of Memphis and New Orleans speak for themselves.

But at the end of the day the complete veracity of the claims of mistreatment and violence are beside the point. If the goal is to discern how the Fourteenth Amendment was understood in 1868 by looking at what spurred its passage, all that really matters is what the framers and ratifiers thought. Even if their views were colored by the politics of the day—and they certainly were—that does not alter the fact that they understood the project of the Fourteenth Amendment as an attempt to prevent a repeat of the horrid events they perceived in the immediate postwar period.

Conclusion

The two gravest problems that led the Nation to adopt section one of the Fourteenth Amendment were the new Black Codes, and violence and other maltreatment meted out to Black people, white loyalists, and Northerners, much of it at the hands of state officials. As for the Black Codes, the framers and ratifiers of the Fourteenth Amendment obviously wanted to prevent any reappearance of race-conscious laws, but their concerns went much farther. Their especial outrage at the South's new vagrancy laws, ironically, seems to have stemmed from the fact that they were race neutral. Race-conscious laws were easy to detect and to fix. By contrast, race-neutral laws such as the vagrancy provisions hid the discrimination of Southern lawmakers in the ocean of discretion afforded to those who enforced the law: sheriffs, constables, police officers, militiamen, and justices of the peace. Thus, the framers and ratifiers of the Amendment were particularly sensitive to laws such as these which were race neutral but afforded so much discretion to law enforcement that they were easily perverted to a discriminatory purpose.

The framers and ratifiers of the Fourteenth Amendment also expressed great concern about the violence being visited upon Black people, loyal whites, and Northerners. They were especially disgusted that many of these outrages went unpunished, which helps explain why the Fourteenth Amendment demands "equal protection of the laws"—literally, equal protection by the government from private acts of violence. But perhaps most horrifying was that it was often government officials themselves—sheriffs, police officers, militias, and citizen patrols—committing acts of violence. The House Committee Report on the Memphis Massacre expressed this horror succinctly:

> The fact that the chosen guardians of the public peace, the sworn executors of the law for the protection of the lives, liberty, and property of the people, and the reliance of the weak and defenceless in time of danger, were found the foremost in the work of murder and pillage, gives a character of infamy to the whole proceeding which is almost without a parallel in all the annals of history.[182]

In Memphis, New Orleans, and places too numerous to list, Black people, loyal whites, and Northerners required constitutional constraints on extralegal violence perpetrated by state agents.

Protection from discriminatory enforcement of neutral laws and extralegal state violence both implicate the requirement of "due process of law." Black people, white loyalists, and Northerners needed assurance that their lives, liberty, and property would be taken by state agents, if at all, only in adherence to state law. And they needed constitutional protection from state agents not only when they were enforcing discriminatory laws but also when they were enforcing laws neutral on their face but that, like the vagrancy laws, allowed for so much discretion that arbitrary and discriminatory enforcement was all but inevitable.

This background sheds great light on the phrase "due process of law" as used in the Fourteenth Amendment. While the phrase had been around for centuries, and was used once before in the Constitution, words always take meaning from their context. In the context of immediate postwar period, "due process of law" meant, among other things, that state agents (1) had to obey the law and (2) must not be given so much discretion as to essentially turn them into lawmakers rather than law-enforcers. We will see in the next two chapters that the framers and ratifiers of the Fourteenth Amendment likely understood it as imposing Fourth Amendment–type restrictions against the States, but they undoubtedly understood these restrictions as serving the overriding goals of ensuring equality and "due process of law."

Seven

Does the Fourteenth Amendment Incorporate the Fourth?

The previous chapter dealt with some of the social ills that the framer and ratifiers of the Fourteenth Amendment wanted to fix. This chapter addresses how they meant to fix them. The overarching question for us is whether and to what extent they understood the Fourth Amendment as applying to the States via the Fourteenth. It is likely that they understood the Fourteenth Amendment as imposing Fourth Amendment–type constraints on state and local officials. However, it is unlikely that they understood that there would be a single corpus of uniform Fourth Amendment law governing the Nation. There are two reasons for this. First, the moderate-to-conservative Republican mainstream, while recognizing the need for protection against lawless, arbitrary, and discriminatory acts by state officials, continued to place a high value on federalism and local control. Second, to the extent that some may have contemplated a national Fourth Amendment standard, such a standard would be quite impossible given the original understanding of the Fourth Amendment. If, as I have suggested, the Fourth Amendment preserves local control of search-and-seizure policy, then the very idea of a national Fourth Amendment standard is oxymoronic.

Rather, as I will suggest in chapter 8, the best way of viewing the original understanding of the Fourteenth Amendment vis-à-vis the Fourth is that security from unreasonable searches and seizures was one of the "privileges or immunities" protected from state infringement, but the specific contours of search-and-seizure policy was to remain largely under state control. However, this state control was constrained by the demands of equal treatment and due process of law: that the law of search and seizure must not discriminate based on race or other invidious classifications; that police and other state agents must follow the law; and that, even where police and other state agents are given legal authority to search and seize, that authority must limit the discretion of those state officials so as to minimize the danger that they will engage in hidden discrimination.

This chapter first introduces the modern debate over incorporation of the Bill of Rights. It then goes back to the Reconstruction period to attempt to tease out whether and to what extent the framers and ratifiers understood the Fourteenth Amendment as applying the Fourth Amendment to the States.

The Incorporation Debate in the Courts

Let's take a step back by moving forward, past the Civil War and into the twentieth century. In a series of cases starting a few years after the Fourteenth Amendment was adopted, the Supreme Court rejected the argument that it applied the Bill of Rights against the States. First, in *The Slaughterhouse Cases* in 1873, the Court narrowly interpreted the Privileges or Immunities Clause to protect only a very limited set of rights of American citizenship.[1] Three years later in *United States* v. *Cruikshank*, the Court rejected the notion that the Fourteenth Amendment applied the Second Amendment's right to bear arms to the States.[2] Later cases continued to reject the idea of "incorporation" of the Bill of Rights into the Fourteenth Amendment.[3]

So what did the Fourteenth Amendment guarantee? Some early cases suggested that as long as a State followed its own laws, the Fourteenth Amendment was satisfied.[4] However, the Court soon adopted the "fundamental fairness" approach. Pursuant to that approach, none of the Bill of Rights applied to the States per se but the Court required that States be fundamentally fair with their residents in their laws and legal processes. The approach was summed up by Justice Benjamin Cardozo writing for the Court in *Palko* v. *Connecticut*, that the Fourteenth Amendment encompassed only those rights that were "of the very essence of a scheme of ordered liberty." To qualify for protection under the Fourteenth Amendment, the claimed right must represent "a 'principle of justice so rooted in the traditions and conscience of our people as to be ranked as fundamental.'"[5] Under the fundamental fairness approach, some aspects of the Bill of Rights applied to the States, although not necessarily in the same way they applied to the federal government, such as the rights to freedom of speech, press, religion, and peaceable assembly, the right not to have private property taken by the State without just compensation, and the rights of an accused to be informed of the charges against him and to the assistance of counsel. But the Court also held that many of the rights protected by the Bill of Rights were not included in the Fourteenth Amendment's scope, such as the right to be indicted by a grand jury, the privilege against self-incrimination, the right to a jury trial in either criminal or civil matters, and the right to confront one's accusers at trial.[6] As Justice Felix Frankfurter, a primary champion of the fundamental fairness approach, described it: "The [Fourteenth] Amendment neither comprehends the specific provisions by which the founders deemed it appropriate to restrict the federal government nor is it confined to them." Rather, the Amendment requires that the States observe "basic liberties."[7]

The Court held in *Wolf* v. *Colorado* in 1949 that the Fourteenth Amendment does indeed incorporate some Fourth Amendment–type protections. Justice Frankfurter wrote for the Court there:

> The security of one's privacy against arbitrary intrusion by the police—which is at the core of the Fourth Amendment—is basic to a free society. It is therefore implicit in "the concept of ordered liberty" and as such enforceable against the States through the [Fourteenth Amendment]. The knock at the door, whether by day or by night, as a prelude to a search, without authority of law but solely on the authority of the police [is] inconsistent with the conception of human rights enshrined in the history and the basic constitutional documents of English-speaking peoples.[8]

Thus, state officials who arrested Wolf in his office and then searched for and seized books there, all without a warrant, violated the Fourteenth Amendment.

However, the Court made clear that just because "the core of the Fourth Amendment" right, freedom from "arbitrary intrusion by the police," applied against the States, this did not sweep into the Fourteenth Amendment every gloss and nuance of the basic Fourth Amendment right that federal courts may discern. Thus, the *Wolf* Court wrote that although a State could not "sanction such police incursion into privacy," it would not dictate everything States must do to protect the basic right:

> [T]he ways of enforcing such a basic right raise questions of a different order. How such arbitrary conduct should be checked, what remedies against it should be afforded, the means by which the right should be made effective, are all questions that are not to be so dogmatically answered as to preclude the varying solutions which spring from an

> allowable range of judgment on issues not susceptible of quantitative solution.[9]

Thus, the Court declined to require that States apply the exclusionary rule, that unconstitutionally acquired evidence must be excluded from a criminal trial.[10]

The opposing view was that the Fourteenth Amendment applied the first eight amendments of the Bill of Rights to the States in toto. The main proponent for this view on the Court was Justice Hugo Black, who set forth this theory in his dissent in *Adamson* v. *California* in 1947. His conclusion from studying the history of framing and ratification of the Fourteenth Amendment was that "one of the chief objects that the provisions of the Amendment's first section, separately, and as a whole, were intended to accomplish was to make the Bill of Rights, applicable to the states."[11] Justice Black was joined by Justice William Douglas, while Justice Frank Murphy penned a separate dissent, joined by Justice Wiley Rutledge, which largely agreed with Black.[12]

By 1961, this four-Justice bloc had grown into a majority. In *Mapp* v. *Ohio*, the Court revisited the exclusionary rule issue in *Wolf* and overruled that case. The Court described *Wolf*, not as holding that "security . . . against arbitrary intrusion by the police" was protected by the Fourteenth Amendment but that the Fourth Amendment itself "was applicable to the States through the" Fourteenth Amendment.[13] The difference is significant. By adopting incorporationist language, the Court suggested that every single aspect of its Fourth Amendment jurisprudence applied to the States in the exact same way it applied to the federal government. The Court confirmed this suggestion two years later in *Ker* v. *California*,[14] and the following year in *Malloy* v. *Hogan* it wrote explicitly that the incorporated provisions of the Bill of Rights "are all to be enforced against the States under the Fourteenth Amendment according to the same standards that protect those personal rights against federal encroachment."[15]

The Court has technically never adopted the total incorporation approach advocated by Justice Black. Instead, it has adopted a "selective incorporation" approach, whereby the Court decides, right-by-right and clause-by-clause, which parts of the Bill of Rights apply to the States. But once a provision is deemed to apply to the States, it applies in precisely the same way as it does to the federal government.[16] Lawyers sometimes refer to this as "jot-for-jot" incorporation. We have ended up with something close to Justice Black's total incorporation view; the Supreme Court has held that the Fourteenth Amendment incorporates virtually all of the Bill of Rights.[17]

Incorporation and Original Understandings

While the incorporation issue appears settled in the courts, the debate in the academic world over the original understanding of the Fourteenth Amendment rages on. Views on that question fall generally into two main camps, the Equal Rights view and the Fundamental Rights view.[18] The Equal Rights view is that the Fourteenth Amendment was understood as imposing no *substantive* constraint on the States but only an *equality* constraint: it ensured that whatever rights States afford must be afforded on an equal basis to everyone. So, for example, a State could permit searches of *all* homes without a warrant. But the State could not permit warrantless searches of the residences of only, say, Republicans or Lutherans. On this view, the Fourteenth Amendment was not understood as incorporating the Bill of Rights. Those who have espoused this view have included Raoul Berger, James Bond, David Currie, Charles Fairman, Philip Hamburger, and Ilan Wurman.[19] I will refer to those who generally support this view as "Incorporation Skeptics."

The Fundamental Rights view is that the Fourteenth Amendment applied certain substantive constraints, including at least some of those in the Bill of Rights, to the States, so that no such right can be taken away by a State even if the State purports to do so on an equal basis for everyone. Under this view, if there is a Fourth Amendment right not to have one's home searched without a warrant, then a State cannot decree it otherwise, even if the majority are willing to sacrifice this freedom. Those in this camp have included Akhil Amar, Chet Antieau, Alfred Avins, Richard Aynes, Randy Barnett and Evan Bernick, William Crosskey, Michael Kent Curtis, Kurt Lash, and Brian Wildenthal.[20] I will refer to those who generally support this view as "Incorporationists."

This, of course, is an oversimplification of the voluminous work of these and other scholars. For example, there is a debate among Incorporationists over whether the Fourteenth Amendment guarantees *only* the rights contained in the Bill of Rights, or all of those rights *plus* other fundamental rights not included in the Bill. Similarly, Incorporation Skeptics disagree among themselves as to the universe of rights triggering the equality requirement.[21] These differences need not detain us long, for Incorporationists generally agree that the Fourth Amendment applies to the States, and Incorporation Skeptics generally agree that any state constraints on searches and seizures must be promulgated and applied equally. Moreover, the Incorporationist position essentially encompasses the Equal Rights view; the former sees the Fourteenth Amendment as requiring equal treatment within a State but views it as requiring more than just equality.

Many books and law review articles have been written examining each side in this debate. Of necessity, the discussion of the incorporation question in this chapter is more summary in form. I don't intend the following to even definitively pick sides. I will suggest that even if the Fourteenth Amendment was understood as an absolute constraint on state searches or seizures, the result looks much the same as it does under an equality constraint. That is, even if the Incorporationists are correct that the framers and ratifiers understood the Fourteenth Amendment as incorporating the Fourth, for reasons that I will explain, they did not understand this to mean the "jot-for-jot" incorporation that the Supreme Court has adopted.

The task of unearthing the understandings of the framers and the ratifiers of the Fourteenth Amendment is not an easy one. Debates over the Amendment, particularly in the halls of the Thirty-Ninth Congress, which drafted the Fourteenth Amendment, were "opaque, intricate, confusing[,] [and] tedious," and "political strategies were in constant flux."[22] Moreover, while much was said in Congress about the need for the provision, very little is available from the state legislatures tasked with ratifying it.[23] What was said in those fora, moreover, is largely unhelpful. Both the framers and ratifiers of the Amendment rarely if ever engaged in discussion of the nitty-gritty of legal doctrine, so the language they used invariably sounded in very high levels of generality.[24]

Moreover, what became section 1 of the Amendment took a backseat to the more important question of the relative political power in the South of the former rebels and the formerly enslaved. Recall that, paradoxically, abolition of slavery threatened to give disloyal whites in the South even more political power in Congress, because Black people would now count fully in apportionment of representatives but would be unable to vote. Thus, it is not surprising that "[m]ost of the political rhetoric of the day was devoted to the subject of political power," specifically Black suffrage, ultimately dealt with by section 2, and disenfranchisement of former rebels, addressed ultimately by section 3.[25] The former did not go far enough for the Radicals and the latter went too far for conservatives.[26] As a result, relatively little attention was paid to section 1.

Nevertheless, all modern scholars agree that the framers and ratifiers of the Amendment understood it as requiring that the Southern States treat Black people, loyalists, and relocated Northerners equally in their civil rights, including their right to be free from arbitrary governmental searches and seizures. The question is whether they understood the Fourth Amendment itself to now apply to the States, as the Incorporationists would have it, or only that whatever search-and-seizure rights people enjoyed as a matter of state law would have to be enforced equally, as the Incorporation Skeptics say.

Although modern doctrine posits that the Due Process Clause of the Fourteenth Amendment incorporates the Bill of Rights, most scholars agree that, if anything, it is the Privileges or Immunities Clause that does so. It is only because the Court early on rejected this argument that later Courts, bound by precedent, reached out to the Due Process Clause to do the work. So, although the Due Process Clause will become relevant, we will focus for the time being on the Privileges or Immunities Clause.

In arguing that that clause was understood as incorporating the Bill of Rights, most Incorporationist scholars focus on statements made by Representative John Bingham of Ohio and Senator Jacob Howard of Michigan. Both were on the Joint Committee on Reconstruction. Bingham essentially drafted section 1 of the Amendment. Howard was acting chair of the Joint Committee and shepherded the Amendment through the Senate when the original chair, Senator William P. Fessenden of Maine, took ill.

Bingham and Howard were the most explicit about the understanding that section 1 applied the Bill of Rights against the States. Bingham made this claim repeatedly. On February 28, Bingham delivered one of the most important speeches he would give on the Amendment. Two weeks earlier, the Joint Committee had proposed a version of the Amendment, drafted primarily by Bingham, that would give Congress "power to make all laws which shall be necessary and proper to secure to the citizens of each State all privileges and immunities of citizens in the several States; and to all persons in the several States equal protection in the rights of life, liberty, and property."[27] In support of this first draft, Bingham explicitly said that the proposal would give Congress "the power to enforce the bill of rights."[28] He used that phrase—"the bill of rights"—to describe what the Amendment would apply to the States at least thirteen times in a speech that takes up about six pages of the Congressional Globe, with interruptions.[29] Bingham had this speech printed up as a pamphlet to be distributed and printed in newspapers across the Nation. In the very title of that pamphlet, he described his speech as being "[i]n support of the proposed amendment *to enforce the Bill of Rights*."[30] Later, in explaining his vote against the Civil Rights Act on the ground that Congress lacked power to enact it, Bingham assured his more radical Republican colleagues of his "earnest desire to have the bill of rights in your Constitution enforced everywhere."[31] But he believed that Congress must be given the power to do so through the incipient Fourteenth Amendment: "I have advocated here an amendment which would arm Congress with the power to . . . punish all violations by State officers of the bill of rights."[32] And in support of the Amendment in its near-final form, Bingham explicitly mentioned a provision of the Bill of Rights—the Cruel and Unusual Punishments Clause—as an example of "the guarantied privileges of citizens of the United States" which had been "flagrant[ly] violat[ed]" by the rebel States.[33]

Senator Howard introduced the Amendment in its near-final form to the Senate on May 23, 1866, after it had already passed the House. In his lengthy oration explaining what was meant by "privileges and immunities," he first quoted a passage from *Corfield* v. *Coryell*, an 1825 opinion written by Justice Bushrod Washington (nephew of our first President) that had laid out a long list of "privileges and immunities" included in the Constitution's Article IV, section 2, sometimes known as the "Comity Clause."[34] He continued: "To these privileges and immunities . . . should be added *the personal rights guarantied and secured by the first eight amendments of the Constitution*."[35] He proceeded to list some of these rights individually as examples of what he meant, including "the right to be exempt from unreasonable searches and seizures, and from any search or seizure except by virtue of a warrant issued upon a formal oath or affidavit [*sic*]."[36] After Howard spoke, there was only minimal discussion of section 1 in the Senate.[37] This is probably reflective of the fact that, though a Radical, Howard was well respected by moderate and conservative Republican senators as an authority on the Constitution.[38]

Incorporation Skeptics, however, point out that no other members of Congress were as explicit as Bingham and Howard were in stating that the Bill of Rights would henceforth apply to the States. Some did reference the Bill of Rights or some of its provisions. However, most of these statements can be interpreted to support the view that the Bill of Rights itself would not apply to the States but, instead, whatever rights were already protected by state law would now have to be equally protected for all. For example, in support of the final version of section 1 (which he mistakenly referred to as section 2), Representative Martin Thayer of Pennsylvania, a centrist,[39] said that "it simply brings into the Constitution what is found in the bill of rights of every State of the Union."[40] This could be understood as supporting either view. Likewise, Incorporationists sometimes point to Radical Pennsylvania Representative Thaddeus Stevens's statement in support of section 1 that "the Constitution limits only the action of Congress, and is not a limitation on the States. This amendment supplies [*sic*] that defect." However, Stevens's comments could be used to support the equality-based view, for he goes on to say that Amendment "allows Congress to correct the unjust legislation of the States, so far that the law which operates upon one man shall operate *equally* upon all."[41]

Incorporationists counter that Bingham's and Howard's understanding would have been known to, and probably shared by, the American general public, given the broad newspaper coverage of the Congressional debates on the Amendment. The debates in Congress were well publicized throughout the Nation in as close to real time as the technology of 1866 would permit. From 1789 to the 1860s, there was about a tenfold increase in the number of daily newspapers in the country, from twenty-four to about 250. In addition, transportation and communications technology had advanced with the railroad, steamship, and telegraph.[42] As a result of the confluence of these changes, newspapers and other writings were far more accessible to the general public than they had been eighty years earlier, and the respective views of the Republicans and Democrats on the proposed Amendment were both highly coordinated and widely disseminated. "The Press reported major speeches in the House and Senate, and the country received a steady stream of newspaper editorials commenting on the policies of the Thirty-Ninth Congress."[43]

Incorporationists point to the fact that the *New York Times* and the *New York Herald* (the best-selling newspaper in the Nation) both printed Bingham's February 26 speech in which he referred to "this immortal bill of rights embodied in the Constitution,"[44] expressing his belief that the Comity Clause already imposed the Bill of Rights on the States (more on that in a moment). The *Times* also reported Bingham's speech two days later which mentioned the Bill of Rights over a dozen times and was reprinted in pamphlet form as a speech "in support of the proposed amendment to enforce the Bill of Rights." In addition, the *Times* printed Bingham's March 9 speech in which he observed that "the enforcement of the bill of rights is the want of the Republic."[45] The *Times* also printed New York Representative Robert S. Hale's February 27 response to Bingham's speech from the day before, in which Hale, a conservative Unionist, expressed the view that the Bill of Rights already bound the States.[46]

Moreover, Howard's explanation of section 1 of the Amendment on May 23 was reprinted in full by at least four leading newspapers, including the *New York Times* and the *New York Herald*, and on their front pages no less.[47] It was in this speech that Howard said that the Privileges or Immunities Clause encompassed "the personal rights guarantied and secured by the first eight amendments of the Constitution," and then listed out individual provisions of the First, Second, Third, Fourth, Sixth, and Eighth Amendments. A *Times* editorial two days later praised Howard for his speech as "frank and satisfactory," and "clear and cogent."[48] During the ratification process, the Amendment came to be known as "the Howard Amendment."[49] Although coverage of debates in the House leading to passage was less extensive, this evidence suggests that the general newspaper-reading public understood the Amendment as applying the Bill of Rights to the States.[50]

Incorporationists also point to the congressional campaign of 1866 and its resulting landslide in favor of Republicans as a good proxy for the ratification debates proper. While "[r]elatively little debate on the Amendment took place in the state assemblies [a] great deal of debate took place on the national campaign trail."[51] Virtually all scholars agree that ratification of the Fourteenth Amendment was a key issue, perhaps the key issue, of that campaign.[52] As a result of both the well-publicized workings of Congress as it shaped the Amendment, and the centrality of the ratification question to the 1866 campaign, "the existing archival material suggests that, during the winter and spring and even into the autumn of 1866, questions connected with the adoption of the Fourteenth Amendment were the central political concern of the American people."[53] In effect, the election of 1866 was seen on both sides as "a referendum on the Fourteenth Amendment," and the public debate over the Amendment was "deep and robust."[54] The result of the election—a landslide giving Republicans over three-quarters of the seats of each house of Congress, "every state legislature in the North and . . . every contested governorship"—was tantamount to a national mandate for the Fourteenth Amendment.[55]

During the campaign, Republicans at first cautiously tried to "downplay the potential scope of the Amendment in order to avoid alienating the votes of wavering Republicans in the upcoming elections." Memphis and New Orleans changed the calculus. The New Orleans massacre demonstrated the danger of leaving to the States the duty to protect freedom of speech and freedom of assembly. And both events showed that "it was no longer plausible to claim that the southern states had any interest in providing the rights of due process to loyal southern Unionists."[56] Even the conservative *New York Evening Post* agreed that "[i]t simply was not plausible to believe that the southern states could be trusted to protect individual liberty." President Johnson's defense of the local authorities in New Orleans and his flippant attitude toward the free speech and assembly rights of loyalists there was "politically disastrous."[57] By the fall campaign, Republicans strongly touted the proposed Amendment as a protection for the rights of loyalists in the South, suggesting a belief that at least the Free Speech and Assembly Clauses of the First Amendment[58] would henceforth apply to the States.

As with some of the statements made in the Thirty-Ninth Congress, the statements made on the campaign trail can be interpreted to reflect that understanding. For example, an August 28 speech by centrist Republican Representative Columbus Delano in Coshocton, Ohio, decried the fact that antislavery whites had "'been driven out of the South, when their opinions did not concur with the "chivalry" of the Southern slaveholders.'" He explained that Congress proposed the Fourteenth Amendment because it "'determined that these privileges and immunities of citizenship by this amendment of the Constitution ought to be protected.'" Likewise, Radical Republican General Benjamin Butler of Massachusetts in October said that the Amendment would permit people speak their minds, in contrast to the experience in the South where people could not "'express [their] opinions freely'" there.[59] Radical Republican Representative James Wilson of Iowa said that the Amendment was necessary because "'They must have the same liberty of speech in any part of the South as they always have had in the North.'"[60] Generally, the claim by Republicans that protection of the rights of speech and assembly "would be achieved by ratifying the Fourteenth Amendment" was "repeated and uncontradicted."[61]

One group in particular that seemed to embrace an Incorporationist understanding of the Amendment were Southern loyalists themselves, the victims of the repressive state regimes in the South.[62] In their July 4, 1866, call for a Southern Loyalists' Convention to be held in Philadelphia in September, the organizers began by noting: "The majority in Congress, and its supporters, firmly declare that 'the rights of the citizen *enumerated in the Constitution*, and established by the supreme law, must be maintained inviolate." Much of the discussion at the convention itself centered around deprivation of the constitutional rights of Southern loyalists. Judge Lorenzo Sherwood of Texas opened his address by discussing "the constitutional rights of the citizen; those rights *specified and enumerated* in the great charter of American liberty," including free press, speech, and religion, and the right to trial by jury. Later in the address, he made clear that he considered these rights to apply against the States, stating: "These rights being established by the supreme law of the land, there is no power . . . *State or National*, that has authority to transgress or invade them." Texas Governor A.J. Hamilton said that the convention stood upon "the old platform of the Constitutional rights of every citizen in our land."[63]

A series of post-election editorials in the *New York Times* by the pseudonymous "Madison" also can be read as suggesting that the incipient Fourteenth Amendment would apply the Bill of Rights to the States. On November 10, "Madison" wrote that the Amendment would include "the right to speak and write [one's] sentiments, regardless of localities" and the right "to keep and bear arms in [one's] own defence." Five days later, "Madison" reiterated that the protection of the Amendment "must be coextensive with the whole Bill of Rights in its reason and spirit." And about two weeks after that, Madison observed the resistance to the Amendment in the Southern States, saying that "everywhere among them it is objected that to Congress is given the power to enforce the Bill of Rights."[64]

However, nearly all of these statements suggesting that the Fourteenth Amendment would protect what we would call the First (and Second and Sixth) Amendment rights of Southern loyalists, are subject to different interpretations. They might, as the Incorporationists urge, reflect an understanding of the Privileges or Immunities Clause as essentially applying the First Amendment to the States. However, they could just as well be interpreted to reflect the equality-based understanding: that, assuming the Southern States provide free speech rights to former Confederates, they must equally provide those rights to loyalists as well. The same could be said of the Second Amendment right to bear arms and the Sixth Amendment jury-trial right.

One important datum supporting the Incorporation Skeptics is that the new state constitutions in the South, which had to be accepted by Congress before those States could be readmitted, contained provisions that were not identical with, and pointedly less protective of individual rights than, the Bill of Rights. These provisions were drafted by Republicans in the South who obviously supported the Fourteenth Amendment and they were deemed acceptable to the same Republican congressmen who framed the Amendment. This, Incorporation Skeptics say, is strong evidence that these Republicans did not understand the Fourteenth Amendment as incorporating the Bill of Rights.[65] Relatedly, some non-Southern States that voted for ratification did not adhere to some of the provisions in the Bill of Rights, such as the Fifth Amendment's requirement of indictment by grand jury and the Seventh Amendment's requirement of juries in civil cases involving amounts in controversy over twenty dollars. Incorporation Skeptics argue that had legislators in these States thought that the Fourteenth Amendment incorporated these provisions by reference, thus voiding their own States' laws, they would have said something about it. Instead, there was silence.[66]

Thus, evidence regarding incorporation of the Bill of Rights cuts both ways. However, even assuming that the clause was understood in 1868 as applying all or some of the Bill of Rights against the States, there are two aspects of the framing and ratification debates that cast doubt on jot-for-jot incorporation. First, the widespread Republican belief in natural rights and "higher law" calls into question how literal they were being when they conceived of applying the Bill to the States. Second, as even most Incorporationists acknowledge, the moderate Republican mainstream put a high value on maintaining our federal system even as it tried to modify that system to provide people with federal constitutional rights as against their own States. These circumstances together call for a more nuanced approach to incorporation that, at the end of the day, bridges the gap between the Incorporationists and their critics.

Republicans and the "Higher Law"

To fully appreciate the relationship between "higher law" and the incorporation question, we need to explore one of the most popular arguments of the Incorporation Skeptics. Some of them have tried to detract from Congressman Bingham's reliability by questioning his competence. They highlight the fact that he appeared to have contradicted himself on numerous occasions regarding the Bill of Rights.[67] First, Bingham on some occasions seemed to accept that *Barron* v. *City of Baltimore* held that the Bill of Rights applied only to the federal government, while on other occasions, he seemed either not to know or not to care about *Barron*, stating that the Bill of Rights already applied to the States.[68] Critics also point to Bingham's apparent confusion about exactly what the "Bill of Rights" was. On some occasions, he seemed to go beyond the first eight amendments and include, for example, the Comity Clause in describing "this immortal bill of rights."[69] In his February 28, 1866, speech, Bingham specifically mentioned the Comity Clause and the Fifth Amendment's Due Process Clause as "provisions in the bill of rights."[70]

However, Bingham was neither inconsistent nor confused. He simply had an unorthodox view of the Comity Clause. The conventional juristic reading of the clause was that given by Justice Washington in *Corfield*, that it requires States to treat nonresidents no worse than it treats residents vis-à-vis certain fundamental rights and interests. In essence, it was and is generally interpreted as an interstate equality provision: citizens of State A sojourning in State B must be treated equally as citizens as State B with respect to certain fundamental legal rights.[71]

However, there was a competing view of the Comity Clause that began to gain traction immediately before the Civil War. Both proslavery and antislavery forces began thinking of the Comity Clause as a fundamental-rights guarantee rather than solely as a guarantee of equality. Slaveowners began to view the clause as guaranteeing them the right to travel to free States with their enslaved persons despite local law outlawing slavery. Abolitionists began to read the clause as guaranteeing the right to advocate for abolitionism in slave States, despite censorship laws there.[72] It appears that Bingham took the abolitionist reading of the clause one step further, as neither solely an equality provision nor as a protection solely for out-of-staters but as requiring that States respect the *fundamental rights of its own citizens*. Those fundamental rights, he reasoned, were those enjoyed by people *as citizens of the United States*, including those contained in other part of the Constitution, such as the first eight amendments.[73] To read the clause this way, Bingham had to add language that, to his way of thinking, had been elided by the framers. This has been called the "ellipsis reading" of the Comity Clause, and Bingham explained it this way:

> "The citizens of each State (being *ipso facto* citizens of the United States) shall be entitled to all the privileges and immunities of citizens (*supplying the ellipsis 'of the United States'*) in the several States. . . ." This guarantee of your Constitution applies to every citizen of every State of the Union.[74]

On this view, even before adoption of the Fourteenth Amendment, the Constitution already required States to honor the privileges and immunities of its own citizens, which included the rights enumerated in the first eight amendments. Thus, on Bingham's view, the Bill of Rights already bound the States, *Barron* notwithstanding. The problem was that Congress had no way of enforcing the States' obligation to honor those rights. It was this shortcoming, apparently, that Bingham sought to fix with his proposed amendment.[75]

There is a good deal of academic controversy over how widely shared Bingham's "ellipsis reading" of the Comity Clause was.[76] However, his view that some constitutional rights already applied as against the States was shared widely among Republicans regardless of whether they attributed this to the Comity Clause. As Curtis has written: "Leading framers of the Fourteenth Amendment and most Republicans who spoke on the subject in 1866 believed that the states were already required to obey the Bill of Rights. For them, the Fourteenth Amendment was an affirmation of their own deeply held legal theories."[77]

To be sure, some Republicans who expressed the sentiment that the principles in the Bill of Rights already bound the States were Radicals.[78] But this notion was also "squarely within the mainstream of moderate Republican Reconstruction theory."[79] For example, conservative Republican Representative John Kasson of Iowa apparently agreed that at least the First Amendment applied to the States when he stated that the Comity Clause had been violated for the past twenty-five or thirty years because Southern abolitionists had been driven from their homes for expressing their beliefs.[80] Senator George H. Williams of Oregon, a conservative-centrist Republican and a member of the Joint Committee, appears to have shared this view.[81] Even conservative Unionist Hale, who opposed Bingham's first draft, accepted Bingham's premise that "the bill of rights . . . defin[es] and limit[s] the power of Federal *and State* legislation."[82]

Once again, these statements are susceptible of an interpretation grounded in equality or in fundamental rights. But whether the consensus in 1866 was that the Fourteenth Amendment would guarantee that the States observe the rights contained in the Bill of Rights or merely required that they treat their own citizens equally regarding those rights, leading Republicans believed that *some* constraint grounded in the Bill of Rights—substantive or equality-based—already bound the States and that the Fourteenth Amendment would finally permit recognition and enforcement of those rights against the States. But how could this be, given the holding of *Barron*?

The answer has a lot to do with the "higher law" thinking that pervaded Republican ideology. Republicans tended to view the rights enumerated in the Constitution as God-given natural rights. Natural rights, to them, existed in nature, even prior to and outside of government.[83] Laws and constitutions did not create these rights but merely declared that they exist.[84] Once people entered into organized society, the theory went, those natural rights were kept but, because people had to forfeit some aspects of their natural rights in exchange for the benefit of protection by the State, many were transformed into "civil rights." Civil rights can be understood as the residue of natural rights after that exchange, or, to put it another way, natural rights when subjected to reasonable regulation by the positive law of the State.[85]

On this way of thinking, the Bill of Rights was merely declaratory of natural rights that pre-existed both the federal government and the States.[86] Americans had always had the natural rights protected by the Bill of Rights and other parts of the Constitution—the right to the writ of habeas corpus,[87] for example—even as against their own States, *Barron* notwithstanding. There was general agreement within the Republican Party, and especially its leadership, that the Bill of Rights bound the States despite *Barron* because the Bill was merely declaratory.[88] By Akhil Amar's count, there were at least "thirty Republican statements in the Thirty-eighth and Thirty-ninth Congresses voicing contrarian sentiments," i.e., the belief that *Barron* was either wrong or irrelevant.[89] Even some state court judges, either not knowing or not caring about *Barron*, felt themselves bound by the "declaratory" law of the Bill of Rights.[90] The "higher law" view was expressed by prominent constitutional scholar Timothy Farrar, who wrote in his 1867 treatise that the incipient Fourteenth Amendment could "scarcely be claimed by anybody . . . to prohibit the States from doing any thing which otherwise they might rightfully do."[91] This "higher law" view was a remnant of antebellum antislavery legal thought and was thus dominant in Republican ideology after the war.[92] There was general agreement among Republicans with Bingham's view that *Barron* stood only for the proposition that these natural rights could not be *enforced* against the States, not that they did not exist.

This explains why Bingham's views may sound inconsistent or confused to modern readers.[93] To modern positivists, Bingham's simultaneous recognition of *Barron* and his assertion that the Bill of Rights binds the States makes no sense. To make sense of this position, we must immerse ourselves in the jurisprudence of the mid-nineteenth century instead of prochronistically imbuing Bingham and his colleagues with a way of thinking about law that would mature only several decades later.[94] Bingham and other Republicans "believed that the states were already required to obey the Bill of Rights," because they rejected the modern, "'positivist' notion that the Constitution was merely what the Supreme Court of the moment said it was."[95] Thus, regardless of what the framers and ratifiers thought about "incorporation" of the Bill of Rights, to the extent they did at all, they "stressed that the privileges and immunities provision would protect United States citizens in their natural rights from State deprivation."[96]

The Fourteenth Amendment and the Preservation of Federalism

At the same time that the framers and ratifiers of the Fourteenth Amendment understood that it would fundamentally change the relationship between the States and federal government, there was a strong countercurrent. All but perhaps the most radical Republicans also valued and wanted to preserve to the extent possible federalism as it had existed since 1789, with the bulk of policy-making authority in the States and only the residuum left to the federal government. They expressed the expectation that American federalism would continue mostly unhindered. Typically these expressions came in response to criticisms by Democrats and more conservative Republicans that echoed the Anti-Federalist critique of the proposed Constitution in 1787–88: that the adoption of the Fourteenth Amendment would lead to a despotic centralized government and the annihilation of the States.

Democratic opponents of the Amendment predicted that, if adopted, the result would be a complete and cataclysmic consolidation of power in the central government. Representative John A. Nicholson of Delaware decried the Republican's "mad schemes" that would "take away, one by one, all the powers now exercised by the several States, and make this a consolidated Government, a centralized despotism," a veritable "yoke of oppression."[97] Representative Andrew Rogers of New Jersey, often considered the spokesman for Congressional Democrats, called Bingham's first draft "another attempt to consolidate the power of the States in the Federal Government" and "another step to an imperial despotism."[98] Erstwhile conservative Republican Senator James Doolittle of Wisconsin, who would switch parties in 1868, warned of "the wiping out of the States, the destruction of the rights of the States."[99] Kentucky Representative George S. Shanklin said that section 1 would "strike down the reserved rights of the States . . . and invest all power in the General Government."[100] Senator Thomas Hendricks of Indiana, a moderate Democrat, argued that section 5 of the Amendment, giving Congress power to enforce the other sections, would "crown the Federal Government with absolute and despotic power."[101] Democratic Representative Aaron Harding of Kentucky argued that section 5 would "transfer[] all powers from the State governments over the citizens of a State to Congress."[102]

Had only Democrats expressed these concerns, one might dismiss them as sore-loser Chicken Littles. But conservative and even moderate Republicans expressed some of these same concerns. New Jersey Representative William Newell, just after criticizing the proponents of "State rights and State sovereignty" for seeking "to deprive the people of their liberties," also spoke out against "all unnecessary and sweeping amendments" to the Constitution that would lead to "a consolidated democracy," in contrast to "State individuality in accordance with national unity."[103] Conservative Republican Senator William M. Stewart of Nevada disapproved of Bingham's first draft because it would allow "Congress to legislate fully upon all subjects affecting life, liberty, and property" and "there would not be much left for the State Legislatures." This, he said, "would work an entire change in our form of government."[104] Representative Thomas Davis, a Unionist from New York, in opposing Bingham's first draft, said: "I will not accept any theory which shall concede the right of the Federal Government to erect a despotism upon the ruins of the States."[105] Representative Delano expressed the conventional view that rights are primarily "to be guarantied and sustained and enforced by the laws of the States under the constitutions of the States" before warning that the "pendulum of public opinion," which had swung too far in the direction of State rights, could swing too far back the other way, which would be "an error about as great and dangerous."[106]

Moderate and conservative Republicans insisted on "maintain[ing] the basic federalist structure of the Constitution."[107] After all, federalism in the antebellum era had provided a useful, if ultimately unsuccessful, device to help protect the rights of alleged fugitives from slavery through the adoption of state "personal liberty" laws as a counter to the federal Fugitive Slave Acts of 1793 and 1850.[108] The 1860 Republican Party platform embraced the values of federalism,[109] and the affinity for states rights lingered among mainstream Republicans after the war.[110] In early 1866, although Radical Republicans made up about 50 percent of the House, moderate Republicans constituted the next largest group. Conservative Republicans were particularly strong in the Senate.[111] The Radicals knew that they needed the moderates and some conservatives on board to get the supermajority in Congress necessary to send the Amendment to the States.[112] With the elections only months away, the party strove to present a united front.

Perhaps the most significant comments—because they caused Bingham to withdraw his first draft from consideration—came from mainstream Republican Representative Giles Hotchkiss of New York, and Representative Hale, a conservative Unionist. Just after Bingham spoke in support of his first draft on February 28, 1866, Hotchkiss said that he opposed it because it would "authorize Congress to establish uniform laws throughout the United States upon . . . the protection of life, liberty, and property."[113] The previous day, Hale had similarly objected that the proposal would effect a "radical change in the system of this Government," and complained that, under the proposal, "all State legislation, in its codes of civil and criminal jurisprudence and procedure . . . may be overridden."[114] Hale reminded his colleagues that "our decentralized system" was founded on the notion that "individual freedom and the protection of personal rights" were primarily the domain of the States.[115] But neither Hotchkiss nor Hale, though voicing these federalism concerns, was "opposed to enforcing the Bill of Rights against the states"[116]—indeed, Hale believed the Bill already applied to the States—and both ultimately supported the final draft of the Fourteenth Amendment.

To those who did not share Bingham's unusual reading of the Comity

Clause, the first draft of the Amendment purported to sweep within the federal purview all of the rights mentioned by Justice Washington in *Corfield*, including "the right to acquire and possess property of every kind, and to pursue and obtain happiness and safety," as well as "many others which might be mentioned."[117] Thus understood, the proposal threatened to "vastly expand[] the scope of federal power to regulate civil rights in the States—a possibility applauded by radical Republicans but strongly opposed by all conservative Republicans and most moderates."[118] Thus, the first draft ran into stiff opposition from fellow Republicans who read it as endowing the federal government with the power to control the common-law rights that had heretofore been the exclusive domain of the States.[119]

Because of the political realities of the day, proponents of the Amendment had to be sensitive to these concerns. As William Nelson put it, they

> made it clear that they did not intend such vast power for Congress. Most Republican supporters of the amendment . . . feared centralized power and did not want to see state and local power substantially curtailed. They recognized that the "doctrine of the rights of the States justly construed is as important to the preservation of the republic as any other fundamental political doctrine."[120]

Radical Republican Pennsylvania Representative John H. Broomall, for example, assured his more conservative colleagues by acknowledging that "by far the largest portion of the business of government is done in the States," and that the Amendment preserves "local government."[121] Bingham, in particular, agreed that federalism must be preserved. While his proposed amendment would "punish all violations by State officers of the bill of rights," it would also "leav[e] those officers to discharge the duties enjoined upon them as citizens of the United States by th[eir] oath and th[e] Constitution." He stated his belief that protection of persons and property lie primarily with the States.[122]

Bingham, no radical himself but a moderate-to-conservative Republican, was speaking in good faith. Radicals may have seen Bingham's first draft as giving Congress the power over the entire litany of common-law rights spelled out in *Corfield*, but Bingham disagreed both descriptively and normatively. Those rights, he believed, were and should remain protected by the States. Bingham, in fact, had opposed the Civil Rights Bill, not only because he believed Congress lacked power to enact it, but also because he believed that civil rights generally were properly the purview of the States. According to him, "the substance of state-level common law rights were matters rightfully left to state control under the Tenth Amendment."[123] Thus, like many of his colleagues, Bingham opposed federalizing these common-law rights; he just did not read his proposal as doing so.[124]

Because Bingham believed that the rights already contained in the Constitution, such as the Bill of Rights, were appropriate for federal protection, he answered the charge that his first draft would lead to consolidation of power by repeating his claim that the Bill of Rights already bound the States.[125] He denied that the proposal would "take from the States [any] rights that belong to the States" because they could not and did not reserve to themselves "the right . . . to withhold from any citizen of the United States within its limits . . . any of the privileges of a citizen of the United States."[126] But beyond that, States retained all their sovereign powers. As an example, Bingham reminded his House colleagues that the Bill of Rights protected "property," but that this protection rose or fell with a particular States' definition of "property." He asked rhetorically: "[W]ho ever heard it intimated that anybody could have property protected in any State until he owned or acquired property there according to its local law or according to the law of some other State which he may have carried thither?"[127] But once a person acquired what a State considered property, they were entitled, as a matter of federal constitutional law, "to be equally protected in the enjoyment of it."[128]

Thus, Bingham and his moderate Republican colleagues sought an accommodation between the extreme centralization sought by some Radicals and the extreme decentralization advocated by Democrats. As Lash has put it:

> Bingham threaded the needle by rejecting both unduly narrow and unduly broad readings of the proposed amendment. . . . [H]e sought nothing less than the enforcement of the Bill of Rights against the states. On the other hand, his amendment had nothing to do with radical efforts to nationalize the countless common law and natural rights traditionally regulated by the states.[129]

This explains why Bingham tabled indefinitely his first proposal, ultimately replacing it with something closer to the version of section 1 that we have today.[130] Less than two weeks earlier, he had witnessed the spectacle of eight Senators who had voted for the Second Freedmen's Bureau Bill switch sides to block an override of Johnson's veto.[131] An earlier version of section 2 of the Fourteenth Amendment relating to Black suffrage had also failed in the Senate for much the same reason.[132] These two experiences showed Bingham that "only those civil rights measures that received virtually unanimous support from mainstream Republicans could be adopted."[133] The moderate and conservative Republican responses to his first draft apparently caused him to realize that those who did not share his "ellipsis reading" of the Comity Clause read the proposal as permitting federal intrusion into virtually every aspect of life, dooming the proposal as unacceptable to moderate and conservative Republicans.[134]

The Republican majority on the Joint Committee, knowing that any amendment to the Constitution would have to meet these federalism concerns by more conservative members of their own party, replaced Bingham's first draft, which used the language of the Comity Clause ("privileges and immunities of citizens *in* the several States"), with the words that were ultimately adopted: "No State shall make or enforce any law which shall abridge the privileges or immunities of citizens *of* the United States."[135] Regardless of whether this was understood as protecting fundamental rights of American citizens absolutely or merely on an equal basis for all, it likely was understood as leaving other "common law civil rights in the hand of local government, subject only to the requirements of due process and equal protection."[136]

The replacement by the Joint Committee of Bingham's first draft with the language in what we know as section 1 "clearly reflects the moderate origin of the current language of section one," because "[t]he more moderate and conservative elements of the committee were virtually unanimous in their support of the proposal." This raises the inference that the second draft's more modest language was a direct response to the federalism concerns raised by the House's more conservative Republicans.[137] This inference is greatly strengthened by the fact that in the debate on the Amendment in its final form, the more conservative Republicans' federalism concerns virtually disappeared. The change in language "apparently mollified conservative mainstream Republicans," given that "only two nominal Republicans . . . argued that . . . section one intruded unduly on states' rights": Senator Edgar Cowan, who became a Democrat the following year, and Representative Charles Phelps of Maryland, of the conservative, pro-Johnson Union Party, whose objections were not strong enough to keep him from voting for the Amendment.[138] Even Democratic Representative Rogers, who still opposed the Amendment in its final form, damned with faint praise when he called it "not so rabid as some of the propositions agreed to be submitted by [the Joint] committee."[139]

The Fourteenth Amendment as proposed by Congress was thus a moderate compromise, not a radical restructuring of the Nation's political system. As Senator Fessenden explained the Joint Committee's work:

> [W]e have been obliged to take into consideration a great many things: first, what it would be wise and just to do, and next what, if it is wise and just, we can do; what would be acceptable in the first place to Congress, and in the next place what would be acceptable to the people. Unquestionably in the committee there was very considerable difference of opinion. That difference of opinion had to be reconciled. I do not suppose that the scheme as presented would be exactly in all particulars what would suit perhaps a large number; . . . and the committee, after much deliberation, came to the conclusion that its duty was to agree upon that which seemed to be the best scheme with regard to reconstruction upon which they could come to a unanimous or nearly unanimous agreement.[140]

As a result, neither radical nor conservative Republicans were truly enthusiastic about the Amendment.[141]

During the campaign of 1866, the Democratic opposition to the Amendment again raised fierce federalism concerns.[142] They had a powerful spokesman in President Johnson. Democrats widely circulated a letter from Secretary of the Interior O.H. Browning, with Johnson's blessing, that came to be seen as Johnson's official position on the Amendment.[143] The letter blasted the proposed amendment on federalism grounds. The effect of section 1, Browning warned, would be to

> subordinate the State judiciaries in all things to Federal supervision and control; to totally annihilate the independence and sovereignty of State judiciaries in the administration of State laws, and the authority and control of the States over matters of purely domestic and local concern. If the State judiciaries are subordinated, all the departments of the State Governments will be equally subordinated, for all State laws, let them relate to what department of Government they may, or to what domestic or local interest, will be equally open to criticism, interpretation and adjudication by the Federal tribunals, whose judgments and decrees will be supreme, and will override the decisions of the State Courts and leave them utterly powerless.[144]

In response, Republicans avoided any mention of the Amendment's operation in the North, apparently on the theory that the Amendment would have no effect in States that recognized the natural rights of its citizens.[145] As Governor Jacob Cox put it: "If these rights are in good faith protected by

State laws and State authorities, there will be no need of federal legislation on the subject, and the power will remain in abeyance."[146] Republicans also generally "disavow[ed] all Radical influence in the framing of" the Amendment in order to further reassure mainstream Americans.[147] The Republican landslide in the 1866 elections suggests that Americans were assuaged by Republican assurances that the Amendment tempered a guarantee of fundamental constitutional rights in the South with a continuation of the American tradition of federalism and localism.

In short, the Fourteenth Amendment was a triumph of moderation. There was a wide diversity of Republican views, but the position that could enjoy consensus support was a "moderate Republican balance between protecting rights and preserving federalism."[148] As Kurt Lash put it: "Time and again, the Thirty-Ninth Congress considered whether to embrace a form of revolutionary nationalism or maintain the original constitutional structure of federalism and dual sovereignty. [A]t every critical fork in the road, a majority held onto the Constitution's dualist structure."[149] Radical Senator Richard Yates of Illinois summed it up nicely:

> While gentlemen upon the other side of the Chamber are opposed to these measures as too radical, I am opposed to them, so far as I might present points of opposition, because they are not radical enough. At all events, therefore, we have the medium between extremes; we have moderation. . . . [I]n the whole history of the world there never were such terms of moderation and of magnanimity proposed to a vindictive foe as by these resolutions which have been reported by the committee of fifteen.[150]

Conclusion

It is possible that the framers and ratifiers of the Fourteenth Amendment understood it to apply the Fourth Amendment to the States, based on the idea that freedom from unreasonable searches and seizures was one of the fundamental, natural-law rights that existed even prior to the formation of government. On the other hand, the framers and ratifiers of the Fourteenth Amendment understood that it left largely intact the federal structure that had existed before, that it did not create power in the federal government to create a uniform national civil and criminal code, and that it left protection of most common-law rights to each State, provided that it do so on an equal basis for all and that it observe due process of law.

The notion of incorporating the Fourth Amendment against the States, then, leaves us with a three-sided conundrum. First, how could the framers and ratifiers of the Fourteenth Amendment have understood it as applying the Fourth Amendment to the States, placing all the subtleties, nuances, and shifting common-law rules we saw in previous chapters under the control of Congress and the federal courts, while simultaneously holding fast to the federal structure created at the founding, with its strict preservation of local control? Second, how do we reconcile the "higher law" naturalism that was the basis for the Republicans' Fourteenth Amendment with the hardheaded proto-Realism that was at the heart of the Anti-Federalists' Fourth Amendment? Finally, how do we fit together what is essentially a federalism provision, carving out search-and-seizure policy for state control, with a provision that is about rights against the States themselves? Attempting to resolve this conundrum is the challenge of the next chapter.

Eight

Applying Constitutional Search-and-Seizure Constraints to the States through the Fourteenth Amendment

We saw in chapter 7 that the Reconstruction-era Republicans may have understood the Fourteenth Amendment as applying the Fourth Amendment against the States. But we saw also that they wished to preserve our basic federal structure and the States' primary responsibility for making decisions of local policy. And as we saw in earlier chapters, the Fourth Amendment itself was understood originally as preserving the profoundly local character of search-and-seizure law. Thus, it is extraordinarily difficult to conceive of the Fourteenth Amendment as imposing nationwide search-and-seizure rules. Determining the way in which the Fourth Amendment can be applied to the States requires a deeper, more nuanced analysis in the face of the seeming paradox of incorporation.

This chapter attempts to provide such an analysis. It first examines closely three reasons that incorporation of the Fourth Amendment against the States presents us with a seemingly insoluble paradox. It then proposes a solution to that paradox by means of what Akhil Amar dubbed "refined incorporation": distilling out the individual-rights core of the Fourth Amendment—freedom from unbridled executive officer discretion—and leaving behind its federalism-based encasement, which gave us only one particular method of securing the core right. Finally, it reads the "due process of law" language of the Fourteenth Amendment in conjunction with the view of freedom from unbridled executive officer discretion as a privilege or immunity of federal citizenship to give us a representation-reinforcing model of the Fourth Amendment. On this model, most search-and-seizure rules are up to the

States so long as politically accountable decision-makers, not individual executive officers, are making the rules.

The Central Paradox of Incorporating the Fourth Amendment

The incorporation of the Fourth Amendment creates a paradox for three overlapping reasons.

Ensuring Rights While Preserving Federalism

First, we must reconcile two undeniable but seemingly inconsistent goals of the framers and ratifiers of the Fourteenth Amendment. On the one hand, the Fourteenth Amendment unquestionably altered the relationship between the federal government, the States, and the people, by "nationaliz[ing] questions about individual rights and depriv[ing] the states of either exclusive or final authority on those questions."[1] On the other hand, the framers and ratifiers also wanted to preserve our essential federal structure.

Consider how mutually inconsistent these seem with respect to the Fourth Amendment. Recall from chapter 5 the complexity and diversity of search-and-seizure rules. The law of search and seizure as of 1791 was highly reticulated, with rules and sub-rules regarding, for example, the proper bases for warrantless arrests, the ability to break doors to make arrests, authority to search incident to arrest, consequences of a fruitless forcible entry, nocturnal entries to search or arrest, guilt of the arrestee as an absolute defense, whether private papers could be seized even with a warrant, and the search warrant requirement in non-dwelling premises. Not only were these rules highly technical in nature, they differed across jurisdictions and over time. Whether a felony in fact was a necessary element for a warrantless arrest, for example, was very much a moving target during the framing period.

The complexity and diversity of the law of search and seizure had only increased by 1868. The state- or region-specific justice of the peace manuals had mostly faded from view, replaced by more modern treatises that set out general views on search-and-seizure law. However, these treatises did not purport to offer straightforward, nationwide standards for all search-and-seizure questions. Quite the contrary, one of the foremost nineteenth-century American authorities on criminal procedure, Joel Prentiss Bishop, writing in 1866, began his chapter on arrests this way: "The subject of this chapter is one of considerable delicacy, and not quite free from difficulty. Its leading doctrines are plain and well established; but there are places at which its minuter lines are indistinct and even uncertain." In particular, Bishop noted later in the same chapter, "[t]he right of arrest by officers of the peace is more or less enlarged by statutory regulations in the several States," and he admonished his readers to "carefully examine questions of this sort in connection with the statute book of his own State." Moreover, as was true at the founding, Bishop found "a considerable degree of intricacy and confusion in the authorities which relate to th[e] subject" of breaking of doors to make an arrest. On the topic of what we call search incident to arrest, Bishop candidly admitted that "[t]here is but little to be found in the books, relating to th[at] matter," and that it was "not easy to lay down a general doctrine on this subject, with any great assurance of its being everywhere accepted as sound."[2]

In this context, it is easy to see why there is so much tension between incorporating the Fourth Amendment against the States and preserving federalism. The law of search and seizure consisted of finely detailed state codes of criminal procedure, carefully balancing in every instance the need for law enforcement and public order, on the one hand, with personal security, privacy, property, and liberty on the other. Yet the framers of the Fourteenth Amendment sharply disclaimed any intention to impose such a unform national code on the States.[3] Indeed, the framers repeatedly claimed that the Amendment would not even have any applicability in States that already afforded its citizens their fundamental rights, downplaying the effect of the Amendment in the North. Incorporation Skeptic Raoul Berger noted the inconsistency in Representative John Bingham's rhetoric in particular, inveighing against federal takeover of the States' civil and criminal codes, on the one hand, and claiming that the Bill of Rights bound, or should bind, the States, on the other.[4] And the ratifiers, taking the framers at their word, almost certainly did not understand the Amendment as taking these finely tuned policy decisions out of their hands. Berger correctly noted: "It is inconceivable, given attachment to State sovereignty over local matters, that the North would tamely have accepted drastic curtailment of its own control of criminal administration."[5] Yet the framers' and ratifiers' attachment to state sovereignty and their desire for the federal government to guarantee rights against arbitrary searches and seizures—whether absolutely or on a basis of equality—existed simultaneously. The difficult task, then, is to "heed the[] dual command to protect rights and to leave legislatures unfettered to adopt laws for the public good."[6]

Meshing the Anti-Federalists' "Proto-Realism" with the Republicans' "Higher Law" Philosophy

We also have to contend with the fact that the framers and ratifiers of the Fourteenth Amendment had a very different view of the nature of law than the Anti-Federalists of the founding generation did. The difference stems from the two disparate ideas at the heart of the Declaration of Independence that we explored in chapter 3: on the one hand, all people enjoy the natural and "unalienable rights[] [of] life, liberty and the pursuit of happiness"; on the other hand, "secur[ing] these rights" requires positive acts of democratically elected assemblies, "governments . . . deriving their just powers from the consent of the governed." While the Reconstruction-era Republicans, like their Federalist forebears, stressed the former, natural rights aspect of the law, the Anti-Federalists, and their Democratic descendants, stressed the latter, positive law requirement.

"Antifederalists, while believing in natural rights, were also hardheaded realists when it came to the issue of securing inalienable rights in law."[7] They knew that natural rights were useless unless reduced to some positive-law manifestation. The idea of rights as "higher law," binding irrespective of positive law, "would have been foreign to many of the men who had clamored for a bill of rights in the 1780s." For the Anti-Federalists, "[t]he word *right* had no talismanic natural law significance." Instead, as discussed earlier in this book, they foreshadowed the rise of modern Legal Realism, "intuit[ing] the idea Hohfeld would resurrect" in the twentieth century, by which "[p]articularistic customs, charters, and the like gave distinct persons or entities distinct rights or privileges against distinct entities, but not others."[8] Recall, for example, Maryland Farmer's admonition that one cannot cite "Locke, Sydney, or Montesquieu" to a judge.

This explains why Democrats, ideological heirs of the Anti-Federalists, generally derided the "higher law" way of thinking. In the antebellum period, "antislavery thought was . . . dependent on natural law theory, while proslavery thought . . . (at least at times) rejected the concept of natural law."[9] This is not to say that Democratic proslavery ideologies did not encompass the idea of natural law and natural rights.[10] But like the Anti-Federalists before them, they viewed democratic majorities as having virtually unfettered power to translate these natural rights into positive law—"secur[ing] these rights" through government by the "consent of the governed."[11] To be sure, the positive law had to "adequately secure[] the inalienable preexisting [natural] rights of the people."[12] But that could be accomplished in any number of ways; a natural right to trial by jury in criminal cases, for example, did not necessarily require a unanimous verdict of twelve people. The Democratic position was summed up in a South Carolina newspaper in 1867:

> Human or natural rights, doubtless exist. They are described generally in the American Declaration of Independence as being the right to "life, liberty and the pursuit of happiness," but how and by what means these natural rights shall be enjoyed or preserved, is under the absolute discretion and will of all, established for their common benefit, by their common government.[13]

This strict separation between natural law and positive law led Democrats to scorn the Republicans' theory that the Bill of Rights already bound the States as "surprising evidence of stolid ignorance of Constitutional law, or of a shameless effort to impose upon the ignorant."[14]

By contrast, Republicans generally embraced the "higher law" way of thinking about rights without specifying, even in their own minds, how those rights would be operationalized.[15] They never really bothered thinking about the relationship between natural law and positive law because they saw the boundary between the two as being porous. According to Howard Graham, Republicans inherited from their abolitionist forebears a

> confusion of moral with civil rights—the failure to distinguish between socially desirable ends and the steps and means necessary for their legal or constitutional attainment. Rights were interchangeably regarded as preexistent human ideals and as socially implemented and enforceable privileges or immunities . . . [W]hat ought to be was mistaken and substituted for what was. Abolitionist theory was a monument to this imprecision. The underlying dualism worked its greatest confusion where constitutional rights were at issue. . . . This confusion persisted and reached its climax in 1866.[16]

As a result, Republican lawyers saw no problem with citing higher law to judges, as when Salmon P. Chase, later Chief Justice of the United States, argued in the Supreme Court in *Jones* v. *Van Zandt*: "The law of the Creator, which invests every human being with an inalienable title to freedom, cannot be repealed by any inferior law, which asserts that man is property."[17] It would be almost unthinkable for any lawyer in the twenty-first century—much less one prominent enough to one day be named to the Supreme Court—to tell the Court that God's law trumped man's law. But the Republicans inherited from their ideological ancestors, the Federalists,[18] a way of thinking about rights as if they existed "in the air," as it were, instead of in the more modern, Hohfeldian sense of rights as a system of rules and sub-rules governing the relationships between and among specific persons and entities. In this way, the Republicans were essentially the mirror image of the Anti-Federalists. The incorporation of the Fourth Amendment is complex precisely because it calls for the reconciliation of these two very different ways of thinking about rights.

Structure vs. Rights

The final aspect of the paradox of incorporating the Fourth Amendment is that the Anti-Federalists and the Republicans had two very different understandings of the Fourth Amendment itself. As we saw in Part I, the Anti-Federalists saw the Amendment as a structural provision that preserved local control while also protecting rights by requiring that federal officers obey state law. These ideas lived on in the rhetoric of the Reconstruction-era Democrats. Indiana Representative Michael C. Kerr, for example, argued that the Bill of Rights—not the Tenth Amendment, mind you, but the entire Bill—secured state authority by inhibiting federal power to "dictate to [a State] how it shall protect its citizens in their right not to be deprived of life, liberty, or property without due process of law." As Kerr put it, the Bill of Rights "simply say[s] that Congress shall not invade the rights of the States of this Union to do things that are forbidden to be done by the first eleven amendments of the Constitution."[19]

The Republicans obviously read the Fourth Amendment very differently, given that many of them believed that it already bound the States, which would be completely nonsensical had they seen the Amendment as primarily a federalism provision. Republican framers and ratifiers of the Fourteenth Amendment saw the Fourth Amendment as imposing on the States general fundamental principles regarding searches and seizures. Moreover, they were profoundly ambivalent about localism. On the one hand, localism in the antebellum period had meant state "personal liberty laws," which sought to protect free persons of color alleged to be fugitives from slavery by providing stringent procedures for the recapture of fugitive slaves.[20] On the other hand, localism in 1866 meant de facto slavery through vagrancy provisions, as well as torture, rape, arson, and murder of Black people and loyal whites committed with impunity.

One could argue that, to the extent that the framers and ratifiers of the Fourteenth Amendment misunderstood the Fourth as being solely about rights, any attempt to incorporate it against the States fails: the Fourth Amendment, as a federalism provision like the Tenth, simply cannot be incorporated. However, this conclusion would do a disservice to the original understanding of the Fourth Amendment, which was not just about federalism but about using federalism principles to preserve individual rights. This conclusion would also do a disservice to the original understanding of the Fourteenth Amendment as encompassing some protections against arbitrary searches and seizures by state officials. If they incorrectly understood that the Fourth Amendment defined the metes and bounds of those protections, that does not negate the fact that *some* type of protection was understood as applying. "[T]he relevant question to determine intent is what the framers of the Fourteenth Amendment believed and intended, not whether their intent was based on a historically correct view of the Constitution."[21] But our task of defining that protection becomes much more difficult.

In short, the goals of the framers and ratifiers of the Fourteenth Amendment were almost the mirror image of those of the framers and ratifiers of the Fourth. Both believed that the States were the primary guarantor of rights, but that's where the agreement ended. The Anti-Federalists' view of the States as the first line of defense against tyranny led them to insist on explicit constraints in a bill of rights that calibrated protection of rights against the federal government to the way the States protected those rights. The Republicans' view of the States as the primary guardians of liberty led them to add a mechanism for the federal government to step in when the States did not do their job.[22]

Incorporating the Fourth Amendment implicates what Bruce Ackerman termed "the problem of multigenerational synthesis." We "have to identify which aspects of the earlier Constitution had survived Republican reconstruction [and] synthesize them into a new doctrinal whole that [gives] expression to the new ideals affirmed by the Republicans in the name of the People." This requires a more nuanced analysis than the two antagonistic positions that dominated twentieth-century discourse on the Bill of Rights: total incorporation and no incorporation. Each of these elides the fundamental tensions between the Anti-Federalists and the Reconstruction-era Republicans. Instead, we must "confront[] th[os]e tensions . . . and . . . elaborate[e] doctrinal principles which harmonize the conflict in a way that does justice to the deepest aspirations of each."[23]

Resolving the Paradox through Refined Incorporation

The first step in tackling the seeming paradox of incorporation of the Fourth Amendment is to engage in a form of what Akhil Amar dubbed "refined incorporation" by distilling the liberty-enhancing principles from the Fourth Amendment and applying those to the States, while leaving behind its federalism components. The idea of "refined incorporation" recognizes that even if "all of the privileges and immunities of citizens recognized in the Bill of Rights became 'incorporated' against states by dint of the Fourteenth Amendment," which we can assume for sake of argument, "not all of the provisions of the original Bill of Rights were indeed rights of citizens [but] instead were at least in part rights of states, and as such, awkward to fully incorporate against states."[24]

The Fourteenth Amendment, after all, does not speak simply of "privileges or immunities," but "privileges or immunities *of citizens of the United States*." According to Amar's key textualist insight, this wording "is remarkably sensitive to [a] more complicated reality . . . requir[ing] us to ask whether a given provision of the Constitution or the Bill really does declare a privilege or immunity of citizens rather than, for example, a right of states."[25] It is also sensitive to Senator Jacob Howard's remark, sometimes overlooked, that the Privileges or Immunities Clause encompassed "*the personal rights* guarantied and secured by the first eight amendments of the Constitution."[26] In effect, the term "privileges or immunities of citizens of the United States" "filter[s] out" the federalism components of the Bill.[27]

The Fourth Amendment, I have suggested, is one place where such filtering must occur. In Amar's evocative phrase, structural rights of the States and personal rights of individuals are "marbled together" there. The Amendment guarantees a personal right against certain kinds of intrusions by the federal government, but it does so in a way that preserves States' rights, by calibrating those personal rights to the policy of each respective State. Where individual rights and States' rights are intertwined in a provision of the Bill of Rights, such an "alloyed provision[] . . . may need to undergo refinement and filtration before the[] citizen-right elements can be absorbed by the Fourteenth Amendment." This approach is true to the mainstream Republican belief that the Bill already applied to the States, a view that "self-consciously sought to distill the pure essence of [individual] rights . . . that had been blended with structural issues in the Bill."[28]

The key, then, is to identify the core liberty-enhancing principles at the heart of the Fourth Amendment, divorced from its federalism aspect.

Whether one reads the Fundamental Rights view or the Equal Rights view into the Reconstruction Republicans' understanding of the Privileges or Immunities Clause, it is clear that they considered freedom from arbitrary searches and seizures as a "privilege or immunity" of American citizenship. That is, the framers and ratifiers of the Fourteenth Amendment almost certainly understood it as limiting the power of the State to search and seize, whether as a substantive constraint or one based purely on principles of equality.[29] During the framing and ratification of the Fourteenth Amendment, "it was overwhelmingly recognized that freedom from unreasonable searches and seizures was a precious, fundamental right deserving of federal protection from State negations."[30] When Members of Congress mentioned specific rights that would henceforth be enforceable against the States, they almost invariably included those protected by the Fourth Amendment. Representative Roswell Hart of New York quoted the language of the Fourth Amendment in describing the rights that inhered in any republican government.[31] Senator James Nye of Nevada, in his list of rights that he believed already applied to the States, mentioned "'security of person,'"[32] in obvious reference to the Fourth Amendment. Kansas Senator Samuel Pomeroy listed only three rights as "indispensable" as "safeguards of liberty": the right to bear arms, the right to vote, and "the right to acquire and hold [a homestead], and *the right to be safe and protected in that citadel of his love.*"[33] One of the earliest proposals for a Fourteenth Amendment included in its second section that all citizens would be "protected[] from unreasonable search and seizure."[34]

Of the natural rights considered to be most fundamental, the right to be free from unreasonable searches and seizures ranked among the most widespread in state constitutions as of 1866. Thirty-four of the thirty-seven state constitutions contained such a provision, and all but one contained a provision forbidding the issuance of warrants on less than probable cause.[35] As Amar wrote: "The Fourth Amendment . . . offers a rather easy case for incorporation, all the more so because its words banning unreasonable intrusions and overbroad warrants track those of so many state constitutions already in place in 1866."[36]

And for good reason. The authority of the government to arbitrarily conduct searches and seizures is a badge and incident of slavery wholly incompatible with freedom. Again, think about the two biggest complaints about the postbellum treatment of Black Southerners: arbitrary arrests for vagrancy and other petty crimes, and violence exacted against Black people as well as loyalists—including domiciliary searches—by state actors. The petty criminal statutes ostensibly applied equally to both races, but it was an open secret that, because of the vast amount of discretion these laws provided police—in part because they were routinely violated by people of both races alike—Black people were overwhelmingly arrested for committing these crimes. And the violence exacted against Black people and loyal whites by state actors always included a literal seizure of the victim's person[37] and often included indiscriminate and suspicionless searches of Black dwellings for arms and stolen property. Recall, finally, the "pass system" during the antebellum period that was designed precisely to seize enslaved persons and prevent their free passage from one place to another. This pass system saw a resurgence after the war, now designed to seize free people of color. The Fourteenth Amendment was, in part, a reaction to "the broad, discretionary search and seizure powers that Southern governments were using to subject Black people to intrusive searches, pretextual arrests, and violent seizures."[38] As Andy Taslitz summarized it, "the overwhelming weight of historians' opinions leaves little doubt that the framers, and probably the ratifiers, of the Fourteenth Amendment understood that it would apply the Fourth Amendment to the states, protection against unreasonable searches and seizures being among the 'privileges and immunities' of U.S. citizens."[39]

Both the founding-era Anti-Federalists and the Reconstruction-era Republicans would agree that at the very core of the Fourth Amendment is ***freedom from unbridled executive officer discretion***, the ability of government officials to arbitrarily choose where, when, why, and whom to search or seize. The Anti-Federalists and the Republicans also sought to control that discretion in the same general way: through ***local democratic control***. To the Anti-Federalists, this meant that whatever search-and-seizure rules bound executive officers at the state and local level would govern across the board, even for federal officers. The Republicans, while obviously more skeptical that executive officer-discretion should be left to the unfettered choices of state and local legislatures, still strove to preserve the basic structure of federalism. So long as the States recognized the core privilege to be free from arbitrary searches and seizures in some form, whether absolutely or on an equal basis for all, States were free to "regulate in diverse manners the form in which [the privilege] existed or the mode in which [it] could be exercised."[40]

So far, this sounds a lot like Justice Felix Frankfurter's "fundamental fairness" approach.[41] Recall that in *Wolf* v. *Colorado*, he wrote for the Court: "The security of one's privacy against arbitrary intrusion by the police—which is at the core of the Fourth Amendment—is basic to a free society. It is therefore implicit in 'the concept of ordered liberty' and as such enforceable against the States through the [Fourteenth Amendment]."[42] But the flabby, toothless doctrine that "fundamental fairness" became could not have been what the framers and ratifiers of the Fourteenth Amendment contemplated. It is true that mainstream Republicans "understood that the states would continue to be the primary guarantors of their citizens' rights, and that the states enjoyed substantial latitude in defining the scope [and] incidents of those rights."[43] But while the Republicans accepted local prerogatives in drawing up detailed criminal procedure codes, they surely were not sanguine about a regime where former Confederate soldiers had virtually unlimited discretion in policing former enslaved persons, even when the laws themselves were race neutral. The experience with the vagrancy laws tells us that much. The framers and ratifiers of the Fourteenth Amendment had to have been thinking of a Fourth Amendment applicable to the States that left room for local variation but that also shaped the nebulous bar on arbitrary incursions on privacy, security, liberty, and property with guideposts that made the promise of fairness and equality real and not illusory.[44]

Amar advocated incorporation of the Fourth Amendment in a way that was sensitive to the evils that gave birth to the Fourteenth, particularly the "Black Codes that had designated blacks as special targets for various searches and seizures." For Amar, this meant a focus on equality:

> [I]n the Fourteenth Amendment, unlike the Fourth, the privacy privilege of the citizen sits next to an explicit guarantee of equal protection. As our society gives meaning to the notion that searches and seizures must not be "unreasonable," the Fourteenth Amendment reminds us that equality values must supplement privacy values. A relatively unintrusive search might not be "unreasonable" in terms of privacy alone; but if, say, blacks are being singled out without good cause, such a search may well offend reconstructed reasonableness.[45]

This is a good start. But an equality proviso is not enough to give full effect to the framers' and ratifiers' understandings. While it was not hard in 1866 to show that "blacks [we]re being singled out without good cause," the Fourteenth Amendment was built for our time as well as theirs. We no longer have former enslaved persons policed by former Confederates. While the presence of white supremacists in law enforcement is still a problem, the bigger problem is that police officers, like the rest of us, suffer from blind spots and implicit bias. Today, there is no crime for which only Black people are arrested, and there is no place where Black people are the only victims of police violence.

The core Fourth Amendment right—freedom from unbridled executive officer discretion—in fact has much more to do with the Due Process Clause than with the Equal Protection Clause. The Due Process Clause, read most naturally, limits the executive.[46] The most obvious of those limits, the core, irreducible meaning of "due process of law," is that of a rule of law / separation of powers constraint: executive officials must obey the law. As Nathan Chapman and Michael McConnell have written: "The first, central, and largely uncontroversial meaning of 'due process of law,' . . . was that the executive may not seize the property or restrain the liberty of a person within the realm without legal authority arising either from established common law or from statute."[47] This was still the core meaning of due process in 1868.[48]

A careful rereading of *Wolf* shows us that the Court was sensitive to the requirement of "due process of law" in this sense of the term. After the passage quoted above, the Court continued: "The knock at the door, whether by day or by night, as a prelude to a search, *without authority of law but solely on the authority of the police* [is] inconsistent with the conception of human rights enshrined in the history and the basic constitutional documents of English-speaking peoples."[49] The emphasized words seem to have gotten lost entirely in the tumultuous debate over incorporation. But they show the main concern of Frankfurter and his colleagues, and why the entry into a home without a warrant, to them, was fundamentally unfair. It was not the absence of a warrant per se that was offensive to "English-speaking peoples," but what that absence signified: one branch of government (the executive) running riot with no constraints placed on it by the other two. Separation-of-powers constraints are the essence of due process of law.

Thus, the separate clauses of section 1 work together synergistically. The Privileges or Immunities Clause recognizes pre-existing rights, already binding on the States per Republican ideology, but it forbids the States from "abridg[ing]" not the rights themselves but only "the contingently-existing set of constitutional, statutory, and common-law rights given to its citizens" to effectuate those rights.[50] Thus, for example, Howard's reference to the Bill of Rights may have been, not to the actual Bill but rather to those same rights "as guaranteed in state bills of rights."[51] The other two clauses provide the parameters within which States must protect these rights, or have the federal government step in and do it for them: on an equal basis for all and with due process of law. As Bond put it, section 1 "preserved the state's traditional authority to define both the rights of its citizens and the procedures by which those rights would be protected," but it "obliged the state to exercise that authority in ways that preserved the privileges and immunities of citizenship for all by commanding that all persons should receive both due process and the equal protection of the laws."[52]

To whatever extent the Incorporationists are correct, we might say that the Privileges or Immunities Clause distills the core of the Fourth Amendment—freedom from arbitrary infringements on liberty, privacy, property, and security—as a privilege or immunity afforded all Americans. The Equal Protection Clause creates an affirmative obligation on state governments to protect those interests equally, rather than allowing one group to suffer infringements on those legal interests without legal recourse, as was the case for Black people, loyal white people, and relocated Northerners in the South in the immediate postwar period.[53] And the Due Process Clause provides a separation of powers / rule of law constraint to further the core right when the government itself infringes on liberty, privacy, property, and security: state officers may do so only if they obey the law rather than making it up as they go along. A State's network of search-and-seizure principles, as constrained by the twin guideposts of due process and equality, operationalizes the key privilege or immunity of being free from arbitrary incursion on liberty, privacy, property, and security.

This way of looking at the application of the Fourth Amendment to the States is the best way of honoring both of the Republicans' seemingly contradictory goals in adopting section 1: protecting certain basic rights while also preserving federalism. When the Republicans referred to the federal structure that had sustained the Nation through nearly eight decades and a Civil War, they surely were not thinking of local executive officials running rampant. To them, federalism meant state and local ***lawmaking***. Steeped in the Blackstonian tradition, they saw law as "a rule; not a transient sudden order from a superior, to or concerning a particular person; but something permanent, uniform, and universal."[54] Lawmaking is the job of legislators, not police, sheriffs, or militias.

And the Republicans were optimistic—too optimistic, it turned out—that Black Americans would soon be involved in that lawmaking process, through which they would be able to protect themselves. Carl Schurz wrote in his influential report on conditions in the South: "In the right to vote [Black men] would find the best permanent protection against oppressive class-legislation, as well as against individual persecution."[55] As James Bond wrote: "Republicans anticipated that Southern blacks would be able to protect themselves in the rough-and-tumble of the political process, especially after they were guaranteed the right to vote. Blacks themselves routinely insisted that they could take care of themselves if they were only given the vote."[56] Earl Maltz explained that, for those who advocated Black suffrage, it would "provide[] a mechanism by which the basic rights of freedmen could be protected at the same time the basic federal structure was preserved," because they "could use their political power to protect *themselves* against white oppression."[57] Representative James G. Blaine later recalled: "In enacting the Reconstruction Laws Congress proceeded upon the basis of faith in Republican government, as defined so tersely by Mr. Lincoln— *of the people, by the people, for the people*."[58]

To be clear, no one believed that Black suffrage would be a panacea. They expected that section 1 would place constraints on legislatures and would continue to do so even after the advent of Black suffrage. But they also thought that once Black people had a hand in lawmaking, they would be, as Schurz wrote, "far less exposed to violation" of their rights than if they were "completely subject to the will of others."[59]

Refined incorporation of the Fourth Amendment also helps us mesh the hardheaded realism of the Anti-Federalists and the lofty naturalism of the Republicans. Both the Anti-Federalists and the Republicans believed that natural-law principles acted as the backdrop for the common law.[60] Both believed that the "customs, practices, and laws" that the common-law method looked to were not ends in themselves but simply "evidence of larger principles of freedom to be applied to present-day circumstances."[61] And both understood that, because these larger principles governed States that were very different from one another in a variety of ways, with "different climates, different geographies, and different economic situations," the everyday, nitty-gritty application of these principles—the "low-level legal rules and judicial decisions"—would be different in different States.[62]

But the Anti-Federalists, "hardheaded realists"[63] that they were, saw that form and representation were inseparable, that abstract principle without concrete manifestation was useless. The Anti-Federalists knew that when push came to shove—when the federal revenue officer came knocking—what mattered were cases, not principles.[64] When the Anti-Federalists thought of search-and-seizure law, they not only thought of the general principle of freedom from arbitrary constraint on liberty, security, privacy, and property. They also thought of the specific common-law practices that changed over time and across borders in response to new insights and understandings, and local policy preferences. When they demanded what became the Fourth Amendment, they did so with particular search-and-seizure practices in mind, which they wanted explicitly carved out of federal power and placed under state control. For them, the principle and the practice were inseparable.

By contrast, when mainstream Republicans of 1866 thought of the rights protected by the Fourth Amendment, they did not have particular practices in mind as if "itemizing a simple contract."[65] They saw natural-law principles as existing separately from the common-law cases, which were mere representations of those principles.[66] They understood the Fourth Amendment as a broad, general protection of personal liberty, security, property, and privacy, not a code of specific regulations set forth in a manual or treatise. They had in mind high-sounding political rhetoric, not "the resolution of specific legal issues."[67] Because, for them, natural-law principles existed outside of and independently from common-law cases, they were able to advocate for the former without the burden of thinking about the latter. While the Anti-Federalists emphasized the "customs, practices, and laws" of the common law, Republicans emphasized the "larger principles of freedom."[68]

But the common denominator between them was the recognition that the larger natural rights principles—"universal, immutable, and unconditional"—would be translated *by the States* into "particularistic, organic, and contingent" rules.[69] Republicans understood that the States must have wide latitude in interpreting the former into the latter, taking higher-law precepts and turning them into usable rules of conduct for government agents. States could implement the privileges and immunities of national citizenship in a way that took account of local norms. What they could not do is "blunt national privileges in an inappropriate manner or negate the abstract principles sustaining them."[70] As William Nelson put it, "even if fundamental rights were derived from higher law or were the entitlement of citizens independent of state law, those rights could be enjoyed only if state legislatures created rules and mechanisms for their enjoyment." State legislatures enjoyed latitude in formulating those rules and mechanisms.[71]

The dichotomy between the fundamental principle and its execution explains the Republicans' claims that the Fourteenth Amendment would not lead to consolidation of power and that the Amendment would have little effect in the North. Both claims rest on the "assumption that states would conform their laws to the moral precepts incorporated into the amendment so that conflict between state and federal authorities would not arise."[72] Accordingly, the States would retain "the most important of their powers: the power to enact specific, detailed regulations of the conditions under which rights would be enjoyed." The difference now is that Congress and the federal courts would have the power to make certain that States' regulation of rights was equal and fair.[73] The twin edicts of due process and equal treatment would act as guardrails against disparate application of even neutral laws, such as the vagrancy provisions of the Black Codes, ensuring they be enforced equally and fairly or not at all.

This way of thinking about the Fourteenth Amendment vis-à-vis the Bill of Rights provides an accommodation between the Fundamental Rights and the Equal Rights views. To whatever extent the framers and ratifiers of the Fourteenth Amendment understood it as "incorporating" parts of the Bill, they understood that incorporation as operating only to secure absolutely the very core of any particular provision of the Bill, which no State was likely to abandon with respect to its most favored citizens anyway. Any further federal guarantee of rights took the form of the dictates of equality and due process: that those rights be enjoyed by all, not subject to the whims of executive officials.

A Representation-Reinforcing Fourteenth Amendment

The wide latitude that mainstream Republicans would give to the States in regulating even the "privileges and immunities" of their own residents, and the Republicans' faith in the democratic process once Black suffrage was to be adopted, puts one in mind of modern process-based, or representation-reinforcing, approaches to the Constitution. Political process theories of constitutional law, pioneered by John Hart Ely in his classic work *Democracy and Distrust*, start from the premise that most policy issues in a representative democracy should be decided in a democratic fashion.[74] For purposes of the Fourth Amendment, as summarized by Silas Wasserstrom and Louis Seidman: "Ely would argue that the tradeoff between privacy and law enforcement produced by our political institutions should stand, provided that everyone's interests are equally represented in the making of these political decisions."[75]

It is only where the specter of imperfections in the political system threaten process failure that courts should step in. Process failure can occur when irrational discrimination against certain subgroups prevents their fair and equal participation by gumming up the gears of ordinary political deal-making, or when it results in laws that "deny[] that minority the protection afforded other groups by a representative system."[76] Apropos of the latter defect, process theory seeks to ensure, as Justice Robert H. Jackson famously put it, "that the principles of law which officials would impose upon a minority must be imposed generally," foreclosing the ability of those officials to "escape the political retribution that might be visited upon them."[77] In the Fourth Amendment context, this means ensuring that the majority does not obtain the benefit of enhanced security and order on the backs of the minority who suffer a loss in privacy, liberty, property, and dignity. Judgments about this cost/benefit balance are constitutionally legitimate only if the majority shares equally in the costs or would strike the same balance if they had to do so.[78] If so, the fact that the majority is willing to bear the burden of law enforcement intrusions suggests that the interests of the minority have not been undervalued.[79]

Accordingly, Ely was particularly concerned with legislatures providing executive officials with outsized discretion because, by doing so, they "provide[] a buffer to ensure that they and theirs will not effectively be subjected to" the laws.[80] By controlling and guiding discretion, we can ensure that elected officials who represent the members of the majority "internalize[] the costs of law enforcement" and that law enforcement, unable to smuggle in too many low-level discretionary decisions, remains accountable to the populace.[81] Thus, according to Ely, judicial review, at least when construing unclear constitutional text such as section 1, should be focused on policing the political process for process failures, such as the delegation of excessive discretionary power.

A process-based approach to state searches and seizures is particularly attractive where broad swaths of people are the potential targets. In such cases, "[c]itizens can protect themselves in the same way that they protect themselves against most kinds of government misconduct—they can throw the rascals out."[82] This is true of the types of intrusions that states implement proactively in order to detect and deter crime, such as sobriety checkpoints and general electronic surveillance, rather than reactively in response to suspicion of a particular crime. Reliance on judicial enforcement of strictures on searches and seizures becomes less pressing when everyone is affected because we can rely on the political process to strike an acceptable balance between liberty and security.

Based on this process-oriented perspective, a school of scholarship has emerged that is centered around the idea that Fourth Amendment reasonableness is primarily about setting standards for democratic controls over policing. Daphna Renan has argued that "Fourth Amendment reasonableness has [a] structural and more systemic dimension [and] is in part about the institutional dynamics through which surveillance is authorized, conducted, and superintended."[83] Chris Slobogin has explicitly applied Ely's political process theory to the Fourth Amendment, arguing that "the political process is often well-situated to deal with panvasive searches and seizures," those that gather large amounts of data pursuant to a widespread regulatory scheme rather than as a result of individualized suspicion, precisely "because these searches and seizures affect wide swaths of the population that can have access to the legislature."[84] And Barry Friedman has set forth a powerful argument that some form of a democratic policing model, "one in which the people must debate and decide—and take responsibility for—the actual practices that will be used to keep us safe," is required by the Constitution.[85] According to these views, constitutional constraints on search-and-seizure authority that has been vetted through the democratic process, with no signs of process failure, including excessive discretion, would be at their ebb. By contrast, constitutional constraints on search-and-seizure authority exercised by executive officials with few or no democratic controls would be robustly enforced.

Political process theory is generally less attractive with respect to reactive, suspicion-based policing. In a very technical sense, such policing potentially affects everyone because every citizen is always a potential target of searches and seizures. Yet we know in a practical sense that this is not true. Our system of highly discretionary law enforcement exacerbates the systemic inequalities of our criminal justice system, leading police to concentrate their energies on "the usual suspects." And because legislatures systemically undervalue the rights of these suspects, they often shirk their responsibility for creating any search-and-seizure rules at all, foisting that responsibility onto the courts.[86] But one can imagine a system that *requires* legal authorization before police can act, at least if they are to act in ways the rest of us cannot.[87] Legislatures would no longer enjoy the luxury of inertia. And given the restrictions on police discretion that I will suggest are embodied in the Fourteenth Amendment, legislatures would have every incentive to draft such rules in ways that they and their constituents can live with if they happen to end up as a target of investigation.

But is this process-based approach the best way of operationalizing the original meaning of the Fourteenth Amendment? The ambiguity of section 1 and the apparent paradoxes involved in incorporating the Bill of Rights make an originalist account of the Amendment extraordinarily difficult.[88] But this does not justify our throwing up our hands and abjuring an originalist methodology completely. Instead, fidelity to the Constitution requires that we make our best estimation of what the Amendment meant in this context given the clues that we have of original meaning. As non-originalist Barry Friedman put it, reconstructing history is essentially an exercise in empiricism, and as any empiricist knows, finding a single explanation for all phenomena is impossible. The best we can do is to construct an explanation that "provides the best account of all the points in the past," to "take a set of data points and do the best job [we] can fitting a straight line to it," attempting to "minimize[] the overall deviation from" those data points.[89] Or, as originalists Randy Barnett and Evan Bernick put it, under-determinacy of the text and history requires use of "constitutional heuristics," that is, "a set of doctrinal tools" that can help us implement the text of section 1 "in a manner that is faithful to its letter and spirit."[90]

Originalists typically understand the importance of focusing on a higher level of generality than the specific applications of an under-determinate constitutional text that were expected in 1791 or 1868. Using what Lee Strang dubbed "abduced-principle originalism," rather than resting upon the conclusion that the framers and ratifiers meant to forbid, allow, or require a "discrete set of practices," modern originalism requires that we go further and "abduce the rule, standard, or principle that best fits" the prohibition, condonation, or requirement of those practices.[91] In trying to recreate the original understanding of the Fourth Amendment in the first part of this book, I downplayed the specific aspects of search-and-seizure policy extant at the founding in favor of the primary structural mechanism, federalism, in which the founding generation placed their faith in preserving liberty. Likewise here, originalist methodology permits us to home in on the structural hallmarks of our Constitution—federalism and separation of powers both—that the Reconstruction-era Republicans so clearly wanted to maintain even as they imposed constitutional constraints on the States in response to the Black Codes and the reprehensible violence against Black Southerners. They contemplated that these structural principles would be the fulcrum upon which the newly protected rights would hinge. Something close to Ely's process-based approach can thus "be defended on a theory of imputed intent" of the Fourteenth Amendment's framers and ratifiers.[92]

In essence, on an original understanding of the Fourteenth Amendment, to whatever extent a State would have to provide a basic right to be free from arbitrary searches and seizures, it would generally be free to tailor its own search-and-seizure regimes within some fairly broad parameters.[93] The nature of the parameters required by the Fourteenth Amendment corresponded to the history behind it. Because discrimination against Black people, loyalists, and Northerners was the main concern, state search-and-seizure provisions that are nondiscriminatory on their face, in their intent, and in their operation should be largely immune from constitutional attack. However, rooting out discriminatory searching and seizing is extraordinarily difficult because this activity is carried out by executive officials of the State, and there is vast room for arbitrariness and bias if those officials are not tightly constrained through democratic controls. There is also the danger that those officials will simply disobey the law. Recognition of the Republicans' emphasis not only on rights but on popular sovereignty, tinged with the hope of Black suffrage, provides us with a useful constitutional heuristic: recognition of freedom from arbitrary searches and seizures as a privilege or immunity of American citizenship, but one that can be protected in many disparate ways by state positive law, bounded by antidiscrimination and rule-of-law constraints. Thus, we come to the heart of constitutional constraints on search-and-seizure activity that, I suggest, are imposed by the Fourteenth Amendment: such activity must be (1) authorized by laws that are (2) nondiscriminatory and that (3) limit executive officer discretion.[94]

Conclusion

If the Incorporationist Skeptics are correct and the Privileges or Immunities Clause merely requires States to treat their citizens equally with regard to certain rights, that equality of treatment must be not only in form but in substance as well. If, on the other hand, the Incorporationists are correct that the framers and ratifiers of the clause understood it as applying the Bill of Rights to the States, that understanding must be tempered by the difficulties of applying to the States a provision so heavily laced with federalism principles as the Fourth Amendment is. Either way, we wind up in much the same place: States have primary responsibility for structuring search-and-seizure law in a way that is responsive to each polity's respective balancing of security and liberty, but they must do so in a way that respects rule-of-law and equality principles. In a sense, each State establishes the rules of the road, but the Fourteenth Amendment maintains the guardrails of due process and equal treatment.

PART III

Original Understandings and Modern Policing

Nine

The Principles of Nondiscrimination, Legality, and Nondelegation

The previous part of the book addressed the best way of thinking about how constitutional search-and-seizure constraints operate on the States. I suggested there that the best way to operationalize the original understanding of the Fourteenth Amendment vis-à-vis applying Fourth Amendment–type constraints to the States is to recognize that the States maintain primary authority for promulgating search-and-seizure policy, subject to equality and rule-of-law/separation-of-powers constraints. Those constraints can be called the principles of "nondiscrimination," "legality," and "nondelegation."

This part of the book switches gears and considers how recognition of these three principles as the constitutional lodestars could change the way the courts think about constraints on policing. This chapter fleshes out the general nature of these principles and suggests some general ideas as to how they might apply in the Fourth Amendment area, using the example of sobriety checkpoints as an illustration of the principles at work. And it addresses one loose thread: how to apply these same constraints to the *federal* government. Chapter 10 then uses our three principles to question some of the orthodoxy of Fourth Amendment jurisprudence. Finally, chapter 11 addresses how a Fourth Amendment more sensitive to these three principles could address four specific problems currently plaguing modern policing.

The Three Principles

First, and most obviously, search-and-seizure practices must not discriminate based on race or other forbidden characteristics, either in the way they are defined by law or the way they are carried out by state agents. We can call this the ***principle of nondiscrimination***. Second, state agents must follow the law; they may search and seize only under circumstances where, and only to the extent that, they are authorized by state and local law. We can call this the ***principle of legality***. Finally, even where certain conduct is authorized by law, state agents must not be granted excessive discretion, for a grant of discretion that is too broad is little better than having no legal authorization at all. We can call this the ***principle of nondelegation***.

Nondiscrimination

The nondiscrimination principle need not detain us long, for it is so obvious. The framers and ratifiers of the Fourteenth Amendment understood that all people had a natural right to be equally free from the types of bodily restraints and governmental intrusions we think of as "unreasonable searches and seizures." This means that at the very least, search-and-seizure law must be written and applied equally.[1] Even Incorporationist Skeptics accept this much.

It might be argued that this constraint goes no further than modern Equal Protection Clause doctrine, pursuant to which any policy or practice, not just those touching on searching and seizing activity, that discriminates on a forbidden basis is suspect. But searching and seizing activity is singled out in the Bill of Rights and was likely meant for special treatment by the framers and ratifiers of the Fourteenth Amendment. The fact that this activity is so fraught with the peril of oppressive government conduct means that we should be particularly sensitive to claims of discrimination in this area. Thus, although such claims typically require proof of intentional discrimination, a more synergistic approach to the Fourth and Fourteenth Amendments might mean that we ought not require such proof where there are disparate and unexplained outcomes in search-and-seizure activity.

Legality

The legality principle tracks the central insight of Anthony Amsterdam in his seminal work *Perspectives on the Fourth Amendment*: "Unless a search or seizure is conducted pursuant to and in conformity with either legislation or police departmental rules and regulations, it is an unreasonable search and seizure prohibited by the fourth amendment."[2] Though Amsterdam was decidedly a non-originalist, there is considerable originalist support for his suggestion, given the postbellum experience with police, sheriffs, militias, and citizen patrols acting lawlessly against Black people and loyal whites. These government agents committed an untold number of criminal and tortious acts. At its most basic level, the requirement of due process of law is a requirement that government officials obey the law. Texan and loyalist George Paschal perhaps had Southern abuses in mind when he wrote of the Fourth Amendment in 1868: "'SEARCHES AND SEIZURES,' are always unreasonable when they are *without authority of law*."[3]

As Amsterdam suggested, administrative guidelines should be considered "law" in the "due process of law" formulation. As a practical matter, legislation can only be so specific in authorizing search-and-seizure activity; administrative rulemaking is required to fill in the details. Where legislation cannot be specific enough to sufficiently narrow police officer discretion, as discussed below, police-issued guidelines are necessary to perform this narrowing function. From the mid-1960s through the 1970s, scholars such as Amsterdam and Kenneth Culp Davis, among others, advocated for a constitutional requirement of police rulemaking in order to limit individual officer discretion.[4] Some modern scholars have picked up that baton and run with it.[5] If, as I will suggest, they are correct, then a necessary concomitant of constitutionally required rulemaking is a constitutional requirement that executive officials obey those rules.[6]

This is not to say, however, that any statutory or regulatory violation related to a search or seizure should be thought to implicate the Fourteenth Amendment. Due process rights are implicated only if the law violation has some causal connection to a deprivation of "life, liberty, or property." Suppose, for example, a police officer were to violate departmental regulations by having a beer at lunch and then immediately make an otherwise lawful arrest. We would say that the officer violated the law and also that the arrestee was deprived of liberty, but the deprivation of liberty was not without due process because the law violation had no causal relationship to the arrest. If, on the other hand, the officer were able to make the arrest only because she identified the suspect using facial recognition technology that was barred by regulation or statute, then we could say that the arrestee may have been deprived of liberty without due process of law. This is true even though the use of such technology would likely not be considered a "search" under current law.

To Amsterdam's edict we should add that police conformity with common-law search and seizure rules also satisfies the legality principle. As discussed in chapter 4, the common law itself is in many ways a democratic institution, whereby time-tested rules enjoying consistent support by multiple generations become part of the landscape of the law, while those that do not are sloughed off. Moreover, although codification of criminal procedure was well underway in 1868, much of the law of search and seizure was still based on common-law principles. Thus, the framers and ratifiers of the Fourteenth Amendment would have understood "due process of law" as incorporating those principles. Whether police violate a democratically enacted statute, a common-law principle, or their own guidelines, "due process of law" is implicated.

As Amsterdam perceived, due process requires that police act not only "in conformity with" but also "pursuant to" the law. Even if police do not violate some statute, common-law rule, or guideline, their conduct must be authorized by law. The framers and ratifiers of the Fourteenth Amendment would have understood the natural right of freedom from arbitrary governmental intrusions to belong to us unless and until our community has decided that we must sacrifice some aspect of that right in the name of collective security. Where no law, rule, or guideline affirmatively authorizes a type of official conduct implicating the security of persons and property, that conduct has not been vetted by the democratic process. In such cases, the Privileges or Immunities Clause puts a thumb on the scale on the side of individual liberty. Moreover, under the centuries-old meaning of the term "due process of law," an executive's acts are beyond the scope of legal authority—*ultra vires*, as lawyers put it—unless they are affirmatively authorized by law.[7] As Davis put it: "A most astounding fact about police policy-making is that much of it is unauthorized by statute or by ordinance, that some of it is directly contrary to statutes or ordinances, and that the strongest argument for legality rests upon legislative inaction in the face of long-continued police practices."[8]

This is not to say, however, that every single investigative tool must specifically be authorized by law before the police can use it. It is simply to say that the police are subject to the same laws as everyone else. Only if they want to go beyond this baseline do they need specific statutory authorization. Thus, if thermal imaging devices are available to all, police may use them unless barred from doing so by law. But because we generally cannot expect there to have been legislative action regarding a technology, technique, or procedure not available to the general public, there must be specific legal authorization for state agents to use it. This is the key insight of the Supreme Court in *Kyllo v. United States*, discussed in chapter 4, that police need a warrant in order to use intrusive technology that is available only to them, but they need no judicial authorization if the technology is available to the general public.[9]

Beyond new technology, we can say more broadly that legal norms governing interactions between private individuals should be the default to which state actors are also bound unless the law gives state agents special dispensation. Take, for example, rules regarding the manner of executing warrants. First, police must generally knock and announce their presence before forcibly entering a premises to execute a warrant.[10] Moreover, they generally may execute a warrant only during daylight hours.[11] As far as the legality principle is concerned, if state law either specifically allows or condemns no-knock or nocturnal entries, that is the end of the matter (although the nondelegation principle might have something to say about it). But if the relevant state law and guidelines are silent as to how and when warrants can be executed, what are the correct default rules?

The legality principle suggests that we base the default rules on what an ordinary person can legally do. At first blush, it seems difficult to draw the analogy because ordinary people lack the power to execute warrants. But there are situations where a private person would have the right to enter another person's premises. In a landlord-tenant relationship, for example, both landlord and tenant have a property interest in the dwelling: the tenant has a right to use and possession for a given term and that interest reverts back to the landlord at the end of the term. The typical lease agreement reflects this arrangement by requiring a tenant to allow a landlord access to a rented dwelling to inspect it, make necessary repairs, or show the dwelling to a prospective tenant. But state law typically requires a landlord to give a tenant advance notice before entering and to enter only during reasonable hours, at least in the absence of an emergency.[12] Absent legislation giving the police special dispensation to deviate from conduct we expect from other private individuals, police must act in an analogous fashion. This is not because, as the Supreme Court has held, these were the rules in 1791; it is because police must abide by "due process of law."

Nondelegation

Legality is a necessary but not a sufficient element of due process when it comes to searches and seizures. A law expressly authorizing police to conduct warrantless searches of any place that they suspect might hold evidence of a crime is hardly consistent with due process of law. Such a law would grant so much discretion to police that it is little different from having no law at all.[13] Not only is excessive discretion inconsistent with rule-of-law principles, but it is extremely effective at masking discrimination. As Kim Forde-Mazrui put it: "As the degree of discretion tends toward absolute, the effectiveness of antidiscrimination review tends toward zero."[14] A nondelegation principle, in Ely's words, "reduce[s] the likelihood that a different set of rules is effectively being applied to the comparatively powerless."[15] The nondelegation principle thus backs up the legality principle as an essential separation-of-powers/rule-of-law aspect of due process. While due process requires the legislature to make the law, this must be true in a factual, not just a formal, sense. When statutes too broadly delegate authority to enforce the law, there comes a point where police have so much discretion as to where to search or what or whom to seize, they are no longer enforcing the law. They are legislating.[16]

We know that the framers and ratifiers of the Fourteenth Amendment wanted to target undue delegation to executive officials, given their outrage over the vagrancy laws. The primary defect of these laws was not their substance, for they were race-neutral and had been around, in one form or another, for centuries. The big problem with the vagrancy laws was in the way that they were enforced: predominantly if not exclusively against Black people. This was possible, in part, because of how vaguely the laws were written. But that was not the only problem with such laws, as demonstrated by the other petty offenses for which Black people were disproportionately arrested. Laws against trespassing, petty theft, and other such crimes were written clearly enough. The problem was their breadth: everyone, at one time or another, commits them. This, like the vagueness of the vagrancy statutes, vested police with too much discretion as to whom to arrest.

The postbellum experience in the South instructs that the main danger of excessive discretion is selective enforcement or, to be precise, *under*-enforcement. The problem of under-enforcement deserves special attention because it is so easily hidden[17] and because "the power to be lenient is the power to discriminate."[18] In the main, we would expect the political process to weed out unpopular laws or curb oppressive enforcement practices. But when criminal laws are either so vague or so broad that they could be enforced against almost anyone, there is a danger that they will not be enforced much against the dominant group. When that is the case, we cannot rely on the political process because those with the political clout to change the laws have no incentive to do so. The result is "unequal justice, for whenever the evidence of an offense is clear, the decisive point in the entire criminal process is usually whether or not an arrest is made."[19]

Yet under-enforcement is inevitable because police cannot possibly arrest all lawbreakers. The level of enforcement thus necessarily becomes a policy decision.[20] When that policy decision is made by executive officials, particularly those who are unelected, rather than by a representative democratic institution, it is, as Davis bluntly put it, "an unlawful assumption of power" and a "reject[ion] [of] the central idea of the rule of law." When that policy is made by an individual officer on the beat, we have the opposite of the rule of law. Again, Davis:

> The system is atrociously unsound under which an individual policeman has unguided discretionary power to weigh social values in an individual case and make a final decision as to governmental policy for that case, despite a statute to the contrary, without review by any other authority, without recording the facts he finds, without stating reasons, and without relating one case to another.[21]

An early Fourteenth Amendment case shows the nondelegation principle at work. In *Yick Wo* v. *Hopkins*, a Chinese national in San Francisco challenged a fine he incurred for violating a city ordinance making it an offense for anyone to operate a laundry in any building not made of brick or stone unless he had the permission of the board of supervisors. Yick Wo alleged that over 150 Chinese nationals operating wooden laundries had been denied permission, while permission had been withheld from only one of the "eighty odd" non-Chinese owners of wooden laundries. The Court reversed Yick Wo's conviction. It acknowledged that the purpose of the ordinance, protecting against fires, was legitimate. However, the Court held that the absolute power vested in the board of supervisors to grant or withhold permission to operate a laundry was inconsistent with due process of law. The ordinances

> confer, not a discretion to be exercised upon a consideration of the circumstances of each case, but a naked and arbitrary power to give or withhold consent. [T]he law had conferred upon them authority to withhold their assent, without reason and without responsibility. The power given to them is not confided to their discretion in the legal sense of that term, but is granted to their mere will. It is purely arbitrary, and acknowledges neither guidance nor restraint.

The Court acknowledged that democratically enacted laws must be implemented by some state agent. But rule-of-law principles dictated that

> the very idea that one man may be compelled to hold his life, or the means of living, or any material right essential to the enjoyment of

> life, at the mere will of another, seems to be intolerable in any country where freedom prevails, as being the essence of slavery itself.

A legislative act purporting to delegate that much power to executive agents of the State is inconsistent with "due process *of law*" because "an ordinance which clothes a single individual with such power hardly falls within the domain of law" at all.[22]

Since *Yick Wo*, the Supreme Court has recognized a constitutional problem with improper delegations only in two cases, both decided in 1935, and only at the federal level. In those cases, the Court declared federal regulations unconstitutional because they were the result of delegations of power to executive agencies without sufficiently narrow legislative guidance.[23] This guidance need not be very detailed; the bare minimum requirement is that the legislation provide the executive officer or agency some "intelligible principle" upon which to act.[24] The nondelegation doctrine has been essentially moribund since that time, given that the Court has deemed the "intelligible principle" standard to have been satisfied by legislative directives that executive agencies issue regulations "in the public interest"[25] and that "set 'fair and equitable' prices and 'just and reasonable' rates."[26] However, there has been a renewed interest on the Supreme Court in reviving the doctrine.[27]

Although this nondelegation doctrine has been justified on separation-of-powers grounds, it could just as easily be characterized as an instantiation of due process principles. "[W]hatever the sources of the doctrine, its application to the States . . . is merely a reflection of . . . fundamental principles of due process." The Court's cases suggest "that due process places limits on the manner and extent to which a state legislature may delegate to others powers which the legislature might admittedly exercise itself."[28] A number of scholars have recognized in the nondelegation context the inherent connections between separation-of-powers and due process principles, "two constitutional bases for nondelegation [that] represent[] mutually reinforcing elements of the Constitution's republican order."[29] For example, Evan Criddle has shown that the Court's reasoning in its early nondelegation cases, although they are nominally based on separation-of-powers concerns, is nearly indistinguishable from the due process principles enunciated in *Yick Wo*.[30]

In a second prominent area, the Court has utilized the principle of nondelegation to strike down both state and federal laws deemed insufficiently clear. This "void-for-vagueness" doctrine is founded in large part on the notion that unduly vague statutes delegate too much legislative power to police, prosecutors, judges, and juries to decide what a statute forbids or requires.[31] Thus, the Court has recognized that there are due process constraints on delegating legislative power to executive officials. And implicit in the nondelegation concerns undergirding the void-for-vagueness doctrine is the danger that excessive discretion is so effective at masking discrimination.[32]

The Court has not explicitly connected the problem of undue delegation to constitutional constraints on searches and seizures. As Davis noted, that omission is difficult to understand. He called it "[e]xtremely incongruous" that the nondelegation doctrine coexists "in the same legal system of enormous undelegated power long exercised by the police without legislative guides of any kind."[33] Even the Court's vagueness cases, which explicitly discuss undue delegation to police as one of the primary rationales of the doctrine, are not Fourth Amendment cases.[34]

Academics have filled this gap. Scholars have noted the problem of undue delegation to police since at least the mid-1960s. In Amsterdam's *Perspectives* article, he recognized the problem of delegation in his second principle, after what I have been calling the principle of legality: "The legislation or police-made rules must be reasonably particular in setting forth the nature of the searches and seizures and the circumstances under which they should be made."[35] Around the same time, Davis suggested in his masterful monograph *Police Discretion* that the nondelegation doctrine's requirement of intelligible principles to guide administrators should apply to "the selective enforcement power of the police." He and a number of other scholars advocated that, in the absence of meaningful legislative standards, police rulemaking should be required in order to cure the problem of undue delegations. As Davis put it: "Any administrator with unguided discretionary power violates due process if he fails to confine and structure his discretion to the extent required to avoid unnecessary arbitrariness in the choices made."[36]

This "first rulemaking moment largely fizzled by the 1980s," but more recently scholars have created "a rulemaking renaissance," producing an impressive body of work reviving the idea that excessive discretion to police should be viewed as type of delegation problem.[37] Renan, for example, has contended that as to "metadata collection program[s]"—those that cull data such as cell phone numbers called—"[t]here are powerful . . . arguments for the proposition that only Congress, not an agency, can create [such] a . . . program inside the United States."[38] She also addressed what agencies must themselves do with that delegated authority, suggesting that courts address the Fourth Amendment reasonableness of "programmatic" searches, those not based on individualized suspicion, by looking at whether the executive authority has "engaged in a deliberate and transparent process to conclude that the privacy intrusions are warranted" and whether "there [are] participatory opportunities in place to identify the relevant tradeoffs."[39] Slobogin explicitly invoked the nondelegation doctrine in asserting that, at least as to "panvasive" surveillance, legislatures ought to be required "to provide relatively detailed instructions to the executive branch," and that, in turn, police departments should be "required to develop, in a transparent fashion, judicially enforceable rules."[40]

As this discussion suggests, the nondelegation principle has two parts. First, it forbids unduly broad delegations from legislatures to law enforcement agencies. Second, it forbids unduly broad delegations from law enforcement agencies to individual officers. Because due process requires that police practices have some basis in the democratic process, such practices are inconsistent with due process if they are authorized only in the most general way by legislation or common-law principles. An "intelligible principle" constraint would likely be enough, particularly if it were applied more robustly than the Court has done. But the ultimate goal of due process in this context is limiting the discretion of the officer in the field. Thus, even where legislation is sufficiently detailed to provide authority for a law enforcement activity, "due process of law" should be understood as requiring that even more detailed police guidelines be promulgated (and, of course, adhered to) in order to limit individual officer discretion.[41]

It remains to be seen what that rulemaking process must look like. There is perhaps some minimal constitutional requirement of public participation in the rulemaking process in order to make the finished product worthy of the appellation "law." Some have called for notice-and-comment rulemaking such as that which takes place pursuant to the Administrative Procedures Act[42] and its state-law analogues, though it is sometimes unclear whether its advocates mean to suggest that such a procedure is constitutionally required.[43] Perhaps it is enough if the rulemaking process is transparent and those responsible for making the rules are either directly accountable to the voters or at least have to answer to other public officials who themselves are politically accountable.[44] However, if, on a political-process theory, democratic policing is going to be largely beyond judicial review, it is extremely important that the communities that are most affected by policing policies have a real say in what those policies are. It is constitutionally unacceptable for the majority to impose burdens on the minority that they are not willing to bear themselves.[45]

It is important at this point to recognize the difference between *limiting* police discretion, which I suggest is constitutionally required, and *minimizing* police discretion, which is not.[46] I do not deny that there are serious administrative and institutional difficulties in determining in a given case how much individual-officer discretion is too much. I cannot pretend that it is easy to draw distinctions to cover all different varieties of police activity between acceptable and unacceptable levels of individual officer discretion. My goal here is to suggest that the Constitution requires that that line be drawn somewhere. If due process of law requires limits on individual-officer discretion, courts cannot shirk their responsibility to try to formulate those limits through the conventional common-law method.

Not only is such line-drawing possible but the Supreme Court has already shown itself quite adept at drawing lines in this area. For example, in the context of police inventory searches of impounded vehicles, it has held that specific police guidelines to limit police discretion are essential to render a search or seizure constitutional, and it has suggested the extent to which such discretion must be limited. The Court held in *South Dakota* v. *Opperman* that such searches are constitutional if conducted "pursuant to standard police procedures."[47] The police department there required "[a] complete 'inventory report,'" following a "survey of the vehicle's exterior—windows, fenders, trunk, and hood—apparently for damage, and its interior, to locate 'valuables' for storage." Further, "*all* impounded vehicles [we]re searched, [and] the search *always* include[d] the glove compartment."[48] In *Colorado* v. *Bertine*, the Court upheld auto inventory search procedures that required officers to open closed containers found in the car.[49] And in *Florida* v. *Wells*, the Court held unconstitutional an auto inventory search of a closed container found in a car where the relevant policy gave officers complete discretion as to whether to open such a container.[50] Justice Harry Blackmun's separate opinion in that case suggested that a State could adopt a policy of either requiring or forbidding the opening of any containers, or some other blanket policy, such as "requir[ing] the opening of all containers that are not locked, or . . . the opening of all containers over or under a certain size." What the State could not do is to leave the decision to the "discretion by an individual officer," perhaps unless such discretion could be "measured against objective, standard criteria."[51] Overall, the automobile inventory cases reflect, perhaps imperfectly, the notion that sufficiently detailed search-and-seizure guidelines that leave little room for individual officer discretion are both necessary and sufficient to satisfy constitutional standards, even if the guidelines are promulgated by the police themselves.[52]

Legality and Nondelegation: The Example of Sobriety Checkpoints

The use of sobriety checkpoints—temporary seizures of motorists on the highways to find intoxicated drivers—can help further explicate the legality and nondelegation principles and the relationship between the two. The Court's approach to vehicle checkpoints represents a process-based Fourth Amendment in action. As Wasserstrom and Seidman pointed out, by requiring that roadblocks stop all motorists, or at least some fixed proportion of motorists with no discretion on the part of officers to pick and choose, "the cost of law enforcement is more widely distributed, and there is less reason to fear that the governmental decisions to trade off privacy for law enforcement are being made without considering everyone's interests equally."[53] The Court has taken a mostly hands-off approach to regulating such checkpoints on just these grounds, noting that democratic controls can largely be trusted in this area because "[p]ractical considerations—namely, limited police resources and community hostility to related traffic tieups—seem likely to inhibit any . . . proliferation" of such checkpoints.[54]

In *Michigan Dep't of State Police* v. *Sitz*, the Supreme Court upheld sobriety checkpoints for reasons to be discussed more fully in the next chapter. The Court explained that the program there was established by the Michigan Department of State Police, an executive agency, which created an advisory committee composed of representatives of various stakeholders and experts. The advisory committee promulgated guidelines regarding selection of sites for the checkpoints, publicizing the checkpoints, and the operation of the checkpoints themselves. Pursuant to those guidelines, "[a]ll vehicles passing through a checkpoint would be stopped and their drivers briefly examined for signs of intoxication." Drivers who showed no such signs would be permitted to go on their way, while drivers manifesting signs of intoxication would be diverted for further examination. In upholding the scheme, the Court emphasized that the guidelines "minimize[d] the discretion of the officers on the scene." It distinguished an earlier case, *Prouse* v. *Delaware*, involving random stops by officers on patrol to check for compliance with license and registration requirements, writing that "random stops involved the 'kind of standardless and unconstrained discretion [which] is the evil the Court has discerned when in previous cases it has insisted that the discretion of the official in the field be circumscribed.'"[55]

The Court was correct to emphasize that the guidelines in *Sitz*, unlike those in *Prouse*, limited officer discretion. It is also noteworthy that the guidelines were created with community input. However, it does not appear that there was any Michigan legislation authorizing the sobriety checkpoint program in the first place. The only possible authorization came from a Michigan statute providing the officers of the Department of State Police with "all the powers of deputy sheriffs in the execution of the criminal laws of the state and of all laws for the discovery and prevention of crime . . . including laws designed for the protection of the public in the use of the highways of the state."[56] But this grant of law enforcement authority is far too general to sustain a very specific type of seizure such as a sobriety checkpoint program.[57] This statute contains no inkling that the people of Michigan have made a determination that the safety and security that comes with highway checkpoints are worth the infringement on liberty, much less a determination about *sobriety* checkpoints in particular. Thus, the checkpoint in *Sitz* fails the principle of legality.[58]

Some States do authorize sobriety checkpoints by statute. For example, New Hampshire law provides that such a checkpoint can be conducted if a "law enforcement officer or agency petitions the superior court and the court issues an order authorizing the sobriety checkpoint after determining that the sobriety checkpoint is warranted and the proposed method of stopping vehicles satisfies constitutional guarantees."[59] A sobriety checkpoint in New Hampshire, assuming it is authorized by a court, would thus pass the legality principle: the people of the State have decided not only that highway checkpoints are an appropriate way of enforcing the law, but they have specifically authorized *sobriety* checkpoints.

Whether a sobriety checkpoint in New Hampshire would pass the nondelegation principle is far more doubtful. By requiring a court order, the legislature has at least not left control of checkpoints in the unfettered hands of the police. However, the direction it has given the police and the courts is virtually nonexistent. The New Hampshire legislation is silent about when, where, and under what circumstances sobriety checkpoints should be conducted, other than that they must be "warranted." That provides no standard whatsoever and would likely fail a robustly applied "intelligible principle" test. Without further direction, the legislature has essentially left it up to the police and the courts to make policy about the use of sobriety checkpoints, a legislative duty.

By contrast, Utah's statute is far more detailed. Like the New Hampshire law, it specifies sobriety checks as one authorized purpose of a checkpoint, though there are others.[60] Like New Hampshire's, Utah's statute involves judicial oversight. Unlike the New Hampshire law, however, the Utah law provides a checklist of items that must be contained in any plan for a checkpoint before it can be approved. It must be submitted by "a command level officer," and it must describe:

> (i) the location of the checkpoint including geographical and topographical information;
> (ii) the date, time, and duration of the checkpoint;
> (iii) the sequence of traffic to be stopped;
> (iv) the purpose of the checkpoint, including the inspection or inquiry to be conducted;
> (v) the minimum number of personnel to be employed in operating the checkpoint, including the rank of the officer or officers in charge at the scene;
> (vi) the configuration and location of signs, barriers, and other means of informing approaching motorists that they must stop and directing them to the place to stop;
> (vii) any advance notice to the public at large of the establishment of the checkpoint; and
> (viii) the instructions to be given to the enforcement officers operating the checkpoint.[61]

In addition, the magistrate may approve any given checkpoint only after she determines that the plan appropriately

> (i) minimizes the length of time the motorist will be delayed;
> (ii) minimizes the intrusion of the inspection or inquiry;
> (iii) minimizes the fear and anxiety the motorist will experience;
> (iv) minimizes the degree of discretion to be exercised by the individual enforcement officers operating the checkpoint; and
> (v) maximizes the safety of the motorist and the enforcement officers.[62]

This is a vast improvement over the New Hampshire statute. It includes the policy goals that the Utah legislature has determined are important, such as minimizing the intrusion on the individual to the extent possible. It also requires the police to think about and decide in advance certain basic characteristics of the seizure—where, when, how, and for how long. Of course, it does leave some discretion to police departments. But it would be unrealistic to demand legislation that specifies, for example, that checkpoints can take place only on certain days, at certain times, on certain highways, or that every third car be stopped, or that each stop take no longer than forty-five seconds.

Notice that discretion that is acceptable for legislatures to grant to police agencies would be unacceptable if granted to individual officers. Thus, the Utah legislation's edict that a checkpoint plan must include "the sequence of traffic to be stopped" is sufficient guidance for police agencies in promulgating guidelines to carry out that requirement. But police guidelines that allowed individual officers to determine for themselves "the sequence of traffic to be stopped" would leave them with free rein to stop every car, or every third or tenth car. Such a rule would fail the nondelegation principle. This highlights the two aspects of nondelegation: legislation must require that police agencies limit individual officer discretion in some way, and police agencies must actually limit that discretion. And the legality principle requires that officers abide by those limits.

Granted, courts must be sensitive to the prospect of "process failure" in the creation of regimes such as checkpoint programs. For example, police agencies must have discretion not only to determine how such checkpoints are conducted but where. They will obviously be inclined to set up checkpoints in places where they are needed, such as main arteries with numerous taverns. But if the process-based justification for the general constitutionality of such checkpoints is that they ideally spread the cost of order and security to the entire citizenry, that justification falters if checkpoints are placed only in the "bad" parts of town.[63] In that case, we run the risk that wealthier, whiter citizens, who tend to have disproportionate political power, are internalizing the benefits and externalizing the costs of safer roads. On the other hand, those living in areas with a high incidence of drunk drivers might welcome the police attention. Courts must therefore scrutinize such decisions to ensure that they are being made by public officials who are politically accountable, not just to the public at large, but to the specific community affected.[64]

"Reverse Incorporation"

One loose end needs tying up. Is the federal government, like the States, bound by the nondiscrimination, legality, and nondelegation principles? A textualist approach suggests not. After all, the operative language of section 1 of the Fourteenth Amendment begins: "No State shall . . ." By contrast, the Fifteenth Amendment, adopted only two years later, provides: "The right of citizens of the United States to vote shall not be denied or abridged *by the United States* or by any State on account of race, color, or previous condition of servitude." It would have been fairly easy to similarly bind the federal government explicitly in the Fourteenth Amendment. That it is not so bound suggests that section 1 was not understood as applying to the federal government.[65]

Even if this textual argument is correct, I have suggested that the Fourth Amendment, as originally understood, required federal officials to abide by state law when searching and seizing. If the States are now bound by the nondiscrimination, legality, and nondelegation principles by virtue of the Fourteenth Amendment, and if federal officials must abide by state law in searching and seizing, then federal officials, by the transitive property, are bound by these three principles. This is akin to the concept of "reverse incorporation," by which the federal government is said to be bound by equal protection principles even though the Equal Protection Clause textually applies only to the States. The reasoning behind that doctrine is that the Due Process Clause of the Fifth Amendment incorporates the Fourteenth Amendment's Equal Protection Clause to apply to the federal government as well. The U.S. Supreme Court reflected this idea in *Bolling* v. *Sharpe*, a companion case to *Brown* v. *Board of Education*, declaring segregation in schools in the District of Columbia to be unconstitutional. Because it was not dealing with a State, the Court could not rely on the Equal Protection Clause as it did in *Brown*. But the Court wrote that the concepts of due process and equal protection overlapped, so that "discrimination may be so unjustifiable as to be violative of due process." The Court declared: "In view of our decision [in *Brown*] that the Constitution prohibits the states from maintaining racially segregated public schools, it would be unthinkable that the same Constitution would impose a lesser duty on the Federal Government."[66]

John Hart Ely famously called the concept of "reverse incorporation" "gibberish both syntactically and historically."[67] After all, how could a provision enacted in 1791 "incorporate" a provision enacted seventy-seven years later? And *Bolling*'s dictum that it is "unthinkable" to permit segregation in the District of Columbia but forbid it in the States is pretty weak sauce—where, one might ask, is the Constitution's "Unthinkability Clause?" But Ely defended the result in *Bolling* on other grounds. He opined that the Ninth Amendment does the trick by preserving some federal constitutional rights unnamed in the document, and that this includes a right to equal treatment akin to that which is required by the States.[68] Our discussion of the Fourth Amendment suggests a similar account. If that Amendment requires the federal government to abide by state law, then changes in state law will apply to federal officials as well. Irrespective of whether those changes come about from legislative alteration or constitutional mandate, they are still changes that bind state officials and, by dint of the Fourth Amendment, federal officials as well.

Some commentators get to much the same destination through an alternate route: by claiming that the Fourteenth Amendment itself changed the Fourth, even as it applies to the federal government.[69] Kurt Lash has made the broader point that adoption of the Fourteenth Amendment altered the Bill of Rights as a whole: "[T]he passage of the Fourteenth Amendment amounts to a second adoption of the Bill of Rights. That being the case, the privileges and immunities that bind the federal government are the same privileges or immunities that bind the States."[70] I would suggest that it is more accurate to say that the Fourteenth Amendment binds the federal government in the same ways it binds the States, *over and above the ways in which the Fourth Amendment continues to constrain it.* The federalism-based constraints placed on the federal government in 1791 have never been lifted.[71]

Despite these quibbles, all agree that the federal government is, for all intents and purposes, bound by the Fourteenth to at least the same extent that the States are. Thus, we are left with two fairly easily stated rules regarding searches and seizures: state officials must follow state law, with the nondiscrimination and nondelegation principles as corollaries; and federal officials must follow both state and federal law, again with the nondiscrimination and nondelegation corollaries. This means that the Fourth Amendment binds the federal government more strictly than the Fourteenth constrains the States; while the States are free to regulate searches and seizures so long as they abide by the three principles embodied in the Fourteenth Amendment, the feds are bound not only by those principles but also by any other limitations that the States impose on themselves.

Conclusion

This way of thinking about the "incorporated" Fourth Amendment distills the essence of the Amendment—freedom from unbounded executive discretion to conduct searches and seizures—while preserving federalism by subjecting that discretion to local democratic controls. Instead of imposing a uniform and highly complex web of common-law search-and-seizure rules on the States, which would be exactly the sort of incursion on federalism that mainstream Reconstruction-era Republicans wanted to avoid, the incorporated Fourth Amendment relies primarily on the democratic process to formulate those rules. The original understanding of the Fourteenth Amendment, with its emphasis on local, democratic controls of executive discretion, bounded by equality and rule-of-law principles, dovetails with the more modern idea of "democratic policing." The final two chapters test modern Fourth Amendment doctrine—which has alternated between judicial micromanagement and judicial abdication—against a model of the Fourteenth Amendment that emphasizes local democratic controls on police discretion.

Ten

Rethinking Constitutional Constraints on Searches and Seizures

Scholars have long criticized the state of Fourth Amendment jurisprudence. At least part of the problem is the Supreme Court's focus on the wrong amendment.[1] Most policing takes place at the state and local levels: state officers enforcing bread-and-butter criminal law, from murder down to spitting on the sidewalk. Even much of the criminal activity that ends up being prosecuted in federal court is initially investigated by state agents, as when police stop a motorist for a traffic infraction resulting in the discovery of drugs or guns whose possession is forbidden by federal law. The appropriate lodestar in these cases is the Fourteenth Amendment's proscription against discrimination, lawlessness, and undue discretion, inspired by the immediate post–Civil War experience: official state violence against Black people, loyal whites, and Northerners; and law enforcement's nearly unbounded discretion to enforce vagrancy and other laws predominantly against the formerly enslaved. Yet our cases are replete with references to the concerns of a much earlier generation—general warrants, writs of assistance, and the common law of search and seizure as of 1791[2]—and hand-wringing over whether there was even a "search"[3] or "seizure"[4] rather than asking where there was a deprivation of "life, liberty, or property without due process of law."

This chapter rethinks conventional Fourth Amendment doctrine with a greater emphasis on the concerns of 1868 than those of 1791. Of course, the overarching goal in both time periods was limiting police officer discretion.[5] But, as we have seen, that goal was sought in different ways by the founding-era Anti-Federalists and the Reconstruction-era Republicans, the former by tying federal authority to state law and the latter by requiring that state officials obey their own law.

The Court has done neither of these things. Instead, it has sought to limit officer discretion through the warrant-preference rule, that police should generally obtain a warrant when possible in order to render a search or seizure reasonable. In so doing, the Court has recognized that the key to limiting executive discretion is to subject their actions to oversight by a different branch of government, in this case the judiciary. But the Court has mistakenly posited the warrant-preference rule as the *primary* method of controlling police officer discretion. The key insight of both the Anti-Federalists and the Republicans was that executive officer discretion should be subjected to local, democratic controls. They knew that discretion is best curbed by spreading decisions across multiple institutions. The Court has largely overlooked the most obvious institutional roles in our democracy for controlling police discretion: legislators and administrators. As Barry Friedman wrote: "Rather than cluttering up policing with a lot of ill-considered constitutional rules, courts should force democratic deliberation and legislative action."[6]

This chapter starts by looking at what the Court has gotten right: using the warrant-preference rule as a device to limit police officer discretion. It then looks at the Court's "special needs" cases, which show that warrants are not the only way to limit individual-officer discretion. Instead, in these cases, the Court has recognized a role for legislative and administrative controls. In this chapter, I argue that the Court has gotten things backwards and that there is nothing "special" about the special needs cases: legislative and administrative controls should in fact be viewed as the default method of controlling individual-officer discretion, with the probable cause and warrant regime serving as a necessary backup when legislative and administrative controls are infeasible. This chapter then shows how reliance on such controls in the context of searches and seizures that are ancillary to the law enforcement function—for example, searches incident to arrest—would serve the overriding goal of limiting officer discretion. Finally, this chapter discusses how federal searches should be treated differently than state searches, given that the former must not only adhere to the three principles derived from the Fourteenth Amendment but must also be consistent with state law.

The Warrant-Preference Rule as a Device to Limit Police Officer Discretion

As discussed in chapter 1, the warrant-preference rule emerged in the Court's Fourth Amendment jurisprudence in the twentieth century as the primary method of controlling individual-officer discretion. The rule is simply stated:

"[T]he police must, whenever practicable, obtain advance judicial approval of searches and seizures through the warrant procedure."[7] The classic statement of the rule's rationale is still Justice Robert H. Jackson's from 1948:

> The point of the Fourth Amendment . . . is not that it denies law enforcement the support of the usual inferences which reasonable [people] draw from evidence. Its protection consists in requiring that those inferences be drawn by a neutral and detached magistrate instead of being judged by the officer engaged in the often competitive enterprise of ferreting out crime.[8]

Arguably, a strict warrant-preference rule is inconsistent with what I have called the principle of legality. That is, suppose a state legislature were to pass a statute permitting police officers to search and seize without warrants, and even without probable cause. Based only on the legality principle, so long as that decision is reached through the democratic process, any police activity conducted pursuant to law satisfies the requirement of due process of law.

However, a scheme of completely warrantless and suspicionless searches would be inconsistent with the nondelegation principle. While white, middle-class legislators and their constituents would be equally subject to such searches as a formal matter, the real-world experience of 1866 tells us otherwise. Remember that John Hart Ely identified outsized executive discretion as a species of process failure. The requirement of probable cause performs a singling-out function, significantly limiting police officer discretion by distinguishing the few cases where there are good grounds to believe a person has committed a crime from the many cases where there are not. A probable cause threshold, it could be argued, approximates what would be demanded by the majority if they were truly subject to governmental intrusions on the same basis as the minority: high enough to block capricious interferences with liberty but low enough to guarantee sufficient security from unlawful behavior.[9]

But would legislatively decreed warrantless searches and seizures based on probable cause be consistent with nondelegation? A state statute could, for example, permit warrantless entry into a home to make an arrest so long as the police have probable cause, as was the case in *Payton* v. *New York*. Incorrect judgments on the part of the police as to whether they had probable cause could be addressed through ex post civil judgments by a jury, just as at the founding. This, recall, is essentially the argument of adherents of the Reasonableness Model of the Fourth Amendment. Yet the *Payton* Court rejected that argument and held that a warrant was generally required for a forcible, in-home arrest.[10]

The history behind the Fourteenth Amendment militates toward a warrant-preference rule absent more specific legislative authorization and suggests that *Payton* was decided correctly. The problem with the view of Reasonableness Model adherents such as the *Payton* dissenters is that it is anchored in 1791. By 1868, the premise that juries were sufficient to keep executive officials in line had weakened considerably. The juries extolled by the Anti-Federalists, and by today's Reasonableness Model enthusiasts, were *local* juries deciding the fates of *federal* officials. But now we are talking about *local* juries deciding the fates of *local* officials, and there was every reason in 1868 to be skeptical of that process. Much of the testimony taken by the Joint Congressional Committee on Reconstruction, and many other reports coming in from the South, concerned the inability of Black people and loyal whites to get justice from Southern juries. The questioning by the members of the Joint Committee reveals a deep cynicism over the entire concept of the jury trial, with casual comments about "packing" juries as the only way to achieve some measure of justice.[11] However sanguine the Anti-Federalists were about the benefits of jury trials, the Reconstruction-era Republicans were far too skeptical to rely on juries to keep Black Southerners and loyalists safe.

The preference for warrants helps further the nondelegation principle by bringing in another branch of government to provide an ex ante judicial confirmation of the executive officer's initial determination that probable cause exists.[12] While the probable cause standard might be sufficient to perform a singling-out function, the facts arguably giving rise to probable cause are often ambiguous enough to warrant a second look by a judicial officer.[13] Here, the traditional judicial function comes into play: applying the general rules set down by legislation and common law to concrete factual allegations to determine whether a law violation has probably occurred. Because violations of criminal law are intensely fact specific, it is precisely this type of situation that legislation cannot cover with sufficient particularity to give guidance to executive officials. Thus, judicial engagement through the warrant process must take the place of legislation in order to satisfy separation-of-powers and rule-of-law constraints.

True, the Reconstruction-era Republicans had almost as little faith in Southern magistrates as they had in Southern juries. However, liberty is best protected by diffusing power; a system that involves police, juries, *and* judges will be better than one that cuts judges out of the equation.[14] This was far from a perfect system in 1868, but it was the best the Republicans could hope for given the realities of the time and the Republicans' twin aims of protecting individual freedom while adhering to basic principles of federalism.

On this view, current doctrine is insufficient in at least one respect. Warrants are generally required for searches and in-home arrests but not for arrests outside the home. The Court permitted warrantless felony arrests in public in *United States* v. *Watson*, relying primarily on the long pedigree of the common-law rule permitting public arrests without a warrant if based on probable cause.[15] If, as I have suggested, the touchstone is not the specific rule on arrests in 1791 or even 1868, but on the Reconstruction-era Republicans' mistrust of individual-officer discretion, arrests should be treated like searches, whether they occur inside or outside the home.

Warrantless arrests would still be permitted in the many cases where police witness a crime and the offender must be apprehended quickly. Likewise, the exigency exception to the warrant requirement also makes sense. If we require police to act pursuant to warrants or detailed statutory or administrative guidelines in the run of cases, we need the exigency exception to account for cases where those sources of constraint are unavailable. Typically, this will occur where the officer is acting pursuant only to a broad mandate to enforce the law, maintain order, or provide for public safety, and there is no opportunity to consult a member of the judiciary.

Lessons from the "Special Needs" Cases: Legislative and Administrative Controls on Officer Discretion

Recognition that there are times where getting a warrant would be impracticable because of the exigencies of the field has, in turn, led the Court to cobble together a number of areas in which the State acts where the probable cause and warrant requirements simply do not fit. In these cases, individual-officer discretion can be curbed through precise statutory and administrative guidelines. These cases demonstrate the Court's instinct that searches and seizures conducted pursuant to schemes that sufficiently limit individual-officer discretion do not offend the Constitution, even where there is no warrant or even probable cause. The Court has treated these areas almost as constitutional oddities. A warrant backed by probable cause is seen as the default,[16] and the Court permits a detailed statutory or administrative scheme to act as a substitute only in a set of seemingly isolated areas grouped together for categorization purposes only as "special needs" cases: health and safety inspections of homes and commercial buildings,[17] roadway checkpoints (discussed in chapter 9),[18] drug-testing regimes for public-school students, hospital patients, and government employees,[19] other searches of students and government employees,[20] searches at the international border (or the functional equivalent, such as an airport receiving international flights),[21] searches of parolees and probationers,[22] inventorying of personal items of arrestees and items found in impounded automobiles (also discussed in chapter 9),[23] and other administrative steps for securing and identifying those detained in jails.[24] These are unlike cases where police are reactively investigating ordinary crime or are acting in the face of an exigency. In those kinds of cases, the facts facing police are so variegated that detailed rules governing them are all but impossible and police must be authorized to exercise their own discretion or, when possible, seek specific authorization from a judge who has been informed of and can make a judgment about the "special facts" and whether they provide sufficient cause to deprive someone of liberty.[25]

While the Court's emphasis on democratic controls of officer discretion in the "special needs" cases is well taken, it has things backwards. The real Fourth Amendment default rule should be the requirement of democratic controls over search-and-seizure regimes: legislative controls specific enough either to directly control police officer discretion or to at least guide administrators in promulgating their own rules, which themselves are specific enough to cabin individual officer discretion. That is to say, the Court's "special needs" doctrine mistakenly treats the warrant and probable cause requirements as the default, and a deviation from those requirements as "exceptional."[26] But it is not that a detailed statutory or administrative scheme can stand in for a warrant backed by probable cause when individualized suspicion is irrelevant; ***it is that a warrant backed by probable cause can stand in for a detailed statutory or administrative scheme when such a scheme is impossible.***[27]

The confusion began with *Camara* v. *Municipal Court*[28] and *See* v. *City of Seattle*,[29] where the Court held that state health and safety inspections of dwellings and commercial premises conducted pursuant to a statutory scheme must be supported by probable cause and a warrant. However, the Court reinterpreted "probable cause" to mean, not individualized suspicion of wrongdoing, but rather satisfaction of "reasonable legislative or administrative standards for conducting an area inspection . . . with respect to a particular [building]." These standards could be "based upon the passage of time, the nature of the building . . . or the condition of the entire area."[30] Thus, an "administrative search" requires an "administrative warrant."

This is nonsense. Given that the impetus for the Fourth Amendment's Warrant Clause was an abhorrence of general warrants, the framers and ratifiers of that provision would have been aghast if "probable cause" were defined in such a way as to permit what amount to general warrants to search entire areas based on nothing more than the nature of the area and the buildings it contains. Faced with the conflict between the Fourth Amendment's textual imperative that "*no* warrant shall issue but upon probable cause," on the one hand, and the need for state and local health and safety inspections even without individualized evidence of dangerous conditions in a specific building, on the other, the Court redefined "probable cause" into oblivion.[31]

The better approach would be to acknowledge that, because these cases involved inspections by *States*, the "no warrant" language of the Fourth Amendment is wholly inapplicable. Instead, the inspection schemes are governed by the due process principles of the Fourteenth Amendment. Since both schemes were authorized by legislation, the legality principle was easily satisfied. The problem was with nondelegation. The city Housing Code in *Camara* allowed inspectors "'to enter, at reasonable times, any building, structure, or premises,'" "'so far as may be necessary for the performance of their duties.'"[32] The city fire code in *See* similarly permitted the fire chief to "'enter all buildings and premises . . . as often as may be necessary.'"[33] The Court appropriately recognized that it was critical that "the decision to enter and inspect . . . not be the product of the unreviewed discretion of the enforcement officer in the field."[34] However, the Court's solution—to require administrative warrants on a case-by-case basis—is only one possibility. More detailed statutory or administrative guidelines instructing inspectors as to how often and according to what criteria to enter, created by an entity more politically accountable than a magistrate, would be even better.

One potential problem with this view is that regulatory search or seizure regimes are typically not so general that they apply to the populace at large but instead apply only to some subpopulation.[35] For example, certain business may be more highly regulated than others. However, as long as the affected sub-group is (1) not the target of irrational discrimination and (2) has a legitimate opportunity to participate in the political process, it should not bother us that a particular search or seizure regime is limited to that sub-group.[36] Certainly, alcohol distributors cannot complain that they somehow have less access to the political process than, say, hoteliers.

The drug-testing cases present this "sub-population problem" in stark relief. The Supreme Court's cases have dealt with drug-testing of Treasury Department employees, railroad workers, political candidates, pregnant women, and high-schoolers.[37] But for the last two, it would be difficult to say that the drug-testing regime was the result of process failure. And high school children, though they obviously have no official say in local politics, have always been thought adequately represented by their parents.[38] On the other hand, even if the drug-testing of pregnant women in *Ferguson* v. *City of Charleston* had been legislatively authorized, it still arguably ought to have been struck down on the ground that it was motivated by irrational prejudice against a constitutionally protected class, especially given that it was obviously aimed at a particular sub-group of pregnant women: poor pregnant women of color.[39]

Another potential objection to a representation-reinforcing approach to constitutional constraints on searches and seizures is the fact that law enforcement interests tend to be very organized, highly motivated, and well funded in the legislative arena.[40] This arguably makes problematic the suggestion that legislatures should be able to create special statutory exemptions for police, for example, to use certain technologies unavailable to the general public or to have more flexibility in using deadly force in law enforcement than private citizens can in self-defense (both discussed more fully in the next chapter). This is a genuine concern. However, political-process theory assumes that some groups will have greater access to the political process than others, and courts should not step in unless a group finds itself "in a state of persistent inability to protect" itself in the political process "from pervasive forms of discriminatory treatment."[41] This is obviously a controversial proposition and it is generally eschewed by those who reject Ely's process-based interpretation of the Constitution, particularly those who focus on the distorting effects of interest groups. But a general defense of Ely's political-process theory, and a corresponding critique of interest-group theory, would take us too far afield. Suffice it say in that regard that, as I argued in chapter 8, Ely's views provide a particularly attractive way of thinking about the original understanding of the Fourteenth Amendment.

Moreover, it is not obvious that the political power of law enforcement will always win the day. Privacy interests may well be strong enough that nongovernmental organizations that favor greater restrictions on policing can at least come close to matching that power. A bevy of nonprofit organizations have sprung up to advocate for enhanced privacy protections, particularly when it comes to electronic surveillance: not just the usual suspects (the American Civil Liberties Union, National Association of Criminal Defense Lawyers, and Public Citizen, for example) but bipartisan, nonpartisan, and conservative groups such as Americans for Prosperity, the Due Process Institute, the Electronic Frontier Foundation, FreedomWorks, the Project for Privacy & Surveillance Accountability, and Restore the Fourth.

Beyond these potential pitfalls of the approach advocated here, there is what one might call the "1984 problem." Suppose a polity, through a fully functioning democratic process, were to decree that all homes be searched once a year (or month, or week), top to bottom, for evidence of nefarious activities. Or suppose the polity were to decide democratically that all homes will be equipped with sufficient apparatus to provide surveillance on a 24/7, 360-degree basis, so that members of the polity are always under the watchful eye of Big Brother. These schemes would pass all three of our principles: they would be legally authorized and nondiscriminatory, and would leave no individual-officer discretion.

Ely wrote that "[i]t is an entirely legitimate response" to such "hypothesizing [of] absurdities" to observe that such a law "couldn't pass and [to] refuse to play any further." He continued, however, closing his book with these words: "[I]t can only deform our constitutional jurisprudence to tailor it to laws that couldn't be enacted, since constitutional law appropriately exists for those situations where representative government cannot be trusted, not those where we know it can."[42] My answer is the same. If such a polity were to exist that sacrifices so much liberty and privacy for additional security and order, its denizens would be free to make that choice. But it is worth asking whether we have ever met anyone who would want to live in such a place. Even those most inclined toward authoritarianism generally take a "privacy for me but not for thee" attitude, one sharply at odds with representation-reinforcement. This should give us some confidence that such a polity will never exist in this country.

Making the "Special Needs" Cases Less Special: Three Errors in the Doctrine

The "special needs" cases, spawned by *Camara* and *See*, essentially provide a blueprint for what much of Fourth Amendment law should look like. But, as noted, the reasoning in those cases is backwards, viewing them as exceptions to a supposed default requirement of a (real) warrant based on (real) probable cause. Instead, they are simply situations where operation of the *real* default constitutional rule—specific legislative and administrative controls to limit officer discretion—is possible. Although the results in *Camara* and *See* are essentially sound, the Court's faulty reasoning in these cases has skewed the "special needs" doctrine in three separate ways.

Ordinary Crime Control vs. "Special Needs"

First, the Court has forbidden searches and seizures conducted for ordinary crime control purposes even if they are conducted pursuant to sufficiently detailed guidelines. For example, in *City of Indianapolis* v. *Edmond*, the city set up a checkpoint not unlike the sobriety checkpoints discussed in chapter 9: cars were stopped and officers approached the motorists pursuant to written guidelines that strictly cabined individual-officer discretion. But in *Edmond*, the police were seeking not drunk drivers but motorists possessing illegal narcotics. To the Court, the purpose of the checkpoint made all the difference. The Court held that the Fourth Amendment is violated by "a checkpoint program whose primary purpose [i]s to detect evidence of ordinary criminal wrongdoing."[43]

The distinction the Court drew in *Edmond* between ordinary crime-fighting and community caretaking is deeply problematic.[44] First, from the perspective of the motorist, the distinction is silly.[45] When I am stopped at a checkpoint, my experience of that seizure is exactly the same whether the police are checking for drugs or impaired driving. Second, the distinction is "razor thin."[46] When police are looking for a dangerous condition or behavior that could harm the public, the condition or behavior is very often criminal. In looking to ensure public safety by detecting drunk drivers, police are simultaneously and necessarily looking for lawbreakers.[47] Third, the Court's holding is incredibly difficult to apply, not only because of the lack of daylight in many cases between public safety and crime control, but also because it may be hard to identify a checkpoint's primary purpose. If the checkpoint has two purposes, what makes one or the other "primary?" What if both purposes are motivating the police conduct? Should we really treat differently a checkpoint whose primary purpose is highway safety with an ancillary purpose of catching lawbreakers from a checkpoint whose primary and ancillary purposes are the reverse?[48] This arbitrary distinction led the Court in *Maryland* v. *King* to stretch and strain to characterize DNA collection from arrestees pursuant to a highly detailed statutory scheme that left virtually no discretion in the hands of the police as a "way to process and identify" the arrestee and not as a way of solving past crimes, which it obviously was.[49] This characterization, Justice Antonin Scalia wryly observed in dissent, "taxes the credulity of the credulous."[50]

But the central flaw in *Edmond* is that the distinction between crime-fighting and community caretaking is nowhere to be found in the original understanding of either the Fourth or the Fourteenth Amendment.[51] The primary targets of the Fourth Amendment were federal customs and revenue collectors. But having uncustomed goods or unaccounted-for revenue is not necessarily a criminal act. At the least, the connection between having possession of uncustomed goods and being a smuggler subject to criminal punishment is about the same as the connection between being a road hazard due to intoxicated driving and being criminally liable as a drunk driver.[52] Likewise, the framers and ratifiers of the Fourteenth Amendment did not seem to care whether citizen patrols and militias checking Black persons for passes were enforcing criminal laws, and they deplored the ransacking of freedmen's homes regardless of whether the purpose was to prosecute the freedmen for unlawfully possessing guns, to seize the guns without a prosecution, or just for the hell of it.

Several scholars have tried to better explain through different verbal formulae the distinction between proactive searches and seizures that are part of a regulatory scheme covering groups of individuals not suspected of wrongdoing, and those conducted reactively, based on one-off events that might create individualized suspicion of wrongdoing or suggest the presence of an exigency. Barry Friedman and Cynthia Stein called these, respectively, "suspicion-less" and "suspicion-based" searches. Daphna Renan distinguished between "programmatic" and "transactional" searches and seizures. For Chris Slobogin, searches were either "panvasive" or "suspicion-based." Scott Sundby divided intrusions into the "initiatory" and the "responsive."[53]

These attempts get much closer to the distinction the Court should be making, which is not between ordinary crime-fighting and community caretaking, but between those situations where a detailed statutory or administrative scheme is possible and those where it is not. Such a scheme, if it sufficiently cabins individual-officer discretion, should be permissible even its goal is ordinary crime-fighting. By the same token, even a detailed administrative scheme conducted for a non-crime-fighting purpose, and which limits individual-officer discretion, should not pass muster if no democratic, politically accountable institution has authorized it. That was the real problem with *Edmond*; the checkpoint was the brainchild of the police, not the legislature.[54]

The Superfluous "Reasonableness" Test

The second problem with the "special needs" jurisprudence is that the Court has required even those regulatory search-and-seizure schemes that can be characterized as "special needs" to pass an additional hurdle of "reasonableness." The *Camara* Court wrote that "there can be no ready test for determining reasonableness other than by balancing the need to search against the invasion which the search entails."[55] The Court typically invokes the three-part test first enunciated in *Brown* v. *Texas*, requiring courts to balance "[1] the gravity of the public concerns served by the [search or] seizure, [2] the degree to which the [search or] seizure advances the public interest, and [3] the severity of the interference with individual liberty."[56]

But these factors, especially the first two, are paradigmatic considerations for politically accountable legislators and administrators, not judges insulated from the political process. As Slobogin put it, "the inquiry into the strength of the government's objectives sends judges into a morass," while "assessment[] of whether suspicion-based searches and seizures or some other 'less restrictive' alternative can achieve the government's goal . . . presents even more of a quandary . . . because it requires evaluation of variables that courts are ill-equipped to assess."[57] Observe that if a search or seizure is authorized by a warrant issued by a magistrate after a finding of probable cause, there is typically no additional requirement of "reasonableness."[58] So too, as long as a detailed statutory or administrative scheme sufficiently limits individual-officer discretion and is the product of a functioning democratic process, the inquiry should generally be at an end.

Fortunately, the Court tends to apply these factors in a way that is highly deferential to the government.[59] In only one case, *Chandler* v. *Miller*,[60] mentioned in the Introduction, has the Court deemed a true special needs search or seizure to fail this three-part test. In *Michigan Dept. of State Police* v. *Sitz*, the Court offered a process-oriented rationale for this deference, at least as to the second factor, the effectiveness of the search or seizure. This part of the test, the *Sitz* Court wrote, is "not meant to transfer from politically accountable officials to the courts the decision as to which among reasonable alternative law enforcement techniques should be employed to deal with a serious public danger."[61] This deferential, process-oriented approach has been compared to the "rational basis" test that the Court uses to determine whether ordinary legislation violates the Fourteenth Amendment's Due Process or Equal Protection Clauses.[62] This is fitting given that in state cases it is the Fourteenth Amendment, not the Fourth, that actually applies. Although I suggest that a search or seizure that is conducted according to specific statutory or administrative guidelines that tightly cabin executive officer discretion ought not to be subject to any additional constraint, evaluating such a search or seizure using a standard that has essentially devolved into a rational-basis test is at least consistent with other areas where the Fourteenth Amendment applies.

Special Treatment for "Closely Regulated" Businesses

The third problem with the "special needs" doctrine is that the Court has distinguished "closely regulated" businesses from others. Because some enterprises have "'a history of government oversight'" occasioned by "'pervasive[] and regular[] regulation," they are deemed "closely regulated" businesses, and administrative searches can occur even without an administrative warrant.[63] The Court has applied this doctrine to auto junkyards, coal mines, gun dealers, and purveyors of alcohol,[64] but has declined to apply it to hotels and other ordinary businesses.[65] But if the true touchstone of the Fourteenth Amendment is the control of officer discretion, why is there one rule for a few "closely regulated" businesses and one for all the others? The better question to ask is not whether an industry is regularly and pervasively regulated in general, but whether the statutory or administrative search-and-seizure regime itself is "sufficiently comprehensive and defined" to tightly control officer discretion.

A dichotomy between administrative schemes detailed enough to constrain executive discretion without judicial supervision and those that are authorized by statute but not sufficiently detailed makes some sense. But the "closely regulated business" label should be used to describe the level of reticulation of a particular State's search-and-seizure regime for a particular industry: if the State provides a detailed enough statutory or administrative scheme for searches and seizures within a particular industry, that industry is "closely regulated," meaning that judicial superintendence is not required; if the industry is regulated by a search-and-seizure regime that leaves too much individual-officer discretion, then judicial superintendence is required. This leaves the people, not the courts, in charge of whether a given business will fall into the "closely regulated" category.[66] That is to say, the question is not whether a particular business is, in general, closely regulated, but whether the business is subject to sufficient statutory and administrative controls *in a particular State* to justify dispensing with judicial oversight.

Intrusions Ancillary to the Law Enforcement Function: The Example of Searches Incident to Arrest

The lesson of the "special needs" cases, that sufficiently specific legislative and administrative guidelines render suspicion-based warrants unnecessary, can be applied to ordinary policing activities. Among the most vexing of areas are those that straddle the line between suspicion-based searches and seizures and those that are suspicionless. I am speaking of searches and seizures that are ancillary to the police crime-fighting function, those that are themselves not motivated by suspicion of wrongdoing but which take place as an adjunct to a suspicion-based search or arrest. I will discuss in some detail the search-incident-to-lawful-arrest, or SILA, rule, which permits police when making an arrest to search the person of the arrestee and her surrounding area. But the law governing these ancillary intrusions also includes the "protective sweep" doctrine, which permits police when making an in-home arrest to look in rooms beyond where the arrest takes place in order to protect themselves from a potential attack;[67] the rule of *Michigan v. Summers*, which allows police conducting a search of a premises to detain persons found there;[68] and rules permitting police to require drivers and their passengers to exit their automobiles during routine traffic stops.[69] In each area, the Court has posited a false choice between judicial micromanagement and judicial abdication, demonstrating the Court's blind spot when it comes to the place of democratic controls on policing that are at the heart of the Fourteenth Amendment.

Each of these doctrines addresses conduct that is ancillary to an often-repeated and easily defined rubric of police activity. And each is essentially exigency-based because each permits police to act in the face of potential dangers to their safety, destruction of evidence, or some other operational necessity. In each area, conventional Fourth Amendment doctrine, which posits probable-cause-based warrants as the default and officer discretion in the face of exigency as the principal exception, left the Court with two options. First, it could require a showing of exigency on a case-by-case basis as a way of demonstrating that obtaining a warrant in a particular case was impracticable. Or, because each area is an easily identifiable rubric of police activity, it could dispense with any need to show exigency, so that as long as the police activity fell within a particular rubric, police were given virtually unbounded discretion to make the associated intrusion. Essentially, the Court saw its choice as one between after-the-fact judicial superintendence to make certain that an exigency existed or wide-open police discretion. In almost every instance, the Court has taken the latter approach. But this is a false choice. The Court has failed to see the adequacy of detailed legislative or administrative guidelines in the crime-fighting context as a third option.

Let us take SILA as an example, because the case law here is the most well developed. The exigency-based justifications for SILA are the danger that the arrestee will either destroy evidence or gain access to a weapon to harm the arresting officer, justifying a search of the arrestee's person and the immediately surrounding area.[70] The Court decided in the companion cases of *United States* v. *Robinson*[71] and *Gustafson* v. *Florida*[72] that no actual exigency, or even suspicion of an exigency, need exist in any particular case for the SILA exception to kick in. Instead, the Court created, in essence, an irrebuttable presumption that one or both of these exigencies exists in all cases. So even if police arrest a motorist for driving without a license, which by definition does not entail any evidence that can be destroyed, and where the danger of violence is infinitesimally small—imagine that the motorist is a frail octogenarian with an "I Love Being a Quaker" bumper sticker—they can still conduct a SILA.

What is missing in most SILA cases is (1) legal authorization for the SILA and (2) statutory or administrative guidance on the parameters of the SILA. First, under the principle of legality, police should not be able to conduct a SILA unless it is authorized by law. Arguably, a statute is unnecessary. It is conventional wisdom that the SILA exception is well rooted in centuries of common-law practice. However, there are indications, discussed in chapter 5, that the conventional wisdom is overblown and that SILA was not as well settled in common law as is sometimes thought to be the case. If so, then statutory authorization would be needed.

Even after one satisfies the legality principle, there is still nondelegation to worry about. On the one hand, SILAs are a type of search that will ordinarily not present the typical dangers of broad individual-officer discretion. First, the universe of potential targets of a search will have already been narrowed significantly: there must be probable cause to arrest. Although the Court has justified the SILA exception in part because of the "arrestee's reduced privacy interests upon being taken into police custody,"[73] the proper focus, I submit, is instead the fact that the arrest separates the arrestee out from the populace at large, thus greatly reducing police discretion. (While police discretion to arrest for minor offenses is incredibly broad under current law, that is a separate problem that will be addressed in chapter 11.) Moreover, there is very little danger of *under*-enforcement of authority to search the person of the arrestee and her immediate surroundings, especially given the officer-safety rationale. This means that if a SILA of those areas is authorized, it will occur in almost every case, with little exercise of discretion on the part of the police.

However, that leaves the question of *how* the officer will conduct the SILA, in terms of both how far afield from the arrestee the officer may search and how intensively into the person of the arrestee or a particular item she may search. Left to their own discretion, officers are likely in some cases to choose the largest area possible in terms of both breadth and depth as incident to the arrest, perhaps on a hunch that evidence is more likely to be found in those cases. But an officer is likely to choose a smaller area in other cases, given the diminishing marginal utility of a broader search. Both breadth and depth can and should be addressed through statute or departmental regulations that leave little or no discretion as to how far afield and how deeply to conduct the search.[74] Specific guidelines would also be far more helpful to the police themselves than the vagaries of the standard from *Chimel* v. *California*, that a SILA is limited to "the arrestee's person and the area 'within his immediate control,'" meaning "the area from within which he might gain possession of a weapon or destructible evidence."[75]

The Supreme Court had a golden opportunity in *Robinson* and *Gustafson* to distinguish between SILAs conducted pursuant to specific administrative guidelines, as in the former case, and SILAs performed freeform by the officer, as in the latter. Professor Anthony Amsterdam declared shortly after the decisions: "If the Court had distinguished the two cases on this ground, it would . . . have made by far the greatest contribution to the jurisprudence of the fourth amendment since James Otis argued against the writs of assistance." Instead, "the Court kicked the chance away."[76]

This is not to say that there should be no limits to what those guidelines may prescribe. But those limits should be dictated by whether the guidelines afford unacceptably expansive police officer discretion, not whether the privacy interests at stake outweigh the government's interest in performing the search. Consider a statute or administrative rule requiring plenary searches of the contents of all items taken from the arrestee. Such a rule might be unobjectionable when only a few levels of searching are possible, as when an officer opens a closed container obtained from the arrestee. The Court has allowed officers to search down several levels of physical space, as in *Robinson* and *Gustafson*; in each case the officer opened a cigarette pack obtained from the arrestee and found illegal narcotics.

But modern technology complicates matters. The Court in *Riley* v. *California* balked at deep-level searching of modern "containers" of information such as laptops, smartphones, and tablets, and generally required a warrant based on probable cause for such searches.[77] The Court reasoned that, given the huge trove of information contained in electronic devices, the individual's privacy interest in the contents of such a device was far greater than in the contents of a more conventional physical container. This interest was not overcome by the twin rationales of the SILA doctrine, preserving evidence and protecting the police officer, because the latter was not really implicated and the former could be served through less intrusive means.

The *Riley* decision is sound but for different reasons. Rather than focus on the greatly enhanced privacy interest the arrestee has in the information contained on an electronic device, the Court should have stressed the fact that this enormous amount of information expands individual-officer discretion exponentially. While any officer would be expected to open a cigarette pack pursuant to a mandatory guideline, no officer would be physically capable of examining the entire contents of a cell phone or laptop for evidence of a crime, even if a guideline required (rather than merely permitted) her to do so. Rather, police will do as they did in *Riley*: pick and choose where on the device, and how deeply, to look. In *Riley*, police focused on photos and videos that suggested Riley's gang membership. In the companion case of *United States* v. *Wurie*, police focused on the most recent calls in the call log and a single item in the contact list. Other officers, looking for other evidence, might have looked in other places. Without any statutory or administrative guidelines in place requiring a search of some smaller portion of this information, officers are free to roam wherever they choose through the vast reaches of information on an electronic device.

It does not appear from either the Supreme Court opinion in *Riley* or the opinions of the lower courts that the SILAs there were either authorized or limited by either statute or police agency guidelines.[78] Such authorization and limitations should be required under the legality and nondelegation principle, respectively. The United States in *Wurie* suggested such a limitation, "that officers should always be able to search a phone's call log."[79] The Court was correct to reject the invitation to draw ad hoc distinctions that are inherently legislative in character. But Justice Samuel Alito was also correct in his separate opinion that, although a SILA of an electronic device in the absence of any statutory or administrative guidance violates the Constitution, "legislation that draws reasonable distinctions based on categories of information or perhaps other variables" should pass constitutional muster. He pointed out that courts, as unrepresentative bodies, are at an institutional disadvantage in passing on the privacy interests involved in searches of electronic devices, and how those interests compare to law enforcement necessities. "Legislatures, elected by the people," he wrote, are better positioned than courts "to assess and respond to the [technological] changes that have already occurred and those that almost certainly will take place in the future."[80]

One could argue that tying constitutional law to administrative regulations, such that the former is implicated every time the latter are violated, is problematic because this will discourage regulators from promulgating rules that go beyond the bare minimum statutory requirements. However, unless those minimum statutory requirements themselves adequately constrain police discretion, regulators will have no choice but to promulgate more specific rules. Without them, the nondelegation principle would be violated and additional regulation would be constitutionally required to fill the gap. It is true that if the statutory bare minimum is itself sufficient to constrain individual-officer discretion, regulators might be averse to imposing rules that narrow discretion further, for fear that every regulatory violation would also present a problem of constitutional proportions. But that assumes that it is easy to determine before the fact what a court will determine to be "too much" discretion in the hands of the police. Risk-averse regulators would be wise to add discretion-limiting rules to statutes that may or may not already be sufficient for constitutional purposes. Finally, as discussed below, depending on the remedies available under state law for violations of regulations, such regulatory violations might not ripen as easily into due process violations and potentially trigger the exclusionary rule.

In the SILA context, as in the other areas where the Court has said that intrusions ancillary to the law enforcement function can be conducted without individualized suspicion, the problem of under-enforcement would be addressed by detailed regulations requiring police to search or seize under particular circumstances. But that raises the significant issue of how to enforce rules against under-enforcement. Where suspect A is properly searched incident to arrest pursuant to detailed regulations, can she claim that the search was nevertheless constitutionally problematic because police wrongfully declined to search suspect B on a different occasion under similar circumstances? And how would suspect A ever know about the failure to search suspect B? The answer to the first, I submit, is yes. Someone subjected to constraints conforming to the letter of the law would still have cause to complain if she is nonetheless being treated less favorably than others, just as the Black criminal defendant who is factually guilty still has a good selective prosecution defense if she can show that similarly situated white people are not prosecuted.[81]

The answer to the second is trickier. However, information about police practices such as SILAs could readily be recorded and made available. Departmental guidelines typically require that an arrest report be completed for every arrest made. Such reports include, or could easily be modified to include, information about a SILA and the items thereby recovered.[82] And although constitutional and statutory entitlements for discovery for criminal defendants in individual cases are notoriously stingy, "transparency litigation"—lawsuits designed to disgorge information about police practices—has grown in recent years.[83] Indeed, the strides made toward greater transparency in policing are part and parcel of the more general idea of democratic policing that I have argued is, at some level, a constitutional requirement.

Suspicion-Based Searches Subject to Democratic Controls: The Example of Implied-Consent Laws

Consider how the lessons of the "special needs" cases can apply even when the police are engaged in crime control and acting based on individualized suspicion of wrongdoing. Perhaps the best example is police collection of breath or blood samples from drivers suspected of being intoxicated. Every State in the Union authorizes police by statute to collect such samples.[84] These so-called "implied consent" laws typically require drivers who either have been arrested for driving while intoxicated or impaired, or about whom the police have probable cause to believe they have committed such an offense, to submit to a breath, blood, or urine test in order to confirm the person's blood alcohol concentration (BAC). The legal fiction employed is that in exchange for a driver's license, the motorist has impliedly consented to such a search. Refusal results in civil consequences, such as temporary loss of driving privileges, or even criminal penalties.

Are such statutes constitutional? The path of the Supreme Court's decision-making in this area somewhat resembles the path of an intoxicated driver. Way back in 1966, in *Schmerber* v. *California*, which did not involve an implied-consent law, the Court held that police could collect a blood sample from a suspected intoxicated driver without a warrant based on an exigent-circumstances theory: the BAC, which is critical evidence of the driver's intoxicated state, dissipates over time, requiring that police act quickly to have it measured.[85] Many read *Schmerber* as announcing a per se rule of exigency in those circumstances.[86] In 2013, however, the Court held to the contrary in *Missouri* v. *McNeely* and determined that whether exigency existed in any particular intoxicated driving case, as in any case, depends on the totality of the circumstances.[87]

Three years later, in *Birchfield* v. *North Dakota*, the Court was asked to bless the warrantless collection of breath and blood samples based on two other exceptions to the so-called warrant requirement: consent and search incident to arrest. The Court held that breath tests, but not blood tests, could be administered as a part of a SILA, because both furthered significant law enforcement interests but breath tests were far less intrusive and no less effective than blood tests.[88] In the same case, the Court held that neither blood tests nor breath tests were reasonable when conducted without a warrant based on a consent theory when refusal triggered criminal penalties, but suggested that consent might be a valid theory where only civil penalties are at stake.[89] Three years after that, the Court agreed to decide in *Mitchell* v. *Wisconsin* whether the Constitution permitted blood draws from intoxicated, unconscious drivers on a theory of consent. The Court ducked the question and decided that a warrantless blood draw when the driver is unconscious is "almost always" justified based on exigency. That view, however, attracted only four votes; Justice Clarence Thomas would have held that exigency is always present under those circumstances.[90]

For those keeping score at home, warrantless breath tests are justified as SILAs but warrantless blood draws are not. However, warrantless blood draws are "almost always" justified by exigent circumstances when the driver is unconscious, but only sometimes when she is not, and may or may not be justified on an implied-consent theory when refusal triggers civil consequences but not when refusal is a criminal offense, except maybe when the driver is unconscious. Got it?

How much clearer and more consistent with the democratic principles that undergird our Constitution if the Court were to simply say this: "The democratically elected, politically accountable legislature of the State has not only authorized but mandated blood testing when there is probable cause to arrest a motorist for drunk driving. The blood draw must be performed by a trained professional in a medical setting using conventional procedures. Because virtually everyone drives, there is no reason to think that this legislation was the result of discrimination against a particular group or that the interests of motorists were not taken into consideration in enacting it. Because testing is triggered upon probable cause of a crime having been committed, the individual tested has properly been singled out as the target of a search. Because testing is mandatory, there is no room for police discretion. Because drunk driving is a serious offense, there is little danger of under-enforcement. Although we acknowledge that the danger of under-enforcement in exceptional cases always exists—for example, when the motorist is a local celebrity or a fellow police officer—we cannot formulate a rule of law around the exceptional case. We are satisfied that blood testing pursuant to this statute adheres to due process of law."

Federal Searches and Seizures

One additional significant change to current doctrine that would result from paying heed to original understandings is that we would treat federal searches and seizures differently from state searches and seizures. As noted in chapter 9, the federal government should be viewed as bound by the search-and-seizure law of the respective States, both those that the States impose on themselves and those imposed on the States by dint of the Fourteenth Amendment. In this context, the legality principle still applies because the federal government is bound by its own Due Process Clause—the one in the Fifth Amendment[91]—requiring that federal officers act only pursuant to law. Thus, the authority to search and seize, and the limits on and guidelines for that search-and-seizure authority, will come from the federal government. But the scheme must also not violate state law. That was the core understanding of the Fourth Amendment by the Anti-Federalists who demanded it as a constraint on the federal government: whatever search-and-seizure regimes the feds established must generally leave federal officers open to state tort actions if they violated state or local norms; and the scheme must not provide for warrants to immunize those officers except under the circumstances spelled out in the Warrant Clause.

This would not mean, however, that Congress and the Justice Department are without power to implement their own laws and rules regarding federal law enforcement. Indeed, Congress could enact legislation governing federal *and state* law enforcement, assuming it otherwise has power under the Constitution to do so. For example, Title III of the Omnibus Crime Control and Safe Streets Act of 1968, also known as the federal Wiretap Act, imposes restrictions relating to electronic surveillance on both state and federal law enforcement.[92] Given Congress's power under the Constitution's Commerce Clause[93] to regulate electronic communications, the constitutionality of the Wiretap Act has not been seriously questioned.

But the Fourth Amendment requires that the federal rules not be inconsistent with state law. This does not mean that the States must affirmatively authorize the kinds of searches and seizures authorized by federal law. The principle of legality is satisfied by federal legal authorization. Nor may States place requirements on federal law enforcement that they do not place on their own agents; the doctrine of intergovernmental immunity dictates that the States may not "'discriminat[e] against the Federal Government.'"[94] Thus, for example, a State that disagrees with robust federal enforcement of immigration or narcotics laws would be able to hamper that enforcement only by placing limits on its own ability to enforce state criminal law generally. But it does mean that the States can impose the same requirements on federal officials that it imposes on its own officials, even if federal law otherwise authorizes federal agents to act. That is to say, there can be "reverse preemption" of federal law by state law.

This admittedly sounds odd based on modern understandings of federal-state relations, by which federal law can often preempt state law but not vice versa. But even with this understanding in place, States have sometimes taken the initiative to try to "preempt" federal search-and-seizure practices. For example, in 2011, when it became known that federal Transportation Security Administration (TSA) officials were engaging in arguably unnecessarily invasive frisks of airline passengers in airport screening, Texas legislators considered making it a criminal act for a

> public servant . . . acting under color of the person's office or employment without probable cause to believe the other person committed an offense [to] perform[] a search for the purpose of granting access to a publicly accessible building or form of transportation; and intentionally, knowingly, or recklessly touch[] the anus, sexual organ, buttocks, or breast of the other person, including touching through clothing; or touch[] the other person in a manner that would be offensive to a reasonable person.[95]

While the move was criticized by many, it represents the spirit of the original Fourth Amendment: a State attempting to provide its citizens with a level of security in their "persons" as against an overreaching (literally) central government.

The States' authority in this area is hardly unlimited. For example, the proposed Texas legislation probably violated the intergovernmental immunity doctrine, given that it was transparently directed at the practices of the TSA instead of being a neutral regulation governing all frisks in the State, most of which are obviously performed by state officials.[96] Even putting that flaw to one side, the federal government is not without power to try to persuade the States not to adopt restrictions that conflict with federal rules. This is particularly true in an area of extensive federal regulation, such as air travel, which is certainly covered by the Commerce Clause. Thus, in the Texas example, the federal government threatened that if the proposed legislation were enacted, the TSA could be constrained to essentially halt all commercial airline flights in and out of the State.[97] This led to the proposed legislation's being scuttled. In areas where the federal government does not have that type of leverage, this model might require more negotiation between federal and state authorities. But given that the state/federal relationship on law enforcement has generally been a cooperative one, there is no reason to think that "reverse preemption" by States would pose a serious threat to effective federal law enforcement.

In other areas, this added constraint on the federal government obviously would place hurdles in the way of any number of federal regulatory schemes. But that is precisely why we have the Fourth Amendment. The Anti-Federalists proponents of that Amendment wanted to make it difficult for the federal government to pursue regulatory objectives that they saw as being within the purview of the States. Consider *Marshall* v. *Barlow's, Inc.*, which involves searches of ordinary businesses to further the workplace health and safety goals of the federal Occupational Safety and Health Act of 1970.[98] It is precisely such a comprehensive national scheme of pursuing traditionally state concerns that the Anti-Federalists would have abjured. Just as they feared, the Supreme Court has read the Commerce Clause broadly to permit this type of federal regulatory scheme. Even if the Court was correct to do so, the Fourth Amendment was adopted to make it difficult for the feds to enforce such a scheme without the cooperation of state officials.

Due Process of Law and the Exclusionary Rule

As noted in the Introduction, the modern Court sees the right to be free from unlawful searches and seizures separately from remedies for the violation of that right such as the exclusion of ill-gotten evidence from the prosecution's case-in-chief at trial against the victim of the unlawful search or seizure. While the right is dictated by the Constitution, the exclusionary rule is seen as a judge-made remedy, to be applied only when needed to achieve deterrence of unlawful police conduct.[99]

When we frame the issue as one of due process of law, the picture changes, although the results might be much the same. Since the idea of due process of law binds all state actors, not just the police, it is impossible to speak of the police alone as depriving a suspect of liberty without due process of law. Instead, we have to speak of a due process violation as the police misconduct *coupled with a failure on the part of the State to provide an adequate response to that misconduct* through its own legal system, thus encouraging lawless behavior to continue. State law itself might require exclusion, in which case exclusion would be required also by the notion of "due process of law." If state law does not provide for exclusion, however, it would have to provide for some other mechanism equally capable of punishing and deterring police misconduct. It is only if the state legal system does not provide an adequate mechanism to prevent lawbreaking by government agents that the exclusionary rule should be constitutionally required. The exclusionary rule should thus be thought of as a constitutional default rule. The Court has described the rule in those very terms. In *Wolf* v. *Colorado*, after declining to apply the exclusionary rule to the States, the Court, emphasizing the sub-constitutional nature of the rule, mused that it was arguable whether the rule would even apply to the federal government if Congress were to legislate otherwise: "We would then be faced with the problem of the respect to be accorded the legislative judgment on an issue as to which, in default of that judgment, we have been forced to depend upon our own."[100]

As a formal matter, perhaps whatever mechanism a State comes up with would suffice to constitute "due process of law." And the federalism concerns of the Thirty-Ninth Congress counsel deference to state legal systems. However, courts should ensure themselves that States are acting robustly and in good faith to ensure that their officers obey state law. Members of the Thirty-Ninth Congress did not accept state prosecutions of whites guilty of assaulting and slaughtering Black Southerners that yielded fines measured in pennies and jail terms measured in minutes.[101]

What would be an adequate state-law mechanism to prevent official lawbreaking will depend on the circumstances. In some instances, it is very unlikely that any state-law response would even be available. Suppose police act in a way that is unauthorized but neither tortious nor criminal, for example by using a technology unavailable to the general public in a way that is unauthorized by law, such as the thermal imaging device in *Kyllo* v. *United States*.[102] As I will argue in the next chapter, the Court in that case was correct to hold, in essence, that police violated Kyllo's liberty interest by using such a device to determine how much heat was being emitted by different parts of his home. However, assume that that conduct was neither a crime nor a tort in Oregon where it occurred. In such a case, even assuming Oregon would not provide for exclusion of the resulting evidence as a matter of state law, exclusion might be the only way to prevent such misconduct from occurring. The same would likely be true anytime a state agent's conduct violates the nondelegation principle. If an officer's conduct is authorized by state law, but the law provides her with too much discretion, there will by definition be no adequate state-law mechanism to curb such conduct, given that the conduct is perfectly lawful under state law.

It is only where a state agent's conduct is clearly forbidden by state law that an adequate state-law mechanism to control such behavior might exist, thereby satisfying the requirement of "due process of law."[103] This would be true, for example, where an officer snoops through a suspect's garbage in violation of a local criminal ordinance, or stops vehicles pursuant to a checkpoint unauthorized by statute, which could be the crime of false imprisonment if engaged in by anyone else. If the officer is treated like any ordinary lawbreaker, including the real prospect of criminal prosecution, then due process of law would be satisfied and exclusion would be unnecessary. Yet we know in the real world that this almost never happens. It would be farcical to think that police officers are routinely subjected to criminal prosecutions when they break the law even in circumstances where criminal charges would be brought against ordinary people.[104] Unless and until these circumstances change, exclusion may well be necessary to pick up the slack caused by non-enforcement of ordinary criminal law principles against police.

Indeed, the lack of adequate state-law responses to law violation by police largely explains the switch from *Wolf* v. *Colorado* in 1949, in which the Supreme Court declined to apply the exclusionary rule to the States, to *Mapp* v. *Ohio*, in which it changed course twelve years later. The *Wolf* Court had invoked "other means of protection" for police misconduct, including civil and criminal liability provided by common law or statute, and "internal discipline of the police."[105] By the time *Mapp* was decided, it had become apparent that those alternative remedies were "worthless and futile," and the Court quoted from the California Supreme Court's conclusion that "'other remedies have completely failed to secure compliance with the'" Constitution.[106]

Where a state agent violates an agency or departmental regulation, on the other hand, due process might require only that the misconduct be addressed through internal departmental discipline in order to avoid the exclusionary sanction. Once again, however, the threat of discipline must be real, not illusory. It must be sufficient to provide a realistic deterrent to state agents to refrain from violating the law as expressed through administrative regulations. Though it might prove more difficult in this context, courts should compare how police are treated when they violate rules to how ordinary people are treated in analogous situations.

Conclusion

Unchecked executive officer discretion was a primary evil the Fourteenth Amendment was designed to address. The Court's focus on controlling police discretion through a warrant-preference rule is thus consistent with the original understanding of that Amendment. But the Court's refusal to see a place for specific legislative and administrative guidelines outside of the "special needs" context has impoverished Fourth Amendment jurisprudence, and its artificial distinction between crime-fighting and "special needs" has exacerbated the problem.

Consider this: As a search incident to arrest, a police officer may decide, free from any constraint, whether to open a closed container obtained from an arrestee. If that container contains another container, the officer can open it, too, continuing until she finds something inside, as if opening Russian nesting dolls. Or not; at any point in this process, the officer can decide that their curiosity has been sated and stop searching. But if the officer waits too long and arrives at the police station not having searched the item, this "search incident to arrest" morphs into an "inventory search." Then the officer can open closed containers only if done pursuant to a policy that requires a specific procedure to be followed in all cases or in some subset of them.

What sense does this make? It is the same officer and the same container. The only thing that has changed is the time and the place. When the officer's discretion is limited, we should not care about where and when the search takes place. All we should care about—what due process is primarily concerned with—is whether she has followed the rules.

Eleven

Original Understandings and Four Problems of Modern Policing

We have seen that the Court's hyper-focus on the language and history of the Fourth Amendment and its relative inattention to the Fourteenth has resulted in a search-and-seizure jurisprudence that is both too forgiving and too strict at the same time. On the one hand, the Court has permitted wide police discretion in some areas that are insufficiently regulated by legislative and administrative guidelines, such as searches incident to arrest, or even unauthorized by law, such as sobriety checkpoints. On the other hand, it has inflexibly posited the warrant backed by probable cause as the gold standard when police are fighting crime, when specific legislative and administrative guidelines can adequately limit police officer discretion, as with checkpoints to interdict illegal narcotics or blood-draw procedures for intoxicated motorists. The Court has failed to see that specific legislative and administrative guidelines that cabin individual officer discretion are generally both necessary and sufficient to satisfy the requirements of due process.

This chapter focuses on four prominent problems of modern policing that are directly traceable to these flaws. First, the Court has failed to recognize the critical role the legality principle should play in the "What is a search?" question, a problem of increasing importance as advancing technologies make it easier for police to conduct investigations in ways that would not be considered searches under current law but which are unauthorized by law or would even be forbidden if undertaken by private citizens. Second, by condoning broad police power to make traffic stops and to arrest for minor crimes the Court has vastly enhanced police officer discretion, in contravention of the demands of due process of law. Third, the Court has also greatly increased police officer discretion by creating a lower tier of permissible stops based on mere reasonable suspicion even outside of emergent situations. Finally, by essentially displacing state law on the use of force with a nebulous and too-forgiving standard, the Court has exacerbated the problem of unjustified police violence.

The overarching flaw is that the Court has largely ignored the part that democratic controls should play in the constitutional law of policing. By setting up a false dichotomy in most areas between judicial regulation of police and no regulation at all, the Court has shunted off to the side the primary policymakers in our democracy: politically accountable legislators and administrators. In chapter 10, we saw fragments of the Court's work in the development of its "special needs" jurisprudence that reflect the promise of democratic policing that was contemplated in 1868. By piecing together and building upon these fragments, this chapter offers a vision of what the constitutional law of policing in these four critical areas might look like if it were more sensitive to the original understandings of the Fourth and Fourteenth Amendments.

The Panopticon Problem: Searches and the Legality Principle

One of the great dangers of current Fourth Amendment jurisprudence is that it is inching us closer and closer to a surveillance state, in which government agents can monitor more and more of our formerly private lives. The danger arises primarily from newer technologies and techniques that are difficult to characterize as "searches" under current doctrine. Recall that the Court has limited the concept of a "search" to police conduct undertaken for the purpose of obtaining information that either (1) entrenches on a property interest or (2) violates a "reasonable expectation of privacy." Only when we decide that a search has occurred, the threshold of the Fourth Amendment is passed and the next question is whether the search was "reasonable."

Consider, under this framework, law enforcement use of pole cameras, video cameras attached to utility poles or lighting fixtures in public places that are owned either by the government or by a private entity, such as a utility company, that has allowed government agents access. Although devices to capture moving images have obviously been around for over a century, only recently has the technology developed to make such devices that are cheap, relatively unobtrusive, and fully usable without a human operator present.[1] Modern technology also permits such innovations as "continuous recording, zooming and tilting, real-time viewable footage, and storing footage for later review," as well as more exotic features such as "ultra-low light capacity or LED lights to illuminate dark spaces, 360-degree field of vision, infrared cameras, weatherproof exterior, solar power, . . . large data storage capacity [and] the ability to detect and track movement."[2] Difficult questions arise when police surreptitiously aim a pole camera at someone's front door to record their comings and goings over a lengthy period of time. While the Supreme Court has not ruled on this issue, several federal appeals courts have held that this does not constitute a Fourth Amendment search on the theory that the camera captures nothing more than the subject exposing themselves to public view.[3] Other courts and some commentators have disagreed.[4] But if use of pole cameras is not a search, current doctrine raises the specter of a future in which *every* house has a camera aimed at it. Moreover, placing cameras in public places is indisputably not a search under current doctrine. Therefore, *every* street and sidewalk could be monitored, perhaps even *every* person followed by a drone equipped with camera.[5] Welcome to the panopticon.

One possibility is for courts to address this problem by adopting what has been termed the "mosaic theory" under the auspices of the reasonable expectation of privacy approach.[6] Under the mosaic theory, law enforcement is entitled to capture snippets of our lives that are exposed to the public but only until the government can piece together those snippets and form a clear picture of a person's activities, like the tiles of a mosaic, in a way that ordinary people would be unable to do. That is to say, we have a reasonable expectation of privacy in a certain quantity of information even if we do not have an expectation of privacy in each constituent piece. A majority of the Court has suggested acceptance of some form of the mosaic theory, though not in name, in two cases. In *United States* v. *Jones*, involving the unwarranted attachment of a GPS device to a suspect's car, Justice Sonia Sotomayor in a concurring opinion, and Justice Samuel Alito joined by Justices Ruth Bader Ginsburg, Stephen Breyer, and Elena Kagan, concurring only in the judgment, each expressed the view that government surveillance of one's location, even in public, becomes a search if it continues for too long.[7] In *Carpenter* v. *United States*, a majority held that government acquisition of cell site location information from one's cell service provider constitutes a search if it discloses location information for too long a period of time.[8] However, the mosaic theory, aside from the obvious administrability problems of any standard that asks whether the government is going "too far," makes no pretense of having any connection to the text and original meaning of the Fourth or Fourteenth Amendment.

So how would the text- and original-meaning-based approach laid out in this book address the panopticon problem? Observe first that the current two-step approach—asking first whether there was a search and second whether the search was reasonable—quite easily maps onto the language of the Fourteenth Amendment, where our attention should lie. Here, the relevant question is whether a person was deprived of "life, liberty, or property without due process of law." The first part of this formulation, which asks whether a person's interest in liberty or property was even implicated—"life" is easy enough to understand—tracks the "search" question. Recall from chapter 4 that the search question should also be answered with reference to state law, which could refer either to (1) positive statutory or common law or (2) a cognizable legal right or interest that has not yet found expression in positive law. Liberty and property interests also are defined largely by state law.[9] When police act adversely to a person's interests in life, liberty, or property in a way that would be unlawful if done by private actors, they have implicated the person's due process rights. The next question is whether police were authorized to take that action and thus acted pursuant to "due process of law," an inquiry that mirrors the Fourth Amendment "reasonableness" question. Together, these questions manifest what I have called the legality principle.[10]

But because the Court has asked the wrong question, it does not recognize legality as necessary to validate police conduct. For example, in *California* v. *Greenwood*, the Court held that the Constitution was not violated when local police rummaged through the defendant's trash to find incriminating evidence, despite the fact that (1) local ordinances forbade the same conduct when committed by private citizens, thus giving Greenwood a property interest in his own trash, and (2) the California constitution affirmatively forbade such police conduct.[11] Perhaps in the absence of positive law to the contrary, one's garbage abandoned outside the curtilage of the home cannot be considered "property" for purposes of the Due Process Clause. However, positive law in effect gives homeowners a property interest in their trash until it is taken by the garbage collector. In addition, any receptacle in which the trash is placed, if it is owned by the homeowner, constitutes property on any view. Likewise, in *Oliver* v. *United States*, the Court held that there was no constitutional violation where state police officers discovered illegal activity after committing what would have been a trespass onto the landowner's property if done by private citizens.[12] Under the legality principle, these become easy cases. One of the key features of the right to property is the right to exclude others from it. Police infringement of the landowner's right to exclude others, whether from his land or from his trash, deprived the landowner of "property"; that police were unauthorized to do so means they did it "without due process of law."

As this discussion suggests, where the law is silent about police use of a particular investigative tool, neither authorizing nor forbidding it, we should fall back upon the general principle of legality: police can do whatever ordinary citizens can do. If a particular technology or investigative technique is available for use by the general public and state law is silent on its use—as with, say, binoculars—we can assume that the polity has spoken by its silence and our ability to conduct ourselves without being observed with binoculars is not deemed by the majority to be a "property" or "liberty" interest protectible by law. Police then have the same authority to use the technology as ordinary citizens do. But when only the State itself has access to a particular technology, democratic controls fail because we cannot always expect the polity to make rules about such a technology or even know about it. Under those circumstances, we cannot be confident that the polity's failure to speak should be taken as a judgment that our interests in liberty or property are not implicated by the technology rather than as a failure to consider the issue at all.

Take, for example, cell site simulators (CSSs).[13] These devices mimic the cellular base stations, such as cell towers, that send and receive cellular telephone signals, forming the backbone of our cellular network. When activated, CSSs gather information typically shared with one's cell provider, such as the cell phone number of the device making contact with the CSS and even the content of the communication contained in phone calls, texts, and internet activity. Moreover, CSSs can block access to other nearby cellular base stations and thus deceive nearby devices into accepting the CSS as the best available cellular base station, forcing all devices within range to share information with that CSS. As David Gray wrote: "It is hard to imagine a surveillance technology more suited to broad and indiscriminate surveillance than cell site simulators."[14] But CSS technology is generally used only by law enforcement, partly because of prohibitive costs, and partly because of its limited utility for ordinary people.[15] Moreover, because this technology, which impersonates the cellular technology we rely on for our daily communication, is hidden from view, most people are likely unaware that it even exists. As a result, CSS technology is almost virtually unregulated.

In such circumstances, even if they know about CSSs, political insiders might be confident that no rules are necessary to protect themselves because of the unlikelihood that they will become a target of the technology, whereas they might not be so sanguine when it comes to use of the technology by their fellow citizens. Because democratic controls cannot be trusted to work when the politically powerful have no reason to think that such a technology will be used against them, principles of political accountability suggest that we presume that people would consider their ability to go about their lives without their cell site information being constantly and automatically disclosed as a liberty interest. Thus, the principle of legality tells us that law enforcement use of such technology must be affirmatively authorized. This is close to what the Supreme Court said in *Kyllo* v. *United States*, where it made much of the fact that the technology there was not in general public use in holding that police conducted a search when using the technology to determine details about the inside of the home.[16]

Kyllo, however, is incomplete because it applies only to information obtained from the home. Moreover, *Kyllo* incorrectly focuses on the technology itself rather than the particular way in which the technology is used. Again, think of binoculars, which are both in general public use and generally unregulated. But using binoculars to peer inside someone's home and see things not observable to the public without visual enhancement technology would generally be considered a tort[17] and, at least in some States, a crime.[18] This distinction is relevant for our pole camera issue. Although video cameras are indeed ubiquitous in our society, aiming one at a neighbor's home to conduct nonstop surveillance, even if the camera picks up only images viewable to anyone passing by the home, may well be a tort or even a crime. If it is, then we have a liberty interest in not being so filmed.

Even if private use of a camera in this fashion would be problematic, police might be given special legislative authorization exempting them from this general rule. Legislation giving the police special dispensation to use technology unavailable to ordinary citizens represents a democratic judgment that, although the technology implicates a liberty or property interest, its use by the government can—subject to the principles of nondiscrimination and nondelegation—satisfy "due process of law." Where a legislative body specifically authorizes use of a particular kind of technology by the police but no one else, the danger that police are getting too far out in front of social norms is lessened because the decision has been vetted through the democratic process. Because everyone is equally vulnerable to searches using the new technology, at least formally, legislative approval represents a considered judgment by the community that the added security is worth the diminished privacy.

True, there is a danger that police will exercise too much discretion in deciding whom to investigate with technology over which they have a monopoly. If that is the case, the costs of added surveillance may not be borne equally throughout the community. But that concern is not technology-specific. In order for due process to be satisfied under the nondelegation principle, even if the police have a monopoly on a certain technology, a legislative or administrative body must still provide sufficiently detailed guidance on how and when to use the technology and police must adhere to those guidelines.[19] Special dispensation to use CSSs or pole cameras, for example, is not a blank check to use them whenever, wherever, and against whomever police choose. They would still be subject to the same kinds of controls as more conventional technology, such as listening devices, which are largely governed by statute. To the extent that legislatively approved technologies are used in areas where police now have excessive discretion, the solution is to curb that discretion, not to judicially limit the use of the technology. That the investigative tool is a technology unavailable to ordinary citizens poses no *incremental* danger of abuse of discretion over and above that which already exists without the technology.

Thus, suggestions that investigative uses of new technology should be generally guided by legislation, not the courts, are well taken. In *United States* v. *Jones*, Justice Alito, writing for himself and three others, expressed the notion that courts should generally defer to legislatures when it comes to the balancing of privacy and security interests implicated by new technologies: "In circumstances involving dramatic technological change, the best solution to privacy concerns may be legislative. A legislative body is well situated to gauge changing public attitudes, to draw detailed lines, and to balance privacy and public safety in a comprehensive way."[20] Orin Kerr, the leading commentator on the Fourth Amendment and new technologies, has said much the same.[21] These sentiments aptly express the position endorsed here, with one difference. Those who have advocated deference to legislatures typically have Congress in mind. However, as noted in chapter 10, federal legislation would also have to be consistent with *state* law.

As observed in chapter 4, recognition of liberty and property interests should primarily come from legislatures, not courts. This is all the more true when it comes to determining those interests in the context of new technologies. Because courts will have to stretch and strain to construe existing schemes, designed to regulate older investigative techniques, to cover newer technologies, courts should be especially insistent that such technologies be specifically governed by legislation before law enforcement can use them. And because such technologies are unlikely to be in the hands of the general public, legislatures will need a nudge from the courts.

Newer technologies are also the least amenable to common-law rulemaking by juries of the type discussed in chapter 4. While we rely on juries to make the common-sense judgments that fall within the interstices of traditional tort- and property-law rules that have accreted over the centuries, it is questionable whether we should entrust to them the power to make similar judgments about technologies that are difficult for laypeople even to understand. Accordingly, legislation and administrative regulations are critical here.

There are legitimate concerns about the growing power of government surveillance because of developing new technologies. This is particularly so given that some surveillance techniques are not "searches" under current law, and thus evade Fourth Amendment review. Asking whether these techniques implicate our legally created interests in "liberty" or "property," and then asking whether police followed "due process of law" in infringing these interests, makes clear where we should primarily look for the answer: state law. If we are to live in a panopticon, the Constitution requires that we put it to a vote.[22]

The Problem with Traffic Stops and Warrantless Arrests for Minor Offenses

One source of virtually unlimited discretion on the part of police officers is that they can stop motorists for traffic violations and arrest for minor offenses almost indiscriminately. In *Whren* v. *United States*, the Court held that probable cause that a motorist was committing a traffic infraction is sufficient for police to make a forcible stop, irrespective of whether they were motivated by a desire to investigate a more serious crime for which they lacked individualized suspicion.[23] In *Atwater* v. *City of Lago Vista*, the Court held that a warrantless arrest is permitted under the Fourth Amendment for minor offenses, even for an offense that cannot be punished by any jail time.[24] That the police have uncanalized discretion to arrest for minor offenses and, in particular, to stop for traffic violations is deeply problematic. When it comes to arrests for major crimes, discretion plays a minimal role because we can expect that the seriousness of the offense will almost always dictate that an arrest will be made. Not so with more minor offenses.[25] As Whren and his codefendant argued, because

> the use of automobiles is so heavily and minutely regulated that total compliance with traffic and safety rules is nearly impossible, a police officer will almost invariably be able to catch any given motorist in a technical violation. This creates the temptation to use traffic stops as

> a means of investigating other law violations, as to which no probable cause or even articulable suspicion exists.[26]

It also creates the opportunity for discrimination, conscious or otherwise. Bernard Harcourt and Tracey Meares helpfully summarized numerous studies that collectively suggest that the evidence that Blacks and Latinos are disproportionately stopped is "overwhelming."[27]

Granting police the complete discretion to decide whether to stop someone for a traffic infraction or ignore it, and to arrest for a minor offense or issue a citation, permits them, through selective enforcement, to essentially make law rather than simply enforce it. This is in serious tension with the fact that the outsized discretion to arrest for vagrancy and other minor offenses, which was used essentially to re-enslave Black people in the South, was one of the main driving forces behind adoption of the Fourteenth Amendment.[28] The Court has put such expansive powers in the hands of petty officers that we can no longer call such stops and arrests "due process of law."

As mentioned in chapter 9, the Court has taken seriously in one area—vague statutes—the problem of virtually unbounded police discretion to arrest. The void-for-vagueness doctrine is based largely on the rationale that such statutes delegate too much discretion to police, as well as prosecutors, judges, and juries, to decide who the lawbreakers are. Yet courts have failed to see any connection between the police-discretion concerns raised by vague statutes and those implicated by the Fourth Amendment as filtered through the Fourteenth. Consider the situation where police seize someone based on individualized suspicion of commission of a crime defined by an unduly vague statute, but the individual is ultimately charged with a more serious and more clearly articulated crime based on the discovery of evidence stemming from the initial seizure. For example, the traffic stop for failure to "'give full time and attention to the operation of the vehicle'" in *Whren*[29] turned into a prosecution for possession of drugs found as a result, leading to prison sentences of fourteen years.[30] In such a case, the outsized police discretion afforded by the arguably vague law that was the basis for the initial intrusion goes completely unchallenged, because the defendant can mount a vagueness challenge only to the statute he is prosecuted for violating.[31]

In addition, statutes so vague as to violate due process are rare. Statutes that are clear but broad, leaving police with virtually unfettered discretion whether and when to enforce them, are legion. Traffic infractions are a prime example. One study of a section of the New Jersey Turnpike in the early 1990s, for example, found that 98.1 percent of motorists drove at an excessive rate of speed.[32] How many of us can claim truthfully that they do not occasionally speed or, say, turn "'without giving an appropriate signal?'"[33] And how many can truthfully claim that they never commit a minor offense—say, jaywalking or littering—punishable by a small fine?

As a result, police have tremendous discretion because they have a virtually limitless universe of people they can stop or arrest for these minor offenses.[34] A police officer patrolling the New Jersey Turnpike in the early 1990s could pick virtually anyone to stop, minus the tiny sliver—1.9 percent—of the exceedingly law-abiding. While a void-for-vagueness challenge might be made to some traffic laws, "fifty-five miles per hour" is perfectly clear. The ability of executive officials to decide, without constraint, who among this virtually limitless pool will be stopped or arrested is the antithesis of due process because it results in executive officials "making up the criminal law as they go along."[35] And because, as in *Whren*, traffic stops often lead to discovery of violation of more serious crimes, arbitrary enforcement of traffic laws inevitably leads to arbitrary enforcement of laws proscribing more serious criminal conduct. As one state court put it over a century ago: "Any law which vests in the discretion of administrative officers the power to determine whether the law shall or shall not be enforced with reference to individuals in the same situation, without any rules or limitations for the exercise of such discretion, is unconstitutional."[36]

That is why some scholars have argued that the same principles that drive the void-for-vagueness doctrine ought to apply to statutes that are clear but broad. As Kim Forde-Mazrui put it: "The degree of discretion delegated to law enforcement through specific laws in the traffic context appears to be as great as has ever been accomplished through vague laws and . . . borders on making police discretion to stop, search, and arrest motorists essentially unfettered."[37] Some, such as Kiel Brennan-Marquez, have even explicitly compared overly broad laws to general warrants: "Like general warrants, [extremely broad laws] equip enforcement officials with a tool . . . that provides automatic legal justification for widespread, and potentially discriminatory, intrusion into private life."[38]

This is not to say that these sorts of laws should go unenforced. Laws creating traffic infractions and forbidding other low-level, quality-of-life offenses, serve useful purposes. Moreover, such laws often protect the interests of, and are favored by, the very people who can easily become the victims of overly discretionary policing: poor people of color. In this sense, the paradox that existed in 1866 is still with us; poor and minority communities are prone to both over-policing and under-policing simultaneously. They are over-policed when they are disproportionately targeted for low-level crimes committed by large swaths of people. They are under-policed when crimes against them, including quality-of-life crimes that have seriously adverse effects on their communities, go unaddressed.[39] Particularly in an age where communities of color have amassed political power, especially in urban areas, we need to be sensitive to the fact that many people in these communities favor aggressive enforcement of low-level crimes while they are also "the same ones who are exposed to the risk that [police] discretion will be abused."[40] Empirical studies have suggested that there is a value to the police addressing not just serious crimes but also community disorder—the so-called "broken windows" theory of policing—but only when denizens of the area perceive the police to be acting in ways that are fair and unbiased, and pursuant to police policies in which they have had a voice.[41]

The solution, then, is not to make these laws unenforceable but to recognize that, as Kenneth Culp Davis put it, "vagueness in an enforcement policy can be just as unfair as vagueness in a statute."[42] Courts should therefore require legislative or administrative guidelines for enforcing such statutes so as not to leave enforcement discretion wholly in the hands of the individual officer.[43] Guidelines might dictate that traffic infractions be enforced through traffic stops only when certain objective conditions exist suggesting that the driver is truly a clear and present danger to others. For example, they might forbid the police from stopping speeders unless the motorist is going a certain number of miles per hour over the legal limit; they might permit stops of those who fail to use turn signals only when the car is within a certain distance of other motorists or pedestrians; or they might forbid stopping for any traffic infraction unless the total number of infractions observed could lead to a certain number of "points" being added to the motorist's license. On the other hand, a community might go all in and develop a zero-tolerance policy for, say, speeders: anyone caught going even one mile per hour over the limit *must* be stopped and cited. If police follow such a guideline, their discretion is reduced to zero.

The almost fully unbounded discretion police now have under the federal Constitution to make traffic stops is especially incongruous with the fact that modern technology will soon make the need for traffic stops virtually obsolete. Red-light cameras and speed cameras have been used in some places to take a picture of the traffic transgressor and their license plate number in order to automatically ticket anyone going through a red light or a certain speed over the posted limit.[44] Stops might still be beneficial in some cases to provide specific deterrence—that is, to get the driver to (at least temporarily) slow down and drive more carefully after the stop—or in more extreme cases such as reckless driving to serve the incapacitationist purpose of taking the driver into custody. But, again, the democratic and administrative organs of local government can determine those cases where a purpose above and beyond the notice achieved through automatic citations justifies the infringement on liberty occasioned by a traffic stop.

One could argue that the administrative regulations I propose would essentially result in the executive branch changing the law. For example, forbidding traffic stops of motorists unless they go a certain number of miles per hour over the speed limit would effectively change the speed limit. However, there are often other ways of enforcing the law than by seizing offenders, particularly in the traffic offense context where, as discussed above, technology is fast making traffic stops unnecessary. Thus, the speed limit would still be what the legislature decrees regardless of which speeders are seized and which simply get a ticket in the mail. Moreover, as Davis recognized long ago, the executive branch is "making law" no matter what. The question is whether law should be made by executive officials at a higher, more politically accountable level so that it applies equally to all, or by the individual officer in the field on an ad hoc, arbitrary basis.

Notice that automatic citations and zero-tolerance policies would result in a dramatic increase in the volume of motorists cited for routine traffic infractions. It is odd to think of this as somehow liberty-enhancing.[45] But such a scheme is entirely consistent with the localized and process-based model of the Fourteenth Amendment that approximates the original understanding of 1868. When enough local denizens get tired of being pulled over for going thirty-six miles per hour on the way to the grocery store because of a community's zero-tolerance policy, one of two things will change: either the zero-tolerance policy or the speed limit. Either way, change will occur through the democratic process.[46] Indeed, we have already seen clamorous popular rejection of red-light and speed cameras in many places, precisely because they eliminate police discretion and because the usual beneficiaries of that discretion—the white and well-to-do—have the political clout to reject discretionless policing in favor of business as usual, with the burden of traffic stops falling disproportionately on poor people of color. Only if the courts were to take "business as usual" off the table would we see policing policies that are truly democratic.

In this light, the Court's own attempt to justify the result in *Atwater* on process-based grounds rings hollow. There, the Court surmised that warrantless arrests for misdemeanors need not be subject to constitutional constraints because the political process is adept at limiting the use of such arrests. The Court noted that some States have imposed their own restrictions on warrantless arrest authority, and that local governments have an interest in limiting warrantless misdemeanor arrests because they "carry costs that are simply too great to incur without good reason." The Court also pointed to the "dearth of horribles demanding redress," observing that Atwater and her amici could point to only "a handful" of "comparably foolish, warrantless misdemeanor arrests," concluding that "the country is not confronting anything like an epidemic of [such] arrests." The Court concluded that a constitutional rule was unnecessary because we can rely on "the good sense (and, failing that, the political accountability) of most local lawmakers and law-enforcement officials."[47]

The main flaw in this process-based argument is that political accountability can be relied upon only when a significant number of citizens are actually inconvenienced by police practices. But while the "dearth of horribles" and lack of "an epidemic" suggest that most police and local officials are acting responsibly, they also suggest that less than a critical mass of citizens are being adversely affected by the incredibly broad police discretion to arrest for minor offenses. That is precisely the problem of under-enforcement: large swaths of citizens unaffected by police practices, who consequently have no motive to demand change through the political process, dotted with cases of adversely affected citizens, with little power to achieve political change. Indeed, evidence now suggests that discretionary-arrest authority might fall heaviest on minority communities, whose stories flew under the *Atwater* Court's radar and who also typically lack the political influence to effect change.[48] Understood this way, the Court's reliance on the lack of "an epidemic of unnecessary minor-offense arrests" to conclude that courts need not step in is positively perverse; it is precisely when practices are *not* widespread that democratic controls cannot be expected to work.[49]

The Court's reliance on the political process to constrain traffic stops and minor-offense arrests rings particularly hollow in light of (1) the *Whren* Court's refusal to take into account local police guidelines—there, "police regulations which permit[ted] plainclothes officers in unmarked vehicles to enforce traffic laws 'only in the case of a violation that is so grave as to pose an immediate threat to the safety of others'"—in determining the reasonableness of a traffic stop[50] and (2) the Court's later decision in *Virginia* v. *Moore*—discussed in the Introduction—that a minor-offense arrest made in violation of state law does not violate the Constitution.[51] The Court grounded these decisions in a refusal to interpret the Fourth Amendment in a way that depends on "police enforcement practices [that] vary from place to place and from time to time." The Court rejected the view that the Fourth Amendment was "so variable, and . . . made to turn upon such trivialities."[52]

Had the Court looked at cases such as *Moore*, *Whren*, and *Atwater* through the lens of the Fourteenth Amendment instead of the Fourth, the results could have been different. The officers' failure to abide by Virginia law in *Moore* should have been determinative as to whether Moore's arrest was consistent with "due process of law." As for *Whren*, the police agency there complemented state law by promulgating internal rules on when arrests should or must be made.[53] If due process of law at its core means that police have to obey the law, then police failure to follow the regulations they themselves set forbidding traffic enforcement by plainclothes officers in unmarked cars also could qualify as a deprivation of liberty without due process of law.[54] Such a bright-line rule would ensure a sturdier guidepost than a test involving, as the *Whren* Court put it, either "the actual motivations of the individual officers" or "whether the officer's conduct deviated materially from usual police practices, so that a reasonable officer in the same circumstances would not have made the stop for the reasons given."[55] Rather than attempting to plumb the depths of an individual officers' consciousness (or subconscious) or ask what was "usual" or "reasonable," we simply have to look at whether the police followed the rules. And, in *Atwater*, the complete absence of any such rules limiting officer discretion itself means that Atwater's arrest was inconsistent with "due process of law." Of course, this means that the outcomes of cases could differ based on the laws and rules in place in each jurisdiction. But that is a product of the fact that the "law" in "due process of law" refers primarily to the underlying positive law of the State. The Court's aversion to a "variable" Fourth Amendment is thus unfounded; as we have seen throughout this book, variability is baked into the Fourth and the Fourteenth Amendments.

Whren in particular provides a poignant example of the hazards of ignoring the Fourteenth Amendment and the deep connections between racial discrimination and discretionary search-and-seizure authority. The specter lurking behind *Whren*, obviously, is racial profiling; as the Court pointed out, both Whren and his codefendant were Black. The Court's answer to this concern was that although "the Constitution prohibits selective enforcement of the law based on considerations such as race . . . the constitutional basis for objecting to intentionally discriminatory application of laws is the Equal Protection Clause, not the Fourth Amendment."[56] But showing intentional discrimination is virtually impossible, short of a brazen admission by someone who (by hypothesis) has already shown no compunction about discriminating and therefore probably has no compunction about lying about it.[57] And intentional discrimination is quite beside the point when the decision to seize is infected with implicit bias of which the officer might be wholly unaware.[58]

Had the Court seen that every Fourth Amendment case is also a Fourteenth Amendment case, it could have seen that the dichotomy it drew between the two provisions was illusory.[59] The Court's artificial separation of the Fourth Amendment from the Fourteenth ignored the fact that the two work together synergistically. As a result, instead of requiring police to obey local regulations designed to limit their discretion, as a way of flushing out unconscious or otherwise undetectable discrimination, the Court sent claims of racially disparate policing off to face an almost insurmountable hurdle.

The Stop-and-Frisk Problem

One of the greatest expansions of police discretionary authority took place as a result of the Supreme Court's 1968 decision in *Terry* v. *Ohio*. There, a police officer forcibly seized and frisked three men whom he spotted engaging in activity that made him reasonably believe that the men were about to rob a store. Specifically, he watched each man individually walk back and forth past the store over a dozen times, looking in each time, and then meet up again with his cohorts. The Supreme Court held that, although the officer lacked probable cause for a full-scale arrest or search, he had "reasonable suspicion," a lower tier of individualized suspicion, and that was enough for him to temporarily seize the men and pat them down for weapons.[60]

Terry has blossomed into a widely used investigative tool for police; nearly every cognizant American adult is likely familiar with the term "stop and frisk." Where police lack probable cause, but have reasonable suspicion, that "criminal activity may be afoot"—that is, that a crime has been, is being, or is about to be committed—they have the authority to forcibly, though temporarily, detain individuals to investigate. If there is reasonable suspicion that the person is "armed and presently dangerous," police may also frisk them for their own safety and the safety of others. Reasonable suspicion exists when police can "point to specific and articulable facts which, taken together with rational inferences from those facts, reasonably warrant [an] intrusion."[61] This is not a difficult standard to meet. The fact that a person runs from police in a "high-crime area," for example, is enough to constitute reasonable suspicion to stop.[62]

The Court's *Terry* jurisprudence has been roundly criticized. While the *Terry* opinion could have been interpreted narrowly, it "contained the seeds of enormous discretion for law enforcement."[63] This discretion, it is argued, has been used disproportionately to initiate street encounters with young Black men in economically depressed urban areas.[64] Bennett Capers identifies *Terry* as the fount of a Fourth Amendment jurisprudence that ignores the equal citizenship promise of the Fourteenth Amendment.[65] As with traffic stops, as Harcourt and Meares put it, the evidence of racial disparities in police decisions to make *Terry* stops is "overwhelming."[66] Devon Carbado has contended that *Terry* has facilitated police violence against Black people.[67]

These criticisms are well taken. *Terry* and its sequelae give the police inordinate discretion to decide whether and when to intrude upon the liberty of civilians, or to refrain from doing so, whenever the low barrier of "reasonable suspicion" is met. Unlike probable cause, which itself means something lower than "more likely than not," police quite often encounter objective, articulable facts from which one could infer that something nefarious is occurring in circumstances that, to other reasonable police officers, are innocuous. As Bill Stuntz pointed out: "Reasonable suspicion of drug activity might cover a large fraction—sometimes, a large majority—of the young males hanging around on the street in communities where drug sales happen."[68]

Courts have applied the "reasonable suspicion" standard in a way that is highly deferential to police expertise. Although *Terry* required "specific and articulable facts" that crime "may be afoot," it often seems that courts find reasonable suspicion whenever officers can "point to specific and articulable facts," full stop. Judge Jacques Wiener of the U.S. Court of Appeals for the Fifth Circuit sardonically summarized a list of twenty or so facts that courts have relied upon in concluding that reasonable suspicion to stop a motorist existed, where half of those facts contradict the other half; that a "vehicle was suspiciously dirty and muddy," for example, gave rise to reasonable suspicion but so, too, did the fact that a "vehicle was suspiciously squeaky-clean."[69] Judge George Pratt of the U.S. Court of Appeals for the Second Circuit engaged in a similar exercise regarding facts that courts had held sufficient to create reasonable suspicion to stop a traveler at an airport: for example, that one suspect "[w]alked rapidly through [the] airport" and another "[w]alked aimlessly through [the] airport" provided reasonable suspicion as to both.[70] That so many contradictory circumstances might give rise to reasonable suspicion that crime is afoot allows police to pick and choose among them to initiate forcible investigative detentions. The *Terry* doctrine is problematic because even those who are entirely innocent of crime often do or say things that get them to the level of reasonable suspicion.[71]

Yet the problem is not so much the reasonable suspicion standard. When police face the potential of a truly dangerous situation or other exigency, we want them to at least investigate and protect the public, and themselves, on lesser facts than would justify a full-blown arrest or search. That is why the Court has strongly hinted that the exigent circumstances exception to the warrant requirement kicks in whenever police have mere reasonable suspicion, not probable cause, to think that the exigency exists.[72] Indeed, the *Terry* case itself fits this paradigm: the officer there, outnumbered three to one, had reasonable suspicion that the suspects were about to commit a daytime robbery of a store, which often involves deadly, concealed weapons. Waiting to develop probable cause—much less to obtain a warrant—could have had deadly consequences for the shop owner, its patrons, the suspects, and the officer himself.[73]

The real problem with *Terry* is that it has expanded in two different directions far beyond this initial exigency-based rationale. First, it has been extended to apply even to offenses that, in their ordinary commission, are not dangerous.[74] Not long after it was decided, the Court wrote that reasonable suspicion was sufficient for a stop of a vehicle near the border to check for undocumented aliens.[75] Later, in *Florida* v. *Royer*, a plurality of the Court, though finding the detention there unlawful, assumed that *Terry* applied where "the public interest involved is the suppression of illegal transactions in drugs or of any other serious crime."[76] Though it has never addressed this issue head on, the Court has applied *Terry* for decades in numerous cases of suspected drug trafficking or possession, serious offenses but hardly crimes dangerous in themselves.[77]

Second, *Terry* has been stretched to cover offenses, dangerous or not, that have already occurred. In *United States* v. *Hensley*, the Court held that "a *Terry* stop may be made to investigate [reasonable] suspicion" that a person has already committed a felony, in that case twelve days prior to the stop.[78] But the stop in *Terry* was justified not to investigate a past, completed offense but to head off an incipient and imminent one. In the latter case, we afford police the discretion to act precipitously only because there is no other choice. In the former case, police discretion can and should be channeled by legislative and administrative guidelines and, where necessary, warrants based on probable cause.

Bill Stuntz aptly summed up the problem: "[I]nstead of *Terry* stops being an exceptional police tactic used to combat an exceptional crime, they are a very common tactic used to combat a very common crime."[79] It need not have been this way. Read carefully, *Terry* itself is limited to dangerous crimes that are imminent or that have just occurred. The *Terry* Court limited its holding to cases where police have reasonable suspicion "that criminal activity may be afoot *and that the persons with whom he is dealing may be armed and presently dangerous.*"[80] Courts have generally read the italicized language as limited to the "frisk" part of "stop and frisk." But the *Terry* opinion focuses on the frisk, treating the stop merely as an incident thereto, so there is reason to believe that *Terry* meant that even the stop may occur *only* upon reasonable suspicion of danger.[81] Prominent Second Circuit Judge Henry Friendly read *Terry* as thus limited to dangerous crimes that are imminent or that have just occurred:

> Terry v. Ohio was intended to free a police officer from the rigidity of a rule that would prevent his doing anything to a man reasonably suspected of being about to commit or having just committed *a crime of violence*, no matter how grave the problem or impelling the need for swift action, unless the officer had what a court would later determine to be probable cause for arrest. *It was meant for the serious cases of imminent danger or of harm recently perpetrated to persons or property*, not the conventional ones of possessory offenses.[82]

These words were echoed by Justice William Brennan in dissent when Judge Friendly's position was rejected by the Supreme Court.[83] This potential limitation on *Terry* has now been buried under five decades of cases.

It ought to be disinterred. *Terry* today provides police with as much discretion to intrude upon civilian liberty as the postbellum vagrancy laws did.[84] To cabin police discretion in a way faithful to the understandings of the framers and ratifiers of the Fourteenth Amendment, we ought to go back to *Terry*'s roots: allow the police discretion to intrude upon the private affairs of citizens on less than probable cause and a warrant, and unguided by specific statutory or administrative guidelines, only when necessary to investigate dangerous conduct that is about to occur or that has just occurred.[85]

The Problem of Unjustified Police Violence

It is in the regulation of police violence that the failure of Fourth Amendment doctrine has been most profound, most disappointing, and most tragic.[86] One of the primary impetuses behind the Fourteenth Amendment was the horrific violence exacted against Black people and, to a lesser extent, loyal whites and Northerners in the postbellum South, often by state agents. Thus, it is in protecting citizens from the unjustified use of violence by state officials that constitutional doctrine should be particularly robust.[87] Unfortunately, just the opposite is true. Today, studies all but uniformly suggest that people of color are disproportionately affected by police violence.[88]

One problem is that the Fourth Amendment has been deemed to protect against police violence only when it constitutes a "seizure" of the person. Thus, the Fourth Amendment has been considered inapplicable to unsuccessful attempts to use force (as when a police officer shoots at but misses another person), intended physical force against an unintended target (as when a police officer shoots at one person but hits another), and physical force used for some reason other than to restrain (as when police fire projectiles into a crowd to get them to disperse).[89] Instead, such cases are governed by a different "substantive due process" standard, which is satisfied only if the officer acted with "a purpose to cause harm unrelated to [any] legitimate object," so that his conduct is "shocking to the conscience."[90]

To make matters worse, the Court held in *Graham* v. *Conner*, discussed in more detail below, that where the Fourth Amendment applies, the Due Process Clause of the Fourteenth Amendment does not. Where the Fourth Amendment "provides an explicit textual source of constitutional protection against [a particular] sort of physically intrusive governmental conduct, that Amendment, not the more generalized notion of 'substantive due process,' must be the guide for analyzing the[] claim[]."[91] Thus, rather than recognize the roots of the Fourteenth Amendment in the post–Civil War use of state violence against Black Southerners, the *Graham* Court took the Fourteenth Amendment entirely out of the equation of police violence where there is a "seizure." Rather than working together, after *Graham*, the Fourth and Fourteenth Amendments are mutually exclusive.[92]

Even where the Fourth Amendment is deemed to apply, its treatment of police violence is out of whack. Let's start with Max Weber's premise that, in a liberal democracy, the State has a monopoly on legitimizing the use of violence against its citizens.[93] Individuals can lawfully engage in violence of the type relevant here in two circumstances. First, the State grants a very limited license to private citizens to use violence on those rare occasions defined by law when violence that would otherwise be criminal is deemed justified, for example when used in self-defense.[94] Second, because the State must operate through individuals, it must give agents of the State the authority to use violence on occasion, so it creates special defenses for those enforcing the law.[95] Police use of force would, if committed by an ordinary person and not for law enforcement purposes, be a crime or tort: from harassment for a simple shove, to assault for more injurious but nonlethal conduct, to homicide. Thus, state-law defenses—special law enforcement defenses as well as defenses that apply to all people—usually protect police officers in their use of force.[96] In particular, most if not all justifiable police use of force fits within one or more of three state-law defenses: self-defense; defense of others; and the public authority defense, which typically permits force in making an arrest, preventing an escape, preventing crime, or otherwise keeping order.[97]

The legality principle demands that state agents obey these laws when using violence. Based on that principle, police should be considered to be acting within the confines of due process of law only when and only to the extent that they would be justified under state law by these three justification defenses. If police have a valid defense under state law, then the target of the violence has not been deprived of liberty without due process of law. Where a state agent's use of force is unjustified under state law, however, the Due Process Clause is implicated.[98]

It is black-letter law that defenses involving use of force can ordinarily be satisfied only if, and only to the extent that, the use of force was necessary.[99] "In justification defenses, this [necessity] requirement is essential: if the force used is not necessary in both its *nature* and *degree* to respond adequately to a threat to one of the recognized interests, it is a crime."[100] As a result, state laws always limit the use of force, deadly or not, in self-defense or defense of others to situations where the type and amount of force was necessary. And virtually all States require that force be used only when, and only to the extent that, it is necessary to enforce the law, particularly when it comes to deadly force.[101] Thus, police in virtually every State would be violating state law—and, under the legality principle, potentially the Fourteenth Amendment—if they used unnecessary force.

Likewise, state self-defense and defense-of-others statutes typically limit these defenses, or even bar them completely, for those who "provoke" the violence against them or are the "initial aggressors." This means that if A commits an aggressive or provocative act toward B and B responds with force, A's right to continue to use, or to escalate, violence against B in response is restricted or even eliminated. Although what qualifies as "provocation" or "aggression" is extraordinary unclear, some form of this rule applies in every State.[102] Thus, if a police officer claims to have used force in self-defense or defense of others, the claim should not be analyzed solely as of the instant of the use of force. One must look to what, if anything, the officer did to precipitate the violence. For example, where police violate knock-and-announce or daytime-search requirements when serving a warrant, and the homeowner, thinking she is being burglarized, responds with deadly force, we cannot evaluate the deadly force used by police in response without considering whether their initial unlawful entry made them the initial aggressors. Moreover, even state public-authority-defense statutes sometimes require, or could be interpreted to require, that the totality of police conduct prior to the need to use force be reasonable before an officer is entitled to the defense. This means that, as with the "initial aggressor" rule, if the officer culpably created the conditions under which she then found it reasonably necessary to use force to make an arrest, her entitlement to the defense should be limited or even barred completely.[103]

Unfortunately, Fourth Amendment doctrine on police violence has diverged from state law. Rather than having the Constitution follow state law, essentially the reverse has occurred; the Supreme Court has set a Fourth Amendment standard wholly divorced from state law, and state legislatures, courts, and police agencies have then incorporated that standard into their own laws and guidelines. In effect, the Court should have incorporated state law into the constitutional standard, but it has instead in many places displaced state law with a watered-down version that permits force, even deadly force, by police even when such force is unnecessary.

The process began in *Tennessee* v. *Garner*, where an officer shot and killed a teenaged boy trying to elude police after a suspected burglary. In fashioning a Fourth Amendment rule, the Court looked to state laws on the defense of use of deadly force to effectuate an arrest. The Tennessee statute authorized an officer to "'use all the necessary means to effect [an] arrest'" for *any* felony. The Court noted that this common-law rule was the law in about twenty-one States. By contrast, other States limited the use of deadly force to those situations where it was necessary to arrest someone suspected of committing a *violent* felony or who was likely to be a serious danger to others if not apprehended immediately. The Court rejected the common-law rule as a constitutional standard and held that the Fourth Amendment permits the use of deadly force to seize a fleeing felon only when "the officer has probable cause to believe that the suspect poses a threat of serious physical harm, either to the officer or to others," so long as deadly force is "necessary to prevent escape, and . . . where feasible, some warning has been given."[104]

Notice that, in *Garner*, the only question was about what Paul Robinson called a "triggering condition," a fact that had to exist to justify the use of physical force.[105] The question was whether the potential escape of any felon, or instead only some subset of felons, triggers the authorization to use deadly force in law enforcement. Whichever formulation was appropriate, neither had anything to do with what Robinson called a "limitation," a rule restricting the use of deadly force in law enforcement once the authorization for the use of force has been triggered. One key limitation under state law, *Garner* itself recognized, is that deadly force be "*necessary to prevent escape*."[106]

Four years later, in *Graham* v. *Connor*, the Court held that the Fourth Amendment governs all use of force, not just deadly force, in making an arrest. The Court wrote that, because the Fourth Amendment demands reasonableness, the question whether excessive force was used "requires a careful balancing of the nature and quality of the intrusion on the individual's Fourth Amendment interests against the countervailing governmental interests at stake." This balancing should take into account "the facts and circumstances of each particular case, including the severity of the crime at issue, whether the suspect poses an immediate threat to the safety of the officers and others, and whether he is actively resisting arrest or attempting to evade arrest by flight."[107] Thus, *Graham* decided that a loose Fourth Amendment reasonableness analysis applied to excessive force cases involving nondeadly force, with many factors relevant and none dispositive. One such factor is "whether the suspect poses an immediate threat to the safety of the officers and others." But this factor would generally be a triggering condition for a state-law claim of self-defense or defense of others. Another such factor, "whether [the suspect] is actively resisting arrest or attempting to evade arrest by flight," would generally be a triggering condition for a state-law public-authority defense. Thus, *Graham* downgraded the triggering conditions for these defenses—each essential under state law for an actor to claim the respective defense—to mere "facts and circumstances" to be weighed with everything else.[108] *Graham* used some form of the word "necessary" only once, and only then in emphasizing how much leeway police should be given in determining "the amount of force that is necessary in a particular situation."[109] The essential state-law limitation of necessity was lost in *Graham*, awash in a sea of reasonableness.

The final act in this play occurred in 2007 in *Scott* v. *Harris*, where a police officer had executed a maneuver to stop a motorist who was evading arrest and driving recklessly at a very high rate of speed. The maneuver caused the motorist to crash, rendering him a quadriplegic, and he sued, claiming a violation of the Fourth Amendment. Although hitting a speeding motorist from behind while traveling at very great speeds certainly constituted deadly force, the Court declined to apply *Garner*. Instead, the Court "reimagined the *Garner* holding," and held that even in cases where deadly force is used, the heavily fact-intensive test from *Graham* applies.[110] Whether the force used was deadly or nondeadly, courts must "slosh [their] way through the factbound morass of 'reasonableness'" by balancing the government's interest in effecting the seizure against the individual's interest to be free from the type of force used.[111]

Having ignored the necessity limitation in *Graham*, the Court affirmatively rejected it in a footnote in *Scott*. In response to the plaintiff's argument that *Garner* established that deadly force is constitutionally permissible only if "necessary to prevent escape," the Court wrote:

> The necessity described in *Garner* was, in fact, the need to prevent "serious physical harm, either to the officer or to others." By way of example only, *Garner* hypothesized that deadly force may be used "if necessary to prevent escape" when the suspect is known to have "committed a crime involving the infliction or threatened infliction of serious physical harm," so that his mere being at large poses an inherent danger to society.[112]

This is nonsense. The *Garner* Court did not use commission of "a crime involving the infliction or threatened infliction of serious physical harm" as an example of when it is "necessary" to use deadly force "to prevent escape." It was positing the triggering condition for use of deadly force to prevent escape. But the triggering condition has nothing to do with the traditional state-law limitations on the use of deadly force, including the necessity requirement.

Having thus dispatched the state-law necessity requirement, the Court reiterated *Graham*'s holding that no single factor was essential in evaluating police use of deadly force: "*Garner* did not establish a magical on/off switch that triggers rigid preconditions whenever an officer's actions constitute 'deadly force.'"[113] While that statement is literally true—no one can possibly predict the infinite variety of factual scenarios that could give rise to a need to use deadly force—under the black-letter state law of justification defenses, there is a "rigid precondition" to the use of deadly force: necessity.[114]

As a result, lower courts have come to the troubling conclusion that the use of force, even deadly force, does not violate the Constitution even in cases where its use may have been unnecessary. As Rachel Harmon found,

> a number of federal courts have effectively ruled that the relationship between the amount of nondeadly force an officer used and the amount that was necessary is irrelevant so long as some force was justified. Others have suggested that so long as *Garner*'s test for deadly force is satisfied, it is irrelevant whether less deadly force would have achieved the same end.[115]

In effect, it is widely believed, even among lawyers, that the Supreme Court's jurisprudence in this area displaces the state law that it is supposed to instead reflect.[116] Thus, many police guidelines appear to ignore their own state-law limitations on the use of force. As discussed above, virtually all States include a necessity limitation in their law enforcement justification defense. And use of force is one area where law enforcement agencies have already promulgated a web of regulations that address the issue on a more granular level than does state law.[117] Yet Brandon Garrett and Seth Stoughton, in their review of the use-of-force policies of the Nation's fifty largest police departments, found that "[f]ew policies speak to any overall view that the need to use force should be minimized and that force should be avoided, when it is possible to do so." Specifically, only about half "counseled minimizing the need to use force, or that officers use the minimum force necessary." In addition, providing a verbal warning prior to the use of force is an important aspect of necessity, but while most agencies required a verbal warning prior to the use of deadly force, only about half required such a warning prior to the use of nondeadly force.[118] The findings of Osagie Obasogie and Zachary Newman, who examined the use-of-force policies of the police departments of the seventy-five largest American cities, are even more startling. According to their study, only 31 percent of the policies required exhaustion of alternatives before resorting to force, only 19 percent required continuous reassessment of the situation, only 17 percent required proportioning force to resistance, and only about half emphasized the importance of de-escalation.[119] Each of these is an aspect of necessity.

Instead of reflecting each State's constraints on the use of force, the policies reviewed in these studies often restate the *Graham* v. *Connor* standard of overall reasonableness, either alone or in conjunction with other guidelines. About half of the policies in the Garrett and Stoughton study "relied upon language from *Graham* and the Supreme Court's Fourth Amendment cases when setting out their general requirements for the use of force."[120] Every policy studied by Obasogie and Newman at least mentioned the *Graham* reasonableness standard, and many did not provide much more guidance. Obasogie and Newman concluded: "Most policies foster symbolic compliance with *Graham*'s statement on reasonableness instead of providing specific rules and processes for officers to engage when deciding whether to use force." Thus, rather than attempting to concretize the Supreme Court's vague *Graham* reasonableness standard into usable, localized norms, these agencies merely reiterate that standard. These policies fail to provide "meaningful guidance on what type of force is in or out of bounds" and what tactics police must take in order to obviate the necessity of using force.[121]

Graham has even infected state law itself. Some state courts, in interpreting statutes or common-law rules on police use of force, will use as their guide, not state common law, but *Graham*, "with some explicitly incorporating constitutional jurisprudence into state law." Seth Stoughton's impressive fifty-State survey found that in thirty-one States, courts have "referenced" *Graham* in "applying or discussing state law," and a few have even "explicitly adopt[ed] part or all of the constitutional framework as a matter of state law."[122] State prosecutors, too, have mistakenly applied *Graham* in determining whether to bring criminal charges against police.[123] This has it exactly backwards. State law ought to set the standards by which police must act, and the Constitution must ensure that they do so. Instead, state law in many places reflects a national model imposed from above by *Graham*, and police "agencies may be adopting generic standards in lieu of engaging in collaborative, stakeholder-informed policymaking that is responsive to local circumstances and concerns."[124]

Notice how far removed this state of affairs is from the original understanding of the Fourteenth Amendment. The framers and ratifiers of that Amendment looked first to the use of state law to cabin state violence against the formerly enslaved. The Due Process Clause requires first and foremost that state officials obey state law. Thus, we should look to the States' own regulation of the use of force by police through their statutory and common-law rules on the justification defenses of self-defense, defense of others, and the law enforcement defense. These rules are detailed enough to address common issues involving the use of force—for example, reasonable belief, necessity, imminence, proportionality, and provocation—flexible enough to be applied in varying factual scenarios, and, if properly applied, narrow enough to strictly limit the use of violence by state agents. In addition, state law and local regulations sometimes go further and forbid particular uses of force, such as chokeholds or tear gas, either altogether or in particular circumstances.[125] It is this law that police should have to follow.

Instead, *Graham* has pushed state law offstage and replaced it with a vague "reasonableness under the totality of circumstances" standard, totally divorced from any statutory detail or common-law accretions of state justification defenses. If state law were as vague as *Graham*, the nondelegation principle would *require* police agencies to provide more specific guidelines about de-escalation, exhaustion of alternatives, proportionate use of force, warnings, and so on. Instead, many police agencies simply mimic *Graham*, leaving police an enormously wide range of discretion on whether and to what extent to use force, deadly or not, in any given situation. Instead of reflecting state law back on itself, Fourth Amendment doctrine replaces it, giving police far less guidance and far more discretion than they otherwise would have. Instead of state policymakers constraining that discretion with specific guidelines on the use of force, the Supreme Court has created "a negative feedback loop,"[126] whereby the Court issues a vague national standard and local agencies simply adopt that standard as their own with no elaboration or local customization.

In an ideal world, state agents would be bound, as a matter of federal constitutional law, to obey state law, including the law regarding the use of force. This does not mean, however, that every unjustifiable use of force should also be considered a violation of due process. Recall from Chapter 10 that it is the failure to follow the law by the State itself, not just by a single agent, that constitutes a deprivation of "life, liberty, or property without due process of law." After all, it was not just the horrific violence exacted against Black Southerners that spurred the Reconstruction-era Republicans to enact the Fourteenth Amendment; it was the fact that this violence went unpunished. Where the State properly holds police accountable for their unjustified acts of violence, then due process has been provided. Unfortunately, although things are improving on that score, we still often hear of police going unindicted, acquitted, or under-punished in ways all too reminiscent of the immediate postwar South.

Conclusion

Mainstream Republicans of the Reconstruction era wanted to protect Americans from arbitrary searches and seizures by States but they were also big believers in federalism. They did not contemplate that the Fourteenth Amendment would make the minutiae of search-and-seizure rules uniform across the Nation. Instead, they understood the Amendment as imposing something like a process-based constraint. As long as state legislation on searching and seizing did not discriminate on its face, in its intent, or in its application, as long as state officials actually followed the law, and as long as officials were not given excessive discretion that would permit arbitrary and discriminatory practices, the federal government would not interfere with the States' search-and-seizure activities.

Today, state officials can violate ordinances that prohibit the rest of us from snooping through other people's trash but they cannot go up to a person's front door and remain for ninety seconds without knocking even if that would not be considered a trespass by a local jury. Individual officers, with no guidelines or controls, can interdict drugs by choosing one motorist among hundreds who are going at least one mile per hour over the speed limit when the officer has an inarticulable hunch—perhaps unconsciously tainted with racial bias—that the driver might be transporting drugs. But a state or locality beleaguered by drugs cannot conduct narcotics interdiction by making a collective decision to allow themselves to be stopped at checkpoints in a way that virtually eliminates individual officer discretion and spreads the pain equally. And police can violate state law by using even deadly force without regard to centuries-old limitations on justified use of force: necessity, imminence, and proportionality.

None of this makes sense. If the idea of "due process of law" means anything, it means that the police must, as the Court once said in a different context, "obey the law while enforcing the law."[127] When police act with no legal authorization, or they go beyond that authorization or the guidelines that they themselves set up, or they act pursuant to purported legal authority that grants them virtually unfettered discretion, they are neither obeying nor enforcing the law. They are making it.

Notes

Introduction

1. Anthony G. Amsterdam, *Perspectives on the Fourth Amendment*, 58 Minn. L. Rev. 349, 416 (1974).

2. Barry Friedman, Unwarranted: Policing Without Permission 27 (2017); *see also* Barry Friedman and Maria Ponomarenko, *Democratic Policing*, 90 N.Y.U. L. Rev. 1827 (2015); The Policing Project / NYU School of Law, "Statement of Principles on Democratic Policing" (2015); Megan Quattlebaum et al., Principles of Procedurally Just Policing 12–15 (2018). For a stimulating examination and critique of the recent movement toward democratic policing, *see generally* David A. Sklansky, Democracy and the Police (2008). Scholarship on democratic policing is only a part of a much larger literature advocating greater democratization of the criminal legal process in general. *See generally* Joshua Kleinfeld et al., *White Paper of Democratic Criminal Justice*, 111 Nw. U. L. Rev. 1693 (2017).

3. U.S. Const., amend. IV.

4. U.S. Const., amend. XIV, sec. 1.

5. 553 U.S. 164 (2008).

6. 520 U.S. 305 (1997).

7. Cooper v. California, 386 U.S. 58, 61 (1967).

8. Barry Friedman, Unwarranted: Policing Without Permission 110 (2017). *See also* Barry Friedman and Cynthia Benin Stein, *Redefining What's "Reasonable": The Protections for Policing*, 84 Geo. Wash. L. Rev. 281, 298 (2016) (characterizing *Chandler* as "mystifying").

9. 277 U.S. 438 (1928).

10. 138 S. Ct. 2206 (2018).

11. 138 S. Ct. at 2272 (Gorsuch, J., dissenting).

12. Kenneth Culp Davis, Discretionary Justice 42 (1969).

13. *See generally* Nathan S. Chapman & Michael W. McConnell, *Due Process as Separation of Powers*, 121 Yale L.J. 1672 (2012); Heather K. Gerken, *Windsor's*

Mad Genius: The Interlocking Gears of Rights and Structure, 95 B.U. L. Rev. 587 (2015).

14. Mapp v. Ohio, 367 U.S. 643, 660 (1961).

15. *See, e.g.*, Collins v. Virginia, 138 S.Ct. 1663, 1675–80 (2018) (Thomas, J., concurring) (expressing a desire to either eliminate the rule or decline to apply it in state cases).

Chapter 1

1. United States v. Rabinowitz, 339 U.S. 56, 70 (1950) (Frankfurter, J., dissenting).

2. California v. Acevedo, 500 U.S. 565, 582 (1991) (Scalia, J., concurring in the judgment). *Compare* United States v. Lefkowitz, 285 U.S. 452, 464 (1932) ("[T]he informed and deliberate determinations of magistrates empowered to issue warrants as to what searches and seizures are permissible under the Constitution are to be preferred over the hurried action of officers and others who may happen to make arrests.") *with* Harris v. United States, 331 U.S. 145, 150 (1947) ("The test of reasonableness cannot be stated in rigid and absolute terms. . . . The Fourth Amendment has never been held to require that every valid search and seizure be effected under the authority of a search warrant."), *and with* Johnson v. United States, 333 U.S. 10, 14 (1948) (declaring that "[w]hen the right of privacy must reasonably yield to the right of search is, as a rule, to be decided by a judicial officer, not by a policeman or Government enforcement agent," unless "exceptional circumstances" exist), *and with Rabinowitz*, 339 U.S. at 66 ("The relevant test is not whether it is reasonable to procure a search warrant, but whether the search was reasonable. That criterion in turn depends upon the facts and circumstances—the total atmosphere of the case.").

3. 576 U.S. 409, 419 (2015) (cleaned up).

4. 576 U.S. at 431 (Scalia, J., dissenting).

5. Payton v. New York, 445 U.S. 573, 581–82 (1980); United States v. Watson, 423 U.S. 411, 418 (1976).

6. Kentucky v. King, 563 U.S. 452, 460 (2011).

7. United States v. Robinson, 414 U.S. 218 (1973); Chimel v. California, 395 U.S. 752 (1969).

8. California v. Carney, 471 U.S. 386, 391–92 (1985); Chambers v. Maroney, 399 U.S. 42 (1970); Carroll v. United States, 267 U.S. 132, 153 (1925).

9. Schneckloth v. Bustamonte, 412 U.S. 218 (1973).

10. *Rabinowitz*, 339 U.S. at 69 (Frankfurter, J., dissenting).

11. Akhil Reed Amar, *Fourth Amendment First Principles*, 107 Harv. L. Rev. 757 (1994); Akhil Reed Amar, The Constitution and Criminal Procedure: First Principles (1997); Akhil Amar, *The Fourth Amendment, Boston, and the Writs of Assistance*, 30 Suffolk U. L. Rev. 53, 55–60 (1996); Akhil Amar, Terry *and Fourth Amendment First Principles*, 72 St. John's L. Rev. 1097, 1106–11 (1998).

12. Akhil Reed Amar, *Fourth Amendment First Principles*, 107 Harv. L. Rev. 757, 761 (1994).

13. Akhil Reed Amar, *Fourth Amendment First Principles*, 107 HARV. L. REV. 757, 774 (1994); see also TELFORD TAYLOR, TWO STUDIES IN CONSTITUTIONAL INTERPRETATION: SEARCH, SEIZURE, AND SURVEILLANCE AND FAIR TRIAL AND FREE PRESS 43 (1969) (asserting that the Fourth Amendment was designed "to prohibit the oppressive use of warrants" and leave warrantless searches and seizures unregulated).

14. *See* Akhil Reed Amar, *Fourth Amendment First Principles*, 107 HARV. L. REV. 757, 764–67 (1994). There is a good deal of dispute over this last proposition. *Compare* Thomas Y. Davies, *Recovering the Original Fourth Amendment*, 98 MICH. L. REV. 547, 647–48 (1999) (taking issue with Amar's account), *with* Fabio Arcila, Jr., *The Death of Suspicion*, 51 WM. & MARY L. REV. 1275, 1316–24 (2010) (supporting Amar's account).

15. Akhil Reed Amar, *Fourth Amendment First Principles*, 107 HARV. L. REV. 757, 776 (1994) (quoting PENNSYLVANIA AND THE FEDERAL CONSTITUTION 1787–1788, at 154 (J. McMaster and F. Stone, eds. 1888)). A shift was a loose-fitting undergarment.

16. Akhil Reed Amar, *Fourth Amendment First Principles*, 107 HARV. L. REV. 757, 772, 776 (1994). *Accord* Fabio Arcila, Jr., *The Death of Suspicion*, 51 WM. & MARY L. REV. 1275, 1284 (2010) ("[T]he Framers sought to limit access to warrants because they immunized officers from suits challenging the propriety of their searches.").

17. *See* Thomas Y. Davies, *Recovering the Original Fourth Amendment*, 98 MICH. L. REV. 547, 589 (1999) ("Like modern judges, the Framers understood that no post-search remedy could adequately restore the breached security of the house.").

18. *See* JOSIAH QUINCY, JR., REPORTS OF CASES ARGUED AND ADJUDGED IN THE SUPERIOR COURT OF JUDICATURE OF THE PROVINCE OF MASSACHUSETTS BAY, BETWEEN 1761 AND 1772, at 490 (1865) (reprinting the column and speculating that Otis had written it); *see also* Thomas Y. Davies, *Recovering the Original Fourth Amendment*, 98 MICH. L. REV. 547, 561 n.20 (1999) (surmising that Otis wrote the column).

19. Ronald J. Allen and Ross M. Rosenberg, *The Fourth Amendment and the Limits of Theory: Local Versus General Theoretical Knowledge*, 72 ST. JOHN'S L. REV. 1149, 1176–77 (1998).

20. 95 Eng. Rep. 807, 818 (C.P. 1765).

21. *Rabinowitz*, 339 U.S. at 70 (Frankfurter, J., dissenting).

22. Olmstead v. United States, 277 U.S. 438, 474 (1928) (Brandeis., J., dissenting) (quoting Otis's argument against writs of assistance).

23. Hon. M. Blane Michael, *Reading the Fourth Amendment: Guidance from the Mischief That Gave It Birth*, 85 N.Y.U. L. REV. 905, 921–22 (2010); *see also* Tracey Maclin, *The Central Meaning of the Fourth Amendment*, 35 WM. & MARY L. REV. 197, 229 (1993) ("The framers declared a broad principle about governmental power in guaranteeing freedom from unreasonable search and seizure. Under that broad principle, government authority and discretion would not go unchecked.").

24. Tracey Maclin, *The Central Meaning of the Fourth Amendment*, 35 WM. & MARY L. REV. 197, 213 (1993) (quoting Jacob W. Landynski, *In Search of Jus-*

tice Black's Fourth Amendment, 45 FORDHAM L. REV. 453, 462 (1976) (alteration added)). In a variation on this theme, Prof. Thomas Davies has contended that the Reasonableness Clause referred only to the inherent illegality of searches pursuant to general warrants, *see* Thomas Y. Davies, *Recovering the Original Fourth Amendment*, 98 MICH. L. REV. 547, 551 (1999), but that warrantless searches and arrests were understood as being regulated by the Due Process Clause of the Fifth Amendment, *see* Thomas Y. Davies, *Correcting Search-and-Seizure History: Now-Forgotten Common-Law Warrantless Arrest Standards and the Original Understanding of "Due Process of Law,"* 77 MISS. L.J. 1, 7–8 (2007). In another variation, Professor David Steinberg has asserted that the Fourth Amendment was intended to require warrants, but only with respect to searches of houses. *See* David E. Steinberg, *The Original Understanding of Unreasonable Searches and Seizures*, 56 FLA. L. REV. 1051, 1053 (2004) ("[T]he Fourth Amendment was intended to proscribe only a single, discrete activity—physical searches of houses pursuant to a general warrant, or no warrant at all.").

25. However, if a subsequent tort action were brought for false arrest, the defendant was required to introduce "evidence . . . that such fame had some probable ground." JAMES PARKER, CONDUCTOR GENERALIS: OR, THE OFFICE, DUTY AND AUTHORITY OF JUSTICES OF THE PEACE, HIGH-SHERIFFS, UNDER-SHERIFFS, CORONERS, CONSTABLES, GAOLERS, JURY-MEN, AND OVERSEERS OF THE POOR 26 (Woodbridge, James Parker 1764) (New Jersey).

26. Edward Hartnett, *A "Uniform and Entire" Constitution; Or, What if Madison Had Won?*, 15 CONST. COMMENT. 251, 252–53, 258–59 (1998); *see also* THE COMPLETE BILL OF RIGHTS: THE DRAFTS, DEBATES, SOURCES, AND ORIGINS 223 (Neil H. Cogan ed., 1997); Laura K. Donohue, *The Original Fourth Amendment*, 83 U. CHI. L. REV. 1181, 1301 (2016).

27. Akhil Reed Amar, *Foreword: Lord Camden Meets Federalism—Using State Constitutions to Counter Federal Abuses*, 27 RUTGERS L.J. 845, 849–50 (1996).

Chapter 2

1. *See* LEONARD LEVY, ORIGINS OF THE BILL OF RIGHTS 161 (1999) ("[T]he Wilkes cases filled the columns of American newspapers from Boston to Charleston."); Akhil Reed Amar, *Fourth Amendment First Principles*, 107 HARV. L. REV. 757, 772 (1994) (asserting that the Wilkes case "was *the* paradigm search and seizure case for Americans"). These cases are: Wilkes v. Halifax, 19 Howell's State Trials 1406 (C.P. 1769); Money v. Leach, 97 Eng. Rep. 1075 (K.B. 1765); Entick v. Carrington, 95 Eng. Rep. 807 (C.P. 1765); Beardmore v. Carrington, 95 Eng. Rep. 790 (C.P. 1764); Wilkes v. Wood, 98 Eng. Rep. 489 (C.P. 1763); and Huckle v. Money, 95 Eng. Rep. 768 (C.P. 1763). The term "Wilkesite cases" to describe them collectively appears to have been coined by Thomas Y. Davies, *Recovering the Original Fourth Amendment*, 98 MICH. L. REV. 547, 563 n.21 (1999). For a concise yet complete description of the background of the Wilkesite cases, *see* Laura K. Donohue, *The Original Fourth Amendment*, 83 U. CHI. L. REV. 1181, 1196–1207 (2016).

2. *See* LEONARD LEVY, ORIGINS OF THE BILL OF RIGHTS 159, 161 (1999). I calculated this amount using https://www.bankofengland.co.uk/monetary-policy/inflation/inflation-calculator and https://dollars2pounds.com/

3. 98 Eng. Rep. at 498–99. *See also Entick*, 95 Eng. Rep. at 818 (declaring the general warrant there "wholly illegal and void").

4. 97 Eng. Rep. at 1088.

5. 97 Eng. Rep. at 1088; *see also Entick*, 95 Eng. Rep. at 817 ("[W]e can safely say there is no law in this country to justify the defendants in what they have done. . . ."); *see also* LEONARD LEVY, ORIGINS OF THE BILL OF RIGHTS 161 (1999) (observing that "Parliament had often authorized searches and arrests on the basis of general warrants," but in the case of Wilkes and his cohorts "no act of Parliament was involved").

6. 98 Eng. Rep. at 490. Of course, Britain had no written constitution; the "constitution" referred to by Pratt meant the unwritten rules that were supposed to govern Parliament, the Crown, and the courts.

7. Laura K. Donohue, *The Original Fourth Amendment*, 83 U. CHI. L. REV. 1181, 1207–21 (2016).

8. LEONARD LEVY, ORIGINS OF THE BILL OF RIGHTS 163 (1999). *See also* Silas J. Wasserstrom, *The Incredible Shrinking Fourth Amendment*, 21 AM. CRIM. L. REV. 257, 286 n.157 (1984) ("Under a system of parliamentary supremacy, general warrants would have been valid if they were authorized by statute.").

9. 16 THE PARLIAMENTARY HISTORY OF ENGLAND, FROM THE EARLIEST PERIOD TO THE YEAR 1803, at 209–10 (1813).

10. *See* WILLIAM J. CUDDIHY, THE FOURTH AMENDMENT: ORIGINS AND ORIGINAL MEANING, 602–1791, at 623–33 (2009).

11. *But see* Akhil Reed Amar, *Fourth Amendment First Principles*, 107 HARV. L. REV. 757, 772 (1994) (asserting that the Wilkesite cases were more important). However, Amar seems later to have acknowledged, at least in part, the significance of the writs-of-assistance controversy in interpreting the Fourth Amendment. *See* Akhil Reed Amar, *The Fourth Amendment, Boston, and the Writs of Assistance*, 30 SUFFOLK U. L. REV. 53, 76–77 (1996) (acknowledging that the "later writs-of-assistance controversies" outside of Massachusetts after 1767 "were . . . more significant at the time than the 1761 Boston case").

12. 2 LEGAL PAPERS OF JOHN ADAMS 107 (L. Kinvin Wroth and Hiller B. Zobel eds., 1965) (quoting Letter from John Adams to William Tudor, Mar. 29, 1817).

13. JOSIAH QUINCY, JR., REPORTS OF CASES ARGUED AND ADJUDGED IN THE SUPREME COURT OF JUDICATURE OF THE PROVINCE OF MASSACHUSETTS BAY BETWEEN 1761 AND 1772, at 471 (1865) (deletion omitted); *see also* LEONARD LEVY, ORIGINS OF THE BILL OF RIGHTS 156 (1999).

14. 97 Eng. Rep. 1075, 1088 (K.B. 1765).

15. LEONARD LEVY, ORIGINS OF THE BILL OF RIGHTS 155 (1999).

16. *See* WILLIAM J. CUDDIHY, THE FOURTH AMENDMENT: ORIGINS AND ORIGINAL MEANING, 602–1791, at 386–94 (2009); *see also* LEONARD LEVY, ORI-

GINS OF THE BILL OF RIGHTS 157 (1999) ("Otis's argument compounded mistakes and misinterpretations.").

17. JOSIAH QUINCY, JR., REPORTS OF CASES ARGUED AND ADJUDGED IN THE SUPREME COURT OF JUDICATURE OF THE PROVINCE OF MASSACHUSETTS BAY BETWEEN 1761 AND 1772, at 493–94 (1865).

18. ANDREW E. TASLITZ, RECONSTRUCTING THE FOURTH AMENDMENT: A HISTORY OF SEARCH & SEIZURE, 1789–1868, at 29 (2006).

19. ANDREW E. TASLITZ, RECONSTRUCTING THE FOURTH AMENDMENT: A HISTORY OF SEARCH & SEIZURE, 1789–1868, at 4–5, 35 (2006).

20. WILLIAM J. CUDDIHY, THE FOURTH AMENDMENT: ORIGINS AND ORIGINAL MEANING, 602–1791, at 574 (2009); *see also* LEONARD LEVY, ORIGINS OF THE BILL OF RIGHTS 166 (1999).

21. ANDREW E. TASLITZ, RECONSTRUCTING THE FOURTH AMENDMENT: A HISTORY OF SEARCH & SEIZURE, 1789–1868, at 34 (2006).

22. ANDREW E. TASLITZ, RECONSTRUCTING THE FOURTH AMENDMENT: A HISTORY OF SEARCH & SEIZURE, 1789–1868, at 34–35 (2006).

23. LEONARD LEVY, ORIGINS OF THE BILL OF RIGHTS 172 (1999); ANDREW E. TASLITZ, RECONSTRUCTING THE FOURTH AMENDMENT: A HISTORY OF SEARCH & SEIZURE, 1789–1868, at 42 (2006).

24. ANDREW E. TASLITZ, RECONSTRUCTING THE FOURTH AMENDMENT: A HISTORY OF SEARCH & SEIZURE, 1789–1868, at 4 (2006).

25. WILLIAM J. CUDDIHY, THE FOURTH AMENDMENT: ORIGINS AND ORIGINAL MEANING, 602–1791, at 403 (2009). For the text of the bill, see JOSIAH QUINCY, JR., REPORTS OF CASES ARGUED AND ADJUDGED IN THE SUPREME COURT OF JUDICATURE OF THE PROVINCE OF MASSACHUSETTS BAY BETWEEN 1761 AND 1772, at 495–96 (1865).

26. WILLIAM J. CUDDIHY, THE FOURTH AMENDMENT: ORIGINS AND ORIGINAL MEANING, 602–1791, at 403–04 (2009).

27. *See* WILLIAM J. CUDDIHY, THE FOURTH AMENDMENT: ORIGINS AND ORIGINAL MEANING, 602–1791, at 513, 526 (2009); *accord* Joseph R. Frese, Writs of Assistance in the American Colonies: 1660–1776, at 246 (1951) (unpublished Ph.D. dissertation, Harvard University) (on file with author); *see also* O.M. Dickerson, *Writs of Assistance as a Cause of the Revolution*, *in* THE ERA OF THE AMERICAN REVOLUTION 40, 62 (Richard B. Morris ed., 1939) (observing that Maryland court expressed willingness to issue writ but not until the need arose in a particular case).

28. *See* WILLIAM J. CUDDIHY, THE FOURTH AMENDMENT: ORIGINS AND ORIGINAL MEANING, 602–1791, at 514, 524 (2009); O.M. Dickerson, *Writs of Assistance as a Cause of the Revolution*, *in* THE ERA OF THE AMERICAN REVOLUTION 40, 50–51 (Richard B. Morris ed., 1939).

29. *Accord* JOSIAH QUINCY, JR., REPORTS OF CASES ARGUED AND ADJUDGED IN THE SUPREME COURT OF JUDICATURE OF THE PROVINCE OF MASSACHUSETTS BAY BETWEEN 1761 AND 1772, at 501–04 (1865); O.M. Dickerson, *Writs of Assistance as a Cause of the Revolution*, *in* THE ERA OF THE AMERICAN REVOLUTION 40, 52–53 (Richard B. Morris ed., 1939); *see* WILLIAM J. CUDDIHY, THE FOURTH AMENDMENT: ORIGINS AND ORIGINAL MEANING, 602–1791, at 514–15 (2009); Joseph R.

Frese, Writs of Assistance in the American Colonies: 1660–1776, at 239–40 (1951) (unpublished Ph.D. dissertation, Harvard University) (on file with author).

30. *See* WILLIAM J. CUDDIHY, THE FOURTH AMENDMENT: ORIGINS AND ORIGINAL MEANING, 602–1791, at 515–16, 519–21, 525 (2009); O.M. Dickerson, *Writs of Assistance as a Cause of the Revolution*, *in* THE ERA OF THE AMERICAN REVOLUTION 40, 58–60 (Richard B. Morris ed., 1939); Joseph R. Frese, Writs of Assistance in the American Colonies: 1660–1776, at 264–68, 277, 286 (1951) (unpublished Ph.D. dissertation, Harvard University) (on file with author).

31. *See* WILLIAM J. CUDDIHY, THE FOURTH AMENDMENT: ORIGINS AND ORIGINAL MEANING, 602–1791, at 521–22, 525–26 (2009); O.M. Dickerson, *Writs of Assistance as a Cause of the Revolution*, *in* THE ERA OF THE AMERICAN REVOLUTION 40, 67–72 (Richard B. Morris ed., 1939). Both JOSIAH QUINCY, JR., REPORTS OF CASES ARGUED AND ADJUDGED IN THE SUPREME COURT OF JUDICATURE OF THE PROVINCE OF MASSACHUSETTS BAY BETWEEN 1761 AND 1772, at 510 & n.14 (1865), and Joseph R. Frese, Writs of Assistance in the American Colonies: 1660–1776, at 270 (1951) (unpublished Ph.D. dissertation, Harvard University) (on file with author), mistakenly referred to these as specific writs. However, an essential feature of a specific warrant is a "prior designation of a particular person or location to whom or which the warrant [i]s confined." WILLIAM J. CUDDIHY, THE FOURTH AMENDMENT: ORIGINS AND ORIGINAL MEANING, 602–1791, at 313 (2009). It is this essential feature that was lacking in the writs issued in Virginia pursuant to the Townshend Act. *See* Joseph R. Frese, Writs of Assistance in the American Colonies: 1660–1776, at 270 (1951) (unpublished Ph.D. dissertation, Harvard University) (on file with author) (quoting writ as permitting entry "into *any* House, Shop, Cellar, Warehouse or Room *or other place* where the said Goods are suspected to be concealed" (emphasis added)).

32. *See* Joseph R. Frese, Writs of Assistance in the American Colonies: 1660–1776, at 279 (1951) (unpublished Ph.D. dissertation, Harvard University) (on file with author); *see also* WILLIAM J. CUDDIHY, THE FOURTH AMENDMENT: ORIGINS AND ORIGINAL MEANING, 602–1791, at 523, 525 (2009); O.M. Dickerson, *Writs of Assistance as a Cause of the Revolution*, *in* THE ERA OF THE AMERICAN REVOLUTION 40, 65–66 (Richard B. Morris ed., 1939).

33. *See* WILLIAM J. CUDDIHY, THE FOURTH AMENDMENT: ORIGINS AND ORIGINAL MEANING, 602–1791, at 518, 524–25 (2009); O.M. Dickerson, *Writs of Assistance as a Cause of the Revolution*, *in* THE ERA OF THE AMERICAN REVOLUTION 40, 66–67 (Richard B. Morris ed., 1939); Thomas Y. Davies, *Can You Handle the Truth? The Framers Preserved Common-Law Criminal Arrest and Search Rules in "Due Process of Law"—"Fourth Amendment Reasonableness" Is Only a Modern, Destructive, Judicial Myth*, 43 TEX. TECH L. REV. 51, 88 (2010); Joseph R. Frese, Writs of Assistance in the American Colonies: 1660–1776, at 289 (1951) (unpublished Ph.D. dissertation, Harvard University) (on file with author).

34. *See* WILLIAM J. CUDDIHY, THE FOURTH AMENDMENT: ORIGINS AND ORIGINAL MEANING, 602–1791, at 513, 523, 526 (2009); O.M. Dickerson, *Writs of Assistance as a Cause of the Revolution*, *in* THE ERA OF THE AMERICAN REVOLUTION 40, 54, 58 (Richard B. Morris ed., 1939); Joseph R. Frese, Writs of Assistance in the

American Colonies: 1660–1776, at 263–64, 276–77, 285–86 (1951) (unpublished Ph.D. dissertation, Harvard University) (on file with author). JOSIAH QUINCY, JR., REPORTS OF CASES ARGUED AND ADJUDGED IN THE SUPREME COURT OF JUDICATURE OF THE PROVINCE OF MASSACHUSETTS BAY BETWEEN 1761 AND 1772, at 507–08, 511 n.15 (1865), first observed that writs were issued in New York, but later asserted that the writs in New York were issued as specific warrants. This latter assertion appears to be incorrect. The form of the writ issued in New York is reproduced in full in O.M. Dickerson, *Writs of Assistance as a Cause of the Revolution*, *in* THE ERA OF THE AMERICAN REVOLUTION 40, 54–55 (Richard B. Morris ed., 1939), and it is phrased as a general warrant. *See also* WILLIAM J. CUDDIHY, THE FOURTH AMENDMENT: ORIGINS AND ORIGINAL MEANING, 602–1791, at 513 (2009) (showing that the writs issued in New York were "phrased as general search warrants"). Moreover, the court's order, reproduced in Joseph R. Frese, Writs of Assistance in the American Colonies: 1660–1776, at 243 (1951) (unpublished Ph.D. dissertation, Harvard University) (on file with author), demonstrates the breadth of the authority granted:

> [Y]ou are hereby authorized . . . in the Day time to enter . . . *any* Ship Boat or other Vessell as also into *any* House Warehouse Shop Cellar or other place in this Colony . . . and to seize . . . *any* kind of Goods or Merchandizes whatsoever prohibited to be imported or Exported or whereof the Customs or other Duties have not been and shall not be duly paid. (emphasis added)

35. It is unclear whether writs were ever issued in New Jersey, but the preponderance of scholarly weight indicates that they were not. *Compare* WILLIAM J. CUDDIHY, THE FOURTH AMENDMENT: ORIGINS AND ORIGINAL MEANING, 602–1791, at 512 (2009) ("At least one writ of assistance . . . operated in New Jersey during the post-Townshend period."), *with* JOSIAH QUINCY, JR., REPORTS OF CASES ARGUED AND ADJUDGED IN THE SUPREME COURT OF JUDICATURE OF THE PROVINCE OF MASSACHUSETTS BAY BETWEEN 1761 AND 1772, at 508 (1865) ("[T]he records of the court [in New Jersey] which are in quite a perfect state, contain no evidence of any writs having been issued. . . ."), *and* O.M. Dickerson, *Writs of Assistance as a Cause of the Revolution*, *in* THE ERA OF THE AMERICAN REVOLUTION 40, 49 (Richard B. Morris ed., 1939) ("There is no evidence that writs were ever applied for in New Jersey. . . ."), *and* Joseph R. Frese, Writs of Assistance in the American Colonies: 1660–1776, at 244 (1951) (unpublished Ph.D. dissertation, Harvard University) (on file with author) ("We have no record of a general writ issued in New Jersey."). It appears that writs of assistance were not requested in the two remaining colonies, Delaware and North Carolina. *See* WILLIAM J. CUDDIHY, THE FOURTH AMENDMENT: ORIGINS AND ORIGINAL MEANING, 602–1791, at 511–12 (2009).

36. *See* Joseph R. Frese, Writs of Assistance in the American Colonies: 1660–1776, at 237–39 (1951) (unpublished Ph.D. dissertation, Harvard University) (on file with author); WILLIAM J. CUDDIHY, THE FOURTH AMENDMENT: ORIGINS AND ORIGINAL MEANING, 602–1791, at 514 (2009).

37. Joseph R. Frese, Writs of Assistance in the American Colonies: 1660–1776, at 242, 245, 269 (1951) (unpublished Ph.D. dissertation, Harvard University) (on file with author).

38. Joseph R. Frese, Writs of Assistance in the American Colonies: 1660–1776, at 259–60 (1951) (unpublished Ph.D. dissertation, Harvard University) (on file with author).

39. Andrew E. Taslitz, Reconstructing the Fourth Amendment: A History of Search & Seizure, 1789–1868, at 29, 58 (2006).

40. 24 J. Cont. Cong. 1774–1789, at 256, 256–57 (1783) *reprinted in* The Resolution of Congress of the 18th of April, 1783: Recommending the States to Invest Congress with the Power to Levy an Impost, for the Use of the States; and the Laws of the Respective States Passed in Pursuance of the Said Recommendation, Together with Remarks on the Resolutions of Congress, and Laws of the Different States 4 (1787) [hereinafter Impost Laws].

41. 24 J. Cont. Cong. 256, 256–59 (1783), *reprinted in* Impost Laws at 7, 10, 12–13, 30–31, 40, 42, 44–45, 48.

42. Impost Laws at 7, 10, 40, 44, 48 (emphasis omitted).

43. Impost Laws at 31.

44. Impost Laws at 13, 42 (Rhode Island: "any . . . other building"; North Carolina: "any other place").

45. Impost Laws at 13 (emphasis omitted).

46. Impost Laws at 42 (emphasis omitted).

47. Impost Laws at 32.

48. Impost Laws at 37.

49. *See* William J. Cuddihy, The Fourth Amendment: Origins and Original Meaning, 602–1791, at 663–64 (2009).

50. Impost Laws at 16 (emphasis omitted). Although general warrants were later deemed illegal in Connecticut, *see* Frisbie v. Butler, 1 Kirby 213 (Conn. 1787), ("[T]he warrant in the present case, being general, to search all places, and arrest all persons, the complainant should suspect, is clearly illegal. . . ."), at the time the Connecticut impost ratification legislation was adopted in May 1784, it appears that general warrants may still have been consistent with Connecticut law. *See* William J. Cuddihy, The Fourth Amendment: Origins and Original Meaning, 602–1791, at 644 (2009).

51. Impost Laws at 17–22.

52. In addition to those whose impost-ratifying legislation expressly required warrants issued only upon oath, both the Maryland and Delaware constitutions, incorporated by reference in those States' legislation, contained this requirement. *See* The Complete Bill of Rights: The Drafts, Debates, Sources, and Origins 234 (Neil H. Cogan ed., 1997).

53. *See* William J. Cuddihy, The Fourth Amendment: Origins and Original Meaning, 602–1791, at 747 (2009) ("Delaware's legislation after 1776 ignored [nighttime searches], neither allowing nor prohibiting.").

54. Impost Laws at 66–67 (determining that the New York legislation "so essentially varies from the system of impost recommended by the United States in Congress assembled on the 18th day of April, 1783, that the said act is not, and cannot be considered as a compliance with the same, so as to enable Congress, consistently with the acts of the other states to bring the system into operation").

55. Judiciary Act of 1789, ch. 20, § 33, 1 Stat. 73, 91 (1789) (emphasis added).

56. William J. Cuddihy, The Fourth Amendment: Origins and Original Meaning, 602–1791, at 753 (2009); *see also* Thomas Y. Davies, *Can You Handle the Truth? The Framers Preserved Common-Law Criminal Arrest and Search Rules in "Due Process of Law"—"Fourth Amendment Reasonableness" Is Only a Modern, Destructive, Judicial Myth*, 43 Tex. Tech L. Rev. 51, 104 (2010).

57. Militia Act of 1792, ch. 28, § 9, 1 Stat. 264, 265, (1792). Thomas Davies has set forth the claim that section 9 of the 1792 Militia Act did no more than confer upon federal marshals the power that local sheriffs had under common law "to call out a posse comitatus of citizens (that is, the local militia) to suppress riots or insurrections." *See* Thomas Y. Davies, *Recovering the Original Fourth Amendment*, 98 Mich. L. Rev. 547, 611 (1999); *see also* Thomas Y. Davies, *Correcting Search-and-Seizure History: Now-Forgotten Common-Law Warrantless Arrest Standards and the Original Meaning of Due Process of Law*, 77 Miss. L.J. 1, 157 n.491 (2007); Thomas Y. Davies, *The Fictional Character of Law-and-Order Originalism: A Case Study of the Distortions and Evasions of Framing-Era Arrest Doctrine in* Atwater *v.* Lago Vista, 37 Wake Forest L. Rev. 239, 355–56 (2002). However, the plain meaning of section 9 is that federal marshals and their deputies were granted "the same powers" as local law enforcement. This comprehends, but goes well beyond, the posse comitatus power. The Supreme Court has consistently interpreted this provision as granting federal officers *all* the law enforcement powers of a local sheriff. *See* United States v. Watson, 423 U.S. 411, 420 (1976); Atwater v. City of Lago Vista, 532 U.S. 318, 339 (2001). Scholars generally agree with this interpretation. *See, e.g.*, Akhil Reed Amar, *Fourth Amendment First Principles*, 107 Harv. L. Rev. 757, 764 (1994).

58. As discussed more fully later in this chapter, the 1789 Judiciary Act and the 1792 Militia Act are much more reflective of the limits placed on federal search and seizure authority by the Fourth Amendment than are the Collection Act of 1789 and the Excise Act of 1791. The latter two Acts, and particularly the 1791 Act, were highly partisan pieces of legislation representing the political dominance of the Federalists in Congress in the very early days of the Republic. As such, one cannot infer from these statutes any consensus view of the Fourth Amendment.

59. *See* Thomas Y. Davies, *Correcting Search-and-Seizure History: Now-Forgotten Common-Law Warrantless Arrest Standards and the Original Meaning of Due Process of Law*, 77 Miss. L.J. 1, 157 (2007); Thomas Y. Davies, *The Fictional Character of Law-and-Order Originalism: A Case Study of the Distortions and Evasions of Framing-Era Arrest Doctrine in* Atwater *v.* Lago Vista, 37 Wake Forest L. Rev. 239, 355 (2002).

60. This appears not to have been the case in North Carolina. *Compare* Fran-

cois X. Martin, The Office and Authority of a Justice of the Peace 280 (1791) ("A search warrant is a justice's order . . . directed to a lawful officer *or any indifferent person*, commanding him to search a house, or houses, therein particularly named, for stolen goods.") (emphasis added), *with* William W. Hening, The New Virginia Justice 403 (1795) (instructing that search warrants "ought to be directed to constable, and other public officers . . . and not to private persons. . . ."), *and* Eliphalet Ladd, Burn's Abridgement, or the American Justice; Containing the Whole Practice, Authority and Duty of Justices of the Peace 358 (2d ed. 1792) (Massachusetts, New Hampshire, and Vermont) (similar), *and* James Parker, The Conductor Generalis: Or, the Office, Duty and Authority of Justices of the Peace 324 (1792) (New Jersey, New York, and Pennsylvania) (similar), *and* The South-Carolina Justice of Peace 425 (1788) (similar).

61. Eliphalet Ladd, Burn's Abridgement, or the American Justice; Containing the Whole Practice, Authority and Duty of Justices of the Peace 40–41 (2d ed. 1792).

62. Eliphalet Ladd, Burn's Abridgement, or the American Justice; Containing the Whole Practice, Authority and Duty of Justices of the Peace 44 (2d ed. 1792); *accord* Akhil Reed Amar, *The Fourth Amendment, Boston, and the Writs of Assistance*, 30 Suffolk U. L. Rev. 53, 57 (1996). One might quibble that these provisions mention only "constables," while the 1792 Militia Act gives federal marshals the same powers as local "sheriffs." However, the sheriff was denominated as the "principal conservator of the peace" for the county. *See, e.g.*, Eliphalet Ladd, Burn's Abridgement, or the American Justice; Containing the Whole Practice, Authority and Duty of Justices of the Peace 384 (2d ed. 1792). As such, he could "apprehend . . . all persons who break the peace, or attempt to break it." Like all conservators of the peace, part of his duty was "in suppressing . . . affrays." 1 William Blackstone, Commentaries on the Laws of England 343, 354 (9th ed. 1783). Accordingly, sheriffs enjoyed the same power of halting affrays and arresting affrayers as did constables.

63. Eliphalet Ladd, Burn's Abridgement, or the American Justice; Containing the Whole Practice, Authority and Duty of Justices of the Peace 43 (2d ed. 1792); *see also* Akhil Reed Amar, *The Fourth Amendment, Boston, and the Writs of Assistance*, 30 Suffolk U. L. Rev. 53, 57 (1996). Again, while the manual uses the word "constable," sheriffs were undoubtedly entitled to the same justification. After all, the rationale behind allowing constables such a justification was that they could be punished if they refused to perform their duties while private persons had the authority to arrest but in most cases were not compelled to. But sheriffs, in this respect, were in the same position as constables. *See* Eliphalet Ladd, Burn's Abridgement, or the American Justice; Containing the Whole Practice, Authority and Duty of Justices of the Peace 41 (2d ed. 1792) ("The warrant is ordinarily directed to the *sheriff or constable*, and they are indictable, and subject thereupon to a fine and imprisonment, if they neglect or refuse it.") (emphasis added).

64. *See, e.g.*, Act of June 18, 1934, ch. 595, 48 Stat. 1008, 1008; Act of June 15, 1935, ch. 259, § 2, 49 Stat. 377, 378.

65. Act of July 31, 1789, ch. 5, § 24, 1 Stat. 29, 43 (1789).

66. Act of Aug. 4, 1790, ch. 35, § 31, 1 Stat. 145 (1790); *see also* Act of Feb. 18, 1793, ch. 8, § 27, 1 Stat. 305, 315 (1793).

67. Act of Mar. 3, 1791, ch. 15, § 29, 1 Stat. 199, 206 (1791).

68. *See, e.g.*, United States v. Villamonte-Marquez, 462 U.S. 579, 585 (1983) ("[T]he enactment of [a] statute by the same Congress that promulgated the . . . Bill of Rights gives the statute an impressive historical pedigree."); Boyd v. United States, 116 U.S. 616, 623 (1886) ("As [the Collection Act] was passed by the same congress which proposed for adoption the original amendments to the constitution, it is clear that the members of that body did not regard searches and seizures of this kind as 'unreasonable' . . . ."); WILLIAM J. CUDDIHY, THE FOURTH AMENDMENT: ORIGINS AND ORIGINAL MEANING, 602–1791, at 737–38 (2009) ("The Collection Act explicated the Fourth Amendment for both documents expressed the thoughts of the same persons upon the same subject at the same time."); Akhil Reed Amar, *The Fourth Amendment, Boston, and the Writs of Assistance*, 30 SUFFOLK U. L. REV. 53, 59 (1996) ("[H]istorical exceptions to a blanket requirement come from the First Congress—the same body that drafted the Fourth Amendment itself."); Fabio Arcila, Jr., *The Death of Suspicion*, 51 WM. & MARY L. REV. 1275, 1289–90 (2010) ("[N]umerous federal statutes from the Framers' era authoriz[ing] warrantless civil searches . . . evidence that neither the Framers nor other political leaders from their generation believed that a warrant was usually required for a valid search.").

69. 5 U.S. (1 Cranch) 137 (1803).

70. *See* Vasan Kesavan and Michael Stokes Paulsen, *The Interpretive Force of the Constitution's Secret Drafting History*, 91 GEO. L.J. 1113, 1170 (2003) (providing several other examples).

71. Lee v. Weisman, 505 U.S. 577, 626 (1992) (Souter, J., concurring).

72. In re Booth, 3 Wis. 1, 36 (1854) (opinion of Smith, J.), *rev'd sub nom* Ableman v. Booth, 62 U.S. (21 How.) 506 (1858).

73. Marsh v. Chambers, 463 U.S. 783, 815–16 (1983) (Brennan, J., dissenting) (footnotes and citations omitted).

74. Gerard V. Bradley, *The Constitutional Theory of the Fourth Amendment*, 38 DEPAUL L. REV. 817, 834–35 (1989).

75. Fabio Arcila, Jr., *The Death of Suspicion*, 51 WM. & MARY L. REV. 1275, 1302 (2010); *see also* WILLIAM J. CUDDIHY, THE FOURTH AMENDMENT: ORIGINS AND ORIGINAL MEANING, 602–1791, at 591 (2009).

76. Thomas Y. Davies, *Recovering the Original Fourth Amendment*, 98 MICH. L. REV. 547, 605–08 (1999).

77. Thomas Y. Davies, *Recovering the Original Fourth Amendment*, 98 MICH. L. REV. 547, 607 (1999).

78. Fabio Arcila, Jr., *The Death of Suspicion*, 51 WM. & MARY L. REV. 1275, 1308 (2010) (emphasis omitted).

79. FRANCIS WHARTON, STATE TRIALS OF THE UNITED STATES DURING THE ADMINISTRATIONS OF WASHINGTON AND ADAMS 102 (1849).

80. 1 Annals of Cong. 1844, 1846 (1791).

81. The Daily Advertiser, June 22, 1790, at 1; *see* Fabio Arcila, Jr., *The Death of Suspicion*, 51 Wm. & Mary L. Rev. 1275, 1308 n.117 (2010). These remarks do not appear in the Annals of Congress.

82. William J. Cuddihy, The Fourth Amendment: Origins and Original Meaning, 602–1791, at 743 (2009).

83. Francis Wharton, State Trials of the United States During the Administrations of Washington and Adams 102 (1849).

84. Francis Wharton, State Trials of the United States During the Administrations of Washington and Adams 102 (1849).

85. *Pittsburgh, Sept. 10*, Indep. Gazeteer, Sept. 24, 1791, at 3; *see* Fabio Arcila, Jr., *The Death of Suspicion*, 51 Wm. & Mary L. Rev. 1275, 1308–09 (2010).

86. *Extract from observations, in a North-Carolina paper "on the Assumption and Excise Laws,"* New York Daily Gazette, Feb. 2, 1793, at 3; *see* Fabio Arcila, Jr., *The Death of Suspicion*, 51 Wm. & Mary L. Rev. 1275, 1308 (2010).

87. Francis Wharton, State Trials of the United States During the Administrations of Washington and Adams 105, 110–17 (1849).

88. *See* John H. Aldrich and Ruth W. Grant, *The Antifederalists, the First Congress, and the First Parties*, 55 J. Pol. 295, 296, 313 (1993). *See also Lee*, 505 U.S. 577, 626 (1992) (Souter, J., concurring) ("[L]ike other politicians, [the framers] could raise constitutional ideals one day and turn their backs on them the next."); Ex Parte Bushnell, 9 Ohio St. 77, 257 (1859) (Sutliff, J., dissenting) (observing that the Second Congress was "of the same political character, and many of the same members, with a subsequent Congress which passed the acts respecting aliens and seditious persons" and whose "political views evidently inclined them to accord much larger powers to Congress than at a later period were claimed by their successors").

89. *See* John H. Aldrich and Ruth W. Grant, *The Antifederalists, the First Congress, and the First Parties*, 55 J. Pol. 295, 310 (1993) ("All of the major issues facing the First Congress had been anticipated before and during the ratification campaign, and they provoked arguments in the House along Federalist-antifederalist lines.").

90. John H. Aldrich and Ruth W. Grant, *The Antifederalists, the First Congress, and the First Parties*, 55 J. Pol. 295, 299–300 (1993) (observing that Anti-Federalists "formed a significant proportion of the opposition forces that Hamilton's supporters were barely able to defeat").

91. Tracey Maclin, *When the Cure for the Fourth Amendment Is Worse Than the Disease*, 68 S. Cal. L. Rev. 1, 11 (1994).

92. Judiciary Act of 1789, ch. 20, § 34, 1 Stat. 73, 92 (1789).

93. One might argue that the omission means nothing because the Fourth Amendment was not yet part of the Constitution when the Judiciary Act was enacted. However, the Judiciary Act went into effect on Sept. 24, 1789, and the Fourth Amendment was proposed by Congress the very next day. It is inconceivable that this incipient restriction on federal searches and seizures would not have been on the minds of legislators when it authorized federal seizures in section 33.

94. Thomas Y. Davies, *Recovering the Original Fourth Amendment*, 98 MICH. L. REV. 547, 661 (1999).

Chapter 3

1. Robin Brooks, *Alexander Hamilton, Melancton Smith, and the Ratification of the Constitution in New York*, 24 WM. & MARY Q. 339, 339 (1967).

2. *See* JACKSON TURNER MAIN, THE ANTIFEDERALISTS: CRITICS OF THE CONSTITUTION, 1781–1788, at 288 app. D (1961) (showing that initial votes in Massachusetts, New Hampshire, New York, and North Carolina were against ratification, while Virginia's convention was tied); Arthur E. Wilmarth, Jr., *The Original Purpose of the Bill of Rights: James Madison and the Founders' Search for a Workable Balance Between Federal and State Power*, 26 AM. CRIM. L. REV. 1261, 1288 (1989) (observing that Federalists were in the minority in Massachusetts, New Hampshire, New York, and Virginia); *see also* Laura K. Donohue, *The Original Fourth Amendment*, 83 U. CHI. L. REV. 1181, 1284 n.589 (2016) (observing that these five States, plus Pennsylvania and Rhode Island, were critical).

3. *See* Forrest McDonald, *The Anti-Federalists, 1781–1789*, *in* THE REINTERPRETATION OF THE AMERICAN REVOLUTION 1763–1789, at 365, 373 (Jack P. Greene ed., 1968); *see also* WILLIAM J. CUDDIHY, THE FOURTH AMENDMENT: ORIGINS AND ORIGINAL MEANING, 602–1791, at 702 (2009) ("The New York convention commenced with a huge majority of its members opposing the Constitution.").

4. WILLIAM J. CUDDIHY, THE FOURTH AMENDMENT: ORIGINS AND ORIGINAL MEANING, 602–1791, at 701 (2009); *accord* THE STATES RIGHTS DEBATE: ANTIFEDERALISM AND THE CONSTITUTION 91 (Alpheus Thomas Mason ed., 2d ed. 1972) (recounting that opponents of the Constitution in Massachusetts, including Samuel Adams and John Hancock, eventually assented on the condition that amendments be recommended).

5. WILLIAM J. CUDDIHY, THE FOURTH AMENDMENT: ORIGINS AND ORIGINAL MEANING, 602–1791, at 702 (2009).

6. WILLIAM J. CUDDIHY, THE FOURTH AMENDMENT: ORIGINS AND ORIGINAL MEANING, 602–1791, at 702 (2009); Laura K. Donohue, *The Original Fourth Amendment*, 83 U. CHI. L. REV. 1181, 1287 (2016); *accord* THE STATES RIGHTS DEBATE: ANTIFEDERALISM AND THE CONSTITUTION 92 (Alpheus Thomas Mason ed., 2d ed. 1972) (observing that when the ratification debate moved to Virginia, the advocates of ratification adopted "[t]he Massachusetts formula" of promising that amendments be recommended in exchange for ratification).

7. Laura K. Donohue, *The Original Fourth Amendment*, 83 U. CHI. L. REV. 1181, 1289 (2016) ("Had [New York and Virginia] not ratified the Constitution, the experiment would have failed. . . . About one quarter of the population lived in the two states. A lack of their presence would have threatened geographic continuity." (citation omitted)).

8. Richard B. Morris, *John Jay and the Adoption of the Federal Constitution in New York: A New Reading of Persons and Events*, 63 N.Y. HIST. 133, 149 (1982);

see also Linda Grant De Pauw, *E. Wilder Spaulding and New York History*, 49 N.Y. Hist. 142, 152 (1968) ("[T]he Antifederalist program [in New York] was not to reject the Constitution, but to adopt it with previous amendments."); David E. Narrett, *A Zeal for Liberty: The Antifederalist Case Against the Constitution in New York*, 69 N.Y. Hist. 285, 297 (1988) ("[M]ost Antifederalists [at the New York convention] favored the reform rather than the rejection of the Constitution.").

9. David E. Narrett, *A Zeal for Liberty: The Antifederalist Case Against the Constitution in New York*, 69 N.Y. Hist. 285, 291 (1988).

10. Robin Brooks, *Alexander Hamilton, Melancton Smith, and the Ratification of the Constitution in New York*, 24 Wm. & Mary Q. 339, 350 (1967).

11. David E. Narrett, *A Zeal for Liberty: The Antifederalist Case Against the Constitution in New York*, 69 N.Y. Hist. 285, 289 (1988); *see also* Robin Brooks, *Alexander Hamilton, Melancton Smith, and the Ratification of the Constitution in New York*, 24 Wm. & Mary Q. 339, 350 (1967).

12. Robin Brooks, *Alexander Hamilton, Melancton Smith, and the Ratification of the Constitution in New York*, 24 Wm. & Mary Q. 339, 339 (1967); *see also* Richard B. Morris, *John Jay and the Adoption of the Federal Constitution in New York: A New Reading of Persons and Events*, 63 N.Y. Hist. 133, 162 (1982); David E. Narrett, *A Zeal for Liberty: The Antifederalist Case Against the Constitution in New York*, 69 N.Y. Hist. 285, 289 (1988).

13. William J. Cuddihy, The Fourth Amendment: Origins and Original Meaning, 602–1791, at 705, 706 (2009); *accord* Richard E. Ellis, *The Persistence of Antifederalism After 1789*, *in* Beyond Confederation: Origins of the Constitution and American National Identity 295, 298 (Richard Beeman, Stephen Botein and Edward C. Carter II eds., 1987) (asserting that Madison "recognized that failure to amend the Constitution would fuel the movement for a second constitutional convention, which was in many ways a more dangerous alternative"); The States Rights Debate: Antifederalism and the Constitution 94–95 (Alpheus Thomas Mason ed., 2d ed. 1972) (discussing Madison's concern that a second convention would lead to crisis).

14. Linda Grant De Pauw, *E. Wilder Spaulding and New York History*, 49 N.Y. Hist. 142, 153 (1968).

15. The States Rights Debate: Antifederalism and the Constitution 96 (Alpheus Thomas Mason ed., 2d ed. 1972) (quoting Letter from James Madison to Thomas Jefferson (Mar. 29, 1789), *in* 15 The Papers of Thomas Jefferson 6–7 (Julian P. Boyd ed., 1958)) (internal quotation marks omitted). *See also* Speech of James Madison in the House of Representatives (June 8, 1789), reprinted in 1 The Founders' Constitution 480 (Philip B. Kurland and Ralph Lerner, eds. 1987) (advocating adoption of the Bill of Rights in part to appease "the great body of the people . . . who at present feel much inclined to join their support to the cause of federalism, if they were satisfied in this one point").

16. William J. Cuddihy, The Fourth Amendment: Origins and Original Meaning, 602–1791, at 704 (2009).

17. William J. Cuddihy, The Fourth Amendment: Origins and Original Meaning, 602–1791, at 706–07 (2009); *see also* Steven R. Boyd, The Poli-

TICS OF OPPOSITION: ANTIFEDERALISTS AND THE ACCEPTANCE OF THE CONSTITUTION 157–58 (1979) ("[D]uring the campaign for a seat in the House of Representatives, Madison pledged to work for prompt congressional amendment of the Constitution.").

18. *See* WILLIAM J. CUDDIHY, THE FOURTH AMENDMENT: ORIGINS AND ORIGINAL MEANING, 602–1791, at 704 (2009); *see also* THE STATES RIGHTS DEBATE: ANTIFEDERALISM AND THE CONSTITUTION 95 (Alpheus Thomas Mason ed., 2d ed. 1972) (discussing a letter from Madison to Jefferson "lamenting North Carolina's failure to ratify the Constitution"). North Carolina finally ratified in November 1789, after Madison had proposed the Bill of Rights in Congress. Less than a year earlier, North Carolina had voted against ratification 184 to 83. *See* Michael Lienesch, *North Carolina: Preserving Rights*, *in* RATIFYING THE CONSTITUTION 343, 363–64 (Michael Allen Gillespie and Michael Lienesch eds., 1989).

19. *See* Speech of James Madison in the House of Representatives (June 8, 1789), reprinted in 1 THE FOUNDERS' CONSTITUTION 480 (Philip B. Kurland and Ralph Lerner, eds. 1987) (proposing the Bill in part "to provide those securities for liberty which are required by . . . those two states who have not thought fit to throw themselves into the bosom of the confederacy").

20. WILLIAM J. CUDDIHY, THE FOURTH AMENDMENT: ORIGINS AND ORIGINAL MEANING, 602–1791, at 706 (2009).

21. Murray Dry, *The Anti-Federalists and the Constitution*, *in* PRINCIPLES OF THE CONSTITUTIONAL ORDER: THE RATIFICATION DEBATES 63, 80 (Robert L. Utley, Jr. ed., 1989). *See also* Hon. Andrew S. Oldham, *The Anti-Federalists: Past as Prologue*, 12 N.Y.U. J.L. & LIBERTY 451, 454–55 (2019) ("As numerous scholars have recognized, we owe our first 10 constitutional amendments to the Anti-Federalists.").

22. Saul A. Cornell, *The Changing Historical Fortunes of the Anti-Federalists*, 84 NW. U. L. REV. 39, 67 (1989); *see also* Robert G. Natelson, *The Original Meaning of the Establishment Clause*, 14 WM. & MARY BILL RTS. J. 73, 84–88 (2005) (discussing the "Gentlemen's Agreement" between the Federalists and moderate Anti-Federalists).

23. Aaron Zelinsky, *Misunderstanding the Anti-Federalist Papers: The Dangers of Availability*, 63 ALA. L. REV. 1067, 1080 (2012). *See, e.g.*, District of Columbia v. Heller, 554 U.S. 570, 598–99 (2008) (Second Amendment); Crawford v. Washington, 541 U.S. 36, 48–49 (2004) (Confrontation Clause); Blakely v. Washington, 542 U.S. 296, 306 (2004) (Jury Trial Clause); Minneapolis Star & Tribune Co. v. Minn. Comm'r of Revenue, 460 U.S. 575, 584 (1983) (Free Press Clause); Timbs v. Indiana, 139 S. Ct. 682, 695–96 (2019) (Thomas, J., concurring in the judgment) (Excessive Fines Clause); Maryland v. King, 569 U.S. 435, 467 (2013) (Scalia, J., joined by Ginsburg, Sotomayor, and Kagan, JJ., dissenting) (Fourth Amendment); United States v. Hubbell, 530 U.S. 27, 53 (2000) (Thomas, J., joined by Scalia, J., concurring) (Self-Incrimination Clause); McIntyre v. Ohio Elections Comm'n, 514 U.S. 334, 365–66 (1995) (Thomas J., concurring in the judgment) (Free Speech Clause). *See also* Gerics v. Trevino, 974 F.3d 798, 805 n.5 (6th Cir. 2020) ("Although

the Anti-Federalists obviously did not prevail on the ultimate question of whether the Constitution should be adopted, they did prevail on the question of whether there ought to be a Bill of Rights. So we look to their work for evidence on the original meaning of the Bill of Rights." (citation omitted)).

24. See Robert C. Palmer, *Liberties as Constitutional Provisions: 1776–1791*, *in* LIBERTY AND COMMUNITY: CONSTITUTION AND RIGHTS IN THE EARLY AMERICAN REPUBLIC 55, 105 (William E. Nelson and Robert C. Palmer eds., 1987) (footnote omitted).

25. Robert C. Palmer, *Liberties as Constitutional Provisions: 1776–1791*, *in* LIBERTY AND COMMUNITY: CONSTITUTION AND RIGHTS IN THE EARLY AMERICAN REPUBLIC 55, 115 (William E. Nelson & Robert C. Palmer eds., 1987); Harry N. Scheiber, *Federalism and the Constitution: The Original Understanding*, *in* AMERICAN LAW AND THE CONSTITUTIONAL ORDER: HISTORICAL PERSPECTIVES 85, 87 (Lawrence M. Friedman and Harry N. Scheiber eds., 1978); George C. Thomas III, *When Constitutional Worlds Collide: Resurrecting the Framers' Bill of Rights and Criminal Procedure*, 100 MICH. L. REV. 145, 180 (2001); Arthur E. Wilmarth, Jr., *The Original Purpose of the Bill of Rights: James Madison and the Founders' Search for a Workable Balance Between Federal and State Power*, 26 AM. CRIM. L. REV. 1261, 1281 (1989).

26. Eleven of the thirteen States—all but Connecticut and Rhode Island—had drafted new constitutions following independence. *See* Steven G. Calabresi, Sarah E. Agudo, and Kathryn L. Dore, *State Bills of Rights in 1787 and 1791: What Individual Rights Are Really Deeply Rooted in American History and Tradition?*, 85 S. CAL. L. REV. 1451, 1465 tbl.3 (2012). These constitutions guaranteed anywhere from nine (in South Carolina) to fifty (in New Hampshire) individual rights, with a median of thirty-five (in Delaware).

27. *See* THE STATES RIGHTS DEBATE: ANTIFEDERALISM AND THE CONSTITUTION 81 (Alpheus Thomas Mason ed., 2d ed. 1972) ("The combined effect of the supremacy clause and the necessary-and-proper clause seemed especially dangerous to the rights of the states and their citizens."); Harry N. Scheiber, *Federalism and the Constitution: The Original Understanding*, *in* AMERICAN LAW AND THE CONSTITUTIONAL ORDER: HISTORICAL PERSPECTIVES 85, 90 (Lawrence M. Friedman and Harry N. Scheiber eds., 1978) ("The means for . . . oppression were ready at hand in the Constitution: its supremacy clause would support nearly any attack on state sovereignty; [and] the necessary-and-proper and general-welfare clauses comprised practically unlimited writs of authority. . . ."); Herbert J. Storing, *What the Anti-Federalists Were* For, *in* 1 THE COMPLETE ANTI-FEDERALIST 3, 28 (Herbert J. Storing ed., 1981) ("The broad grants of power, taken together with the 'supremacy' and the 'necessary and proper' clauses, amounted, the Anti-Federalists contended, to an unlimited grant of power to the general government to do whatever it might choose to do.").

28. AKHIL REED AMAR, THE BILL OF RIGHTS: CREATION AND RECONSTRUCTION 128 (1998) ("[The] point is not that substantive rights are unimportant, but that these rights were intimately intertwined with structural considerations.");

Saul Cornell, The Other Founders: Anti-Federalism and the Dissenting Tradition in America, 1788–1828, at 6 (1999) ("Cast in modern terms, states' rights and individual rights were not antithetical in Anti-Federalist constitutionalism, but intimately bound together."); Michael Lienesch, *North Carolina: Preserving Rights*, *in* Ratifying the Constitution 343, 355 (Michael Allen Gillespie and Michael Lienesch, eds., 1989) ("For them, the rights of the people were inseparable from the rights of their states."); The States Rights Debate: Antifederalism and the Constitution 98 (Alpheus Thomas Mason ed., 2d ed. 1972) ("Spurring the Antifederalist campaign was the unshakeable conviction that the proposed Constitution would enthrone a consolidated government, thereby rendering *state* protection of individual rights insecure.").

29. George Mason, *Objections to the Constitution of Government Formed by the Convention* (1787), *reprinted in* 2 The Complete Anti-Federalist 11 (Herbert J. Storing ed., 1981).

30. Robert A. Rutland, *Framing and Ratifying the First Ten Amendments*, *in* The Framing and Ratification of the Constitution 305, 305 (Leonard W. Levy and Dennis J. Mahoney eds., 1987).

31. Saul Cornell, The Other Founders: Anti-Federalism and the Dissenting Tradition in America, 1788–1828, at 29 (1999).

32. George Mason, *Objections to the Constitution of Government Formed by the Convention* (1787), *reprinted in* 2 The Complete Anti-Federalist 11, 11 (Herbert J. Storing ed., 1981).

33. Pennsylvania and the Federal Constitution 1787–1788, at 287 (John Bach McMaster and Frederick D. Stone eds., 1888); *see also* Robert C. Palmer, *Liberties as Constitutional Provisions: 1776–1791*, *in* Liberty and Community: Constitution and Rights in the Early American Republic 55, 109 (William E. Nelson and Robert C. Palmer eds., 1987) (recounting fear of a minority of the Pennsylvania ratifying convention "that the federal government would absorb the states, and that the federal Constitution would supersede completely the rights specifications in state constitutions").

34. Letter of Centinel (Oct. 24, 1787), *reprinted in* 2 The Complete Anti-Federalist 143, 152 (Herbert J. Storing ed., 1981). This letter was among the most widely circulated Anti-Federalist tracts, having been reprinted eleven times during the ratification period. *See* Saul Cornell, The Other Founders: Anti-Federalism and the Dissenting Tradition in America, 1788–1828, at 46 (1999).

35. Patrick Henry, Speech in the Virginia State Ratifying Convention (June 16, 1788), *reprinted in* 5 The Complete Anti-Federalist 246, 247 (Herbert J. Storing ed., 1981).

36. 2 The Debates in the Several State Conventions on the Adoption of the Federal Constitution 401 (Jonathan Elliot ed., 1876).

37. Speech of James Wilson in the Pennsylvania Ratifying Convention (Dec. 4, 1787), reprinted in 1 The Founders' Constitution 454 (Philip B. Kurland and Ralph Lerner, eds. 1987).

38. Speech of James Wilson in the Pennsylvania Ratifying Convention (Nov. 28, 1787), reprinted in 1 THE FOUNDERS' CONSTITUTION 454 (Philip B. Kurland and Ralph Lerner, eds., 1987).

39. *See* THE FEDERALIST No. 84, at 445 (Alexander Hamilton) (George W. Carey and James McClellan eds., 2001) ("[A] minute detail of particular rights, is certainly far less applicable to a constitution like that under consideration, which is merely intended to regulate the general political interests of the nation, than to one which has the regulation of every species of personal and private concerns. * * * I go further, and affirm, that bills of rights . . . are not only unnecessary in the proposed constitution, but would even be dangerous. They would . . . afford a colourable pretext to claim more [powers] than were granted. For why declare that things shall not be done, which there is no power to do?"). *See also* THE STATES RIGHTS DEBATE: ANTIFEDERALISM AND THE CONSTITUTION 83 (Alpheus Thomas Mason ed., 2d ed. 1972); Arthur E. Wilmarth, Jr., *Elusive Foundation: John Marshall, James Wilson, and the Problem of Reconciling Popular Sovereignty and Natural Law Jurisprudence in the New Federal Republic*, 72 GEO. WASH. L. REV. 113, 171 (2003) (observing that Wilson's arguments were repeated by "Federalist leaders throughout the nation").

40. 2 THE RECORDS OF THE FEDERAL CONVENTION OF 1787, at 588 (Max Farrand ed., 1911).

41. 3 THE DEBATES IN THE SEVERAL STATE CONVENTIONS ON THE ADOPTION OF THE FEDERAL CONSTITUTION 468 (Jonathan Elliot ed., 1876) (emphasis added). Though Randolph, like Mason, had refused to sign the Constitution at the Constitutional Convention, he favored ratification in the Virginia ratifying convention.

42. Letter from Agrippa to the Massachusetts Convention (Feb. 5, 1788), *reprinted in* THE ESSENTIAL ANTI-FEDERALIST 54, 57 (W.B. Allen and Gordon Lloyd eds., 2d ed. 2002).

43. 2 THE DEBATES IN THE SEVERAL STATE CONVENTIONS ON THE ADOPTION OF THE FEDERAL CONSTITUTION 409–10 (Jonathan Elliot ed., 1876); *see* 1 THE DEBATES IN THE SEVERAL STATE CONVENTIONS ON THE ADOPTION OF THE FEDERAL CONSTITUTION 331 (Jonathan Elliot ed., 1876).

44. George Mason, *Objections to the Constitution of Government Formed by the Convention* (1787), *reprinted in* 2 THE COMPLETE ANTI-FEDERALIST 11 (Herbert J. Storing ed., 1981).

45. Laura K. Donohue, *The Original Fourth Amendment*, 83 U. CHI. L. REV. 1181, 1269–76 (2016).

46. Southern Pac. Co. v. Jensen, 244 U.S. 205, 222 (1917) (Holmes, J., dissenting).

47. Antonin Scalia, *Common-Law Courts in a Civil-Law System: The Role of United States Federal Courts in Interpreting the Constitution and Laws*, *in* A MATTER OF INTERPRETATION: FEDERAL COURTS AND THE LAW 3, 10 (Amy Gutmann ed., 1997).

48. U.S. Decl. of Ind., para. 2 (July 4, 1776) (emphasis added).

49. See David S. Bogen, *The Transformation of the Fourteenth Amendment: Reflec-*

tions from the Admission of Maryland's First Black Lawyers, 44 MD. L. REV. 939, 949–50 (1985) (footnotes omitted). *See also* Trisha Olson, *The Natural Law Foundation of the Privileges or Immunities Clause of the Fourteenth Amendment*, 48 ARK. L. REV. 347, 375 n.118 (1995) ("From the beginning of the Republic, two theories of state vied for dominance. Conflicting with republicanism which 'enshrined the law of a [sic] nature, [as] a rule of right and reason,' was a second theory of republicanism that asserted the will of the people was the source of law." (quoting ROBERT FERGUSON, LAW AND LETTERS IN AMERICAN CULTURE 278–79 (1984) (alteration in original))). An earlier commentator similarly wrote:

> In the speculations of political philosophy the claim may be made that rights are not dependent upon constitutions and laws; that all men are endowed by their Creator with certain inalienable rights . . . ; but unfortunately it remains true, that to secure these rights governments must be instituted among men. . . .

Charles R. Pence, *The Construction of the Fourteenth Amendment*, 25 AM. L. REV. 536, 546 (1891).

50. *See* David S. Bogen, *The Transformation of the Fourteenth Amendment: Reflections from the Admission of Maryland's First Black Lawyers*, 44 MD. L. REV. 939, 950 (1985).

51. 2 THE DEBATES IN THE SEVERAL STATE CONVENTIONS ON THE ADOPTION OF THE FEDERAL CONSTITUTION 162 (Jonathan Elliot ed., 1876).

52. AKHIL REED AMAR, THE BILL OF RIGHTS: CREATION AND RECONSTRUCTION 152 (1998).

53. David A. Sklansky, *The Fourth Amendment and Common Law*, 100 COLUM. L. REV. 1739, 1788 (2000). *See also* Bernadette Meyler, *Towards a Common Law Originalism*, 59 STAN. L. REV. 551, 557 (2006) ("A certain self-consciousness . . . characterized common law jurisprudence of the seventeenth and eighteenth centuries, a self-consciousness that undermines the view . . . that we became aware only with the legal realists that judges made rather than discovered law."); Trisha Olson, *The Natural Law Foundation of the Privileges or Immunities Clause of the Fourteenth Amendment*, 48 ARK. L. REV. 347, 375 n.118 (1995) ("Positivism . . . had a strong hold during the founding.").

54. AKHIL REED AMAR, THE BILL OF RIGHTS: CREATION AND RECONSTRUCTION 152–53 (1998). Amar refers to the legal classic, Wesley Newcomb Hohfeld, *Some Fundamental Legal Conceptions as Applied in Judicial Reasoning*, 23 YALE L.J. 16 (1913).

55. Thomas B. McAffee, *The Original Meaning of the Ninth Amendment*, 90 COLUM. L. REV. 1215, 1273 (1990) ("Antifederalists, while believing in natural rights, were also hardheaded realists when it came to the issue of securing inalienable rights in law. . . .").

56. *See* RANDY E. BARNETT AND EVAN D. BERNICK, THE ORIGINAL MEANING OF THE 14TH AMENDMENT: ITS LETTER AND SPIRIT 49 (2021) (noting the founding-era idea that "British law 'regards, asserts, and preserves' by tried-and-true positive-law guarantees, natural rights that [we]re neglected by the positive law of 'most other countries of the world'"). *See also* 1 BLACKSTONE, COMMENTAR-

IES ON THE LAWS OF ENGLAND 126–27 (9th ed. 1783) (contrasting Britain, where civil liberties "flourish in their highest vigour . . . fall[ing] little short of perfection," with the "[v]ery different . . . modern constitutions of other states, on the continent of Europe . . . which in general are calculated to vest an arbitrary and despotic power, of controlling the actions of the subject, in the prince, or in a few grandees").

57. George Mason, *Objections to the Constitution of Government Formed by the Convention* (1787), *reprinted in* 2 THE COMPLETE ANTI-FEDERALIST 11 (Herbert J. Storing ed., 1981) (emphasis added); *see also* THE STATES RIGHTS DEBATE: ANTIFEDERALISM AND THE CONSTITUTION 89 (Alpheus Thomas Mason ed., 2d ed. 1972) (observing that Anti-Federalists believed that "common law rights stood on no higher law foundation [and] were inherently subject to legislative alteration").

58. Essay by A [Maryland] Farmer No. I (Feb. 15, 1788), *reprinted in* 5 THE COMPLETE ANTI-FEDERALIST 9, 13 (Herbert J. Storing ed., 1981) (emphasis added).

59. Herbert J. Storing, *Commentary to Essays by A Farmer*, 5 THE COMPLETE ANTI-FEDERALIST 3, 70 n.8 (Herbert J. Storing ed., 1981) (internal quotation marks omitted).

60. United States v. Worrall, 2 U.S. (2 Dall.) 384 (1798).

61. FRANCIS WHARTON, STATE TRIALS OF THE UNITED STATES DURING THE ADMINISTRATIONS OF WASHINGTON AND ADAMS 197 (1849); *see also* 1 WILLIAM E. NELSON, THE COMMON LAW IN COLONIAL AMERICA: THE CHESAPEAKE AND NEW ENGLAND, 1607–1660, at 129–31 (2008) (observing that, by 1660, significant differences had emerged between the New England and Chesapeake colonies regarding the reception of English common law); Julius Goebel, Jr., Ex Parte *Clio*, 54 COLUM. L. REV. 450, 464–65 (1954) (documenting "some very bold and drastic divagations from the common law practice [that] were pursued" in the colonies); Henry Paul Monaghan, *Supremacy Clause Textualism*, 110 COLUM. L. REV. 731, 774 (2010) ("Americans understood that the common law varied from state to state, and Republicans in particular thought that there was no room for a national common law. . . ." (footnote omitted)).

62. 8 ANNALS OF CONG. 2137 (1798).

63. Letter from Thomas Jefferson to Edmund Randolph (Aug. 18, 1799), reprinted in 4 THE WRITINGS OF THOMAS JEFFERSON 301, 301–02 (H.A. Washington ed. 1859).

64. Letter from Thomas Jefferson to Gideon Granger (Aug. 13, 1800), reprinted in PROCEEDINGS OF THE MASSACHUSETTS HISTORICAL SOCIETY 1871–1873, at 138 (1873).

65. Instruction from the General Assembly of Virginia to the Senators from that State in Congress (Jan. 11, 1800), reprinted in PETER S. DU PONCEAU, A DISSERTATION ON THE NATURE AND EXTENT OF THE JURISDICTION OF THE COURTS OF THE UNITED STATES 225 (1824).

66. *Mr. Madison's Report on the Virginia Resolutions*, *reprinted in* THE VIRGINIA AND KENTUCKY RESOLUTIONS OF 1798 AND '99, at 21, 31 (Washington, Jonathan Elliot 1832).

67. Arthur E. Wilmarth, Jr., *Elusive Foundation: John Marshall, James Wilson, and the Problem of Reconciling Popular Sovereignty and Natural Law Jurisprudence in the New Federal Republic*, 72 GEO. WASH. L. REV. 113, 187 (2003).

68. *See* Stewart Jay, *Origins of Federal Common Law: Part One*, 133 U. PA. L. REV. 1003, 1101 (1985) ("Republicans could point to wide discrepancies among the various states with respect to the content of their common law, a consequence of the divergent conditions in the respective jurisdictions and the fact that the colonies were settled at differing times when English common law itself was changing.").

69. 1 ST. GEORGE TUCKER, BLACKSTONE'S COMMENTARIES: WITH NOTES OF REFERENCE, TO THE CONSTITUTION AND LAWS, OF THE FEDERAL GOVERNMENT OF THE UNITED STATES; AND OF THE COMMONWEALTH OF VIRGINIA 405 (1803) (emphasis omitted).

70. *United States v. Hudson*, 11 U.S. (7 Cranch) 32, 33 (1812).

71. David A. Sklansky, *The Fourth Amendment and Common Law*, 100 COLUM. L. REV. 1739, 1788 (2000) (quoting Charles W. Wolfram, *The Constitutional History of the Seventh Amendment*, 57 MINN. L. REV. 639, 736 (1973)).

72. *See* TRIAL OF WILLIAM BUTLER FOR PIRACY 24 (1813) ("[T]he adoption of the Common Law, depended upon the voluntary act of the legislative power of the several States, as much as the passage of any positive law.").

73. Letter from The Federal Farmer (Oct. 12, 1787), *reprinted in* 2 THE COMPLETE ANTI-FEDERALIST 245, 249 (Herbert J. Storing ed., 1981); *see also* Thomas K. Clancy, *The Framers' Intent: John Adams, His Era, and the Fourth Amendment*, 86 IND. L.J. 979, 1040 (2011) ("[A] significant focus was . . . on general warrants.").

74. WILLIAM J. CUDDIHY, THE FOURTH AMENDMENT: ORIGINS AND ORIGINAL MEANING, 602–1791, at 690 (2009); *see also* Thomas K. Clancy, *The Framers' Intent: John Adams, His Era, and the Fourth Amendment*, 86 IND. L.J. 979, 1032 (2011) ("Some have claimed that the commentary addressed solely a concern with general warrants. The historical record, however, does not support that view." (footnote omitted)).

75. Essay by A [Maryland] Farmer No. I, *reprinted in* 5 THE COMPLETE ANTI-FEDERALIST 9, 13–14 (Herbert J. Storing ed., 1981).

76. 3 THE DEBATES IN THE SEVERAL STATE CONVENTIONS ON THE ADOPTION OF THE FEDERAL CONSTITUTION 58 (Jonathan Elliot ed., 1876).

77. *See* Michael J.Z. Mannheimer, *Self-Government, the Federal Death Penalty, and the Unusual Case of Michael Jacques*, 36 VT. L. REV. 131, 148–55 (2011) (exploring Anti-Federalist view of accountability deficits flowing from a large-scale Republic).

78. 3 THE DEBATES IN THE SEVERAL STATE CONVENTIONS ON THE ADOPTION OF THE FEDERAL CONSTITUTION 57 (Jonathan Elliot ed., 1876).

79. 3 THE DEBATES IN THE SEVERAL STATE CONVENTIONS ON THE ADOPTION OF THE FEDERAL CONSTITUTION 412 (Jonathan Elliot ed., 1876).

80. 3 THE DEBATES IN THE SEVERAL STATE CONVENTIONS ON THE ADOPTION OF THE FEDERAL CONSTITUTION 58 (Jonathan Elliot ed., 1876) (emphasis added).

81. John DeWitt, Essay to the Free Citizens of the Commonwealth of Mas-

sachusetts No. IV (Dec. 1787), *reprinted in* 4 THE COMPLETE ANTI-FEDERALIST 29, 33 (Herbert J. Storing ed., 1981) (emphasis added).

82. Coke reproduced this provision as follows: "No Freeman shall be taken or imprisoned, or be disseised of his Freehold, or Liberties, or free Customs, or be outlawed, or exiled, or any other wise destroyed; nor will We not pass upon him,nor condemn him,but by lawful judgment of his Peers, or by the Law of the Land" (2 THE SELECTED WRITINGS OF SIR EDWARD COKE 848 (Steve Sheppard ed. 2003)).

83. Letter from The Federal Farmer (Jan. 20, 1788), *reprinted in* 2 THE COMPLETE ANTI-FEDERALIST 323, 328 (Herbert J. Storing ed., 1981) (emphasis added). The Federal Farmer's essays have been described as "[t]he best known of the Antifederalist pamphlets," "[a]mong the most important writings published by Antifederalists in the contest over ratification," and "a key resource for the Constitution's opponents." Robert H. Webking, *Melancton Smith and the* Letters from the Federal Farmer, 44 WM. & MARY Q. 510, 510 (1987).

84. *See, e.g.*, THE BODY OF LIBERTIES OF 1641, *reprinted in* THE COLONIAL LAWS OF MASSACHUSETTS 33 (William H. Whitmore ed., 1889) ("expresse law of the Country"); THE CHARTER OF LIBERTYES AND PRIVILEDGES GRANTED BY HIS ROYALL HIGHNESSE TO THE INHABITANTS OF NEW YORKE AND ITS DEPENDENCYES (Oct. 30, 1683), *reprinted in* 1 THE COLONIAL LAWS OF NEW YORK: YEAR 1664 TO THE REVOLUTION 111, 113 (James B. Lyon ed., 1894) ("the Law of this province"); AN ACT DECLARING WHAT ARE THE RIGHTS AND PRIVILEDGES, OF HIS MAJESTY'S SUBJECTS, INHABITING WITHIN THIS PROVINCE OF EAST NEW JERSEY (1698), *reprinted in* AARON LEAMING AND JACOB SPICER, THE GRANTS, CONCESSIONS, AND ORIGINAL CONSTITUTIONS OF THE PROVINCE OF NEW JERSEY 368, 371 (Philadelphia, W. Bradford, 1881) (same); Act of Nov. 27, 1700, ch. 19, § 1, 1700 Pa. Stat. 18, ("the laws of this province and territories thereof"). *See* Ryan C. Williams, *The One and Only Substantive Due Process Clause*, 120 YALE L.J. 408, 435 (2010) ("For the most part, these enactments . . . paraphrased 'law of the land' to refer specifically to the duly enacted law of the colony itself.").

85. Ryan C. Williams, *The One and Only Substantive Due Process Clause*, 120 YALE L.J. 408, 439 (2010).

86. *See* Robert H. Webking, *Melancton Smith and the* Letters from the Federal Farmer, 44 WM. & MARY Q. 510, 511 (1987); Gordon S. Wood, *The Authorship of the* Letters from the Federal Farmer, 31 WM. & MARY Q. 299 (1974). *But see* David E. Narrett, *A Zeal for Liberty: The Antifederalist Case Against the Constitution in New York*, 69 N.Y. HIST. 285, 291 n.9 (1988) (expressing skepticism that Smith was "Federal Farmer").

87. 95 Eng. Rep. 807 (K.B. 1765). *See also* Akhil Reed Amar, *Fourth Amendment First Principles*, 107 HARV. L. REV. 757, 782 (1994) (asserting that a warrant issued on probable cause "justified searches only for items akin to contraband or stolen goods, not 'mere evidence'").

88. *See* WILLIAM J. CUDDIHY, THE FOURTH AMENDMENT: ORIGINS AND ORIGINAL MEANING, 602–1791, at 363 (2009); Tracey Maclin, *The Central Meaning of the Fourth Amendment*, 35 WM. & MARY L. REV. 197, 219 (1993); *see also* WILLIAM

J. Cuddihy, The Fourth Amendment: Origins and Original Meaning, 602–1791, at 683 (2009) (explaining that Henry was concerned about federal excisemen searching "without warrant").

89. *See* Tracey Maclin, *The Central Meaning of the Fourth Amendment*, 35 Wm. & Mary L. Rev. 197, 222–23 (1993).

90. *See* Saul Cornell, The Other Founders: Anti-Federalism and the Dissenting Tradition in America, 1788–1828, at 31 (1999).

91. 3 The Debates in the Several State Conventions on the Adoption of the Federal Constitution 58 (Jonathan Elliot ed., 1876).

92. Gerard V. Bradley, *The Constitutional Theory of the Fourth Amendment*, 38 DePaul L. Rev. 817, 862 (1989).

93. *See* Akhil Reed Amar, *Fourth Amendment First Principles*, 107 Harv. L. Rev. 757, 818 (1994) (observing that local juries are optimally situated "to decide, in any given situation, whom it fears more, the cops or the robbers," and that "[t]his judgment . . . will vary from place to place and over time").

Chapter 4

1. *See* Brendlin v. California, 551 U.S. 249, 254–55 (2007).

2. *See* Katz v. United States, 389 U.S. 347, 360 (1967) (Harlan, J. concurring).

3. Georgia v. Randolph, 547 U.S. 103, 121 (2006).

4. 277 U.S. 438, 464 (1928).

5. 316 U.S. 129 (1942).

6. 365 U.S. 505 (1961).

7. 365 U.S. at 505–07, 509, 510–11.

8. 277 U.S. at 474 (Brandeis, J., dissenting).

9. 389 U.S. at 352.

10. 389 U.S. at 361 (Harlan, J., concurring).

11. United States v. Miller, 425 U.S. 435, 442 (1976); United States v. White, 401 U.S. 745, 752 (1971) (plurality opinion).

12. 565 U.S. 400, 402–03 & n.1 (2012). Although agents had obtained a warrant, they did not comply with its terms in attaching the device, so the Government argued that the attachment and subsequent monitoring did not require a warrant at all because this conduct did not amount to a Fourth Amendment search.

13. 565 U.S. at 404 (majority opinion); *see also* 565 U.S. at 406–07 n.3 (holding that a search occurs "[w]here . . . the Government obtains information by physically intruding on a constitutionally protected area"); 565 U.S. at 414 (Sotomayor, J., concurring) ("When the government physically invades personal property to gather information, a search occurs.").

14. 565 U.S. at 409 (majority opinion).

15. Florida v. Jardines, 569 U.S. 1, 6, 8, 9 (2013) (quoting Kentucky v. King, 563 U.S. 452, 469 (2011)).

16. *See* Orin S. Kerr, *The Curious History of Fourth Amendment Searches*, 2012 Sup. Ct. Rev. 1, 82–83.

17. 365 U.S. at 511–12. *See also* 365 U.S. at 513 (Douglas, J., concurring) ("Our concern should not be with the trivialities of the local law of trespass, as the opinion of the Court indicates.").

18. 343 U.S. 747, 751–52 (1952).

19. *See generally* Laurent Sacharoff, *Constitutional Trespass*, 81 TENN. L. REV. 877 (2014).

20. 486 U.S. 35, 37–43 (1988).

21. 533 U.S. 27 (2001).

22. Rakas v. Illinois, 439 U.S. 128, 143 n.12 (1978). *See also* Robbins v. California, 453 U.S. 420, 428 (1981) ("Expectations of privacy are established by general social norms. . . .").

23. Georgia v. Randolph, 547 U.S. 103, 111, 120–21 (2006). Randolph is a case about third-party consent, where the question is whether one person's consent to search a shared premises is binding on the co-occupants. Such cases indisputably involve Fourth Amendment searches, but they share a methodology with the "search" cases, relying on social norms and understandings. *See* 547 U.S. at 112–13 (observing that expectations of privacy help determine consent).

24. Jeffrey Bellin, *Fourth Amendment Textualism*, 118 MICH. L. REV. 233, 238 (2019); *see also* Akhil Reed Amar, *Fourth Amendment First Principles*, 107 HARV. L. REV. 757, 769 (1994) ("A search is a search, whether with Raybans or x-rays.").

25. Minnesota v. Carter, 525 U.S. 83, 97 (1998) (Scalia, J., concurring) ("[T]hat self-indulgent test . . . has no plausible foundation in the text of the Fourth Amendment."); *see also* Carpenter v. United States, 138 S. Ct. 2206, 2236 (2018) (Thomas, J., dissenting) ("The *Katz* test has no basis in the text or history of the Fourth Amendment.").

26. Kyllo v. United States, 533 U.S. 27, 34 (2001) (Scalia, J.) ("The *Katz* test . . . has often been criticized as circular, and hence subjective and unpredictable."); *see also Carpenter*, 138 S. Ct. at 2245 (Thomas, J., dissenting) (observing that viewing the *Katz* test as descriptive "risks 'circular[ity]'" (quoting *Kyllo*, 533 U.S. at 34 (alteration in original))).

27. *Carter*, 525 U.S. at 97 (Scalia, J., concurring) ("[T]he only thing the past three decades have established about the *Katz* test . . . is that, unsurprisingly, those 'actual (subjective) expectation[s] of privacy' 'that society is prepared to recognize as "reasonable"' bear an uncanny resemblance to those expectations of privacy that this Court considers reasonable." (citation omitted) (alteration in original)); *see also Carpenter*, 138 S. Ct. at 2246 (Thomas, J., dissenting) ("[T]his Court's precedents . . . bear the hallmarks of subjective policymaking instead of neutral legal decisionmaking."); 138 S. Ct. at 2256 (Gorsuch, J., dissenting) (asserting that legislators are better able than judges to discern what expectations of privacy are reasonable).

28. *See Carter*, 525 U.S. at 97–98 (Scalia, J., concurring) (citations omitted).

29. JERRY L. MASHAW, CREATING THE ADMINISTRATIVE CONSTITUTION: THE LOST ONE HUNDRED YEARS OF AMERICAN ADMINISTRATIVE LAW 76 (2012); *see also* William Baude & James Y. Stern, *The Positive Law Model of the Fourth Amendment*, 129 HARV. L. REV. 1821, 1840 (2016) ("At the time it was ratified, the only

way to enforce rights against unlawful searches and seizures was through private law remedies, such as . . . trespass and false imprisonment actions. . . .").

30. JERRY L. MASHAW, CREATING THE ADMINISTRATIVE CONSTITUTION: THE LOST ONE HUNDRED YEARS OF AMERICAN ADMINISTRATIVE LAW 66 (2012).

31. Kyllo v. United States, 533 U.S. 27, 40 (2001).

32. *Randolph*, 547 U.S. at 144 (Scalia, J., dissenting).

33. *See* 1 F. A. HAYEK, LAW, LEGISLATION AND LIBERTY 88, 95 (1973).

34. CARLTON K. ALLEN, LAW IN THE MAKING 28 (2d ed. 1930).

35. *See* R.H. Helmholz, *Christopher St. German and the Law of Custom*, 70 U. CHI. L. REV. 129, 131 (2003) (quoting 1 THE DIGEST OF JUSTINIAN 13 (Theodor Mommsen, Paul Krueger, & Alan Watson eds., 1985) (translation of *Digestum Justiniani* 1.3.32)).

36. HENRY DE BRACTON, ON THE LAWS AND CUSTOMS OF ENGLAND (1250); RANULF DE GLANVILL, THE TREATISE ON THE LAWS AND CUSTOMS OF THE KINGDOM OF ENGLAND (1189). *See also* E.K. Braybrooke, *Custom as a Source of English Law*, 50 MICH. L. REV. 71, 72 (1951) (discussing Bracton); R.H. Helmholz, *Christopher St. German and the Law of Custom*, 70 U. CHI. L. REV. 129, 134 (2003) (discussing Bracton and Glanvill); Albert Kiralfy, *Custom in Mediaeval English Law*, 9 J. LEG. HIST. 26, 27 (1988) (discussing Bracton); Gerard J. Postema, *Classical Common Law Jurisprudence (Part I)*, 2 OXFORD U. COMMONWEALTH L.J. 155, 168 (2002) (discussing Bracton and Glanvill).

37. *See* R.H. Helmholz, *Christopher St. German and the Law of Custom*, 70 U. CHI. L. REV. 129, 134 (2003) ("What St. German described as 'general customs of old time used throughout all the realm, which have been accepted and approved by [the English Kings] and all their subjects' were for him an immediate source of English law.") (quoting ST. GERMAN'S DOCTOR AND STUDENT 45 (T.F.T. Plucknett & J.L. Barton eds., 1974) (alteration in original)).

38. *See* Harold J. Berman, *The Origins of Historical Jurisprudence: Coke, Selden, Hale*, 103 YALE L.J. 1651, 1686 (1994).

39. Harold J. Berman, *The Origins of Historical Jurisprudence: Coke, Selden, Hale*, 103 YALE L.J. 1651, 1687 (1994); Gerard J. Postema, *Classical Common Law Jurisprudence (Part I)*, 2 OXFORD U. COMMONWEALTH L.J. 155, 169 (2002) (observing that Coke "put the notion of immemorial usage at the centre of [his] conception of common law" (emphasis omitted)); *see also* Gerard J. Postema, *Classical Common Law Jurisprudence (Part II)*, 3 OXFORD U. COMMONWEALTH L.J. 1, 21 (2003) ("[T]he history to which Coke and others like him appealed bordered on the mythological.").

40. Harold J. Berman, *The Origins of Historical Jurisprudence: Coke, Selden, Hale*, 103 YALE L.J. 1651, 1695 (1994); *see also* Gerard J. Postema, *Classical Common Law Jurisprudence (Part I)*, 2 OXFORD U. COMMONWEALTH L.J. 155, 173 (2002) ("Selden showed through painstaking historical research that English law had gone through vast changes. . . ."). *See* MATTHEW HALE, THE HISTORY OF THE COMMON LAW OF ENGLAND 2 (3d ed. 1739).

41. 1 WILLIAM BLACKSTONE, COMMENTARIES ON THE LAWS OF ENGLAND 67, 68, 73 (9th ed. 1783).

42. Carol Rose, *The Comedy of the Commons: Custom, Commerce and Inherently Public Property*, 53 U. CHI. L. REV. 711, 742 (1986). *See, e.g.*, THEODORE F.T. PLUCKNETT, A CONCISE HISTORY OF THE COMMON LAW 307 (5th ed. 1956) ("[T]he principal element in most legal systems was custom."); FREDERICK POLLOCK, A FIRST BOOK OF JURISPRUDENCE FOR STUDENTS OF THE COMMON LAW 280 (3d ed. 1911) ("Another use of the term 'custom' is to denote rules that once formed an exceptional body of law, but have been adopted within historical times as part of the Common Law.").

43. 1 WILLIAM BLACKSTONE, COMMENTARIES ON THE LAWS OF ENGLAND 64, 67 (9th ed. 1783).

44. 2 THE SELECTED WRITINGS OF SIR EDWARD COKE 701 (Steve Sheppard ed. 2003).

45. Gerard J. Postema, *Classical Common Law Jurisprudence (Part I)*, 2 OXFORD U. COMMONWEALTH L.J. 155, 170 (2002). *See also* Harold J. Berman, *The Origins of Historical Jurisprudence: Coke, Selden, Hale*, 103 YALE L.J. 1651, 1692 (1994) ("[T]he artificial reason of the English common law was the unique reason, logic, sense, and purposes of the historically rooted law of the English nation, a repository of the thinking and experience of the English common lawyers over many centuries.").

46. 2 THE SELECTED WRITINGS OF SIR EDWARD COKE 701 (Steve Sheppard ed. 2003).

47. Gerard J. Postema, *Classical Common Law Jurisprudence (Part II)*, 3 OXFORD U. COMMONWEALTH L.J. 1, 24 (2003) ("Consent is evidenced in, indeed constituted by, long usage. . . ."). *See also* Harold J. Berman, *The Origins of Historical Jurisprudence: Coke, Selden, Hale*, 103 YALE L.J. 1651, 1699 (1994) (observing that Selden viewed "the binding force of customary law . . . as essentially consensual in nature"); Andrea C. Loux, Note, *The Persistence of the Ancient Regime: Custom, Utility, and the Common Law in the Nineteenth Century*, 79 CORNELL L. REV. 183, 202 (1993) (observing that the "legitimacy" of custom as a form of law "rested on the consent of the people").

48. 1 WILLIAM BLACKSTONE, COMMENTARIES ON THE LAWS OF ENGLAND 73 (9th ed. 1783); *see also* THEODORE F.T. PLUCKNETT, A CONCISE HISTORY OF THE COMMON LAW 308 (5th ed. 1956) (observing that custom "proceeded from the people").

49. Gerard J. Postema, *Classical Common Law Jurisprudence (Part I)*, 2 OXFORD U. COMMONWEALTH L.J. 155, 175 (2002) (observing that rules "are refined over time, softened to fit the contours of the community's daily life").

50. Gerard J. Postema, *Classical Common Law Jurisprudence (Part I)*, 2 OXFORD U. COMMONWEALTH L.J. 155, 175 (2002).; *see also* Gerard J. Postema, *Classical Common Law Jurisprudence (Part II)*, 3 OXFORD U. COMMONWEALTH L.J. 1, 24 (2003) ("The laws are approved or accepted by the whole people in virtue of and manifested in that law's integration . . . into their daily lives. . . .").

51. 1 WILLIAM BLACKSTONE, COMMENTARIES ON THE LAWS OF ENGLAND 74 (9th ed. 1783).

52. Lon L. Fuller, *Human Interaction and the Law*, 14 AM. J. JURIS. 1, 4 (1969).

53. E.P. Thompson, Customs in Common 97 (1991) (quoting Samuel Carter, Lex Custumaria (1696)).

54. *See* Carlton K. Allen, Law in the Making 105 (2d ed. 1930); *see also* Andrea C. Loux, Note, *The Persistence of the Ancient Regime: Custom, Utility, and the Common Law in the Nineteenth Century*, 79 Cornell L. Rev. 183, 210 (1993) ("Custom arose from ancient community praxis. . . .").

55. *See* Richard A. Epstein, *The Path to* The T.J. Hooper*: The Theory and History of Custom in the Law of Tort*, 21 J. Legal Stud. 1, 6 (1992).

56. *See* 1 F. A. Hayek, Law, Legislation and Liberty 77 (1973); *see also* Carlton K. Allen, Law in the Making 56 (2d ed. 1930) ("[C]ustom grows by the force of concrete example. . . ."); E.K. Braybrooke, *Custom as a Source of English Law*, 50 Mich. L. Rev. 71, 73 (1951) ("[C]ustom is made 'by the frequent iteration and multiplication of th[e] act.'" (quoting Davis Rep. (Ir.) 28, 32–33, 80 Eng. Rep. 516 (1608)); Richard A. Epstein, *The Path to* The T.J. Hooper*: The Theory and History of Custom in the Law of Tort*, 21 J. Legal Stud. 1, 12 (1992) ("Customs arise . . . from widespread imitation and adaptation of past practice.").

57. Carlton K. Allen, Law in the Making 60–61 (2d ed. 1930); *see also* Carlton K. Allen, Law in the Making 60–61 (2d ed. 1930) ("To be singular in the ordinary matters of use and wont is worth neither the effort nor the discomfort.").

58. Lon L. Fuller, *Human Interaction and the Law*, 14 Am. J. Juris. 1, 9 (1969).

59. E.P. Thompson, Customs in Common 102 (1991) ("Agrarian custom was . . . a lived environment comprised of practices, inherited expectations, rules which both determined limits to usages and disclosed possibilities, norms and sanctions both of law and neighbourhood pressures.").

60. Carlton K. Allen, Law in the Making 104 (2d ed. 1930); *see also* Frederick Schauer, *The Jurisprudence of Custom*, 48 Tex. Int'l L.J. 523, 532 (2013) ("[A]ctual human practices make customs normative."); Stephen E. Sachs, *Finding Law*, 107 Cal. L. Rev. 527, 540 (2019) ("[C]ustomary law has long been said to demand two things: that there be widespread practice, and that the practice be followed from a sense of obligation. . . .").

61. R.H. Helmholz, *Christopher St. German and the Law of Custom*, 70 U. Chi. L. Rev. 129, 132 (2003) ("Custom was not simply a 'background norm.' For many purposes it was treated as binding law."). *See also* E.P. Thompson, Customs in Common 98 (1991) ("[C]ustom was sharply defined [and] enforceable at law."); Carlton K. Allen, Law in the Making 28 (2d ed. 1930) ("[Customs] are 'legal' in this sense, that they are binding and obligatory, and the breach of them is a breach of *duty*.").

62. John Hudson, The Formation of the English Common Law: Law and Society in England from the Norman Conquest to Magna Carta 21 (1996).

63. E.P. Thompson, Customs in Common 104 (1991).

64. Carlton K. Allen, Law in the Making 29–30 (2d ed. 1930) ("[C]ustoms . . . are essentially non-litigious in origin. They arise not from any

conflict of rights adjusted by a supreme arbiter . . . but from practices prompted by the convenience of society and of the individual. . . .").

65. *See* Albert Kiralfy, *Custom in Mediaeval English Law*, 9 J. LEG. HIST. 26, 27 (1988) ("[M]ost cases, like cases today, were settled out of court, or dropped, or decided on technicalities of proof or procedure, so that there are few 'leading cases' to operate as a logical basis for the system.").

66. Frederick Schauer, *The Jurisprudence of Custom*, 48 TEX. INT'L L.J. 523, 524 (2013).

67. Gerard J. Postema, *Classical Common Law Jurisprudence (Part II)*, 3 OXFORD U. COMMONWEALTH L.J. 1, 3 (2003) (quoting Matthew Hale, *Reflections by the Lord Chief Justice Hale on Mr. Hobbes His Dialogue of the Law*, *in* 5 WILLIAM HOLDSWORTH, A HISTORY OF ENGLISH LAW 503 (7th ed. 1956) (alteration added)).

68. Frederick Schauer, *The Jurisprudence of Custom*, 48 TEX. INT'L L.J. 523, 526 (2013) (citing JOHN AUSTIN, THE PROVINCE OF JURISPRUDENCE DETERMINED 34–36, 141–42, 238–39 (Wilfrid E. Rumble, Cambridge Univ. Press, 5th ed. 1995) (1832)); *see also* Andrea C. Loux, Note, *The Persistence of the Ancient Regime: Custom, Utility, and the Common Law in the Nineteenth Century*, 79 CORNELL L. REV. 183, 201–02 (1993) ("According to Bentham, spontaneous custom gives rise to legitimate expectations, but cannot create a binding legal obligation until it is legalized by a common law court." (citing JEREMY BENTHAM, A COMMENT ON THE COMMENTARIES: A CRITICISM OF WILLIAM BLACKSTONE'S COMMENTARIES ON THE LAWS OF ENGLAND 221–23 (1928)).

69. CARLTON K. ALLEN, LAW IN THE MAKING 28 (2d ed. 1930).

70. CARLTON K. ALLEN, LAW IN THE MAKING 87 (2d ed. 1930); *see also* Harold J. Berman, *The Origins of Historical Jurisprudence: Coke, Selden, Hale*, 103 YALE L.J. 1651, 1711 n.161 (1994) ("Law . . . is developed first by custom and by popular belief, and only then by juristic activity." (citing FRIEDRICH CARL VON SAVIGNY, OF THE VOCATION OF OUR AGE FOR LEGISLATION AND JURISPRUDENCE (Abraham Hayward trans., 3d. ed. 1831) (1813)). More modern positivists, notably H.L.A. Hart and Hans Kelsen, have accepted the notion of custom as a source of law even prior to formal adoption by judges or legislators. *See* Frederick Schauer, *The Jurisprudence of Custom*, 48 TEX. INT'L L.J. 523, 529 (2013) ("Hart insists that many norms and sources can have the status of law. . . ." (citing H.L.A. HART, THE CONCEPT OF LAW 97–98 (Penelope A. Bulloch & Joseph Raz eds., Clarendon Press, 2d ed. 1994) (1961)); Frederick Schauer, *The Jurisprudence of Custom*, 48 TEX. INT'L L.J. 523, 529 (2013) ("Kelsen . . . recognized that 'norms created by custom do not differ radically from norms created by acts of will.'" (quoting Richard Tur, *The Kelsenian Enterprise*, *in* ESSAYS ON KELSEN 149, 153 (Richard Tur & William Twining eds., 1986)).

71. HAROLD J. BERMAN, LAW AND REVOLUTION: THE FORMATION OF THE WESTERN LEGAL TRADITION 441 (1983).

72. Stephen E. Sachs, *Finding Law*, 107 CAL. L. REV. 527, 536 (2019); *see also* Gregory M. Duhl, *Property and Custom: Allocating Space in Public Places*, 79 TEMP. L. REV. 199, 202 (2006) ("Members of communities abide by customs as normative

and binding, even though they are neither reflected in positive law . . . nor in the common law." (footnote omitted)).

73. Paul Finkelman, *Fugitive Baseballs and Abandoned Property: Who Owns the Home Run Ball?*, 23 CARDOZO L. REV. 1609, 1621–24 (2002).

74. Popov v. Hayashi, No. 400545, 2002 WL 31833731, at *5 (Cal. Super. Ct. Dec. 18, 2002).

75. *Jones*, 565 U.S. at 402–03.

76. *Jardines*, 569 U.S. at 3–4.

77 . *Jones*, 565 U.S. at 425 (Alito, J., concurring in the judgment) ("Attaching such an object is generally regarded as so trivial that it does not provide a basis for recovery under modern tort law."). Notice that Justice Alito assumed that only *actionable* torts are relevant for these purposes but it is unclear why that would be. Any intermeddling with another person's property is a trespass to chattel, *see* RESTATEMENT (SECOND) OF TORTS § 217(b) (AM. LAW INST. 1965), while only a smaller universe of such trespasses, those that damage or destroy the property or deprive the owner of its use, give rise to a tort action for damages, *see* RESTATEMENT (SECOND) OF TORTS § 218 (AM. LAW INST. 1965); *see also* Laurent Sacharoff, *Constitutional Trespass*, 81 TENN. L. REV. 877, 906–7 (2014). But even a non-actionable trespass gives the property owner certain legal rights such as the right to use reasonable force to protect her interest in the property.

78. 569 U.S. at 8 (quoting McKee v. Gratz, 260 U.S. 127, 136 (1922) (alteration added)). McKee had involved whether there was an implicit license to trawl for mussels in a riverbed on another's property. *McKee*, 260 U.S. at 134–36.

79. *Jardines*, 569 U.S. at 8–9. *See also* 569 U.S. at 9 n.3 ("We think a typical person would find it a cause for great alarm . . . to find a stranger snooping about his front porch with or without a dog." (internal quotation marks and emphasis omitted)); 569 U.S. at 9 n.4 ("[N]o one is impliedly invited to enter the protected premises of the home in order to do nothing but conduct a search."); 569 U.S. at 9 (opining that no implied license would include a "visitor exploring the front path with a metal detector").

80. 569 U.S. at 20–21 (Alito, J., dissenting).

81. 529 U.S. 334, 338–39 (2000).

82. 547 U.S. 103.

83. 547 U.S. at 111, 113, 121.

84. 277 U.S. at 468–69.

85. 365 U.S. at 512.

86. 486 U.S. at 43.

87. *Jardines*, 569 U.S. at 9; *see also* William Baude & James Y. Stern, *The Positive Law Model of the Fourth Amendment*, 129 HARV. L. REV. 1821, 1835 (2016) (observing that *Jones* and *Jardines* "treated the Fourth Amendment as borrowing the general look and feel of trespassory actions, not as formally incorporating the background law of property").

88. 1 WILLIAM BLACKSTONE, COMMENTARIES ON THE LAWS OF ENGLAND 63, 74 (9th ed. 1783) (emphasis omitted).

89. William Baude & James Y. Stern, *The Positive Law Model of the Fourth Amendment*, 129 HARV. L. REV. 1821, 1874 (2016).

90. Note, *The Fourth Amendment's Third Way*, 120 HARV. L. REV. 1627, 1645 (2007).

91. *Carpenter*, 138 S. Ct. at 2270 (Gorsuch, J., dissenting).

92. *White*, 401 U.S. at 752 (plurality opinion); Lopez v. United States, 373 U.S. 427, 429–32 (1963); *On Lee*, 343 U.S. at 749–50.

93. 260 U.S. at 136.

94. *Country*, LAIRD & LEE'S WEBSTER'S NEW STANDARD DICTIONARY OF THE ENGLISH LANGUAGE 86 (1920) (defining "country" as "region" or "rural region").

95. "In suits at common law, where the value in controversy shall exceed twenty dollars, the right of trial by jury shall be preserved, and no fact tried by a jury, shall be otherwise reexamined in any court of the United States, than according to the rules of the common law." U.S. CONST., amend. VII.

96. *See* 1 WILLIAM BLACKSTONE, COMMENTARIES ON THE LAWS OF ENGLAND 76–79 (9th ed. 1783).

97. Matthew Tokson & Ari Ezra Waldman, *Social Norms in Fourth Amendment Law*, 120 MICH. L. REV. 265, 279 (2021) ("[N]orms rarely permanently stabilize but rather undergo frequent contestation and change.").

98. David J. Bederman, *The Curious Resurrection of Custom: Beach Access and Judicial Takings*, 96 COLUM. L. REV. 1375, 1385 (1996) ("[T]he legal finding of a custom applied only to that court; it did not operate as precedent within a conception of stare decisis.").

99. Steven Hetcher, *The Jury's Out: Social Norms' Misunderstood Role in Negligence Law*, 91 GEO. L.J. 633, 634 (2003) ("Legal centralists wrongly focus on top-down, formal explanations of the source of entitlements at the expense of bottom-up explanations that would take into account the causal impacts of informal social norms, such as those that might flow from the deliberations of juries."); *see also* David J. Bederman, *The Bederman Lecture on Law and Jurisprudence: Public Law and Custom*, 61 EMORY L.J. 949, 949–50 (2012) ("Custom . . . is a bottom-up dynamic, where legal rules are being made by the actual participants in the relevant legal community."); Carol Rose, *The Comedy of the Commons: Custom, Commerce and Inherently Public Property*, 53 U. CHI. L. REV. 711, 742 (1986) ("[C]ustom is the method through which an otherwise unorganized public can order its affairs authoritatively.").

100. *See, e.g.*, AKHIL REED AMAR, THE BILL OF RIGHTS: CREATION AND RECONSTRUCTION 81–118 (1998); LAURA I. APPLEMAN, DEFENDING THE JURY: CRIME, COMMUNITY, AND THE CONSTITUTION 13–38 (2015); Nathan Chapman, *The Jury's Constitutional Judgment*, 67 ALA. L. REV. 189, 201–04, 237–38 (2015); Lauren M. Ouziel, *Beyond Law and Fact: Jury Evaluation of Law Enforcement*, 92 NOTRE DAME L. REV. 691, 729–33 (2016).

101. *See, e.g.*, Ronald J. Bacigal, *A Case for Jury Determination of Search and Seizure Law*, 15 U. RICH. L. REV. 791 (1981); Erik Luna, *The* Katz *Jury*, 41 U.C. DAVIS L. REV. 839, 850–56 (2008); Meghan J. Ryan, *Juries and the Criminal Constitution*,

65 Ala. L. Rev. 849, 877–87 (2014); George C. Thomas III & Barry S. Pollack, *Saving Rights from a Remedy: A Societal View of the Fourth Amendment*, 73 B.U. L. Rev. 147, 150–51 (1993).

102. George C. Thomas III & Barry S. Pollack, *Saving Rights from a Remedy: A Societal View of the Fourth Amendment*, 73 B.U. L. Rev. 147, 182–87 (1993); *see also* Erik Luna, *The* Katz *Jury*, 41 U.C. Davis L. Rev. 839, 865–70 (2008) (exploring but not advocating this idea). Again, I leave consideration of the exclusionary rule for another day, but if we are to maintain it, I see no reason not to involve juries.

103. The Supreme Court: A C-SPAN Book Featuring the Justices in Their Own Words 45 (Brian Lamb, Susan Swain, & Mark Farkas eds., 2010) (interview of Justice Scalia).

104. 1 William Blackstone, Commentaries on the Laws of England 75 (9th ed. 1783); *see also* Theodore F.T. Plucknett, A Concise History of the Common Law 314 (5th ed. 1956) (observing that the law merchant "became the unified custom of a particular class, that of the merchants").

105. *See* I. Trotter Hardy, *The Proper Legal Regime for "Cyberspace,"* 55 U. Pitt. L. Rev. 993, 1019–25 (1994); David R. Johnson & David Post, *Law and Borders—The Rise of Law in Cyberspace*, 48 Stan. L. Rev. 1367, 1389 (1996); Joel R. Reidenberg, *Lex Informatica: The Formulation of Information Policy Rules Through Technology*, 76 Tex. L. Rev. 553, 553–54 (1998). It is true that the conventional view of a uniform *lex mercatoria* has recently come under attack as a misreading of history. *See, e.g.*, Emily Kadens, *The Myth of the Customary Law Merchant*, 90 Tex. L. Rev. 1153, 1158 (2012) (asserting that custom in the commercial world was, like custom generally, primarily local in nature); Stephen E. Sachs, *From St. Ives to Cyberspace: The Modern Distortion of the Medieval "Law Merchant,"* 21 Am. U. Int'l L. Rev. 685, 768–80 (2006) ("*Lex Mercatoria* does not present mercantile law as an entirely independent legal system, [but] instead, . . . was highly dependent on the English common law. . . ."). However, it still provides a useful model for the recognition of a set of norms that revolves around a particular subject matter rather than geography and that can inform Fourth Amendment search doctrine.

106. Steven Hetcher, *The Jury's Out: Social Norms' Misunderstood Role in Negligence Law*, 91 Geo. L.J. 633, 634–35 n.10 (2003). One problem with this view is that it arguably places too much power in the hands of the corporate interests that design and control our online activity. The economic model for online business places a premium on the extraction and monetization of personal data. As a result, deference to online norms generated and perpetuated by corporate interests in determining the metes and bounds of Fourth Amendment protections can privilege the economic interests in data extraction over individual interests in privacy. *See* Matthew Tokson & Ari Ezra Waldman, *Social Norms in Fourth Amendment Law*, 120 Mich. L. Rev. 265, 298–301 (2021). However, it is important to remember that such corporate-generated norms would govern only in the absence of federal and state laws. *See* Matthew Tokson & Ari Ezra Waldman, *Social Norms in Fourth Amendment Law*, 120 Mich. L. Rev. 265, 310–13 (2021) (seeing a role for administrators, lawmakers, and local communities in developing limits on the use of new technologies for surveillance).

Chapter 5

1. *See, e.g.*, Torres v. Madrid, 141 S. Ct. 989 (2021); California v. Hodari D., 499 U.S. 621, 623–29 (1991).

2. David A. Sklansky, *The Fourth Amendment and Common Law*, 100 COLUM. L. REV. 1739, 1744 (2000); *see also* Thomas K. Clancy, *The Framers' Intent: John Adams, His Era, and the Fourth Amendment*, 86 IND. L.J. 979, 1014 (2011) (observing that "search and seizure principles were [not] fully formed" during the framing period and that treatises during that time demonstrated no "consensus as to proper practices").

3. Thomas K. Clancy, *The Framers' Intent: John Adams, His Era, and the Fourth Amendment*, 86 IND. L.J. 979, 1053 (2011).

4. Morgan Cloud, *Searching Through History; Searching for History*, 63 U. CHI. L. REV. 1707, 1716 (1996). *See also* Donald A. Dripps, *Responding to the Challenges of Contextual Change and Legal Dynamism in Interpreting the Fourth Amendment*, 81 MISS. L.J. 1085, 1121 (2012) ("The Framers . . . knew that common-law doctrine could change . . . judicially [or] by the legislature. . . .").

5. David A. Sklansky, *The Fourth Amendment and Common Law*, 100 COLUM. L. REV. 1739, 1795 (2000).

6. Thomas Y. Davies, *The Fictional Character of Law-and-Order Originalism: A Case Study of the Distortions and Evasions of Framing-Era Arrest Doctrine in* Atwater v. Lago Vista, 37 WAKE FOREST L. REV. 239, 278 n.121 (2002).

7. Thomas Y. Davies, *The Fictional Character of Law-and-Order Originalism: A Case Study of the Distortions and Evasions of Framing-Era Arrest Doctrine in* Atwater v. Lago Vista, 37 WAKE FOREST L. REV. 239, 280 (2002).

8. John A. Conley, *Doing It by the Book: Justice of the Peace Manuals and English Law in Eighteenth Century America*, 6 J. LEGAL HIST. 257, 265 (1985).

9. *See* Thomas Y. Davies, *The Fictional Character of Law-and-Order Originalism: A Case Study of the Distortions and Evasions of Framing-Era Arrest Doctrine in* Atwater v. Lago Vista, 37 WAKE FOREST L. REV. 239, 280 n.122 (2002). For a helpful summary of the American justice of the peace manuals, organized by place of publication, *see* John A. Conley, *Doing It by the Book: Justice of the Peace Manuals and English Law in Eighteenth Century America*, 6 J. LEGAL HIST. 257, 293–95 (1985). By contrast, Conley lists only four English Justice of the Peace Manuals in use from 1581 to 1869, only two of which overlap temporally.

10. Two slightly different versions of this manual were published, one by Hugh Gaine and the other by John Patterson. References to this manual will generally be to the Gaine version unless I state otherwise.

11. This manual was published anonymously but has been attributed to John F. Grimké. *See* John A. Conley, *Doing It by the Book: Justice of the Peace Manuals and English Law in Eighteenth Century America*, 6 J. LEGAL HIST. 257, 280 (1985); Thomas Y. Davies, *The Fictional Character of Law-and-Order Originalism: A Case Study of the Distortions and Evasions of Framing-Era Arrest Doctrine in* Atwater v. Lago Vista, 37 WAKE FOREST L. REV. 239, 281 n.122 (2002).

12. Samuel v. Payne, 99 Eng. Rep. 230, 231 (K.B. 1780).

13. Thomas Y. Davies, *Recovering the Original Fourth Amendment*, 98 MICH. L. REV. 547, 635 (1999).

14. *Samuel*, 99 Eng. Rep. at 231 n.7.

15. *Samuel*, 99 Eng. Rep. at 231 n.7; *see also* Thomas Y. Davies, *Recovering the Original Fourth Amendment*, 98 MICH. L. REV. 547, 634–36 (1999) (contrasting trial court ruling adopting "felony in fact" requirement from appellate court's ruling allowing an arrest "on charge" of felony (internal quotation marks omitted)).

16. *See* WILLIAM WALLER HENING, THE NEW VIRGINIA JUSTICE 34 (1795).

17. *See* THE CONDUCTOR GENERALIS: OR, THE OFFICE, DUTY AND AUTHORITY OF JUSTICES OF THE PEACE, HIGH-SHERIFFS, UNDER-SHERIFFS, CORONERS, CONSTABLES, GAOLERS, JURY-MEN, AND OVERSEERS OF THE POOR 25 (Robert Campbell 1792); ELIPHALET LADD, BURN'S ABRIDGEMENT, OR THE AMERICAN JUSTICE; CONTAINING THE WHOLE PRACTICE, AUTHORITY AND DUTY OF JUSTICES OF THE PEACE 40 (2d ed. 1792).

18. Wakely v. Hart, 6 Binn. 316, 318 (Pa. 1814).

19. 3 Wend. 350, 353 (N.Y. Sup. Ct. 1829).

20. *See* SIR EDWARD COKE, THE FOURTH PART OF THE INSTITUTES OF THE LAWS OF ENGLAND 177 (1644); 2 WILLIAM HAWKINS, A TREATISE OF THE PLEAS OF THE CROWN 139 (6th ed. 1788); 1 RICHARD BURN, THE JUSTICE OF THE PEACE, AND PARISH OFFICER 87 (6th ed. 1758); MICHAEL FOSTER, CROWN LAW 321 (1762); *see also* Thomas Y. Davies, *Correcting Search-and-Seizure History: Now-Forgotten Common-Law Warrantless Arrest Standards and the Original Understanding of "Due Process of Law,"* 77 MISS. L.J. 1, 65 (2007) ("Coke insisted that only a post-indictment felony arrest warrant, but not a pre-indictment warrant, could justify breaking a house.").

21. *See* THE CONDUCTOR GENERALIS: OR, THE OFFICE, DUTY AND AUTHORITY OF JUSTICES OF THE PEACE, HIGH-SHERIFFS, UNDER-SHERIFFS, CORONERS, CONSTABLES, GAOLERS, JURY-MEN, AND OVERSEERS OF THE POOR 27 (1788) (emphasis omitted); THE CONDUCTOR GENERALIS: OR, THE OFFICE, DUTY AND AUTHORITY OF JUSTICES OF THE PEACE, HIGH-SHERIFFS, UNDER-SHERIFFS, CORONERS, CONSTABLES, GAOLERS, JURY-MEN, AND OVERSEERS OF THE POOR 27 (1792) (emphasis omitted); JOSEPH GREENLEAF, AN ABRIDGEMENT OF BURN'S JUSTICE OF THE PEACE AND PARISH OFFICER 24–25 (1773) (omitting the word "of") (emphasis omitted); ELIPHALET LADD, BURN'S ABRIDGEMENT, OR THE AMERICAN JUSTICE; CONTAINING THE WHOLE PRACTICE, AUTHORITY AND DUTY OF JUSTICES OF THE PEACE 42–43 (2d ed. 1792) (same) (emphasis omitted); JAMES PARKER, CONDUCTOR GENERALIS: OR, THE OFFICE, DUTY AND AUTHORITY OF JUSTICES OF THE PEACE, HIGH-SHERIFFS, UNDER-SHERIFFS, CORONERS, CONSTABLES, GAOLERS, JURY-MEN, AND OVERSEERS OF THE POOR 29 (1764) (emphasis omitted).

22. *See* THE CONDUCTOR GENERALIS: OR, THE OFFICE, DUTY AND AUTHORITY OF JUSTICES OF THE PEACE, HIGH-SHERIFFS, UNDER-SHERIFFS, CORONERS, CONSTABLES, GAOLERS, JURY-MEN, AND OVERSEERS OF THE POOR 27 (1788) (emphasis omitted); THE CONDUCTOR GENERALIS: OR, THE OFFICE, DUTY AND AUTHORITY OF JUSTICES OF THE PEACE, HIGH-SHERIFFS, UNDER-SHERIFFS,

Coroners, Constables, Gaolers, Jury-Men, And Overseers of the Poor 27 (1792) (emphasis omitted); Joseph Greenleaf, An Abridgement of Burn's Justice of the Peace and Parish Officer 25 (1773) (emphasis omitted); Eliphalet Ladd, Burn's Abridgement, or the American Justice; Containing the Whole Practice, Authority and Duty of Justices of the Peace 43 (2d ed. 1792) (spelling "break" as "brake") (emphasis omitted); James Parker, Conductor Generalis: Or, the Office, Duty and Authority of Justices of the Peace, High-Sheriffs, Under-Sheriffs, Coroners, Constables, Gaolers, Jury-Men, and Overseers of the Poor 29 (1764) (emphasis omitted).

23. 2 Matthew Hale, The History of the Common Law of England 116–17 (3d ed. 1739).

24. William Simpson, The Practical Justice of the Peace and Parish-Officer, of His Majesty's Province of South-Carolina 25 (1761); *accord* The South-Carolina Justice of Peace 20 (1788).

25. 4 William Blackstone, Commentaries on the Laws of England 292 (9th ed. 1783).

26. Richard Starke, The Office and Authority of a Justice of Peace Explained and Digested, Under Proper Titles 17 (1774). To add to this complexity, the 1795 Virginia manual, without choosing sides, provided both this more lenient rule and the stricter one requiring an indictment before doors could be broken. *See* William Waller Hening, The New Virginia Justice 37 (1795) ("[W]here one lies under a probable suspicion only, and is not indicted . . . no one can justify the breaking open doors in order to apprehend him. . . .").

27. John Adams, Minutes of the Argument in Petition of Lechmere (Feb. 24, 1761), *in* 2 Legal Papers of John Adams 123, 130 (L. Kinvin Wroth & Hiller B. Zobel eds., 1965); *see also* David A. Sklansky, *The Fourth Amendment and Common Law*, 100 Colum. L. Rev. 1739, 1761 n.143 (2000).

28. James Parker, Conductor Generalis: Or, the Office, Duty and Authority of Justices of the Peace, High-Sheriffs, Under-Sheriffs, Coroners, Constables, Gaolers, Jury-Men, and Overseers of the Poor 457 (1764) (emphasis omitted) (citation omitted); *accord* The Conductor Generalis: Or, the Office, Duty and Authority of Justices of the Peace, High-Sheriffs, Under-Sheriffs, Coroners, Constables, Gaolers, Jury-Men, and Overseers of the Poor 366–67 (1788); The Conductor Generalis: Or, the Office, Duty and Authority of Justices of the Peace, High-Sheriffs, Under-Sheriffs, Coroners, Constables, Gaolers, Jury-Men, And Overseers of the Poor 366–67 (1792); Joseph Greenleaf, An Abridgement of Burn's Justice of the Peace and Parish Officer 372 (1773); Eliphalet Ladd, Burn's Abridgement, or the American Justice; Containing the Whole Practice, Authority and Duty of Justices of the Peace 418–19 (2d ed. 1792); The South-Carolina Justice of Peace 492–93 (1788).

29. William Simpson, The Practical Justice of the Peace and Parish-Officer, of His Majesty's Province of South-Carolina 258 (1761); *accord* Richard Starke, The Office and Authority of a Justice of Peace Explained and Digested, Under Proper Titles 351 (1774).

30. 2 William Hawkins, A Treatise of the Pleas of the Crown 76 (6th ed. 1788).

31. *See* James Parker, Conductor Generalis: Or, the Office, Duty and Authority of Justices of the Peace, High-Sheriffs, Under-Sheriffs, Coroners, Constables, Gaolers, Jury-Men, and Overseers of the Poor 26 (1764); The Conductor Generalis: Or, the Office, Duty and Authority of Justices of the Peace, High-Sheriffs, Under-Sheriffs, Coroners, Constables, Gaolers, Jury-Men, and Overseers of the Poor 24 (1788); The Conductor Generalis: Or, the Office, Duty and Authority of Justices of the Peace, High-Sheriffs, Under-Sheriffs, Coroners, Constables, Gaolers, Jury-Men, And Overseers of the Poor 24 (1792); Joseph Greenleaf, An Abridgement of Burn's Justice of the Peace and Parish Officer 21 (1773); William Waller Hening, The New Virginia Justice 33 (1795); Eliphalet Ladd, Burn's Abridgement, or the American Justice; Containing the Whole Practice, Authority and Duty of Justices of the Peace 39 (2d ed. 1792); The South-Carolina Justice of Peace 17 (1788).

32. *See* James Davis, The Office and Authority of a Justice of Peace 14–16 (1774); William Simpson, The Practical Justice of the Peace and Parish-Officer, of His Majesty's Province of South-Carolina 23 (1761); Richard Starke, The Office and Authority of a Justice of Peace Explained and Digested, Under Proper Titles 16 (1774).

33. *See* Joseph Greenleaf, An Abridgement of Burn's Justice of the Peace and Parish Officer 23 (1773) ("[A] watchman may arrest a night walker, without any warrant from a magistrate."); *accord* William Waller Hening, The New Virginia Justice 35 (1795); Eliphalet Ladd, Burn's Abridgement, or the American Justice; Containing the Whole Practice, Authority and Duty of Justices of the Peace 40 (2d ed. 1792); The South-Carolina Justice of Peace 18 (1788).

34. *See* The Conductor Generalis: Or, the Office, Duty and Authority of Justices of the Peace, High-Sheriffs, Under-Sheriffs, Coroners, Constables, Gaolers, Jury-Men, and Overseers of the Poor 25–26 (1788); The Conductor Generalis: Or, the Office, Duty and Authority of Justices of the Peace, High-Sheriffs, Under-Sheriffs, Coroners, Constables, Gaolers, Jury-Men, And Overseers of the Poor 25–26 (1792); James Davis, The Office and Authority of a Justice of Peace 14–16 (1774); James Parker, Conductor Generalis: Or, the Office, Duty and Authority of Justices of the Peace, High-Sheriffs, Under-Sheriffs, Coroners, Constables, Gaolers, Jury-Men, and Overseers of the Poor 27–28 (1764); William Simpson, The Practical Justice of the Peace and Parish-Officer, of His Majesty's Province of South-Carolina 23–24 (1761); Richard Starke, The Office and Authority of a Justice of Peace Explained and Digested, Under Proper Titles 16 (1774).

35. *See* George C. Thomas III, *Stumbling Toward History: The Framers' Search and Seizure World*, 43 Tex. Tech L. Rev. 199, 226 (2010).

36. William Simpson, The Practical Justice of the Peace and Parish-Officer, of His Majesty's Province of South-Carolina 23 (1761) (permitting arrest of those "living an idle, vagrant and disorderly life, without having any visible means to support it"); *accord* The Conductor Generalis: Or, the Office, Duty and Authority of Justices of the Peace, High-Sheriffs, Under-Sheriffs, Coroners, Constables, Gaolers, Jury-Men, and Overseers of the Poor 25 (1788); The Conductor Generalis: Or, the Office, Duty and Authority of Justices of the Peace, High-Sheriffs, Under-Sheriffs, Coroners, Constables, Gaolers, Jury-Men, And Overseers of the Poor 25 (1792); Joseph Greenleaf, An Abridgement of Burn's Justice of the Peace and Parish Officer 22 (1773); William Waller Hening, The New Virginia Justice 34 (1795); Eliphalet Ladd, Burn's Abridgement, or the American Justice; Containing the Whole Practice, Authority and Duty of Justices of the Peace 40 (2d ed. 1792); James Parker, Conductor Generalis: Or, the Office, Duty and Authority of Justices of the Peace, High-Sheriffs, Under-Sheriffs, Coroners, Constables, Gaolers, Jury-Men, and Overseers of the Poor 26 (1764); The South-Carolina Justice of Peace 18 (1788); *see also* James Davis, The Office and Authority of a Justice of Peace 120 (1774) (observing that the constable "must endeavour to apprehend Rogues, Vagabonds, and idle Persons, wandring, or begging, or found loitering within his Precinct").

37. *See* Richard Starke, The Office and Authority of a Justice of Peace Explained and Digested, Under Proper Titles 16–17, 103–05 (1774) (omitting such grounds).

38. *See* 4 William Blackstone, Commentaries on the Laws of England 289 (9th ed. 1783); 1 Edward Hyde East, A Treatise of the Pleas of the Crown § 71, at 303 (London, A. Strahan 1803). Blackstone and East are admittedly ambiguous, however, because they wrote only that breach of the peace was a sufficient, not a necessary, condition for warrantless arrest authority for a misdemeanor.

39. 2 Matthew Hale, The History of the Common Law of England 88 (3d ed. 1739).

40. 2 William Hawkins, A Treatise of the Pleas of the Crown 78 (6th ed. 1788).

41. *See* James Parker, Conductor Generalis: Or, the Office, Duty and Authority of Justices of the Peace, High-Sheriffs, Under-Sheriffs, Coroners, Constables, Gaolers, Jury-Men, and Overseers of the Poor 111–24 (1764); Conductor Generalis: Or the Office, Duty and Authority of Justices of the Peace, High-Sheriffs, Under-Sheriffs, Coroners, Constables, Goalers, Jury-Men, and Overseers of the Poor 109–24 (New York, John Patterson 1788).

42. *See, e.g.*, Thornton v. United States, 541 U.S. 615, 630–31 & 631 n.2 (2004) (Scalia, J., concurring in the judgment).

43. *See* James Parker, Conductor Generalis: Or, the Office, Duty

and Authority of Justices of the Peace, High-Sheriffs, Under-Sheriffs, Coroners, Constables, Gaolers, Jury-Men, and Overseers of the Poor 117 (1764).

44. *See* The Conductor Generalis: Or, the Office, Duty and Authority of Justices of the Peace, High-Sheriffs, Under-Sheriffs, Coroners, Constables, Gaolers, Jury-Men, And Overseers of the Poor 97–100 (1792); James Davis, The Office and Authority of a Justice of Peace 115–23 (1774); Joseph Greenleaf, An Abridgement of Burn's Justice of the Peace and Parish Officer 102 (1773) (no entry for "Constable"); William Waller Hening, The New Virginia Justice 135–37 (1795); Eliphalet Ladd, Burn's Abridgement, or the American Justice; Containing the Whole Practice, Authority and Duty of Justices of the Peace 110 (2d ed. 1792) (no entry for "Constable"); William Simpson, The Practical Justice of the Peace and Parish-Officer, of His Majesty's Province of South-Carolina 84–87 (1761); Richard Starke, The Office and Authority of a Justice of Peace Explained and Digested, Under Proper Titles 103–05 (1774); The South-Carolina Justice of Peace 117–22 (1788).

45. James Parker, Conductor Generalis: Or, the Office, Duty and Authority of Justices of the Peace, High-Sheriffs, Under-Sheriffs, Coroners, Constables, Gaolers, Jury-Men, and Overseers of the Poor iii (1764).

46. *See* Wayne A. Logan, *An Exception Swallows a Rule: Police Authority to Search Incident to Arrest*, 19 Yale L. & Pol'y Rev. 381, 385 (2001) (observing the obscurity of "the historical provenance and contours" of the search-incident-to-arrest doctrine); George C. Thomas III, *The Common Law Endures in the Fourth Amendment*, 27 Wm. & Mary Bill Rts. J. 85, 101–04 (2018) (discussing whether search-incident-to-arrest authority was widespread at common law). As will be discussed in chapter 10, the Supreme Court has permitted broad search-incident-to-arrest authority.

47. James Parker, Conductor Generalis: Or, the Office, Duty and Authority of Justices of the Peace, High-Sheriffs, Under-Sheriffs, Coroners, Constables, Gaolers, Jury-Men, and Overseers of the Poor 29 (1764); *accord* The Conductor Generalis: Or, the Office, Duty and Authority of Justices of the Peace, High-Sheriffs, Under-Sheriffs, Coroners, Constables, Gaolers, Jury-Men, and Overseers of the Poor 27 (1788); The Conductor Generalis: Or, the Office, Duty and Authority of Justices of the Peace, High-Sheriffs, Under-Sheriffs, Coroners, Constables, Gaolers, Jury-Men, And Overseers of the Poor 27 (1792); Joseph Greenleaf, An Abridgement of Burn's Justice of the Peace and Parish Officer 25 (1773); William Waller Hening, The New Virginia Justice 37 (1795); Eliphalet Ladd, Burn's Abridgement, or the American Justice; Containing the Whole Practice, Authority and Duty of Justices of the Peace 43 (2d ed. 1792); The South-Carolina Justice of Peace 20 (1788).

48. James Parker, Conductor Generalis: Or, the Office, Duty and

Authority of Justices of the Peace, High-Sheriffs, Under-Sheriffs, Coroners, Constables, Gaolers, Jury-Men, and Overseers of the Poor 29 (1764) (emphasis omitted); *accord* The Conductor Generalis: Or, the Office, Duty and Authority of Justices of the Peace, High-Sheriffs, Under-Sheriffs, Coroners, Constables, Gaolers, Jury-Men, and Overseers of the Poor 27 (1788); The Conductor Generalis: Or, the Office, Duty and Authority of Justices of the Peace, High-Sheriffs, Under-Sheriffs, Coroners, Constables, Gaolers, Jury-Men, And Overseers of the Poor 27 (1792); Joseph Greenleaf, An Abridgement of Burn's Justice of the Peace and Parish Officer 25 (1773); William Waller Hening, The New Virginia Justice 37 (1795); Eliphalet Ladd, Burn's Abridgement, or the American Justice; Containing the Whole Practice, Authority and Duty of Justices of the Peace 43 (2d ed. 1792); The South-Carolina Justice of Peace 20 (1788).

49. *See* James Davis, The Office and Authority of a Justice of Peace 15–16 (1774); William Simpson, The Practical Justice of the Peace and Parish-Officer, of His Majesty's Province of South-Carolina 25–26 (1761); Richard Starke, The Office and Authority of a Justice of Peace Explained and Digested, Under Proper Titles 17 (1774).

50. *See* William Waller Hening, The New Virginia Justice 37 (1795); The South-Carolina Justice of Peace 20 (1788).

51. James Parker, Conductor Generalis: Or, the Office, Duty and Authority of Justices of the Peace, High-Sheriffs, Under-Sheriffs, Coroners, Constables, Gaolers, Jury-Men, and Overseers of the Poor 28 (1764); *accord* The Conductor Generalis: Or, the Office, Duty and Authority of Justices of the Peace, High-Sheriffs, Under-Sheriffs, Coroners, Constables, Gaolers, Jury-Men, and Overseers of the Poor 26 (1788); The Conductor Generalis: Or, the Office, Duty and Authority of Justices of the Peace, High-Sheriffs, Under-Sheriffs, Coroners, Constables, Gaolers, Jury-Men, And Overseers of the Poor 26 (1792); James Davis, The Office and Authority of a Justice of Peace 15 (1774); Joseph Greenleaf, An Abridgement of Burn's Justice of the Peace and Parish Officer 24 (1773); William Waller Hening, The New Virginia Justice 36 (1795); Eliphalet Ladd, Burn's Abridgement, or the American Justice; Containing the Whole Practice, Authority and Duty of Justices of the Peace 42 (2d ed. 1792); Richard Starke, The Office and Authority of a Justice of Peace Explained and Digested, Under Proper Titles 17 (1774).

52. *See* William Simpson, The Practical Justice of the Peace and Parish-Officer, of His Majesty's Province of South-Carolina 25–27 (1761).

53. *See* The South-Carolina Justice of Peace 19 (1788).

54. James Davis, The Office and Authority of a Justice of Peace 308 (1774) (citing 2 Matthew Hale, The History of the Common Law of England 150 (3d ed. 1739)).

55. James Parker, Conductor Generalis: Or, the Office, Duty and Authority of Justices of the Peace, High-Sheriffs, Under-Sheriffs, Coroners, Constables, Gaolers, Jury-Men, and Overseers of the Poor 385–86 (1764) (emphasis and citation omitted); *accord* The Conductor Generalis: Or, the Office, Duty and Authority of Justices of the Peace, High-Sheriffs, Under-Sheriffs, Coroners, Constables, Gaolers, Jury-Men, and Overseers of the Poor 323–24 (1788); Joseph Greenleaf, An Abridgement of Burn's Justice of the Peace and Parish Officer 323 (1773); The South-Carolina Justice of Peace 425 (1788).

56. *See* The Conductor Generalis: Or, the Office, Duty and Authority of Justices of the Peace, High-Sheriffs, Under-Sheriffs, Coroners, Constables, Gaolers, Jury-Men, And Overseers of the Poor 323–24 (1792); Eliphalet Ladd, Burn's Abridgement, or the American Justice; Containing the Whole Practice, Authority and Duty of Justices of the Peace 358 (2d ed. 1792).

57. Richard Starke, The Office and Authority of a Justice of Peace Explained and Digested, Under Proper Titles 351 (1774) (emphasis added).

58. *See* William Waller Hening, The New Virginia Justice 402 (1795).

59. *See* William Simpson, The Practical Justice of the Peace and Parish Officer, of His Majesty's Province of South-Carolina 225–27 (1761).

60. Thomas Y. Davies, *Recovering the Original Fourth Amendment*, 98 Mich. L. Rev. 547, 631 (1999); *see also* Akhil Reed Amar, *Fourth Amendment First Principles*, 107 Harv. L. Rev. 757, 767 (1994).

61. James Parker, Conductor Generalis: Or, the Office, Duty and Authority of Justices of the Peace, High-Sheriffs, Under-Sheriffs, Coroners, Constables, Gaolers, Jury-Men, and Overseers of the Poor 26 (1764) (emphasis added); *accord* The Conductor Generalis: Or, the Office, Duty and Authority of Justices of the Peace, High-Sheriffs, Under-Sheriffs, Coroners, Constables, Gaolers, Jury-Men, and Overseers of the Poor 24 (1788); The Conductor Generalis: Or, the Office, Duty and Authority of Justices of the Peace, High-Sheriffs, Under-Sheriffs, Coroners, Constables, Gaolers, Jury-Men, And Overseers of the Poor 24 (1792); Joseph Greenleaf, An Abridgement of Burn's Justice of the Peace and Parish Officer 22 (1773); William Waller Hening, The New Virginia Justice 33 (1795); Eliphalet Ladd, Burn's Abridgement, or the American Justice; Containing the Whole Practice, Authority and Duty of Justices of the Peace 39 (2d ed. 1792); The South-Carolina Justice of Peace 17 (1788).

62. *See* Richard Starke, The Office and Authority of a Justice of Peace Explained and Digested, Under Proper Titles 16 (1774) (emphasis added).

63. (1765) 95 Eng. Rep. 807 (K.B.); 2 Wils. K.B. 275. For a discussion of this aspect of *Entick*, *see* Donald A. Dripps, *"Dearest Property": Digital Evidence and the*

History of Private "Papers" as Special Objects of Search and Seizure, 103 J. CRIM. L. & CRIMINOLOGY 49, 65–66 (2013).

64. WILLIAM WALLER HENING, THE NEW VIRGINIA JUSTICE 404 (1795).

65. Donald A. Dripps, *"Dearest Property": Digital Evidence and the History of Private "Papers" as Special Objects of Search and Seizure*, 103 J. CRIM. L. & CRIMINOLOGY 49, 76 (2013).

66. *See* THE CONDUCTOR GENERALIS: OR, THE OFFICE, DUTY AND AUTHORITY OF JUSTICES OF THE PEACE, HIGH-SHERIFFS, UNDER-SHERIFFS, CORONERS, CONSTABLES, GAOLERS, JURY-MEN, AND OVERSEERS OF THE POOR 324 (1792); ELIPHALET LADD, BURN'S ABRIDGEMENT, OR THE AMERICAN JUSTICE; CONTAINING THE WHOLE PRACTICE, AUTHORITY AND DUTY OF JUSTICES OF THE PEACE 359 (2d ed. 1792). Although Ladd did cite *Entick*, he did so only for the proposition that "[g]eneral search warrants are illegal." ELIPHALET LADD, BURN'S ABRIDGEMENT, OR THE AMERICAN JUSTICE; CONTAINING THE WHOLE PRACTICE, AUTHORITY AND DUTY OF JUSTICES OF THE PEACE 357 (2d ed. 1792). This might be read as forbidding searches and seizures of private papers. *See* Donald A. Dripps, *"Dearest Property": Digital Evidence and the History of Private "Papers" as Special Objects of Search and Seizure*, 103 J. CRIM. L. & CRIMINOLOGY 49, 76 (2013).

67. Act of Nov. 5, 1781, ch. 40, § 11, 1781 Va. Acts 151.

68. *See* Thomas Y. Davies, *Recovering the Original Fourth Amendment*, 98 MICH. L. REV. 547, 682 n.374 (1999) (observing that the North Carolina statute "provided the same search authority as that of Virginia").

69. Act of Jan. 22, 1784, ch. 84, § 7.

70. Act of Dec. 23, 1780, ch. 190, §§ 10–11, in LAWS OF THE FIRST SITTING OF THE FIFTH GENERAL ASSEMBLY OF THE COMMONWEALTH OF PENNSYLVANIA 409, 411–12 (1785) (emphasis added).

71. An Act Laying Duties of Impost and Excise, on Certain Goods, Wares, and Merchandize, 19–20 (July 10, 1783) (emphasis added).

72. Thomas Y. Davies, *Recovering the Original Fourth Amendment*, 98 MICH. L. REV. 547, 706 (1999).

73. Thomas Y. Davies, *Correcting Search-and-Seizure History: Now-Forgotten Common-Law Warrantless Arrest Standards and the Original Understanding of "Due Process of Law,"* 77 MISS. L.J. 1, 73 n.220 (2007) (observing that CONDUCTOR GENERALIS, the 1773 Massachusetts manual, the 1774 Virginia manual, and the 1788 South Carolina manual all derived from Burn); *see also* Thomas Y. Davies, *Can You Handle the Truth? The Framers Preserved Common-Law Criminal Arrest and Search Rules in "Due Process of Law"—"Fourth Amendment Reasonableness" Is Only a Modern, Destructive, Judicial Myth*, 43 TEX. TECH L. REV. 51, 64 n.46 (2010) (observing that CONDUCTOR GENERALIS, the 1773 Massachusetts manual, the 1788 South Carolina manual, the 1792 New England manual, and the 1795 Virginia manual all derived from Burn). The only exception from among the works I have referred to is the 1774 North Carolina manual. *See* Thomas Y. Davies, *The Fictional Character of Law-and-Order Originalism: A Case Study of the Distortions and Evasions of Framing-Era Arrest Doctrine in* Atwater v. Lago Vista, 37 WAKE FOREST L. REV. 239, 281 n.122 (2002).

74. John A. Conley, *Doing It by the Book: Justice of the Peace Manuals and English Law in Eighteenth Century America*, 6 J. LEGAL HIST. 257, 265 (1985).

75. Thomas Y. Davies, *The Fictional Character of Law-and-Order Originalism: A Case Study of the Distortions and Evasions of Framing-Era Arrest Doctrine in* Atwater v. Lago Vista, 37 WAKE FOREST L. REV. 239, 282 n.124 (2002).

76. *See* Thomas Y. Davies, *Can You Handle the Truth?: The Framers Preserved Common-Law Criminal Arrest and Search Rules in "Due Process of Law"—"Fourth Amendment Reasonableness" Is Only a Modern, Destructive, Judicial Myth*, 43 TEX. TECH L. REV. 51, 75 n.105 (2010).

77. John A. Conley, *Doing It by the Book: Justice of the Peace Manuals and English Law in Eighteenth Century America*, 6 J. LEGAL HIST. 257, 276, 278, 279, 280, 293 n.154, 290 n.94 (1985).

78. ELIPHALET LADD, BURN'S ABRIDGEMENT, OR THE AMERICAN JUSTICE; CONTAINING THE WHOLE PRACTICE, AUTHORITY AND DUTY OF JUSTICES OF THE PEACE v–vi (2d ed. 1792).

79. John A. Conley, *Doing It by the Book: Justice of the Peace Manuals and English Law in Eighteenth Century America*, 6 J. LEGAL HIST. 257, 269, 288 n.61 (1985).

80. THE CONDUCTOR GENERALIS: OR, THE OFFICE, DUTY AND AUTHORITY OF JUSTICES OF THE PEACE, HIGH-SHERIFFS, UNDER-SHERIFFS, CORONERS, CONSTABLES, GAOLERS, JURY-MEN, AND OVERSEERS OF THE POOR 24–29 (1792) (using the terms "the king's will," "the king's peace," "the suit of the king," "king's bench," "forfeiture to the king," and "the king's name," and citing An Ordinance of the Forest, 1306, 34 Edw. 1, c. 1; Apprehension of Endorsed Warrants Act, 1750, 24 Geo. 2, c. 55; and the Statute of Winchester, 1285, 13 Edw. 1, c. 1–6).

81. John A. Conley, *Doing It by the Book: Justice of the Peace Manuals and English Law in Eighteenth Century America*, 6 J. LEGAL HIST. 257, 263 (1985).

82. Bernadette Meyler, *Towards a Common Law Originalism*, 59 STAN. L. REV. 551, 578 (2006).

83. 532 U.S. 318, 323 (2001).

84. 392 U.S. 1 (1968). Both *Atwater* and *Terry* are discussed in Chapter 11.

85. *Compare* Minnesota v. Dickerson, 508 U.S. 366, 381 (1993) (Scalia, J., concurring) (analogizing the rule announced in *Terry* to the common-law power to arrest nightwalkers) *with* David A. Sklansky, *The Fourth Amendment and Common Law*, 100 COLUM. L. REV. 1739, 1804 (2000) ("[T]he treatment of night-walkers is weak precedent for *Terry* stops."). For an interesting discussion of whether the nightwalker statutes provide support for *Terry* on originalist grounds, see Lawrence Rosenthal, *Pragmatism, Originalism, Race, and the Case Against* Terry v. Ohio, 43 TEX. TECH L. REV. 299, 330–33 (2010).

86. JOSEPH GREENLEAF, AN ABRIDGEMENT OF BURN'S JUSTICE OF THE PEACE AND PARISH OFFICER 323 (1773).

87. *See* Kentucky v. King, 563 U.S. 452, 470 (2011) (assuming without deciding that sounds of movement in an apartment known to contain drugs after a knock on the door went unanswered gave rise to exigent circumstances).

88. *See* Richards v. Wisconsin, 520 U.S. 385 (1997) (holding that reason-

able suspicion of exigency is sufficient for police to dispense with the "knock and announce" requirement).

89. *Compare* United States v. Gorman, 314 F.3d 1105, 1111–15 (9th Cir. 2002) (requiring probable cause to believe defendant is on the premises), *with* Valdez v. McPheters, 172 F.3d 1220, 1224–25 (10th Cir. 1999) (permitting such entry on less than probable cause to believe defendant is on the premises).

90. *See, e.g.*, Spinelli v. United States, 393 U.S. 410, 414 (1969) (characterizing the allegation that the suspect was generally known "as a bookmaker, an associate of bookmakers, a gambler, and an associate of gamblers" as "but a bald and unilluminating assertion of suspicion that is entitled to no weight").

91. Payton v. New York, 445 U.S. 573 (1980).

Chapter 6

1. 32 U.S. (7 Pet.) 243 (1833).

2. U.S. CONST., amend XIV, § 1.

3. ANDREW E. TASLITZ, RECONSTRUCTING THE FOURTH AMENDMENT: A HISTORY OF SEARCH AND SEIZURE, 1789–1868, at 11 (2006) (observing that "[i]n interpreting the Fourth Amendment, courts and commentators consistently focus solely on the events surrounding the Framers' drafting, and the People's ratifying, the Bill of Rights in 1791," rather than Reconstruction).

4. ANDREW E. TASLITZ, RECONSTRUCTING THE FOURTH AMENDMENT: A HISTORY OF SEARCH AND SEIZURE, 1789–1868, at 12 (2006).

5. MICHAEL KENT CURTIS, NO STATE SHALL ABRIDGE: THE FOURTEENTH AMENDMENT AND THE BILL OF RIGHTS 12–13 (1986).

6. *See* David H. Gans, *"We Do Not Want to Be Hunted": The Right to Be Secure and Our Constitutional Story of Race and Policing*, 11 COLUM. J. RACE & LAW 239, 269 (2021) ("The Fourteenth Amendment was framed against the backdrop of . . . vagrancy laws that gave white police officers sweeping power to seize and arrest Black Americans for failing to sign a work contract, refusing to obey an employer's order, or leaving a plantation; warrantless home invasions to seize weapons belonging to Black persons; and police killings and other forms of state-sponsored violence.").

7. *See* Cong. Globe, 39th Cong., 1st Sess., 1093 (Rep. Bingham) (Feb. 28, 1866) ("[W]hen the [rebel] State shall be restored, and the troops of the Government withdrawn, they will have no security in the future except by force of national laws giving them protection against those who have been in arms against them."); Cong. Globe, 39th Cong., 1st Sess., 1833 (Rep. Lawrence of Ohio) (Apr. 7, 1866) ("It is partly because there is no . . . law [protecting civil rights] that the Freedmen's Bureau now . . . interposes military authority to secure the civil rights of the white Union population, and of the freedmen. . . ."). *See also* ERIC FONER, RECONSTRUCTION: AMERICA'S UNFINISHED REVOLUTION, 1863–1877, at 258 (1988) (noting that Congress preferred for the federal judiciary to enforce civil rights, rather than "maintaining indefinitely a standing army in the South, or establishing a permanent national bureaucracy empowered to oversee Reconstruction").

8. The political reality was more nuanced and complex; then, as now, some politicians were not so easily pigeonholed. EARL M. MALTZ, CIVIL RIGHTS, THE CONSTITUTION, AND CONGRESS, 1863–1869, at 42 (1990). The labels "conservative," "moderate," and "radical" should be understood as a rough categorization, not a hard-and-fast typology.

9. The override vote in the Senate can be found at Cong. Globe., 39th Cong., 1st Sess. 943 (Feb. 20, 1866).

10. KURT T. LASH, THE FOURTEENTH AMENDMENT AND THE PRIVILEGES AND IMMUNITIES OF AMERICAN CITIZENSHIP 137 (2014) ("Johnson's veto of the Civil Rights Act . . . signaled an irreparable breach with the Republicans in the Thirty-Ninth Congress."). For Johnson's veto message, *see* Cong. Globe., 39th Cong., 1st Sess. 1679–81 (Mar. 27, 1866).

11. Kurt T. Lash, *The Origins of the Privileges or Immunities Clause, Part III: Andrew Johnson and the Constitutional Referendum of 1866*, 101 GEO. L.J. 1275, 1279 (2013) ("The Democratic Party . . . played the role[] once played by Anti-Federalists. . . . The Republican Party . . . stepped into the role[] once played by Federalists. . . .").

12. JOSEPH B. JAMES, THE RATIFICATION OF THE FOURTEENTH AMENDMENT 304 (1984) ("Ratification was reluctantly accepted [in the South] as the price required for other developments deemed absolutely necessary.").

13. *See* RAOUL BERGER, THE FOURTEENTH AMENDMENT AND THE BILL OF RIGHTS 144 (1989) ("A long-standing guide to construction is: what was the mischief the draftsmen sought to remedy.").

14. Carl Schurz, *Report on the Condition of the South*, in 1 SPEECHES, CORRESPONDENCE AND POLITICAL PAPERS OF CARL SCHURZ 279 *et seq.* (1913).

15. *See, e.g.*, SIDNEY ANDREWS, THE SOUTH SINCE THE WAR (1866); JOHN RICHARD DENNETT, THE SOUTH AS IT IS: 1865–1866 (2010); WILLIAM HEPWORTH DIXON, THE NEW AMERICA (1867); WHITELAW REID, AFTER THE WAR: A SOUTHERN TOUR, MAY 1, 1865 TO MAY 1, 1866 (1866); DAVID THOMAS, MY AMERICAN TOUR (1868); J.T. TROWBRIDGE, A PICTURE OF THE DESOLATED STATES (1868); J.T. TROWBRIDGE, THE SOUTH: A TOUR OF ITS BATTLE-FIELDS AND RUINED CITIES (1866).

16. *See* RAOUL BERGER, THE FOURTEENTH AMENDMENT AND THE BILL OF RIGHTS 144 (1989) (observing that both the Civil Rights Bill and the Fourteenth Amendment were "fueled by the Black Codes' attempt to return the emancipated slaves to serfdom, accompanied by a campaign of flogging, murder, and terrorism.").

17. *See* An Act Concerning Vagrants and Vagrancy, Acts of Alabama 1865–66, at 119–20 (Dec. 15, 1865) [hereinafter Alabama Vagrancy Law]; An Act to Punish Vagrants and Vagabonds, Law of Florida, 1865, ch. 1,467 [No. 4] (Jan. 12, 1866) [hereinafter Florida Vagrancy Law]; An Act to Alter and Amend the 4435th Section of the Penal Code of Georgia, Public Laws of Georgia, 1866, No. 240 (Mar. 12, 1866) [hereinafter Georgia Vagrancy Law]; An Act to Amend the Vagrant Laws, Kentucky 1866, at 765–67 (Feb. 17, 1866) [hereinafter Kentucky Vagrancy Law]; An Act to Amend and Reenact the One Hundred and Twenty-First Section of an

Act Entitled "An Act Relative to Crimes and Offences," Approved March 14, 1855, Louisiana Session Laws—Extraordinary Session, 1865, No. 12, at 16–20 (Dec. 20, 1865) [hereinafter Louisiana Vagrancy Law]; An Act to Amend the Vagrant Laws of the State, Laws of Mississippi, 1865, ch. VI, at 90–93 (Nov. 24, 1865); An Act to Punish Vagrancy, Laws of North Carolina, 1866, chap. 42, at 111 (Mar. 2, 1866) [hereinafter North Carolina Vagrancy Law]; An Act to Establish and Regulate the Domestic Relations of Persons of Color, and to Amend the Law in Relation to Paupers and Vagrancy, Statutes at Large of South Carolina, 1865, No. 4733, § 96 (Dec. 21, 1865) [hereinafter South Carolina Vagrancy Law]; An Act to Define the Offense of Vagrancy, and to Provide for the Punishment of Vagrants, Gen. Laws of Texas, 1866, ch. 111, at 102–04 (Nov. 8, 1866) [hereinafter Texas Vagrancy Law]; An Act Providing for the Punishment of Vagrants, Virginia, 1866, ch. 28, at 91–93 (Jan. 15, 1866) [hereinafter Virginia Vagrancy Law].

18. Florida Vagrancy Law, § 1.

19. Georgia Vagrancy Law, § 1.

20. Kentucky Vagrancy Law, § 1.

21. North Carolina Vagrancy Law, § 1. *See also* South Carolina Vagrancy Law, § 96 ("wandering from place to place"); Texas Vagrancy Law, § 1 ("persons who stroll idly about the streets").

22. W.E.B. DuBois, Black Reconstruction in America: An Essay Toward a History of the Part Which Black Folk Played in the Attempt to Reconstruct Democracy in America, 1860–1880, at 178 (1935); *see also* William Cohen, *Negro Involuntary Servitude in the South, 1865–1940: A Preliminary Analysis*, 42 J. South. Hist. 32, 47 (1976) ("Defining vagrancy in sweeping terms, these nine states gave local authorities a virtual mandate to arrest any poor man who did not have a labor contract."); David H. Gans, *"We Do Not Want to Be Hunted": The Right to Be Secure and Our Constitutional Story of Race and Policing*, 11 Colum. J. Race & Law 239, 271 (2021) ("The vagrancy laws . . . were astounding in their sweep and in the discretion they afforded.").

23. *See* Report of Brevet Brig. Gen. J.S. Fullerton to Maj. Gen. O.O. Howard, Comm'r, Dec. 2, 1865, reprinted in H.R. Exec. Doc. No. 39-70, at 393, 396.

24. *See* Douglas A. Blackmon, Slavery by Another Name: The Re-Enslavement of Black Americans from the Civil War to World War II 53 (2008) ("Few laws specifically enunciated their applicability only to blacks, but it was widely understood that these provisions would rarely if ever be enforced on whites."); W.E.B. DuBois, Black Reconstruction in America: An Essay Toward a History of the Part Which Black Folk Played in the Attempt to Reconstruct Democracy in America, 1860–1880, at 173 (1935) (noting that, although "drawn in general terms," vagrancy provisions were "evidently designed to fit the Negro's condition and to be enforced particularly with regard to Negroes"); Freedom: A Documentary History of Emancipation, 1861–1867, Sr. 3, Vol. 2: Land and Labor, 1866–1867, at 500 (Rene Hayden et al. eds., 2013) (noting that vagrancy "laws were often enforced against freedpeople while white workers in identical circumstances went unmolested"); Risa Goluboff, Vagrant

NATION: POLICE POWER, CONSTITUTIONAL CHANGE, AND THE MAKING OF THE 1960S 116 (2016) ("From citizen patrol to sheriff to jury to judge, the whites who enforced vagrancy laws knew they were aimed at African Americans."); HOWARD N. RABINOWITZ, RACE RELATIONS IN THE URBAN SOUTH 1865–1890, at 35 (1978) ("Although they did not mention race, the vagrancy acts became the chief statutes for disciplining the freedmen."); Barry A. Crouch, *"All the Vile Passions": The Texas Black Code of 1866*, 97 SW. HIST. Q. 13, 31 (1993) ("Everyone understood what they attempted to do with the codes."); 2 REPORT OF THE JOINT COMMITTEE ON RECONSTRUCTION AT THE FIRST SESSION, 39TH CONGRESS 35 (1866) ("They are passing vagrant laws on purpose to oppress the colored people and to keep them in vassalage. . . .") (testimony of Jonathan Roberts).

25. Report of Wager Swayne, Maj. Gen. and Ass't Comm'r, Freedman's Bureau, Montgomery, Ala., dated Oct. 31, 1866, reprinted in SEN. EXEC. DOC. NO. 39-6, at 3, 7. *See also* William Cohen, *Negro Involuntary Servitude in the South, 1865–1940: A Preliminary Analysis*, 42 J. SOUTH. HIST. 32, 34 (1976) ("Most of the laws . . . made no mention of race, but southerners knew that they were intended to maintain white control of the labor system, and local enforcement authorities implemented them with this in mind."); THEODORE BRANTNER WILSON, THE BLACK CODES OF THE SOUTH 108 (1965) (observing that the North Carolina law "was so written that no discrimination appears, yet it in fact opened the way to as much discrimination as any county court judge cared to exercise"); FREEDOM: A DOCUMENTARY HISTORY OF EMANCIPATION, 1861–1867, SR. 3, VOL. 2: LAND AND LABOR, 1866–1867, at 12 (Rene Hayden et al. eds., 2013) ("Such capacious categories left much to the discretion of local authorities, who were far more likely to prosecute freedpeople than similarly situated white people.").

26. 2 REPORT OF THE JOINT COMMITTEE ON RECONSTRUCTION AT THE FIRST SESSION, 39TH CONGRESS 85 (1866) (testimony of Jaquelin M. Wood). This is consistent with a report of Col. E. Whittlesey, Assistant Commissioner of the Freedmen's Bureau in North Carolina, that "a much larger amount of vagrancy exists among the whites than among the blacks." 2 REPORT OF THE JOINT COMMITTEE ON RECONSTRUCTION AT THE FIRST SESSION, 39TH CONGRESS 189 (1866).

27. LEON F. LITWACK, BEEN IN THE STORM SO LONG: THE AFTERMATH OF SLAVERY 370 (1979).

28. *See, e.g.*, Alabama Vagrancy Law, § 4, 7; Florida Vagrancy Law, § 1; Georgia Vagrancy Law, § 1; Louisiana Vagrancy Law, § 1; South Carolina Vagrancy Law, § 98; Virginia Vagrancy Law, § 1. Kentucky's statute even adverted to the vagrant's former status as an enslaved person, providing that he or she should be hired out, preferably "to those having heretofore owned the service of such convicted person." Kentucky Vagrancy Law, § 3.

29. William Cohen, *Negro Involuntary Servitude in the South, 1865–1940: A Preliminary Analysis*, 42 J. SOUTH. HIST. 32, 55 (1976); *see, e.g.*, EDWARD MCPHERSON, POLITICAL MANUAL FOR 1866, at 34 (Alabama), 38 (Florida) (1866).

30. Joe M. Richardson, *Florida Black Codes*, 47 FLA. HIST. Q. 365, 374 (1969).

31. WILLIAM COHEN, AT FREEDOM'S EDGE: BLACK MOBILITY AND THE SOUTHERN WHITE QUEST FOR RACIAL CONTROL 1861–1915, at 34 (1991).

32. Howard N. Rabinowitz, Race Relations in the Urban South 1865–1890, at 35–36 (1978); *see* Report of Brevet Brig. Gen. J.R. Lewis, to Maj. Gen. O.O. Howard, Comm'r, dated Nov. 1, 1866, reprinted in Sen. Exec. Doc. No. 39-6, at 126, 129 (recounting this incident).

33. Eric Foner, Reconstruction: America's Unfinished Revolution, 1863–1877, at 205 (1988).

34. U.S. Const., amend. XII (emphasis added). *See* Eric Foner, The Second Founding: How the Civil War and Reconstruction Remade the Constitution 49 (2019) (quoting a Congressman as stating: "'Cunning rebels' . . . were using 'the exceptional clause' to reduce freed persons to slavery").

35. Freedom: A Documentary History of Emancipation, 1861–1867, Sr. 3, Vol. 2: Land and Labor, 1866–1867, at 15 (Rene Hayden et al. eds., 2013); *see also* Barry A. Crouch, *"All the Vile Passions": The Texas Black Code of 1866*, 97 Sw. Hist. Q. 13, 30 (1993) (observing that the Texas "Legislature provided for the beginning of convict leasing, no doubt realizing that blacks would be sentenced to the penitentiary in droves").

36. Douglas A. Blackmon, Slavery by Another Name: The Re-Enslavement of Black Americans from the Civil War to World War II 64 (2008).

37. *See* Eric Foner, The Second Founding: How the Civil War and Reconstruction Remade the Constitution 48 (2019) ("[V]agrancy laws go back to the premodern era and were widely used throughout the country before the Civil War to punish able-bodied persons who appeared to be unwilling to work."); Risa Goluboff, Vagrant Nation: Police Power, Constitutional Change, and the Making of the 1960s 15 (2016) (tracing vagrancy laws back to the mid-fourteenth-century English Statute of Laborers, and observing that "the English vagrancy laws of the sixteenth and seventeenth centuries" were "[t]he more direct antecedents" of those adopted in America); *see also* W.E.B. DuBois, Black Reconstruction in America: An Essay Toward a History of the Part Which Black Folk Played in the Attempt to Reconstruct Democracy in America, 1860–1880, at 179 (1935); Eric Foner, Reconstruction: America's Unfinished Revolution, 1863–1877, at 208 (1988); William C. Harris, Presidential Reconstruction in Mississippi 128 (1967); Joseph A. Ranney, In the Wake of Slavery: Civil War, Civil Rights, and the Reconstruction of Southern Law 46 (2006).

38. *See* William Cohen, At Freedom's Edge: Black Mobility and the Southern White Quest for Racial Control 1861–1915, at 32 (1991) (observing that although all these States had vagrancy laws before the war, "Alabama, Mississippi, and Louisiana replaced their prewar laws with statutes that were clearly harsher than the old ones"); Freedom: A Documentary History of Emancipation, 1861–1867, Sr. 3, Vol. 2: Land and Labor, 1866–1867, at 12 (Rene Hayden et al. eds., 2013) (noting the "harsher punishments" imposed by the new statutes).

39. Theodore Brantner Wilson, The Black Codes of the South 78

(1965); *see* Theodore Brantner Wilson, The Black Codes of the South 98–99 (1965) (discussing Florida law); William Cohen, *Negro Involuntary Servitude in the South, 1865–1940: A Preliminary Analysis*, 42 J. South. Hist. 34, 47 (1976).

40. William Cohen, At Freedom's Edge: Black Mobility and the Southern White Quest for Racial Control 1861–1915, at 33 (1991).

41. Eric Foner, The Second Founding: How the Civil War and Reconstruction Remade the Constitution 48 (2019); *see also* Risa Goluboff, Vagrant Nation: Police Power, Constitutional Change, and the Making of the 1960s 115 (2016) (describing Southern vagrancy laws as "deeply embedded . . . within a system of racial subordination"); Barry A. Crouch, *"All the Vile Passions": The Texas Black Code of 1866*, 97 Sw. Hist. Q. 13, 34 (1993) (contending that "[t]he Texas black code went far beyond any of the Northern laws" and was designed to "mak[e] blacks forever legally subservient").

42. *What's to be Done With the Negroes*, De Bow's Review, June 1866, at 577, 579.

43. William Cohen, At Freedom's Edge: Black Mobility and the Southern White Quest for Racial Control 1861–1915, at 28 (1991) (quoting Diary of J.B. Moore, June 3, 1865).

44. James E. Bond, No Easy Walk to Freedom: Reconstruction and the Ratification of the Fourteenth Amendment 214 (1997).

45. Barry A. Crouch, *"All the Vile Passions": The Texas Black Code of 1866*, 97 Sw. Hist. Q. 13, 18 (1993) (quoting James M. Smallwood, Time of Hope, Time of Despair: Black Texans During Reconstruction 54 (1981)) (alteration added). *See also* Barry A. Crouch, *"All the Vile Passions": The Texas Black Code of 1866*, 97 Sw. Hist. Q. 13, 22 (1993) ("They never mentioned race, but the freedmen had been their sole focus.").

46. James E. Bond, No Easy Walk to Freedom: Reconstruction and the Ratification of the Fourteenth Amendment 36 (1997) (discussing the view expressed later by Mississippi Governor Benjamin Humphreys that the freedmen "'abandoned all pursuits of industry, and prowled at large . . . subsisting on game and plunder'" [quoting P.L. Rainwater, ed., *"The Autobiography of Benjamin Grubb Humphreys,"* Miss. Valley Hist. Rev. 21 (Sept. 1934): 231, 247 (alteration added)]); Report of William E. Strong, Insp. Gen. to Maj. Gen. O.O. Howard, Comm'r, Jan. 1, 1866, reprinted in H.R. Exec. Doc. No. 39-70, at 308, 310 (reporting that white Texas planters believed "that the negroes . . . showed no disposition to work, and were wandering about the country . . . plundering and stealing indiscriminately from the citizens"). *See also* Joe M. Richardson, *Florida Black Codes*, 47 Fla. Hist. Q. 365, 367 (1969) (describing views of many Floridians that Black people were "criminally inclined" and "disposed to steal").

47. Freedom: A Documentary History of Emancipation, 1861–1867, Sr. 3, Vol. 2: Land and Labor, 1866–1867, at 14 (Rene Hayden et al. eds., 2013).

48. Freedom: A Documentary History of Emancipation, 1861–1867, Sr. 3, Vol. 2: Land and Labor, 1866–1867, at 14 (Rene Hayden et al. eds., 2013); *see also* Eric Foner, Reconstruction: America's Unfinished Revolution, 1863–

1877, at 202 (1988) ("[L]egislators moved to bolster whites' hold upon their property by sharply increasing the penalty for petty larceny.").

49. Barry A. Crouch, *"All the Vile Passions": The Texas Black Code of 1866*, 97 Sw. Hist. Q. 13, 29 (1993).

50. 3 Report of the Joint Committee on Reconstruction at the First Session, 39th Congress 8 (1866) (testimony of Brevet Brig. Gen. George E. Spencer).

51. Joe M. Richardson, The Negro in the Reconstruction of Florida, 1865–77, at 47 (1965).

52. Steven Hahn, *Hunting, Fishing, and Foraging: Common Rights and Class Relations in the Postbellum South*, in Crime And Capitalism: Readings in Marxist Criminology 142, 143–46 (David F. Greenberg ed., rev. ed. 1993); *see also* Freedom: A Documentary History of Emancipation, 1861–1867, Sr. 3, Vol. 2: Land and Labor, 1866–1867, at 14 (Rene Hayden et al. eds., 2013) ("Swamps, woods, and other uncultivated expanses had previously been regarded as open to all for hunting, foraging, and livestock grazing. . . .").

53. Steven Hahn, *Hunting, Fishing, and Foraging: Common Rights and Class Relations in the Postbellum South*, in Crime And Capitalism: Readings in Marxist Criminology 142, 149–50 (David F. Greenberg ed., rev. ed. 1993); *see also* Freedom: A Documentary History of Emancipation, 1861–1867, Sr. 3, Vol. 2: Land and Labor, 1866–1867, at 14 (Rene Hayden et al. eds., 2013) ("[W]hite Southerners began to assert notions of private property that were designed to close off such uses, at least for former slaves."); Eric Foner, Reconstruction: America's Unfinished Revolution, 1863–1877, at 203 (1988) ("Rights such as hunting, fishing, and the free grazing of livestock, which whites took for granted and many blacks had enjoyed as slaves, were now, in some areas, transformed into crimes.").

54. Eric Foner, Reconstruction: America's Unfinished Revolution, 1863–1877, at 203 (1988); *see also* Eric Foner, Nothing but Freedom: Emancipation and Its Legacy 65–67 (1983).

55. Steven Hahn, *Hunting, Fishing, and Foraging: Common Rights and Class Relations in the Postbellum South*, in Crime And Capitalism: Readings in Marxist Criminology 142, 151 (David F. Greenberg ed., rev. ed. 1993).

56. James E. Bond, No Easy Walk to Freedom: Reconstruction and the Ratification of the Fourteenth Amendment 172 (1997); Eric Foner, Reconstruction: America's Unfinished Revolution, 1863–1877, at 203 (1988); Joe M. Richardson, The Negro in the Reconstruction of Florida, 1865–77, at 44 (1965).

57. Howard N. Rabinowitz, Race Relations in the Urban South 1865–1890, at 49 (1978).

58. J.T. Trowbridge, The South: A Tour of its Battle-Fields and Ruined Cities 436 (1866).

59. Eric Foner, Reconstruction: America's Unfinished Revolution, 1863–1877, at 203 (1988) ("Whites staffed urban police forces as well as state

militias, intended, as a Mississippi white put it in 1865, to 'keep good order and discipline amongst the negro population.'"); David H. Gans, *"We Do Not Want to Be Hunted": The Right to Be Secure and Our Constitutional Story of Race and Policing*, 11 Colum. J. Race & Law 239, 277 n.155 (2021) ("Southern militia, like the police, were charged with the responsibility 'to apprehend criminals, suppress crime, and protect the inhabitants.'" (quoting Otis A. Singletary, Negro Militias and Reconstruction 5 (1957)); *see also* William C. Harris, Presidential Reconstruction in Mississippi 71–74 (1967).

60. 4 Report of the Joint Committee on Reconstruction at the First Session, 39th Congress 91 (1866) (testimony of John T. Allen).

61. 4 Report of the Joint Committee on Reconstruction at the First Session, 39th Congress 126 (1866) (testimony of Dr. James M. Turner).

62. 4 Report of the Joint Committee on Reconstruction at the First Session, 39th Congress 61 (1866) (testimony of D.E. Haynes).

63. 3 Report of the Joint Committee on Reconstruction at the First Session, 39th Congress 24 (1866) (testimony of Ezra Hienstadt).

64. 2 Report of the Joint Committee on Reconstruction at the First Session, 39th Congress 206 (1866) (testimony of Rev. Hope Bain).

65. William McKee Evans, Ballots and Fence Rails: Reconstruction on the Lower Cape Fear 68 & n.16, 80–81, 128–29 (1967); Cong. Globe, 39th Cong., 1st Sess., 2083 (Rep. Perham) (Apr. 21, 1866).

66. Memorial of John Schimmler et al., to Joint Congressional Committee on Reconstruction, Jan. 9, 1866, reprinted in 1 Report of the Joint Committee on Reconstruction at the First Session, 39th Congress 91, 93 (1866) (loyal members of the Tennessee legislature complaining "that the bushwacker and guerilla can defeat the most respectable Union man for constable or justice of the peace"); 3 Report of the Joint Committee on Reconstruction at the First Session, 39th Congress 65 (1866) (testimony of David C. Humphreys) ("All the officers for th[e] [Alabama] militia were appointed from those who had been in the rebel service."); 3 Report of the Joint Committee on Reconstruction at the First Session, 39th Congress 115 (1866) (testimony of Brevet Lt. Col. Hunter Brook) (testifying that the elected sheriff of Madison County, Alabama was a former Confederate ranger under sentence for the murder of a Union general); 3 Report of the Joint Committee on Reconstruction at the First Session, 39th Congress 10 (1866) (testimony of Brevet Brig. Gen. George E. Spencer) (same); 2 Report of the Joint Committee on Reconstruction at the First Session, 39th Congress 61 (1866) (testimony of D.B. White) (testifying that a deputy sheriff in Virginia expressed his desire "to drive out of that part of the country every Union man, whether of the south or of the north"); 4 Report of the Joint Committee on Reconstruction at the First Session, 39th Congress 10 (1866) (testimony of Rev. L.M. Hobbs) (describing Florida "constables and justices of the peace" as "bad set of men, bitter and treacherous," who vowed to kill northerners, white loyalists, and Black people as soon as the military left); Report of W.F. Denton, Former Lieut., 12th Kentucky Cavalry, to Maj. Gen.

Palmer, Dec. 29, 1865, reprinted in H.R. Exec. Doc. No. 39-70, at 234, 235 ("The civil law [in Kentucky] is in the hands of the rebels.").

67. 3 Report of the Joint Committee on Reconstruction at the First Session, 39th Congress 175 (1866).

68. *See, e.g.*, Cong. Globe, 39th Cong., 1st Sess. 517 (Rep. Eliot) (Jan. 30, 1866) (describing a schedule of wages set by agreement of a group of farmers on the James River in Henrico County, Virginia); *see also* Cong. Globe, 39th Cong., 1st Sess., 589 (Rep. Donnelly) (Feb. 1, 1866) ("He shall work at a rate of wages to be fixed by a county judge or a Legislature made up of white masters, or by combinations of white masters, and not in any case by himself.").

69. *See* Letter from Maj. Gen. and Comm'r O.O. Howard to Hon. E.M. Stanton, Sec'y of War, Dec. 21, 1866, reprinted in Sen. Exec. Doc. No. 39–6, at 2–3. *See also* W.E.B. DuBois, Black Reconstruction in America: An Essay Toward a History of the Part Which Black Folk Played in the Attempt to Reconstruct Democracy in America, 1860–1880, at 167 (1935).

70. Gen. Order No. 4, Richmond, Va., Jan. 24, 1866, reprinted in Edward McPherson, Political Manual for 1866, at 42.

71. Freedom: A Documentary History of Emancipation, 1861–1867, Sr. 3, Vol. 2: Land and Labor, 1866–1867, at 12 (Rene Hayden et al. eds., 2013).

72. Eric Foner, The Second Founding: How the Civil War and Reconstruction Remade the Constitution 49 (2019); *see, e.g.*, J.T. Trowbridge, The South: A Tour of its Battle-Fields and Ruined Cities 372–73 (1866) ("The design of all such enactments is . . . to reorganize slavery under a new name."); 2 Report of the Joint Committee on Reconstruction at the First Session, 39th Congress 243 (1866) (testimony of J.W. Alvord) (asserting that the design of the vagrancy acts was "to re-establish a *quasi* slavery among the blacks"); Douglas R. Egerton, The Wars of Reconstruction: The Brief, Violent History of America's Most Progressive Era 179 (2014) (quoting a U.S. soldier stationed in Mississippi that "'under the guise of vagrant laws,' legislators proposed 'to restore all of slavery but its name'"); Leon F. Litwack, Been in the Storm So Long: The Aftermath of Slavery 368 (1979) ("To many in the North, the Codes smacked of the old bondage. . . ."); Carl Schurz, "The Logical Results of the War," Speech Delivered Sept. 8, 1866, in Philadelphia, Pa., reprinted in 1 Speeches, Correspondence and Political Papers of Carl Schurz 377, 387 (1913) (describing Virginia's vagrancy law as "calculated to make the freedman a vagrant, and the vagrant a slave again").

73. Cong. Globe, 39th Cong., 1st Sess., 383 (Jan. 23, 1866); *see also* Cong. Globe, 39th Cong., 1st Sess., 91 (Dec. 20, 1865) (Sen. Sumner) ("Slavery must be abolished not in form only, but in substance, so that there shall be no Black Code"); Cong. Globe, 39th Cong., 1st Sess., App. 155 (Sen. Morrill) (Mar. 8, 1866) ("[T]he contest for chattel slavery is over, but the struggle for the possession of the negro as a forced laborer goes on. . . .").

74. Theodore Brantner Wilson, The Black Codes of the South 139 (1965); *see also* James B. Browning, *The North Carolina Black Code*, 15 J. Negro

Hist. 461, 471 (1930) ("In the North the black codes were generally regarded as a deliberate expression of defiance on the part of the Southerners to nullify the results of the four-year struggle, by revitalizing slavery").

75. *See* Raoul Berger, The Fourteenth Amendment and the Bill of Rights 52 (1989) ("Outraged by the Black Codes, the North set out to protect a set of fundamental rights that would enable emancipated slaves to exist."); William Cohen, At Freedom's Edge: Black Mobility and the Southern White Quest for Racial Control 1861–1915, at 30 (1991) ("By the fall of 1866 it was clear that northern public opinion would not tolerate southern statutes that smacked of reenslavement."); Douglas R. Egerton, The Wars of Reconstruction: The Brief, Violent History of America's Most Progressive Era 199 (2014) (observing that the Civil Rights Act was "designed to nullify the Black Codes"); Joseph B. James, The Framing of the Fourteenth Amendment 76 (1965) ("Undoubtedly [section 7 of the Freedmen's Bureau Bill] had been stimulated by the so-called black codes, which were being enacted as security measures in the Southern states."); William E. Nelson, The Fourteenth Amendment: From Political Principle to Judicial Doctrine 48 (1998) (observing that the Civil Rights Act was passed to counteract the Black Codes); William J. Stuntz, The Collapse of American Criminal Justice 102 (2011) (observing that "[t]he conventional wisdom" is that the Fourteenth Amendment "was designed to undo the South's Black Codes").

76. *See* David H. Gans, *"We Do Not Want to Be Hunted": The Right to Be Secure and Our Constitutional Story of Race and Policing*, 11 Colum. J. Race & Law 239, 275–76 (2021).

77. *See, e.g.*, Cong. Globe, 39th Cong., 1st Sess., 588–89 (Rep. Donnelly) (Feb. 1, 1866) (reviewing the Black Codes of South Carolina, Mississippi, Alabama, Tennessee, and Virginia, and noting particularly the provisions that permitted blacks to be "punished as a vagrant" and thus "sold to the highest bidder for a term of years"); Cong. Globe, 39th Cong., 1st Sess., 603 (Sen. Wilson) (Feb. 2, 1866) (characterizing as "atrocious" and "wholly incompatible with the freedom of these freedmen" the new Black Codes in "at least six of the reorganized States"); Cong. Globe, 39th Cong., 1st Sess., 340 (Sen Wilson) (Jan. 22, 1866) (observing that the laws "practically make the freedman a peon or serf"); Cong. Globe, 39th Cong., 1st Sess., 1123 (Rep. Cook) (Mar. 1, 1866) (citing the vagrancy laws "which, under the pretense of selling these men as vagrants, are calculated and intended to reduce them to slavery again," and the "laws which provide for selling these men into slavery in punishment of crimes of the slightest magnitude"); Cong. Globe, 39th Cong., 1st Sess., 783 (Rep. Ward) (Feb. 10, 1866) (criticizing southern courts that "have sold the freedmen into slavery . . . under some pretense of punishing him for vagrancy or something else equally absurd"); Cong. Globe, 39th Cong., 1st Sess., 1151 (Rep. Thayer) (Mar. 2, 1866) (opining that Civil Rights Bill was necessary because the former rebel States "declare [the freedmen] vagrants because they have no homes and because they have no employment"); Cong. Globe, 39th Cong., 1st Sess., 1160 (Rep. Windom) (Mar. 2, 1866) ("In Virginia the laws and customs reduce the negro

to vagrancy, and then seize and sell him as a vagrant."); 39th Cong., 1st Sess., 1621 (Rep. Myers) (Mar. 24, 1866) (citing vagrancy laws of Alabama, Florida, and Virginia); 39th Cong., 1st Sess., 1629 (Rep. Hart) (Mar. 24, 1866) ("[T]hey enact laws which practically reënslave the freedmen"); Cong. Globe, 39th Cong., 1st Sess., 3170 (June 14, 1866) (Rep. Windom) ("They have demonstrated . . . by the reënactment of vagrant laws and slave codes for freedmen . . . how readily [slavery], abolished in name, may be reëstablished in fact and with increased cruelty."); Cong. Globe, 39th Cong., 1st Sess., App. 155 (Sen. Morrill) (Mar. 8, 1866) (declaring that the former rebel states had "enacted black codes and vagrant laws to take possession and control of these 'freedmen'"); Cong. Globe, 39th Cong., 1st Sess. 1839 (Rep. Clarke) (Apr. 7, 1866) (citing the Kentucky vagrancy law, by which "[a] negro adult, if it be decided that he appears to have nothing to do, can be sold to forced labor for one year").

78. "Legislative Enactments," *New York Times*, Mar. 11, 1866; *see also* REMBERT W. PATRICK, THE RECONSTRUCTION OF THE NATION 46 (1967) ("Northern newspapers printed excerpts of the laws along with critical comments and repeatedly used 'odious,' 'vicious,' and 'terrible' in describing the codes.").

79. 1 ELLIS P. OBERHOLTZER, A HISTORY OF THE UNITED STATES SINCE THE CIVIL WAR 137 (1917) (quoting *N.Y. Tribune*, Nov. 15, 1865).

80. JAMES E. BOND, NO EASY WALK TO FREEDOM: RECONSTRUCTION AND THE RATIFICATION OF THE FOURTEENTH AMENDMENT 3 (1997); W.E.B. DUBOIS, BLACK RECONSTRUCTION IN AMERICA: AN ESSAY TOWARD A HISTORY OF THE PART WHICH BLACK FOLK PLAYED IN THE ATTEMPT TO RECONSTRUCT DEMOCRACY IN AMERICA, 1860–1880, at 179–80 (1935); DOUGLAS R. EGERTON, THE WARS OF RECONSTRUCTION: THE BRIEF, VIOLENT HISTORY OF AMERICA'S MOST PROGRESSIVE ERA 197 (2014); ERIC FONER, RECONSTRUCTION: AMERICA'S UNFINISHED REVOLUTION, 1863–1877, at 200 (1988); WILLIAM E. NELSON, THE FOURTEENTH AMENDMENT: FROM POLITICAL PRINCIPLE TO JUDICIAL DOCTRINE 45 (1998); JOEL WILLIAMSON, AFTER SLAVERY: THE NEGRO IN SOUTH CAROLINA DURING RECONSTRUCTION 77 (1965); *see, e.g.*, Cong. Globe, 39th Cong., 1st Sess., 88 (Sen. Sumner) (Dec. 20, 1865) (introducing a petition "from citizens of Massachusetts" imploring the Senate "that emancipation is not complete as long as the black codes exist," and "present[ing] similar petitions from citizens of the States of Missouri, New York, New Jersey, Kentucky, Indiana, Ohio, and Illinois").

81. EARL M. MALTZ, THE FOURTEENTH AMENDMENT AND THE LAW OF THE CONSTITUTION 63 (2003); *see also* James B. Browning, *The North Carolina Black Code*, 15 J. NEGRO HIST. 461, 471 (1930) (noting the "increasing sentiment" in the North that "soon stirred up to action Congressional leaders").

82. James B. Browning, *The North Carolina Black Code*, 15 J. NEGRO HIST. 461, 473 (1930) ("[I]t seems highly probable that if the black codes had not been enacted, the leaders in Congress like Sumner and Stevens would have had an exceedingly difficult task in securing the necessary votes to pass the Civil Rights Bill, the Fourteenth and the Fifteenth Amendment.").

83. Cong. Globe, 39th Cong., 1st Sess., 77 (Dec. 19, 1865) (emphasis added).

84. Cong. Globe, 39th Cong., 1st Sess., 603 (Feb. 2, 1866) (emphasis added).

85. Cong. Globe., 39th Cong., 1st Sess. 914 (Feb. 19, 1866) (alteration and emphases added).

86. Cong. Globe, 39th Cong., 1st Sess., 632 (Feb. 3, 1866).

87. Cong. Globe, 39th Cong., 1st Sess., 1124 (Mar. 1, 1866).

88. Horace Edgar Flack, The Adoption of the Fourteenth Amendment 148 (1908) (emphasis added).

89. Chester James Antieau, The Intended Significance of the Fourteenth Amendment 402 (1997) (quoting Robert Harris, The Quest for Equality 40 (1960) (emphasis added).

90. Although the focus of Northern ire was violence in the South, Northerners also recognized that some of the worst racial violence took place in their own backyards. The worst massacre of Black people in American history took place during the so-called Draft Riot in New York City in July 1863 in which hundreds were murdered and thousands left homeless. *See, e.g.*, Cong. Globe, 39th Cong., 1st Sess., App. 140 (Sen. Wilson) (Mar. 2, 1866) (adverting to "the fires of riot and arson in the city of New York"); Cong. Globe, 39th Cong., 1st Sess., 1073 (Sen. Nye) (Feb. 28, 1866) (mentioning the July 1863 New York City massacre). *See generally* Report of the Merchants Committee for the Relief of Colored People Suffering From the Riots in the City of New York (1863) (documenting the massacre).

91. Frederick Douglass, *An Appeal to Congress for Impartial Suffrage*, reprinted in 19 The Atlantic Monthly 112, 113 (1867).

92. Eric Foner, The Second Founding: How the Civil War and Reconstruction Remade the Constitution 60 (2019); Eric Foner, Reconstruction: America's Unfinished Revolution, 1863–1877, at 225 (1988).

93. Carl Schurz, *Report on the Condition of the South*, in 1 Speeches, Correspondence and Political Papers of Carl Schurz 279, 292 (1913); *see also* Carl Schurz, "The Logical Results of the War," Speech Delivered Sept. 8, 1866, in Philadelphia, Pa., reprinted in 1 Speeches, Correspondence and Political Papers of Carl Schurz 377, 388 (1913) (observing that "the reactionary movement" of the South "malignantly turned upon those Southern men who had refused to espouse the cause of the rebellion").

94. Report of J.W. Sprague, Ass't Comm'r, to Maj. Gen. O.O. Howard, Comm'r, dated Oct. 18, 1866, reprinted in Sen. Exec. Doc. No. 39-6, at 22, 24 (reporting that persecution of loyalists in Arkansas had "rapidly increased" during the previous six months); 1 Ellis P. Oberholtzer, A History of the United States Since the Civil War 138 (1917) (citing *New York Tribune* report that "[i]n Tennessee one hundred 'rebels' [i.e., loyalists] and negroes [were] butchered" between June and December 1865); Report of Brevet Maj. Gen. R.K. Scott, to Maj. Gen. O.O. Howard, Comm'r, dated Nov. 1, 1866, reprinted in Sen. Exec. Doc. No. 39-6, at 112, 113 (reporting that loyal whites had their houses burned or were otherwise "driven from their homes"); Carl Schurz, *Report on the Condition of the South*, in 1 Speeches, Correspondence and Political Papers of Carl Schurz 279, 293

(1913) (recounting the "murder of a Union man by a gang of lawless persons, in Jackson [Mississippi]."). Carl Schurz, "The Logical Results of the War," Speech Delivered Sept. 8, 1866, in Philadelphia, Pa., reprinted in 1 SPEECHES, CORRESPONDENCE AND POLITICAL PAPERS OF CARL SCHURZ 377, 389 (1913) ("Houses were burned to smoke out men of loyal sentiments."); 2 REPORT OF THE JOINT COMMITTEE ON RECONSTRUCTION AT THE FIRST SESSION, 39TH CONGRESS 7 (1866) (testimony of John C. Underwood), (testimony that a loyalist was gunned down in Alexandria "by a returned rebel surgeon"); Report of Brevet Brig. Gen. J.R. Lewis, to Maj. Gen. O.O. Howard, Comm'r, dated Nov. 1, 1866, reprinted in SEN. EXEC. DOC. No. 39-6, at 126, 129 (reporting that three counties in Tennessee were essentially ruled by a notorious Confederate guerilla and his "band of armed men . . . who perpetrate[d] outrages so numerous and revolting as to strike terror to all unorganized and unprotected citizens, whether black or white, who entertain[ed] Union sentiments").

95. Carl Schurz, *Report on the Condition of the South*, in 1 SPEECHES, CORRESPONDENCE AND POLITICAL PAPERS OF CARL SCHURZ 279, 289 (1913) (relating that the driver for Major Miller of the Freedmen's Bureau in Alabama "was brutally murdered" while Miller was on an inspection tour.); *see* Report of Brevet Maj. Gen. Davis Tillson, Ass't Comm'r, to Maj. Gen. O.O. Howard, Comm'r, dated Nov. 1, 1866, reprinted in SEN. EXEC. DOC. No. 39-6, at 48, 48 (reporting the murder of a bureau officer in Georgia); Report of Maj. Gen. P.H. Sheridan, to Maj. Gen. O.O. Howard, Comm'r, dated Oct. 31, 1866, reprinted in SEN. EXEC. DOC. No. 39-6, at 68, 68 (reporting murder of bureau officer in Louisiana); Report of Brevet Maj. Gen. Th. J. Wood, to Maj. Gen. O.O. Howard, Comm'r, dated Oct. 31, 1866, reprinted in SEN. EXEC. DOC. No. 39-6, at 94, 96 (reporting that "roaming bands of desperadoes . . . chiefly the debris of the rebel army" made "the freedmen and northern men their particular objects of murder and rapine"); Cong. Globe, 39th Cong., 1st Sess., 339 (Sen. Creswell) (Jan. 22, 1866) (reporting receipt of letters from reliable sources that former rebels in his State had conspired to cruelly beat and in some cases murder Black soldiers). *See also* Carl Schurz, "The Logical Results of the War," Speech Delivered Sept. 8, 1866, in Philadelphia, Pa., reprinted in 1 SPEECHES, CORRESPONDENCE AND POLITICAL PAPERS OF CARL SCHURZ 377, 388–89 (1913) (describing death threats to Union soldiers and observing that some in the South turned against "those Northerners who, during and after the war, imported into the South their capital, intelligence, enterprise and civilization").

96. Carl Schurz, *Report on the Condition of the South*, in 1 SPEECHES, CORRESPONDENCE AND POLITICAL PAPERS OF CARL SCHURZ 279, 363 (1913); Carl Schurz, "The Logical Results of the War," Speech Delivered Sept. 8, 1866, in Philadelphia, Pa., reprinted in 1 SPEECHES, CORRESPONDENCE AND POLITICAL PAPERS OF CARL SCHURZ 377, 385–86 (1913).

97. ERIC FONER, RECONSTRUCTION: AMERICA'S UNFINISHED REVOLUTION, 1863–1877, at 119 (1988). While some violence ran the other way, Schurz reported that "[t]he acts of violence perpetrated by freedmen against white persons do not stand in any proportion to those committed by whites against negroes." Carl

Schurz, *Report on the Condition of the South*, in 1 SPEECHES, CORRESPONDENCE AND POLITICAL PAPERS OF CARL SCHURZ 279, 339 (1913).

98. Report of Brevet Thomas Smith and Lt. Stuart Eldridge, to Capt. Bamberger, Acting Ass't Adj. Gen., dated Dec. 28, 1865, reprinted in H.R. EXEC. Doc. No. 39-70, at 257, 258–59; Report of Jef. C. Davis, Ass't Comm'r, to Maj. Gen. O.O. Howard, Comm'r, dated Nov. 5, 1866, reprinted in SEN. EXEC. Doc. No. 39-6, at 60, 67; Report of Brevet Brig. Gen. J.R. Lewis, to Maj. Gen. O.O. Howard, Comm'r, dated Nov. 1, 1866, reprinted in SEN. EXEC. Doc. No. 39-6, at 126, 133.

99. Carl Schurz, *Report on the Condition of the South*, in 1 SPEECHES, CORRESPONDENCE AND POLITICAL PAPERS OF CARL SCHURZ 279, 316 (1913); Report of Brevet Maj. Gen. R.K. Scott, to Maj. Gen. O.O. Howard, Comm'r, dated Nov. 1, 1866, reprinted in SEN. EXEC. Doc. No. 39-6, at 112, 112, 121.

100. ERIC FONER, RECONSTRUCTION: AMERICA'S UNFINISHED REVOLUTION, 1863–1877, at 119–21 (1988); Carl Schurz, *Report on the Condition of the South*, in 1 SPEECHES, CORRESPONDENCE AND POLITICAL PAPERS OF CARL SCHURZ 279, 314, 317 (1913); Report of Brevet Maj. Gen. R. Saxton, Ass't Comm'r, to Maj. Gen. O.O. Howard, Comm'r, dated Jan. 15, 1866, reprinted in H.R. EXEC. Doc. No. 39-70, at 248, 249; Report of J.W. Sprague, Ass't Comm'r, to Maj. Gen. O.O. Howard, Comm'r, dated Oct. 18, 1866, reprinted in SEN. EXEC. Doc. No. 39-6, at 22, 24; Report of Maj. Gen. P.H. Sheridan, to Maj. Gen. O.O. Howard, Comm'r, dated Oct. 31, 1866, reprinted in SEN. EXEC. Doc. No. 39-6, at 68, 86, 87; Report of Brevet Maj. Gen. R.K. Scott, to Maj. Gen. O.O. Howard, Comm'r, dated Nov. 1, 1866, reprinted in SEN. EXEC. Doc. No. 39 6, at 112, 112, 121.

A particularly horrendous series of atrocities is detailed in the report of a special inspector for the Freedmen's Bureau in eastern Kentucky in March 1866. *See* Report of P. Bonesteel, Spec. Insp. For Ky. and Tenn., to Maj. Gen. O.O. Howard, Comm'r, Mar. 5, 1866, reprinted in H.R. EXEC. Doc. No. 39-70, at 201. Black Union soldiers were perhaps the most despised of all. In the Bonesteel report, at least twenty of the victims were soldiers or the daughters or wives of soldiers. Report of P. Bonesteel, Spec. Insp. For Ky. and Tenn., to Maj. Gen. O.O. Howard, Comm'r, Mar. 5, 1866, reprinted in H.R. EXEC. Doc. No. 39-70, at 203–7; *see also* Report of Clinton B. Fisk, Brevet Maj. Gen., to Maj. Gen. O.O. Howard, Comm'r, Feb. 14, 1866, reprinted in H.R. EXEC. Doc. No. 39-70, at 236, 237 ("'A great many colored men are beaten, their lives threatened, and they [sic] refused the privilege of returning home, *because they have been in the army*.'" (quoting Judge Samuel A. Spencer, Green County, Kentucky)); Report of Clinton B. Fisk, Brevet Maj. Gen., to Maj. Gen. O.O. Howard, Comm'r, Feb. 14, 1866, reprinted in H.R. EXEC. Doc. No. 39-70, at 236, 237–38 (reporting several cases of Black soldiers and their families being murdered, assaulted, or driven from their homes).

101. *See* ANDREW E. TASLITZ, RECONSTRUCTING THE FOURTH AMENDMENT: A HISTORY OF SEARCH AND SEIZURE, 1789–1868, at 13 (2006) (observing that postwar violence was "sometimes overtly state-sanctioned, sometimes by 'private' mobs often led by state officials").

102. 2 REPORT OF THE JOINT COMMITTEE ON RECONSTRUCTION AT THE FIRST

SESSION, 39TH CONGRESS 185 (1866) (testimony of Col. E. Whittlesey).

103. 2 REPORT OF THE JOINT COMMITTEE ON RECONSTRUCTION AT THE FIRST SESSION, 39TH CONGRESS 209 (1866).

104. 2 REPORT OF THE JOINT COMMITTEE ON RECONSTRUCTION AT THE FIRST SESSION, 39TH CONGRESS 209–10 (1866).

105. WILLIAM MCKEE EVANS, BALLOTS AND FENCE RAILS: RECONSTRUCTION ON THE LOWER CAPE FEAR 84 (1967).

106. 4 REPORT OF THE JOINT COMMITTEE ON RECONSTRUCTION AT THE FIRST SESSION, 39TH CONGRESS 79 (1866) (testimony of Thomas Conway).

107. 4 REPORT OF THE JOINT COMMITTEE ON RECONSTRUCTION AT THE FIRST SESSION, 39TH CONGRESS 80 (1866).

108. WILLIAM MCKEE EVANS, BALLOTS AND FENCE RAILS: RECONSTRUCTION ON THE LOWER CAPE FEAR 70 (1967).

109. 2 REPORT OF THE JOINT COMMITTEE ON RECONSTRUCTION AT THE FIRST SESSION, 39TH CONGRESS 271–72 (1866) (testimony of Brevet Lt. Col. W.H.H. Beadle); *see also* WILLIAM MCKEE EVANS, BALLOTS AND FENCE RAILS: RECONSTRUCTION ON THE LOWER CAPE FEAR 84 (1967).

110. Report of Clinton B. Fisk, Brevet Maj. Gen., to Maj. Gen. O.O. Howard, Comm'r, Feb. 14, 1866, reprinted in H.R. EXEC. DOC. No. 39-70, at 236, 238.

111. WILLIAM J. STUNTZ, THE COLLAPSE OF AMERICAN CRIMINAL JUSTICE 104 (2011) ("Slave patrols and similar entities were functional agents of the government. . . .").

112. Carl Schurz, *Report on the Condition of the South*, in 1 SPEECHES, CORRESPONDENCE AND POLITICAL PAPERS OF CARL SCHURZ 279, 315 (1913) (quoting Capt. Poillon).

113. 2 REPORT OF THE JOINT COMMITTEE ON RECONSTRUCTION AT THE FIRST SESSION, 39TH CONGRESS 222 (1866) (testimony of Gen. Rufus Saxton); Report of Capt. J.H. Matthews, Jan. 12, 1866, reprinted in 3 REPORT OF THE JOINT COMMITTEE ON RECONSTRUCTION AT THE FIRST SESSION, 39TH CONGRESS 146 (1866).

114. Carl Schurz, *Report on the Condition of the South*, in 1 SPEECHES, CORRESPONDENCE AND POLITICAL PAPERS OF CARL SCHURZ 279, 350–51 (1913); *see also* 3 REPORT OF THE JOINT COMMITTEE ON RECONSTRUCTION AT THE FIRST SESSION, 39TH CONGRESS 122 (1866) (testimony of B.H. Grierson).

115. Carl Schurz, *Report on the Condition of the South*, in 1 SPEECHES, CORRESPONDENCE AND POLITICAL PAPERS OF CARL SCHURZ 279, 351 (1913); *see also* 3 REPORT OF THE JOINT COMMITTEE ON RECONSTRUCTION AT THE FIRST SESSION, 39TH CONGRESS 10 (1866) (testimony of Brevet Brig. Gen. George E. Spencer) ("The arming of the militia is only for the purpose of intimidating the Union men, and enforcing upon the negroes a species of slavery. . . .").

116. Cong. Globe., 39th Cong., 1st Sess. 914 (Feb. 19, 1866) (alteration added).

117. Cong. Globe., 39th Cong., 1st Sess. 914 (Feb. 19, 1866) (alteration added).

118. Cong. Globe., 39th Cong., 1st Sess. 914 (Feb. 19, 1866) (alteration added).

119. Cong. Globe., 39th Cong., 1st Sess. 914 (Feb. 19, 1866) (alteration added).

120. Report of Capt. James H. Mathews, to Maj. George D. Reynolds, Nov. 27,

1865, reprinted in 3 Report of the Joint Committee on Reconstruction at the First Session, 39th Congress 185 (1866).

121. William C. Harris, Presidential Reconstruction in Mississippi 75 (1967) (quoting letter dated Sept. 4, 1865).

122. 3 Report of the Joint Committee on Reconstruction at the First Session, 39th Congress 142 (1866) (testimony of Capt. J.H. Matthews).

123. Report of Capt. J.H. Matthews, Jan. 12, 1866, reprinted in 3 Report of the Joint Committee on Reconstruction at the First Session, 39th Congress 146 (1866).

124. Report of Capt. J.H. Matthews, Jan. 12, 1866, reprinted in 3 Report of the Joint Committee on Reconstruction at the First Session, 39th Congress 146 (1866).

125. *See* Report of Brevet Brig. Gen. C.H. Howard to Maj. Gen. O.O. Howard, Comm'r, Dec. 30, 1865, reprinted in H.R. Exec. Doc. No. 39-70, at 350, 358.

126. Carl Schurz, *Report on the Condition of the South*, in 1 Speeches, Correspondence and Political Papers of Carl Schurz 279, 352 (1913).

127. Eric Foner, Reconstruction: America's Unfinished Revolution, 1863–1877, at 204 (1988); *see* Report of J.W. Sprague, Ass't Comm'r, to Maj. Gen. O.O. Howard, Comm'r, dated Oct. 18, 1866, reprinted in Sen. Exec. Doc. No. 39-6, at 22, 24 (noting "[t]he neglect of the civil authorities to make an effort to bring . . . to justice" murderers of at least twenty-nine Black people in Arkansas in July and August 1866); Report of Brevet Brig. Gen. C.H. Howard, Ass't Comm'r, to Maj. Gen. O.O. Howard, Comm'r, dated Oct. 22, 1866, reprinted in Sen. Exec. Doc. No. 39-6, at 33, 35 (noting the "refusal of constables to make arrest of whites, where freedmen are involved" in Maryland); *see* Report of Brevet Maj. Gen. J.G. Foster, Ass't Comm'r, to Maj. Gen. O.O. Howard, Comm'r, dated Oct. 1866, reprinted in Sen. Exec. Doc. No. 39-6, at 43, 44 ("[T]he arrest[s] of criminals guilty of outrages and murderous assaults upon freedmen have been so delayed [in Florida] as to permit the escape of the criminal and cause a failure of justice."); Report of Brevet Brig. Gen. O. Brown, to Maj. Gen. O.O. Howard, Comm'r, dated Oct. 27, 1866, reprinted in Sen. Exec. Doc. No. 39-6, at 157, 167 ("Justices of the peace have frequently refused to entertain complaints made by the freedmen, and also have in some cases given decisions manifestly partial.").

128. Report of Jef. C. Davis, Ass't Comm'r, to Maj. Gen. O.O. Howard, Comm'r, dated Nov. 5, 1866, reprinted in Sen. Exec. Doc. No. 39-6, at 60, 67; *see also* Report of Clinton B. Fisk, Brevet Maj. Gen., to Maj. Gen. O.O. Howard, Comm'r, Feb. 14, 1866, reprinted in H.R. Exec. Doc. No. 39-70, at 236, 238 (quoting Maj. Lawrence, 17th Kentucky Cavalry) ("The judges and justices of the peace [in Russellville, Kentucky] in almost every instance are rebels of very strong prejudices, who will not even take notice of the most *hideous outrages*. . . ."); Report of Brevet Brig. Gen. J.R. Lewis, to Maj. Gen. O.O. Howard, Comm'r, dated Nov. 1, 1866, reprinted in Sen. Exec. Doc. No. 39-6, at 126, 128 (reporting that when five white men shot and killed a Black man in Tennessee in July 1866, a magistrate issued an arrest warrant but the sheriff refused to execute it).

129. JOE M. RICHARDSON, THE NEGRO IN THE RECONSTRUCTION OF FLORIDA, 1865–77, at 45–47 (1965).

130. REPORT OF THE JOINT COMMITTEE ON RECONSTRUCTION AT THE FIRST SESSION, 39TH CONGRESS 17 (1866).

131. Report of Brevet Maj. Gen. R.K. Scott, to Maj. Gen. O.O. Howard, Comm'r, dated Nov. 1, 1866, reprinted in SEN. EXEC. DOC. No. 39-6, at 112, 117.

132. JOE M. RICHARDSON, THE NEGRO IN THE RECONSTRUCTION OF FLORIDA, 1865–77, at 41, 46, 48 (1965); Report of Brevet Brig. Gen. J.R. Lewis, to Maj. Gen. O.O. Howard, Comm'r, dated Nov. 1, 1866, reprinted in SEN. EXEC. DOC. No. 39-6, at 126, 128. *See also* ERIC FONER, RECONSTRUCTION: AMERICA'S UNFINISHED REVOLUTION, 1863–1877, at 204 (1988).

133. 2 REPORT OF THE JOINT COMMITTEE ON RECONSTRUCTION AT THE FIRST SESSION, 39TH CONGRESS 7 (1866); *see also* 2 REPORT OF THE JOINT COMMITTEE ON RECONSTRUCTION AT THE FIRST SESSION, 39TH CONGRESS 32 (1866) (testimony of Joseph Stiles) (declaring that a "Union or northern man" had "[n]o chance at all" in the courts); 2 REPORT OF THE JOINT COMMITTEE ON RECONSTRUCTION AT THE FIRST SESSION, 39TH CONGRESS 33 (1866) (testimony of Sheriff Jonathan Roberts of Fairfax, Virginia that when a former rebel soldier shot a Union man in Falls Church, the jury of nine former rebels and three Union men reached a compromise verdict of manslaughter with one year of imprisonment, despite the evidence being "just as plain and positive as it could be").

134. THE SOUTHERN LOYALISTS' CONVENTION 48 (1866).

135. 2 REPORT OF THE JOINT COMMITTEE ON RECONSTRUCTION AT THE FIRST SESSION, 39TH CONGRESS 55 (1866) (testimony of Madison Newby) (relating incident where patrols in Surrey County, Virginia "search[ed] the houses of colored people, turning them out and beating them").

136. *See* EDWARD MCPHERSON, POLITICAL MANUAL FOR 1866, at 32 (Mississippi), 33 (Alabama), 35 (South Carolina), 40 (Florida); *see also* JOE M. RICHARDSON, THE NEGRO IN THE RECONSTRUCTION OF FLORIDA, 1865–77, at 43 (1965).

137. Report of Brevet Maj. Gen. Wager Swayne, Ass't Comm'r, to Maj. Gen. O.O. Howard, Comm'r, Jan. 31, 1866, reprinted in H.R. EXEC. DOC. No. 39-70, at 285, 289; *see also* 3 REPORT OF THE JOINT COMMITTEE ON RECONSTRUCTION AT THE FIRST SESSION, 39TH CONGRESS 140 (1866) (testimony of Brevet Maj. Gen. Wager Swayne).

138. 2 REPORT OF THE JOINT COMMITTEE ON RECONSTRUCTION AT THE FIRST SESSION, 39TH CONGRESS 128 (1866) (testimony of Col. Orlando Brown).

139. 3 REPORT OF THE JOINT COMMITTEE ON RECONSTRUCTION AT THE FIRST SESSION, 39TH CONGRESS 32 (1866) (testimony of Maj. Gen. Clinton B. Fisk that "local militia[s] were ordered by the adjutant general of [Mississippi] to disarm the negroes").

140. WILLIAM MCKEE EVANS, BALLOTS AND FENCE RAILS: RECONSTRUCTION ON THE LOWER CAPE FEAR 71, 80–81 (1967); *see, e.g.*, Report of P. Bonesteel, Spec. Insp. For Ky. and Tenn., to Maj. Gen. O.O. Howard, Comm'r, Mar. 5, 1866, reprinted in H.R. EXEC. DOC. No. 39-70, at 205–06 (documenting instance in

January 1866, in which a Lexington, Kentucky, police officer entered the home of Armstead Fowler, a Black man, to seize a pistol, which was kept by the officer even after Fowler paid $14 in fines and costs).

141. Report of Clinton B. Fisk, Brevet Maj. Gen., to Maj. Gen. O.O. Howard, Comm'r, Feb. 14, 1866, reprinted in H.R. Exec. Doc. No. 39-70, at 236, 237.

142. William McKee Evans, Ballots and Fence Rails: Reconstruction on the Lower Cape Fear 71–72 (1967); *see also* Dan T. Carter, *The Anatomy of Fear: The Christmas Day Insurrection Scare of 1865*, 42 J. Southern Hist. 345, 361 (1976) ("On the assumption that blacks could not have acquired property except by thievery, valuables were taken without justification or explanation."); David H. Gans, *"We Do Not Want to Be Hunted": The Right to Be Secure and Our Constitutional Story of Race and Policing*, 11 Colum. J. Race & Law 239, 277 (2021) ("Police, militia, and armed vigilantes ransacked the homes of Black people . . . to steal their arms [and] rob them. . . ." (footnote omitted)).

143. William C. Harris, Presidential Reconstruction in Mississippi 91 (1967); *see also* Cong. Globe. 39th Cong., 1st Sess. 40 (Dec. 13, 1865) (Sen. Wilson) ("In Mississippi rebel State forces . . . are traversing the State, visiting the freedmen, disarming them[] [and] perpetrating murders and outrages upon them. . . .").

144. 2 Report of the Joint Committee on Reconstruction at the First Session, 39th Congress 272 (1866) (testimony of Brevet Lt. Col. W.H.H. Beadle); *see also* William McKee Evans, Ballots and Fence Rails: Reconstruction on the Lower Cape Fear 73 (1967); Eric Foner, Reconstruction: America's Unfinished Revolution, 1863–1877, at 203 (1988) (noting that white militiamen "ransack[ed] homes to seize shotguns and other property"); Dan T. Carter, *The Anatomy of Fear: The Christmas Day Insurrection Scare of 1865*, 42 J. Southern Hist. 345, 361 (1976) ("More often than not . . . the raids degenerated into a moblike attack in which freedmen were abused and threatened, furniture overturned, and locked chests smashed.").

145. Report of C.W. Buckley, Dist. Insp., to Brevet Maj. Gen. W. Swayne, Ass't Comm'r, dated Jan. 5, 1866, reprinted in H.R. Exec. Doc. No. 39-70, at 291, 292; 3 Report of the Joint Committee on Reconstruction at the First Session, 39th Congress 140 (1866) (testimony of Brevet Maj. Gen. Wager Swayne).

146. 4 Report of the Joint Committee on Reconstruction at the First Session, 39th Congress 49–50 (1866) (testimony of Lt. Col. H.S. Hall).

147. William McKee Evans, Ballots and Fence Rails: Reconstruction on the Lower Cape Fear 130–31 (1967) (quoting Wilmington *Daily Journal*, Dec. 22, 1865).

148. 3 Report of the Joint Committee on Reconstruction at the First Session, 39th Congress 8 (1866) (testimony of Brevet Brig. Gen. George E. Spencer).

149. Cong. Globe., 39th Cong., 1st Sess. 941 (Feb. 20, 1866). Trumbull also claimed to have other letters to the same effect from other parts of the South.

150. Joseph B. James, The Framing of the Fourteenth Amendment 158 (1965).

151. Mass. House Rep. No. 149, at 18–20 (Feb. 28, 1867).

152. Theodore Brantner Wilson, The Black Codes of the South 136 (1965).

153. Cong. Globe, 39th Cong., 1st Sess., App. 58 (Rep. Julian) (Jan. 29, 1866) (adverting to "the testimony of the great cloud of concurring witnesses whose voices are now filling the land, respecting the popular feeling in the South"); Cong. Globe, 39th Cong., 1st Sess., 633 (Rep. Moulton) (Feb. 3, 1866) ("The testimony which will be published that has been exhibited before the committee of fifteen will astonish the world as to . . . the condition of things in the South."); Cong. Globe, 39th Cong., 1st Sess., 1617 (Rep. Moulton) (Mar. 24, 1866) (reporting that "[t]he testimony taken by the reconstruction committee" demonstrates that Southerners' "hatred toward the Union and northern people is intense" and, that the "constant and barbarous outrages committed by rebels in the South against the Union men and freedmen would fill volumes"); Cong. Globe, 39th Cong., 1st Sess., 1267 (Rep. Schenck) (Mar. 8, 1866) (stating that the stories of attitudes in the South were "proved by the evidence laid before the House by the committee on reconstruction"). *See also* Cong. Globe, 39th Cong., 1st Sess., 1629 (Rep. Hart) (Mar. 24, 1866) (quoting testimony); Cong. Globe, 39th Cong., 1st Sess., 1833 (Rep. Lawrence of Ohio) (Mar. 24, 1866) (same); Cong. Globe, 39th Cong., 1st Sess., 2092 (Rep. Thomas) (Apr. 21, 1866) (same).

154. Jacobus tenBroek, The Antislavery Origins of the Fourteenth Amendment 187 (1951).

155. Cong. Globe, 39th Cong., 1st Sess., 79 (Dec. 19, 1865); *see* Joseph B. James, The Framing of the Fourteenth Amendment 51–52 (1965); *see* 1 Speeches, Correspondence and Political Papers of Carl Schurz 374 n.1 (1913) (reporting that Senator Sumner "proposed to the Senate to have 100,000 copies printed").

156. Joseph B. James, The Framing of the Fourteenth Amendment 51 (1965).

157. *See, e.g.*, Cong. Globe, 39th Cong., 1st Sess., App. 58 (Rep. Julian) (Jan. 29, 1866); Cong. Globe, 39th Cong., 1st Sess., 589 (Rep. Donnelly) (Feb. 1, 1866); Cong. Globe, 39th Cong., 1st Sess. 1839 (Rep. Clarke of Kansas) (Apr. 7, 1866); Cong. Globe, 39th Cong., 1st Sess., 2092 (Rep. Thomas) (Apr. 21, 1866).

158. Joseph B. James, The Framing of the Fourteenth Amendment 51 (1965) ("[T]he document created much excitement."); Earl M. Maltz, Civil Rights, the Constitution, and Congress, 1863–1869, at 38 (1990).

159. *See generally* Stephen V. Ash, A Massacre in Memphis: The Race Riot that Shook the Nation One Year after the Civil War (2013); Marius Carriere, *An Irresponsible Press: Memphis Newspapers and the 1866 Riot*, 60 Tenn. Hist. Q. 2 (2001); Hon. Bernice Bouie Donald, *When the Rule of Law Breaks Down: Implications of the 1866 Memphis Massacre for the Passage of the Fourteenth Amendment*, 98 B.U. L. Rev. 1607 (2018); Kevin R. Hardwick, *"Your Old Father Abe Lincoln Is Dead and Damned": Black Soldiers and the Memphis Race Riot of 1866*, 27 J. South. Hist. 109 (1993); Jack D. L. Holmes, *The Underlying Causes of the Memphis*

Race Riot of 1866, 17 TENN. HIST. Q. 195 (1958); Bobby L. Lovett, *Memphis Riots: White Reaction to Blacks in Memphis, May 1865–July 1866*, 38 TENN. HIST. Q. 9 (1979); Joe M. Richardson, *The Memphis Race Riot and Its Aftermath: Report by a Northern Missionary*, 24 TENN. HIST. Q. 63 (1965); James Gilbert Ryan, *The Memphis Riots of 1866: Terror in a Black Community During Reconstruction*, 62 J. NEGRO HIST. 243 (1977); Altina L. Waller, *Community, Class and Race in the Memphis Riot of 1866*, 18 J. SOUTH. HIST. 233 (1984).

160. *See generally* JAMES G. HOLLANDSWORTH JR., AN ABSOLUTE MASSACRE: THE NEW ORLEANS RACE RIOT OF JULY 30, 1866 (2001); Donald E. Reynolds, *The New Orleans Riot of 1866: Reconsidered*, 5 LA. HIST. 5 (1964); Gilles Vandal, *The Origins of the New Orleans Riot of 1866, Revisited*, 22 LA. HIST. 135 (1981).

161. H.R. Rep. 39–16, at 351 (1867) (quoting dispatch from Maj. Gen. Philip H. Sheridan to Gen. Ulysses S. Grant, dated Aug. 2, 1866).

162. *See* MICHAEL KENT CURTIS, NO STATE SHALL ABRIDGE: THE FOURTEENTH AMENDMENT AND THE BILL OF RIGHTS 137 (1986); Donald E. Reynolds, *The New Orleans Riot of 1866: Reconsidered*, 5 LA. HIST. 5, 14 (1964).

163. Cong. Globe, 39th Cong., 1st Sess., 2468 (Rep. Kelley) (May 8, 1866); Cong. Globe, 39th Cong., 1st Sess., 2544 (Rep. Stevens) (May 10, 1866) ("Let not these friends of secession sing to me their siren song of peace and good will until they can stop my ears to the screams and groans of the dying victims at Memphis.").

164. KURT T. LASH, THE FOURTEENTH AMENDMENT AND THE PRIVILEGES AND IMMUNITIES OF AMERICAN CITIZENSHIP 180 (2014); *see also* JAMES E. BOND, NO EASY WALK TO FREEDOM: RECONSTRUCTION AND THE RATIFICATION OF THE FOURTEENTH AMENDMENT 85 (1997) (observing that Northern Republicans saw the incident "as a deliberate massacre of the blacks and their white supporters, orchestrated perhaps by local officials.").

165. KURT T. LASH, THE FOURTEENTH AMENDMENT AND THE PRIVILEGES AND IMMUNITIES OF AMERICAN CITIZENSHIP 202 (2014).

166. *See* H.R. Rep. 39–101 (1866).

167. H.R. Rep. 39–16 (1867).

168. *See* H.R. Exec. Doc. 39–68 (1867).

169. ERIC FONER, RECONSTRUCTION: AMERICA'S UNFINISHED REVOLUTION, 1863–1877, at 226, 240–41 (1988).

170. ERIC FONER, RECONSTRUCTION: AMERICA'S UNFINISHED REVOLUTION, 1863–1877, at 246 (1988); *see also* JOSEPH A. RANNEY, IN THE WAKE OF SLAVERY: CIVIL WAR, CIVIL RIGHTS, AND THE RECONSTRUCTION OF SOUTHERN LAW 5 (2006) ("The black codes and continuing reports of widespread violence and mistreatment of blacks in the South eventually led many moderates to side with the Radicals").

171. JAMES G. HOLLANDSWORTH JR., AN ABSOLUTE MASSACRE: THE NEW ORLEANS RACE RIOT OF JULY 30, 1866, at 148 (2001); *see* also James E. Bond, *The Original Understanding of the Fourteenth Amendment in Illinois, Ohio, and Pennsylvania*, 18 AKRON L. REV. 435, 444 (1985) ("The Memphis and New Orleans incidents reinforced the view that white Southerners treated the freedmen like ani-

mals." (footnotes omitted)); Donald E. Reynolds, *The New Orleans Riot of 1866: Reconsidered*, 5 LA. HIST. 5, 5 (1964) (observing that the massacre "convinced a majority of Northerners that the South was determined, through intimidation or violence, to keep the Negro in a state of semi-slavery"); Joe M. Richardson, *The Memphis Race Riot and Its Aftermath: Report by a Northern Missionary*, 24 TENN. HIST. Q. 63, 63 (1965) ("The spectacle of white mobs massacring Negroes gave apparent proof of the Republicans' belief in Southern intransigence and the necessity of a more vigorous reconstruction."); Gilles Vandal, *The Origins of the New Orleans Riot of 1866, Revisited*, 22 LA. HIST. 135, 135 (1981) (observing that the massacre "gave plausibility to Republican charges of an unrepentant South").

172. JAMES E. BOND, NO EASY WALK TO FREEDOM: RECONSTRUCTION AND THE RATIFICATION OF THE FOURTEENTH AMENDMENT 85 (1997); *see also* Gilles Vandal, *The Origins of the New Orleans Riot of 1866, Revisited*, 22 LA. HIST. 135, 135 (1981) (noting "the role [the massacre] played in the congressional elections of 1866"). *See also* KURT T. LASH, THE FOURTEENTH AMENDMENT AND THE PRIVILEGES AND IMMUNITIES OF AMERICAN CITIZENSHIP 203 (2014) ("[T]he riots of Memphis and New Orleans became a living lesson to the public regarding the meaning and necessity of Section One of the Fourteenth Amendment.").

173. Carl Schurz, "The Logical Results of the War," Speech Delivered Sept. 8, 1866, in Philadelphia, Pa., reprinted in 1 SPEECHES, CORRESPONDENCE AND POLITICAL PAPERS OF CARL SCHURZ 377, 389 (1913); *see also* Carl Schurz, "The Logical Results of the War," Speech Delivered Sept. 8, 1866, in Philadelphia, Pa., reprinted in 1 SPEECHES, CORRESPONDENCE AND POLITICAL PAPERS OF CARL SCHURZ 377, 400 (1913) ("When the news of the New Orleans riots and the connection of the President with that revolting butchery flashed over the country, the heart of every honest man was palpitating with indignation.").

174. 9 JOURNALS AND DEBATES OF THE GENERAL ASSEMBLY OF THE STATE OF INDIANA 29 (1867).

175. JOURNAL OF THE ASSEMBLY OF WISCONSIN 34 (1867).

176. *See, e.g.*, RAOUL BERGER, THE FOURTEENTH AMENDMENT AND THE BILL OF RIGHTS 85 (1989); EARL M. MALTZ, CIVIL RIGHTS, THE CONSTITUTION, AND CONGRESS, 1863–1869, at 38 (1990).

177. *See, e.g.*, Cong. Globe, 39th Cong., 1st Sess., 96 (Sen. Cowan) (Dec. 20, 1865) (dismissing the anecdotes brought to the floor of Congress as "a series of *ex parte* statements made up by anonymous letter-writers," and saying that "[o]ne man out of ten thousand is brutal to a negro, and that is paraded here as a type of the whole people of the South.").

178. JOSEPH B. JAMES, THE FRAMING OF THE FOURTEENTH AMENDMENT 187 (1965).

179. Cong. Globe, 39th Cong., 1st Sess., 1267 (Rep. Raymond) (Mar. 8, 1866) ("I have not been able as yet to convince myself that the state of the South is so wholly and irredeemably bad as it is thus represented to be").

180. *See, e.g.*, Report of Benjamin C. Truman to Andrew Johnson, President, dated Apr. 9, 1866, reprinted in SEN. EXEC. DOC. NO. 39-43, at 1, 11 ("[T]here have

not been, and are not now, more colored people murdered, in proportion to their whole number, than whites.").

181. *See* Carl Schurz, "The Logical Results of the War," Speech Delivered Sept. 8, 1866, in Philadelphia, Pa., reprinted in 1 SPEECHES, CORRESPONDENCE AND POLITICAL PAPERS OF CARL SCHURZ 377, 391 (1913) ("[T]he President's friends will say that I exaggerate. . . . But let them read the testimony of our military commanders whom a protracted residence in the South has enabled to form a judgment. . . .").

182. H.R. Rep. 39–101, at 34 (July 25, 1866).

Chapter 7

1. 83 U.S. (16 Wall.) 36 (1873).

2. 92 U.S. (2 Otto) 542 (1876).

3. *See, e.g.*, O'Neil v. Vermont, 144 U.S. 323 (1892); Twining v. New Jersey, 211 U.S. 78 (1908).

4. *See, e.g.*, Barrington v. Missouri, 205 U.S. 483 (1907).

5. Palko v. Connecticut, 302 U.S. 319, 325 (1937) (quoting Snyder v. Massachusetts, 291 U.S. 97, 105 (1934)).

6. *Palko*, 302 U.S. at 323–24. *See also Snyder*, 291 U.S. 97; Chicago, B. & Q. R. Co. v. Chicago, 166 U.S. 226 (1896).

7. Adamson v. California, 332 U.S. 46, 66 (1947) (Frankfurter, J., concurring).

8. 338 U.S. 25, 27–28 (1949).

9. 338 U.S. at 28.

10. The Court later held that it would apply the exclusionary rule where police conduct was not only violative of ordinary due process norms but also "shock[ed] the conscience." Rochin v. California, 342 U.S. 165, 172 (1952). *Cf.* Breithaupt v. Abram, 352 U.S. 432, 435–36 (1957) (drawing blood from unconscious suspect did not violate the "community sense of 'decency and fairness' that has been woven by common experience into the fabric of acceptable conduct").

11. *Adamson*, 332 U.S. at 71–72 (Black, J., dissenting).

12. *Adamson*, 332 U.S. at 124 (Murphy, J., dissenting).

13. Mapp v. Ohio, 367 U.S. 643, 655 (1961).

14. 374 U.S. 23, 30–34 (1963).

15. Malloy v. Hogan, 378 U.S. 1, 10 (1964).

16. Louis Henkin, *"Selective Incorporation" in the Fourteenth Amendment*, 73 YALE L.J. 74, 75 (1963) ("Selective incorporation would apply to the states the substantive provisions of the first and fourth amendments, imposing the same limitations that these amendments place on the federal government.").

17. The Court in Walker v. Sauvinet, 92 U.S. 90 (1875), rejected the incorporation of the Seventh Amendment, *see* U.S. CONST., amend. VII ("In Suits at common law, where the value in controversy shall exceed twenty dollars, the right of trial by jury shall be preserved. . . ."). In Hurtado v. California, 110 U.S. 516 (1884), it rejected incorporation of the Fifth Amendment's Grand Jury Clause, *see* U.S.

Const., amend. V ("No person shall be held to answer for a capital, or otherwise infamous crime, unless on a presentment or indictment of a Grand Jury, except in cases arising in the land or naval forces, or in the Militia, when in actual service in time of War or public danger. . . ."). These cases are still good law.

The Court has never held that the Fourteenth Amendment incorporates the Excessive Bail Clause of the Eighth Amendment, which provides: "Excessive bail shall not be required. . . ." U.S. Const., amend. VIII. However, its decision in Timbs v. Indiana, 139 S. Ct. 682 (2019), that the Fourteenth Amendment incorporates the Excessive Fines Clause of the Eighth Amendment ("excessive fines [shall not be] imposed"), suggests that the companion Excessive Bail Clause would likely be held to apply to the States as well. The Third Amendment, which provides that "[n]o Soldier shall, in time of peace be quartered in any house, without the consent of the Owner, nor in time of war, but in a manner to be prescribed by law," U.S. Const., amend. III, has not been applied to the States either, but the situations in which it would arise are extremely rare.

18. Kurt T. Lash, The Fourteenth Amendment and the Privileges and Immunities of American Citizenship 280–87 (2016). There are a number of prominent scholars who have studied the issue of incorporation but remain fairly agnostic. *See, e.g.*, Earl M. Maltz, Civil Rights, the Constitution, and Congress, 1863–1869, at 117–18 (1990); William E. Nelson, The Fourteenth Amendment: From Political Principle to Judicial Doctrine 123 (1988); John Harrison, *Reconstructing the Privileges or Immunities Clause*, 101 Yale L.J. 1385, 1465–66 (1992).

19. Raoul Berger, The Fourteenth Amendment and the Bill of Rights (1989); James E. Bond, No Easy Walk to Freedom: Reconstruction and the Ratification of the Fourteenth Amendment (1997); David P. Currie, The Constitution in the Supreme Court: The First Hundred Years, 1789–1888 (1985); Ilan Wurman, The Second Founding: An Introduction to the Fourteenth Amendment (2020); Charles Fairman, *Does the Fourteenth Amendment Incorporate the Bill of Rights? The Original Understanding*, 2 Stan. L. Rev. 5 (1949); Philip Hamburger, *Privileges or Immunities*, 105 Nw. U. L. Rev. 61 (2011).

20. Akhil Amar, The Bill of Rights: Creation and Reconstruction (1998); Chester James Antieau, The Intended Significance of the Fourteenth Amendment (1997); Randy E. Barnett and Evan D. Bernick, The Original Meaning of the 14th Amendment: Its Letter and Spirit (2021); Michael Kent Curtis, No State Shall Abridge: The Fourteenth Amendment and the Bill of Rights (1990); Kurt T. Lash, The Fourteenth Amendment and the Privileges and Immunities of American Citizenship (2016); Alfred Avins, *Incorporation of the Bill of Rights: The Crosskey-Fairman Debate Revisited*, 6 Harv. J. on Legis. 1 (1968); Richard L. Aynes, *On Misreading John Bingham and the Fourteenth Amendment*, 103 Yale L.J. 57 (1993); William Crosskey, *Charles Fairman, Legislative History, and the Constitutional Limitations on State Authority*, 22 U. Chi. L. Rev. 1 (1954); Bryan Wildenthal, *Nationalizing the*

Bill of Rights: Revisiting the Original Understanding of the Fourteenth Amendment in 1866–67, 68 Ohio St. L.J. 1509 (2007).

21. *See* Randy E. Barnett and Evan D. Bernick, The Original Meaning of the 14th Amendment: Its Letter and Spirit 42 (2021) (summarizing the various views).

22. Barry Friedman, *Reconstructing Reconstruction: Some Problems for Originalists (And Everyone Else, Too)*, 11 U. Pa. J. Const. L. 1201, 1213 (2009).

23. *See* Kurt T. Lash, The Fourteenth Amendment and the Privileges and Immunities of American Citizenship 178–79 (2016) (observing that most scholars have noted the silence of state legislatures in the ratification process); Michael Kent Curtis, No State Shall Abridge: The Fourteenth Amendment and the Bill of Rights 145 (1990) (observing that there are no records of the debates in most States and some perfunctory discussion in others).

24. *See* William E. Nelson, The Fourteenth Amendment: From Political Principle to Judicial Doctrine 7 (1988) ("[T]he meaning the amendment had for them existed on a conceptual level different from the doctrinal level on which most scholars have tended to examine it. . . ."); *see also* Michael Kent Curtis, No State Shall Abridge: The Fourteenth Amendment and the Bill of Rights 16 (1990) ("Because of the number of people involved and the lack of direct evidence as to what many of them thought about the meaning of section 1, absolute certainty is impossible."); Michael J. Perry, The Constitution in the Courts: Law or Politics? 117 (1994) ("There is room for reasonable disagreement about the original meaning of the second sentence of section 1.").

25. Michael Kent Curtis, No State Shall Abridge: The Fourteenth Amendment and the Bill of Rights 14 (1990); *see* Joseph B. James, The Framing of the Fourteenth Amendment 55–73 (1965). *See also* James E. Bond, *The Original Understanding of the Fourteenth Amendment in Illinois, Ohio, and Pennsylvania*, 18 Akron L. Rev. 435, 438 (1985) (observing that during ratification, "[t]he principal issue in [some] states was control of the national government," implicated by sections 2 and 3).

26. Akhil Amar, The Bill of Rights: Creation and Reconstruction 203 (1998); Earl M. Maltz, Civil Rights, the Constitution, and Congress, 1863–1869, at 91, 93 (1990); David T. Hardy, *Original Popular Understanding of the Fourteenth Amendment as Reflected in the Print Media of 1866–1868*, 30 Whittier L. Rev. 695, 699 (2009). *See, e.g.*, Cong. Globe, 39th Cong., 1st Sess., 2459 (May 8, 1866) (Rep. Stevens) (calling section 2 "the most important in the article"); Cong. Globe, 39th Cong., 1st Sess., 2504 (May 9, 1866) (Rep. McKee) (observing that section 3 had "generated more opposition . . . than any other."); *see also* Cong. Globe, 39th Cong., 1st Sess., 2503 (Rep. Raymond) (May 9, 1866) (expressing support for all but section 3); Cong. Globe, 39th Cong., 1st Sess., 2537 (Rep. Beaman) (May 10, 1866) (expressing support for Amendment despite "serious objections to the third section"); Cong. Globe, 39th Cong., 1st Sess., 2539 (Rep. Farnsworth) (May 10, 1866) ("I intend to vote for this amendment in the form reported, with the exception of the third section."); Cong. Globe, 39th Cong.,

1st Sess., 2540 (Rep. Dawes) (May 10, 1866) ("I give [the Amendment], with the exception of the third section, my hearty support.").

27. Cong. Globe, 39th Cong., 1st Sess., 806 (Feb. 13, 1866).

28. Cong. Globe, 39th Cong., 1st Sess., 1088 (Feb. 28, 1866).

29. Akhil Amar, The Bill of Rights: Creation and Reconstruction 182 (1998).

30. One Country, One Constitution, One People: Speech of Hon. John A. Bingham of Ohio, in the House of Representatives, February 28, 1866, In support of the proposed amendment to enforce the Bill of Rights (1866) (emphasis added).

31. Cong. Globe, 39th Cong., 1st Sess., 1291 (Mar. 9, 1866).

32. Cong. Globe, 39th Cong., 1st Sess., 1292 (Mar. 9, 1866).

33. Cong. Globe, 39th Cong., 1st Sess., 2542 (May 10, 1866).

34. *See* U.S. Const., art. IV, § 2, cl. 1 ("The Citizens of each State shall be entitled to all Privileges and Immunities of Citizens in the several States.").

35. Cong. Globe, 39th Cong., 1st Sess., 2765 (May 23, 1866) (emphasis added).

36. Cong. Globe, 39th Cong., 1st Sess., 2765 (May 23, 1866) (emphasis added).

37. Michael Kent Curtis, No State Shall Abridge: The Fourteenth Amendment and the Bill of Rights 89 (1990).

38. Michael Kent Curtis, No State Shall Abridge: The Fourteenth Amendment and the Bill of Rights 87 (1990); Earl M. Maltz, The Fourteenth Amendment and the Law of the Constitution 70 (2003). Unless otherwise indicated, my characterization of Republicans as radical, moderate, or conservative is drawn from Michael Les Benedict, A Compromise of Principle: Congressional Republicans and Reconstruction, 1863–1869, at 348–53 (1974).

39. Michael Kent Curtis, No State Shall Abridge: The Fourteenth Amendment and the Bill of Rights 79 (1990).

40. Cong. Globe, 39th Cong., 1st Sess., 2465 (May 8, 1866).

41. Cong. Globe, 39th Cong., 1st Sess., 2459 (May 8, 1866).

42. Kurt T. Lash, The Fourteenth Amendment and the Privileges and Immunities of American Citizenship 177 n.9 (2016); David T. Hardy, *Original Popular Understanding of the Fourteenth Amendment as Reflected in the Print Media of 1866–1868*, 30 Whittier L. Rev. 695, 696–97 (2009).

43. Kurt T. Lash, The Fourteenth Amendment and the Privileges and Immunities of American Citizenship 184 (2016); *see* Kurt T. Lash, The Fourteenth Amendment and the Privileges and Immunities of American Citizenship 177–78 (2016). *See also* Chester James Antieau, The Intended Significance of the Fourteenth Amendment 60–61 (1997) (noting that speeches in Congress referring to "natural rights" "were widely read and there is good reason to believe that they were generally understood and approved by the people of the States which effectuated the Amendment by ratification."); James E. Bond, No Easy Walk to Freedom: Reconstruction and the Ratification of the Fourteenth Amendment 21–22 (1997) (noting newspaper coverage in the South).

44. Cong. Globe, 39th Cong., 1st Sess., 1034 (Feb. 26, 1866).

45. Cong. Globe, 39th Cong., 1st Sess., 1291 (Mar. 9, 1866).

46. Kurt T. Lash, The Fourteenth Amendment and the Privileges and Immunities of American Citizenship 184–85 (2016); Michael Kent Curtis, No State Shall Abridge: The Fourteenth Amendment and the Bill of Rights 128 (1990); David T. Hardy, *Original Popular Understanding of the Fourteenth Amendment as Reflected in the Print Media of 1866–1868*, 30 Whittier L. Rev. 695, 711–13 (2009).

47. Kurt T. Lash, The Fourteenth Amendment and the Privileges and Immunities of American Citizenship 187–88 (2016); *see* Akhil Amar, The Bill of Rights: Creation and Reconstruction 187 (1998); David T. Hardy, *Original Popular Understanding of the Fourteenth Amendment as Reflected in the Print Media of 1866–1868*, 30 Whittier L. Rev. 695, 713–16 (2009).

48. "The Reconstruction Committee's Amendment in the Senate," *New York Times*, May 25, 1866. *See also* Michael Kent Curtis, No State Shall Abridge: The Fourteenth Amendment and the Bill of Rights 128 (1990); Kurt T. Lash, The Fourteenth Amendment and the Privileges and Immunities of American Citizenship 188 (2016).

49. Kurt T. Lash, The Fourteenth Amendment and the Privileges and Immunities of American Citizenship 227 (2016).

50. Kurt T. Lash, The Fourteenth Amendment and the Privileges and Immunities of American Citizenship 187 (2016); *see also* Chester James Antieau, The Intended Significance of the Fourteenth Amendment 124 (1997) ("[I]t can be inferred that the people probably knew of what had been said by the aforementioned Congressmen and accepted the fact."); Horace Edgar Flack, The Adoption of the Fourteenth Amendment 142 (1908) (observing that in his May 23 speech "Mr. Howard said that one of the purposes of the first section was to give Congress power to enforce the Bill of Rights," and that "[b]y declarations of this kind, by giving extracts or digests of the principal speeches made in Congress, the people were kept informed as to the objects and purposes of the Amendment").

51. Kurt T. Lash, The Fourteenth Amendment and the Privileges and Immunities of American Citizenship 178 (2016). *See also* Joseph B. James, The Framing of the Fourteenth Amendment 158 (1965) (observing that speeches during the campaign of 1866 and the Report of the Joint Committee "constituted the more or less official evidence available to the average voter").

52. William E. Nelson, The Fourteenth Amendment: From Political Principle to Judicial Doctrine 59 (1988) ("The amendment was . . . a central issue in the congressional elections in the autumn of 1866, and the Northern electorate gave it a hearty approval."); James E. Bond, *The Original Understanding of the Fourteenth Amendment in Illinois, Ohio, and Pennsylvania*, 18 Akron L. Rev. 435, 436 (1985) ("[R]atification of the 14th Amendment was the major election issue in 1866."). *But see* Joseph B. James, The Ratification of the Fourteenth Amendment 3 (1984) ("The amendment . . . was not a singular, burning issue;

other topics figured in the campaign, and many speakers did not even refer to the amendment.").

53. William E. Nelson, The Fourteenth Amendment: From Political Principle to Judicial Doctrine 60 (1988).

54. Kurt T. Lash, The Fourteenth Amendment and the Privileges and Immunities of American Citizenship 176, 179 (2016); *see also* James E. Bond, No Easy Walk to Freedom: Reconstruction and the Ratification of the Fourteenth Amendment 4–5 (1997); Eric Foner, Reconstruction: America's Unfinished Revolution, 1863–1877, at 267 (1988); James E. Bond, *The Original Understanding of the Fourteenth Amendment in Illinois, Ohio, and Pennsylvania*, 18 Akron L. Rev. 435, 436 (1985) (observing that "th[e] sharp and bitter clash" of parties in the 1866 campaign "insured a thorough analysis of the amendment"); 9 Journals and Debates of the General Assembly of the State of Indiana 44 (1867) (Sen. Bennett) (Jan. 16, 1867) (observing that the Amendment "ha[d] been discussed from every stump and school house"); 9 Journals and Debates of the General Assembly of the State of Indiana 28 (1867) (message of Gov. Oliver P. Morton) ("No public measure was ever more fully discussed before the people, better understood by them or received a more distinct and intelligent approval."); Journal of the Assembly of Wisconsin 33 (1867) (message of Gov. Lucius Fairchild) ("This resolution has for many months been before the people, and during that time its several sections have been made the subject of earnest discussion.").

55. Kurt T. Lash, The Fourteenth Amendment and the Privileges and Immunities of American Citizenship 176, 208, 215 (2016); James E. Bond, No Easy Walk to Freedom: Reconstruction and the Ratification of the Fourteenth Amendment 5 (1997) ("[V]oters overwhelmingly . . . returned candidates who favored ratification of the Fourteenth Amendment."); William E. Nelson, The Fourteenth Amendment: From Political Principle to Judicial Doctrine 59 (1988); *see* 2 Messages of the Governors of Michigan 586 (George N. Fuller ed. 1926) (remarks of Michigan Governor Henry H. Crapo); Journal of the Assembly of Wisconsin 33 (1867) (remarks of Wisconsin Governor Lucius Fairchild); Journal of the Senate of the Commonwealth of Pennsylvania 16 (1867) (message of Gov. A.G. Curtin) ("By the election of a large majority of members openly favoring and advocating the amendments, th[e] opinion [of the people] seems to me to have been abundantly expressed."). *See also* Horace Edgar Flack, The Adoption of the Fourteenth Amendment 176, 178 (1908).

56. Kurt T. Lash, The Fourteenth Amendment and the Privileges and Immunities of American Citizenship 191, 212 (2016). *See also* Earl M. Maltz, Civil Rights, the Constitution, and Congress, 1863–1869, at 123 (1990) ("[N]ew instances of mistreatment of southern freedmen highlighted the continuing need to provide for their protection. The most visible demonstrations were the race riots in Memphis and New Orleans. . . ."); Michael Kent Curtis, No State Shall Abridge: The Fourteenth Amendment and the Bill of

Rights 146 (1990) (observing that Gov. Paul Dillingham of Vermont cited the Memphis and New Orleans massacres as showing the need for the Amendment).

57. Kurt T. Lash, The Fourteenth Amendment and the Privileges and Immunities of American Citizenship 203, 213 (2016).

58. "Congress shall make no law . . . abridging the freedom of speech . . . or the right of the people peaceably to assemble. . . ." U.S. Const., amend. I.

59. Kurt T. Lash, The Fourteenth Amendment and the Privileges and Immunities of American Citizenship 209 (2016) (alteration added) (emphasis omitted).

60. Michael Kent Curtis, No State Shall Abridge: The Fourteenth Amendment and the Bill of Rights 144 (1990).

61. Kurt T. Lash, The Fourteenth Amendment and the Privileges and Immunities of American Citizenship 210 (2016); *see also* Michael Kent Curtis, No State Shall Abridge: The Fourteenth Amendment and the Bill of Rights 133 (1990) ("The idea that First Amendment rights, protected against state as well as federal invasion, are among the rights of all American citizens in every state was a recurring theme in the campaign. . . .").

62. Michael Kent Curtis, No State Shall Abridge: The Fourteenth Amendment and the Bill of Rights 133 (1990).

63. The Southern Loyalists' Convention 1, 6, 25, 33 (1866) (emphasis added) (some emphasis omitted). Although the convention material was not widely published, Kurt T. Lash, The Fourteenth Amendment and the Privileges and Immunities of American Citizenship 208 (2016), maintains that "the[se] proceedings . . . illustrate the common conception of the proposed Fourteenth Amendment as guarding against state-sponsored abridgement of constitutionally enumerated rights such as speech and assembly."

64. "The National Question," *New York Times*, Nov. 10, 1866; "Political Affairs," *New York Times*, Nov. 15, 1866; "The National Question," *New York Times*, Nov. 28, 1866; *see also* Kurt T. Lash, The Fourteenth Amendment and the Privileges and Immunities of American Citizenship 216–17 (2016) (alteration added); David T. Hardy, *Original Popular Understanding of the Fourteenth Amendment as Reflected in the Print Media of 1866–1868*, 30 Whittier L. Rev. 695, 717–19 (2009).

65. *See* James E. Bond, No Easy Walk to Freedom: Reconstruction and the Ratification of the Fourteenth Amendment 259 (1997); Charles Fairman, *Does the Fourteenth Amendment Incorporate the Bill of Rights? The Original Understanding*, 2 Stan. L. Rev. 5, 126–32 (1949). Another point in favor of the Incorporation Skeptics is that incorporation of the Fifth Amendment's Due Process Clause would render the Fourteenth Amendment's Due Process Clause superfluous. *See* Charles Fairman, *Does the Fourteenth Amendment Incorporate the Bill of Rights? The Original Understanding*, 2 Stan. L. Rev. 5, 58–59 (1949).

66. *See* Charles Fairman, *Does the Fourteenth Amendment Incorporate the Bill of Rights? The Original Understanding*, 2 Stan. L. Rev. 5, 82–126 (1949). *See also* Philip Hamburger, *Privileges or Immunities*, 105 Nw. U. L. Rev. 61, 132 (2011)

("If the Fourteenth Amendment were understood to have incorporated the Bill of Rights, so profound a change would have been directly, candidly, and clearly discussed.").

67. *See, e.g.*, Raoul Berger, The Fourteenth Amendment and the Bill of Rights 130–31 (1989).

68. *See, e.g.*, Raoul Berger, The Fourteenth Amendment and the Bill of Rights 87–88, 95 (1989) (contending that it was unclear whether Bingham was unaware of *Barron* or just disagreed with it, and commenting on "Bingham's muddleheadedness"); Raoul Berger, Government by Judiciary: The Transformation of the Fourteenth Amendment 163–64 (2d ed. 1997); Joseph B. James, The Framing of the Fourteenth Amendment 86 (1965) (stating that Bingham misunderstood "the essential nature of the first ten amendments" as directed only to the federal government); Charles Fairman, *Does the Fourteenth Amendment Incorporate the Bill of Rights? The Original Understanding*, 2 Stan. L. Rev. 5, 66 (1949) ("Bingham said inconsistent things, and was very unsatisfactory when pressed for clarification."). For a similar contemporaneous criticism, *see* S.S. Nicholas, *The Civil Rights Act*, in 3 Conservative Essays, Legal and Political 47, 48–49 (1867).

69. Cong. Globe, 39th Cong., 1st Sess., 1034 (Feb. 26, 1866).

70. Cong. Globe, 39th Cong., 1st Sess., 1089 (Feb. 28, 1866); *see* Kurt T. Lash, The Fourteenth Amendment and the Privileges and Immunities of American Citizenship 94–95 (2016). *See also* Jacobus tenBroek, The Antislavery Origins of the Fourteenth Amendment 197 (1951) (explaining that by "Bill of Rights," Bingham meant the Comity Clause, the Due Process Clause of the Fifth Amendment, and "the requirement 'that all shall be protected alike in life, liberty, and property,' not explicitly mentioned in either body or amendments").

71. 6 F.Cas. 546, 551–52 (E.D. Pa. 1823). *See* Randy E. Barnett and Evan D. Bernick, The Original Meaning of the 14th Amendment: Its Letter and Spirit 61–65 (2021) (observing that this was the dominant antebellum reading of the Comity Clause among jurists); Kurt T. Lash, The Fourteenth Amendment and the Privileges and Immunities of American Citizenship 23–26 & n.86 (2016) (same).

72. Randy E. Barnett and Evan D. Bernick, The Original Meaning of the 14th Amendment: Its Letter and Spirit 65–88 (2021); David R. Upham, *The Meanings of the "Privileges or Immunities of Citizens" on the Eve of the Civil War*, 91 Notre Dame L. Rev. 1117, 1129–63 (2016).

73. Kurt T. Lash, The Fourteenth Amendment and the Privileges and Immunities of American Citizenship 105 (2016) (explaining that Bingham viewed the Comity Clause as applying the Bill of Rights to the States).

74. Cong. Globe, 39th Cong., 1st Sess. 158 (Jan. 9, 1866); *see also* Cong. Globe, 39th Cong., 1st Sess., 430 (Rep. Bingham) (Jan. 25, 1866) ("I believe that the free citizens of each State were guarantied . . . all—not some, 'all'—the privileges of citizens *of the United States* in every State." (emphasis added)); Cong. Globe, 39th Cong., 1st Sess., 1090 (Rep. Bingham) (Feb. 28, 1866) ("[T]he citizens of each

State, being citizens of the United States, should be entitled to all the privileges and immunities of citizens of the United States in every State. . . ."). *See* Randy E. Barnett and Evan D. Bernick, The Original Meaning of the 14th Amendment: Its Letter and Spirit 129–30 (2021); Kurt T. Lash, The Fourteenth Amendment and the Privileges and Immunities of American Citizenship 86 (2016).

75. *See* Cong. Globe, 39th Cong., 1st Sess., 429 (Rep. Bingham) (Jan. 25, 1866) (observing that his initial proposal would give "power to the Congress . . . to enforce in behalf of every citizen of every State . . . *the rights which were guarantied to him from the beginning*, but which guarantee has unhappily been disregarded by more than one State of this Union . . . because of a want of power in Congress to enforce that guarantee" (emphasis added)); Cong. Globe, 39th Cong., 1st Sess. 1034 (Rep. Bingham) (Feb. 26, 1866) ("Every word of the proposed amendment is to-day in the Constitution . . . save the words conferring the express grant of power upon the Congress. . . . [I]t has been the want of the Republic that there was not an express grant of power in the Constitution to enable the whole people of every State, by congressional enactment, to enforce obedience to these requirements of the Constitution."). *See also* Michael Kent Curtis, No State Shall Abridge: The Fourteenth Amendment and the Bill of Rights 63–64 (1990); Kurt T. Lash, The Fourteenth Amendment and the Privileges and Immunities of American Citizenship 82, 85, 91–93 (2016); Earl M. Maltz, The Fourteenth Amendment and the Law of the Constitution 38 (2003).

76. *Compare* Kurt T. Lash, The Fourteenth Amendment and the Privileges and Immunities of American Citizenship 103 (2016) ("Bingham's 'ellipsis' theory of Article IV was so odd and idiosyncratic that it appears that no other Republican followed his argument."), *and* Earl M. Maltz, The Fourteenth Amendment and the Law of the Constitution 32, 38 (2003) (observing that "Bingham's invocation of the Comity Clause as a limitation on the ability of states to deal with their own citizenry was truly novel," and "had little support in the case law"), *with* Michael Kent Curtis, No State Shall Abridge: The Fourteenth Amendment and the Bill of Rights 47–48 (1990) ("Leading Republicans read the [Comity] clause to protect the fundamental rights of American citizens against hostile state action" and to provided "a body of national rights that states were required to respect.").

77. Michael Kent Curtis, No State Shall Abridge: The Fourteenth Amendment and the Bill of Rights 91 (1990).

78. Cong. Globe, 39th Cong., 1st Sess., App. 157 (Mar. 8, 1866) (Rep. Wilson) (stating that the formerly enslaved were "entitled to certain rights as citizens of the United States," and that the authority of Congress to protect those rights was "necessarily implied from the entire body of the Constitution, which was made for the protection of these rights"); Cong. Globe, 39th Cong., 1st Sess., 1054 (Feb. 27, 1866) (Rep. Higby) (observing that Bigham's first draft would "only have the effect to give vitality and life to portions of the Constitution that probably were intended from the beginning to have life and vitality, but which have received such a con-

struction that they have been entirely ignored and have become as dead matter"); Cong. Globe, 39th Cong., 1st Sess., 1294 (Mar. 9, 1866) (Rep. Wilson of Iowa) (asserting that "the great fundamental rights embraced in the bill of rights" already belonged to every citizen); Cong. Globe, 39th Cong., 1st Sess., App. 256 (July 9, 1866) (Rep. Baker) ("What business is it of any State . . . to rob the American citizen of *rights thrown around him by the supreme law of the land*?" (emphasis added)).

Some Radicals mentioned specific rights in the Bill of Rights as if they already bound the States. Representative Sidney Clarke of Kansas, for example, after observing that Black men had been stripped of their arms in Alabama and Mississippi, quoted a portion of the Second Amendment, and noted: "I shall insist that the reconstructed rebels of Mississippi respect the Constitution in their local laws, before I will even consider their claims to representation in Congress." Cong. Globe, 39th Cong., 1st Sess. 1838 (Apr. 7, 1866). At least two referred to the Fourth Amendment. *See* Cong. Globe, 39th Cong., 1st Sess., 1072 (Feb. 28, 1866) (Sen. Nye) ("In the enumeration of natural and personal rights to be protected, the framers of the Constitution apparently specified everything they could think of—'life,' 'liberty,' 'property,' 'freedom of speech,' 'freedom of the press,' 'freedom in the exercise of religion,' '*security of person*.'" (emphasis added)); Cong. Globe, 39th Cong., 1st Sess., 1629 (Mar. 24, 1866) (Rep. Hart) (describing a "republican form of government" as being one where "'no law shall be made prohibiting the free exercise of religion; where 'the right of the people to keep and bear arms shall not be infringed;' where '*the right of the people to be secure in their persons, houses, papers, and effects, against unreasonable searches and seizures, shall not be violated*,' and where 'no person shall be deprived of life, liberty, or property without due process of law.'" (emphasis added)). *See also* Randy E. Barnett and Evan D. Bernick, The Original Meaning of the 14th Amendment: Its Letter and Spirit 194 (2021) (observing that "the right to be free from unreasonable searches and seizures" was mentioned in Congressional debates "less frequently" than some other enumerated rights, such as the right to free speech, but that it "did not inspire controversy" when it was brought up).

79. Earl M. Maltz, Civil Rights, the Constitution, and Congress, 1863–1869, at 59 (1990); Richard L. Aynes, *On Misreading John Bingham and the Fourteenth Amendment*, 103 Yale L.J. 57, 74 (1993).

80. Cong. Globe, 38th Cong., 2d Sess. 193 (Jan. 12, 1865) (stating that Southern abolitionists had been "driven from the States in the south where they had a right to live as citizens, because of the tyranny which this institution exercised over public feeling and public opinion, and even over the laws of those States").

81. Joseph B. James, The Framing of the Fourteenth Amendment 63–64 (1965).

82. Cong. Globe, 39th Cong., 1st Sess., 1063, 1064 (Feb. 27, 1866) (emphasis added). Hale elaborated that if one believed that the laws of a State were "inconsistent with the bill of rights contained in the Constitution of the United States, then . . . his remedy is [that] the courts may be appealed to to vindicate the rights of the citizens, both under civil and criminal procedure"). Cong. Globe, 39th Cong.,

1st Sess. 1065 (Feb. 27, 1866). *See* KURT T. LASH, THE FOURTEENTH AMENDMENT AND THE PRIVILEGES AND IMMUNITIES OF AMERICAN CITIZENSHIP 101 (2016) (observing that Hale assumed the Bill of Rights bound the States); MICHAEL KENT CURTIS, NO STATE SHALL ABRIDGE: THE FOURTEENTH AMENDMENT AND THE BILL OF RIGHTS 69 (1990).

83. KURT T. LASH, THE FOURTEENTH AMENDMENT AND THE PRIVILEGES AND IMMUNITIES OF AMERICAN CITIZENSHIP 82 (2016); *see also* MICHAEL KENT CURTIS, NO STATE SHALL ABRIDGE: THE FOURTEENTH AMENDMENT AND THE BILL OF RIGHTS 41 (1990); Robert J. Kaczorowski, *Revolutionary Constitutionalism in the Era of the Civil War and Reconstruction*, 61 N.Y.U. L. REV. 863, 890–93 (1986).

84. KURT T. LASH, THE FOURTEENTH AMENDMENT AND THE PRIVILEGES AND IMMUNITIES OF AMERICAN CITIZENSHIP 82 (2016) ("Like most of his Republican colleagues, John Bingham accepted the concept of natural rights—the idea that some freedoms were so foundational that they belonged to all persons regardless of their status in society.").

85. *See* RANDY E. BARNETT, RESTORING THE LOST CONSTITUTION: THE PRESUMPTION OF LIBERTY 61 (2004) (explaining that the term "civil rights" includes "the legally protected rights one received in return for surrendering to the government the natural right, or 'executive power,' to enforce one's own rights"); WILLIAM E. NELSON, THE FOURTEENTH AMENDMENT: FROM POLITICAL PRINCIPLE TO JUDICIAL DOCTRINE 82 (1988) ("[P]roponents of the Fourteenth Amendment conceded that rights derived from higher law or from the nature of citizenship in a republic were not absolute but were subject to reasonable regulation by government, including the states.").

86. AKHIL AMAR, THE BILL OF RIGHTS: CREATION AND RECONSTRUCTION 148 (1998) (observing that many in the nineteenth century, particularly "*Barron* contrarians" such as Bingham, viewed the Bill of Rights as merely declaratory of pre-existing "natural or fundamental rights"); Howard J. Graham, *Our "Declaratory" Fourteenth Amendment*, reprinted in HOWARD JAY GRAHAM, EVERYMAN'S CONSTITUTION: HISTORICAL ESSAYS ON THE FOURTEENTH AMENDMENT, THE "CONSPIRACY THEORY," AND AMERICAN CONSTITUTIONALISM 295, 300 (1968) (noting that the Fourteenth Amendment "was regarded by its framers and ratifiers as declaratory of the previously existing law and Constitution").

87. "The Privilege of the Writ of Habeas Corpus shall not be suspended, unless when in Cases of Rebellion or invasion the public Safety may require it." U.S. CONST., art. I, § 9, cl. 2.

88. AKHIL AMAR, THE BILL OF RIGHTS: CREATION AND RECONSTRUCTION 204–5 (1998).

89. AKHIL AMAR, THE BILL OF RIGHTS: CREATION AND RECONSTRUCTION 186 (1998); *see also* Trisha Olson, *The Natural Law Foundation of the Privileges or Immunities Clause of the Fourteenth Amendment*, 48 ARK. L. REV. 347, 356 (1995) ("Congressional members steadily reiterated that the [Civil Rights] Act only declared the *pre-existing* constitutional privileges and immunities of citizens *notwithstanding* Congress's lack of enforcement power.").

90. Akhil Amar, The Bill of Rights: Creation and Reconstruction 146–47, 149 & n.* (1998). *Cf.* Joseph B. James, The Framing of the Fourteenth Amendment 190 (1965) ("Bingham's confusion on the nature of the Bill of Rights . . . does not show greater ignorance . . . than that of the average lawyer of his day.").

91. Timothy Farrar, Manual of the Constitution of the United States of America § 448, at 402 (1867); *see also* Bryan H. Wildenthal, *Nationalizing the Bill of Rights: Scholarship and Commentary on the Fourteenth Amendment in 1867–1873*, 18 J. Contemp. Legal Issues 153, 229–33 (2009) (summarizing Farrar's views).

92. *See generally* Howard J. Graham, *The Early Antislavery Backgrounds of the Fourteenth Amendment*, reprinted in Howard Jay Graham, Everyman's Constitution: Historical Essays on the Fourteenth Amendment, the "Conspiracy Theory," and American Constitutionalism 151, 157–241 (1968).

93. Michael Kent Curtis, No State Shall Abridge: The Fourteenth Amendment and the Bill of Rights 100 (1990) ("Much of what Republicans had to say does seem confused if read without an understanding of the antislavery background, and in light of modern legal ideas").

94. Trisha Olson, *The Natural Law Foundation of the Privileges or Immunities Clause of the Fourteenth Amendment*, 48 Ark. L. Rev. 347, 397 (1995); *See also* Michael Kent Curtis, No State Shall Abridge: The Fourteenth Amendment and the Bill of Rights 15 (1990) (suggesting sensitivity to "legal thought long forgotten and . . . what legal theories meant to Republicans in 1866 instead of what they mean to us today"); Howard J. Graham, *The Early Antislavery Backgrounds of the Fourteenth Amendment*, reprinted in Howard Jay Graham, Everyman's Constitution: Historical Essays on the Fourteenth Amendment, the "Conspiracy Theory," and American Constitutionalism 151, 160 (1968) ("[W]e must . . . beware of that sort of hindsight which inverts perspective and makes it easy to dismiss an entire Congress or generation as inept because its views and purposes are *today* less than clear. The confusion and the difficulties may be partially ours.").

95. Michael Kent Curtis, No State Shall Abridge: The Fourteenth Amendment and the Bill of Rights 130 (1990).

96. Chester James Antieau, The Intended Significance of the Fourteenth Amendment 61 (1997).

97. Cong. Globe, 39th Cong., 1st Sess., 434–35 (Jan. 25, 1866). *See also* Cong. Globe, 39th Cong., 1st Sess. 2081 (Apr. 21, 1866) (Rep. Nicholson) (claiming that Bingham's first draft would "strike down the power of the States and consolidate the Government into a centralized despotism").

98. Cong. Globe, 39th Cong., 1st Sess., App. 134 (Feb. 26, 1866). While Rogers acknowledged that the later draft was "not so rabid," he continued to rail against it on federalism grounds. *See* Cong. Globe, 39th Cong., 1st Sess., 2538 (May 10, 1866) ("[I]t consolidates everything into one imperial despotism; it annihilates all the rights which lie at the foundation of the Union of the States. . . .").

99. Cong. Globe, 39th Cong., 1st Sess., 2493 (May 9, 1866).

100. Cong. Globe, 39th Cong., 1st Sess., 2500 (May 9, 1866).

101. Cong. Globe, 39th Cong., 1st Sess. 2940 (June 4, 1866).

102. Cong. Globe, 39th Cong., 1st Sess. 3147 (June 13, 1866). *See* Michael Kent Curtis, No State Shall Abridge: The Fourteenth Amendment and the Bill of Rights 100 (1990) (observing that the concern for opponents of Bingham's first draft was "that the amendment would give Congress power to legislate generally on matters of state law—such as the status of married women"); Christopher R. Green, Equal Citizenship, Civil Rights, and the Constitution: The Original Sense of the Privileges or Immunities Clause 108 (2015) ("The Fourteenth Amendment was, of course, a major inroad on federalism. Charges were made, not implausibly, that the clause would destroy local control by homogenizing the rights of American citizens."); William E. Nelson, The Fourteenth Amendment: From Political Principle to Judicial Doctrine 108 (1988) ("[T]he claim of the opponents of the Fourteenth Amendment was that its adoption would destroy the American constitutional tradition of local self-rule.").

103. Cong. Globe, 39th Cong., 1st Sess., 868 (Feb. 15, 1866).

104. Cong. Globe, 39th Cong., 1st Sess., 1082 (Feb. 28, 1866).

105. Cong. Globe, 39th Cong., 1st Sess., 1085 (Feb. 28, 1866).

106. Cong. Globe, 39th Cong., 1st Sess., App. 157 (Mar. 8, 1866).

107. Kurt T. Lash, The Fourteenth Amendment and the Privileges and Immunities of American Citizenship 79 (2016). *See also* Raoul Berger, The Fourteenth Amendment and the Bill of Rights 52–53 (1989) (discussing Republican commitment to federalism); James E. Bond, No Easy Walk to Freedom: Reconstruction and the Ratification of the Fourteenth Amendment 4 (1997) ("[M]any—probably a majority—of Republicans still believed in the basic tenets of federalism."); William E. Nelson, The Fourteenth Amendment: From Political Principle to Judicial Doctrine 7 (1988) ("[T]he Republicans remained dedicated to traditional values of federalism and did not . . . want to undermine state power in any drastic fashion."); Donald A. Dripps, About Guilt and Innocence: The Origins, Development, and Future of Constitutional Criminal Procedure 34 (2003) ("[R]espect for federalism was as integral to Republican thought as was respect for individual rights."); Phillip S. Paludan, Covenant with Death: The Constitution, Law, and Equality in the Civil War Era 59 (1975) (noting that even Republicans sought to maintain the basic federal structure). These sentiments were echoed in the moderate Republican press. *See* Joseph B. James, The Framing of the Fourteenth Amendment 87 (1965). According to Howard J. Graham, *Our "Declaratory" Fourteenth Amendment*, reprinted in Howard Jay Graham, Everyman's Constitution: Historical Essays on the Fourteenth Amendment, the "Conspiracy Theory," and American Constitutionalism 295, 312 (1968), "even the extreme Radicals" were devoted to federalism.

108. *See generally* Thomas D. Morris, Free Men All: The Personal Liberty Laws of the North, 1780–1861 (1974); *see also* Kurt T. Lash, The Four-

teenth Amendment and the Privileges and Immunities of American Citizenship 79 (2016). Representative Clarke of Kansas noted with some irony: "Those who supported [the fugitive slave laws] and could see no infringement of the reserved rights of the States, now build many an argument upon the very principles they then so scornfully rejected." Cong. Globe, 39th Cong., 1st Sess., 1838 (Apr. 7, 1866).

109. Kurt T. Lash, The Fourteenth Amendment and the Privileges and Immunities of American Citizenship 80 (2016).

110. William E. Nelson, The Fourteenth Amendment: From Political Principle to Judicial Doctrine 35 (1988).

111. Michael Kent Curtis, No State Shall Abridge: The Fourteenth Amendment and the Bill of Rights 37 (1990) (citing Michael Les Benedict, A Compromise of Principle: Congressional Republicans and Reconstruction, 1863–1869, at 348–51 (1974)); Kurt T. Lash, The Fourteenth Amendment and the Privileges and Immunities of American Citizenship 7 (2016); Joseph B. James, The Framing of the Fourteenth Amendment 84, 87 (1965).

112. Kurt T. Lash, The Fourteenth Amendment and the Privileges and Immunities of American Citizenship 81 (2016); *see also* Raoul Berger, The Fourteenth Amendment and the Bill of Rights 64 (1989) (noting the "conservative-moderate majority which . . . controlled the Thirty-Ninth Congress"); William E. Nelson, The Fourteenth Amendment: From Political Principle to Judicial Doctrine 53–54 (1988) (citing sentiment among Republicans that compromise among radical and more moderate Republicans was essential, lest the party lose power to the Democrats).

113. Cong. Globe, 39th Cong., 1st Sess., 1095 (Feb. 28, 1866).

114. Cong. Globe, 39th Cong., 1st Sess., 1063 (Feb. 27, 1866). *See* Kurt T. Lash, The Fourteenth Amendment and the Privileges and Immunities of American Citizenship 100–102 (2016) (discussing Hale's extensive federalism concerns). As a Radical, Hotchkiss's concern was that a later, more conservative Congress could claim extensive federal power to detract from the rights provided by some States. *See* Randy E. Barnett and Evan D. Bernick, The Original Meaning of the 14th Amendment: Its Letter and Spirit 135 (2021).

115. Cong. Globe, 39th Cong., 1st Sess., 1065 (Feb. 28, 1866). He also complained about "the extremely vague, loose, and indefinite provisions of the proposed amendment." Cong. Globe, 39th Cong., 1st Sess., 1064 (Feb. 28, 1866).

116. Kurt T. Lash, The Fourteenth Amendment and the Privileges and Immunities of American Citizenship 99 (2016); *see also* Kurt T. Lash, The Fourteenth Amendment and the Privileges and Immunities of American Citizenship 109 (2016).

117. Corfield v. Coryell, 6 F.Cas. 546, 551–52 (E.D. Pa. 1825); *see* Kurt T. Lash, The Fourteenth Amendment and the Privileges and Immunities of American Citizenship 73, 87–88 (2016).

118. Kurt T. Lash, The Fourteenth Amendment and the Privileges and Immunities of American Citizenship 73 (2016).

119. Kurt T. Lash, The Fourteenth Amendment and the Privileges and Immunities of American Citizenship 112 (2016). *See also* Earl M. Maltz, The Fourteenth Amendment and the Law of the Constitution 95 (2003) (discussing "the concerns of conservative Republicans such as Roscoe Conkling, Thomas T. Davis, Robert Hale, and William M. Stewart, whose fears regarding undue expansion of congressional authority led to the modification of the Fourteenth Amendment").

120. William E. Nelson, The Fourteenth Amendment: From Political Principle to Judicial Doctrine 114 (1988) (quoting "Centralization," *Boston Daily Evening Voice*, May 9, 1866, p. 1, col. 1); *see also* Eric Foner, Reconstruction: America's Unfinished Revolution, 1863–1877, at 242 (1988) (observing that moderate Republicans "did not believe the legitimate rights of the states had been destroyed, or the traditional principles of federalism eradicated"); Douglas G. Smith, *Natural Law, Article IV, and Section One of the Fourteenth Amendment*, 47 Am. U. L. Rev. 351, 410 (1997) ("Republicans forcefully demonstrated their intent that the states retain their power of regulation and that the Fourteenth Amendment not mandate a uniform civil or criminal code for the states.").

121. Cong. Globe, 39th Cong., 1st Sess., 2499 (May 9, 1866).

122. Cong. Globe, 39th Cong., 1st Sess., 1292–93 (Mar. 9, 1866).

123. Kurt T. Lash, The Fourteenth Amendment and the Privileges and Immunities of American Citizenship 129 (2016) (emphasis omitted); *see also* Earl M. Maltz, Civil Rights, the Constitution, and Congress, 1863–1869, at 59 (1990).

124. Michael Kent Curtis, No State Shall Abridge: The Fourteenth Amendment and the Bill of Rights 58–59 (1990); Kurt T. Lash, The Fourteenth Amendment and the Privileges and Immunities of American Citizenship 73, 112 (2016).

125. Kurt T. Lash, The Fourteenth Amendment and the Privileges and Immunities of American Citizenship 103 (2016).

126. Cong. Globe, 39th Cong., 1st Sess., 1089–90 (Feb. 28, 1866).

127. Cong. Globe, 39th Cong., 1st Sess., 1089 (Feb. 28, 1866).

128. Cong. Globe, 39th Cong., 1st Sess., 1089 (Feb. 28, 1866); *see* Earl M. Maltz, The Fourteenth Amendment and the Law of the Constitution 68 (2003); Trisha Olson, *The Natural Law Foundation of the Privileges or Immunities Clause of the Fourteenth Amendment*, 48 Ark. L. Rev. 347, 428–29 (1995); Douglas G. Smith, *Natural Law, Article IV, and Section One of the Fourteenth Amendment*, 47 Am. U. L. Rev. 351, 411 (1997).

129. Kurt T. Lash, The Fourteenth Amendment and the Privileges and Immunities of American Citizenship 104 (2016).

130. Kurt T. Lash, The Fourteenth Amendment and the Privileges and Immunities of American Citizenship 113 (2016); Earl M. Maltz, Civil Rights, the Constitution, and Congress, 1863–1869, at 60 (1990).

131. Kurt T. Lash, The Fourteenth Amendment and the Privileges and Immunities of American Citizenship 97 (2016).

132. Earl M. Maltz, Civil Rights, the Constitution, and Congress, 1863–1869, at 52 (1990) ("[T]he critical factor was the opposition of conservative Republicans. . . .").

133. Earl M. Maltz, Civil Rights, the Constitution, and Congress, 1863–1869, at 60 (1990).

134. Kurt T. Lash, The Fourteenth Amendment and the Privileges and Immunities of American Citizenship 108–09 (2016); Earl M. Maltz, Civil Rights, the Constitution, and Congress, 1863–1869, at 60 (1990).

135. Kurt T. Lash, The Fourteenth Amendment and the Privileges and Immunities of American Citizenship 70, 104 (2016); Earl M. Maltz, Civil Rights, the Constitution, and Congress, 1863–1869, at 49 (1990). *See also* Jacobus tenBroek, The Antislavery Origins of the Fourteenth Amendment 200 (1951) (noting that the Amendment's final wording was consistent with federalism, unlike Bingham's first draft, which would have injected Congress into every facet of state law).

136. Kurt T. Lash, The Fourteenth Amendment and the Privileges and Immunities of American Citizenship 73 (2016).

137. Earl M. Maltz, Civil Rights, the Constitution, and Congress, 1863–1869, at 90 (1990).

138. Earl M. Maltz, Civil Rights, the Constitution, and Congress, 1863–1869, at 94 (1990); Earl M. Maltz, The Fourteenth Amendment and the Law of the Constitution 69 (2003).

139. Cong. Globe, 39th Cong., 1st Sess., 2538 (May 10, 1866).

140. Cong. Globe, 39th Cong., 1st Sess., 2332–33 (May 2, 1866). *See also* Joseph B. James, The Framing of the Fourteenth Amendment 152 (1965) ("Disharmony within Republican ranks, executive opposition, pressure of public opinion, and the proximity of approaching elections had finally resulted in the adoption of a constitutional amendment far less radical than many had desired.").

141. *See* Cong. Globe, 39th Cong., 1st Sess. 3148 (June 13, 1866) (Rep. Stevens) (urging his fellow Radicals to "take what we can get now, and hope for better things in further legislation"); Cong. Globe, 39th Cong., 1st Sess., 3037–38 (June 8, 1866) (Sen. Yates) (deriding the "timid and cowardly conservatism which will not risk a great people to take their destiny in their own hands," but pledging his support of the Amendment because "I cannot get the position for which I have so earnestly contended"); Cong. Globe, 39th Cong., 1st Sess., 2498 (Rep. Broomall) (May 9, 1866) ("I want every man to come to the conclusion to which I have come, to vote, if not for that which he wants, for the best that he can get. . . ."); Cong. Globe, 39th Cong., 1st Sess., 2964 (Sen. Stewart) (June 5, 1866) ("While it is not the plan that I would have adopted . . . still it is the best that I can get, and contains many excellent provisions.").

142. See Horace Edgar Flack, The Adoption of the Fourteenth Amendment 161–207 (1908).

143. "Secretary Browning's Letter—The President and the Amendment," *New York Times*, Oct. 25, 1866 (stating that the letter was issued with "an explicit dec-

laration of the President's approval, as a statement of his views and purposes"). *See also* Joseph B. James, The Framing of the Fourteenth Amendment 165 (1965); Kurt T. Lash, The Fourteenth Amendment and the Privileges and Immunities of American Citizenship 211 (2016).

144. "The Political Situation," *New York Times*, Oct. 24, 1866; *see* Joseph B. James, The Framing of the Fourteenth Amendment 165–66 (1965); *see also* Horace Edgar Flack, The Adoption of the Fourteenth Amendment 146 (1908).

145. Joseph B. James, The Framing of the Fourteenth Amendment 167 (1965).

146. 1 Message and Annual Reports for 1866, Made to the Fifty-Seventh General Assembly, of the State of Ohio 282 (1867).

147. Joseph B. James, The Framing of the Fourteenth Amendment 167 (1965).

148. Kurt T. Lash, The Fourteenth Amendment and the Privileges and Immunities of American Citizenship 114 (2016); *see also* Raoul Berger, The Fourteenth Amendment and the Bill of Rights 99 (1989); Trisha Olson, *The Natural Law Foundation of the Privileges or Immunities Clause of the Fourteenth Amendment*, 48 Ark. L. Rev. 347, 425 (1995) ("[A]s much as Section One sought to constrain the states, it also sought to preserve federalism.").

149. Kurt T. Lash, The Fourteenth Amendment and the Privileges and Immunities of American Citizenship 69 (2016).

150. Cong. Globe, 39th Cong., 1st Sess., 3038 (June 8, 1866); *see also* Cong. Globe, 39th Cong., 1st Sess., 2964 (Sen. Poland) (June 5, 1866) ("It seems to me that this plan, as a whole, is characterized by so much moderation and forbearance that it cannot fail to commend itself to the people of these States so that they will readily and freely give it their sanction.").

Chapter 8

1. James E. Bond, No Easy Walk to Freedom: Reconstruction and the Ratification of the Fourteenth Amendment 267 (1997).

2. 1 Joel Prentiss Bishop, Commentaries on the Law of Criminal Procedure § 612, at 437, § 641, at 452–53, § 651, at 461, § 667, at 470, § 668, at 471 (1866). Others also recognized the lack of clarity in some of these areas. *See* 1 John H. Colby, A Practical Treatise Upon the Criminal Law Practice of the State of New York 68 (1868) (noting that the question whether a person could be arrested for a misdemeanor without a warrant was still unsettled); 1 Thomas W. Waterman, A Complete Practical Treatise on Criminal Procedure, Pleading, and Evidence in Indictable Cases 29 to 29-1 n.[1] (1853) (noting differing views over authority to break doors to arrest).

3. Raoul Berger, The Fourteenth Amendment and the Bill of Rights 125–26 (1989) ("[T]he framers had no intention of displacing State control of . . . local rights by a national 'equal' standard.").

4. Raoul Berger, The Fourteenth Amendment and the Bill of Rights 28–30 (1989).

5. Raoul Berger, The Fourteenth Amendment and the Bill of Rights 39 (1989) (footnote omitted); *see also* William E. Nelson, The Fourteenth Amendment: From Political Principle to Judicial Doctrine 119 (1988) ("The economic and personal rights for which they were advocating federal protection were coextensive with rights in the domain of state legislative jurisdiction. . . .").

6. William E. Nelson, The Fourteenth Amendment: From Political Principle to Judicial Doctrine 11 (1988).

7. Thomas B. McAffee, *The Original Meaning of the Ninth Amendment*, 90 Colum. L. Rev. 1215, 1273 (1990).

8. Akhil Amar, The Bill of Rights: Creation and Reconstruction 152–53 (1998). Amar is referring to Wesley Newcomb Hohfeld's classic article *Some Fundamental Legal Conceptions as Applied in Judicial Reasoning*, 23 Yale L.J. 16 (1913).

9. Earl M. Maltz, The Fourteenth Amendment and the Law of the Constitution 51 (2003); *see also* Michael Kent Curtis, No State Shall Abridge: The Fourteenth Amendment and the Bill of Rights 100 (1990) ("[T]he Republicans and Democrats adhered to different legal philosophies.").

10. *See* Earl M. Maltz, The Fourteenth Amendment and the Law of the Constitution 51 (2003) ("[B]oth antislavery and proslavery analysis generally rested on a theory of absolute rights belonging to every member of the community. . . ."); *see also* William E. Nelson, The Fourteenth Amendment: From Political Principle to Judicial Doctrine 23 (1988) (noting that "higher law" arguments were sometimes made by defenders of slavery).

11. *See* Trisha Olson, *The Natural Law Foundation of the Privileges or Immunities Clause of the Fourteenth Amendment*, 48 Ark. L. Rev. 347, 375 (1995) ("[T]he Jacksonians . . . trumpeted the People's will as the fundamental source of law.").

12. Randy E. Barnett and Evan D. Bernick, The Original Meaning of the 14th Amendment: Its Letter and Spirit 199 (2021).

13. James E. Bond, No Easy Walk to Freedom: Reconstruction and the Ratification of the Fourteenth Amendment 127–28 (1997) (quoting Charleston (S.C.) Mercury, Apr. 18, 1867); *see also* James E. Bond, *The Original Understanding of the Fourteenth Amendment in Illinois, Ohio, and Pennsylvania*, 18 Akron L. Rev. 435, 445–46 (1985) ("In this view a man had no rights by virtue of his humanity alone; rather, man had only those rights which a majority of his fellows deemed he could exercise wisely."); Speeches of John C. Calhoun Delivered in the Congress of the United States from 1811 to the Present Time 219 (1843) (distinguishing between "the means of enjoying or securing rights" and "rights themselves").

14. S.S. Nicholas, *The Civil Rights Act*, in 3 Conservative Essays, Legal and Political 47, 48–49 (1867).

15. Howard J. Graham, *Our "Declaratory" Fourteenth Amendment*, reprinted in

Howard Jay Graham, Everyman's Constitution: Historical Essays on the Fourteenth Amendment, the "Conspiracy Theory," and American Constitutionalism 295, 303 (1968) ("Probably few framers or ratifiers of 1866–68 . . . faced the problem of implementation squarely or presciently."); *see also* Robert J. Kaczorowski, *Revolutionary Constitutionalism in the Era of the Civil War and Reconstruction*, 61 N.Y.U. L. Rev. 863, 922–23 (1986) (observing that Attorney General "Edward Bates noted in 1862 that 'learned lawyers and able writers' refer to the rights of citizens without explaining what they are").

16. Howard J. Graham, *The Early Antislavery Backgrounds of the Fourteenth Amendment*, reprinted in Howard Jay Graham, Everyman's Constitution: Historical Essays on the Fourteenth Amendment, the "Conspiracy Theory," and American Constitutionalism 152, 188 (1968). *See also* Howard J. Graham, *The Early Antislavery Backgrounds of the Fourteenth Amendment*, reprinted in Howard Jay Graham, Everyman's Constitution: Historical Essays on the Fourteenth Amendment, the "Conspiracy Theory," and American Constitutionalism 152, 227 (1968) (noting the abolitionists' "confusion of abstract moral rights with enforceable constitutional ones"); Randy E. Barnett and Evan D. Bernick, The Original Meaning of the 14th Amendment: Its Letter and Spirit 155 (2021) ("[C]ongressional Republicans did not always cleanly separate civil rights from natural rights [and] sometimes referred to natural-rights-protective positive rights . . . as natural rights.").

17. Argument for the Defendant in Jones v. Vanzandt [*sic*] by S.P. Chase at 84 (1847), reprinted in 1 Fugitive Slaves and American Courts: The Pamphlet Literature 424 (Paul Finkelman ed., 2007); *see also* William E. Nelson, The Fourteenth Amendment: From Political Principle to Judicial Doctrine 22 (1988) (discussing Chase's view of natural rights).

18. The relationship between the Federalists and the Republicans was not lost on Democrats of this era. *See* S.S. Nicholas, *The Civil Rights Act*, in 3 Conservative Essays, Legal and Political 47, 49–50 (1867) (deriding the Federalists as "the New England party of 1798" and the Republicans as "the New England party of the present day").

19. Cong. Globe, 39th Cong., 1st Sess., 1270 (Mar. 8, 1866) (emphasis omitted).

20. *See generally* Thomas D. Morris, Free Men All: The Personal Liberty Laws of the North, 1780–1861 (1974).

21. Richard L. Aynes, *On Misreading John Bingham and the Fourteenth Amendment*, 103 Yale L.J. 57, 68 n.62 (1993).

22. Earl M. Maltz, Civil Rights, the Constitution, and Congress, 1863–1869, at 65 (1990) ("[M]ainstream Republicans in the Thirty-ninth Congress viewed the state governments as the primary bulwarks of fundamental rights, with the federal government stepping in only when the states failed to live up to their obligations.").

23. 1 Bruce Ackerman, We the People: Foundations 88–89, 94 (1991).

24. Akhil Amar, The Bill of Rights: Creation and Reconstruction xiv (1998) (emphasis omitted). *See also* Kurt T. Lash, The Fourteenth Amendment and the Privileges and Immunities of American Citizenship 292

(2014) ("It is possible . . . that not all of the provisions in the Bill of Rights constitute 'personal rights' covered by the [Privileges or Immunities] Clause."); Henry Brannon, A Treatise on the Rights and Privileges Guaranteed by the Fourteenth Amendment to the Constitution of the United States 72 (1901) (contending that whether a provision of the Bill of Rights is included as a "privilege or immunity" "depends on the nature of the right, not on the fact that it is mentioned in those amendments").

25. Akhil Amar, The Bill of Rights: Creation and Reconstruction 180 (1998) (emphasis omitted).

26. Cong. Globe, 39th Cong., 1st Sess., 2765 (May 23, 1866) (emphasis added). Of course, there is some ambiguity here, as the word "personal" might have been meant as a limitation on the word "rights" or it might have simply been meant as a descriptor of that word. Richard L. Aynes, *Refined Incorporation and the Fourteenth Amendment*, 33 U. Rich. L. Rev. 289, 302 n.86 (1999).

27. Akhil Amar, The Bill of Rights: Creation and Reconstruction 190 (1998) (emphasis omitted).

28. Akhil Amar, The Bill of Rights: Creation and Reconstruction xiv, 153, 222 (1998).

29. *See* Earl M. Maltz, Civil Rights, the Constitution, and Congress, 1863–1869, at 117 (1990) (contending that "there can be little doubt that the privileges and immunities clause was intended to incorporate *some* of the Bill of Rights," such as the Free Speech and Free Exercise Clauses, the Takings Clause, and the Second, Fourth, and Eighth Amendments); *see* Richard L. Aynes, *Refined Incorporation and the Fourteenth Amendment*, 33 U. Rich. L. Rev. 289, 295–96 (1999) (listing provisions of Bill of Rights specifically mentioned by members of Congress during debate).

30. Chester James Antieau, The Intended Significance of the Fourteenth Amendment 290 (1997); *see also* Andrew E. Taslitz, Reconstructing the Fourth Amendment: A History of Search and Seizure, 1789–1868, at 13 (2006) ("The Fourteenth Amendment is best understood . . . as in important part serving to fix th[e] problem[s] [of Reconstruction] by applying the Fourth Amendment to the states.").

31. Cong. Globe, 39th Cong., 1st Sess., 1629 (Mar. 24, 1866).

32. Cong. Globe, 39th Cong., 1st Sess., 1072 (Feb. 28, 1866).

33. Cong. Globe, 39th Cong., 1st Sess., 1182 (Mar. 5, 1866) (emphasis added).

34. Cong. Globe, 39th Cong., 1st Sess., 20 (Dec. 14, 1865) (introduced by Rep. Lovejoy).

35. Steven G. Calabresi and Sarah E. Agudo, *Individuals Rights under State Constitutions When the Fourteenth Amendment Was Ratified in 1868: What Rights Are Deeply Rooted in American History and Tradition*, 87 Tex. L. Rev. 7, 57–58 (2008). *See also* Chester James Antieau, The Intended Significance of the Fourteenth Amendment 290 (1997) ("By 1866 . . . twenty-five of the twenty-seven States that effectuated the Amendment had specific Constitutional clauses recognizing as natural and fundamental the right to be free from unreasonable searches and seizures.").

36. Akhil Amar, The Bill of Rights: Creation and Reconstruction 267–68 (1998).

37. David H. Gans, *"We Do Not Want to Be Hunted": The Right to Be Secure and Our Constitutional Story of Race and Policing*, 11 Colum. J. Race & Law 239, 290 (2021) ("[T]he Fourteenth Amendment was centrally concerned, in a way the original Fourth Amendment was not, with police violence.").

38. David H. Gans, *"We Do Not Want to Be Hunted": The Right to Be Secure and Our Constitutional Story of Race and Policing*, 11 Colum. J. Race & Law 239, 289 (2021).

39. Andrew E. Taslitz, Reconstructing the Fourth Amendment: A History of Search and Seizure, 1789–1868, at 248 (2006). Interestingly, the Report of the House of Representatives of Massachusetts, while agreeing that section 1 encompassed parts of the existing Constitution, believed that these were limited to the Preamble, the Comity Clause, the First, Second, Sixth, and Seventh Amendments, and the Due Process Clause of the Fifth Amendment. Mass. House Rep. No. 149 at 2–3 (Feb. 28, 1867); Horace Edgar Flack, The Adoption of the Fourteenth Amendment 187 (1908). This omission of the Fourth Amendment by a single state legislative committee perhaps signals that some ratifiers did not understand that it would apply against the States, but, if so, that understanding goes against the preponderance of the evidence.

40. Douglas G. Smith, *Natural Law, Article IV, and Section One of the Fourteenth Amendment*, 47 Am. U. L. Rev. 351, 406 (1997).

41. Trisha Olson, *The Natural Law Foundation of the Privileges or Immunities Clause of the Fourteenth Amendment*, 48 Ark. L. Rev. 347, 421 (1995) (opining that Justice Frankfurter's "concept of ordered liberty may have been closer to the mark than any other reading of the Amendment").

42. 338 U.S. 25, 27–28 (1949).

43. James E. Bond, No Easy Walk to Freedom: Reconstruction and the Ratification of the Fourteenth Amendment 259 (1997).

44. *See* Donald A. Dripps, About Guilt and Innocence: The Origins, Development, and Future of Constitutional Criminal Procedure xix (2003) ("[T]he old fundamental fairness standard describes the governing values too generally, while selective incorporation describes the governing norms too particularly.").

45. Akhil Amar, The Bill of Rights: Creation and Reconstruction 268 (1998).

46. Randy E. Barnett, Restoring the Lost Constitution: The Presumption of Liberty 203 (2004) ("Whereas the Privileges or Immunities Clause protects a broad set of rights—including life, liberty, and property—of all citizens from improper *laws*, the Due Process Clause protects the life, liberty, or property of all persons from an improper *application* of an otherwise proper law.").

47. Nathan S. Chapman and Michael W. McConnell, *Due Process as Separation of Powers*, 121 Yale L.J. 1672, 1782 (2012); *see also* Nathan S. Chapman and Michael W. McConnell, *Due Process as Separation of Powers*, 121 Yale L.J. 1672,

1679 (2012) ("Fundamentally, 'due process' meant that the government may not interfere with established rights without legal authorization and according to law, with 'law' meaning the common law as customarily applied by courts and retrospectively declared by Parliament, or as modified prospectively by general acts of Parliament."); HENRY BRANNON, A TREATISE ON THE RIGHTS AND PRIVILEGES GUARANTEED BY THE FOURTEENTH AMENDMENT TO THE CONSTITUTION OF THE UNITED STATES 141–42 (1901) (observing that due process requires "'[a] general public law equally binding on all,'" not "unusual or arbitrary action" (quoting Bank v. State, 24 Am. D. 517 (alteration added))); ILAN WURMAN, THE SECOND FOUNDING: AN INTRODUCTION TO THE FOURTEENTH AMENDMENT 23 (2020) (opining that "due process of law" historically meant that "deprivations of life, liberty, or property required express warrant in law" (emphasis omitted)).

48. Nathan S. Chapman and Michael W. McConnell, *Due Process as Separation of Powers*, 121 YALE L.J. 1672, 1778 (2012) ("Fourteenth Amendment due process was understood to mean nothing different than what due process and the law of the land had meant up to that point.").

49. 338 U.S. 25, 28 (1949) (emphasis added). *See* SARAH A. SEO, POLICING THE OPEN ROAD: HOW CARS TRANSFORMED AMERICAN FREEDOM 161 (2019) ("It was not per se the entry into a home . . . that was reminiscent of Nazi Germany and totalitarian rule. It was police action carried out without the *authority of law*.").

50. CHRISTOPHER R. GREEN, EQUAL CITIZENSHIP, CIVIL RIGHTS, AND THE CONSTITUTION: THE ORIGINAL SENSE OF THE PRIVILEGES OR IMMUNITIES CLAUSE 107 (2015).

51. Philip Hamburger, *Privileges or Immunities*, 105 NW. U. L. REV. 61, 131 (2011). *See also* JOHN NORTON POMEROY, AN INTRODUCTION TO THE CONSTITUTIONAL LAW OF THE UNITED STATES § 230, at 145 (1868) (observing that the States are "subject to restraints of the same general nature as those expressed in" the federal Bill of Rights).

52. JAMES E. BOND, NO EASY WALK TO FREEDOM: RECONSTRUCTION AND THE RATIFICATION OF THE FOURTEENTH AMENDMENT 266–67 (1997). A different way of reading the three clauses together is that, while the Privileges or Immunities Clause protects the rights in the Bill of Rights absolutely from abridgement by the States, the other two clause permit the States to deprive someone of *other* common-law rights so long as they provide due process of law and equal protection. *See, e.g.*, KURT T. LASH, THE FOURTEENTH AMENDMENT AND THE PRIVILEGES AND IMMUNITIES OF AMERICAN CITIZENSHIP 73 (2014) (asserting that section 1 "protect[s] the Bill of Rights against state abridgement as 'privileges or immunities of citizens of the United States,' but le[aves] common law civil rights in the hands of local government, subject only to the requirements of due process and equal protection"); *see also* KURT T. LASH, THE FOURTEENTH AMENDMENT AND THE PRIVILEGES AND IMMUNITIES OF AMERICAN CITIZENSHIP 106 (2014) (distinguishing "rights listed in the Constitution" from "common law rights in the states"). This view is problematic because it conceives of a sharp delineation between rights in the Bill of Rights and other "common law civil rights." But the right to be free

from unreasonable searches and seizures was seen as nothing more than a bundle of "common law civil rights" such as those contained in the justice of the peace manuals. Trisha Olson, *The Natural Law Foundation of the Privileges or Immunities Clause of the Fourteenth Amendment*, 48 Ark. L. Rev. 347, 371 (1995) ("[T]he nineteenth century legal mind conceived of the Bill of Rights as protecting entitlements that sprang from the common law.").

53. Randy E. Barnett and Evan D. Bernick, The Original Meaning of the 14th Amendment: Its Letter and Spirit 34–35 (2021).

54. 1 William Blackstone, Commentaries on the Laws of England 44 (9th ed. 1783) (emphasis omitted).

55. Carl Schurz, *Report on the Condition of the South*, in 1 Speeches, Correspondence and Political Papers of Carl Schurz 366 (1913).

56. James E. Bond, No Easy Walk to Freedom: Reconstruction and the Ratification of the Fourteenth Amendment 267 (1997).

57. Earl M. Maltz, Civil Rights, the Constitution, and Congress, 1863–1869, at 37 (1990); *see also* William E. Nelson, The Fourteenth Amendment: From Political Principle to Judicial Doctrine 43 (1988) (noting that freedmen "argued that it was the 'solemn duty' of the federal government to provide 'for our protection' until it 'grant[s] us the right to protect ourselves by means of the ballot'") (quoting "The Voice of the Freedmen of North Carolina," Wash. *Sunday Chronicle*, May 13, 1866, p.1 col. 2 (alteration in original)).

58. 2 James G. Blaine, Twenty Years of Congress: From Lincoln to Garfield 466–67 (1886).

59. Carl Schurz, *Report on the Condition of the South*, in 1 Speeches, Correspondence and Political Papers of Carl Schurz 366 (1913).

60. *See* Stephen M. Feldman, *From Premodern to Modern American Jurisprudence: The Onset of Positivism*, 50 Vand. L. Rev. 1387, 1407 (1997) ("From this perspective, natural law principles provided a metaphysical foundation for the American legal system, including the common law."); Douglas G. Smith, *Natural Law, Article IV, and Section One of the Fourteenth Amendment*, 47 Am. U. L. Rev. 351, 377 (1997) ("The common law . . . was a body of positive law developed over time that reflected principles of natural law or natural reason.").

61. Jack M. Balkin, Living Originalism 199 (2011).

62. Stephen M. Feldman, *From Premodern to Modern American Jurisprudence: The Onset of Positivism*, 50 Vand. L. Rev. 1387, 1415 (1997).

63. Thomas B. McAffee, *The Original Meaning of the Ninth Amendment*, 90 Colum. L. Rev. 1215, 1273 (1990).

64. *See* Stephen M. Feldman, *From Premodern to Modern American Jurisprudence: The Onset of Positivism*, 50 Vand. L. Rev. 1387, 1407–08 (1997) ("[I]n concrete judicial disputes, the principles needed to be specifically interpreted and applied. . . .").

65. Howard J. Graham, *Our "Declaratory" Fourteenth Amendment*, reprinted in Howard Jay Graham, Everyman's Constitution: Historical Essays on the Fourteenth Amendment, the "Conspiracy Theory," and American Constitutionalism 295, 304 (1968).

66. *See* Trisha Olson, *The Natural Law Foundation of the Privileges or Immunities Clause of the Fourteenth Amendment*, 48 ARK. L. REV. 347, 413 (1995) ("[T]his era considered the question of what the law was and the question of the authority to declare it to be two distinct questions. . . ." (emphasis omitted)).

67. WILLIAM E. NELSON, THE FOURTEENTH AMENDMENT: FROM POLITICAL PRINCIPLE TO JUDICIAL DOCTRINE 61 (1988). *See also* 1 BRUCE ACKERMAN, WE THE PEOPLE: FOUNDATIONS 92 (1991) ("[T]he impact of [Reconstruction's] new ideals on a host of . . . traditional principles has not yet been worked out in a thoroughgoing and considered way."); Howard J. Graham, *Our "Declaratory" Fourteenth Amendment*, reprinted in HOWARD JAY GRAHAM, EVERYMAN'S CONSTITUTION: HISTORICAL ESSAYS ON THE FOURTEENTH AMENDMENT, THE "CONSPIRACY THEORY," AND AMERICAN CONSTITUTIONALISM 295, 314 n.80 (1968) ("[T]he natural rights thinking and theories of the day obscured the problem [of incorporation] and probably precluded a precise intent with reference to full incorporation."); WILLIAM E. NELSON, THE FOURTEENTH AMENDMENT: FROM POLITICAL PRINCIPLE TO JUDICIAL DOCTRINE 111 (1988) ("[E]ven though many congressmen had been trained as lawyers, they usually did not address the Fourteenth Amendment in the standard fashion of lawyers seeking to identify the doctrinal issues that would arise when the amendment was placed in operation."); Richard L. Aynes, *Refined Incorporation and the Fourteenth Amendment*, 33 U. RICH. L. REV. 289, 294 (1999) ("[P]eople did not think clearly and carefully about the intricacies of the general principle."); Douglas G. Smith, *Natural Law, Article IV, and Section One of the Fourteenth Amendment*, 47 AM. U. L. REV. 351, 407 (1997) (arguing that "substantive guarantee[s]" in the Privileges or Immunities Clause were "not intended to mandate a certain set of regulations accompanying these fundamental rights").

68. JACK BALKIN, LIVING ORIGINALISM 199 (2011).

69. Trisha Olson, *The Natural Law Foundation of the Privileges or Immunities Clause of the Fourteenth Amendment*, 48 ARK. L. REV. 347, 360 (1995).

70. Trisha Olson, *The Natural Law Foundation of the Privileges or Immunities Clause of the Fourteenth Amendment*, 48 ARK. L. REV. 347, 429 (1995). *See also* Douglas G. Smith, *Natural Law, Article IV, and Section One of the Fourteenth Amendment*, 47 AM. U. L. REV. 351, 412 (1997) (observing that Republicans recognized a "distinction between the *regulation* of a right and its *destruction* or *abridgement*"); Charles R. Pence, *The Construction of the Fourteenth Amendment*, 25 AM. L. REV. 536, 542 (1891) (distinguishing between "a reasonable regulation of [a] right," which the Fourteenth Amendment permitted, and "its denial or abridgement," which it did not.); GEORGE W. PASCHAL, THE CONSTITUTION OF THE UNITED STATES DEFINED AND CAREFULLY ANNOTATED § 279, at 290 (1868) (explaining that the federal Bill of Rights had been adopted in most state constitutions "in *general* terms," and that "the *general* principles" of the Bill of Rights would henceforth apply to the States via the Fourteenth Amendment (emphasis added)).

71. WILLIAM E. NELSON, THE FOURTEENTH AMENDMENT: FROM POLITICAL PRINCIPLE TO JUDICIAL DOCTRINE 119 (1988); *see also* Douglas G. Smith, *Natural Law, Article IV, and Section One of the Fourteenth Amendment*, 47 AM. U. L. REV. 351, 359 (1997) (observing that the Privileges or Immunities Clause protected

fundamental rights but that it would be "the province of the state legislatures" to prescribe "the mode or manner in which these [rights] could be exercised.").

72. William E. Nelson, The Fourteenth Amendment: From Political Principle to Judicial Doctrine 111 (1988); *see also* Eric Foner, Reconstruction: America's Unfinished Revolution, 1863–1877, at 259 (1988) ("[F]ew Republicans wished to break completely with the principles of federalism. Only if state governments failed to protect citizens' rights would federal action become necessary."); James E. Bond, *The Original Understanding of the Fourteenth Amendment in Illinois, Ohio, and Pennsylvania*, 18 Akron L. Rev. 435, 460 (1985) (observing that during ratification, Republicans insisted that federal government would not exercise its power under the Fourteenth Amendment as long as "'rights are in good faith protected by State laws and State authorities'") (quoting Ohio Exec. Doc., Part I 282 (1867)).

73. William E. Nelson, The Fourteenth Amendment: From Political Principle to Judicial Doctrine 121 (1988).

74. John Hart Ely, Democracy and Distrust: A Theory of Judicial Review 103 (1980) ("In a representative democracy value determinations are to be made by our elected representatives, and if in fact most of us disapprove we can vote them out of office.").

75. Silas J. Wasserstrom and Louis Michael Seidman, *The Fourth Amendment as Constitutional Theory*, 77 Geo. L.J. 19, 93 (1988).

76. John Hart Ely, Democracy and Distrust: A Theory of Judicial Review 103 (1980).

77. Railway Express Agency, Inc. v. New York, 336 U.S. 106, 112 (1949) (Jackson, J., concurring).

78. Silas J. Wasserstrom and Louis Michael Seidman, *The Fourth Amendment as Constitutional Theory*, 77 Geo. L.J. 19, 94 (1988). *See also* Dan M. Kahan and Tracey L. Meares, *Foreword: The Coming Crisis of Criminal Procedure*, 86 Geo. L.J. 1153, 1172 (1998) (arguing that courts should step in when "the coercive incidence of a particular policy is being visited on a powerless minority").

79. Dan M. Kahan and Tracey L. Meares, *Foreword: The Coming Crisis of Criminal Procedure*, 86 Geo. L.J. 1153, 1172 (1998); *see also* Christopher Slobogin, *Is the Fourth Amendment Relevant in a Technological Age?*, *in* Constitution 3.0: Freedom and Technological Change 11, 29 (Jeffrey Rosen and Benjamin Wittes eds., 2013) ("If the authorizing legislation applies evenly to the entire group . . . the full costs of the program are likely to be considered in enacting it.").

80. John Hart Ely, Democracy and Distrust: A Theory of Judicial Review 177 (1980); *see also* Donald A. Dripps, *Criminal Procedure, Footnote Four, and the Theory of Public Choice; Or, Why Don't Legislatures Give a Damn About the Rights of the Accused?*, 44 Syracuse L. Rev. 1079, 1090 (1993) ("Executive discretion . . . operates as an important shock-absorber that protects legislatures from hostile reaction to law enforcement operations."); Silas J. Wasserstrom, *The Incredible Shrinking Fourth Amendment*, 21 Am. Crim. L. Rev. 257, 292 n.185 (1984) (observing that pursuant to "a 'representation-reinforcing' theory of judicial review,"

it should "make[] no difference whether the otherwise uncontrolled discretion of law enforcement officials results from legislative action or legislative default").

81. Dan M. Kahan and Tracey L. Meares, *Foreword: The Coming Crisis of Criminal Procedure*, 86 GEO. L.J. 1153, 1183 (1998).

82. William J. Stuntz, *Implicit Bargains, Government Power, and the Fourth Amendment*, 44 STAN. L. REV. 553, 588 (1992).

83. Daphna Renan, *The Fourth Amendment as Administrative Governance*, 68 STAN. L. REV. 1039, 1081–82 (2016); *see also* John Rappaport, *Second-Order Regulation of Law Enforcement*, 103 CALIF. L. REV. 205, 263–65 (2015) (advocating "second-order regulation," i.e., constitutional requirements aimed at policymakers rather than individual law enforcement officers, across a broad spectrum of contexts).

84. Christopher Slobogin, *Panvasive Surveillance, Political Process Theory, and the Nondelegation Doctrine*, 102 GEO. L.J. 1721, 1738 (2014).

85. BARRY FRIEDMAN, UNWARRANTED: POLICING WITHOUT PERMISSION 318 (2017). *See also* BARRY FRIEDMAN, UNWARRANTED: POLICING WITHOUT PERMISSION 19 (2017) ("*[A]s a matter of constitutional law*, policing without permission is altogether illegitimate."). It is true that it is difficult to justify reliance on the political process where the government engages in secret surveillance. *See* Eve Brensike Primus, *Disentangling Administrative Searches*, 111 COLUM. L. REV. 254, 294 (2011). But if, as I suggest, any surveillance regime that permits government agents to do what ordinary people cannot must be affirmatively authorized by legislation, this objection vanishes.

86. *See* Donald A. Dripps, *Criminal Procedure, Footnote Four, and the Theory of Public Choice; Or, Why Don't Legislatures Give a Damn About the Rights of the Accused?*, 44 SYRACUSE L. REV. 1079, 1100 (1993).

87. Donald A. Dripps, *Criminal Procedure, Footnote Four, and the Theory of Public Choice; Or, Why Don't Legislatures Give a Damn About the Rights of the Accused?*, 44 SYRACUSE L. REV. 1079, 1082 (1993) (observing that legislatures will impose limits on policing where "certain law enforcement techniques [are] constitutional if and only if these techniques are subjected to legislative regulations").

88. Barry Friedman, *Reconstructing Reconstruction: Some Problems for Originalists (and Everyone Else, Too)*, 11 U. PA. J. CONST. L. 1201, 1210–11 (2009) ("The first problem with incorporating Reconstruction into the originalist canon is the sheer difficulty of doing so."); Lawrence Rosenthal, *The New Originalism Meets the Fourteenth Amendment: Original Public Meaning and the Problem of Incorporation*, 18 J. CONTEMP. LEGAL ISSUES 361, 401–08 (2009) (rejecting an originalist approach to incorporation given the ambiguity of the evidence of original understanding).

89. Barry Friedman, *Reconstructing Reconstruction: Some Problems for Originalists (and Everyone Else, Too)*, 11 U. PA. J. CONST. L. 1201, 1206 (2009).

90. RANDY E. BARNETT AND EVAN D. BERNICK, THE ORIGINAL MEANING OF THE 14TH AMENDMENT: ITS LETTER AND SPIRIT 233 (2021).

91. Lee J. Strang, *Originalism and the "Challenge of Change": Abduced-Principle Originalism and Other Mechanisms by Which Originalism Sufficiently Accommodates Changed Social Conditions*, 60 HASTINGS L.J. 927, 973 (2009).

92. Earl M. Maltz, *Federalism and the Fourteenth Amendment: A Comment on Democracy and Distrust*, 42 Ohio St. L.J. 209, 211–12 (1981).

93. *See* Jack B. Weinstein, *Local Responsibility for Improvement of Search and Seizure Practices*, 34 Rocky Mntn. L. Rev. 150, 150, 152 (1962) (predicting, after *Mapp*, the onset of a search-and-seizure regime with broad, national mandates but with enough play in the joints to accommodate "our system of federalism as a unique check on the threat to liberty from centralized authority and . . . the opportunities of legislative and administrative experiment, assumption of local responsibility, and widespread participation in important affairs of government").

94. *See* Christopher Slobogin, *Is the Fourth Amendment Relevant in a Technological Age?*, in Constitution 3.0: Freedom and Technological Change 11, 29–30 (Jeffrey Rosen and Benjamin Wittes eds., 2013) ("As conceptualized by Ely, judicial deference would be mandated only if the search and seizure program were established pursuant to legislation (as opposed to executive fiat), adequately constrained the executive branch (by, for instance, instructing police to search everyone, or everyone who meets predefined criteria), and avoided discriminating against a discrete and insular minority or any other group that is not adequately represented in the legislature.").

Chapter 9

1. David H. Gans, *"We Do Not Want to Be Hunted": The Right to Be Secure and Our Constitutional Story of Race and Policing*, 11 Colum. J. Race & Law 239, 291 (2021) (observing that the Fourteenth Amendment "prohibited . . . all forms of discriminatory policing").

2. Anthony G. Amsterdam, *Perspectives on the Fourth Amendment*, 58 Minn. L. Rev. 349, 416 (1974).

3. George W. Paschal, The Constitution of the United States Defined and Carefully Annotated § 251, at 257 (1868) (emphasis added).

4. Anthony G. Amsterdam, *Perspectives on the Fourth Amendment*, 58 Minn. L. Rev. 349, 417 (1974); Kenneth Culp Davis, Discretionary Justice: A Preliminary Inquiry 58 (1969); Kenneth Culp Davis, Police Discretion 121–38 (1975); Kenneth Culp Davis, *An Approach to Legal Control of the Police*, 52 Tex. L. Rev. 703, 708–12 (1974); *see also* Gerald M. Caplan, *The Case for Rulemaking by Law Enforcement Agencies*, 36 Law & Contemp. Probs. 500, 502–06 (1971); Herman Goldstein, *Police Policy Formulation: A Proposal for Improving Police Performance*, 65 Mich. L. Rev. 1123, 1130–35 (1967); Samuel Walker, *Controlling the Cops: A Legislative Approach to Police Rulemaking*, 63 U. Det. L. Rev. 361, 382–91 (1986). Also starting around this time, various authorities advocated a sub-constitutional requirement that police promulgate regulations in order to limit individual-officer discretion. *See* 1 American Bar Association, Standards for Criminal Justice § 1–4.3 (2d ed. supp. 1986); American Law Institute, A Model Code of Pre-Arraignment Procedure § 10.3 (1975); The President's Commission on Law Enforcement and Administration of Justice, The Challenge of

Crime in a Free Society 104 (1967). Maria Ponomarenko has referred to this era as "policing's first 'rulemaking moment.'" Maria Ponomarenko, *Rethinking Police Rulemaking*, 114 Nw. L. Rev. 1, 2 (2019).

5. *See, e.g.*, John Rappaport, *Second-Order Regulation of Law Enforcement*, 103 Calif. L. Rev. 205, 268 (2015) ("In the second-order model, search-and-seizure activity must be undertaken pursuant to adequate guidelines to pass constitutional muster."). Scholars have also advocated police rulemaking based on administrative law principles without claiming that such rulemaking is a constitutional necessity. *See, e.g.*, Kami Chavis Simmons, *New Governance and the New Paradigm of Police Accountability: A Democratic Approach to Police Reform*, 59 Cath. U. L. Rev. 373, 400–02 (2010). I pay less attention to these sub-constitutional policy arguments because my claim is that some police rulemaking is constitutionally required.

6. *See* United States v. Caceres, 440 U.S. 741, 758 (1979) (Marshall, J., dissenting) ("Where individual interests are implicated, the Due Process Clause [of the Fifth Amendment] requires that an executive agency adhere to the standards by which it professes its action to be judged."). The Supreme Court in *Caceres* rejected this position. *See* 440 U.S. at 751–52 ("[T]he violations of agency regulations . . . do not raise any constitutional questions.").

7. Nathan S. Chapman and Michael W. McConnell, *Due Process as Separation of Powers*, 121 Yale L.J. 1672, 1785 (2012) (arguing that "the due process presumption" is against executive action). *See also* Kim Forde-Mazrui, *Ruling Out the Rule of Law*, 60 Vand. L. Rev. 1495, 1500 (2007) ("[T]he rule of law requires that government officials exercise coercive power over people only when authorized by laws previously enacted by politically legitimate institutions."); Daphna Renan, *The Fourth Amendment as Administrative Governance*, 68 Stan. L. Rev. 1039, 1082 (2016) (arguing that the Court "is wrong to decouple the question of Fourth Amendment reasonableness from the question whether the search at issue is ultra vires"); Christopher Slobogin, *Panvasive Surveillance, Political Process Theory, and the Nondelegation Doctrine*, 102 Geo. L.J. 1721, 1751 (2014) ("It is a basic administrative law principle that agency actions that are not authorized by statute are ultra vires and that courts have the authority to nullify such actions.").

8. Kenneth Culp Davis, Discretionary Justice: A Preliminary Inquiry 84 (1969). *See also* Barry Friedman, Unwarranted: Policing Without Permission 107 (2017) (observing that failing to ask "whether what the police did was authorized by law . . . is strange in a country like ours that's so full of pride about its democratic heritage, so ostensibly reliant on the will of the people"). The Fourth Amendment itself was understood for many years as requiring that executive officers have affirmative legal authorization to conduct searches and seizures, a requirement that has gotten lost. Orin S. Kerr, *Cross-Enforcement of the Fourth Amendment*, 132 Harv. L. Rev. 471, 500 (2018) (observing that the legal authorization requirement is "utterly foreign" to modern lawyers).

9. 533 U.S. 27 (2001).

10. Wilson v. Arkansas, 514 U.S. 927, 930, 931–36 (1995).

11. Payton v. New York, 445 U.S. 573, 617 (1980) (White, J., dissenting).

12. *See, e.g.*, Uniform Residential Landlord and Tenant Act of 1972 § 701(b) (rev. 2015).

13. *See* Kim Forde-Mazrui, *Ruling Out the Rule of Law*, 60 Vand. L. Rev. 1495, 1506 (2007) ("Legislative supremacy in the criminal law requires judicial checks on delegating discretion. . . ."); *see also* Christopher Slobogin, *Panvasive Surveillance, Political Process Theory, and the Nondelegation Doctrine*, 102 Geo. L.J. 1721, 1725 (2014) ("If political process theory is to have teeth in the panvasive-surveillance context, maintaining some version of the nondelegation doctrine is crucial to ensuring that law enforcement officers do not depart from the electorate's conception of how their discretion should be exercised.").

14. Kim Forde-Mazrui, *Ruling Out the Rule of Law*, 60 Vand. L. Rev. 1495, 1504–05 (2007).

15. John Hart Ely, Democracy and Distrust: A Theory of Judicial Review 177 (1980).

16. Nathan S. Chapman and Michael W. McConnell, *Due Process as Separation of Powers*, 121 Yale L.J. 1672, 1679, 1785 (2012).

17. Joseph Goldstein, *Police Discretion Not to Invoke the Criminal Process: Low-Visibility Decisions in the Administration of Justice*, 69 Yale L.J. 543, 552 (1960) ("[P]olice decisions not to invoke the criminal process, except when reflected in gross failures of service, are not visible to the community.").

18. Kenneth Culp Davis, Discretionary Justice: A Preliminary Inquiry 170 (1969) (emphasis omitted). *See also* Kim Forde-Mazrui, *Ruling Out the Rule of Law*, 60 Vand. L. Rev. 1495, 1522 23 (2007) (noting the problem of under-enforcement of traffic laws and other minor offenses).

19. Kenneth Culp Davis, Discretionary Justice: A Preliminary Inquiry 90 (1969); *see also* Joseph Goldstein, *Police Discretion Not to Invoke the Criminal Process: Low-Visibility Decisions in the Administration of Justice*, 69 Yale L.J. 543, 543 (1960) (observing that the initial decision not to make a stop or arrest "define[s] the ambit of discretion throughout the process of other decisionmakers—prosecutor, grand and petit jury, judge, probation officer, correction authority, and parole and pardon boards").

20. Kenneth Culp Davis, Discretionary Justice: A Preliminary Inquiry 81–82 (1969) ("With respect to law enforcement, the problems of policy as to whether and when to refrain in some degree from full enforcement are enormous, sometimes involving broad social problems, and often raising difficult problems about justice to the individual.").

21. Kenneth Culp Davis, Discretionary Justice: A Preliminary Inquiry 87–88 (1969) (emphasis omitted). *See also* Michael R. Gottfredson and Don M. Gottfredson, Decision Making in Criminal Justice: Toward the Rational Exercise of Discretion 73 (2d ed. 1988) (observing that "it is the patrol officer who, by default, is the real policymaker within police departments with respect to when to arrest" and that "[t]he absence of clearly articulated policies for the exercise of arrest discretion that can be monitored . . . raises serious issues of accountability"); Robert M. Igleburger and Frank A. Schubert, *Policy Making for*

the Police, 58 Am. B. Ass'n J. 307, 308 (1972) ("A consequence of th[e] absence of formal policy development by police administrators has been that police officers have had to determine intuitively how they should exercise their discretion to arrest or not to arrest in given types of situations.").

22. 118 U.S. 356, 359, 366–67, 370, 373 (1886). *See* Evan J. Criddle, *When Delegation Begets Domination: Due Process of Administrative Lawmaking*, 46 Ga. L. Rev. 117, 160–61 (2011) (describing *Yick Wo* as "[a]n early example" of "[t]he emergence of substantive due process as a constraint on legislative delegations").

23. *See* A. L. A. Schechter Poultry Corp. v. United States, 295 U.S. 495 (1935); Panama Ref. Co. v. Ryan, 293 U.S. 388 (1935).

24. J. W. Hampton, Jr., & Co. v. United States, 276 U.S. 394, 409 (1928).

25. National Broadcasting Co. v. United States, 319 U.S. 190, 216 (1943).

26. Gundy v. United States, 139 S. Ct. 2116, 2129 (2019) (plurality opinion) (quoting Yakus v. United States, 321 U.S. 414, 422, 427 (1944); FPC v. Hope Natural Gas Co., 320 U.S. 591 (1944)).

27. 139 S. Ct. at 2131 (Alito, J., concurring in the judgment) ("If a majority of this Court were willing to reconsider the approach we have taken for the past 84 years, I would support that effort."); 139 S. Ct. at 2133–42 (Gorsuch, J., joined by Roberts, C.J., and Thomas, J., dissenting) (urging a return to a more robust form of the doctrine); Paul v. United States, 140 S. Ct. 342, 342 (2019) (Kavanaugh, J., respecting denial of certiorari) ("Justice Gorsuch's thoughtful *Gundy* opinion raised important points that may warrant further consideration in future cases."). Justice Amy Coney Barrett has not officially weighed in but in her prior career as an academic, she expressed a skepticism of broad delegations in another context. *See generally* Amy Coney Barrett, *Suspension and Delegation*, 99 Cornell L. Rev. 251 (2014).

28. McGautha v. California, 402 U.S. 183, 271–72 & n.22 (1971) (Brennan, J., dissenting).

29. Evan J. Criddle, *When Delegation Begets Domination: Due Process of Administrative Lawmaking*, 46 Ga. L. Rev. 117, 163 (2011). *See also* Rebecca L. Brown, *Separated Powers and Ordered Liberty*, 139 U. Pa. L. Rev. 1513, 1555 (1991) ("[T]he evils of excessive delegation include the possibility of conferring 'unlimited power,' 'unfettered discretion,' and 'uncontrolled legislative power' on the Executive Branch, [which] pose the threat of arbitrary enforcement of the law—an injury that *due process* is supposed to prevent." (footnotes omitted)); Kenneth Culp Davis, *A New Approach to Delegation*, 36 U. Chi. L. Rev. 713, 730 (1969) (predicting that "[t]he non-delegation doctrine will merge with the concept of due process"); Robert E. Cushman, *Constitutional Status of the Independent Regulatory Commissions*, 24 Cornell L. Q. 13, 33 (1938) ("[T]he effective rule against the delegation of legislative power as that rule is now construed exists . . . for the purpose of surrounding private rights with a protection just as easily and logically available under the due process clause."); Kevin M. Stack, *The Constitutional Foundations of* Chenery, 116 Yale L.J. 952, 988 n.149 (2007) ("[T]o the extent that the nondelegation doctrine and the due process protections both aim to check arbitrary government

action, it makes sense that their application and requirements may overlap."); Ann Woolhandler, *Delegation and Due Process: The Historical Connection*, 2008 Sup. Ct. Rev. 223 (showing that due process and the nondelegation doctrine are historically intertwined). *But see* Harold I. Abramson, *A Fifth Branch of Government: The Private Regulators and Their Constitutionality*, 16 Hastings Const. L.Q. 165, 208–10 (1989) (criticizing the "commingling" of the nondelegation doctrine and due process principles by judges and commentators).

30. Evan J. Criddle, *When Delegation Begets Domination: Due Process of Administrative Lawmaking*, 46 Ga. L. Rev. 117, 163–67 (2011).

31. *See* Kolender v. Lawson, 461 U.S. 352, 358 (1983); Michael J.Z. Mannheimer, *Vagueness as Impossibility*, 98 Tex. L. Rev. 1049, 1055–57 (2020); *see also Gundy*, 139 S. Ct. at 2142 (Gorsuch, J., dissenting) ("[I]t seems little coincidence that our void-for-vagueness cases became much more common soon after the Court began relaxing its approach to legislative delegations."); John Hart Ely, Democracy and Distrust: A Theory of Judicial Review 177 (1980) (observing that the void-for-vagueness doctrine is evidence of the Court's general suspicion of systems granting too much discretion to executive officials). Although there is a second rationale based on the lack of fair notice that vague statutes provide for potential wrongdoers, the Court has written that the nondelegation principle is "the more important aspect of the vagueness doctrine." *Kolender*, 461 U.S. at 358.

32. Kim Forde-Mazrui, *Ruling Out the Rule of Law*, 60 Vand. L. Rev. 1495, 1505 (2007).

33. Kenneth Culp Davis, Discretionary Justice: A Preliminary Inquiry 84 (1969).

34. *See* Tracey Maclin, *What Can Fourth Amendment Doctrine Learn from Vagueness Doctrine*, 3 U. Pa. J. Const. L. 398 (2001) (observing tension between the void-for-vagueness doctrine's emphasis on controlling police discretion and Fourth Amendment cases permitting broad police discretion); *see also* Kenneth Culp Davis, Police Discretion 136–37 (1975) (observing that vague enforcement policies should be considered unconstitutional for the same reason that vague statutes are).

35. Anthony G. Amsterdam, *Perspectives on the Fourth Amendment*, 58 Minn. L. Rev. 349, 416 (1974).

36. Kenneth Culp Davis, Police Discretion 122, 134 (1975). *See also* Carl McGowan, *Rule-Making and the Police*, 70 Mich. L. Rev. 659, 676–89 (1972) (advocating for self-regulation by police agencies through a rulemaking process and suggesting that a failure of police to make and follow rules that implicate life, liberty, and property "would in itself raise due process concerns."); Wayne R. LaFave, *Controlling Discretion by Administrative Regulations: The Use, Misuse, and Nonuse of Police Rules and Policies in Fourth Amendment Adjudication*, 89 Mich. L. Rev. 442, 447–51 (1990); James Vorenberg, *Narrowing the Discretion of Criminal Justice Officials*, 1976 Duke L.J. 651, 662–66.

37. Maria Ponomarenko, *Rethinking Police Rulemaking*, 114 Nw. L. Rev. 1, 3–4 (2019).

38. Daphna Renan, *The Fourth Amendment as Administrative Governance*, 68 Stan. L. Rev. 1039, 1086 (2016).

39. Daphna Renan, *The Fourth Amendment as Administrative Governance*, 68 Stan. L. Rev. 1039, 1083 (2016).

40. Christopher Slobogin, *Panvasive Surveillance, Political Process Theory, and the Nondelegation Doctrine*, 102 Geo. L.J. 1721, 1759, 1761 (2014). *See also* Kim Forde-Mazrui, *Ruling Out the Rule of Law*, 60 Vand. L. Rev. 1495, 1550–51 (2007) (analogizing potential constitutional constraints on police discretion to the conventional nondelegation doctrine); Richard C. Worf, *The Case for Rational Basis Review of General Suspicionless Searches and Seizures*, 23 Touro L. Rev. 93, 143–58 (2007) (arguing that a search or seizure should be subject to strict scrutiny if the legislative authorization for it provides too much executive discretion in how to carry it out). Other scholars have touted the benefits of democratic accountability in police rulemaking without necessarily suggesting that it is a constitutional requirement. *See, e.g.*, Erik Luna, *Principled Enforcement of Penal Codes*, 4 Buff. Crim. L. Rev. 515, 590–623 (2000). It should be acknowledged that there have always been some notable dissents from the proposition that police rulemaking is advisable, even by advocates of democratic policing or of increased legal control of the police more generally. *See generally* Ronald J. Allen, *Police and Substantive Rulemaking: Reconciling Principle and Expediency*, 125 U. Pa. L. Rev. 62 (1976); Charles D. Breitel, *Controls in Criminal Law Enforcement*, 27 U. Chi. L. Rev. 427 (1960); Maria Ponomarenko, *Rethinking Police Rulemaking*, 114 Nw. L. Rev. 1 (2019); Samuel Walker, *Governing the American Police: Wrestling with the Problems of Democracy*, 2016 U. Chi. Legal F. 615.

41. *See* Kenneth Culp Davis, *A New Approach to Delegation*, 36 U. Chi. L. Rev. 713, 730 (1969) ("Some courts have . . . held that due process forbids the administrators to exercise their discretionary power in particular cases without first creating administrative standards or guides."); Carl McGowan, *Rule-Making and the Police*, 70 Mich. L. Rev. 659, 680 (1972) (advocating the transfer of policy-making from "the single patrolman on the beat . . . to the highest echelons of leadership where it belongs"); Eric J. Miller, *Challenging Police Discretion*, 58 Howard L.J. 521, 535–36 (2015) (distinguishing between "departmental discretion" and "the on-the-street discretion of individual officers to make policy on the fly"); Christopher Slobogin, *Panvasive Surveillance, Political Process Theory, and the Nondelegation Doctrine*, 102 Geo. L.J. 1721, 1725 (2014).

42. 5 U.S.C. § 551 et seq.

43. *See* Kenneth Culp Davis, Police Discretion 106 (1975) ("Clearly the police should learn about notice-and-comment rulemaking procedure, and clearly they should experiment with it."); Carl McGowan, *Rule-Making and the Police*, 70 Mich. L. Rev. 659, 682 (1972) (observing that "public participation" in the rulemaking process "would add a democratic element to law enforcement which has long been absent"); Eric J. Miller, *Challenging Police Discretion*, 58 Howard L.J. 521, 544–45 (2015) (laying out a vision of community participation in law-enforcement policymaking); Christopher Slobogin, *Policing as Administration*, 165 U. Pa. L. Rev. 91, 96 (2016) (asserting that "notice-and-comment or analogous

procedures that ensure public input into police rulemaking" should be required). *See also* Evan J. Criddle, *When Delegation Begets Domination: Due Process of Administrative Lawmaking*, 46 Ga. L. Rev. 117, 123–24 (2011) (suggesting that some form of notice-and-comment rulemaking by administrative agencies might be constitutionally required).

In its "special needs" cases, discussed in more detail in the next chapter, the Court has sometimes relied in part on the existence of a participatory rulemaking process in upholding some searches. *See* Nat'l Treas. Emps. Union v. Von Raab, 489 U.S. 656, 661 n.1 (1989) (observing that the drug-testing policy adopted by U.S. Customs Service had to comply with government regulations adopted through notice-and-comment rulemaking (citing 53 Fed. Reg. 11979 (Apr. 11, 1988))); Skinner v. Ry. Labor Execs. Ass'n, 489 U.S. 602, 607–08 (1989) (detailing the notice-and-comment period that preceded promulgation of regulations by the Federal Railroad Administration requiring drug and alcohol testing); *see also* Bd. of Ed. of Indep. Sch. Dist. No. 92 of Pottawatomie Cnty. v. Earls, 536 U.S. 822, 841 (2002) (Breyer, J., concurring) (describing the "democratic, participatory process" by which a local school board developed its student drug-testing policy).

44. Anthony G. Amsterdam, *Perspectives on the Fourth Amendment*, 58 Minn. L. Rev. 349, 422 (1974) (suggesting that it is enough if "[d]epartmental rules [are] subject to . . . scrutiny by the community and by local political organs"); Gerald M. Caplan, *The Case for Rulemaking by Law Enforcement Agencies*, 36 Law & Contemp. Probs. 500, 508–09 (1971) (remaining agnostic on public participation in police rulemaking); Final Report of the President's Task Force on 21st Century Policing 15 (2015) ("In order to achieve external legitimacy, law enforcement agencies should involve the community in the process of developing and evaluating policies and procedures."); Megan Quattlebaum, Tracey Meares, and Tom Tyler, Principles of Procedurally Just Policing 14 (2018) ("When writing policies, departments should seek community input through one or more structured processes that provide community members with meaningful opportunities to be heard."); Robert M. Igleburger and Frank A. Schubert, *Policy Making for the Police*, 58 Am. B. Ass'n J. 307, 309 (1972) (advocating formulation of enforcement policy "at the police administrative level where it would be more visible to citizens" and open to "community influence on police practices").

45. *See* Railway Express Agency v. New York, 336 U.S. 106, 112 (1949) (Jackson, J., concurring) ("[T]here is no more effective practical guaranty against arbitrary and unreasonable government than to require that the principles of law which officials would impose upon a minority must be imposed generally.").

46. Kenneth Culp Davis, *An Approach to Legal Control of the Police*, 52 Tex. L. Rev. 703, 706 (1974) ("The objective in rulemaking is not to minimize discretion. It is to provide for the optimum degree of discretion."); *see also* Michael R. Gottfredson and Don M. Gottfredson, Decision Making in Criminal Justice: Toward the Rational Exercise of Discretion 51 (2d ed. 1988) ("[I]t is both unrealistic and ill-advised to argue that discretion in arrest decisions be eliminated.").

47. 428 U.S. 364, 372 (1976).

48. 428 U.S. 364, 380 n.6 (1976) (Powell, J., concurring) (emphasis added).

49. 479 U.S. 367, 374 n.6 (1987) ("We emphasize that . . . the Police Department's procedures *mandated* the opening of closed containers and the listing of their contents." (emphasis added)).

50. 495 U.S. 1, 4–5 (1990).

51. 495 U.S. 1, 11 (1990) (Blackmun, J., concurring in the judgment).

52. *See* Eve Brensike Primus, *Disentangling Administrative Searches*, 111 COLUM. L. REV. 254, 305–06 (2011) (reporting that "lower courts assessing inventory searches rigorously analyze whether the government has standardized criteria that limit officers' discretion"). *Cf.* Barry Friedman and Cynthia Benin Stein, *Redefining What's "Reasonable": The Protections for Policing*, 84 GEO. WASH. L. REV. 281, 322–23 (2016) (arguing that police ought to have no discretion when it comes to auto inventories); Wayne R. LaFave, *Controlling Discretion by Administrative Regulations: The Use, Misuse, and Nonuse of Police Rules and Policies in Fourth Amendment Adjudication*, 89 MICH. L. REV. 442, 451–63 (1990) (providing a valuable critique of this line of cases).

53. Silas J. Wasserstrom and Louis Michael Seidman, *The Fourth Amendment as Constitutional Theory*, 77 GEO. L.J. 19, 95 (1988). *See also* I. Bennett Capers, *Rethinking the Fourth Amendment: Race, Citizenship, and the Equality Principle*, 46 HARV. C.R.-C.L. L. REV. 1, 44 (2011) ("[N]on-discretionary searches such as checkpoints . . . spread the cost of law enforcement to everyone. [They] are by definition egalitarian."); Dan M. Kahan and Tracey L. Meares, *Foreword: The Coming Crisis of Criminal Procedure*, 86 GEO. L.J. 1153, 1172–73 (1998) (observing that, because intrusions such as sobriety checkpoints "burden average members of the community, there is much less reason for courts to doubt the determination of politically accountable officials that these policies strike a fair balance between liberty and order"); William J. Stuntz, *Implicit Bargains, Government Power, and the Fourth Amendment*, 44 STAN. L. REV. 553, 588 (1992) ("The likeliest explanation for giving greater leeway to group stops is that politics provides an adequate remedy for overzealous police action. . . .").

54. Illinois v. Lidster, 540 U.S. 419, 426 (2004). There is some empirical support for this assertion. *Id.* (citing James C. Fell, Susan A. Ferguson, Allan F. Williams and Michele Fields, *Why Aren't Sobriety Checkpoints Widely Adopted as an Enforcement Strategy in the United States?* 35 ACCIDENT ANALYSIS & PREVENTION 897 (Nov. 2003)).

55. 496 U.S. 444, 447, 452, 454 (1990) (quoting Delaware v. Prouse, 440 U.S. 648, 661 (1979) (alteration in original)). *See also* United States v. Brignoni-Ponce, 422 U.S. 873, 882–83 (1975) (holding unconstitutional suspicionless vehicle stops by roving patrols looking for undocumented immigrants near the border).

56. MICH. COMP. LAWS ANN. 28.6(5).

57. BARRY FRIEDMAN, UNWARRANTED: POLICING WITHOUT PERMISSION 59–60 (2017) ("The typical enabling statute of a policing agency simply authorizes it to enforce the criminal laws on the books in the broadest of terms, saying little or nothing about what methods the police are permitted to use in doing so.").

58. *See* Christopher Slobogin, *Panvasive Surveillance, Political Process Theory,*

and the Nondelegation Doctrine, 102 GEO. L.J. 1721, 1743 (2014) ("[S]everal of the roadblocks and drug-testing programs the Court considered were instituted by law enforcement agencies; neither state legislatures nor municipal or other local elective bodies were involved in the authorization of the executive branch's investigative actions."); *see also* Barry Friedman, *Lawless Surveillance*, 97 N.Y.U. L. REV. 1143, 1186 (2022) (discussing state court cases rejecting "general grants of authority" as proper authorization for sobriety checkpoints).

59. N.H. REV. STAT. ANN. § 265:1-a.

60. UTAH CODE ANN. § 77-23-104(2)(c). The statute might delegate too much authority here inasmuch as it permits checkpoints for any other purpose other than "a general interest in crime control." However, this affirmative authority at least signals a policy choice that Utahns are willing to give up some liberty in exchange for protection on the highways from danger arising out of virtually any source.

61. UTAH CODE ANN. § 77-23-104(2)(a).

62. UTAH CODE ANN. § 77-23-104(2)(b). A similar Iowa statute does not require judicial superintendence. IOWA CODE ANN. § 321K.1. To be clear, involvement of the judiciary should not be necessary. *See* United States v. Martinez-Fuerte, 428 U.S. 543, 564–66 (1976).

63. Silas J. Wasserstrom, *The Incredible Shrinking Fourth Amendment*, 21 AM. CRIM. L. REV. 257, 309 n.246 (1984) ("Even roadblocks . . . do not ensure even-handed criminal law enforcement, for . . . their location may be chosen in a discriminatory way.").

64. Christopher Slobogin, *Panvasive Surveillance, Political Process Theory, and the Nondelegation Doctrine*, 102 GEO. L.J. 1721, 1753–54 (2014). *See also* Tracey L. Meares, Terry *and the Relevance of Politics*, 72 ST. JOHN'S L. REV. 1343, 1348 (1998) ("[W]hen it can be said that the relevant political community internalizes the burden of a particular enforcement procedure, courts should relax scrutiny of the judgments about the balance between liberty and order produced by the political process.").

65. JOHN HART ELY, DEMOCRACY AND DISTRUST: A THEORY OF JUDICIAL REVIEW 33 (1980).

66. 347 U.S. 497, 499, 500 (1954).

67. JOHN HART ELY, DEMOCRACY AND DISTRUST: A THEORY OF JUDICIAL REVIEW 32 (1980).

68. JOHN HART ELY, DEMOCRACY AND DISTRUST: A THEORY OF JUDICIAL REVIEW 32 (1980). *See* U.S. CONST., amend. IX ("The enumeration in the Constitution, of certain rights, shall not be construed to deny or disparage others retained by the people.").

69. *See, e.g.*, I. Bennett Capers, *Rethinking the Fourth Amendment: Race, Citizenship, and the Equality Principle*, 46 HARV. C.R.-C.L. L. REV. 1, 36 (2011) (asserting that the Fourth Amendment's "meaning was indelibly changed in 1868 by ratification of the Fourteenth Amendment"); ANDREW E. TASLITZ, RECONSTRUCTING THE FOURTH AMENDMENT: A HISTORY OF SEARCH AND SEIZURE, 1789–1868 at 12 (2006) ("The Fourteenth Amendment . . . mutated the meaning of the constitutional rules governing search and seizure.").

70. Kurt T. Lash, The Fourteenth Amendment and the Privileges and Immunities of American Citizenship 295 (2014); *cf.* Randy E. Barnett and Evan D. Bernick, The Original Meaning of the 14th Amendment: Its Letter and Spirit 202–04 (2021) (justifying "reverse incorporation" on somewhat different grounds).

71. *See* Donald A. Dripps, About Guilt and Innocence: The Origins, Development, and Future of Constitutional Criminal Procedure 186 (2003) (suggesting a broader interpretation of some of the provisions of the Bill of Rights when applied against the federal government).

Chapter 10

1. *See* I. Bennett Capers, *Rethinking the Fourth Amendment: Race, Citizenship, and the Equality Principle*, 46 Harv. C.R.-C.L. L. Rev. 1, 36 (2011) ("[T]o interpret the Fourth Amendment based solely on *its* historical context and antecedents, and the so-called intent of the founding fathers, is to ignore the sea change ushered in by the Fourteenth Amendment."); David H. Gans, *"We Do Not Want to Be Hunted": The Right to Be Secure and Our Constitutional Story of Race and Policing*, 11 Colum. J. Race & Law 239, 336 (2021) ("The Supreme Court's collective amnesia about the Fourteenth Amendment's text, history, and values has produced a deeply flawed constitutional jurisprudence."); *see also* Akhil Amar, The Bill of Rights: Creation and Reconstruction 223 (1998) ("[W]hen we 'apply' the Bill of Rights against the states today, we must first and foremost reflect on the meaning and the spirit of the amendment of 1866, not the Bill of 1789."); Donald A. Dripps, About Guilt and Innocence: The Origins, Development, and Future of Constitutional Criminal Procedure xiv (2003) ("The Warren Court's decision to rely in state cases on the Bill of Rights, rather than on due process and equal protection, lies at the root of modern law's incoherence and dysfunction"). For a critique of this problem more generally, *see* Josh Blackman, *Response: Originalism at the Right Time?*, Tex. L. Rev. See Also 269, 275 (2012).

The most ambitious and cogent attempt to turn our attention from the specific provisions of the Bill of Rights to the language of the Fourteenth Amendment has been Donald A. Dripps, About Guilt and Innocence: The Origins, Development, and Future of Constitutional Criminal Procedure 131–73 (2003), which viewed the Fourteenth Amendment as a device favoring fair and proportional law enforcement procedures and reliable trial outcomes.

2. *See, e.g.*, Virginia v. Moore, 553 U.S. 164, 168–69 (2008) ("The immediate object of the Fourth Amendment was to prohibit the general warrants and writs of assistance that English judges had employed against the colonists."); Atwater v. City of Lago Vista, 532 U.S. 318, 326–40 (2001) (taking up thirteen pages of the U.S. Reports addressing the authority to make warrantless arrests for minor offenses at the time of the framing of the Fourth Amendment.); Wilson v. Arkansas, 514 U.S. 927, 931 (1995) (adverting to "the traditional protections against unreasonable searches and seizures afforded by the common law at the time of the framing" of the Fourth Amendment).

3. *See* chapter 4.

4. *See, e.g.*, Torres v. Madrid, 141 S. Ct. 989 (2021) (holding that intentionally shooting a target who then flees constitutes a seizure); California v. Hodari D., 499 U.S. 621, 623–29 (1991) (holding that a seizure does not occur upon police show of authority until the suspect submits). As Donald Dripps pointed out, it is certainly more natural to think of a police killing of a civilian as a deprivation of life (with or without due process) than as a "seizure." DONALD A. DRIPPS, ABOUT GUILT AND INNOCENCE: THE ORIGINS, DEVELOPMENT, AND FUTURE OF CONSTITUTIONAL CRIMINAL PROCEDURE 60 (2003).

5. *See, e.g.*, Brown v. Texas, 443 U.S. 47, 51 (1979) (noting that "[a] central concern" of the Fourth Amendment "has been to assure that an individual's reasonable expectation of privacy is not subject to arbitrary invasions solely at the unfettered discretion of officers in the field"). *See also* Tracey Maclin, *The Central Meaning of the Fourth Amendment*, 35 WM. & MARY L. REV. 197, 201 (1993) ("[T]he central meaning of the Fourth Amendment is distrust of police power and discretion.").

6. BARRY FRIEDMAN, UNWARRANTED: POLICING WITHOUT PERMISSION 107 (2017).

7. Terry v. Ohio, 392 U.S. 1, 20 (1968).

8. Johnson v. United States, 330 U.S. 10, 13–14 (1948).

9. Silas J. Wasserstrom and Louis Michael Seidman, *The Fourth Amendment as Constitutional Theory*, 77 GEO. L.J. 19, 95 (1988) ("Probable cause can . . . be seen as a rough proxy for what a fully participational community would insist upon over the range of cases before a search is conducted."); *see also* Brinegar v. United States, 338 U.S. 160, 176 (1949) ("Requiring more [than probable cause] would unduly hamper law enforcement. To allow less would be to leave law-abiding citizens at the mercy of the officers' whim or caprice."); JOHN HART ELY, DEMOCRACY AND DISTRUST: A THEORY OF JUDICIAL REVIEW 173 (1980) ("The probable cause requirement . . . requires that persons not be singled out for arrest or search in the absence of strong indication of guilt. . . .").

10. Payton v. New York, 445 U.S. 573, 577 & n.6 (1980).

11. The questioning by Sen. Jacob Howard of Michigan of loyalist Virginia Judge John C. Underwood is typical:

> Question. Could [Jefferson Davis] be convicted of treason in Virginia?
> Answer. Oh, no; unless you had a packed jury.
> Question. Could you manage to pack a jury there?
> Answer. I think it would be very difficult, but it could be done; I could pack a jury to convict him. . . .

2 REPORT OF THE JOINT COMMITTEE ON RECONSTRUCTION 10 (1866).

12. BARRY FRIEDMAN, UNWARRANTED: POLICING WITHOUT PERMISSION 117 (2017). ("Before the police burst into someone's home, or seize them or their property, another branch of government—the judiciary—checks to make sure that the facts justify what is about to occur.").

13. EGON BITTNER, ASPECTS OF POLICE WORK 21 (1990).

14. *See* William J. Stuntz, The Collapse of American Criminal Justice 304 (2011) (arguing that where one entity necessarily has large discretionary powers, "giving other decisionmakers discretion promotes consistency, not arbitrariness," because "[d]iscretion limits discretion [and] institutional competition curbs excess and abuse").

15. 423 U.S. 411, 418–21 (1976).

16. South Dakota v. Opperman, 428 U.S. 364, 370 n.5 (1976) (observing that the probable cause and warrant requirements are "unhelpful when analysis centers upon the reasonableness of routine administrative caretaking functions"); Illinois v. Lidster, 540 U.S. 419, 424 (2004) (upholding traffic checkpoint designed to find witnesses to an earlier traffic fatality because in that context "individualized suspicion has little role to play").

17. Michigan v. Clifford, 464 U.S. 287, 294–95 (1984) (plurality); Donovan v. Dewey, 452 U.S. 594 (1981); Michigan v. Tyler, 436 U.S. 499 (1978); United States v. Biswell, 406 U.S. 311 (1972); Colonnade Catering Corp. v. U.S., 397 U.S. 72 (1970); See v. City of Seattle, 387 U.S. 541 (1967); Camara v. Municipal Ct., 387 U.S. 523 (1967).

18. *Lidster*, 540 U.S. 419; Mich. Dept. of State Police v. Sitz, 496 U.S. 444 (1990); United States v. Martinez-Fuerte, 428 U.S. 543 (1976).

19. Board of Educ. of Indep. Sch. Dist. No. 92 of Pottawatomie Cnty. v. Earls, 536 U.S. 822, 825 (2002); Ferguson v. City of Charleston, 532 U.S. 67 (2001); Chandler v. Miller, 520 U.S. 305, 318–22 (1997); Vernonia Sch. Dist. 47J v. Acton, 515 U.S. 646 (1995); Nat'l Treas. Emps. Union v. Von Raab, 489 U.S. 656 (1989); Skinner v. Ry. Labor Execs. Ass'n, 489 U.S. 602, 606 (1989).

20. City of Ontario v. Quon, 560 U.S. 746 (2010); Safford Unified Sch. Dist. No. 1 v. Redding, 557 U.S. 364 (2009); O'Connor v. Ortega, 480 U.S. 709 (1987); New Jersey v. T.L.O., 469 U.S. 325 (1985).

21. United States v. Flores-Montano, 541 U.S. 149 (2004); United States v. Montoya de Hernandez, 473 U.S. 531 (1985); United States v. Villamonte-Marquez, 462 U.S. 579 (1983); United States v. Ramsey, 431 U.S. 606 (1977).

22. Samson v. California, 547 U.S. 843 (2006); United States v. Knights, 534 U.S. 112 (2001); Griffin v. Wisconsin, 483 U.S. 868 (1987).

23. Florida v. Wells, 495 U.S. 1 (1990); Colorado v. Bertine, 479 U.S. 367 (1987); Illinois v. Lafayette, 462 U.S. 640 (1983); *Opperman*, 428 U.S. 364.

24. Maryland v. King, 569 U.S. 435 (2013) (collection of DNA); Florence v. Board of Chosen Freeholders, 566 U.S. 318 (2012) (invasive body search). It is true that the Court in *King* disclaimed the "special needs" label. 569 U.S. at 463 ("The special needs cases, though in full accord with the result reached here, do not have a direct bearing on the issues presented in this case, because unlike the search of a citizen who has not been suspected of a wrong, a detainee has a reduced expectation of privacy."). However, it is difficult to classify *King* in any other way.

25. *See Opperman*, 428 U.S. at 383 (Powell, J., concurring) ("Inventory searches are conducted in accordance with established police department rules or policy and occur whenever an automobile is seized. *There are thus no special facts for a neutral magistrate to evaluate.*" (emphasis added)).

26. *See, e.g.*, *T.L.O.*, 469 U.S. at 351 (Blackmun, J., concurring in the judgment) (opining that the doctrine applies "[o]nly in those exceptional circumstances in which special needs, beyond the normal need for law enforcement, make the warrant and probable-cause requirement impracticable"); *Chandler*, 520 U.S. at 309 (characterizing as "closely guarded" the "category of constitutionally permissible suspicionless searches"). *See also* Eve Brensike Primus, *Disentangling Administrative Searches*, 111 COLUM. L. REV. 254, 266 (2011) (noting that, at least initially, the Court preferred "individualized suspicion regimes" to suspicionless searches and viewed the latter as "justified only if they were absolutely necessary").

27. *See* Daphna Renan, *The Fourth Amendment as Administrative Governance*, 68 STAN. L. REV. 1039, 1081 (2016) ("The question for a court under programmatic reasonableness review is not whether any particular encounter requires a warrant, but whether structures and processes are in place to adequately protect Fourth Amendment interests in the aggregate. . . ."); Christopher Slobogin, *Panvasive Surveillance, Political Process Theory, and the Nondelegation Doctrine*, 102 GEO. L.J. 1721, 1737 (2014) ("[L]aw enforcement targeting of a particular individual cannot be addressed through the legislative process. In th[at] situation, the warrant, probable cause, and particularity requirements of the Fourth Amendment apply."); Richard C. Worf, *The Case for Rational Basis Review of General Suspicionless Searches and Seizures*, 23 TOURO L. REV. 93, 176 (2007) (arguing that the "presumption against general suspicionless searches and seizures . . . is unjustified").

28. 387 U.S. 523.

29. 387 U.S. 541. These cases overruled Frank v. Maryland, 359 U.S. 360, 367 (1959), which held that "[i]nspection without a warrant, as an adjunct to a regulatory scheme for the general welfare of the community and not as a means of enforcing the criminal law," did not violate the Due Process Clause of the Fourteenth Amendment.

30. *Camara*, 387 U.S. at 538; *see also See*, 387 U.S. at 545 (re-characterizing "probable cause to issue a warrant" as a "flexible standard of reasonableness that takes into account the public need for effective enforcement of the particular regulation involved").

31. *See* Scott E. Sundby, *An Ode to Probable Cause: A Brief Response to Professors Amar and Slobogin*, 72 ST. JOHN'S L. REV. 1133, 1134 (1998) ("*Camara* twisted the Warrant Clause into a pretzel. . . ."); *see also* Barry Friedman and Cynthia Benin Stein, *Redefining What's "Reasonable": The Protections for Policing*, 84 GEO. WASH. L. REV. 281, 313 (2016) (highlighting the Fourth Amendment's text and concluding that the "new definition" of probable cause "was odd indeed").

32. 387 U.S. at 526 (quoting San Francisco Housing Code § 503).

33. 387 U.S. at 541 (quoting City of Seattle Ordinance No. 87870, § 8.01.050 (alteration added)).

34. *See*, 387 U.S. at 545; *see Camara*, 387 U.S. at 532 (reasoning that a constitutional regime must not "leave the occupant subject to the discretion of the official in the field").

35. Barry Friedman and Cynthia Benin Stein, *Redefining What's "Reasonable": The Protections for Policing*, 84 GEO. WASH. L. REV. 281, 327–28 (2016); Eve Bren-

sike Primus, *Disentangling Administrative Searches*, 111 COLUM. L. REV. 254, 294–95 & n.223 (2011).

36. Christopher Slobogin, *Is the Fourth Amendment Relevant in a Technological Age?*, *in* CONSTITUTION 3.0: FREEDOM AND TECHNOLOGICAL CHANGE 11, 29–30 (Jeffrey Rosen and Benjamin Wittes eds., 2013) (arguing that, to be constitutional, a legislatively authorized search or seizure regime must "avoid[]discriminating against a discrete and insular minority or any other group that is not adequately represented in the legislature."); *see also* Barry Friedman and Cynthia Benin Stein, *Redefining What's "Reasonable": The Protections for Policing*, 84 GEO. WASH. L. REV. 281, 335–36 (2016) (observing that regulatory searches based on suspect classifications should be unconstitutional unless they are narrowly tailored to effect a compelling government interest).

37. *Von Raab*, 489 U.S. 656; *Skinner*, 489 U.S. at 606; *Chandler*, 520 U.S. at 318–22; *Ferguson*, 532 U.S. 67; *Earls*, 536 U.S. at 825; *Acton*, 515 U.S. 646.

38. *Cf.* Christopher Slobogin, *Government Dragnets*, 73 J.L. & CONTEMP. PROBS. 107, 135–36 (2010) (questioning this approach).

39. *See* Scott E. Sundby, *Protecting the Citizen Whilst He Is Quiet: Suspicionless Searches, Special Needs and General Warrants*, 74 MISS. L.J. 501, 545–47 (2004). This is arguably also true of surveillance regimes that target parolees and probationers, *see, e.g.*, *Samson*, 547 U.S. 843; *Knights*, 534 U.S. 112; *Griffin*, 483 U.S. 868, because the target population is generally shut out of the democratic process by felon disenfranchisement laws. *See* Christopher Slobogin, *Government Dragnets*, 73 J.L. & CONTEMP. PROBS. 107, 135 (2010).

40. *See* Christopher Slobogin, *Government Dragnets*, 73 J.L. & CONTEMP. PROBS. 107, 135 (2010) ("[L]aw enforcement . . . is the ideal collective-action group: small and cohesive, with easy access to legislators.").

41. JOHN HART ELY, DEMOCRACY AND DISTRUST: A THEORY OF JUDICIAL REVIEW 84 (1980).

42. JOHN HART ELY, DEMOCRACY AND DISTRUST: A THEORY OF JUDICIAL REVIEW 182–83 (1980).

43. 531 U.S. 32, 34–35, 41 (2000). *See also Ferguson*, 532 U.S. at 82 (striking down state hospital policy of drug testing pregnant women and referring women testing positive for arrest and prosecution where "throughout the development and application of the policy, the . . . prosecutors and police were extensively involved in the day-to-day administration of the policy").

44. BARRY FRIEDMAN, UNWARRANTED: POLICING WITHOUT PERMISSION 176 (2017) ("When it comes to figuring out whether a search without cause is permissible, the concern for arbitrary and discriminatory policing is what should matter—and not the Supreme Court's impenetrable distinction between 'ordinary law enforcement' and the 'special needs of law enforcement.'"); *see also* I. Bennett Capers, *Rethinking the Fourth Amendment: Race, Citizenship, and the Equality Principle*, 46 HARV. C.R.-C.L. L. REV. 1, 44 (2011) (criticizing the distinction); Daphna Renan, *The Fourth Amendment as Administrative Governance*, 68 STAN. L. REV. 1039, 1081 (2016) (same).

45. Christopher Slobogin, *Panvasive Surveillance, Political Process Theory, and

the Nondelegation Doctrine, 102 GEO. L.J. 1721, 1730 (2014) ("In objective terms, the intrusiveness of a seizure at a roadblock does not vary depending on whether the government is after a drug trafficker or drunk driver. . . ."); Scott E. Sundby, *A Return to Fourth Amendment Basics: Undoing the Mischief of* Camara *and* Terry, 72 MINN. L. REV. 383, 411 (1988) ("[W]hatever the inspection's purpose, the intrusion still invades the individual's privacy.").

46. Christopher Slobogin, *Panvasive Surveillance, Political Process Theory, and the Nondelegation Doctrine*, 102 GEO. L.J. 1721, 1728 (2014).

47. BARRY FRIEDMAN, UNWARRANTED: POLICING WITHOUT PERMISSION 172 (2017) (observing that both drivers caught driving drunk and those caught with drugs are "headed to jail for violating the law"); Ric Simmons, *Searching for Terrorists: Why Public Safety Is Not a Special Need*, 59 DUKE L.J. 843, 891 (2010) ("Antiterrorism searches are designed to prevent individuals from intentionally committing acts of violence, and to apprehend those who attempt to commit these acts; to claim that this is a public safety purpose rather than a law-enforcement or crime-control purpose is simply disingenuous."); Christopher Slobogin, *Policing as Administration*, 165 U. PA. L. REV. 91, 109 (2016) (observing that "virtually all panvasive searches and seizures," even those the Court has included in the "special needs" category, "are aimed at crime control"); Scott E. Sundby, *A Return to Fourth Amendment Basics: Undoing the Mischief of* Camara *and* Terry, 72 MINN. L. REV. 383, 409–10 (1988) ("[E]ven if the government's primary purpose is regulatory, penal sanctions often do attach when violations are found. . . .").

48. *Compare* 531 U.S. at 47 n.2 ("[W]e need not decide whether the State may establish a checkpoint program with the primary purpose of checking licenses or driver sobriety and a secondary purpose of interdicting narcotics.") *with* Wayne R. LaFave, *The Fourth Amendment as a "Big Time TV" Fad*, 53 HASTINGS L.J. 265, 274 (2001) (ridiculing this reasoning). *See generally* Brooks Holland, *The Road 'Round* Edmond*: Steering through Primary Purposes and Crime Control Agendas*, 111 PENN ST. L. REV. 293 (2006) (evaluating "'multi-purpose' checkpoints").

49. 569 U.S. at 449.

50. 569 U.S. at 466 (Scalia, J., dissenting).

51. *See Frank*, 359 U.S. at 376 (Douglas, J., dissenting) ("The Court misreads history when it relates the Fourth Amendment primarily to searches for evidence to be used in criminal prosecutions.").

52. *See Frank*, 359 U.S. at 379 (1959) (Douglas, J., dissenting) ("Some of the statutes which James Otis denounced did not involve criminal proceedings. They in the main regulated customs and allowed forfeitures of goods shipped into the Colonies in violation of English shipping regulations."); Christopher Slobogin, *Government Dragnets*, 73 J.L. & CONTEMP. PROBS. 107, 130 (2010) ("[T]he revenue and customs laws that led to many of the general-warrant searches [the founders] maligned were at most quasi-criminal in nature.").

53. Barry Friedman and Cynthia Benin Stein, *Redefining What's "Reasonable": The Protections for Policing*, 84 GEO. WASH. L. REV. 281, 286 (2016); Daphna Renan, *The Fourth Amendment as Administrative Governance*, 68 STAN. L. REV. 1039, 1041–42 (2016); Christopher Slobogin, *Policing as Administration*, 165 U. PA. L. REV.

91, 92 (2016); Scott E. Sundby, *A Return to Fourth Amendment Basics: Undoing the Mischief of* Camara *and* Terry, 72 MINN. L. REV. 383, 418 (1988).

54. *See also Ferguson*, 532 U.S. at 71 (striking down state hospital policy of drug testing pregnant women and referring women testing positive for arrest and prosecution where policy was developed, with no legislative authorization, by city prosecutor in conjunction with representatives of the hospital, "the police, the County Substance Abuse Commission and the Department of Social Services"); Richard C. Worf, *The Case for Rational Basis Review of General Suspicionless Searches and Seizures*, 23 TOURO L. REV. 93, 164–73 (2007) (rejecting the distinction on similar grounds).

55. 387 U.S. at 536–37. *See also* Anthony G. Amsterdam, *Perspectives on the Fourth Amendment*, 58 MINN. L. REV. 349, 409 (1974) (opining that "legislation or police-made rules and regulations" must both "tolerably confine[]" police discretion and also be "subject to judicial review for reasonableness").

56. 443 U.S. at 50–51. Although *Brown* specifically mentions only seizures, the Court has used essentially the same test for special needs searches. *See, e.g.*, *Chandler*, 520 U.S. at 318–22; *Lafayette*, 462 U.S. at 644.

57. Christopher Slobogin, *Policing as Administration*, 165 U. PA. L. REV. 91, 114–15 (2016); *see also* Barry Friedman and Cynthia Benin Stein, *Redefining What's "Reasonable": The Protections for Policing*, 84 GEO. WASH. L. REV. 281, 297 (2016) ("Isn't the very point of having elected legislative bodies precisely to decide which interests are worth pursuing and which are not?"); Christopher Slobogin, *Panvasive Surveillance, Political Process Theory, and the Nondelegation Doctrine*, 102 GEO. L.J. 1721, 1732 (2014) (asserting that the *Brown* "factors raise issues the courts are not well-equipped to answer" and "that legislatures and administrative agencies are ideally set up to" address); Daphna Renan, *The Fourth Amendment as Administrative Governance*, 68 STAN. L. REV. 1039, 1081 (2016) (arguing that for "programmatic" searches and seizures, the primary question is "whether and pursuant to what protections . . . a balance has been struck by the political branches").

58. I say "typically" because, as the Court recognized in Whren v. United States, 517 U.S. 806, 818 (1996), if a search or seizure authorized by probable cause and a warrant is conducted in a particularly intrusive manner, it might still be deemed unreasonable. *See, e.g.*, *Wilson*, 514 U.S. 927 (unannounced entry into a home was unreasonable even when the entry was authorized by warrant based on probable cause); Tennessee v. Garner, 471 U.S. 1 (1985) (arrest effectuated with excessive force was unreasonable even if supported by probable cause); Winston v. Lee, 470 U.S. 753 (1985) (unconsented-to surgery requiring general anesthesia in order to obtain evidence embedded in suspect's chest would be unreasonable even if supported by probable cause and a warrant). But these are precisely the types of ancillary issues surrounding searches and seizures—whether and to what extent invasive surgery is permitted, announcement is required, or force is authorized—that can be addressed by specific legislative and administrative guidelines. A constitutional requirement of police compliance with guidelines on the use of force is explored in chapter 11.

59. Christopher Slobogin, *Panvasive Surveillance, Political Process Theory, and*

the Nondelegation Doctrine, 102 Geo. L.J. 1721, 1726 (2014) ("When asked to assess the constitutionality of panvasive actions, the courts usually defer to the legislative and executive branches."); I. Bennett Capers, *Crime, Surveillance, and Communities*, 40 Fordham Urb. L.J. 959, 975 (2013) ("The Court has held that . . . special needs searches are almost by default reasonable."); Barry Friedman and Cynthia Benin Stein, *Redefining What's "Reasonable": The Protections for Policing*, 84 Geo. Wash. L. Rev. 281, 297 (2016) ("[T]he Court's idea of 'balancing' is illusory—the test is rigged such that the government almost always wins.").

60. 520 U.S. 305. It is ironic that *Chandler* is a paradigmatic case where there was no process defect: the drug-testing scheme there was authorized by statute and it targeted only those running for political office, hardly a group bereft of political clout. *See* Christopher Slobogin, *Government Dragnets*, 73 J.L. & Contemp. Probs. 107, 136 (2010).

61. 496 U.S. at 453.

62. *See, e.g.*, William J. Stuntz, *The Substantive Origins of Criminal Procedure*, 105 Yale L.J. 393, 445 (1995) (observing that in the "special needs" cases, "the Court has consistently declined to apply ordinary Fourth Amendment standards, adopting instead a kind of rational basis scrutiny that holds the (non-police) search legal unless it was outrageous"). *See also* Christopher Slobogin, *Panvasive Surveillance, Political Process Theory, and the Nondelegation Doctrine*, 102 Geo. L.J. 1721, 1731 (2014) (comparing the *Brown* test to the standards used under the Fourteenth Amendment, which look to the strength of the government interest and the tailoring of the program to that interest). For a process-based argument that rational basis review is appropriate, *see generally* Richard C. Worf, *The Case for Rational Basis Review of General Suspicionless Searches and Seizures*, 23 Touro L. Rev. 93 (2007).

The classic statement of the rational basis test is in Williamson v. Lee Optical of Oklahoma Inc., 348 U.S. 483, 487–88 (1955): "[T]he law need not be in every respect logically consistent with its aims to be constitutional. It is enough that there is an evil at hand for correction, and that it might be thought that the particular legislative measure was a rational way to correct it."

63. New York v. Burger, 482 U.S. 691, 700, 701 (1987) (quoting Marshall v. Barlow's, Inc., 436 U.S. 307, 313 (1978); *Donovan*, 452 U.S. at 600, 606 (alteration added)).

64. *Burger*, 482 U.S. 691; *Donovan*, 452 U.S. 594; *Biswell*, 406 U.S. 311; *Colonnade Catering Corp.*, 397 U.S. 72.

65. City of Los Angeles v. Patel, 576 U.S. 409 (2015); *Marshall*, 436 U.S. 307. Even searches of a closely regulated business are subjected to a *Brown* v. *Texas*–style test: A warrantless administrative search regime for a "closely regulated" business will be upheld if (1) it is based on "a 'substantial' government interest'"; (2) "warrantless inspections [are] 'necessary to further [the] regulatory scheme'"; and (3) the "'inspection program . . . provide[s] a constitutionally adequate substitute for a warrant." This last element is satisfied if the regulatory regime is "'sufficiently comprehensive and defined that the owner of commercial property cannot help but

be aware that his property will be subject to periodic inspections undertaken for specific purposes.'" *Burger*, 482 U.S. at 702–03 (quoting *Donovan*, 452 U.S. at 600, 602, 603 (first and third alterations added)). Again, there is a strong argument that this test is surplusage.

66. *But see Burger*, 482 U.S. at 720 (Brennan, J., dissenting) (noting the "obvious bootstrapping" involved where the pervasiveness of regulations dictates the constraints on state inspections of businesses); *Donovan*, 452 U.S. at 612 (Stewart, J., dissenting) ("Under the peculiar logic of today's opinion, the scope of the Fourth Amendment diminishes as the power of governmental regulation increases.").

67. *See* Maryland v. Buie, 494 U.S. 325, 334 (1990).

68. 452 U.S. 692, 705 (1981).

69. *See* Maryland v. Wilson, 519 U.S. 408 (1997); Pennsylvania v. Mimms 434 U.S. 106 (1977) (per curiam).

70. Chimel v. California, 395 U.S. 752, 766 (1969).

71. 414 U.S. 218, 235 (1973).

72. 414 U.S. 260, 266 (1973).

73. Riley v. California, 573 U.S. 373, 391 (2014). *See also King*, 569 U.S. at 463 (upholding statute requiring the taking of DNA samples of those arrested for violent crimes on the ground that "a detainee has a reduced expectation of privacy").

74. *See, e.g.*, *Robinson*, 414 U.S. at 221 n.2 (quoting District of Columbia Metropolitan Police guideline that, when making a custodial arrest for driving after license revocation, the entire car should not be searched but only those areas of the car within the arrestee's "'immediate control'").

75. 395 U.S. at 763.

76. Anthony G. Amsterdam, *Perspectives on the Fourth Amendment*, 58 MINN. L. REV. 349, 416 (1974) (footnote omitted). *See Robinson*, 414 U.S. at 221 n.2 (determining that the presence of guidelines was "not . . . determinative of the constitutional issues presented"); *Gustafson*, 414 U.S. at 265 ("Though . . . there did not exist a departmental policy establishing the conditions under which a full-scale body search should be conducted, we do not find th[is] difference[] determinative of the constitutional issue."). *See also* Wayne R. LaFave, *Controlling Discretion by Administrative Regulations: The Use, Misuse, and Nonuse of Police Rules and Policies in Fourth Amendment Adjudication*, 89 MICH. L. REV. 442, 488 (1990) (suggesting that "the control of police discretion in *Robinson* and the absence of control in *Gustafson* was the dominant characteristic in the cases—one which should have produced different results in the two decisions").

77. 573 U.S. at 386–98.

78. *See* People v. Riley, D059840, 2013 WL 475242, at *6 (Cal. Ct. App. Feb. 8, 2013), *rev'd*, 573 U.S. 373 (2014); United States v. Wurie, 612 F.Supp.2d 104, 109–11 (D. Mass. 2009), *rev'd*, 728 F.3d 1 (1st Cir. 2013), *aff'd*, 573 U.S. 373 (2014).

79. 573 U.S. at 400.

80. 573 U.S. at 408 (Alito, J., concurring in part and concurring in the judgment). *See generally* Orin S. Kerr, *The Fourth Amendment and New Technologies: Constitutional Myths and the Case for Caution*, 102 MICH. L. REV. 801 (2004) (arguing

that, at least with respect to new technologies, legislative rules regarding police searches and seizures should generally displace the Fourth Amendment).

81. *See* United States v. Armstrong, 517 U.S. 456, 465 (1996).

82. Even Judge Charles Breitel, although generally in favor of broad discretion for the police, advocated controlling individual officer discretion not to arrest by instituting a "formal regulated practice" of keeping a record explaining each such decision. Charles D. Breitel, *Controls in Criminal Law Enforcement*, 27 U. CHI. L. REV. 427, 433 (1960).

83. *See generally* Hannah Bloch-Webbah, *Visible Policing: Technology, Transparency, and Democratic Control*, 109 CAL. L. REV. 917 (2021).

84. *See* Mitchell v. Wisconsin, 139 S. Ct. 2525, 2531 (2019) (plurality); Birchfield v. North Dakota, 579 U.S. 438, 444 (2016); Missouri v. McNeely, 569 U.S. 141, 161 (2013).

85. 384 U.S. 757, 765 (1966).

86. *See, e.g.*, *McNeely*, 569 U.S. at 178 (Thomas, J. dissenting) ("The Court [in *Schmerber*] held that dissipation of alcohol in the blood constitutes an exigency that allows a blood draw without a warrant.").

87. 569 U.S. at 156 (majority opinion).

88. Birchfield v. North Dakota, 579 U.S. 438, 476 (2016).

89. 579 U.S. at 476–77.

90. 139 S. Ct. at 2531 (plurality); 139 S. Ct. at 2539 (Thomas, J., concurring in the judgment). *See also* 139 S. Ct. at 2551 (Gorsuch, J., dissenting) (observing that the Court took the case "to decide whether Wisconsin drivers impliedly consent to blood alcohol tests thanks to a state [implied-consent] statute," and criticizing the Court for answering a different question).

91. "No person shall . . . be deprived of life, liberty, or property, without due process of law. . . ." U.S. CONST., amend. V.

92. 34 U.S.C. § 10101 et seq.; *see* Orin S. Kerr, *The Fourth Amendment and New Technologies: Constitutional Myths and the Case for Caution*, 102 MICH. L. REV. 801, 852 (2004).

93. U.S. CONST., art. 1, § 8, cl. 3 ("The Congress shall have Power [t]o regulate Commerce . . . among the several States. . . .").

94. United States v. Washington, 142 S. Ct. 1976, 1984 (2022) (quoting North Dakota v. United States, 495 U.S. 423, 435 (1990) (plurality opinion) (alteration in original).

95. Tex. H.B. No. 1937.

96. Although the proposed legislation did not mention the TSA by name, it applied only to "a search for the purpose of granting access to a publicly accessible building or form of transportation." Moreover, the proposed legislation went out of its way to define "public servant" to include federal officers and agents. Finally, the Bill Analysis by the Senate cited invasive searches by the TSA as the impetus for the bill.

97. Letter from John E. Murphy, United States Attorney for the Western District of Texas, to Joe Straus, Speaker of the House of Texas et al., dated May 24,

2011, at 2 (on file with author). Murphy wrote on behalf of himself and his counterparts in the Eastern, Northern, and Southern Districts of Texas.

98. 436 U.S. 307. *See* 29 U.S.C. § 651 et seq.

99. *See, e.g.*, Davis v. United States, 564 U.S. 229, 230–32 (2011).

100. Wolf v. Colorado, 338 U.S. 25, 33 (1949). *See also* Nicholas Quinn Rosenkranz, *Federal Rules of Statutory Interpretation*, 115 HARV. L. REV. 2086, 2097–98 (2002) (describing a constitutional default rule as one that is mandatory unless displaced by specific legislation); *see also* Leading Case, *Article I—Stare Decisis for Constitutional Default Rules—Dormant Commerce Clause*—South Dakota v. Wayfair, Inc., 132 HARV. L. REV. 277, 277 (2018) (characterizing exclusionary rule as a constitutional default rule); Tara Mikkilineni, Note, *Constitutional Default Rules and Interbranch Cooperation*, 82 N.Y.U. L. REV. 1403, 1408 (2007) (same).

101. ERIC FONER, RECONSTRUCTION: AMERICA'S UNFINISHED REVOLUTION, 1863–1877, at 204 (1988); JOE M. RICHARDSON, THE NEGRO IN THE RECONSTRUCTION OF FLORIDA, 1865–77, at 41, 46, 48 (1965); Report of Brevet Brig. Gen. J.R. Lewis, to Maj. Gen. O.O. Howard, Comm'r, dated Nov. 1, 1866, reprinted in SEN. EXEC. DOC. No. 39-6, at 126, 128.

102. 533 U.S. 27 (2001).

103. This parallels the way Justice Felix Frankfurter would have interpreted 42 U.S.C. § 1983, which provides a federal remedy for violation of constitutional rights by persons acting "under color of" state law. According to him, official conduct in violation of state law is not done "under color of" law because the statute's drafters intended that such conduct be remediable by the State itself. The drafters, he argued, did not intend "to reach . . . instances of acts in defiance of state law and which no settled state practice, no systematic pattern of official action or inaction, no 'custom, or usage, of any State,' insulates from effective and adequate reparation by the State's authorities." Monroe v. Pape, 365 U.S. 167, 236 (1961) (Frankfurter, J., dissenting in part). It is only where the state agent's conduct is "either in strict pursuance of some specific command of state law or within the scope of executive discretion in the administration of state laws" that the § 1983 remedy is needed because state law would provide no remedy in that instance. 365 U.S. at 213–14 (footnote omitted). The Court rejected that approach on the ground that the drafters of the legislation intended to provide a federal remedy in every case because they knew that "state laws might not be enforced." 365 U.S. at 180 (majority opinion).

104. *See* Wolf v. Colorado, 338 U.S. 25, 42 (1949) (Murphy, J., dissenting) (rejecting out of hand "the possibilities of criminal prosecution" under these circumstances).

105. 338 U.S. at 30–31 & n.1.

106. 367 U.S. at 651–52 (quoting People v. Cahan, 282 P.2d 905, 911 (1955)). Two prominent law review articles published the same year as *Cahan*—halfway between *Wolf* and *Mapp*—addressed the almost complete lack of state-law criminal prosecutions and tort actions, respectively, against police for unlawful searches and seizures. *See generally* Richard A. Edwards, *Criminal Liability for Unreasonable Searches and Seizures*, 41 VA. L. REV. 621 (1955); Caleb Foote, *Tort Remedies for Police Violations of Individual Rights*, 39 MINN. L. REV. 493 (1955).

Chapter 11

1. United States v. Tuggle, 4 F.4th 505, 527 (7th Cir. 2021) ("Eventually, cameras grew so sophisticated, discrete, portable, and inexpensive that they pervaded society."), *cert. denied*, 142 S. Ct. 1107 (2022).

2. Matthew Tokson, *Pole Cameras Under Fourth Amendment Law*, 83 Ohio St. L.J. __ (forthcoming 2022) (draft at 6–7).

3. *Tuggle*, 4 F.4th at 523–29 (use of pole cameras for eighteen months not a search); United States v. Houston, 813 F.3d 282 (6th Cir. 2016) (use of pole camera for ten weeks not a search); United States v. Bucci, 582 F.3d 108, 116–17 (1st Cir. 2009) (use of pole camera for eight months not a search); United States v. Jackson, 213 F.3d 1269, 1282 (10th Cir.) (use of pole camera for undisclosed period of time not a search), *vac. on other grounds*, 531 U.S. 1033 (2000). *See also* United States v. Vankesteren, 553 F.3d 286, 287 (4th Cir. 2009) (use of camera placed in open field not a search). The U.S. Court of Appeals for the First Circuit, sitting en banc, recently split 3-3 on this issue. *See* United States v. Moore-Bush, 36 F.4th 320 (1st Cir.) (en banc), *petition for cert. filed* (U.S. Nov. 22, 2022).

4. *See generally* Matthew Tokson, *Pole Cameras Under Fourth Amendment Law*, 83 Ohio St. L.J. __ (forthcoming 2022).

5. *Tuggle*, 4 F.4th at 509 ("[W]e are steadily approaching a future with a constellation of ubiquitous public and private cameras accessible to the government that catalog the movements and activities of all Americans.").

6. *See generally* Orin S. Kerr, *The Mosaic Theory of the Fourth Amendment*, 111 Mich. L. Rev. 311 (2012) (discussing but not endorsing this view); *see also* David Gray and Danielle Keats Citron, *A Shattered Looking Glass: The Pitfalls and Potential of the Mosaic Theory of Fourth Amendment Privacy*, 14 N.C. J. L. & Tech. 381, 411–28 (2013) (offering a tentative defense of the mosaic theory).

7. 565 U.S. 400, 416 (2012) (Sotomayor, J., concurring); 565 U.S. at 429–31 (2012) (Alito, J., concurring in the judgment).

8. 138 S. Ct. 2206, 2217–20 (2018). *See* Paul Ohm, *The Many Revolutions of* Carpenter, 32 Harv. J.L. & Tech. 357, 373 (2019) ("[T]he [*Carpenter*] Court in effect endorse[d] the mosaic theory of privacy.").

9. *See, e.g.*, Philips v. Washington Legal Found., 524 U.S. 156, 164 (1998) ("Because the Constitution protects rather than creates property interests, the existence of a property interest is determined by reference to 'existing rules or understandings that stem from an independent source such as state law.' (quoting Board of Regents of State Colleges v. Roth, 408 U.S. 564, 577 (1972))); Wilkinson v. Austin, 545 U.S. 209, 221 (2005) ("A liberty interest may arise from the Constitution itself, by reason of guarantees implicit in the word 'liberty,' or it may arise from an expectation or interest created by state laws or policies." (citation omitted)).

10. Barry Friedman, Unwarranted: Policing Without Permission 232 (2017) ("If state law forbids what the cops have done, that should be the end of the matter.").

11. California v. Greenwood, 486 U.S. 35, 37–38 (1988); *see* California v. Rooney, 483 U.S. 307, 325 (1987) (White, J., dissenting); People v. Krivda, 486 P.2d 1262 (Cal. 1971).

12. 466 U.S. 170 (1984).

13. *See* David Gray, The Fourth Amendment in an Age of Surveillance 32–38 (2017).

14. David Gray, The Fourth Amendment in an Age of Surveillance 35 (2017).

15. *See, e.g.*, United States v. Lambis, 197 F.Supp.3d 606, 610 (S.D.N.Y. 2016) ("[T]he cell-site simulator is not a device 'in general public use.'" (quoting Kyllo v. United States, 533 U.S. 27, 40 (2001))).

16. 533 U.S. 27.

17. *See* 3 Restatement (Second) of Torts § 652B, comment (b) (1977) (giving this as an example of the tort of intrusion upon seclusion).

18. *See, e.g.*, Cal. Pen. Code § 647(j)(1) ("A person who . . . views, by means of any instrumentality, including, but not limited to . . . binoculars . . . the interior of a bedroom, bathroom, changing room, fitting room, dressing room, or tanning booth, or the interior of any other area in which the occupant has a reasonable expectation of privacy, with the intent to invade the privacy of a person or persons inside [commits disorderly conduct].").

19. *See* Barry Friedman, Unwarranted: Policing Without Permission 231 (2017) (arguing that courts should "refuse to allow emerging technologies to be used by the police for surveillance until rules are in place to regulate them"); *see generally* Mailyn Fidler, *Local Police Surveillance and the Administrative Fourth Amendment*, 36 Santa Clara High Tech. L.J. 481 (2020). *But see* Andrew Guthrie Ferguson, *Surveillance and the Tyrant Test*, 110 Geo. L.J. 205, 259–62 (2021) (offering a critique of the view that "technocratic" controls are sufficient).

20. *Jones*, 565 U.S. at 429–30 (Alito, J., concurring in the judgment).

21. Orin Kerr, *The Fourth Amendment and New Technologies: Constitutional Myths and the Case for Caution*, 102 Mich. L. Rev. 801, 850–851 (2004).

22. *See* Barry Friedman, *Lawless Surveillance*, 97 N.Y.U. L. Rev. 1143, 1146–57 (2022) (opining that regulation of government "digital surveillance, particularly bulk surveillance . . . is absolutely mandatory as a matter of constitutional law").

23. 517 U.S. 806, 810 (1996). As a federal case arising from the District of Columbia, *Whren* is the atypical modern case where the Fourth Amendment does apply directly to a police officer. However, because of what we have inelegantly termed "reverse incorporation," the Fourteenth Amendment applies also, so we will treat *Whren* as we would any state case.

24. 532 U.S. 318 (2001).

25. *See* Egon Bittner, Aspects of Police Work 192–98 (1990); Michael R. Gottfredson and Don M. Gottfredson, Decision Making in Criminal Justice: Toward the Rational Exercise of Discretion 60 (2d ed. 1988).

26. 517 U.S. at 810.

27. Bernard E. Harcourt and Tracey L. Meares, *Randomization and the Fourth Amendment*, 78 U. Chi. L. Rev. 809, 854–59 (2011). *See also* Charles R. Epp, Steven Maynard-Moody, and Donald Haider-Markel, Pulled Over: How Police Stops Define Race and Citizenship 3 (2014) ("[I]t is well established that racial minorities are more likely than whites to be stopped by the police."). *See,*

e.g., Emma Pierson et al., *A Large-Scale Analysis of Racial Disparities in Police Stops Across the United States*, 4 NATURE HUM. BEHAVIOUR 736, 740–41 (2020) ("Our analysis provides evidence that decisions about whom to stop and, subsequently, whom to search are biased against black and Hispanic drivers."). For a discussion of racial disparities in policing generally, *see* DAVID COLE, NO EQUAL JUSTICE: RACE AND CLASS IN THE AMERICAN CRIMINAL JUSTICE SYSTEM 16–62 (1999).

28. David H. Gans, *"We Do Not Want to Be Hunted": The Right to Be Secure and Our Constitutional Story of Race and Policing*, 11 COLUM. J. RACE & LAW 239, 308 (2021) (arguing that *Atwater* ignored the concerns of "[t]he Framers of the Fourteenth Amendment . . . that white police officers were arresting Black people for a host of trivial crimes."); Alexandra Natapoff, Atwater *and the Misdemeanor Carceral State*, 133 HARV. L. REV. F. 147, 173–74 (2020) (arguing that the *Atwater* Court should have paid attention to the postbellum use of misdemeanor arrests to re-enslave Black people rather than just the common law of 1791). Of course, limitations on *arrests* for minor crimes are not the same as limitations on *prosecutions* for minor crimes. Arrests are simply one way of beginning the criminal process. *See generally* Rachel A. Harmon, *Why Arrest?*, 115 MICH. L. REV. 307 (2016) (concluding that arrests are unnecessary in many instances to begin the criminal process). Yet, as noted in Chapter Eight, the initial decision *not* to make a stop or arrest altogether binds actors further downstream in the criminal process. Due process protections analogous to the ones described here might be required in order to check outsized discretion in the hands of prosecutors. But because their decisions are not generally seen as implicating the Fourth Amendment, that is a topic for another day.

29. 517 U.S. at 810 (citing 18 D.C. Mun. Regs. § 2213.4 (1995)).

30. *See* United States v. Whren, 53 F.3d 371, 373 (D.C. Cir. 1996), *aff'd*, 517 U.S. 806 (1996).

31. Michigan v. DeFillippo, 443 U.S. 31, 37–38 (1979). For an excellent analysis of this problem, *see generally* Joel S. Johnson, *Vagueness Attacks on Searches and Seizures*, 107 VA. L. REV. 347 (2021).

32. Tracey Maclin, *Race and the Fourth Amendment*, 51 VAND. L. REV. 333, 346–47 (1998).

33. *Whren*, 517 U.S. at 810 (citing 18 D.C. Mun. Regs. § 2204.3). *See* DAVID A. HARRIS, PROFILES IN INJUSTICE: WHY RACIAL PROFILING CANNOT WORK 31 (2002) ("*[N]o* driver can go for even a short drive without violating *some* aspect of the traffic code."); I. Bennett Capers, *Rethinking the Fourth Amendment: Race, Citizenship, and the Equality Principle*, 46 HARV. C.R.-C.L. L. REV. 1, 34 (2011) ("[M]ost drivers routinely violate traffic laws. . . ."); Carissa Byrne Hessick, *Vagueness Principles*, 48 ARIZ. ST. L.J. 1137, 1157 (2016) ("[M]ost drivers will commit an infraction if observed for any appreciable amount of time. . . .").

34. Kim Forde-Mazrui, *Ruling Out the Rule of Law*, 60 VAND. L. REV. 1497, 1514 (2007) ("Because virtually everyone, acting conscientiously and reasonably, violates traffic laws every time they drive, an officer can identify a crime to justify a stop, search, interrogation, and arrest of virtually any motorist he chooses." (footnote omitted)).

35. J. Skelly Wright, *Beyond Discretionary Justice*, 81 YALE L.J. 575, 590 (1972) (book review); *see also* KENNETH CULP DAVIS, DISCRETIONARY JUSTICE: A PRELIMINARY INQUIRY 91 (1969) ("Criminal statutes which overshoot are a prime cause of avoidable injustice, because such statutes inevitably result in selective enforcement, and cases are often selected for enforcement on irrational grounds." (emphasis omitted)).

36. Bd. of Admin. v. Miles, 115 N.E. 841, 842 (Ill. 1917); *see* Evan J. Criddle, *When Delegation Begets Domination: Due Process of Administrative Lawmaking*, 46 GA. L. REV. 117, 162 (2011).

37. Kim Forde-Mazrui, *Ruling Out the Rule of Law*, 60 VAND. L. REV. 1497, 1503 (2007); *see also* Carissa Byrne Hessick, *Vagueness Principles*, 48 ARIZ. ST. L.J. 1137, 1138 (2016) ("[T]he current state of traffic laws and traffic enforcement have led to enforcement that is as arbitrary and discriminatory as the enforcement of vague laws.").

38. Kiel Brennan-Marquez, *Extremely Broad Laws*, 61 ARIZ. L. REV. 641, 655 (2019). *See also* Barbara C. Salken, *The General Warrant of the Twentieth Century? A Fourth Amendment Solution to Unchecked Discretion to Arrest for Traffic Offenses*, 62 TEMP. L. REV. 221, 253 (1989) ("[A]rrests for minor traffic offenses are identical to the unlimited and arbitrary power of the court's messengers and customs inspectors that led to the adoption of the fourth amendment.").

39. *See generally* Alexandra Natapoff, *Underenforcement*, 75 FORDHAM L. REV. 1715 (2006); *see also* I. Bennett Capers, *Crime, Surveillance, and Communities*, 40 FORDHAM URB. L.J. 959, 988 (2013); Sarah L. Swan, *Discriminatory Dualism*, 54 GA. L. REV. 869, 876–78 (2020).

40. Dan M. Kahan and Tracey L. Meares, *Foreword: The Coming Crisis of Criminal Procedure*, 86 GEO. L.J. 1153, 1170 (1998). *See also* Maria Ponomarenko, *Rethinking Police Rulemaking*, 114 NW. L. REV. 1, 12 (2019) ("Often, it is the very same residents who report feeling both underprotected and overpoliced.").

41. *See* Tom Tyler and Tracey Meares, *Revisiting Broken Windows: The Role of the Community and the Police in Promoting Community Engagement*, 76 N.Y.U. ANN. SURV. AM. L. 637, 652 (2021). The "broken windows" theory refers to the controversial hypothesis that small instances of disorder in a community lead to an escalating cycle of greater disorder and serious crime, and ultimately the deterioration of entire neighborhoods. *See generally* George Kelling and James Q. Wilson, *Broken Windows: The Police and Neighborhood Safety*, *reprinted in* CRITICAL ISSUES IN POLICING: CONTEMPORARY READINGS 96 (Roger G. Dunham, Geoffrey P. Alper, and Kyle D. McLean eds., 8th ed. 2021).

42. Kenneth Culp Davis, *An Approach to Legal Control of the Police*, 52 TEX. L. REV. 703, 714 (1974); *accord* Gregory Howard Williams, *Police Rulemaking Revisited: Some New Thoughts on an Old Problem*, 47 L. & CONTEMP. PROBS. 123, 174 (1984).

43. *See* Kim Forde-Mazrui, *Ruling Out the Rule of Law*, 60 VAND. L. REV. 1497, 1542–47 (2007) (suggesting various strategies, such as by requiring higher rates of enforcement or limitations on enforcement to "serious traffic violations"); Dan M. Kahan and Tracey L. Meares, *Foreword: The Coming Crisis of Criminal Procedure*, 86

Geo. L.J. 1153, 1170 (1998) (distinguishing between "general order-maintenance policing" from policing pursuant to ordinances that "jealously guard[] against the diffusion of enforcement authority").

44. *See* Elizabeth E. Joh, *Discretionless Policing: Technology and the Fourth Amendment*, 95 Calif. L. Rev. 199, 216–23 (2007); *see also* I. Bennett Capers, *Crime, Surveillance, and Communities*, 40 Fordham Urb. L.J. 959, 984 (2013).

45. *See* Delaware v. Prouse, 440 U.S. 648, 664 (1979) (Rehnquist, J., dissenting) (deriding such reasoning as "elevat[ing] the adage 'misery loves company' to a novel role in Fourth Amendment jurisprudence").

46. Silas J. Wasserstrom and Louis Michael Seidman, *The Fourth Amendment as Constitutional Theory*, 77 Geo. L.J. 19, 96 (1988) (observing that on a political process theory, where searches are widespread, "there is no reason to doubt that . . . political representatives will respond to the complaints of their constituents"); *see also* Robert M. Igleburger and Frank A. Schubert, *Policy Making for the Police*, 58 Am. B. Ass'n J. 307, 308 (1972) ("It is highly likely that if officers were to arrest persons for being one mile over the speed limit and strictly enforce the curfew, disorderly conduct, and disturbing the peace ordinances, citizens would be clamoring at the city commission chambers and asking whether they have a police force or a gestapo.").

47. 532 U.S. at 352, 353 & n.24.

48. Alexandra Natapoff, Atwater *and the Misdemeanor Carceral State*, 133 Harv. L. Rev. F. 147, 159–64 (2020). *See also* Maria Ponomarenko, *Rethinking Police Rulemaking*, 114 Nw. L. Rev. 1, 28 (2019) ("[T]hose who bear the brunt of excess discretion typically are not in a position to make things politically difficult for [police] chiefs.").

49. Another flawed argument is that the cost of policing minor crimes acts as a political constraint. Given the prevalence of usage fees, civil forfeiture, and other moneymaking schemes associated with policing low-level criminal activity, policing minor crimes has very much become a for-profit enterprise for police agencies and local government. *See* Developments in the Law, *Policing and Profit*, 128 Harv. L. Rev. 1723, 1726–33 (2015).

50. 517 U.S. at 815 (quoting Metropolitan Police Department, Washington, D.C., General Order 303.1, pt. 1, Objectives and Policies (A)(2)(4) (Apr. 30, 1992) (emphasis omitted)).

51. *See* Alexandra Natapoff, Atwater *and the Misdemeanor Carceral State*, 133 Harv. L. Rev. F. 147, 165–66 (2020) (observing this irony).

52. *Whren*, 517 U.S. at 815. *See* Ayesha Bell Hardaway, *The Supreme Court and the Illegitimacy of Lawless Fourth Amendment Policing*, 100 B.U. L. Rev. 1193, 1200–03 (2020) (describing *Whren* and *Moore* as instances of the Court rewarding rule-breaking by police); Eric J. Miller, *Challenging Police Discretion*, 58 Howard L.J. 521, 534 (2015) ("The *Moore* Court, for the most part, regarded itself as re-applying the same sort of rule it established in *Whren*. . . ."); Andrew E. Taslitz, *Fourth Amendment Federalism and the Silencing of the American Poor*, 85 Chi.-Kent L. Rev. 277, 299 (2010) (drawing a connection between *Whren* and *Moore*).

53. *See* Samuel Walker, Taming The System: The Control of Discretion in Criminal Justice 1950–90, at 33–39 (1993) (documenting the rise in policies mandating arrest in domestic violence assault cases).

54. *See* John Rappaport, *Second-Order Regulation of Law Enforcement*, 103 Calif. L. Rev. 205, 269 (2015) ("[E]vidence that officers deviated from agency policy, as the officers in *Whren* allegedly did, should tend to establish a constitutional violation.").

55. *Whren*, 517 U.S. at 813–14.

56. 517 U.S. at 813.

57. *See* Kim Forde-Mazrui, *Ruling Out the Rule of Law*, 60 Vand. L. Rev. 1497, 1535–38 (2007).

58. I. Bennett Capers, *Rethinking the Fourth Amendment: Race, Citizenship, and the Equality Principle*, 46 Harv. C.R.-C.L. L. Rev. 1, 40 (2011); Anthony C. Thompson, *Stopping the Usual Suspects: Race and the Fourth Amendment*, 74 N.Y.U. L. Rev. 956, 983–91 (1999).

59. *See* Albert W. Alschuler, *Racial Profiling and the Constitution*, 2002 U. Chi. Legal F. 163, 193 (characterizing the *Whren* Court as having treated the two provisions as "hermetically sealed units whose principles must not contaminate one another"); I. Bennett Capers, *Rethinking the Fourth Amendment: Race, Citizenship, and the Equality Principle*, 46 Harv. C.R.-C.L. L. Rev. 1, 35 (2011) (criticizing the Court's "acoustic separation" of the two provisions).

60. 392 U.S. 1, 5–7, 21–25 (1968).

61. 392 U.S. at 21, 30.

62. Illinois v. Wardlow, 528 U.S. 119 (2000).

63. Barry Friedman, Unwarranted: Policing Without Permission 149 (2017); *see also* Silas J. Wasserstrom, *The Incredible Shrinking Fourth Amendment*, 21 Am. Crim. L. Rev. 257, 350 (1984) (observing that the *Terry* opinion "emphasized the 'narrowness' of . . . its holding").

64. *See, e.g.*, David A. Harris, *Factors for Reasonable Suspicion: When Black and Poor Means Stopped and Frisked*, 69 Ind. L.J. 659, 677–78 (1994); Tracey Maclin, Terry *v.* Ohio's *Fourth Amendment Legacy: Black Men and Police Discretion*, 72 St. John's L. Rev. 1271, 1278 (1998).

65. I. Bennett Capers, *Rethinking the Fourth Amendment: Race, Citizenship, and the Equality Principle*, 46 Harv. C.R.-C.L. L. Rev. 1, 30 (2011).

66. Bernard E. Harcourt and Tracey L. Meares, *Randomization and the Fourth Amendment*, 78 U. Chi. L. Rev. 809, 854–59 (2011). *See, e.g.*, Andrew Gelman, Jeffrey Fagan, and Alex Kiss, *An Analysis of the New York City Police Department's "Stop-and-Frisk" Policy in the Context of Claims of Racial Bias*, 102 J. Am. Stat. Assn. 813, 822 (2007) (concluding that, even controlling for precinct location and estimated rate of criminal behavior, Blacks and Latinos were stopped "between 1.5 and 2.5 as often as whites . . . for the most common categories of stops").

67. Devon W. Carbado, *From Stop and Frisk to Shoot and Kill:* Terry *v.* Ohio's *Pathway to Police Violence*, 64 UCLA L. Rev. 1508 (2017); Devon W. Carbado, *From Stopping Black People to Killing Black People: The Fourth Amendment Pathways to Police Violence*, 105 Cal. L. Rev. 125 (2017). *See also* Rory Kramer and Brianna

Remster, *Stop, Frisk, and Assault—Racial Disparities in Police Use of Force During Investigatory Stops*, 52 Law & Soc'y Rev. 960, 982 (2018) (concluding that stops of Blacks are significantly more likely to involve the use of force than stops of whites, all other things being equal).

68. William J. Stuntz, Terry *and Substantive Law*, 72 St. John's L. Rev. 1362, 1364 (1998); *see also* David H. Gans, *"We Do Not Want to Be Hunted": The Right to Be Secure and Our Constitutional Story of Race and Policing*, 11 Colum. J. Race & Law 239, 303 (2021) ("*Terry* made it easy for the police to stop and frisk people with virtually no evidentiary foundation."); Scott E. Sundby, *A Return to Fourth Amendment Basics: Undoing the Mischief of* Camara *and* Terry, 72 Minn. L. Rev. 383, 402 n.65 (1988) ("The potential misuse of reasonable suspicion is exacerbated by the laxness of the standard itself. . . .").

69. United States v. Zapata-Ibarra, 223 F.3d 281, 282–83 (5th Cir. 2000) (Wiener, J., dissenting).

70. *See* United States v. Hooper, 935 F.2d 484, 499–500 (2d Cir. 1991) (Pratt, J., dissenting). *See also* David Cole, No Equal Justice: Race and Class in the American Criminal Justice System 47–49 (1999) (listing forty-seven factors that federal agents have claimed to be part of a "drug-courier profile," many of them mutually inconsistent).

71. *See* William J. Stuntz, Terry *and Substantive Law*, 72 St. John's L. Rev. 1362, 1364–65 (1998) (observing that reasonable suspicion of drug crime is so common that *Terry* gives police enormous discretion in deciding whom to stop); *see also* I. Bennett Capers, *Rethinking the Fourth Amendment: Race, Citizenship, and the Equality Principle*, 46 Harv. C.R.-C.L. L. Rev. 1, 32 (2011) ("[I]t is reasonable suspicion's very plasticity that has had lasting implications for the lives of racial minorities, and lasting implications for the goal of equal citizenship.").

72. *See* Brigham City v. Stuart, 547 U.S. 398, 400 (2006) (permitting warrantless entry into a home where police "have an objectively reasonable basis for believing that an occupant is seriously injured or imminently threatened with such injury"); Michigan v. Fisher, 558 U.S. 45, 47 (2009) (same). The point is not entirely free from doubt. *Compare* Kit Kinports, *The Quantum of Suspicion Needed for an Exigent Circumstances Search*, 52 U. Mich. J.L. Ref. 615, 631 (2019) ("The entry and search of premises under the exigent circumstances exception should require probable cause not only to enter, but also to believe that exigent circumstances exist. . . ."), *with* Michael Gentithes, *Exigencies, Not Exceptions: How to Return Warrant Exceptions to Their Roots*, 25 U. Pa. J. Con. L. ___, draft at 31 (forthcoming 2022) (on file with author) (arguing that only "*Terry*-style reasonable suspicion of an exigency" should be required.).

73. Scott E. Sundby, *A Return to Fourth Amendment Basics: Undoing the Mischief of* Camara *and* Terry, 72 Minn. L. Rev. 383, 421–23 (1988) (positing *Terry* as a case about exigent circumstances).

74. *See* 4 Wayne R. LaFave, Search and Seizure: A Treatise on the Fourth Amendment, § 9.2(c) (5th ed. 2012).

75. United States v. Brignoni-Ponce, 422 U.S. 873, 881 (1975). Note that in

Brignoni-Ponce, *Terry* was also stretched to cover stops of motorists as well as pedestrians even though the intrusion on liberty might be greater for the former.

76. 460 U.S. 491, 498–99 (1983) (plurality).

77. *See, e.g.*, Alabama v. White, 496 U.S. 325 (1990); United States v. Sokolow, 490 U.S. 1 (1989); United States v. Mendenhall, 446 U.S. 544 (1980). *See* Sherry F. Colb, *The Qualitative Dimension of Fourth Amendment "Reasonableness,"* 98 COLUM. L. REV. 1642, 1693 (1998) (noting that, following *Terry*, the Court "permitted *Terry* stops and frisks in the case of reasonably suspected narcotics possession offenses, in which there is no necessary safety risk attached to the suspected activity").

78. 469 U.S. 221, 229 (1985). The Court did leave open the question whether *Terry* stops can be made to investigate completed misdemeanors.

79. William J. Stuntz, Terry *and Substantive Law*, 72 ST. JOHN'S L. REV. 1362, 1363–64 (1998); *see also* United States v. Brignoni-Ponce, 422 U.S. 873, 888–89 (1975) (Douglas, J., concurring in the judgment) ("Hopes that [*Terry*] might be employed only in the pursuit of violent crime . . . have now been dashed, as it . . . has come to be viewed as a legal construct for the regulation of a general investigatory police power.").

80. 392 U.S. at 30 (emphasis added).

81. BARRY FRIEDMAN, UNWARRANTED: POLICING WITHOUT PERMISSION 149 (2017).

82. Williams v. Adams, 436 F.2d 30, 39 (2d Cir. 1970) (Friendly, J., dissenting) (emphasis added), *rev'd en banc*, 441 F.2d 394 (2d Cir. 1971), *rev'd*, 407 U.S. 143 (1972).

83. Adams v. Williams, 407 U.S. 143, 151–53 (1972) (Brennan, J., dissenting).

84. *See* David H. Gans, *"We Do Not Want to Be Hunted": The Right to Be Secure and Our Constitutional Story of Race and Policing*, 11 COLUM. J. RACE & LAW 239, 300 (2021) ("Just as vagrancy laws replaced slave patrols, stop-and-frisk replaced vagrancy laws as a means of controlling Black people and enforcing their subordinate status.").

85. *See* Sherry F. Colb, *The Qualitative Dimension of Fourth Amendment "Reasonableness,"* 98 COLUM. L. REV. 1642, 1693 (1998) (asserting that, if the principles behind *Terry* were followed, "[t]he police could . . . only stop and frisk those suspects reasonably suspected of preparing to engage in a potentially violent or otherwise serious crime"); Scott E. Sundby, *An Ode to Probable Cause: A Brief Response to Professors Amar and Slobogin*, 72 ST. JOHN'S L. REV. 1133, 1135 (1998) ("Reduced to its essence, the [*Terry*] holding is a relatively modest one, basically creating a limited right of 'self-defense' for a police officer who in carrying out her duties comes across someone whom she reasonably believes is armed and dangerous."); *cf.* 4 WAYNE R. LAFAVE, SEARCH AND SEIZURE: A TREATISE ON THE FOURTH AMENDMENT, § 9.2(c) at 396 (5th ed. 2012) ("The *Terry* rule should be expressly limited to investigation of serious offenses."). This would necessarily call into question the dicta in United States v. Place, 462 U.S. 696, 708–09 (1983), that police may seize personal property on mere reasonable suspicion that it is evidence of a crime.

86. Following the lead of Seth Stoughton, I use the terms "police violence"

and "police use of force" interchangeably. Because we accept that police will use violence at times in order to perform their jobs effectively, these terms should not be read with any normative connotation unless accompanied by the terms "justified" or "unjustified." Seth W. Stoughton, *Accountability and Enhancement: The Dual Objectives of Use-of-Force Review*, in RETHINKING AND REFORMING AMERICAN POLICING 227, 230–31 (Joseph A. Schafer and Richard W. Myers eds., 2022); Seth W. Stoughton, *The Regulation of Police Violence*, in CRITICAL ISSUES IN POLICING: CONTEMPORARY READINGS 321, 322–23 (Roger G. Dunham, Geoffrey P. Alper, and Kyle D. McLean eds., 8th ed. 2021).

87. Ayesha Bell Hardaway, *The Supreme Court and the Illegitimacy of Lawless Fourth Amendment Policing*, 100 B.U. L. REV. 1193, 1195 (2020) (drawing connection between Reconstruction-era violence against Blacks and modern police use of force).

88. Joshua Correll et al., *Across the Thin Blue Line: Police Officers and Racial Bias in the Decision to Shoot*, 92 J. PERSONALITY & SOC. PSYCHOL. 1006, 1006 (2007) ("Investigators have consistently found evidence that police use greater force, including lethal force, with minority suspects than with White suspects."); Frank Edwards et al., *Risk of Being Killed by Police Use of Force in the United States by Age, Race–Ethnicity, and Sex*, 116 PROC. NAT'L ACAD. SCI. 16793, 16794 (2019) (concluding that Black men and women are 2.5 and 1.4 times more likely, respectively, to be killed by police than white men and women); Justin Nix et al., *A Bird's Eye View of Civilians Killed by Police in 2015*, 16 CRIMINOLOGY & PUB. POL'Y 309, 325 (2017) (finding that nonwhite civilians "were significantly more likely than Whites to have been fatally shot because of an apparent threat perception failure"); Niraj Sekhon, *Blue on Black: An Empirical Assessment of Police Shootings*, 54 AM. CRIM. L. REV. 189, 199–202 (2017) (finding that in Chicago Black persons are disproportionately shot by police compared to other races, and citing studies drawing similar conclusions in Las Vegas, New York, Philadelphia, and San Francisco). *See also* Joshua Correll et al., *The Influence of Stereotypes on Decisions to Shoot*, 37 EUR. J. SOC. PSYCHOL. 1102, 1102 (2007) (observing that "research using computer simulations to investigate the influence of race on shoot/don't-shoot decisions demonstrates a pronounced bias to shoot Blacks"). *Cf.* Roland G. Fryer, Jr., "An Empirical Analysis of Racial Differences in Police Use of Force," at 29–38 (working paper) (last revised Jan. 2018) (finding "sometimes quite large" racial disparities in police use of nonlethal force, "even after controlling for a large set of controls," but no racial disparities in the use of deadly force). At least some studies suggest that bias plays a role. *See* CENTER FOR POLICING EQUITY, THE SCIENCE OF JUSTICE: RACE, ARRESTS, AND POLICE USE OF FORCE 4 (2016) (concluding that "racial disparities in police use of force persist even when controlling for racial distribution of local arrest rates"); Kendra Scott et al., *A Social Scientific Approach Toward Understanding Racial Disparities in Police Shooting: Data from the Department of Justice (1980–2000)*, 73 J. SOC. ISSUES 1, 16 (2017) (concluding "that officers tended to use deadly force more in response to Black compared to White suspects even after criminal activity was equated").

89. Seth Stoughton, *How the Fourth Amendment Frustrates the Regulation of Police Violence*, 70 Emory L.J. 521, 535–42 (2020). Stoughton's fourth category, physical force that fails to restrain (as when a police officer shoots someone in order to stop them but the person flees), now constitutes a seizure. *See* Torres v. Madrid, 141 S. Ct. 989 (2021).

90. Cnty. of Sacramento v. Lewis, 523 U.S. 833, 836 (1998).

91. Graham v. Connor, 490 U.S. 386, 395 (1989).

92. *See* Osagie K. Obasogie and Zachary Newman, *The Endogenous Fourth Amendment: An Empirical Assessment of How Police Understandings of Excessive Force Become Constitutional Law*, 104 Cornell L. Rev. 1281, 1319 (2019) ("[T]he [*Graham*] Court signaled that the only way to think about police excessive force—violence that is often racialized in a manner thought to give rise to Fourteenth Amendment considerations—is through an ambiguous Fourth Amendment."). *See generally* Toni M. Massaro, *Reviving Hugo Black? The Court's "Jot for Jot" Account of Substantive Due Process*, 73 N.Y.U. L. Rev. 1086 (1998) (criticizing *Graham* on these grounds).

93. Robert Leider, *Taming Self-Defense: Using Deadly Force to Prevent Escapes*, 70 Fla. L. Rev. 971, 973 (2019) (quoting Max Weber, Political Writings 310–11 (Peter Lassman and Ronald Spiers eds., 1994)).

94. Robert Leider, *Taming Self-Defense: Using Deadly Force to Prevent Escapes*, 70 Fla. L. Rev. 971, 973 (2019).

95. *See* Rachel A. Harmon, *When Is Police Violence Justified?*, 102 Nw. U. L. Rev. 1119, 1121 (2008) (observing the dual nature of police use of force as both a "form of state coercion" and a "form of justified individual violence").

96. Rachel A. Harmon, *When Is Police Violence Justified?*, 102 Nw. U. L. Rev. 1119, 1146 (2008) ("Self-defense, the defense of others, and the public authority defense, among other defenses—known to the criminal law as 'justification defenses'—are precisely the law's means of differentiating between cases in which the use of force is acceptable and those in which it is simply an exercise of violent will.").

97. Rachel A. Harmon, *When Is Police Violence Justified?*, 102 Nw. U. L. Rev. 1119, 1120 (2008). Not all state statutes that authorize the use of force by police are couched as defenses in a civil or criminal action. Some articulate an affirmative authorization to use force. Either way, the effect is the same: legal authorization of the use of force in the prescribed circumstances. When I discuss use of force as a defense, I am also including affirmative legal authorizations to use force.

98. My approach thus differs from Rachel Harmon's inasmuch as she advocates application of the framework of justificatory defenses to Fourth Amendment use-of-force cases *by analogy*, *see* Rachel A. Harmon, *When Is Police Violence Justified?*, 102 Nw. U. L. Rev. 1119, 1146–50 (2008), whereas I contend that it is that framework, as provided by the laws of each State, that applies *directly* to determine whether a police officer's use of force has resulted in a deprivation of life or liberty without due process. *See also* Jesse Chang, Note, *Who Is the Reasonable Police Officer? A Localized Solution to a Nationwide Problem*, 122 Colum. L. Rev. 87, 112–20

(2022) (advocating that the Fourth Amendment reasonableness inquiry be localized by taking into account state and local law, police policies and training, and other local norms).

99. *See* Paul H. Robinson, *Criminal Law Defenses: A Systematic Analysis*, 82 Colum. L. Rev. 199, 216–17 (1982) (observing that "[a]ll justification defenses have the same internal structure: triggering conditions permit a necessary and proportional response," and that "[t]he necessity requirement demands that the defendant act only when and to the extent necessary to protect or further the interest at stake." (footnotes omitted)); *see also* Brandon Garrett and Seth Stoughton, *A Tactical Fourth Amendment*, 103 Va. L. Rev. 211, 241 (2017) (discussing the "rule of necessity" in tort law).

100. Rachel A. Harmon, *When Is Police Violence Justified?*, 102 Nw. U. L. Rev. 1119, 1172 (2008). Harmon also separately discusses the requirements of imminence and proportionality. *Id.* at 1167–71, 1178–83. To a large extent, these are specific applications of a necessity requirement. For example, if a police officer uses force against an arrestee before the arrestee's escape is imminent, we would say that the use of force was unnecessary. Likewise, a judgment that an officer used disproportionate force in response to one resisting arrest is another way of saying that she used more force than was necessary. Thus, for the sake of brevity, I focus on the necessity requirement.

101. Seth Stoughton, Jeffrey J. Noble, and Geoffrey P. Alpert, Evaluating Police Uses of Force 239–87 (2020) (surveying state law). Several States require only that the force used be "reasonable," but that term could be interpreted to encompass a necessity requirement. *See also* Robert Leider, *Taming Self-Defense: Using Deadly Force to Prevent Escapes*, 70 Fla. L. Rev. 971, 976 (2019) (observing that at common law "courts prohibited an officer from using deadly force unless the force was 'necessary' to effect an arrest; an officer could not use deadly force if he could accomplish the arrest by other means"). To emphasize the necessity requirement, some States specifically require that police exhaust all other means of apprehension before resorting to deadly force. Seth Stoughton, Jeffrey J. Noble, and Geoffrey P. Alpert, Evaluating Police Uses of Force 85 (2020).

102. *See* Cynthia Lee, *Firearms and Initial Aggressors*, 101 N.C. L. Rev. 1, 19 (2022) ("All fifty states and the District of Columbia have placed some limitation on an initial aggressor's ability to justify the use of force in self-defense. . . .").

103. *See generally* Cynthia Lee, *Officer-Created Jeopardy: Broadening the Time Frame for Assessing a Police Officer's Use of Deadly Force*, 89 G.W.U. L. Rev. 1362 (2021). *See also* Seth W. Stoughton, *Accountability and Enhancement: The Dual Objectives of Use-of-Force Review*, in Rethinking and Reforming American Policing 227, 238 (Joseph A. Schafer and Richard W. Myers eds., 2022) (asserting that review of police compliance with law and agency rules should include not only "the 'final frame,' or the moment in which force is used, but must begin with original justification for the police contact").

104. 471 U.S. at 4, 11–12 (quoting Tenn. Code Ann. § 40-7-108 (1982) (alteration added)).

105. Robert Leider, *Taming Self-Defense: Using Deadly Force to Prevent Escapes*, 70 FLA. L. REV. 971, 994 (2019).

106. 471 U.S. at 11 (emphasis added).

107. 490 U.S. 386, 396 (1989) (internal quotation marks omitted).

108. Rachel A. Harmon, *When Is Police Violence Justified?*, 102 NW. U. L. REV. 1119, 1172 (2008) ("[T]he *Graham* factors do not make necessity central or mandatory, since they emphasize the suspect's conduct in isolation rather than tying reasonableness to whether force was required to overcome that conduct and achieve the officer's aims."); Seth Stoughton, *How the Fourth Amendment Frustrates the Regulation of Police Violence*, 70 EMORY L.J. 521, 548–49 (2020) (criticizing these *Graham* factors because they provide "binary answers [that] are useful for determining whether the situation justified *some* amount of force" but "are patently unhelpful in assessing" whether the type or degree of "force is reasonable to use under the circumstances").

109. 490 U.S. at 397.

110. SETH STOUGHTON, JEFFREY J. NOBLE, AND GEOFFREY P. ALPERT, EVALUATING POLICE USES OF FORCE 46 (2020).

111. 550 U.S. 372, 383 (2007).

112. 550 U.S. at 382 n.9 (quoting *Garner*, 471 U.S. at 11). *See* Alice Ristroph, *The Constitution of Police Violence*, 64 UCLA L. REV. 1182, 1207 (2017) ("[T]he Supreme Court . . . ma[d]e clear [in *Scott*] that Fourth Amendment reasonableness does not require a showing that the force used was actually or even apparently necessary.").

113. 550 U.S. at 382. *See* Rachel A. Harmon, *When Is Police Violence Justified?*, 102 NW. U. L. REV. 1119, 1172 (2008) ("In *Scott*, the Court . . . rejected *Garner*'s necessity requirement as a 'precondition' for using force in favor of the broader, vaguer standard of 'reasonableness.'").

114. *See* 550 U.S. at 397 (Stevens, J., dissenting) (observing that "less drastic measures . . . could have avoided such a tragic result"); *see also* Robert Leider, *Taming Self-Defense: Using Deadly Force to Prevent Escapes*, 70 FLA. L. REV. 971, 983 (2019) ("The [*Scott*] Court essentially abandoned any attempt to limit the police use of force in making arrests. The Court replaced *Garner*'s rules with vague standards that do not cabin police violence."); *cf.* Mullenix v. Luna, 577 U.S. 7 (2015) (per curiam) (holding that qualified immunity protected officer who shot an escaping motorist dead instead of waiting to see if spike strips would be effective).

115. Rachel A. Harmon, *When Is Police Violence Justified?*, 102 NW. U. L. REV. 1119, 1173 (2008) (footnotes omitted). *See also* Seth Stoughton, *How the Fourth Amendment Frustrates the Regulation of Police Violence*, 70 EMORY L.J. 521, 581–82 (2020).

116. *See* Chad Flanders and Joseph Welling, *Police Use of Deadly Force: State Statutes 30 Years After* Garner, 35 ST. LOUIS U. PUB. L. REV. 109, 124–28 (2015) (discussing this misconception).

117. *See* SAMUEL WALKER, TAMING THE SYSTEM: THE CONTROL OF DISCRETION IN CRIMINAL JUSTICE 1950–90, at 25–33 (1993); *see also* Maria Ponoma-

renko, *Rethinking Police Rulemaking*, 114 Nw. L. Rev. 1, 31 (2019) ("Most if not all agencies have rules for when force may be used. . . .").

118. Brandon Garrett and Seth Stoughton, *A Tactical Fourth Amendment*, 103 Va. L. Rev. 211, 278, 281 (2017).

119. Osagie K. Obasogie and Zachary Newman, *The Endogenous Fourth Amendment: An Empirical Assessment of How Police Understandings of Excessive Force Become Constitutional Law*, 104 Cornell L. Rev. 1281, 1308 (2019).

120. Brandon Garrett and Seth Stoughton, *A Tactical Fourth Amendment*, 103 Va. L. Rev. 211, 285 (2017).

121. *See* Osagie K. Obasogie and Zachary Newman, *The Endogenous Fourth Amendment: An Empirical Assessment of How Police Understandings of Excessive Force Become Constitutional Law*, 104 Cornell L. Rev. 1281, 1303, 1310, 1312 (2019). *See also* Franklin E. Zimring, When Police Kill 170 (2017) (citing "ambiguous and improperly aggressive departmental regulations" as a cause of the failure to successfully prosecute "unjustified killings"); Brandon Garrett and Seth Stoughton, *A Tactical Fourth Amendment*, 103 Va. L. Rev. 211, 252–78 (2017) (reviewing police tactics designed to minimize need to use force and "force matrices" which can guide police in whether and when to use escalating degrees of force).

122. Seth Stoughton, *How the Fourth Amendment Frustrates the Regulation of Police Violence*, 70 Emory L.J. 521, 527, 564–68 (2020). *See also* Rachel Harmon, The Law of the Police 408 (2021). In a particularly egregious example, the Supreme Court of Ohio recently incorporated the constitutional standard into state law and in doing so appears to have dispensed entirely with the necessity requirement. Citing *Garner*, it wrote that "a police officer acts reasonably in using deadly force when the officer has a reasonable belief that the suspect poses a threat of serious physical harm or death to the officer or to others." It further criticized as "extraneous" the trial court's jury instruction that a police officer "could not avail himself of the affirmative defense if he used 'more force than reasonably necessary.'" State v. White, 29 N.E.3d 939, 952–53 (Ohio 2015). Read literally, this standard would permit police to shoot dead all dangerous suspects rather than go to the trouble of arresting them, abrogating approximately 700 years of Anglo-American law. *See* Joshua Dressler, Understanding Criminal Law 273 (9th ed. 2022) (explaining that the rule that "deadly force" in making an arrest "is permitted only as a last resort" has been the law since the fourteenth century).

123. Seth W. Stoughton, *The Regulation of Police Violence*, in Critical Issues in Policing: Contemporary Readings 321, 326 (Roger G. Dunham, Geoffrey P. Alper, and Kyle D. McLean eds., 8th ed. 2021).

124. Seth Stoughton, *How the Fourth Amendment Frustrates the Regulation of Police Violence*, 70 Emory L.J. 521, 572 (2020); *see also* Brandon Garrett and Seth Stoughton, *A Tactical Fourth Amendment*, 103 Va. L. Rev. 211, 280 (2017) (observing "that there is a real public accountability and transparency problem in this area" because many police use-of-force policies are not accessible to the public); Osagie K. Obasogie and Zachary Newman, *The Endogenous Fourth Amendment: An Empirical Assessment of How Police Understandings of Excessive Force Become Consti-*

tutional Law, 104 CORNELL L. REV. 1281, 1332 (2019) ("[O]ur key recommendation is that use-of-force policies must become radically democratic documents that allow diverse constituencies to participate in their creation."); Osagie K. Obasogie and Zachary Newman, *Constitutional Interpretation Without Judges: Police Violence, Excessive Force, and Remaking the Fourth Amendment*, 105 VA. L. REV. 425, 444 (2019) (advocating that "citizens, stakeholders, and the public . . . work with police" to create Fourth Amendment constraints on the police use of force "from the 'bottom up'"); Jonathan M. Smith, *Closing the Gap between What Is Lawful and What Is Right in Police Use of Force Jurisprudence by Making Police Departments More Democratic Institutions*, 21 MICH. J. RACE & L. 315, 336 (2016) (discussing "the need to democratize the institution of policing through meaningful community participation" in creating local use-of-force policies).

125. *See* Jesse Chang, Note, *Who Is the Reasonable Police Officer? A Localized Solution to a Nationwide Problem*, 122 COLUM. L. REV. 87, 105–06, 113 n.142 (2022) (discussing local bans on police use of tear gas and chokeholds).

126. Brandon Garrett and Seth Stoughton, *A Tactical Fourth Amendment*, 103 VA. L. REV. 211, 290 (2017).

127. Spano v. New York, 360 U.S. 315, 320 (1959).

Table of Cases

Bibliography

Harold I. Abramson, *A Fifth Branch of Government: The Private Regulators and Their Constitutionality*, 16 HASTINGS CONST. L.Q. 165 (1989).

1 BRUCE ACKERMAN, WE THE PEOPLE: FOUNDATIONS (1991).

John H. Aldrich and Ruth W. Grant, *The Antifederalists, the First Congress, and the First Parties*, 55 J. POL. 295 (1993).

CARLTON K. ALLEN, LAW IN THE MAKING (2d ed. 1930).

Ronald J. Allen, *Police and Substantive Rulemaking: Reconciling Principle and Expediency*, 125 U. PA. L. REV. 62 (1976).

Ronald J. Allen and Ross M. Rosenberg, *The Fourth Amendment and the Limits of Theory: Local Versus General Theoretical Knowledge*, 72 ST. JOHN'S L. REV. 1149 (1998).

Albert W. Alschuler, *Racial Profiling and the Constitution*, 2002 U. CHI. LEGAL F. 163 (2002).

AKHIL REED AMAR, THE BILL OF RIGHTS: CREATION AND RECONSTRUCTION (1998).

AKHIL REED AMAR, THE CONSTITUTION AND CRIMINAL PROCEDURE: FIRST PRINCIPLES (1997).

Akhil Reed Amar, *Foreword: Lord Camden Meets Federalism—Using State Constitutions to Counter Federal Abuses*, 27 RUTGERS L.J. 845 (1996).

Akhil Reed Amar, *The Fourth Amendment, Boston, and the Writs of Assistance*, 30 SUFFOLK U. L. REV. 53 (1996).

Akhil Reed Amar, *Fourth Amendment First Principles*, 107 HARV. L. REV. 757 (1994).

Akhil Reed Amar, Terry *and Fourth Amendment First Principles*, 72 ST. JOHN'S L. REV. 1097 (1998).

AMERICAN BAR ASSOCIATION, STANDARDS FOR CRIMINAL JUSTICE (2d ed. supp. 1986).

AMERICAN LAW INSTITUTE, A MODEL CODE OF PRE-ARRAIGNMENT PROCEDURE (1975).

Anthony G. Amsterdam, *Perspectives on the Fourth Amendment*, 58 MINN. L. REV. 349 (1974).

SIDNEY ANDREWS, THE SOUTH SINCE THE WAR (1866).

CHESTER JAMES ANTIEAU, THE INTENDED SIGNIFICANCE OF THE FOURTEENTH AMENDMENT (1997).

LAURA I. APPLEMAN, DEFENDING THE JURY: CRIME, COMMUNITY, AND THE CONSTITUTION (2015).

Fabio Arcila, Jr., *The Death of Suspicion*, 51 WM. & MARY L. REV. 1275 (2010).

STEPHEN V. ASH, A MASSACRE IN MEMPHIS: THE RACE RIOT THAT SHOOK THE NATION ONE YEAR AFTER THE CIVIL WAR (2013).

Alfred Avins, *Incorporation of the Bill of Rights: The Crosskey-Fairman Debate Revisited*, 6 HARV. J. ON LEGIS. 1 (1968).

Richard L. Aynes, *On Misreading John Bingham and the Fourteenth Amendment*, 103 YALE L.J. 57 (1993).

Richard L. Aynes, *Refined Incorporation and the Fourteenth Amendment*, 33 U. RICH. L. REV. 289 (1999).

Ronald J. Bacigal, *A Case for Jury Determination of Search and Seizure Law*, 15 U. RICH. L. REV. 791 (1981).

JACK M. BALKIN, LIVING ORIGINALISM (2011).

RANDY E. BARNETT, RESTORING THE LOST CONSTITUTION: THE PRESUMPTION OF LIBERTY (2004).

RANDY E. BARNETT AND EVAN D. BERNICK, THE ORIGINAL MEANING OF THE 14TH AMENDMENT: ITS LETTER AND SPIRIT (2021).

Amy Coney Barrett, *Suspension and Delegation*, 99 CORNELL L. REV. 251 (2014).

William Baude and James Y. Stern, *The Positive Law Model of the Fourth Amendment*, 129 HARV. L. REV. 1821 (2016).

David J. Bederman, *The Bederman Lecture on Law and Jurisprudence: Public Law and Custom*, 61 EMORY L.J. 949 (2012).

David J. Bederman, *The Curious Resurrection of Custom: Beach Access and Judicial Takings*, 96 COLUM. L. REV. 1375 (1996).

Jeffrey Bellin, *Fourth Amendment Textualism*, 118 MICH. L. REV. 233 (2019).

MICHAEL LES BENEDICT, A COMPROMISE OF PRINCIPLE: CONGRESSIONAL REPUBLICANS AND RECONSTRUCTION, 1863–1869 (1974).

RAOUL BERGER, THE FOURTEENTH AMENDMENT AND THE BILL OF RIGHTS (1989).

RAOUL BERGER, GOVERNMENT BY JUDICIARY: THE TRANSFORMATION OF THE FOURTEENTH AMENDMENT (2d ed. 1997).

HAROLD J. BERMAN, LAW AND REVOLUTION: THE FORMATION OF THE WESTERN LEGAL TRADITION (1983).

Harold J. Berman, *The Origins of Historical Jurisprudence: Coke, Selden, Hale*, 103 YALE L.J. 1651 (1994).

JOEL PRENTISS BISHOP, COMMENTARIES ON THE LAW OF CRIMINAL PROCEDURE (1866).

EGON BITTNER, ASPECTS OF POLICE WORK (1990).

Josh Blackman, *Response: Originalism at the Right Time?*, TEX. L. REV. SEE ALSO 269 (2012).

DOUGLAS A. BLACKMON, SLAVERY BY ANOTHER NAME: THE RE-ENSLAVEMENT OF BLACK AMERICANS FROM THE CIVIL WAR TO WORLD WAR II (2008).

WILLIAM BLACKSTONE, COMMENTARIES ON THE LAWS OF ENGLAND (9th ed. 1783).

JAMES G. BLAINE, TWENTY YEARS OF CONGRESS: FROM LINCOLN TO GARFIELD (1886).

Hannah Bloch-Webbah, *Visible Policing: Technology, Transparency, and Democratic Control*, 109 CAL. L. REV. 917 (2021).

David S. Bogen, *The Transformation of the Fourteenth Amendment: Reflections from the Admission of Maryland's First Black Lawyers*, 44 MD. L. REV. 939 (1985).

JAMES E. BOND, NO EASY WALK TO FREEDOM: RECONSTRUCTION AND THE RATIFICATION OF THE FOURTEENTH AMENDMENT (1997).

James E. Bond, *The Original Understanding of the Fourteenth Amendment in Illinois, Ohio, and Pennsylvania*, 18 AKRON L. REV. 435 (1985).

STEVEN R. BOYD, THE POLITICS OF OPPOSITION: ANTIFEDERALISTS AND THE ACCEPTANCE OF THE CONSTITUTION (1979).

HENRY DE BRACTON, ON THE LAWS AND CUSTOMS OF ENGLAND (1250).

Gerald V. Bradley, *The Constitutional Theory of the Fourth Amendment*, 38 DEPAUL L. REV. 817 (1989).

HENRY BRANNON, A TREATISE ON THE RIGHTS AND PRIVILEGES GUARANTEED BY THE FOURTEENTH AMENDMENT TO THE CONSTITUTION OF THE UNITED STATES (1901).

E.K. Braybrooke, *Custom as a Source of English Law*, 50 MICH. L. REV. 71 (1951).

Charles D. Breitel, *Controls in Criminal Law Enforcement*, 27 U. CHI. L. REV. 427 (1960).

Kiel Brennan-Marquez, *Extremely Broad Laws*, 61 ARIZ. L. REV. 641 (2019).

Robin Brooks, *Alexander Hamilton, Melancton Smith, and the Ratification of the Constitution in New York*, 24 WM. & MARY Q. 339 (1967).

Rebecca L. Brown, *Separated Powers and Ordered Liberty*, 139 U. PA. L. REV. 1513 (1991).

James B. Browning, *The North Carolina Black Code*, 15 J. NEGRO HIST. 461 (1930).

RICHARD BURN, THE JUSTICE OF THE PEACE, AND PARISH OFFICER (London, Henry Lintot 6th ed. 1758).

Steven G. Calabresi, Sarah E. Agudo, and Kathryn L. Dore, *State Bills of Rights in 1787 and 1791: What Individual Rights Are Really Deeply Rooted in American History and Tradition?*, 85 S. CAL. L. REV. 1451 (2012).

I. Bennett Capers, *Crime, Surveillance, and Communities*, 40 FORDHAM URB. L.J. 959 (2013).

I. Bennett Capers, *Rethinking the Fourth Amendment: Race, Citizenship, and the Equality Principle*, 46 HARV. C.R.-C.L. L. REV. 1 (2011).

Gerald M. Caplan, *The Case for Rulemaking by Law Enforcement Agencies*, 36 LAW & CONTEMP. PROBS. 500 (1971).

Devon W. Carbado, *From Stop and Frisk to Shoot and Kill:* Terry *v.* Ohio's *Pathway to Police Violence*, 64 UCLA L. REV. 1508 (2017).

Devon W. Carbado, *From Stopping Black People to Killing Black People: The Fourth Amendment Pathways to Police Violence*, 105 CAL. L. REV. 125 (2017).

Marius Carriere, *An Irresponsible Press: Memphis Newspapers and the 1866 Riot*, 60 TENN. HIST. Q. 2 (2001).

Dan T. Carter, *The Anatomy of Fear: The Christmas Day Insurrection Scare of 1865*, 42 J. Southern Hist. 345 (1976).

Center for Policing Equity, The Science of Justice: Race, Arrests, and Police Use of Force (2016).

Jesse Chang, Note, *Who Is the Reasonable Police Officer? A Localized Solution to a Nationwide Problem*, 122 Colum. L. Rev. 87 (2022).

Nathan S. Chapman, *The Jury's Constitutional Judgment*, 67 Ala. L. Rev. 189 (2015).

Nathan S. Chapman and Michael W. McConnell, *Due Process as Separation of Powers*, 121 Yale L.J. 1672 (2012).

Thomas K. Clancy, *The Framers' Intent: John Adams, His Era, and the Fourth Amendment*, 86 Ind. L.J. 979 (2011).

Morgan Cloud, *Searching Through History; Searching for History*, 63 U. Chi. L. Rev. 1707 (1996).

William Cohen, At Freedom's Edge: Black Mobility and the Southern White Quest for Racial Control 1861–1915 (1991).

William Cohen, *Negro Involuntary Servitude in the South, 1865–1940: A Preliminary Analysis*, 42 J. South. Hist. 32 (1976).

Sir Edward Coke, The Fourth Part of the Institutes of the Laws of England (1644).

Sherry Colb, *The Qualitative Dimension of Fourth Amendment Reasonableness*, 98 Colum. L. Rev. 1642 (1998).

John H. Colby, A Practical Treatise Upon the Criminal Law Practice of the State of New York (1868).

David Cole, No Equal Justice: Race and Class in the American Criminal Justice System (1999).

The Colonial Laws of Massachusetts (Boston, William H. Whitmore 1889).

The Colonial Laws of New York: Year 1664 to the Revolution (Albany, James B. Lyon 1894).

The Complete Anti-Federalist (Herbert J. Storing ed., 1981).

The Complete Bill of Rights: The Drafts, Debates, Sources, and Origins (Neil H. Cogan ed., 1997).

The Conductor Generalis: Or, the Office, Duty and Authority of Justices of the Peace, High-Sheriffs, Under-Sheriffs, Coroners, Constables, Gaolers, Jury-Men, and Overseers of the Poor (New York, Hugh Gaine 1788).

The Conductor Generalis: Or the Office, Duty and Authority of Justices of the Peace, High-Sheriffs, Under-Sheriffs, Coroners, Constables, Goalers, Jury-Men, and Overseers of the Poor 109–24 (New York, John Patterson 1788).

John A. Conley, *Doing It by the Book: Justice of the Peace Manuals and English Law in Eighteenth Century America*, 6 J. Legal Hist. 257 (1985).

Saul A. Cornell, *The Changing Historical Fortunes of the Anti-Federalists*, 84 Nw. U. L. Rev. 39 (1989).

Saul A. Cornell, The Other Founders: Anti-Federalism and the Dissenting Tradition in America, 1788–1828 (1999).

Joshua Correll et al., *Across the Thin Blue Line: Police Officers and Racial Bias in the Decision to Shoot*, 92 J. PERSONALITY & SOC. PSYCHOL. 1006 (2007).
Joshua Correll et al., *The Influence of Stereotypes on Decisions to Shoot*, 37 EUR. J. SOC. PSYCHOL. 1102 (2007).
Evan J. Criddle, *When Delegation Begets Domination: Due Process of Administrative Lawmaking*, 46 GA. L. REV. 117 (2011).
William Crosskey, *Charles Fairman, Legislative History, and the Constitutional Limitations on State Authority*, 22 U. CHI. L. REV. 1 (1954).
Barry A. Crouch, *"All the Vile Passions": The Texas Black Code of 1866*, 97 SW. HIST. Q. 13 (1993).
WILLIAM J. CUDDIHY, THE FOURTH AMENDMENT: ORIGINS AND ORIGINAL MEANING, 602–1791 (2009).
DAVID P. CURRIE, THE CONSTITUTION IN THE SUPREME COURT: THE FIRST HUNDRED YEARS, 1789–1888 (1985).
MICHAEL KENT CURTIS, NO STATE SHALL ABRIDGE: THE FOURTEENTH AMENDMENT AND THE BILL OF RIGHTS (1986).
Robert E. Cushman, *Constitutional Status of the Independent Regulatory Commissions*, 24 CORNELL L. Q. 13 (1938).
THE DAILY ADVERTISER, June 22, 1790.
Thomas Y. Davies, *Can You Handle the Truth? The Framers Preserved Common-Law Criminal Arrest and Search Rules in "Due Process of Law"—"Fourth Amendment Reasonableness" Is Only a Modern, Destructive, Judicial Myth*, 43 TEX. TECH L. REV. 51 (2010).
Thomas Y. Davies, *Correcting Search-and-Seizure History: Now-Forgotten Common-Law Warrantless Arrest Standards and the Original Understanding of "Due Process of Law,"* 77 MISS. L.J. 1 (2007).
Thomas Y. Davies, *The Fictional Character of Law-and-Order Originalism: A Case Study of the Distortions and Evasions of Framing-Era Arrest Doctrine in* Atwater *v.* Lago Vista, 37 WAKE FOREST L. REV. 239 (2002).
Thomas Y. Davies, *Recovering the Original Fourth Amendment*, 98 MICH. L. REV. 547 (1999).
JAMES DAVIS, THE OFFICE AND AUTHORITY OF A JUSTICE OF PEACE (Newbern, James Davis 1774).
Kenneth Culp Davis, *An Approach to Legal Control of the Police*, 52 TEX. L. REV. 703 (1974).
KENNETH CULP DAVIS, DISCRETIONARY JUSTICE: A PRELIMINARY INQUIRY (1969).
Kenneth Culp Davis, *A New Approach to Delegation*, 36 U. CHI. L. REV. 713 (1969).
KENNETH CULP DAVIS, POLICE DISCRETION (1975).
THE DEBATES IN THE SEVERAL STATE CONVENTIONS ON THE ADOPTION OF THE FEDERAL CONSTITUTION (Jonathan Elliot ed., Philadelphia, J.B. Lippincott & Co. 1876).
JOHN RICHARD DENNETT, THE SOUTH AS IT IS: 1865–1866 (Caroline E. Janney ed., 2010; essays originally published in THE NATION).
Linda Grant De Pauw, *E. Wilder Spaulding and New York History*, 49 N.Y. HIST. 142 (1968).

Developments in the Law, *Policing and Profit*, 128 HARV. L. REV. 1723 (2015).
O.M. Dickerson, *Writs of Assistance as a Cause of the Revolution*, in THE ERA OF THE AMERICAN REVOLUTION (Richard B. Morris ed., 1939).
WILLIAM HEPWORTH DIXON, THE NEW AMERICA (1867).
Hon. Bernice Bouie Donald, *When the Rule of Law Breaks Down: Implications of the 1866 Memphis Massacre for the Passage of the Fourteenth Amendment*, 98 B.U. L. REV. 1607 (2018).
Laura K. Donohue, *The Original Fourth Amendment*, 83 U. CHI. L. REV. 1181 (2016).
Frederick Douglass, *An Appeal to Congress for Impartial Suffrage*, reprinted in 19 THE ATLANTIC MONTHLY 112 (1867).
JOSHUA DRESSLER, UNDERSTANDING CRIMINAL LAW (9th ed. 2022).
DONALD A. DRIPPS, ABOUT GUILT AND INNOCENCE: THE ORIGINS, DEVELOPMENT, AND FUTURE OF CONSTITUTIONAL CRIMINAL PROCEDURE (2003).
Donald A. Dripps, *Criminal Procedure, Footnote Four, and the Theory of Public Choice; Or, Why Don't Legislatures Give a Damn About the Rights of the Accused?*, 44 SYRACUSE L. REV. 1079 (1993).
Donald A. Dripps, *"Dearest Property": Digital Evidence and the History of Private "Papers" as Special Objects of Search and Seizure*, 103 J. CRIM. L. & CRIMINOLOGY 49 (2013).
Donald A. Dripps, *Responding to the Challenges of Contextual Change and Legal Dynamism in Interpreting the Fourth Amendment*, 81 MISS. L.J. 1085 (2012).
Murray Dry, *The Anti-Federalists and the Constitution*, in PRINCIPLES OF THE CONSTITUTIONAL ORDER: THE RATIFICATION DEBATES 63 (Robert L. Utley, Jr. ed., 1989).
W.E.B. DUBOIS, BLACK RECONSTRUCTION IN AMERICA: AN ESSAY TOWARD A HISTORY OF THE PART WHICH BLACK FOLK PLAYED IN THE ATTEMPT TO RECONSTRUCT DEMOCRACY IN AMERICA, 1860–1880 (1935).
PETER S. DU PONCEAU, A DISSERTATION ON THE NATURE AND EXTENT OF THE JURISDICTION OF THE COURTS OF THE UNITED STATES (1824).
EDWARD HYDE EAST, A TREATISE OF THE PLEAS OF THE CROWN (London, A. Strahan 1803).
Frank Edwards et al., *Risk of Being Killed by Police Use of Force in the United States by Age, Race–Ethnicity, and Sex*, 116 PROC. NAT'L ACAD. SCI. 16793 (2019).
Richard A. Edwards, *Criminal Liability for Unreasonable Searches and Seizures*, 41 VA. L. REV. 621 (1955).
DOUGLAS R. EGERTON, THE WARS OF RECONSTRUCTION: THE BRIEF, VIOLENT HISTORY OF AMERICA'S MOST PROGRESSIVE ERA (2014).
Richard E. Ellis, *The Persistence of Antifederalism After 1789*, in BEYOND CONFEDERATION: ORIGINS OF THE CONSTITUTION AND AMERICAN NATIONAL IDENTITY 295 (Richard Beeman, Stephen Botein, and Edward C. Carter II eds., 1987).
JOHN HART ELY, DEMOCRACY AND DISTRUST: A THEORY OF JUDICIAL REVIEW (1980).
CHARLES R. EPP, STEVEN MAYNARD-MOODY, AND DONALD HAIDER-MARKEL, PULLED OVER: HOW POLICE STOPS DEFINE RACE AND CITIZENSHIP (2014).

Richard A. Epstein, *The Path to* The T.J. Hooper*: The Theory and History of Custom in the Law of Tort*, 21 J. LEGAL STUD. 1 (1992).

THE ESSENTIAL ANTI-FEDERALIST (W.B. Allen and Gordon Lloyd eds., 2d ed. 2002).

WILLIAM MCKEE EVANS, BALLOTS AND FENCE RAILS: RECONSTRUCTION ON THE LOWER CAPE FEAR (1967).

Extract from Observations in a North-Carolina Paper "On the Assumption and Excise Law," NEW YORK DAILY GAZETTE, Feb. 2, 1793.

Charles Fairman, *Does the Fourteenth Amendment Incorporate the Bill of Rights? The Original Understanding*, 2 STAN. L. REV. 5 (1949).

TIMOTHY FARRAR, MANUAL OF THE CONSTITUTION OF THE UNITED STATES OF AMERICA (1867).

HORACE EDGAR FLACK, THE ADOPTION OF THE FOURTEENTH AMENDMENT (1908).

THE FEDERALIST (Clinton Rossiter ed., 2003).

Stephen M. Feldman, *From Premodern to Modern American Jurisprudence: The Onset of Positivism*, 50 VAND. L. REV. 1387 (1997).

Andrew Guthrie Ferguson, *Surveillance and the Tyrant Test*, 110 GEO. L.J. 205 (2021).

Mailyn Fidler, *Local Police Surveillance and the Administrative Fourth Amendment*, 36 SANTA CLARA HIGH TECH. L.J. 481 (2020).

FINAL REPORT OF THE PRESIDENT'S TASK FORCE ON 21ST CENTURY POLICING (2015).

Paul Finkelman, *Fugitive Baseballs and Abandoned Property: Who Owns the Home Run Ball?*, 23 CARDOZO L. REV. 1609 (2002).

Chad Flanders and Joseph Welling, *Police Use of Deadly Force: State Statutes 30 Years After* Garner, 35 ST. LOUIS U. PUB. L. REV. 109 (2015).

ERIC FONER, NOTHING BUT FREEDOM: EMANCIPATION AND ITS LEGACY (1983).

ERIC FONER, RECONSTRUCTION: AMERICA'S UNFINISHED REVOLUTION, 1863–1877 (1988).

ERIC FONER, THE SECOND FOUNDING: HOW THE CIVIL WAR AND RECONSTRUCTION REMADE THE CONSTITUTION (2019).

Caleb Foote, *Tort Remedies for Police Violations of Individual Rights*, 39 MINN. L. REV. 493 (1955).

Kim Forde-Mazrui, *Ruling Out the Rule of Law*, 60 VAND. L. REV. 1495 (2007).

MICHAEL FOSTER, CROWN LAW (Oxford, Clarendon Press 1762).

THE FOUNDERS' CONSTITUTION (Philip B. Kurland and Ralph Lerner eds., 1987).

FREEDOM: A DOCUMENTARY HISTORY OF EMANCIPATION, 1861–1867, SR. 3, VOL. 2: LAND AND LABOR, 1866–1867 (Rene Hayden et al. eds., 2013).

Joseph R. Frese, Writs of Assistance in the American Colonies: 1660–1776 (1951) (unpublished Ph.D. dissertation, Harvard University).

Barry Friedman, *Lawless Surveillance*, 97 N.Y.U. L. REV. 1143 (2022).

Barry Friedman, *Reconstructing Reconstruction: Some Problems for Originalists (and Everyone Else, Too)*, 11 U. PA. J. CONST. L. 1201 (2009).

BARRY FRIEDMAN, UNWARRANTED: POLICING WITHOUT PERMISSION (2017).

Barry Friedman and Maria Ponomarenko, *Democratic Policing*, 90 N.Y.U. L. REV. 1827 (2015).
Barry Friedman and Cynthia Benin Stein, *Redefining What's "Reasonable": The Protections for Policing*, 84 GEO. WASH. L. REV. 281 (2016).
Roland G. Fryer, Jr., "An Empirical Analysis of Racial Differences in Police Use of Force," (working paper) (last revised Jan. 2018).
FUGITIVE SLAVES AND AMERICAN COURTS: THE PAMPHLET LITERATURE (Paul Finkelman ed., 2007).
Lon L. Fuller, *Human Interaction and the Law*, 14 AM. J. JURIS. 1 (1969).
David H. Gans, *"We Do Not Want to Be Hunted": The Right to Be Secure and Our Constitutional Story of Race and Policing*, 11 COLUM. J. RACE & LAW 239, 308 (2021).
Brandon Garrett and Seth Stoughton, *A Tactical Fourth Amendment*, 103 VA. L. REV. 211 (2017).
Andrew Gelman et al., *An Analysis of the New York City Police Department's "Stop-and-Frisk" Policy in the Context of Claims of Racial Bias*, 102 J. AM. STAT. ASSN. 813 (2007).
Michael Gentithes, *Exigencies, Not Exceptions: How to Return Warrant Exceptions to Their Roots*, 25 U. PA. J. CON. L. (forthcoming 2022).
Heather K. Gerken, *Windsor's Mad Genius: The Interlocking Gears of Rights and Structure*, 95 B.U. L. REV. 587 (2015).
RANULF DE GLANVILL, THE TREATISE ON THE LAWS AND CUSTOMS OF THE KINGDOM OF ENGLAND (1189).
Julius Goebel, Jr., Ex Parte *Clio*, 54 COLUM. L. REV. 450 (1954).
Herman Goldstein, *Police Policy Formulation: A Proposal for Improving Police Performance*, 65 MICH. L. REV. 1123 (1967).
Joseph Goldstein, *Police Discretion Not to Invoke the Criminal Process: Low-Visibility Decisions in the Administration of Justice*, 96 YALE L.J. 543 (1960).
RISA GOLUBOFF, VAGRANT NATION: POLICE POWER, CONSTITUTIONAL CHANGE, AND THE MAKING OF THE 1960S (2016).
MICHAEL R. GOTTFREDSON AND DON M. GOTTFREDSON, DECISION MAKING IN CRIMINAL JUSTICE: TOWARD THE RATIONAL EXERCISE OF DISCRETION (2d ed. 1988).
HOWARD JAY GRAHAM, EVERYMAN'S CONSTITUTION: HISTORICAL ESSAYS ON THE FOURTEENTH AMENDMENT, THE "CONSPIRACY THEORY," AND AMERICAN CONSTITUTIONALISM (1968).
DAVID GRAY, THE FOURTH AMENDMENT IN AN AGE OF SURVEILLANCE (2017).
David Gray and Danielle Keats Citron, *A Shattered Looking Glass: The Pitfalls and Potential of the Mosaic Theory of Fourth Amendment Privacy*, 14 N.C. J. L. & TECH. 381 (2013).
CHRISTOPHER R. GREEN, EQUAL CITIZENSHIP, CIVIL RIGHTS, AND THE CONSTITUTION: THE ORIGINAL SENSE OF THE PRIVILEGES OR IMMUNITIES CLAUSE (2015).
JOSEPH GREENLEAF, AN ABRIDGEMENT OF BURN'S JUSTICE OF THE PEACE AND PARISH OFFICER (Boston, Joseph Greenleaf 1773).
Steven Hahn, *Hunting, Fishing, and Foraging: Common Rights and Class Relations*

in the Postbellum South, in CRIME AND CAPITALISM: READINGS IN MARXIST CRIMINOLOGY 142 (David F. Greenberg ed., rev. ed. 1993).

MATTHEW HALE, THE HISTORY OF THE COMMON LAW OF ENGLAND (3d ed. 1739).

Philip Hamburger, *Privileges or Immunities*, 105 NW. U. L. REV. 61 (2011).

Bernard E. Harcourt and Tracey L. Meares, *Randomization and the Fourth Amendment*, 78 U. CHI. L. REV. 809 (2011).

Ayesha Bell Hardaway, *The Supreme Court and the Illegitimacy of Lawless Fourth Amendment Policing*, 100 B.U. L. REV. 1193 (2020).

Kevin R. Hardwick, *"Your Old Father Abe Lincoln Is Dead and Damned": Black Soldiers and the Memphis Race Riot of 1866*, 27 J. SOUTH. HIST. 109 (1993).

I. Trotter Hardy, *The Proper Legal Regime for "Cyberspace,"* 55 U. PITT. L. REV. 993 (1994).

RACHEL A. HARMON, THE LAW OF THE POLICE (2021).

Rachel A. Harmon, *When Is Police Violence Justified?*, 102 NW. U. L. REV. 1119 (2008).

Rachel A. Harmon, *Why Arrest?*, 115 MICH. L. REV. 307 (2016).

David A. Harris, *Factors for Reasonable Suspicion: When Black and Poor Means Stopped and Frisked*, 69 IND. L.J. 659 (1994).

DAVID A. HARRIS, PROFILES IN INJUSTICE: WHY RACIAL PROFILING CANNOT WORK (2002).

WILLIAM C. HARRIS, PRESIDENTIAL RECONSTRUCTION IN MISSISSIPPI (1967).

John Harrison, *Reconstructing the Privileges or Immunities Clause*, 101 YALE L.J. 1385 (1992).

Edward Hartnett, *A "Uniform and Entire" Constitution; Or, What if Madison Had Won?*, 15 CONST. COMMENT. 251 (1998).

WILLIAM HAWKINS, A TREATISE OF THE PLEAS OF THE CROWN (Thomas Leach ed., London, Eliz. Lynch 6th ed. 1788).

F. A. HAYEK, LAW, LEGISLATION AND LIBERTY (1973).

R.H. Helmholz, *Christopher St. German and the Law of Custom*, 70 U. CHI. L. REV. 129 (2003).

WILLIAM W. HENING, THE NEW VIRGINIA JUSTICE (1795).

Louis Henkin, *"Selective Incorporation" in the Fourteenth Amendment*, 73 YALE L.J. 74 (1963).

Carissa Byrne Hessick, *Vagueness Principles*, 48 ARIZ. ST. L.J. 1137 (2016).

Steven Hetcher, *The Jury's Out: Social Norms' Misunderstood Role in Negligence Law*, 91 GEO. L.J. 633 (2003).

Wesley Newcomb Hohfeld, *Some Fundamental Legal Conceptions as Applied in Judicial Reasoning*, 23 YALE L.J. 16 (1913).

Brooks Holland, *The Road 'Round* Edmond*: Steering through Primary Purposes and Crime Control Agendas*, 111 PENN ST. L. REV. 293 (2006).

JAMES G. HOLLANDSWORTH, JR., AN ABSOLUTE MASSACRE: THE NEW ORLEANS RACE RIOT OF JULY 30, 1866 (2001).

Jack D. L. Holmes, *The Underlying Causes of the Memphis Race Riot of 1866*, 17 TENN. HIST. Q. 195 (1958).

JOHN HUDSON, THE FORMATION OF THE ENGLISH COMMON LAW: LAW AND SOCIETY IN ENGLAND FROM THE NORMAN CONQUEST TO MAGNA CARTA (1996).

Robert M. Igleburger and Frank A. Schubert, *Policy Making for the Police*, 58 Am. B. Ass'n J. 307 (1972).

Joseph B. James, The Framing of the Fourteenth Amendment (1965).

Joseph B. James, The Ratification of the Fourteenth Amendment (1984).

Stewart Jay, *Origins of Federal Common Law: Part One*, 133 U. Pa. L. Rev. 1003 (1985).

Elizabeth E. Joh, *Discretionless Policing: Technology and the Fourth Amendment*, 95 Calif. L. Rev. 199 (2007).

David R. Johnson and David Post, *Law and Borders—The Rise of Law in Cyberspace*, 48 Stan. L. Rev. 1367 (1996).

Joel S. Johnson, *Vagueness Attacks on Searches and Seizures*, 107 Va. L. Rev. 347 (2021).

Kyle Johnson, *A New Frontier for Ending Qualified Immunity: State Civil Rights Acts*, 26 Pub. Int. L. Rep. 55 (2020).

Robert J. Kaczorowski, *Revolutionary Constitutionalism in the Era of the Civil War and Reconstruction*, 61 N.Y.U. L. Rev. 863 (1986).

Emily Kadens, *The Myth of the Customary Law Merchant*, 90 Tex. L. Rev. 1153 (2012).

Dan M. Kahan and Tracey L. Meares, *Foreword: The Coming Crisis of Criminal Procedure*, 86 Geo. L.J. 1153 (1998).

George Kelling and James Q. Wilson, *Broken Windows: The Police and Neighborhood Safety*, reprinted in Critical Issues in Policing: Contemporary Readings 96 (Roger G. Dunham, Geoffrey P. Alper, and Kyle D. McLean eds., 8th ed. 2021).

Orin S. Kerr, *Cross-Enforcement of the Fourth Amendment*, 132 Harv. L. Rev. 471 (2018).

Orin S. Kerr, *The Curious History of Fourth Amendment Searches*, 2012 Sup. Ct. Rev. 1.

Orin S. Kerr, *The Fourth Amendment and New Technologies: Constitutional Myths and the Case for Caution*, 102 Mich. L. Rev. 801 (2004).

Orin S. Kerr, *The Mosaic Theory of the Fourth Amendment*, 111 Mich. L. Rev. 311 (2012).

Vasan Kesavan and Michael Stokes Paulsen, *The Interpretive Force of the Constitution's Secret Drafting History*, 91 Geo. L.J. 1113 (2003).

Kit Kinports, *The Quantum of Suspicion Needed for an Exigent Circumstances Search*, 52 U. Mich. J.L. Ref. 615 (2019).

Albert Kiralfy, *Custom in Mediaeval English Law*, 9 J. Leg. Hist. 26 (1988).

Joshua Kleinfeld et al., *White Paper of Democratic Criminal Justice*, 111 Nw. U. L. Rev. 1693 (2017).

Rory Kramer and Brianna Remster, *Stop, Frisk, and Assault—Racial Disparities in Police Use of Force During Investigatory Stops*, 52 Law & Soc'y Rev. 960 (2018).

Eliphalet Ladd, Burn's Abridgement, or the American Justice; Containing the Whole Practice, Authority and Duty of Justices of the Peace (2d ed. 1792).

Wayne R. LaFave, *Controlling Discretion by Administrative Regulations: The Use, Misuse, and Nonuse of Police Rules and Policies in Fourth Amendment Adjudication*, 89 Mich. L. Rev. 442 (1990).

Wayne R. LaFave, *The Fourth Amendment as a "Big Time TV" Fad*, 53 Hastings L.J. 265 (2001).

WAYNE R. LAFAVE, SEARCH AND SEIZURE: A TREATISE ON THE FOURTH AMENDMENT (5th ed. 2012).

LAIRD & LEE'S WEBSTER'S NEW STANDARD DICTIONARY OF THE ENGLISH LANGUAGE (1920).

KURT T. LASH, THE FOURTEENTH AMENDMENT AND THE PRIVILEGES AND IMMUNITIES OF AMERICAN CITIZENSHIP (2014).

Kurt T. Lash, *The Origins of the Privileges or Immunities Clause, Part III: Andrew Johnson and the Constitutional Referendum of 1866*, 101 GEO. L.J. 1275 (2013).

Leading Case, *Article I—Stare Decisis for Constitutional Default Rules—Dormant Commerce Clause*—South Dakota *v.* Wayfair, Inc., 132 HARV. L. REV. 277 (2018).

AARON LEAMING AND JACOB SPICER, THE GRANTS, CONCESSIONS, AND ORIGINAL CONSTITUTIONS OF THE PROVINCE OF NEW JERSEY (Philadelphia, W. Bradford, 1881).

Cynthia Lee, *Firearms and Initial Aggressors*, 101 N.C. L. REV. 1 (2022).

Cynthia Lee, *Officer-Created Jeopardy: Broadening the Time Frame for Assessing a Police Officer's Use of Deadly Force*, 89 G.W.U. L. REV. 1362 (2021).

LEGAL PAPERS OF JOHN ADAMS (L. Kinvin Wroth and Hiller B. Zobel eds., 1965).

"Legislative Enactments," *New York Times*, Mar. 11, 1866.

Robert Leider, *Taming Self-Defense: Using Deadly Force to Prevent Escapes*, 70 FLA. L. REV. 971 (2019).

LEONARD LEVY, ORIGINS OF THE BILL OF RIGHTS (1999).

Michael Lienesch, *North Carolina: Preserving Rights*, in RATIFYING THE CONSTITUTION 343 (Michael Allen Gillespie and Michael Lienesch eds., 1989).

LEON F. LITWACK, BEEN IN THE STORM SO LONG: THE AFTERMATH OF SLAVERY (1979).

Wayne A. Logan, *An Exception Swallows a Rule: Police Authority to Search Incident to Arrest*, 19 YALE L. & POL'Y REV. 381 (2001).

Andrea C. Loux, Note, *The Persistence of the Ancient Regime: Custom, Utility, and the Common Law in the Nineteenth Century*, 79 CORNELL L. REV. 183 (1993).

Bobby L. Lovett, *Memphis Riots: White Reaction to Blacks in Memphis, May 1865–July 1866*, 38 TENN. HIST. Q. 9 (1979).

Erik Luna, *The* Katz *Jury*, 41 U.C. DAVIS L. REV. 839 (2008).

Erik Luna, *Principled Enforcement of Penal Codes*, 4 BUFF. CRIM. L. REV. 515 (2000).

Tracey Maclin, *The Central Meaning of the Fourth Amendment*, 35 WM. & MARY L. REV. 197 (1993).

Tracey Maclin, *Race and the Fourth Amendment*, 51 VAND. L. REV. 333 (1998).

Tracey Maclin, Terry *v.* Ohio's *Fourth Amendment Legacy: Black Men and Police Discretion*, 72 ST. JOHN'S L. REV. 1271 (1998).

Tracey Maclin, *What Can Fourth Amendment Doctrine Learn from Vagueness Doctrine*, 3 U. PA. J. CONST. L. 398 (2001).

Tracey Maclin, *When the Cure for the Fourth Amendment Is Worse Than the Disease*, 68 S. CAL. L. REV. 1 (1994).

JACKSON TURNER MAIN, THE ANTIFEDERALISTS: CRITICS OF THE CONSTITUTION, 1781–1788 (1961).

EARL M. MALTZ, CIVIL RIGHTS, THE CONSTITUTION, AND CONGRESS, 1863–1869 (1990).

Earl M. Maltz, *Federalism and the Fourteenth Amendment: A Comment on Democracy and Distrust*, 42 OHIO ST. L.J. 209 (1981).

EARL M. MALTZ, THE FOURTEENTH AMENDMENT AND THE LAW OF THE CONSTITUTION (2003).

Michael J.Z. Mannheimer, *The Contingent Fourth Amendment*, 64 EMORY L.J. 1229 (2015).

Michael J.Z. Mannheimer, *Cruel and Unusual Federal Punishments*, 98 IOWA L. REV. 69 (2012).

Michael J.Z. Mannheimer, *Decentralizing Fourth Amendment Search Doctrine*, 107 KY. L.J. 169 (2019).

Michael J.Z. Mannheimer, *The Local-Control Model of the Fourth Amendment*, 108 J. CRIM. L. & CRIMINOLOGY 253 (2018).

Michael J.Z. Mannheimer, *Self-Government, the Federal Death Penalty, and the Unusual Case of Michael Jacques*, 36 VT. L. REV. 131 (2011).

Michael J.Z. Mannheimer, *Vagueness as Impossibility*, 98 TEX. L. REV. 1049 (2020).

FRANCOIS X. MARTIN, THE OFFICE AND AUTHORITY OF A JUSTICE OF THE PEACE (1791).

JERRY L. MASHAW, CREATING THE ADMINISTRATIVE CONSTITUTION: THE LOST ONE HUNDRED YEARS OF AMERICAN ADMINISTRATIVE LAW (2012).

Toni M. Massaro, *Reviving Hugo Black? The Court's "Jot for Jot" Account of Substantive Due Process*, 73 N.Y.U. L. REV. 1086 (1998).

Thomas B. McAffee, *The Original Meaning of the Ninth Amendment*, 90 COLUM. L. REV. 1215 (1990).

Forrest McDonald, *The Anti-Federalists, 1781–1789*, in THE REINTERPRETATION OF THE AMERICAN REVOLUTION 1763–1789, at 365 (Jack P. Greene ed., 1968).

Carl McGowan, *Rule-Making and the Police*, 70 MICH. L. REV. 659 (1972).

EDWARD MCPHERSON, POLITICAL MANUAL FOR 1866 (1866).

Tracey L. Meares, Terry *and the Relevance of Politics*, 72 ST. JOHN'S L. REV. 1343 (1998).

MESSAGES OF THE GOVERNORS OF MICHIGAN (George N. Fuller ed., 1926).

Bernadette Meyler, *Towards a Common Law Originalism*, 59 STAN. L. REV. 551 (2006).

Hon. M. Blane Michael, *Reading the Fourth Amendment: Guidance from the Mischief That Gave It Birth*, 85 N.Y.U. L. REV. 905 (2010).

Tara Mikkilineni, Note, *Constitutional Default Rules and Interbranch Cooperation*, 82 N.Y.U. L. REV. 1403 (2007).

Eric J. Miller, *Challenging Police Discretion*, 58 HOWARD L.J. 521 (2015).

Henry Paul Monaghan, *Supremacy Clause Textualism*, 110 COLUM. L. REV. 731 (2010).

Richard B. Morris, *John Jay and the Adoption of the Federal Constitution in New York: A New Reading of Persons and Events*, 63 N.Y. HIST. 133 (1982).

THOMAS D. MORRIS, FREE MEN ALL: THE PERSONAL LIBERTY LAWS OF THE NORTH, 1780–1861 (1974).

David E. Narrett, *A Zeal for Liberty: The Antifederalist Case Against the Constitution in New York*, 69 N.Y. HIST. 285 (1988).

Alexandra Natapoff, Atwater *and the Misdemeanor Carceral State*, 133 HARV. L. REV. F. 147 (2020).

Alexandra Natapoff, *Underenforcement*, 75 FORDHAM L. REV. 1715 (2006).

Robert G. Natelson, *The Original Meaning of the Establishment Clause*, 14 WM. & MARY BILL RTS. J. 73 (2005).

"The National Question," *New York Times*, Nov. 10, 1866.

"The National Question," *New York Times*, Nov. 28, 1866.

WILLIAM E. NELSON, THE COMMON LAW IN COLONIAL AMERICA: THE CHESAPEAKE AND NEW ENGLAND, 1607–1660 (2008).

WILLIAM E. NELSON, THE FOURTEENTH AMENDMENT: FROM POLITICAL PRINCIPLE TO JUDICIAL DOCTRINE (1988).

S.S. Nicholas, *The Civil Rights Act*, in 3 CONSERVATIVE ESSAYS, LEGAL AND POLITICAL 47 (1867).

Justin Nix et al., *A Bird's Eye View of Civilians Killed by Police in 2015*, 16 CRIMINOLOGY & PUB. POL'Y 309 (2017).

Note, *The Fourth Amendment's Third Way*, 120 HARV. L. REV. 1627 (2007).

Osagie K. Obasogie and Zachary Newman, *Constitutional Interpretation Without Judges: Police Violence, Excessive Force, and Remaking the Fourth Amendment*, 105 VA. L. REV. 425 (2019).

Osagie K. Obasogie and Zachary Newman, *The Endogenous Fourth Amendment: An Empirical Assessment of How Police Understandings of Excessive Force Become Constitutional Law*, 104 CORNELL L. REV. 1281 (2019).

ELLIS P. OBERHOLTZER, A HISTORY OF THE UNITED STATES SINCE THE CIVIL WAR (1917).

Paul Ohm, *The Many Revolutions of* Carpenter, 32 HARV. J.L. & TECH. 357 (2019).

Andrew S. Oldham, *The Anti-Federalists: Past as Prologue*, 12 N.Y.U. J.L. & LIBERTY 451 (2019).

Trisha Olson, *The Natural Law Foundation of the Privileges or Immunities Clause of the Fourteenth Amendment*, 48 ARK. L. REV. 347 (1995).

ONE COUNTRY, ONE CONSTITUTION, ONE PEOPLE: SPEECH OF HON. JOHN A. BINGHAM OF OHIO, IN THE HOUSE OF REPRESENTATIVES, FEBRUARY 28, 1866, IN SUPPORT OF THE PROPOSED AMENDMENT TO ENFORCE THE BILL OF RIGHTS (1866).

Lauren M. Ouziel, *Beyond Law and Fact: Jury Evaluation of Law Enforcement*, 92 NOTRE DAME L. REV. 691 (2016).

Robert C. Palmer, *Liberties as Constitutional Provisions: 1776–1791*, in LIBERTY AND COMMUNITY: CONSTITUTION AND RIGHTS IN THE EARLY AMERICAN REPUBLIC 55 (William E. Nelson and Robert C. Palmer eds., 1987).

PHILLIP S. PALUDAN, COVENANT WITH DEATH: THE CONSTITUTION, LAW, AND EQUALITY IN THE CIVIL WAR ERA (1975).

JAMES PARKER, CONDUCTOR GENERALIS: OR, THE OFFICE, DUTY AND AUTHORITY OF JUSTICES OF THE PEACE, HIGH-SHERIFFS, UNDER-SHERIFFS, CORO-

NERS, CONSTABLES, GAOLERS, JURY-MEN, AND OVERSEERS OF THE POOR (Woodbridge, James Parker 1764).

JAMES PARKER, THE CONDUCTOR GENERALIS: OR, THE OFFICE, DUTY AND AUTHORITY OF JUSTICES OF THE PEACE, HIGH-SHERIFFS, UNDER-SHERIFFS, CORONERS, CONSTABLES, GAOLERS, JURY-MEN, AND OVERSEERS OF THE POOR (Philadelphia, Robert Campbell 1792).

THE PARLIAMENTARY HISTORY OF ENGLAND, FROM THE EARLIEST PERIOD TO THE YEAR 1803 (1813).

GEORGE W. PASCHAL, THE CONSTITUTION OF THE UNITED STATES DEFINED AND CAREFULLY ANNOTATED (1868).

REMBERT W. PATRICK, THE RECONSTRUCTION OF THE NATION (1967).

Charles R. Pence, *The Construction of the Fourteenth Amendment*, 25 AM. L. REV. 536 (1891).

PENNSYLVANIA AND THE FEDERAL CONSTITUTION 1787–1788 (J. McMaster and F. Stone eds., 1888).

MICHAEL J. PERRY, THE CONSTITUTION IN THE COURTS: LAW OR POLITICS? (1994).

Emma Pierson et al., *A Large-Scale Analysis of Racial Disparities in Police Stops Across the United States*, 4 NATURE HUM. BEHAVIOUR 736 (2020).

Pittsburgh, Sept. 10, INDEP. GAZETEER, Sept. 24, 1791.

THEODORE F.T. PLUCKNETT, A CONCISE HISTORY OF THE COMMON LAW (5th ed. 1956).

The Policing Project / NYU School of Law, "Statement of Principles on Democratic Policing" (2015).

"Political Affairs," *New York Times*, Nov. 15, 1866.

"The Political Situation," *New York Times*, Oct. 24, 1866.

FREDERICK POLLOCK, A FIRST BOOK OF JURISPRUDENCE FOR STUDENTS OF THE COMMON LAW (5th ed. 1923).

JOHN NORTON POMEROY, AN INTRODUCTION TO THE CONSTITUTIONAL LAW OF THE UNITED STATES (1868).

Maria Ponomarenko, *Rethinking Police Rulemaking*, 114 NW. L. REV. 1 (2019).

Gerard J. Postema, *Classical Common Law Jurisprudence (Part I)*, 2 OXFORD U. COMMONWEALTH L.J. 155 (2002).

Gerard J. Postema, *Classical Common Law Jurisprudence (Part II)*, 3 OXFORD U. COMMONWEALTH L.J. 1 (2003).

THE PRESIDENT'S COMMISSION ON LAW ENFORCEMENT AND ADMINISTRATION OF JUSTICE, THE CHALLENGE OF CRIME IN A FREE SOCIETY (1967).

Eve Brensike Primus, *Disentangling Administrative Searches*, 111 COLUM. L. REV. 254 (2011).

PROCEEDINGS OF THE MASSACHUSETTS HISTORICAL SOCIETY 1871–1873 (1873).

MEGAN QUATTLEBAUM ET AL., PRINCIPLES OF PROCEDURALLY JUST POLICING (2018).

JOSIAH QUINCY JR., REPORTS OF CASES ARGUED AND ADJUDGED IN THE SUPREME COURT OF JUDICATURE OF THE PROVINCE OF MASSACHUSETTS BAY BETWEEN 1761 AND 1772 (1865).

Howard N. Rabinowitz, Race Relations in the Urban South 1865–1890 (1978).

Joseph A. Ranney, In the Wake of Slavery: Civil War, Civil Rights, and the Reconstruction of Southern Law (2006).

John Rappaport, *Second-Order Regulation of Law Enforcement*, 103 Calif. L. Rev. 205 (2015).

Margaret Raymond, *Penumbral Crimes*, 39 Am. Crim. L. Rev. 1395 (2002).

"The Reconstruction Committee's Amendment in the Senate," *New York Times*, May 25, 1866.

The Records of the Federal Convention of 1787 (Max Farrand ed., 1911).

Whitelaw Reid, After the War: A Southern Tour, May 1, 1865 to May 1, 1866 (1866).

Joel R. Reidenberg, *Lex Informatica: The Formulation of Information Policy Rules Through Technology*, 76 Tex. L. Rev. 553 (1998).

Alexander Reinert, Joanna C. Schwartz, and James E. Pfander, *New Federalism and Civil Rights Enforcement*, 116 Nw. U. L. Rev. 737 (2021).

Daphna Renan, *The Fourth Amendment as Administrative Governance*, 68 Stan. L. Rev. 1039 (2016).

Report of the Joint Committee on Reconstruction at the First Session, 39th Congress (1866).

Report of the Merchants Committee for the Relief of Colored People Suffering From the Riots in the City of New York (1863).

The Resolution of Congress of the 18th of April, 1783: Recommending the States to Invest Congress with the Power to Levy an Impost, for the Use of the States; and the Laws of the Respective States Passed in Pursuance of the Said Recommendation, Together with Remarks on the Resolutions of Congress, and Laws of the Different States (1787).

Restatement (Second) of Torts (1977).

Donald E. Reynolds, *The New Orleans Riot of 1866: Reconsidered*, 5 La. Hist. 5 (1964).

Joe M. Richardson, *Florida Black Codes*, 47 Fla. Hist. Q. 365 (1969).

Joe M. Richardson, *The Memphis Race Riot and Its Aftermath: Report by a Northern Missionary*, 24 Tenn. Hist. Q. 63 (1965).

Joe M. Richardson, The Negro in the Reconstruction of Florida, 1865–77 (1965).

Alice Ristroph, *The Constitution of Police Violence*, 64 UCLA L. Rev. 1112 (2017).

Paul H. Robinson, *Criminal Law Defenses: A Systematic Analysis*, 82 Colum. L. Rev. 199 (1982).

Carol Rose, *The Comedy of the Commons: Custom, Commerce and Inherently Public Property*, 53 U. Chi. L. Rev. 711 (1986).

Nicholas Quinn Rosenkranz, *Federal Rules of Statutory Interpretation*, 115 Harv. L. Rev. 2086 (2002).

Lawrence Rosenthal, *The New Originalism Meets the Fourteenth Amendment: Original Public Meaning and the Problem of Incorporation*, 18 J. Contemp. Legal Issues 361 (2009).

Lawrence Rosenthal, *Pragmatism, Originalism, Race, and the Case Against* Terry v. Ohio, 43 TEX. TECH L. REV. 299 (2010).
Robert A. Rutland, *Framing and Ratifying the First Ten Amendments*, in THE FRAMING AND RATIFICATION OF THE CONSTITUTION 305 (Leonard W. Levy and Dennis J. Mahoney eds., 1987).
James Gilbert Ryan, *The Memphis Riots of 1866: Terror in a Black Community During Reconstruction*, 62 J. NEGRO HIST. 243 (1977).
Meghan J. Ryan, *Juries and the Criminal Constitution*, 65 ALA. L. REV. 849 (2014).
Laurent Sacharoff, *Constitutional Trespass*, 81 TENN. L. REV. 877 (2014).
Stephen E. Sachs, *Finding Law*, 107 CAL. L. REV. 527 (2019).
Stephen E. Sachs, *From St. Ives to Cyberspace: The Modern Distortion of the Medieval "Law Merchant,"* 21 AM. U. INT'L L. REV. 685 (2006).
Barbara C. Salken, *The General Warrant of the Twentieth Century? A Fourth Amendment Solution to Unchecked Discretion to Arrest for Traffic Offenses*, 62 TEMP. L. REV. 221 (1989).
Antonin Scalia, *Common-Law Courts in a Civil-Law System: The Role of United States Federal Courts in Interpreting the Constitution and Laws*, in A MATTER OF INTERPRETATION: FEDERAL COURTS AND THE LAW 3 (Amy Gutmann ed., 1997).
Frederick Schauer, *The Jurisprudence of Custom*, 48 TEX. INT'L L.J. 523 (2013).
Harry N. Scheiber, *Federalism and the Constitution: The Original Understanding*, in AMERICAN LAW AND THE CONSTITUTIONAL ORDER: HISTORICAL PERSPECTIVES 85 (Lawrence M. Friedman and Harry N. Scheiber eds., 1978).
Kendra Scott et al., *A Social Scientific Approach Toward Understanding Racial Disparities in Police Shooting: Data from the Department of Justice (1980–2000)*, 73 J. SOC. ISSUES 1 (2017).
"Secretary Browning's Letter—The President and the Amendment," *New York Times*, Oct. 25, 1866.
Niraj Sekhon, *Blue on Black: An Empirical Assessment of Police Shootings*, 54 AM. CRIM. L. REV. 189 (2017).
THE SELECTED WRITINGS OF SIR EDWARD COKE (Steve Sheppard ed. 2003).
SARAH A. SEO, POLICING THE OPEN ROAD: HOW CARS TRANSFORMED AMERICAN FREEDOM (2019).
Kami Chavis Simmons, *New Governance and the New Paradigm of Police Accountability: A Democratic Approach to Police Reform*, 59 CATH. U. L. REV. 373 (2010).
Ric Simmons, *Searching for Terrorists: Why Public Safety Is Not a Special Need*, 59 DUKE L.J. 843 (2010).
WILLIAM SIMPSON, THE PRACTICAL JUSTICE OF THE PEACE AND PARISH-OFFICER, OF HIS MAJESTY'S PROVINCE OF SOUTH-CAROLINA (Charlestown, Robert Wells 1761).
DAVID A. SKLANSKY, DEMOCRACY AND THE POLICE (2008).
David A. Sklansky, *The Fourth Amendment and Common Law*, 100 COLUM. L. REV. 1739 (2000).
Christopher Slobogin, *Government Dragnets*, 73 J.L. & CONTEMP. PROBS. 107 (2010).
Christopher Slobogin, *Is the Fourth Amendment Relevant in a Technological Age?*,

in CONSTITUTION 3.0: FREEDOM AND TECHNOLOGICAL CHANGE 11 (Jeffrey Rosen and Benjamin Wittes eds., 2013).

Christopher Slobogin, *Panvasive Surveillance, Political Process Theory, and the Nondelegation Doctrine*, 102 GEO. L.J. 1721 (2014).

Christopher Slobogin, *Policing as Administration*, 165 U. PA. L. REV. 91 (2016).

Douglas G. Smith, *Natural Law, Article IV, and Section One of the Fourteenth Amendment*, 47 AM. U. L. REV. 351 (1997).

Jonathan M. Smith, *Closing the Gap between What Is Lawful and What Is Right in Police Use of Force Jurisprudence by Making Police Departments More Democratic Institutions*, 21 MICH. J. RACE & L. 315 (2016).

THE SOUTH-CAROLINA JUSTICE OF PEACE (Philadelphia, R. Aitken & Son 1788).

THE SOUTHERN LOYALISTS' CONVENTION (1866).

SPEECHES, CORRESPONDENCE AND POLITICAL PAPERS OF CARL SCHURZ (1913).

SPEECHES OF JOHN C. CALHOUN DELIVERED IN THE CONGRESS OF THE UNITED STATES FROM 1811 TO THE PRESENT TIME (1843).

Kevin M. Stack, *The Constitutional Foundations of* Chenery, 116 YALE L.J. 952 (2007).

RICHARD STARKE, THE OFFICE AND AUTHORITY OF A JUSTICE OF PEACE EXPLAINED AND DIGESTED, UNDER PROPER TITLES (Williamsburg, Alexander Purdie & John Dixon 1774).

THE STATES RIGHTS DEBATE: ANTIFEDERALISM AND THE CONSTITUTION (Alpheus Thomas Mason ed., 2d ed. 1972).

David E. Steinberg, *The Original Understanding of Unreasonable Searches and Seizures*, 56 FLA. L. REV. 1051 (2004).

Seth W. Stoughton, *Accountability and Enhancement: The Dual Objectives of Use-of-Force Review*, in RETHINKING AND REFORMING AMERICAN POLICING 227 (Joseph A. Schafer and Richard W. Myers eds., 2022).

Seth W. Stoughton, *How the Fourth Amendment Frustrates the Regulation of Police Violence*, 70 EMORY L.J. 521 (2020).

Seth W. Stoughton, *The Regulation of Police Violence*, in CRITICAL ISSUES IN POLICING: CONTEMPORARY READINGS 321 (Roger G. Dunham, Geoffrey P. Alper, and Kyle D. McLean eds., 8th ed. 2021).

SETH W. STOUGHTON, JEFFREY J. NOBLE, AND GEOFFREY P. ALPERT, EVALUATING POLICE USES OF FORCE (2020).

Lee J. Strang, *Originalism and the "Challenge of Change": Abduced-Principle Originalism and Other Mechanisms by Which Originalism Sufficiently Accommodates Changed Social Conditions*, 60 HASTINGS L.J. 927 (2009).

WILLIAM J. STUNTZ, THE COLLAPSE OF AMERICAN CRIMINAL JUSTICE (2011).

William J. Stuntz, *Implicit Bargains, Government Power, and the Fourth Amendment*, 44 STAN. L. REV. 553 (1992).

William J. Stuntz, *The Substantive Origins of Criminal Procedure*, 105 YALE L.J. 393 (1995).

William J. Stuntz, Terry *and Substantive Law*, 72 ST. JOHN'S L. REV. 1362 (1998).

Scott E. Sundby, *An Ode to Probable Cause: A Brief Response to Professors Amar and Slobogin*, 72 ST. JOHN'S L. REV. 1133 (1998).

Scott E. Sundby, *Protecting the Citizen Whilst He Is Quiet: Suspicionless Searches, Special Needs and General Warrants*, 74 MISS. L.J. 501 (2004).

Scott E. Sundby, *A Return to Fourth Amendment Basics: Undoing the Mischief of* Camara *and* Terry, 72 MINN. L. REV. 383 (1988).

THE SUPREME COURT: A C-SPAN BOOK FEATURING THE JUSTICES IN THEIR OWN WORDS (Brian Lamb, Susan Swain, and Mark Farkas eds., 2010).

Sarah L. Swan, *Discriminatory Dualism*, 54 GA. L. REV. 869 (2020).

Andrew E. Taslitz, *Fourth Amendment Federalism and the Silencing of the American Poor*, 85 CHI.-KENT L. REV. 277 (2010).

ANDREW E. TASLITZ, RECONSTRUCTING THE FOURTH AMENDMENT: A HISTORY OF SEARCH AND SEIZURE, 1789–1868 (2006).

TELFORD TAYLOR, TWO STUDIES IN CONSTITUTIONAL INTERPRETATION: SEARCH, SEIZURE, AND SURVEILLANCE AND FAIR TRIAL AND FREE PRESS (1969).

JACOBUS TENBROEK, THE ANTISLAVERY ORIGINS OF THE FOURTEENTH AMENDMENT (1951).

DAVID THOMAS, MY AMERICAN TOUR (1868).

George C. Thomas III, *The Common Law Endures in the Fourth Amendment*, 27 WM. & MARY BILL RTS. J. 85 (2018).

George C. Thomas III, *Stumbling Toward History: The Framers' Search and Seizure World*, 43 TEX. TECH L. REV. 199, 226 (2010).

George C. Thomas III, *When Constitutional Worlds Collide: Resurrecting the Framers' Bill of Rights and Criminal Procedure*, 100 MICH. L. REV. 145 (2001).

George C. Thomas III and Barry S. Pollack, *Saving Rights from a Remedy: A Societal View of the Fourth Amendment*, 73 B.U. L. REV. 147 (1993).

Anthony C. Thompson, *Stopping the Usual Suspects: Race and the Fourth Amendment*, 74 N.Y.U. L. REV. 956 (1999).

E.P. THOMPSON, CUSTOMS IN COMMON (1991).

Matthew Tokson, *The Next Wave of Fourth Amendment Challenges After* Carpenter, 59 WASHBURN L.J. 1 (2020).

Matthew Tokson and Ari Ezra Waldman, *Social Norms in Fourth Amendment Law*, 120 MICH. L. REV. 265 (2021).

TRIAL OF WILLIAM BUTLER FOR PIRACY (1813).

J.T. TROWBRIDGE, A PICTURE OF THE DESOLATED STATES (1868).

J.T. TROWBRIDGE, THE SOUTH: A TOUR OF ITS BATTLE-FIELDS AND RUINED CITIES (1866).

ST. GEORGE TUCKER, BLACKSTONE'S COMMENTARIES: WITH NOTES OF REFERENCE, TO THE CONSTITUTION AND LAWS, OF THE FEDERAL GOVERNMENT OF THE UNITED STATES; AND OF THE COMMONWEALTH OF VIRGINIA (1803).

Tom Tyler and Tracey Meares, *Revisiting Broken Windows: The Role of the Community and the Police in Promoting Community Engagement*, 76 N.Y.U. ANN. SURV. AM. L. 637 (2021).

David R. Upham, *The Meanings of the "Privileges or Immunities of Citizens" on the Eve of the Civil War*, 91 NOTRE DAME L. REV. 1117 (2016).

Gilles Vandal, *The Origins of the New Orleans Riot of 1866, Revisited*, 22 LA. HIST. 135 (1981).

THE VIRGINIA AND KENTUCKY RESOLUTIONS OF 1798 AND '99 (Washington, Jonathan Elliot 1832).

James Vorenberg, *Narrowing the Discretion of Criminal Justice Officials*, 1976 DUKE L.J. 651.

Samuel Walker, *Controlling the Cops: A Legislative Approach to Police Rulemaking*, 63 U. DET. L. REV. 361 (1986).

Samuel Walker, *Governing the American Police: Wrestling with the Problems of Democracy*, 2016 U. CHI. LEGAL F. 615.

SAMUEL WALKER, TAMING THE SYSTEM: THE CONTROL OF DISCRETION IN CRIMINAL JUSTICE 1950–90 (1993).

Altina L. Waller, *Community, Class and Race in the Memphis Riot of 1866*, 18 J. SOUTH. HIST. 233 (1984).

Silas J. Wasserstrom, *The Incredible Shrinking Fourth Amendment*, 21 AM. CRIM. L. REV. 257 (1984).

Silas J. Wasserstrom and Louis Michael Seidman, *The Fourth Amendment as Constitutional Theory*, 77 GEO. L.J. 19 (1988).

THOMAS W. WATERMAN, A COMPLETE PRACTICAL TREATISE ON CRIMINAL PROCEDURE, PLEADING, AND EVIDENCE IN INDICTABLE CASES (1853).

Robert H. Webking, *Melancton Smith and* the Letters from the Federal Farmer, 44 WM. & MARY Q. 510 (1987).

Jack B. Weinstein, *Local Responsibility for Improvement of Search and Seizure Practices*, 34 ROCKY MNTN. L. REV. 150 (1962).

FRANCIS WHARTON, STATE TRIALS OF THE UNITED STATES DURING THE ADMINISTRATIONS OF WASHINGTON AND ADAMS (1849).

What's to Be Done With the Negroes, DE BOW'S REVIEW, June 1866, 577.

Bryan H. Wildenthal, *Nationalizing the Bill of Rights: Revisiting the Original Understanding of the Fourteenth Amendment in 1866–67*, 68 OHIO ST. L.J. 1509 (2007).

Bryan H. Wildenthal, *Nationalizing the Bill of Rights: Scholarship and Commentary on the Fourteenth Amendment in 1867–1873*, 18 J. CONTEMP. LEGAL ISSUES 153 (2009).

Gregory Howard Williams, *Police Rulemaking Revisited: Some New Thoughts on an Old Problem*, 47 L. & CONTEMP. PROBS. 123 (1984).

Ryan C. Williams, *The One and Only Substantive Due Process Clause*, 120 YALE L.J. 408 (2010).

JOEL WILLIAMSON, AFTER SLAVERY: THE NEGRO IN SOUTH CAROLINA DURING RECONSTRUCTION (1965).

Arthur E. Wilmarth, Jr., *Elusive Foundation: John Marshall, James Wilson, and the Problem of Reconciling Popular Sovereignty and Natural Law Jurisprudence in the New Federal Republic*, 72 GEO. WASH. L. REV. 113 (2003).

Arthur E. Wilmarth, Jr., *The Original Purpose of the Bill of Rights: James Madison and the Founders' Search for a Workable Balance Between Federal and State Power*, 26 AM. CRIM. L. REV. 1261 (1989).

THEODORE BRANTNER WILSON, THE BLACK CODES OF THE SOUTH (1965).

Gordon S. Wood, *The Authorship of the* Letters from the Federal Farmer, 31 WM. & MARY Q. 299 (1974).

Ann Woolhandler, *Delegation and Due Process: The Historical Connection*, 2008 SUP. CT. REV. 223.

Richard C. Worf, *The Case for Rational Basis Review of General Suspicionless Searches and Seizures*, 23 TOURO L. REV. 93 (2007).

J. Skelly Wright, *Beyond Discretionary Justice*, 81 YALE L.J. 575 (1972).

THE WRITINGS OF THOMAS JEFFERSON (H.A. Washington ed., New York, H.W. Derby 1859).

ILAN WURMAN, THE SECOND FOUNDING: AN INTRODUCTION TO THE FOURTEENTH AMENDMENT (2020).

Aaron Zelinsky, *Misunderstanding the Anti-Federalist Papers: The Dangers of Availability*, 63 ALA. L. REV. 1067 (2012).

FRANKLIN E. ZIMRING, WHEN POLICE KILL (2017).

Index

Printed and bound by CPI Group (UK) Ltd, Croydon, CR0 4YY
09/11/2026
14999539-0001